COLLECTED WORKS OF ERASMUS

VOLUME 6

THE CORRESPONDENCE OF
ERASMUS

LETTERS 842 TO 992

1518 TO 1519

translated by R.A.B. Mynors and D.F.S. Thomson

annotated by Peter G. Bietenholz

University of Toronto Press

Toronto / Buffalo / London

The research and publication costs of the
Collected Works of Erasmus are supported by the
Social Sciences and Humanities Research Council of Canada
(and previously by the Canada Council).
The publication costs are also assisted by
University of Toronto Press

Canadian Cataloguing in Publication Data
Erasmus, Desiderius, circa 1466–1536.
Collected works of Erasmus
Contents: v. 6. The correspondence of Erasmus,
letters 842 to 992, 1518 to 1519 / translated by
R.A.B. Mynors and D.F.S. Thomson; annotated by
Peter G. Bietenholz.
ISBN 0-8020-5500-1 (v. 6)
1. Erasmus, Desiderius, circa 1466–1536.
I. Mynors, R.A.B., 1903– II. Thomson, D.F.S.,
1919– III. Bietenholz, Peter G., 1933–
IV. Title.
PA8500 1974   876'.04   C74-6326-x

cc

Collected Works of Erasmus

The aim of the Collected Works of Erasmus
is to make available an accurate, readable English text
of Erasmus' correspondence and his
other principal writings. The edition is planned
and directed by an Editorial Board, an Executive Committee,
and an Advisory Committee.

Contents

Illustrations

Preface

The first letters in this volume appear to have been written during Erasmus' journey from Louvain to Basel in May of 1518. Riding an English horse[1] over highways that were far from safe,[2] he went to Basel to assist his publisher and friend Johann Froben during the crucial phases in the production of his revised New Testament.[3] A great deal was at stake. Through the long months of relentless toiling over the text, the notes, and the translation, he had increasingly formed the conviction that he stood at a turning point in his life. The new edition was to be his lasting contribution to the scholarly foundations of the Christian faith; it had to be bold and uncompromising. Once it was in the hands of the public, he could face the approach of old age more calmly, 'singing to himself and the Muses.'[4] Meanwhile, during the summer months spent at Basel he continued to work harder than was good for him and was plagued by ill heath.[5] In September, on the way home to Louvain, the English horse 'simply gave up,' and Erasmus himself fell gravely ill. For four weeks he lay recovering in the house of his other publisher-friend, Dirk Martens. Physicians came and went; two of them, he tells us, diagnosed bubonic plague. As he lay recovering he produced a brilliant account of his homeward journey and his ensuing illness.[6]

By the middle of October he felt well enough to return to his rooms in the College of the Lily and to serious work. The New Testament finally came off the press, and so did lesser publications related to the great work.[7] He did not leave Louvain except in the spring of 1519 for brief visits to Mechelen,[8]

* * * * *

1 Epp 785:51n, 867:30–2
2 Ep 829
3 Ep 864 introduction
4 Cf CWE 5 preface.
5 Epp 847, 860
6 Ep 867
7 Epp 894, 916, 956
8 Ep 926 introduction

Antwerp,[9] and Brussels.[10] But the outward impression of normality that prevails to the end of June, when the last letters in this volume were written, may be deceptive. Experienced astrologers agreed that these were troubled times and pointed to a heavenly cause for human problems.[11] International politics would sometimes stir Erasmus' interest and also his emotions.[12] From July to October, Maximilian I held a diet at Augsburg which was to be his last. Other issues apart,[13] negotiations in Augsburg concerned a papal request for funds in support of a crusade against the unrelenting Turks[14] – a request that aroused the flames of German national sentiment.[15] Moreover the electors' choice of a successor for the ageing emperor was discussed both openly and in private, Maximilian himself having done his share to involve such foreign powers as England and France in addition to his Hispano-Burgundian grandsons, Charles and Ferdinand.[16] Of Erasmus' friends, Pace,[17] Hutten,[18] and Budé[19] were all involved in diplomatic negotiations concerning the imperial succession. The pace of the negotiations quickened after the death of Maximilian on 12 January 1519,[20] which also prompted a war between Ulrich of Württemberg and the Swabian League and led Hutten, the knight, to brandish his sword as well as his pen.[21] The question of Erasmus' own return to active court duties was raised when Prince Ferdinand arrived from Spain and required a tutor. Erasmus declined the position and recommended his new friend, Juan Luis Vives.[22]

There were other worries affecting Erasmus' daily life at Louvain. The Collegium Trilingue progressed, and as it did so it began to arouse the hostility of the conservative theologians and brought Erasmus himself into conflict with some of their leading representatives,[23] while at the same time it heightened his interest in the progress of the new learning in such

* * * * *

9 Epp 934:10n, 964 introduction
10 Epp 970–1
11 Ep 948:19ff
12 Epp 927:10, 954
13 Ep 916 introduction
14 Ep 854, 868
15 Epp 860, 863 introductions, 891
16 Epp 893:36–44, 917 introduction
17 Epp 968 introduction
18 Ep 744:52n
19 Ep 924
20 Epp 915:176–7, 926 introduction
21 Epp 923, 986
22 Epp 917, 927
23 Epp 934, 946

universities as Erfurt, Wittenberg, Oxford, and Cambridge.[24] No longer did he write, with amused excitement, about being co-opted into the theological faculty.[25] In many ways Louvain still proved congenial, but once again he was becoming restless. In the spring of 1519 he sensed among the diehard theologians a conspiracy directed against his person and his work,[26] and explored with renewed determination the conditions and rewards that might await him if he were to move to London[27] or Paris.[28] He came to believe that his problems in Louvain were centred around an Englishman, Edward Lee, who was preparing an attack upon his New Testament – a frivolous and alarming scheme to jeopardize Erasmus' historic gift to his age. He was determined to cut through this web of elusive opposition spreading from Louvain to England[29] and Germany,[30] but only succeeded in escalating the conflict by bringing Lee to the attention of his international readership, albeit without mentioning a name.[31] He privately appealed for help to his friends in England,[32] while Lee broke off all channels of communication with the Erasmian camp.[33] Irritation on both sides was growing to the point of obsession. In the next volume the reader of Erasmus' correspondence will witness the climax and virtual end of the controversy with Lee and will also better understand the issues at stake, which in retrospect can hardly be judged to be fundamental.

Fundamental issues were raised, however, by Erasmus' residence in a town which contained the sole university of the Hapsburg-Burgundian Netherlands and was internationally reputed to be a bastion of orthodox theology. Luther's Ninety-five Theses on indulgences, purgatory, and papal authority led to a flurry of pamphlets and widespread discussion. In Louvain, as elsewhere, the immediate attention and often enthusiastic response given to Luther's ideas lent new emphasis to the question whether Erasmus' own work might have, or indeed was already having, an equally harmful effect: both were innovators, and both insisted that a good deal needed to be changed in the traditional ways of society and the church that controlled it in so many respects. Those who two years earlier had opposed

* * * * *

24 Epp 871, 939–42, 965, 967, 978–80
25 Ep 637:12n
26 Epp 930, 946, 948
27 Epp 886, 964 introductions
28 Ep 926:37n
29 Ep 898A introduction
30 Ep 972
31 Epp 843, 897
32 Epp 886, 936, 973–4
33 Epp 922, 960

Erasmus' New Testament could now hardly fail to oppose Luther too, and to condemn both men in one breath.[34]

Erasmus reacted angrily[35] but was not yet alarmed.[36] In fact he had little reason to be alarmed until the winter of 1519–20, when Luther's heterodoxy became clear beyond doubt, and conservative Christians everywhere began to perceive the tares in their midst and wonder whether it was not Erasmus who had sown the seeds. For the time being, however, Erasmus was prepared to commend Luther, at least in certain quarters,[37] and more generally to defend his right to be critical of the church. It is true that he perceived in Luther's writings a radical commitment which differed from his own[38] and therefore decided that their causes would have to be kept apart – hence his endeavours to suppress the *Julius exclusus*[39] and to prevent his own publishers from printing Luther's works[40] – but his overriding conviction at this time was that he and Luther were both in their separate ways part of the great intellectual and spiritual renewal triumphantly manifest in so many places.[41]

Although his earliest letter to Luther, Ep 980, was promptly printed in Germany without his knowledge, there is little evidence to indicate that at the time he wrote it Erasmus did not himself intend to publish it. He did in fact publish it in the *Farrago* of October 1519, adding Luther's Ep 933, to which Ep 980 was the reply, although Ep 933 had not otherwise been published in Germany. Since Luther's appearance lent a new kind of spiritual and patriotic vigour to the various circles of German humanists, the cult of Erasmus as a hero of German letters became an integral part of that new enthusiasm. Saxony was a centre; during the breaks between academic terms pilgrims set out for Louvain from the University of Erfurt, specifically to set eyes on Erasmus.[42] Some of the messages and gifts they brought came from Frederick the Wise, elector of Saxony, and his chancellor, Spalatinus. Cultural politics were assuming a new significance with the impending election of a new emperor. The tremendous electoral campaign launched by the house of Hapsburg now rendered the dynastic union of Austria and Burgundy, of Germany and the Netherlands, real and positively exciting,

* * * * *

34 Epp 938:5n, 948, 961:36–9; cf CWE 7 preface.
35 Epp 946, 948
36 Ep 968:21n
37 Epp 872, 939, 947
38 Epp 967, 967A, 980, 983
39 Ep 961:42n
40 Ep 904:20n
41 Epp 872, 947
42 Epp 870, 963, 1122 introduction, 1462

whereas in the days of Maximilian it had for the most part remained theoretical and patently ineffectual. And it was not only in Saxony that cultural politics were important. The young archbishop of Mainz, who was also the titular of two Saxon sees, the chancellor of Erfurt University, and a recent convert to the Hapsburg party, had taken Ulrich von Hutten into his service. It could be expected that he shared Hutten's enthusiasm for Reuchlin and Luther,[43] and it was evident that he shared his admiration for Erasmus.[44]

Erasmus' response to the new spring of German humanism was, on the whole, remarkably positive. How positive it was would not be fully demonstrated until the publication of his *Farrago* and other writings of the period of 1519–20.[45] Right now his approbation was reflected in the addition of Ep 858 to Froben's edition of the *Enchiridion* – a move designed to heighten its appeal to the German public – and in the fact that letters to and from Germany account for the greatest share by far of the correspondence contained in this volume.[46] The new climate is also reflected in the wide circulation of the *Julius exclusus*, especially in Germany.[47] In the light of his private statements such as those in Ep 872 it is questionable whether Erasmus was quite as upset about the success of the dialogue as his published statements profess.

In the case of some of the issues mentioned so far the reader of this volume will see no more than the proverbial tip of the iceberg and will have to speculate upon the immense preoccupation they caused Erasmus and the amount of time he was prepared to spend on them. This applies equally to a fundamental issue like Erasmus' new contacts with Luther and the reactions they provoked in Germany and Louvain and to a predominantly personal one like the conflict with Lee. A very different situation arises as the reader turns to the tortuous friendship between Erasmus and Guillaume Budé. Half a dozen major letters[48] and a handful of shorter ones in CWE 5–6 offer very nearly the complete record of a dramatic, even critical, phase in the relationship between the two scholars. There is too much uneasiness in their letters for their stabs to be passed off simply as a display of wit and brilliance.

* * * * *

43 Ep 1033
44 Epp 986, 988
45 Cf Ep 1009 introduction, CWE 8 preface.
46 This volume comprises 152 letters, of which 59 are exchanged with German correspondents (including Alsatian and Swiss), 36 with Netherlanders, 23 with Englishmen, 16 with Frenchmen, 10 with Italians, and 8 with correspondents from other nations.
47 Epp 785:42n, 849:32n, 877:12–13
48 Epp 744, 778, 810, 896, 906, 915

One's judgment on the issues concerned will depend on the importance one is prepared to attach to style as against substance. To readers who are able to take matters of style as seriously as did the two protagonists and their admirers, these letters will appear significant; other readers may find them taxing, a display of endless, if elegant, bickering over points of little weight. It does not appear that then or later the opinions of Erasmus and Budé clashed over such issues as politics or religion; even their assessments of Erasmus' controversy with Lefèvre d'Etaples do not offer evidence of a profound difference of opinion. At the very least, however, these letters will help the reader to appreciate the importance a well-turned Latin phrase had for Erasmus and his friends. To fathom an expression down to the last shade of implied meaning or be able to imply at one's discretion another meaning within the limits of correct Latin was a skill they greatly admired and assiduously perfected. It was a skill both men used in a constant, and possibly novel, effort to explore and define the subtle recesses of their own personality as well as the other's.

The 152 letters contained in this volume are, as always, only part of Erasmus' correspondence at the time. These letters make specific reference to 41 others now missing, and how many more vanished without trace it is impossible to say. For volumes 3 to 5 of this edition the Deventer Letter-book[49] has been an essential source of letters sent and received that Erasmus did not choose to release to his publishers, although he had them copied into the letter-book by his amanuenses. When he went to Basel he took the Deventer book with him because he intended to publish a new collection of his correspondence, and some more letters were recorded in it both at Basel and after his return to Louvain. But Ep 895 of 25 October 1518 is the last text in this edition that is derived from the Deventer book. As its contributions cease the character of the surviving correspondence changes substantially. From that point on the majority of letters known today were published by Erasmus and his associates either in various collections of his correspondence[50] or as prefaces and appendixes to some of his own writings and other books; most were printed in his lifetime and were therefore widely known to his contemporaries. The few letters published by modern scholars from scattered manuscript sources cannot always be relied upon to provide continuous insight into Erasmus' daily life and the thoughts and experiences he desired to keep private. To mention one example, very little is revealed in this volume about Erasmus' financial transactions, in sharp contrast to the

* * * * *

49 Cf Allen 1, appendix 8.
50 Cf Allen 1, appendix 7.

preceding volume, where the Deventer book provided more than half the letters. While in the past not all the letters were copied into the Deventer book, either by accident or by design, and while hereafter a number of indiscreet remarks and trivial notes will continue to be found, from this point on there are appreciably fewer unedited and spontaneous letters than in the preceding volumes.

The termination of the Deventer Letter-book is also reflected in the composition of this volume. In addition to the last 17 letters derived from the Deventer book, no more than 20 others were preserved in manuscript only until they were published by scholars of a more recent period. This leaves 115 letters out of a total of 152 that were published in the sixteenth century: 6 in the *Auctarium*,[51] 81 in the *Farrago* of October 1519, 5 more in later collections, and 23 elsewhere, for the most part in Erasmus' lifetime. Of these only Ep 939 can perhaps be assumed to have been published against Erasmus' wishes, while in the case of Ep 980 an earlier version printed in Germany differs in one important point from the edited version in his *Farrago*. As in the past, P.S. Allen's chronology for letters lacking dates and his attributions for letters lacking addresses have for the most part been accepted. Allen's Ep 705, however, is in this edition Ep 902A, his Ep 912 is here Ep 898A, and his Ep 985 is Ep 967A. Finally, a new addressee is suggested for Ep 880.

The procedure established in preceding CWE volumes, by which readers are informed of the date by which each letter first appeared in print, has been retained here. For letters published in contemporary collections of Erasmus' correspondence, the introduction cites the earliest such collection to print the letter in question. For letters published elsewhere in Erasmus' lifetime, the first edition is cited as well. Where manuscript sources exist, these are also cited provided they carry any weight. When no sources are indicated in the introduction, the letter was copied into the Deventer Letter-book and first published in LB. If a manuscript source alone is cited, the letter was first published by Allen or before him by another scholar of modern times. Where printed letter collections are described by short titles, a full reference is given among the Works Frequently Cited. The footnotes dealing with currency have been supplied by John H. Munro.

The index to this volume, prepared by James Farge CSB, contains references to the persons, places, and works mentioned in the volume, following the plan for the correspondence series. When that series of

* * * * *

51 Ep 886:57n

volumes is completed the reader will also be supplied with an index of classical and scriptural references. A Biographical Register will supplement the biographical information found in the annotation to the letters.

The letters in this volume were translated by R.A.B. Mynors. My notes for this volume and the preceding one were compiled during a year of sabbatical leave for which I wish to record my gratitude to the University of Saskatchewan. I also wish to thank the Warburg Institute, University of London, and the Öffentliche Bibliothek of the University of Basel for hospitality and assistance on many occasions. Finally it should be recalled that the Collected Works of Erasmus could not have been undertaken without the generous assistance of the Social Sciences and Humanities Research Council of Canada.

PGB

Cambridge

•Oxford
London•
Richmond•
Canterbury•

Veere•

Courtrai•
Brussels•
Liège•

Antwerp
Bedburg•
Aachen•

•Utrecht

•Cologne
•Bonn

Wittenberg

•Koblenz
Boppard•
Trier•   Frankfurt
Mainz•

Erfurt•   Leipzig

Wrocław•

Paris•

Worms

Kostelec•

Speyer•

Prague•

Sens•

Strasbourg•
Breisach• •Freiburg
Basel•
Constance
•Nürnberg
Stuttgart
Ingolstadt
•Augsburg

Lake
Constance

Lake
Geneva

Danube

Rhine
Maas
Seine
Rhône
Elbe

Milan•

Montpellier•
Narbonne•

Venice•

Rome•
Nola•

N

Antwerp•

0   25 MILES
0   25 KILOMETRES

•Mechelen

•Brussels   •Louvain
Tienen•
St Truiden• Maastricht•
Tongeren•
•Gembloux   Liège•

Maas

0   150 MILES
0   150 KILOMETRES

THE CORRESPONDENCE OF ERASMUS

LETTERS 842 TO 992

842 / To Helias Marcaeus   [Cologne? 1518?]

At an undetermined date after June 1517 there appeared in Cologne a slim volume with a set of gory illustrations. It contained a text known from the Septuagint, where it is included as book 4 of Maccabees; in the Cologne edition it is, perhaps wrongly, attributed to Josephus and entitled Περὶ αὐτοκράτορος λογισμοῦ, *hoc est de imperatrice ratione liber*, *a D. Erasmo Roterodamo diligenter recognitus ac emendatus* (Cologne: E. Cervicornus, n d). The author uses the story of the Maccabean brothers to illustrate the maxim that human emotions can be mastered with the help of reason. This letter was printed as a preface to the Cologne volume, which also included some extracts from Fathers and other authors about the Maccabees and a letter to Marcaeus from Magdalius Jacobus of Gouda, a Cologne Dominican, 1469–1520 (cf NNBW). Magdalius' letter offers the only date to be found in this volume; it is dated 5 June 1517.

Helias Marcaeus was a native of Jülich (cf ADB). Besides teaching in the Cologne faculty of arts, he was the warden of the convent of Benedictine nuns which possessed the relics of the Maccabees (now in St Andrew's church, Cologne) and took its name from them. He was apparently collecting texts about the Maccabean martyrs, and Magdalius' letter drew his attention to Josephus. Allen suggested that in early May, when Erasmus was passing through Cologne on his way to Basel (cf Ep 843 introduction), the book may have been in preparation and that Erasmus may have obliged his friends by checking either a manuscript or the proofs and by composing this preface. The book may, however, have been published at any time after June 1517. It need not have been in or near Cologne that he looked through the text; and if it was, it could have been while returning to Louvain, when he was resting for five days with Neuenahr (cf Ep 867:79–81). However that may be, he used this letter to relate the popular cult of relics to his own devotional ideals.

ERASMUS OF ROTTERDAM TO THE MOST WORTHY AND LEARNED FATHER HELIAS MARCAEUS OF THE COMMUNITY OF MACCABEANS, WARDEN OF THEIR MOST HONOURABLE CONVENT, GREETING
I have pleasure in dedicating to you, most worthy Father, the slight work of a single day, in which I have revised and (so far as I could) corrected Josephus' 5 book on the martyrdom of the seven Maccabean brethren and their valiant mother. I wish I could have returned a more satisfactory answer to your wishes; but I had no Greek text at hand, and had to make several changes (but not a great number) by reconstructing the Greek out of the Latin. There is much truth in Josephus' assertion that in his command of Greek he has 10

* * * * *

842
10 Josephus' assertion] Josephus *Antiquitates Judaicae* 20.11.263

reached remarkable heights of eloquence; one can see this even from the present small book, in which he displays a singular vigour and abundance of style, so that one feels he has matched a noble deed with splendid utterance. No wonder St Jerome singles this out for special praise as a 'very elegant' book, and Suidas calls it 'most excellent.' From these two authors I have 15 restored the corrupted title Περὶ αὐτοκράτορος λογισμοῦ (*On the sovereign rule of Reason*), for the message of the narrative is that reason can produce any effect in human beings, once it has mastered their desires. The story is to be found in the books of Maccabees, which the Hebrews list among the sacred books, although they do not receive them into the canon.   20

Personally I regard your convent, which is famous on many other grounds as well, as being especially fortunate in its possession of such an outstanding treasure. In fact, I think the whole city of Cologne is to be greatly congratulated: blessed as she is in so many ways, in none is she more so than in providing a home for so many and such remarkable documents of 25 true religion. More blessed still will she be, if she learns to reproduce the virtues of those whose relics she enshrines, and not only holds their bodies but preserves their way of life: imitating in the sincerity of her religion the piety of the Three Kings, emulating in her sobriety of life the purity of the Eleven Thousand Virgins which made them worthy of martyrdom, and by an 30 unbroken constancy of spirit recalling those heroic Maccabees and that invincible heroine their mother. And what is more, this ampler share of blessedness she can bestow upon herself, or double what she has.

Continue then as you have begun: throw light upon the martyrs' glorious history, and so make their courageous example more familiar and 35 your city's fame more brilliant, more inspiring. Farewell.

843 / To Maarten Lips   [On the Rhine?], 7 May 1518

Erasmus left Louvain c 1 May. He may have travelled through Liège (Ep 867:198–9), certainly visited Cologne (Epp 842, 846:4, 852:91–2), and then continued for some distance by boat on the Rhine (line 15). He may then have

* * * * *

14 St Jerome] *De viris illustribus* 13 (PL 23:662)
15 Suidas] An immense Greek lexicon called 'The Suda,' compiled in the tenth century AD, and printed by Aldus in 1514. Erasmus, who thought Suidas was the compiler's name, makes much use of it in the *Adagia*. This entry is I 503.
29 Three Kings] Their relics had been in the cathedral of Cologne since 1164.
30 Virgins] The legend of St Ursula and the eleven thousand (originally just eleven?) virgins developed from the eighth century around a historical kernel dating from the fourth or fifth century. St Ursula is the patron saint of Cologne. The cult, which was highly popular at the time, centred upon the basilica erected in her honour.

passed through Colmar (AK II Ep 616:22–3), and arrived in Basel on 13 May (Epp 847–8).

In this letter Erasmus resumed a controversy destined to remain one of his major concerns throughout the fifteen months covered by this volume (see the preface). The letter answered criticisms of Erasmus' New Testament made by Edward Lee (see Ep 765 introduction), an English scholar then at Louvain, and a future archbishop. Lee's critical notes were brought to Erasmus' attention by Maarten Lips, an Augustinian canon (see Ep 750), who was friendly with both men. This letter was evidently composed for quick publication in the *Auctarium* (cf Epp 861 introduction, 886:57n) and may never have been sent to Lips. Although Lee's name was not mentioned and Lips' name appeared only in the *Opus epistolarum* of 1529 (in the salutation as well as in lines 734, 750), a hint at the critic's British origin (lines 88–9) was no doubt enough to enlighten Louvain's academic community and others who knew Erasmus well. Some people, however, guessed wrongly (see Ep 844 introduction). Lee himself was bound to conclude that Erasmus had made the first step towards publicizing their controversy, and that in insulting language. It is no wonder that Lee returned to the attack with fresh zeal; cf Epp 898A, 936:34–6.

ERASMUS OF ROTTERDAM TO MAARTEN LIPS, GREETING
Do you not think me exceptionally fortunate? There comes to me unasked a blessing which other men scarcely obtain by great effort and expense: everyone offers to instruct Erasmus. And so of necessity, unless I am a mere blockhead, I must some day make progress. In one point, however, I may be   5
thought somewhat unlucky: most of my would-be teachers play the part of hostile critics rather than instructors. Some of them have as their object not to make me a better scholar or a better man, but by joining battle with me to earn, they hope, some pittance of reputation for themselves. All are furious, none more so than those who can teach me absolutely nothing. They are like   10
some schoolmasters, always shouting and clouting and flogging the boys' skin off their backs, and can teach nothing for all that except bad grammar, which they will soon have to unlearn. The man whose pamphlet you have sent me is one of these; it is so illiterate that I could hardly endure to read it, so comical that I could not fail to, though I kept it for a journey by boat. I   15
should be as mad as he is if I tried to answer such malicious falsehoods. But I

* * * * *

843
15 journey by boat] The date suggests that Erasmus composed his answer as he read the letter; cf line 695 and the general lack of exact references, careful argumentation, and organization.

will scribble a word of comment on each chapter of his nonsense, in such a way that, if you like, they can actually be numbered.

1. First of all then, having assured us that ten acute conclusions have validated his constatation (his whole style is gay with such blossoms as   20
these), he assumes as generally accepted that the version of the New Testament now in common use is Jerome's, though it is known to be neither Cyprian's nor Hilary's nor Ambrose's nor Augustine's nor Jerome's, for he has different readings; much less is it the version which he tells us he has corrected, for things are found in it which he condemns, in respect not only   25
of the wording but of the sense. And this is the base of his theological argument.

2. He imagines, and assumes as proved, that I publicly correct and alter the Vulgate text, whereas I leave that intact and untouched and have turned into Latin what is found in the Greek copies, pointing out as I go along the   30
agreements or disagreements of our own text; not seldom preferring what is in these copies of ours, correcting anything corrupt, explaining ambiguities, elucidating obscurities, and changing anything that is notably barbarous in expression, because I understand that very many people are so disgusted by the prodigious errors (which however are nearly always the translator's   35
work and not the authors') that they cannot bring themselves to read the Scriptures. Nor for that matter have all mortals such an iron digestion that they can endure the style of it. But if we simplify our language for the benefit of ignorant and simple folk, should we not help educated readers too by purifying the language? In any case, if this critic of mine wishes nothing   40
whatever to be published that differs from the Vulgate text in common use, it will not be lawful to publish the New Testament in Greek as the Greeks use it, unless it has first been corrected against our published Vulgate, for fear that someone will detect some disagreement. Who is mad enough to say any such thing? We must do away forthwith with St Ambrose's version or   45
paraphrase, whichever it is, of the Pauline Epistles, which differs extensively from our version; we must do away with Jerome's too, which differs from it in a number of places. And then most of our manuscripts must be done away with, because as a rule they differ among themselves. Observe too the disagreement between your friend and Augustine, whom he seems to think   50

* * * * *

23 Jerome's] Following a commission by Pope Damasus I, from 382 Jerome revised the Latin New Testament in the light of Greek texts. Later he translated the Old Testament anew from the Hebrew. In the 'Apologia' prefixed to the 1516 edition of his New Testament Erasmus had correctly pointed out that Jerome was the editor rather than the translator of the New Testament; cf LB VI f**2 recto.

no one else has read. Augustine declares that he has actually been helped by
the difference between copies, since what is obscure in one version is more
clearly rendered in another; we cannot all do all things. This man supposes
that all confidence in Scripture is brought to an end, if the difference in
reading is made public, and would rather the most manifest blunders were   55
left in the sacred text than that two or three foolish old men who are hard to
please should take offence. Yet St Jerome was not in the least deterred from
this line of enquiry by the fact that the change of some small word or other in
the prophet Jonah made almost the whole population rebel against their
bishop, and pours scorn on those gods so dependent on gourds who are   60
shaken by so small a change, although Augustine had written and told
Jerome the story as though it were a serious matter. Why, let that severe critic
of yours answer me just this one question: should we wish on behalf of
God's church that she should read the books of Holy Scripture in a truly
accurate text or no? If he admits that it is desirable, let him tell us whether he 65
admits that sundry errors are imported into those books every day by the
ignorance of correctors or the negligence of scribes. If this cannot be denied,
why does he not welcome these efforts of mine, which contribute more than
anything else to the double object of mending corruptions and preserving
from corruption what is correct? For there is no denying that there are   70
corruptions in most of our manuscripts – in fact, in almost all. Then let him
tell us whether it is important that the Scriptures should be correctly
understood or no. If he thinks it is important, why does he condemn my
efforts, which have explained so many passages that even he, learned as he
is, never understood before? Let him read my work through and deny if he   75
can that what I say is true.

3. He says that many people have tried to undermine and do away with
the Vulgate text, some to add elegance of style, others to exclude error, but
that all attempts have failed. Is the man not ashamed of such palpable

* * * * *

51 Augustine declares] See the beginning of the *Quaestiones in Heptateuchum* 1 (cc
   33:1); *De civitate Dei* 11.19.
53 all things] Virgil *Eclogues* 8.63; *Adagia* II iii 94
59 Jonah] In Jonah 4:6 God provides some shade for the weary prophet in the form
   of a common plant – a gourd, according to the Vulgate. In Jerome's translation
   the plant was an ivy, and Augustine reported that this unaccustomed word,
   when used by a bishop, had caused a disturbance among his flock in the city of
   Oea. In his reply Jerome tried to clarify the nature of that plant for which Latin
   apparently had no name; see Jerome's Ep 112.22, in reply to Augustine's Ep 71
   (CSEL 34:253, 322; 55:392).

nonsense? Let him produce one person who has tried this – unless perhaps   80
he will put forward the sole name of Lefèvre.

4. He writes that among all the Latin and Greek scholars who abound in
Paris and Germany and England and Scotland no one has dared to attempt
this, although Lefèvre has lately made the attempt, criticizing this edition of
mine and carping at it here and there.   85

5. And who can fail to see how openly false it is to say that in these
countries there are so many men skilled in Latin and Greek? – especially in
Scotland, while of Italy he says nothing. This makes me suspect that the man
is a Scot.

6. Then what is more foolish than this line of argument? 'In Paris there   90
are a great many learned philosophers; it is therefore forbidden for this or
that individual to attempt any innovation in philosophy.' Let there be many
thousands of them: even so one person must make a start. And none the less
I suppose that in all that multitude I am not absolutely last, as far as
knowledge of the two tongues is concerned.   95

7. He says that Lorenzo was the start of the trouble; as though Lorenzo
had translated the New Testament, or Jerome had not done the same thing
long before his time.

8. Then he is most foolishly indignant because I subject Christ's words
to the rules of Donatus – just as though Christ had spoken in the exact words 100
used by our translator. On the contrary, as it is known that the apostles
wrote Greek, though not very correctly, I have not changed a single letter in
the language they used; much less have I wished to bring Christ's words
under the rule of law.

9. It is ridiculous too to make me responsible for the rules of grammar, as 105
though it were I who am the authority for good Latin, rather than authors
who wrote before the birth of Christ.

10. 'Erasmus reckons this decree unworthy,' says he. Quite the
contrary: it is the papal decretals which lay down that a document shall be

* * * * *

81 Lefèvre] Jacques Lefèvre d'Etaples; cf Ep 315 introduction.
84 Lefèvre] In his commentary on the Pauline Epistles he had criticized an
   interpretation in Erasmus' New Testament of 1516; see Epp 597:37n, 765.
89 Scot] Cf Allen Ep 993:17.
97 done the same thing] As Lorenzo Valla; cf above line 23n and Ep 182.
100 Donatus] The grammar of Aelius Donatus was so popular in the Middle Ages
   that his name came to connote grammar in general.
109 decretals] Cf 'Apologia' (LB VI f **2 verso; Ep 373:19–20). Erasmus was probably
   recalling *Decreta* part 1 distinctio 9 chs 3–6 in the *Corpus iuris canonici*.
   This quotes Augustine admitting errors in his own works and insisting that, in
   order to be authoritative, the text of Scripture must be freed from errors, using

rejected as spurious if a manifest blunder is detected in it, and another   110
decree carefully legislates for public instruction in the three ancient
languages as being essential for the understanding of Scripture.

11. His standard for the purity of Latin is ancient usage, as Augustine
wrote; as though I used any other standard, or the translator wrote in the
style of his Ancients. The next thing, I suppose, will be a demand that we   115
should all adopt his own flowers of style.

12. And all through this discussion he confuses elegance of language,
which is a question for grammarians, with eloquence and with poetic style,
as though there were no difference, and asserts that the way we should
express ourselves depends entirely on the precedent of Holy Scripture,   120
finding fault in passing with all those sainted authors whose writing is most
unlike the example set by the language of the apostles. If we are not allowed
to write in any other fashion, how dare he write this stammering stuff himself
and use so many monstrous expressions, none of which is to be found in the
writings of the apostles?   125

13. Meanwhile he dreams up the idea that the Latin translator
produced what we now have under the inspiration of the Holy Spirit,
though Jerome himself in his preface openly testifies that each translator
renders to the best of his ability what he is capable of understanding.
Otherwise, Jerome himself would be grossly irreligious, in that he is not   130
afraid to find fault sometimes with what we have in this edition.

14. In order to prove that all eloquence must be sought from Holy
Scripture, he produces Jerome as his authority, although Jerome credits
some of the prophets with uneducated language and Paul with ignorance of
Greek, and that too in more than one passage.   135

15. We believe that Augustine likewise had the assistance of the Holy
Spirit in expounding the books of Scripture; and yet he revises his work and
wishes it to be read with a critical eye.

16. Besides which, the objection he raises against himself, following
Jerome, that the saints were more eloquent in their mother tongue than in   140
any other, is thus dissolved by our expert logician. 'If it is a question,' says

* * * * *

Hebrew and Greek as a basis. Erasmus may also have thought of Jerome's
preface (see below line 447n) which acknowledges the papal request to revise
the New Testament.
110 another decree] It dated from the Council of Vienne, 1311–12, but is slightly
    misrepresented here. See Epp 182:205n, 337:733–5.
128 preface] To the Pentateuch (PL 28:179–84)
134 prophets] *Prologus in Ieremiam* (PL 28:903)
135 more than one passage] Cf Ep 844:91n.
137 revises] In his *Retractationes;* cf Ep 810:132n.

he, 'of the flatulent and windy verbiage admired by the world, I at least do
not refuse to call the saints inarticulate. But if the saints meant rustic
barbarism when they criticized the prophets, it is right in our day to have a
higher opinion of them.' As though the word 'eloquence' changed its   145
meaning when wrongly used, or as though we thought the apostles foolish
and rustic in their statements of principle, in which the most important part
of eloquence is to be found, or as though Cyprian's style must be windy
verbiage because it is unlike the language of the prophets.

   17. He then concludes this elegant syllogism by telling us that all the   150
folly and falsehood of the poets must be rejected, in order to secure the truth
of his conclusion. It goes like this (and I quote the precise words, so let no
one suspect me of fabricating my charges): 'The sole source for purity of
language, for ornament, for elegance or eloquence, lies in Holy Scripture
alone.' But what has eloquence in prose or verse to do with grammar? This is 155
where the amphora started that suddenly turned out to be a storage-jar. St
Augustine on the other hand, to whom he refers, tells his friend Licentius to
return to his familiar Muses. And Jerome makes himself familiar with Cicero's
dialogues to get himself a more abundant style. Did any of the Ancients draw
his style from any other source than the works of orators and poets? Who   160
ever attempted to enrich his vocabulary out of Holy Scripture? Finally, has
anyone by despising the poets immediately achieved eloquence of this
sacred and prophetical variety?

   18. And surely anyone can see that this famous argument of his
contains manifest blasphemy. He says that the only elegance is to be found in 165
Holy Scripture; does this mean that only elegance is to be found there? Yet
what Augustine says, whom he quotes as an authority, is not the same as
what this man meant – although he is too illiterate to express what he did
mean. For Augustine argues, not that eloquence is to be found solely in Holy
Scripture, but that it does not lack eloquence, while possessing wisdom   170
whose handmaid he thinks eloquence should be, although he admits it is
eloquence of a different kind. And yet he calls in question whether Scripture
should be credited with any share of eloquence, though of its other virtues
he has no doubt.

   19. To ignore for the moment that it does not immediately follow, if you   175
      * * * * *

148 Cyprian's style] Cf Allen Ep 1000:65–116.
156 amphora] Horace *Ars poetica* 21, 22
156 St Augustine] Cf *De ordine* 1.8.24 (CC 29:100–1) and Erasmus' *Methodus*,
    prefacing the New Testament in the 1516 edition (*Ausgewählte Werke*, Darm-
    stadt 1967–   , III 50–1).
158 Jerome] Cf *Adversus Rufinum* 1.16 (PL 23:428–9).
167 Augustine] Cf perhaps De *doctrina christiana* 4.6.9–7.21 (CC 32:121–31).

can produce a certain number of rhetorical figures from the writings of the apostles, that perfect eloquence is to be found in them, since Jerome and Origen and Chrysostom are often offended by their inversions, their uncompleted arguments, and the other drawbacks of their style; but in apostles we do not expect Aristotelian or Platonic philosophy, any more 180 than wealth or servants, and equally we do not expect eloquence.

20. After that, he strings together three prodigious lies when he says, pointing at me, 'What then can a man now have in mind who tries to bring back into the daylight the version of Lorenzo Valla that was condemned long ago, except to make the language of Holy Scripture look despicable and 185 inept?' To begin with, everyone knows it to be false that Lorenzo made a version of Holy Scripture. Still more false is it that his annotations were condemned long ago. Falsest of all, his remark that anyone who publishes them is trying to make the language of Holy Scripture look despicable. On the contrary, it is made both more luminous and more attractive by the 190 removal of portentous errors, imported into it by his own old friends.

21. Then he lets fly against me and makes a tremendous fuss because in a proverb somewhere I compared Holy Scripture in passing to those Silenus figures spoken of by Alcibiades, although the same view is held in different language by every orthodox theologian. What comparison could be more 195 appropriate? And this man speaks as though no one but he understands the Scriptures – because he is innocent of anything in the way of culture! – and as though I were incapable of achieving any of the discoveries of which he is so proud.

22. And look at the shameless falsehoods which he aims at me, 200 declaring that by this comparison I make a mock of Holy Scripture! When all that I say there aims at the praise and glory of Christ and of his holy word, as must be obvious to all who read what I write. A fine example of that heavenly eloquence that he and he alone has acquired – without opening the poets, from his studies in Holy Writ! – the virtue of which is to make shameless 205 attacks with a lot of trumped-up charges against another man's reputation.

23. It is the same folly that makes him say I deprive Holy Writ of its eloquence, when in so many passages I speak highly of it. I am concerned with nothing but the translation; and if I have any fault to find with the apostles, I state openly that it lies in their language, and even so, I do not 210 criticize or correct it.

24. Our self-appointed inquisitor ordains that all the poets shall be thrown away, although, as I say, Augustine tells his friends to go back to

* * * * *

193 proverb] *Adagia* III iii 1; cf Ep 337:546–7.
213 as I say] Cf lines 156–8.

them and so often quotes them with respect; nor is he alone in this. And why
mention the poets, as though it was with their aid that I corrected the New 215
Testament rather than on the authority of ancient and orthodox Fathers who
are read with approval by the whole church?

25. After this he invokes all the authority of a certain Thomas (I cannot
think it is Aquinas), who wrote a commentary on Boethius' *Consolation of
Philosophy*, to prove his assertion that all the poets should be thrown away, 220
because Boethius speaks of the torn garments of the Muses. He does not
notice that, ragged as they are, they tell him what he is to write, and that he
relaxes in lyric verse all through his book; nor does he drive away all the
Muses, but only those of the theatre, and not even them completely, but only
while he is in such great grief, which needs a more powerful remedy. I will 225
forgive anyone who looks down on the Muses as Boethius looked down on
them; but this man rejects poetry as gold and jewels are rejected by donkeys.

26. Furthermore, while Boethius called the elegiac Muses 'all in rags'
because they bear all the outward marks of sorrow, our friend adapts the
epithet to poetry as a whole, and says they are called ragged in two ways, 230
actively because they tear men's minds to rags and passively because they
rest on no unbroken basis of reason. Both remarks are equally absurd.

27. He then goes further and, since elegance of style depends not on
reason but on authority, he challenges me to put forward two examples, one
from the poets and one from Holy Scripture, and stand or fall by the result. I 235
therefore put forward that phrase from the Apocalypse 'He that is and was
and is to come' – words which are attributed to St John, so let us have no
quibbling about the translation; and the other from the poets 'Well begun is
half done.'

28. Not but what he has forgotten all this time that Augustine speaks of 240
more eminent authors, meaning classics like Plautus, Sallust, Cicero, and
others like them, and says that elegance of style depends upon their

* * * * *

218 Thomas] The attribution to Aquinas had justly been rejected by Josse Bade; cf
P. Courcelle *La Consolation de philosophie dans la tradition littéraire* (Paris 1967)
322–3. The commentary is found in many old editions of Boethius; and in vol 32
of the Vivès edition of St Thomas (Paris 1871–   ). There is no evidence that
Thomas Wallensis is the author, as Allen thought.
221 Boethius] *De consolatione philosophiae* 1.1.3
236 'He ... to come'] Rev 4:8, a celebrated phrase in which the first and third
members are expressed with participles (which is good grammar) and the
middle one with an imperfect indicative (which is barbarous).
238 'Well ... done'] Horace *Epistles* 1.2.40; succinct elegance has rendered the
expression proverbial – see *Adagia* I ii 39.
240 Augustine] See above line 109n.

authority and not on the Holy Spirit. And yet the language of the apostles does not conform to their authority.

29. Not to mention, at the same time, that when Augustine lays it 245 down, following Quintilian, that good writing has a threefold purpose, to instruct, to entertain, and to move the reader, this man refers it to the authority of St Thomas. And who can deny that we owe this to the Holy Spirit, when he without the Holy Spirit gives so much entertainment – though he does not instruct us, or move us except to laughter? 250

30. He reasons moreover, in his idiot fashion, as follows: 'Hitherto the church has used this version: if the version is done away, the church did not possess the Holy Spirit.' I will now reason in my turn, thus: 'Ambrose did not possess this version: he therefore did not possess the Holy Spirit.'

31. On the contrary, the gift of the Spirit is given more lavishly, the 255 more the church acquires of other good things. In the old days she had no literature and no eloquence, and she lacked wealth and power; now she has both, but it does not follow that Christ has deserted his spouse.

32. That countrified and simple style in which the New Testament was left to us by the apostles suited those early days; nowadays perhaps it is 260 fitting that we should have it in neater dress, provided it be simple still.

33. And all the time, all through this argument, the solecisms which we find in our Latin New Testament, and even the errors which his old friends have introduced in no small number, are ascribed by him to the authority of the Holy Spirit – with barefaced impudence, for it would be improper to do 265 such a thing even with the apostles.

34. Finally, he settles the question with a syllogism more than worthy of Chrysippus. 'Eloquence stems from authority; it is therefore not a science. From the authority of the lesser judges or the greater? Not from the lesser; from the greater therefore. But no man is greater than the Holy Spirit. It is 270 unlawful therefore to make any innovations in the New Testament.' Who can read such stuff and not roar with laughter?

35. Besides this, he makes a malicious attack on a statement in a certain letter of mine to Dorp that the leaders of the church have been more concerned with a knowledge of the ancient tongues than with sophistic or 275 Aristotelian philosophy, since in particular they took steps to encourage the tongues as being absolutely necessary, but did nothing of the sort for

* * * * *

245 Augustine] *De doctrina christiana* 4.12.27 (CC 32:135), but Augustine's quotation is closer to Cicero *Orator* 21.69 than to Quintilian 3.5.2.

268 Chrysippus] Head of the Stoic school of philosophy in the third century BC, whose interest in logic was well-known

274 letter ... to Dorp] Ep 337:733–7, by then repeatedly reprinted

277 but] reading *autem* for *aut*

sophistic philosophy; in fact, it is called in question in the *Decreta*, some great
authorities disapproving of it. At this point, he accused me of a triple
falsehood. 'Not at all,' he says 'every wise man teaches that without   280
philosophy it is impossible to understand the Scriptures.' But out of this
large party, he does not produce a single name. If he did produce one, it
would not touch me, for I am speaking of the warnings conveyed in the
Decreta.

36. Secondly, he admits that the study of philosophy has aroused   285
doubts, but not, he says, disapproval. That is exactly what I say. A subject,
therefore, which has been encouraged by decree and never doubted is much
more reliable.

37. He also denies that the study of philosophy has ever been
disapproved of by eminent authorities. He will not deny it if he reads   290
Origen, Jerome, Ambrose.

38. But then he argues against me on this point as though I condemned
the study of philosophy, when all I did was compare it with practice in the
tongues. At least it cannot be denied that the gift of tongues was given to the
apostles as something essential for the preaching of the Gospel; that they   295
were given a knowledge of the philosophy of Plato or Aristotle is not on
record – although a reasonable study of philosophy has my emphatic
approval.

39. It is absurd that he should expect the interpreter, the man who
makes a translation, to seek his style from the Holy Spirit without any   300
reading of classical authors, and should deny that anyone can compass an
explanation, which is really a more excellent gift of prophecy, except with
the help of Aristotelian philosophy.

40. This first conclusion, as he calls it, he rounds off by saying that all
poets were thieves and robbers, who came later. And yet most of the poets   305
were before Christ; nor does he distinguish what a poet is, so that he seems
to thrust Damasus, Gregory of Nazianzus, and Prudentius down into this
class.

41. Then, as though forgetting what he has just said, he admits that in
the sacred books there is no elegance of style; but thus it seemed good to   310
God, he says, to save the human race by foolishness. Nor did any of the
saints dare, he says, to alter the style of the translators, although that is what
Jerome did, when the Septuagint had already been accepted in the public

* * * * *

307 this class] Prudentius is the greatest poet of Christian antiquity; Gregory did
write many poems, but is better known as a theologian. Pope Damasus I (d 384)
was primarily concerned with placing the text of Scripture, the creed, and the
institution of the papacy on solid foundations.

usage of the church for nearly five hundred years. Besides which he was not
afraid to alter a Hebraism too harsh for modern ears, which we can still see in   315
Augustine's book on the idioms of the Old Covenant.

42. 'The man who denies,' he says, 'that this version is Jerome's flies in
the face of the whole world, of every rank in the ministry, and of the whole
established order. The Roman church herself confesses that her version is
Jerome's, and sets his prefaces at its head.' Those are his words. Let him   320
substantiate what he asserts so boldly. The church of Rome has never
pronounced on this point, and it is the consensus of scholars that this
version is not Jerome's.

43. What then is the point of the abuse he levels at me? 'No doubt they
are all liars, and he alone is speaking the truth.' As though I alone had said   325
what thousands of scholars freely admit.

44. But Jerome's prefaces are added. Is that surprising, they being so
informative? Though some of them are not Jerome's.

45. Then he expects me to make it clear that Jerome disapproves of some
things which are found in my edition. Let him read Jerome for himself and   330
convict me of falsehood if he can.

46. He says that the church cannot err. Is the church in error instantly if
there is a corruption in your copy of the text? And yet some things can
happen to the church of which she has no previous experience. And I
maintain, not that in this translation there is anything that can undermine   335
the orthodox faith, but that there are defects which it is worth while to point
out. Read my own version, and if you do not find hundreds of passages
which you, good scholar as you are, have hitherto misunderstood, have the
law on me to your heart's content.

47. 'You are a stumbling-block to the world,' he says, 'with your   340
innovations in things that all accept.' Not at all: all men of the highest station
and character are grateful to me, and the dogs who barked to begin with bark
no more when they have read my work. A few conceited people take offence,
who would not have it thought that there is anything they did not know.

48. 'Granting,' says he, 'that there are errors in the text, it was not right   345
to publish them for ordinary people.' On the contrary, there is every reason
to publish things that all men ought to know.

49. 'A private person,' he says, 'without authorization cannot make a
new translation or correct an old one.' In the first place, I think that I, like
others, have the right, if I have made any progress in theology, to make it   350

* * * * *

314 five hundred years] The Septuagint translation originated in Alexandria dur-
    ing the third century BC.
316 Augustine's book] *De locutionibus* (PL 34:485–546)

publicly known, having been co-opted into a faculty of theology. Secondly, I am not making a new version; I translate the Greek; and so far as I am concerned, the old version is still there for all men's use, as it always was. Last but not least, let us assume that I have no authority: does this mean that, while the ignorant are free to corrupt the sacred text, I may not correct it   355 unless a synod has been summoned first? Suppose I were a bishop or a cardinal, what has that to do with it? The business in hand calls not for a mitre or a red hat, but for skill in the tongues.

50. There is another absurdity, where he says that this is the version which refuted Jerome Hus and Wycliffe; whereas the former was burnt and   360 not confuted, and the latter's books were not condemned until after his death. And even if what he says were quite true, does it follow that it is unlawful to remove any error that may have crept into the Scriptures?

51. 'If there is any error in them,' he says, 'it should have been corrected in accordance with the ancient testimony of the Fathers.' And yet what he   365 demands is exactly what I have done; only this has escaped his notice, because he has not glanced at my book.

52. 'Leprosy,' he says, 'must be shown to the priest, whose business it is to pass judgment.' Quite right; and that is why I submitted my work to Leo the Tenth, who had encouraged me to undertake it. And he, by the agency of   370 two cardinals, approved my efforts. When he thinks fit, he will entrust to some person of his choice the task of having my books corrected by the learned. This is a province which I do not take upon myself, although I have paved the way to it.

53. As for the point he makes about the seventy separate cells, he does   375 not perceive that the force of this falls on Jerome, who makes fun of them as the constructions of some anonymous forger. If their version is attributed to the Holy Spirit, Jerome is impious, who calls it somewhere a forgery; and yet

* * * * *

351 faculty of theology] At Louvain: see Ep 637:12n.

360 Jerome Hus] A slight confusion: Jerome of Prague (after 1365–30 May 1416) and Jan Hus (1370/1–6 July 1415) were both burned during the Council of Constance.

361 after his death] While five bulls issued by Gregory XI in 1377 suspected John Wycliffe (c 1330–84) of heresy and listed a number of specific statements due to be investigated, a longer list of errors was drawn up by the Council of Constance in 1415, which declared him a heretic and ordered his remains to be dug up and his books to be burned.

368 'Leprosy ... judgment'] Cf Lev 13:49.

371 cardinals] See Ep 835 introduction.

375 separate cells] Occupied by the translators of the Septuagint; see Jerome *Praefatio in Pentateuchum*, also quoted in *Adversus Rufinum* 2.25; cf Ep 326:90–2.

this verdict of Jerome's is accepted by the church in respect of several books
of the Old Covenant.   380

54. The same wisdom is evident in his remark that the Greeks falsified
their texts when they split off from the Roman church. And what, pray, was
the reason why they should corrupt them all? Moreover, their separation
from the Roman church being quite recent, how comes it that their modern
texts and their very ancient ones are in agreement? How comes it that Origen   385
and Basil and Chysostom – and Latin Fathers too, Ambrose, Jerome, Hilary,
Cyprian – are in accord with their falsified texts and disagree with ours? Did
the Greeks falsify at one stroke the texts used by all these authors?

55. Moreover, where I had objected, following the papal decrees, that
the true text of the New Testament ought to be checked against the Greek   390
copies, he admits that in ancient times this was appropriate, but says that
nothing could be less so now. And the reason he gives is their separation. As
though the revolt of the Greeks had made any difference to their text of the
Gospels!

56. But if the fact that the Greeks have split off from the Roman church   395
is a valid reason for mistrusting the Greek text of the Bible, it was equally
illicit in Jerome's day to correct the Old Testament out of the Hebrew texts,
for the Jewish people had already rebelled, not from the Roman church but
from Christ himself, which I consider somewhat more damnable.

57. Last but not least, if we are to put our trust exclusively in the books   400
of Greeks who are not schismatics, it is precisely their texts that I follow for
preference; but they do not differ from the schismatics' copies.

58. But his master-stroke of impudence is that, whereas I had written
that it is more difficult for a Greek text to be corrupted than for one of ours, he
makes out that I said it was impossible for Greek codices to be damaged in   405
any way; and though the reason I adduced was the difficulty of Greek script,
which is made up not merely of letters but of ligatures and accents, this liar
says the reason I gave was that the Greek language allows no scope for
falsehood. What monstrous effrontery – especially as my letter still exists and
has been printed more than once!   410

59. And on this point he maintains that I contradict Augustine, who
wrote that Luke was the only gospel accepted by Greek heretics. What is it to
us, if the Greeks had their heretics? Is it a reason for corruption in Latin texts,
that heretics have arisen among the Latins? I myself in this work follow none

* * * * *

389 papal decrees] See lines 108–112.
403 I had written] In Ep 337:800–5
411 Augustine] Cf De haeresibus 30 (cc 46:304).

but orthodox authorities; and even so, there are places where it would be   415
right to give heretics too a hearing. What new critical spirit have we here?

60. He attacks me for stating that the Greeks do not differ from the
Roman church in those doctrines which are set forth in the books of the New
Testament, and that the only points in dispute are in ancient times the word
homusius and nowadays certain questions of liturgy and the jurisdiction and   420
poverty of the Roman pontiff. 'Let the man read Augustine's *De haeresibus*,'
says he, 'and he will learn what he has been ignorant of hitherto.' What sort
of argument, if you please, is this? Everybody knows that various heresies
arose among the Greeks even before they recognized the Roman church, and
yet in those days they were reputed orthodox. I am talking about schism, and   425
the questions on which those Greeks differ from us who have separated
themselves from the Roman See.

61. If, however, he contends that the Greeks did manipulate their texts,
at least the passages they corrupted were those which appeared to
undermine their schismatic opinions. Then let him produce one single   430
passage which can be suspect on those grounds. In actual fact, if anything
can arouse suspicion in the Greek texts, it will be above all the passages
which were thought to tell in favour of the Arians or the school of Origen; for
the whole of Greece seems to have been united in such hatred or jealousy of
them in particular that, although their authors have taken from Origen as   435
their source almost everything they tell us that is worth having, they seem to
have had nothing so much at heart, none the less, as the complete
destruction of everything he wrote – which would have been enough, even
in isolation, to give us an understanding of Holy Scripture. I overlook for the
moment the way in which he tells me to read Augustine on heresies as   440
though he were the only man who had ever read it, or as though I could not
read it unless instructed to by him, or as though I do not in fact cite evidence
from that work in several places.

62. We have surveyed the keen thinker and the brilliant writer, and I
cannot refrain from giving you at the same time an example of the wit. This is   445
the kind of elegant sally in which this facetious fellow, the Graces' favourite
son, indulges at my expense. 'Jerome remarks,' says he, 'that there are as
many different texts as there are copies. Some men follow one copy and some
another; which is our poor translator to take as his authority? At any rate, my
dear Jerome, saint as you are, it was to no purpose that Pope Damasus drove   450

* * * * *

417 stating] In Ep 337:790–5
435 from Origen] Cf Ep 844:272–4.
447 Jerome] In the preface, addressed to Pope Damasus I, of his edition of the
       Gospels (PL 29:558)

you to work so hard, when there was in existence a Greek copy faultless at all
points, which our translator has now unearthed. O my dear Jerome, what a
blinking night-owl you were, if you could not find such a copy as our friend,
a mere beginner, has now found!' Such are his words, and as I recall them I
think of Hercules at Lindus, and how he enjoyed the flood of abuse as he sat   455
at dinner. In the old days there were as many different texts as there were
copies, and now it is not so. So what did Jerome follow in correcting the text?
And another point: did I really depend on a single copy?

63. Again, repeating his initial assumption that by my new translation I
wish to do away with the old, he recommends to me the rule of Augustine,   460
who 'in the canonical writings follows the authority of the great majority of
churches, which should include of course those which were important
enough to have apostles as their bishops and to have epistles addressed to
them. A man will therefore observe this limitation in the canonical books: he
will prefer those which are accepted by all catholic churches to those which   465
certain of them do not accept, and among those which are not accepted by all
churches he will prefer those received by more numerous and important
churches to those held by churches which are fewer and less authoritative. If
however he finds that some are held by the majority of churches and others
by the more important ones, though such a thing is not easy to find,' and so   470
forth. From all this he infers that my translation can carry no weight at all. But
how am I affected by what is said in this passage about the rejection or
acceptance of books, and not about the correction of the text? Otherwise,
why did Augustine himself accept Jerome's version, which was entirely
new? And besides, what scope will be left for this rule of Augustine's, if the 475
only thing all the churches are allowed to accept is what has already been
accepted by the church of Rome? Not that I am against Augustine, but
because it is clear that he did not recognize the authority of the Roman See
which we now accord it; all the more so as, when writing to Innocent, he
addresses him as brother and gives no hint of his supreme eminence, but   480
treats him as a colleague.

64. After this he proceeds as though I thought there were some
falsehood or folly in those Scriptures in which I admit that there is some

* * * * *

455 Lindus] *Adagia* II v 19. Hercules killed and ate two oxen belonging to a peasant
at Lindus in the island of Rhodes, and maintained that the owner's curses made
his meat taste all the sweeter.
460 Augustine] *De doctrina christiana* 2.8.12 (CC 32:39)
474 Jerome's version] Cf above line 23n.
480 eminence] There is little substance to Erasmus' claim, except that Augustine
and other bishops quite properly addressed Pope Innocent I as brother; see
Augustine Epp 175–7.

obscurity. On the contrary, if there is anything false or foolish in the copies, it is attributable not to the apostles but to the old cronies of this muck-raking   485 critic. And in any case I make no changes that affect the solid basis of the faith.

65. He instructs me therefore that I ought to have sent my book to the supreme pontiff for him to decide whether it should be suppressed or published. On that argument every book ought to be sent to the supreme   490 pontiff, for every book might contain matter of offence for someone. But Thomas never did such a thing, nor did Scotus, nor for that matter did Augustine or Jerome. They published first, and the approval followed, and was not asked for. And furthermore, as I do not uproot the old version, but by publishing a revision of it make it easier for us not only to possess it in a   495 purer form but to understand it better, how could I suspect that there would be malignant critics like this man, ready to take offence at a work that would benefit everyone? If anyone had cause to fear a stumbling-block, it was those that are weak; yet on their side no cause of stumbling has arisen. All this trouble has been stirred up solely by two or three people of the class   500 commonly accounted perfect, who when my book was not yet published poisoned the minds of simple folk everywhere and condemned what as yet they knew nothing of, rousing prejudice against my work before it was known what good it could do. It is their fault, not mine, if any man has been offended.   505

66. Again, that I should have dared to dedicate it to Leo the Tenth, he calls temerity. 'The poets,' he says, 'show brazen temerity in dedicating their worst obscenities to those who are endowed with the highest positions in the church.' And why did our muck-raker suddenly drag the poets in at this point? Or who pray are those poets who dedicate their filth to bishops? Far   510 from that, I dedicated my work to the pope in response to a letter to me from himself; nor did he think it too much to read a large part of it with his own eyes. Men of the greatest authority can testify that having read it he gave it the highest praise in the hearing of the cardinals and scholars who were with him. And, as I said before, he sent me an answer by the agency of two   515 cardinals.

67. In any case, what does he mean by 'authorize'? Put through such tests that there is no error left? If that is the law, nothing we have is authorized outside the canonical Scriptures. Nor is that what I asked of Leo.

* * * * *

501 perfect] Apparently the academic theologians; cf below lines 538–42.
511 in response] This is probably a confusion; see Ep 835 introduction; cf above
    lines 370–1.

I merely draw men's attention, leaving the decision to scholars, if they have   52c
found something more correct.

68. After these declamatory flights he spreads himself in a more
agreeable field and portrays for us the gifts of a translator out of Augustine
and Thomas, but all the time confusing at every point the gift of the tongues
or of interpretation and the gift of prophecy, which according to Paul are   52°
different gifts. He declares that no one can translate Scripture unless he is
provided with the gift of the Holy Ghost. And yet I have shown that St
Jerome's view was different, though he is the translator of both Testaments.

69. Besides this, while there is, I suppose, no one today arrogant
enough to claim that he has the gift of prophecy or of the tongues, it is rash to   530
pass judgment on the spirit of other men. I have striven to convey the very
truth, following in the footsteps of the orthodox Fathers, nor have I set any
goal before me save the reader's profit and Christ's glory. As I toiled, from
time to time I sought the guidance of the Holy Spirit; at least there was no lack
of good intentions. Further, what angel was it gave you the idea that the   53.
Spirit's aid was denied me as I sought to do good, while you fancy he was
one of your privy council as you penned these scurrilous attacks – attacks,
moreover, on a work you had never even seen? Nor is the identity of your
paraclete concealed from me. He who poured calumnies on a work that did
not yet exist – he was your inspiration in criticizing a work you had not read,   54°
if we can call it criticism to spew what filth you please over something you've
never seen.

70. He declares it unlawful for any man to teach without public
authorization. Does it not satisfy him that I have the same authorization that
Thomas had? (Not that I would compare myself with him.) Does it not satisfy   54
him if I do it at the urgent request of the best of prelates and on encouragement from the pope himself? Though Thomas for that matter is not
concerned with publishing texts, but with public sermons or lectures.

71. He maintains that Jerome did not dare undertake a version of Holy

* * * * *

525 Paul] Cf 1 Cor 12:10.
535 you] Here and in line 629 Erasmus lapses inadvertently into the second person,
     as though Lee were addressed directly; corrected in the *Epistolae ad diversos* of
     1521.
538 your paraclete] Here and in lines 571, 633 we find probably the first hints at
     Erasmus' conviction that his growing difficulties in Louvain were caused in the
     first place by Jan Briart of Ath (cf Ep 670 introduction), theologian and chief
     administrative officer of the University of Louvain; cf Epp 948:27n, 998
     introduction, Allen Ep 1029:2–5.
549 Jerome] The dedicatory preface to Damasus (cf line 447n) does not mention his
     translations of books of the Old Testament, but cf Epp 35–6, 56 (CSEL 54:265–85,

Scripture, except on orders from Damasus. What effrontery the man has! On   550
whose authority then did he translate the Pentateuch? At the request of a
certain Desiderius, was it not? Was it Damasus put him up to translate the
books of Esdras? Read his preface, and let this featherpate blush for his
mistakes. And then Tobit: surely he was put up to that by Chromatius and
Heliodorus? But why need I refute his falsehoods one by one, seeing that the   555
New Testament was the only thing Jerome revised at the request of Pope
Damasus?

72. It is known therefore that the New Testament was revised at the
request of Pope Damasus; but it is not known that he approved Jerome's
revision. For you cannot approve something of which you have no   560
knowledge – especially as this fellow thinks everything should be rejected
that has not achieved endorsal (to adapt his own flowers of speech) in
published instruments.

73. Though Damasus does not lay this task upon him by virtue of being
supreme pontiff of the world. Whether he was such a thing I leave an open   565
question; the name at least in those days had not yet been heard, so far as one
can gather from the writings of all the early Fathers. He lays the task as
bishop of Rome upon Jerome as being hitherto a Roman; for it was in Rome
that he was both baptized and ordained to the priesthood.

74. Meanwhile there is another surprising fact: this scandalmonger, or   570
the spirit that suborns him, has never so much as mentioned Lefèvre
d'Etaples, who showed earlier and greater audacity than I ever have, and
that too without authorization either from the pope, whom I had informed by
letter of what I was setting out to do before I set out, or from the authority
conferred on all who are accepted as professors of divinity. From this it is   575
clear that he does not so much dislike the result as wish to attack the man
who produced it.

75. So, having accomplished this to his heart's content, he goes on to
make trouble about a remark in my letter to Dorp that 'Jerome sometimes
cannot refrain from an outburst of indignation against Vigilantius, from   580
levelling insults against Jovinian and bitter invective against Rufinus.' This
he interprets as a savage and wanton attack on Jerome, as though I meant
that he was wrong in so doing, or as though Jerome while still alive was

* * * * *

497–8). The following references to three prefaces inserted in Jerome's Bible
also do not refer to an order from Damasus; cf PL 28:177–9, 1471; 29:23–6.
571 Lefèvre d'Etaples] Cf Ep 337, which had, it seems, been closely scrutinized by
    Lee, especially lines 879–905.
573 by letter] Cf Ep 835 introduction.
579 a remark] Ep 337:54–7

exempt from all human failings, and indeed as though every man of good will
did not sometimes wish that Jerome had a little more of this mildness in him.   585

76. Then again, rejecting a remark of mine that in what I write I never
reflect on any man's reputation, he objects that in a number of passages I
dissent from Thomas, from the Master of the Sentences, from Lyra, from
Hugo of Saint-Cher, as though no one could dissent without insulting or
attacking the reputation of his opponent. Could anything be more idiotic?   590
And yet, if I do dissent, it is with a prior expression of respect for those to
whom such respect is due, among whom I do not reckon Lyra or Saint-Cher.
And if some do accord them less weight than they used to, there was no
reason why to preserve their authority we must always follow a false view.

77. He says they would not tolerate it, if they were still alive. Very well: 595
let him who like a second Elisha has succeeded to their spirit play their part
for them if he can.

78. Then he thinks it an unanswerable argument against me that in my
notes on Jerome I poke fun in passing at a certain Franciscan, while I do this
without naming any names, and there is such a large crowd of Franciscans   600
for whom such fun would be appropriate. If one were to tell a story of a man's
ignorance without mentioning his name, must one be thought to insult all
one's fellow-creatures?

79. What follows, to be quite honest, I simply do not understand, but I
will copy his own words with the bloom still on them: 'I might add,' says he,   605
'that he is wrong in thus attacking this Franciscan. It is men greedy for
position or reputation, hungry for coin, empty-headed, full of words and
wind, who see to it that our text of Jerome should be thus mutilated and
corrupt. If some copies are corrupt through scribal error, let them be
corrected against ancient texts (for I reckon some can still be found that were   610
written in Jerome's own day), and let us not have new ones made which
destroy the elegance of Jerome and his eloquence and meaning.' Those are
his words.

80. My first question is: by these elegant words 'hungry for coin,
empty-headed, full of words and wind' and so forth, does he mean to   615
describe the Franciscans?

81. Secondly, is he saying that I mutilated Jerome, when I have added a

* * * * *

586 remark of mine] Ep 337:63–6
588 dissent from] Thomas Aquinas; Peter Lombard (cf Ep 456:273n); Nicholas
     of Lyra (cf Ep 372:13n); Hugo of Saint-Cher (cf Ep 459:81n) – principal repre-
     sentatives of scholastic theology in the twelfth to fourteenth centuries
596 second Elisha] Cf 2 Kings 2:9.
599 Franciscan] Henry Standish; cf Epp 337:711–17, 608:15n.

great deal to earlier editions and cut away nothing except wrong headings in
a number of places?

82. And then, am I inventing a new Jerome, and not rather restoring the   620
ancient one? Are some people so crass that they think what they are reading
now is Erasmus and not Jerome?

83. Again, do they suppose that I have corrected Jerome from any
source other than very ancient copies, which might well be thought to have
been written in the age of Jerome himself, did any such thing exist? And even   625
so, I have not been satisfied with single copies. In this department at least
very good scholars have done more work than might be thought possible.

84. What are these things that overthrow Jerome's elegance and
eloquence and meaning? Unless you find nothing elegant except what
smacks of your own style.   630

85. After this, like a spider on the warpath, he brings up some of his
venom on passages selected from the *Moria* as well, although I bet my life he
has never read it. But inspired by that guardian angel of his he says I have
never adequately defended that passage where, through the mouth of Folly,
I described the supreme reward of immortality as a kind of foolishness – a   635
statement which I instantly modify in so many words in the same passage in
order to give no offence to anyone. He wishes me to subject what I say to
certain rules. What rules? Not those followed by Augustine or by Jerome or
by Cyprian or by Thomas or by Peter Lombard, men whose wording is
scarcely defended by professional theologians. Shall we derive our rule from   640
the scholastic philosophers of our own day? They do not agree among
themselves. I agree that we should be circumspect in our references to sacred
things; that we should be hypochondriac and hypercritical I do not see.

86. If we are allowed to use no words except those of Holy Scripture,
how did Thomas dare to use so many novelties in both words and things –   645
some taken from Aristotle and some of his own invention – in not merely
expressing an opinion but laying down the law about holy things? Where do
we read in Holy Writ that the church of Christ exists essentially in the
gathering of all the faithful, by representation in the cardinals and virtually
in the Roman pontiff? (To choose this one instance out of many thousands.)   650
If we may use no comparative image that is not in Holy Writ, what shall we
make of all the orthodox Fathers who adduce countless new images to
support their teaching? No one raises loud protests against the work of a
certain Dominican, crassly stupid though it is, which gives a Christian

* * * * *

632 *Moria*] Cf *Moriae encomium*, ASD IV-3 190; Erasmus suggests that Lee is merely
    repeating Ep 337:554–6.

adaptation – distortion, rather – of all the myths in Ovid. Yet they rant on   655
against me for distorting the Sileni to fit Christ and his apostles, though I
show more reverence than they do in their own treatment of Holy Writ.

87. But what is my offence if I do attribute folly to God or to Christ,
as Paul did before me, and after Paul Augustine did in more passages than
one? May I not even use Paul's own words? I only wish that the folly which I   660
attribute to Christ and the apostles could be ascribed in real earnest to all our
bishops!

88. But pray mark this! The man has found something with which he
can simply cut my throat. In order to show how Christ had brought himself
down to the level of our weakness, I had said that there was in Christ   665
something infirm, something subject to our affections; and the blockhead
imagines that I attribute faulty passions of the mind to Christ. Whereupon,
as though he had won the day, he enjoys his triumph, proclaiming that from
time to time I posit a blemish or wrinkle in Christ; and all he says reeks of
blemishes and wrinkles.   670

89. Then, having expounded out of Thomas that the motions of the
mind are one thing in Christ and quite another in the apostles, he sums up
thus: 'Had Erasmus known the distinction between the passions of Christ
and the apostles, he would not have arrived at this opinion.' As though I
have not explained this at length, some twenty years ago, in my disputation   675
with Colet! Or as though I could not have discovered this for myself, even
had Thomas never given that lecture!

90. He goes on to get his teeth into my remark that the ecstasy of godly
men, which Plato calls a holy madness, is a kind of foretaste of future
blessedness, by which we shall be absorbed into God and shall live in future   680

* * * * *

655 Ovid] On the 'moralization' of Ovid's *Metamorphoses* in the Middle Ages, still
amply reflected in the commentaries of early printed editions, see F. Munari
Ovid im Mittelalter (Zürich 1960); J. Engels *Etudes sur l'Ovide moralisé* (Groningen
1943). The reference is probably to the *Ovidius moralizatus* of Pierre Bersuire,
published in Paris (J. Bade) in 1509. This is often ascribed to Thomas Wallensis,
an English Dominican.
656 Sileni] Cf Ep 337:545–7; *Adagia* III iii 1.
658 folly] Cf *Moriae encomium*, ASD IV-3 188; Ep 337:499–501.
659 Paul] 1 Cor 1:18–28; cf ASD IV-3 186.
659 Augustine] Cf eg *Enarratio in Psalmum* 40.1 (CC 38:449).
665 I had said] In *De tedio Iesu* against Colet (LB V 1270B, 1288A–B); cf Ep 108
introduction.
669 blemish] Cf Eph 5:27.
678 my remark] Ep 337:489–91
679 Plato] *Phaedrus* 256b

more in him than in ourselves. Whereupon he goes for me with Turlupins and Beghards, whatever they may be, who taught, it seems, that the soul is absorbed into the divinity as a drop of water put into a wine-cask is absorbed into the wine, and who also hold that all things will be as they were before the creation of the world. What have the ravings of his Turlupins and   685
Beghards to do with me? I said that the soul was absorbed by God because it is wholly rapt into him by love, and the soul exists more truly where it loves than where it gives life. For it is rapt away in such a fashion that it does not disappear but is made perfect.

91. Leaving the *Moria*, he passes to the *Enchiridion*, where, in the course   690
of urging that we should follow the mind and not the body, because it is in the mind that we bear the image of God, I wrote among other things: 'As concerns the soul, we are so far capable of divinity that we are permitted to rise even beyond the minds of the angels and to become one with God.' And again something to this effect (I have not the book handy) 'Had you no mind,   695
you would be a beast; had you no body, you would be a god'; he seems to wish to attack as though I had given it as my opinion that the human soul is a particle of the divine nature. What need is there to refute these barefaced falsehoods?

92. Returning to the *Moria*, he says it does not follow to say 'There is   700
something foolish in God; therefore God is foolish.' I beg you, dear reader, not to take offence at the language, for the meaning is pious enough, and it is on the meaning that he challenges me. But it follows well to say 'There is such a thing as the foolishness of God; therefore God can be called in some way foolish. There is such a thing as the blackness of a crow; therefore a crow   705
is black.' For that 'foolish' there is put for foolishness I have further shown out of the reading of Augustine.

93. But meanwhile he ignores the exaggeration of Paul, who speaks of the foolishness of God in contrast to his eternal and inexpressible wisdom, after showing us that of which we might somehow or other be capable. As   710
Christ took upon himself our infirmity, so he also assumed to some extent our foolishness.

94. Finally, the falsehoods he utters about the ecstasy of the three disciples do not seem to me to be worthy of refutation. He supposes this to mean an ecstasy in which a man is wholly rapt out of his bodily senses. Men   715
lose their reason from both fear and joy, so that they do not know what they

* * * * *

681 Turlupins and Beghards] Heterodox sects of the fourteenth century; cf G. Leff
     Heresy in the Later Middle Ages (Manchester 1967) I 325 and passim.
690 *Enchiridion*] LB V 11F–12E; cf Ep 858 introduction.
708 Paul] See lines 658–662.
713 ecstasy] Matt 17; cf Ep 337:487–92; *Moriae encomium*, ASD IV-3 192.

are saying, or those who are beside themselves from some other reason. It was said of Peter that he knew not what he said. This was good enough for me in a humorous piece, for I was not treating a theological theme, but writing my *Moria*.   72

95. He says that doctors of divinity were instituted to explain things in Jerome and Augustine and not in Erasmus. As though they deserved more lenient treatment because they were greater men than we are! It is the weak who deserve leniency. We are more ready to forgive a boy than a man, and we make more allowances for Augustine and Jerome in the things they   72 published when they were young. A theologian's job would indeed be a pretty one, if the sole object of his labours were to find some pretext on which to defend anything the Ancients may have said. If what they said was right, why may not I speak after the same fashion? Why find fault in me with what is approved in them? If it was not right, why defend them and find fault   73 with me on the same point? And what a policy – to defend whatever the Ancients have said, or at least to turn a blind eye to much of it, and to bring trumped-up charges against everything in the books of the moderns!

You see, my dear Maarten, what a lot of nonsense there is in that small book. Though even so I have noted a few points out of many, and already   73 repent the waste of time. And yet he is so self-confident that he dares to make you the judge whether he has said anything silly, though there are rather more silly things in his book than there are words. Such are the men who set up to teach Erasmus! And yet this is that famous book which he laboriously completed on the basis of those ten conclusions which had passed, he says,   74 through the hands of many men, and which he proposed to dedicate to some outstanding figure; and he tells us to share such valuable material with faithful and right-thinking friends. Then he summons anyone who is willing to take him on into the ring, and demands an antagonist – though we ought to respect the eminent researches of so great a scholar, for they cannot be   74 interrupted without great loss to the world. It would be truer to say that the poor man has a foul itch and wants someone to scratch himself against; and any man of sense will not go near him. I, to be sure, do not yet dislike the man enough to wish to expose him to the jeers of the learned world, though that is what he wants. Pray tell him, my dear Lips, to use his spare time more   75 fruitfully in future. If he is sound at heart, he will accept your warning and amend; if his mind is too far gone, leave him to his distemper. I hope you will devote yourself to reading sacred authors, in preference to wasting your best years on this sort of rubbish.

Farewell. 1518, 7 May   75

* * * * *

718 Peter] Luke 9:33

844 / To Johann Maier von Eck   Basel, 15 May 1518

Dated soon after Erasmus' arrival at Basel (cf Ep 843 introduction), this letter
answers some critical observations regarding his work made in Ep 769 by one of
Germany's leading theologians.

Epp 843–4 were both published in the *Auctarium*. Superficial parallels
between the two letters unfortunately left some German readers with the
incorrect impression that the unnamed critic rebuked in Ep 843 was also Eck; cf
Scheurl's Briefbuch Ep 177. While Erasmus' answer to Lee (Ep 843) shows signs
of impatience, Eck deserved a careful reply in keeping with his academic
reputation and the polite and cogent form in which he had voiced his criticisms.

DESIDERIUS ERASMUS OF ROTTERDAM TO THE DISTINGUISHED
THEOLOGIAN JOHANN ECK, GREETING

I accept with gratitude, my dear Eck, the kindness you have done me, which
is worthy of such a well read and most scholarly person as yourself. You
freely offer me what I was bound to seek with all the energy at my command,   5
and I appreciate it all the more because it comes unasked, to prove that the
proverb Goods given away will soon decay is not always in place. In the
encomiums, however, which you pile upon me with more zeal than reason, I
can accept and welcome nothing except the sincerity of your feelings
towards me. It is for you and your like to strive for the palm of greatness; I am   10
a small man and my themes are small. As for the carping critics (if there can be
any who bear ill will to one so insignificant as myself), what surprises me in
them above all is that none are more unpleasant in their protests against my
work (which, if not very profitable, at least does no harm) than those who
never on any account open what I write, or those who stood to gain most   15
from it, if they would not rather rail at a man than learn from him. But you, in
your scholarly way, spend almost too much time in preparing the ground
before giving me your advice, although you credit me with so much good
nature – if you really mean what you say. Personally, I am never reluctant to
receive advice from any quarter, so far am I from demanding to be advised   20
with deep respect by a man of your distinction. All the same, there is rather
more respect – or should I say, civility? – in your preamble and your
transitional passages than in the advice itself; for you put your matter

* * * * *

844
7 proverb] Cf *Adagia* I ix 53.
11 critics] Erasmus uses the name of Zoilus, an ancient scholar impossible to
please; see *Adagia* II v 8.

forward as though you were reporting mistaken charges made by others and
follow up your points as though you were defending your own opinion.   25

To begin with, in the passage you adduce from my notes on the second
chapter of Matthew, you can see that this is a disjunctive sentence consisting
of two alternatives, although one of its two halves is rejected; your friends
pick on one half only, and that the less acceptable half. But it is forbidden,
you will say, to have any doubts at all on this point. How do you know that I   30
have any? I am quoting other men's opinions. It does not immediately follow
that because a thing is not certain, I regard it as uncertain. And then I quote a
passage, the fifth chapter of Micah, where St Jerome in his commentary
reviews the same opinions as I do – putting them, you say, in someone else's
mouth; I agree, but not a heretic's – and his review ends in not rejecting   35
either side. Nor, in my view, would the authority of the whole of Scripture
be instantly imperilled, as you suggest, if an evangelist by a slip of memory
did put one name for another, Isaiah for instance instead of Jeremiah, for this
is not a point on which anything turns. We do not instantly form a low
opinion of the whole of Peter's life because Augustine and Ambrose affirm   40
that he suffered a few lapses even after he had received the Spirit from
heaven, nor does a book forthwith lose all credence if it contains some
blemish. Augustine and Jerome are great authorities and are read even with
reverence, although no one denies that in their books there are many
departures from the truth; heaven forbid that Christian readers should be so   45
difficult to please. Nor do we immediately deprive them of the Holy Spirit.
But perhaps it is not for us to dictate how that Spirit shall tune the instrument
that he makes of his disciples; however he may have done this, he has done it
in the way that he knew to be most conducive to the salvation of the human
race. He was present in them so far as pertained to the business of the   50
Gospel, but with this limitation, that in other respects he allowed them to be
human none the less. I would not wish to say this because I think the
apostles ever did make mistakes, but because I deny that the presence of
some mistake must needs shake the credit of the whole of Scripture.

Again, if it seems to you unworthy that the apostles should use books   55
to help them, what will you make of Paul, who gives instructions for books

* * * * *

26 passage you adduce] Ep 769:43–68
33 Jerome] *Commentarii in Micheam* 2.5.3. (CC 76:481–2), quoted in LB VI 14D.
   Jerome mentions that in the opinion of some people errors occurred in the
   transmission of the Old Testament. He does so in support of his own view that
   Matthew corrected an inconsistency in Mic 5:2.
34 you say] As in line 78, a hypothetical objection
40 Augustine and Ambrose] Cf *Novum Testamentum*, LB VI 807D–810C; Ep 956:39n.
56 Paul] 2 Tim 4:13

to be sent him with his cloak, 'but especially the parchments'? Nor did Christ
tell them not to read the Scriptures (to the reading of which Paul urges his
beloved Timothy), but not to appear before their judges with speeches
carefully prepared. But on this topic I reply more fully in a later edition of the   60
volume, which I am now getting ready; and so I reckon it unnecessary to
burden a letter with further argument.

In the same way, with the second objection you raise, on the tenth
chapter of Acts, where, putting the case for the apostles, I excuse them on
the ground that they learnt their Greek not from the speeches of Demos-   65
thenes but from the conversation of ordinary people: I do not deny the gift of
tongues, but yet it does not follow that they could not learn their Greek from
ordinary speech. Syriac at any rate they learnt from ordinary speech; why
could they not do the same with Greek as well? For thanks to the victories of
Alexander and the Roman empire, Egypt with most of Syria and the whole of   70
Asia Minor, or rather, almost the whole of the East, as Jerome says, spoke
Greek. For I do not suppose that the Spirit to which you refer drowned in
oblivion what they had previously learnt. If however you maintain that the
Greek which we see in the Apostolic Epistles is a gift from heaven, whence
comes all that clumsiness of language, not to say barbarism, which we cannot   75
attempt to conceal? For the works of the Holy Spirit are more perfect than
those of nature or of human industry, for which Chrysostom is our
authority. But, you say, he gave them just so much skill in the language as he
thought suitable to the simplicity of the Gospel. What if the apostles
possessed that already? Why need they be given it now? We are not told that   80
the apostles spoke Greek by some miracle; we are told that they spoke in
some one language, if I mistake not, and were understood by everyone. Let
this by all means be what happened; there is even so no need to work a
continuing series of miracles in the apostles. As often as the business of the
faith called for it, they possessed the gift of tongues; they did not all have it   85
equally, nor was it always present; we read that it happened to the apostles
only once. There is also the gift of prophecy; the man to whom it was given,
to explain this or that passage, would not have been able at any other time

* * * * *

57 Christ] Cf Matt 10, especially 10:19, cf 10:10. Erasmus treated the problem of
   divine inspiration and human ignorance in the apostles more fully in his notes
   on Matt 2 and Acts 10 (LB VI 12–14, 476–8).
58 Paul urges] 2 Tim 3:14–16
63 second objection] Ep 769:68–83
71 Jerome] See perhaps PL 25:545–59, 26:380–2; cf LB VI 476–8; also for the
   following reference to Chrysostom.
87 only once] Cf LB VI 441F, commenting on Acts 2:8.

you please to explain any other passage. That same Spirit distributed his
gifts according to the measure of faith, as Paul puts it.   90

Finally, how can it be that Jerome in so many places is not afraid to
charge Paul with an imperfect knowledge of Greek? He also asserts that
Luke knew more Greek than Hebrew, because he came from Antioch; and on
the other hand that Paul had a better command of his native language than
he had of Greek, because he was a Cilician. Again, in the second Epistle to   95
the Corinthians he wishes his faithful Titus was present because, he says, he
had greater skill in the language, as the early Greeks understand the
passage. Origen, at any rate, and the Greek commentators find difficulties in
Paul in many places from the uncouthness of his style, and so does Jerome.
So it is not necessary that whatever was in the apostles should at once be   100
attributed to a miracle. Christ allowed his chosen to make mistakes even after
they had received the Paraclete, but not to the extent of imperilling the faith,
just as today we admit that the church can err in places, but short of any risk
to faith and religion. In any case, how do you know whether Christ did not
wish to reserve the credit of being right without exception for himself alone?   105
He said of himself alone 'I am the Truth'; so it may be that he who according
to the opinion of the Fathers is alone innocent without spot is alone without
any exception free from error.

In the third place, you lay on the rod because I express surprise that the
Evangelist should be willing to misuse the word *therapeuein*, which means to   110
cure by the remedies physicians use. To begin with, this is a point more
against the translator than against Matthew, since he is held to have written
in Hebrew. Secondly, the word 'misuse' need not always mean to use for a
wrong purpose; for we also misuse things which we have taken for our own
use from some other source, and when we use a word in a different sense, we   115
misuse it, but to good effect. Finally a man who expresses surprise is not
necessarily critical: we are surprised at things we admire, at new things, at
things the cause of which we do not know – for instance, at the way iron is
attracted by a magnet and the Nile floods at midsummer and the Euripus is in

* * * * *

90 Paul] Rom 12:3
91 Jerome] Cf LB VI 673E–674C, 677F, 788E, 825F, 840F, 842E; PL 30:1042.
93 Luke] Cf LB VI 217A, 673E; PL 24:100, 26:18.
94 Paul] Jerome Ep 121.10 (CSEL 56:41)
96 Corinthians] 2 Cor 2:13; cf LB VI 758B–C.
106 He said] John 14:6
110 misuse] LB VI 25E; cf Ep 769:84n.
119 Euripus] The water in the narrow strait of Euripus (between Boeotia and
    Euboea) was said to rush in and out seven times each day and each night:
    Adagia I ix 62.

such constant ebb and flow. Thus what was not clear to me I put forward for   120
other people to discuss. And you know that some topics are put forward for
discussion in our universities in far more prejudicial terms.

It is now clear enough of itself how far off the mark your invidious
suggestions are, as though I were trying to show the evangelists the way or
to repair the negligence of the Holy Spirit, though I think that in reciting   125
these charges you are recounting other men's malignant attacks and not
conveying your own opinion. Otherwise how could one say anything more
hostile even of an enemy? But the last point that you bring forward you claim
as entirely your own; and so this is the place where you would have your
Erasmus gauge how fair-minded and devoted to him is his old friend Eck. Yet   130
I myself should have supposed this part more than any other to be other
men's work, had you not expressly claimed it as your own. You disapprove
of my judgment, because in the study of Scripture I have such a preference
for Jerome over Augustine that I think it an impertinence to compare one
with the other. To this point, dear Eck my most learned friend, I shall not   135
reply until you have conceded that it is no discredit to be placed second by a
judge who regards both candidates as outstanding. My feelings about
Augustine are such as it is proper to hold of a saintly man endowed with
exceptional gifts. I cast no reflections on his reputation, as you say I do, but I
do not allow Jerome's reputation to be put in the shade; and he would clearly   140
suffer injury if he were placed second to a man whom he far outdistances. I
ask you, would a man insult Peter who set Christ above him? Would one
wrong the archbishop of Canterbury by placing the pope over him? Would a
man tarnish the glory of silver who preferred gold? But suppose there were
still a doubt which of them stands first. If some particular enthusiasm made   145
me prefer Jerome, I should not, I think, lay myself open to attack – for in
these matters Paul is willing that each man should follow his own opinion –
provided that I hold a very high opinion of Augustine, as indeed I do. When
you credit Augustine with supreme authority after the canon of Scripture
and the sacrosanct decrees of the church and in succession to the church's   150
early pillars, who would not agree that this is going rather far? He makes no
such demands on his own behalf, nor has anyone ever made such claims for
him, especially since the first place in this sort of contest of reputation
belongs to the Greeks, as it does in all others.

But let us consider the arguments on which you rest your case against   155
me. You confront me with the authority of Filelfo who (you say), though he

* * * * *

128 the last point] Ep 769:93–114
147 Paul] Cf 1 Cor 7:6–7.
156 Filelfo] Cf Ep 769:100n.

conceded the palm for eloquence to Jerome, set Augustine above him in dialectic, and you add out of your own head that he reckoned him supreme in the whole field of philosophy. For my part, my learned friend, I do not think Filelfo carries such weight, especially as a critic in sacred studies, that I must submit to be silenced by his authority; for even in his own field, if the facts so required, I should not be very ready to give way – to say nothing boastful about myself, though he enlarged so much on his own merits. And what he said was a casual remark made in a private letter to a personal friend, though you now launch it against me like the oracle of Delphi. Everybody knows it is a commonplace of the schools that Augustine among the Fathers is an outstanding theologian, an admirable philosopher, and an invincible dialectician – as though every utterance thrown off in the schools for any casual reason must be regarded as an oracle. Every class of men has its common throng, and the best has always appealed only to the few. I doubt not that you yourself disagree with much that is repeated as of the first importance in our universities. All scholars, according to you, give Augustine the same position in theology that Filelfo gave him in philosophy. Not at all: I understand that there are men of consummate scholarship who think far less well of Augustine than I do. What is more, the reason why the academic fraternity put Augustine above Jerome or Ambrose is partly that he is more frequently quoted by those authors who have acquired a despotic position in our universities, either because they found him easier to understand than them or because his pronouncements are more definite than theirs. Jerome is heavy going in many ways, Ambrose is made somewhat obscure by his allusions; both of them, following Greek precedent, are less willing to lay down the law, the more they know.

As for what follows in your letter, I could not read it, I must admit, with a straight face. '"Every man," you say, "is a good judge of what he knows well," says the Stragirite; and there is no shortcoming in you which your supporters so much regret as your failure to have read Augustine.' I find nothing in myself, good sir, which should make anyone wish to be an Erasmian, and I absolutely loathe these names of factions. We are all Christ's, and it is for his glory alone that we labour each according to his share. But who pray are these Erasmians of yours, so devoted to me that, through excess of affection no doubt, they suppose me never to have set eyes on Augustine's works? If they said I did not understand them, this would

160

165

170

175

180

185

190

* * * * *

169 oracle] Erasmus uses the phrase 'from the tripod' (on which the prophetess at Delphi sat); *Adagia* I vii 90.
184 you say] Ep 769:107–9. Erasmus pointedly repeats Eck's misspelling of Aristotle's birthplace, Stragira for Stagira.

have been abuse of an ordinary kind which I should share with many others. But what impertinence it would be to wish to compare one author with another, when one of the two you simply have not read! How for that matter could such an idea have entered your Erasmians' heads? For they cannot possibly know exactly what I have read or not read. On the contrary, if you were able, while still a young man (so they tell me) to toil assiduously at Durandus and Gabriel and their like in the academic wrestling-schools, and yet to read Augustine, did a man in his fifties like myself, who has always been more devoted to the theologians of Antiquity, never find time to read Augustine of all people? Citing him as I do constantly in books published many years ago, am I thought never to have read anything he wrote? The men you speak of suppose, no doubt, that I had never read Jerome's books before editing his works. On the contrary, Augustine was the author I read first of them all, and now reread daily as often as need arises. And the more I read him, the more I feel satisfied with my estimate of the two of them.

Will you allow me, my most learned friend, to make a conjecture about you in my turn? If what you write is what you think, you have never read anything of mine. In any case, there is scarcely a work of Augustine's which I do not quote as an authority, in more than thirty score places, if I mistake not. And after all that, you recommend me to make the acquaintance of his books! I take a more favourable view of you, in supposing you to have read everything; but all the same I urge you to read Jerome with more attention, and you will vote for my side. But here perhaps we shall find Horace's words apply: 'Three guests I have of wishes quite contrary: / As their tastes differ, so their orders vary,' or that tag in Terence 'Each man has his own opinion.' Let us stick to the facts. No one will deny what great importance lies in birthplace and education. Jerome was born at Stridon, a town so close to Italy that the Italians claim it as their own, and educated in Rome, in a capital city, under the best scholars of the day; Augustine in Africa, a barbarous region where literary studies were at an amazingly low ebb, a fact which Augustine does not conceal in his letters. Jerome, a Christian of Christian stock,

* * * * *

199 Durandus and Gabriel] The names of two popular nominalists are probably selected at random. For Durand de Saint-Pourçain (d 1334) see Ep 396:101n. For Gabriel Biel (d 1495) see Ep 575:35n.
202 in books] This and some of the following statements are corroborated by C. Béné *Erasme et Saint Augustin* (Geneva 1969) 63–4 and passim. Béné shows that Erasmus' interest in Augustine dates back to the time when he entered the service of Bishop Hendrik van Bergen in 1492.
215 vote] Literally 'vote with your feet'; *Adagia* II vii 12
215 Horace's words] *Epistles* 2.2.61–2
217 Terence] *Phormio* 454; cf *Adagia* I iii 7.

imbibed the philosophy of Christ with his mother's milk; Augustine was
already nearly thirty when he sat down to read the Pauline Epistles without   225
a teacher. Jerome with all his abilities devoted thirty-five years to the study of
Holy Scripture; Augustine was diverted at once to the duties of a bishop and
compelled to teach what he had not yet learnt. If you do not believe me, read
his own letter to Bishop Valerianus, in which he begs earnestly for a little
time to learn what he is to teach others.   230

Now suppose, if you like, that birthplace, ability, teachers, and upbringing get equal marks on either side, and let us reckon up how much
better equipped Jerome was when he took up this task – unless perhaps you
regard a good knowledge of Greek and Hebrew as of little moment.
All philosophy and all theology in those days belonged to the Greeks.   235
Augustine knew no Greek; or, if he had acquired a smattering, it was not
much help towards reading the Greek commentators. I am astonished how
some people can credit Augustine with a perfect knowledge of Aristotelian
philosophy, when he himself admits in his *Confessions* that he has read only
one short book of his, and that too in a Latin version. And though in many   240
places he handles questions involving dialectic, for which he seems to have
had a natural aptitude and a strong inclination – for instance, in his *De
doctrina christiana*, in the *De trinitate*, and in several short works which he
wrote as a catechumen – he does not state that he has read anything beyond
Porphyry's *Quinque voces* or *Praedicabilia* and *Decem rerum genera* or *Praedica-* 245
menta and his book *De enunciatione*. Apart from that, show me a single word
that might be thought to be taken from the *Priora* or *Posteriora* or the *Elenchi* or
the *Topica*, to say nothing for the moment of the *Physica* and *Metaphysica* and
the other voluminous works of that philosopher, particularly as in the books
which he wrote as a catechumen he boasts with youthful conceit of any   250
smattering of philosophy he had acquired, and admits himself that those
books still have a touch of academic conceit in them. But what book was there
in the whole library of Greek literature that Jerome had not mastered and did
not have at his fingertips as though he had indexed it all? If you are ready to
judge both by results, take Jerome in operation against Jovinianus, against   255
Rufinus, against Pelagius, against the Luciferians, and tell me whether you
find in him any weakness as a dialectician. If the same arguments were
handled nowadays by men who have grown grey in dialectic, it would then

* * * * *

229 letter] Augustine Ep 21
240 one short book] A questionable reference based, it seems, on *Confessions* 4.16;
     7.9
243 short works] Cf *Retractationes* 1.1 (CSEL 36:11).
250 he boasts] Cf *Retractationes*, prologue (CSEL 36:10).
254 at his fingertips] Literally 'in ready cash'; *Adagia* IV iii 82

be clear how far Jerome stands out, except that their bad Latin and childish
quibbles are beyond him. And yet Augustine calls Cicero a mock philos-   260
opher, being of course the genuine article himself, though Cicero, if I am not
mistaken, had read somewhat more widely in Greek philosophy than
Augustine had in Holy Scripture.

I could adduce many passages specifically which bear on this question
from the works of both Fathers and so continue the discussion. But that   265
would exceed the limits of a letter, and there would be some risk of my
seeming eager to do so, in the eyes of Augustine's passionate supporters;
and I am no less devoted to him than they are and have perhaps read him
with more attention and a deeper understanding of his gifts than they have,
while they, having had no grounding in humane studies, merely collect in   270
the course of desultory reading a few verities, as they call them. Other men's
experience I know not; but in myself at least I find good reason to say that I
learn more of Christian philosophy from a single page of Origen than from
ten of Augustine. And besides Origen, Jerome had so many teachers. All the
same, my love of Augustine is great enough for me to have attempted in an   275
edition of his works to do for him what I did for Jerome.

And so, to draw to a close, most learned Eck, while you urge me not to
dim the glory of Augustine – which I am so far from doing that I would
rather see it enhanced – I in return urge you not to dim the glory of Jerome,
who added lustre to Augustine himself, for it was only after his dispute with 280
Jerome that he began emphatically to make progress. Let us rather with equal
enthusiasm strive to add the greatest possible lustre to them both – better
still, to imitate them. I myself long ago as a young man held the opinion
you do now. I conceive that added years and wider reading have added
something in the way of judgment. I have changed my mind, not because I   285
have a less exalted opinion of Augustine, of whom I think more highly as an
old man than I did in my youth, but because I have watched Jerome at closer
quarters. Maybe you will have the same experience. If you do not, you will
agree with me none the less that I may be allowed to differ from you in places
without impairing our friendship, just as the friendship between Augustine   290
and Jerome was not affected by a difference of opinion on several subjects.

Another point. When you promise to give me advice diligently on other

* * * * *

260 Augustine] *De civitate Dei* 2.27
273 page of Origen] See Bietenholz *History and Biography* 41–6; cf Ep 843:435–6.
275 have attempted] Erasmus' edition of Augustine for Froben's press only
      materialized in 1528–9 (cf Ep 2157; Bietenholz *History and Biography* 77–9), but it
      had a long prehistory; cf Epp 581:22–4, 922:40–1.
283 young man] See above line 202n.
292 When you promise] Cf Ep 769:93–4.

occasions as well, if you find that by this service you have been a help to me, I
have no time, my excellent friend, to answer any and every false accusation –
for who is so illiterate that he cannot somehow invent charges to bring   295
against another man's book? – nor am I so ill disposed to you that I would
have you devote your valuable time to any but the most valuable activities.
Good advice is not unwelcome from any source, but some men are too
ignorant for their advice to be any use to me; and yet they are the severest
critics of them all. Some men I could name give me advice in a way that can   300
only misrepresent me in hopes of getting a small supply of reputation for
themselves. Some again are so carried away by the love of putting others
right that in advising a fellow man they seem to forget that they are men
themselves. And yet the man who finds fault cannot expect us to make
allowances as we do for him who sets out to instruct us.   305

I must thank you for the books you sent me. I admire your fluency and
add my tribute to your triumphant reception. But I shall rejoice with you still
more when you are blessed with leisure and with the spirit to ponder the
secrets of the philosophy of Christ in deepest silence and in your inmost
heart, when the Bridegroom will lead you into his chamber and into his   310
store. When in those essays of yours you pile such tributes on the name of
Erasmus, I can accept none of it except your warm and friendly feelings; the
salvoes of applause and all the prizes I leave to others, for of such glories I
have had all I want. Forgive these hasty sheets: I write under a double
burden of ill health and research. If I fall short of what I owe you now, it shall   315
be made good another day.

Urbanus Rhegius I know as a learned man from the letter he himself
wrote me and suppose him a civilized one from the service he did me; pray
give him my warmest greetings. To the most illustrious Duke Ernest I have
dedicated the Quintus Curtius lately published by Schürer, that there might   320
be some evidence at least that I have not forgotten his kindness to me.
Farewell.

Basel, 15 May 1518

* * * * *

306 books you sent] Cf Ep 769:13n, 128n.
311 store] Song of Solomon 1:3, 2:4 etc
315 ill health] Cf Ep 847.
317 Urbanus Rhegius] Rhegius was Eck's pupil and his junior colleague at the
    University of Ingolstadt. He was now preparing to leave for Constance; see Ep
    386.
319 Ernest] Of Bavaria: Ep 704. The words 'lately published by Schürer' may have
    been added in printing.

845 / From Thomas More   [England, c May 1518]

A fragment printed in Thomas Stapleton *Tres Thomae* (Douai: J. Bogardus 1588)
73, from a collection of More's papers taken to Douai probably by John Harris, a
former secretary of More's. The preface referred to (BRE Ep 72, 23 February
1518) was written by Beatus Rhenanus for the Froben edition of More's
Epigrammata (together with the *Utopia*, etc; cf Epp 634–5) of March 1518. The
tentative date was assigned by Allen in view of More's statement that his
thanks to Beatus were overdue. For Beatus Rhenanus see Ep 327, 596
introductions.

Rhenanus I am especially fond of and I owe him a great debt on account of his
most handsome preface. I would have written to thank him long ago, had not
indomitable lethargy restrained me like the gout.

846 / From Pieter Gillis   Antwerp, 24 May [1518]

This letter was first printed by Allen from the autograph now in the Bodleian
Library, Oxford: MS Lat misc c 20 f 80 (olim MS Autogr c 9 f 74).
    Pieter Gillis (cf Ep 184), secretary of the town of Antwerp, was one of
Erasmus' closest friends; Erasmus was often a guest in his house and relied on
him for the forwarding of letters and money.

TO MASTER ERASMUS FROM P. GILLIS, GREETING
Thanks be to heaven, I am now much better. If all is well with you, I am the
happiest of men. Please let me know how you are and how things are going.
Ever since you left Cologne I have heard no news of you. A bundle of letters
from Budé must have reached you, I have no doubt. Franz the bookseller   5
coming from Paris brought the news that Glareanus has been chosen to
succeed Fausto, who has died. I am very glad for the sake of a man with
poetry in him, of whom you often give me such a charming description.

    * * * * *
    846
    2 much better] After a prolonged state of ill health; cf Ep 597:23–4 and the index
      of CWE 5.
    4 Cologne] See Ep 843 introduction.
    5 Budé] Guillaume Budé was an eminent Greek scholar and promoter of
      humanistic studies at the French court. For the letters in question see Ep 810
      introduction.
    5 Franz] Birckmann, the Cologne bookseller, maintained a store in Antwerp; cf
      Ep 258:14n.
    7 Fausto] Andrelini (cf Ep 84 introduction). For the death of Erasmus' old friend

I beg you to keep a watchful eye on the Athanasius, and not to allow it
to be taken apart. I should be sorry to hurt the canon from whom I borrowed 10
it, for if he did not get it back I do not see what excuse I could possibly offer. I
could wish the New Testament were finished to your satisfaction and that
you were here with us. Everyone likes you beyond question both here and in
Louvain. There are some of our magistrates who constantly ask after your
health; they have your welfare so much at heart. 15

Ferdinand, Charles' brother, is expected among us. Rumour has it that
the heer van Veere, the admiral and commander of the convoy, has landed.
Farewell.

Give my greetings to Beatus Rhenanus, my dearest friend, as of course
he is, especially because he is so dear to you, and I am your best and truest 20
Pylades.

Antwerp, the morrow of Pentecost
To the eminent theologian and master of every branch of learning,

* * * * *

and the appointment of a new poet royal see Ep 810:489n; for the Swiss
humanist Henricus Glareanus see Ep 440 introduction.

9 Athanasius] Erasmus edited some texts by Athanasius in 1527 (cf Ep 1790), but
these can hardly be meant here. No doubt Gillis was concerned about a
manuscript containing a Latin translation of Theophylact's commentary on the
Epistles of Paul, which was often attributed to Athanasius. The manuscript,
which he had borrowed, was apparently then at Froben's press and thus in
danger of being taken apart for the convenience of the compositors. (This
seems the likely sense, but the verb *distrahatur* could also mean 'sold.') Erasmus
made frequent use of Theophylact's commentary for the *Annotationes in Novum
Testamentum*. In the 1518–19 edition he still referred to the author as Vulgarius
on pp 245, 260 of the *Annotationes*. But then comparison with the Greek text of
Theophylact led to the identification of the author, and the correct name
appears on the title page of the volume containing the text and in subsequent
editions of the New Testament. There is an edition of Athanasius' works in
Latin (Strasbourg: J. Knobloch March 1522) that includes the commentary but
states that the attribution to Theophylact was widely accepted (f 236 verso).
12 New Testament] See Ep 864 introduction.
14 Louvain] When leaving Louvain for a summer in Basel, Erasmus may have
anticipated increased opposition in his absence (cf Epp 809 introduction,
843:538n). He was seriously considering a permanent move to England (see
Epp 834, 886 introductions). His fears were partially confirmed by Ep 852:54–7.
17 Veere] Adolph of Burgundy (cf Ep 93 introduction). In 1517 he became admiral
in succession to Philip of Burgundy, bishop of Utrecht, and he was in charge of
the expedition which took Prince Charles to Spain. In the summer of 1518,
when Ferdinand arrived from Spain (see Ep 917 introduction), Adolph
organized a splendid and extravagant welcome for him at Middelburg; cf NNBW
VIII 190–1.
21 Pylades] The proverbial friend of Orestes; cf Ep 849:11–12.

Master Erasmus of Rotterdam, his second father and most respected teacher.
In Basel.   25

847 / To Pierre Barbier   Basel, 31 May 1518

Epp 847–8 are the only ones to be copied into the Deventer Letter-book by
Hand E (cf Allen I 605–6); evidently this was a temporary secretary taken on at
Basel. For Barbier, a chaplain, who was now in Spain with the court of King
Charles, cf Ep 443 introduction.

ERASMUS TO HIS FRIEND BARBIER, GREETING
I reached Basel precisely on Ascension day, after a somewhat unpleasant
journey mainly on account of the heat. Work on my New Testament now
occupies me, and it is being printed. But in these parts a new kind of plague
is spreading throughout Germany, which attacks a great many people with   5
coughs, headache, and internal pains and kills a number of them, but the
majority get over it. It went for me too after ten days, and I have now for some
days been very poorly. I should have got quit of this place within three
months if my health had been favourable. I had brought my work to such a
point; but one must yield to fate. If my excellent Maecenas and you yourself 10
are both well, I have good reason to bear my own misfortune more lightly.
Farewell.
    Basel, the morrow of Trinity Sunday 1518
    I wrote some time ago both to you and to my lord the chancellor from
Louvain, on your instructions. Give Guy my best wishes.   15

848 / To Thomas More   Basel, 31 May [1518]

Cf Ep 847 introduction.

ERASMUS TO HIS FRIEND MORE, GREETING
I reached Basel precisely on Ascension day, after a somewhat unpleasant
journey on account of the heat, but safe and sound none the less. But there is
        * * * * *
847
 2 Ascension] 13 May 1518
 7 some days] Ill health continued to bother Erasmus during most of his stay at
    Basel (cf Epp 844:314–15, 848, 855:19–23, 860:7–12, 869:21), and he fell
    seriously ill on his journey back to Louvain; cf Ep 867.
10 Maecenas] Chancellor Jean Le Sauvage; see Epp 410 introduction, 852:72n.
14 I wrote] Epp 793–4
15 Guy] Morillon; see Ep 532 introduction.

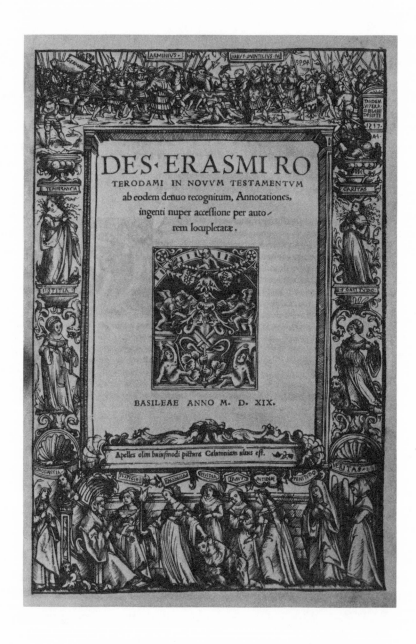

Erasmus, ed and tr, *Novum Testamentum* title page
Basel: Froben 1519
One of three copies printed on vellum;
this copy was owned by Cuthbert Tunstall
The Philip H. and A.S.W. Rosenbach Foundation, Philadelphia

a new kind of plague now spreading all through Germany, the symptoms of
which are cough and headache, in some cases leading to delirium, with   5
internal pains. My friends had written to say it had now passed off, but after
about ten days it got me, and I have now been some days in a poor way. But I
begin to mend. It has killed many people but let the majority go free. The
work on my New Testament is now proceeding. I have given instructions for
three copies to be struck off on vellum. One had been ordered by Tunstall.   10
Had my health been favourable for two months at least, I should have
brought it to a point where it could have been finished even in my absence.
But we are driven by fate, and fate we must obey. If the gods are kind, I shall
return to Brabant next September. But it will be impossible to finish the work
before the next fair. Please let Tunstall too know this. Farewell, dearest of   15
friends.

Basel, Trinity Monday

* * * * *

848
6 My friends] See Ep 801–2; but their answers and Erasmus' inquiry concerned
   the bubonic plague; cf Epp 847:7n, 861:7n.
8 begin to mend] Hypothetical text, since two or three words are missing in the
   Deventer Letter–book; the new secretary may have had some difficulty with
   Erasmus' handwriting.
10 on vellum] Cf Ep 886:22–4. Tunstall's copy passed to the library of York Minster
   and is now in the collection of the Rosenbach Foundation in Philadelphia.
   Another copy was given to Erard de la Marck (cf Allen I 43:40–2, Ep 738
   introduction). Unfortunately it cannot be identified as one or the other of the
   two remaining copies on vellum which have also survived. One is in the
   Lambeth Palace Library, London (**E 1965, 1519), purchased in 1824 from the
   Sir Mark Sykes collection. Its leather binding shows the date of 1579, and on
   the inside cover is a manuscript epitaph on Erasmus by Rumoldus Tutorius
   (Voocht?) of Antwerp. The third copy on vellum, without any indication of its
   provenance, is in Christ's College, Cambridge (CC 3.3).
10 Tunstall] Cuthbert Tunstall (cf Ep 207:25n) had taken an active interest in
   Erasmus' revision of the New Testament when the two met in Brussels in the
   summer of 1517 (cf Epp 571 introduction, 597:18–20). Tunstall was a member of
   an English embassy.
13 fate] Adapted from Seneca Oedipus 980; cf Ep 794:91.
15 fair] In time for the Frankfurt autumn fair; cf Ep 864 introduction.

849 / From Pieter Gillis   Antwerp, 19 June [1518]

This letter was published in the *Farrago*.

TO ERASMUS OF ROTTERDAM FROM PIETER GILLIS, GREETING
I can see you are very busy – four letters from me, and you have not
answered! A courier arrived here lately with a letter from you to Jan de
Neve. Franz was away in England while he was here, and the letter was
eventually delivered to me, with a letter from Froben which was particularly   5
welcome.

Borssele has been given a deanery, as they call it. Passing here on his
way to Zeeland he paid me a visit and told me you had reached Basel, which I
was very glad to hear. Can you wonder that I was glad, when at any mention
of your name I rejoice and jump for joy? Do please, dear Erasmus, if you ever   10
have a chance, find time to send your Pylades (for so you call me with no less
sincerity than truth) something in the way of a letter. I was not a little
surprised that you never let me know you had had the letter from Budé that I
sent you, all the more so as meanwhile you had twice sent a letter to Neve.

Bade has been with us, and we had a merry time. Lefèvre d'Etaples   15
came up in conversation at table; he is sorry that he ever annoyed you and

* * * * *

849
2 four letters] Only Ep 846 survives. The two letters to Neve (line 14) are also
   lost.
4 Neve] The regent of the College of the Lily, Erasmus' residence at Louvain; cf
   Epp 298 introdution, 643:14n.
4 Franz] Birckmann; also line 41.
5 Froben] The Basel printer Johann Froben (cf Ep 419 introduction) had perhaps
   sent a note accompanied by the new *Utopia*; cf Ep 845.
7 Borssele] Thanks to Erasmus' efforts (cf Ep 805), the appointment of Jan Becker
   of Borssele (cf Ep 291 introduction) as professor of Latin to the Collegium
   Trilingue seemed assured (cf Ep 836:9–10), but at the beginning of June it was
   learned in Louvain that he had preferred a comfortable benefice. Exercising a
   right belonging to the family, Anna van Borssele, Lady of Veere, and her son,
   Adolph of Burgundy, nominated him dean of the chapter of Zanddijk or
   Zandenburg, which had recently been transferred to the town of Veere. He
   was now on his way to take up the appointment; cf Ep 932:50–2; de Vocht
   CTL I 263.
11 Pylades] Cf Ep 846:21n.
13 from Budé] See Ep 810 introduction.
15 Bade] Josse Bade, the Paris scholar and printer, was a native of Brabant; cf Ep
   183 introduction.

will never publish a reply till the Greek calends. Paolo Emilio has handed over the remaining books of his histories to Bade to be printed. I understand also that Budé is collecting his letters. I suppose he will get them published to the great admiration and profit of the learned world.   20

We have among us (would you believe it?) that mischief-maker Highstreet, who is as universally popular as any screech-owl. He is now engaged on something entirely unsuited to his Order – selling those perfectly idiotic pamphlets of his which he called his *Apologia*. These are being hawked around by those out-at-elbow itinerant pamphlet-sellers, and   25 the profit such as it is is pocketed by our scrofulous and pitiful friend Highstreet. As for him, no one deigns to talk to him, no one even greets him, except perhaps a few crazy and worn-out bawds, though even they do not think the wretch worthy of their society. He scrapes together money from wherever he can, but it is all gold with a curse on it.   30

A dialogue by an unknown author, but a very well informed one, about Julius is on sale here everywhere. Everybody buys it, people talk about nothing else. I very much wish you had seen it; though no doubt it will be on sale in your part of the world as well. Ferdinand, our most illustrious prince, has made a happy landing accompanied by a few of our own countrymen. He   35 is said on reliable authority to have a friendly and affable disposition and an excellent character, and to be astonishingly good at Latin and quite a good speaker.

* * * * *

17 Greek calends] Never, the Greeks not having calends; cf *Adagia* I v 84. For Lefèvre's intentions see Ep 721 introduction.

18 histories] See Ep 719:7n. Without changing the title page, Bade added to books 1–4 (published c 1517) first books 5–7 and subsequently books 8–9. A tenth book was added in a later edition.

19 published] *Epistolae Gulielmi Budaei* (Paris: J. Bade 20 August 1520)

22 Highstreet] 'Hypsistrotus' in the Latin text refers to the Dominican Jacob of Hoogstraten (cf Ep 290:11n). His journey to the Netherlands – in September 1518 he was at Louvain visiting his old university (cf Ep 1006 introduction), but he subsequently returned to Cologne – came amid the continuing conflicts in faction-ridden Cologne (cf Ep 821:19n). It is little wonder that his opponents, the Reuchlinists, spread some compromising rumours about the motives of his journey (cf Epp 877–8), but there is no doubt that he was campaigning for his cause wherever he went. For his *Apologia* and the after-effects cf Epp 680:28n, 1078 introduction.

30 gold] Literally 'gold of Toulouse'; cf *Adagia* I x 98.

32 Julius] The circulation of the *Julius exclusus* (cf Ep 502 introduction) combined with the presence of Hoogstraten was bound to cause Erasmus some anxiety (cf Epp 821:19n, 877). Martens printed the *Julius* in September 1518 (NK 3283–4).

34 Ferdinand] See Ep 917 introduction.

et amplificet. Itaq optatus ut deus Ihc omnig bonorum om mu-
nificus largitor Successus Matis V. R. In dies magis atq̃ magis secundet factaq̃ et celsitudine. V. R. diu Sospite et incolume
seti p̃servamur.

Desiderio Erasmo Rodendano
oratori et Theologo Summo.
S D

fricatio
curuim

Summa et incredibilis Virtus tua. Friderici singularis ingenij
celsitudo. et eloquentiæ maiestas perfectissime Erasme. quæ partim
lectione tuarum operum partim tam egregia q̃m vera doctorum
hominum commendatione mihi innotuerunt. in causa sunt.
Ut ad te in presentia scribere non dubitarim. Nam cum
omnium qui ingenij laboribus illustris reliquis mortalibus prestant
unquã non fuerim studiosior. tum eorum. qui cum Romana
eloquentia Christianæ fidej puritatem copulauere. observantissimus
videri cupiam. qualem te unũ ex universa mortalitate
hæc etas diuinitus nacta. maioribus suis. et multis retro secu-
lis adeo nihil concedit. Ut quem obijciat Veneranda aliquin
antiquitati summis omnibus eglem reliquis superiorem habeat
ac iure pretendet. Post futuris alus penè spem omnem adimit.
adeo. Ut sibi simile quiddam Vix unquã audeant polliceri Ætas,
ita me dij bene ament, Ut audito Erasmi nolr mirifice
gestire soleo et exultare. fit aut hoc iso msequenter. habes /
n. complures. Vel in his locis eximij ingenij tui miratores
nominisaq̃ tui clarissimi precones perquos. inter qũos Iohannes
Piso extat olim tibi Romæ cognitus. Regis Ludouici p̃ Ungarie
in h̃is preceptor. tum caspar Ursinus Velius Phaleca illui

Letter from Johannes Thurzo to Erasmus, Epistle 850
Bayerische Staatsbibliothek, Munich, MS Clm 965, 349

Dr Marcus Laurinus has been with me for a few days. We talked and
we gossipped about nothing but you, and he sent you most hearty greetings.   40
Sixtinus has written to me. Of More I have no news. Franz has left England
for Paris. If Beatus Rhenanus is in good health and spirits, I am highly
delighted. Farewell, dear Erasmus. My precious wife, who is now near her
time, sends you at least a thousand greetings.

Antwerp, 19 June [1519]   45

850 / From Johannes Thurzo   [Wrocław, c 20 June 1518]

The only source for this letter is a manuscript copy in a collection of papers from
Wrocław, now in the Bayerische Staatsbibliothek, Munich: Clm 965 pp 349–53.
(For the contents and the history of this collection cf Allen's headnote and an
addendum, VI xix–xx; *Catalogus codicum latinorum bibliothecae regiae Monacensis*,
second edition, I-1, Munich 1892, 217–18.) The letter is clearly contemporary
with Ep 851. Answered by Ep 943, it initiated a correspondence which was to
continue until Thurzo's death.

Johannes Thurzo (1464–1520) belonged to an influential family that rose to
prominence under the Jagiełło rulers of Poland and Hungary. After studies in
Cracow and Italy he became bishop of Wrocław in 1506.

TO DESIDERIUS ERASMUS OF ROTTERDAM, THE EMINENT WRITER
AND THEOLOGIAN, GREETING
Your supreme excellence that passes all belief, your extraordinary learning,
your lofty genius and grandeur of style, Erasmus most complete of men, are
known to me partly from the perusal of your works and partly from the praise   5
of learned men which is as true as it is notable; and hence it comes that I write
to you at this moment without hesitation. All those who have won fame by
works of genius and stand above the rest of men have always attracted me,
and those especially who have combined with Roman eloquence the purity
of Christian faith inspire me with the wish to show my admiration. Of this   10
kind you are the one man out of the whole human race vouchsafed by
providence to our generation, which thus falls in no way short of our
ancestors and of many past centuries, for it possesses and can justly put
forward one who is a match for that Antiquity otherwise so venerable, equal

* * * * *

39 Laurinus] Canon at Bruges and a close friend of Erasmus; see Ep 651
   introduction.
41 Sixtinus] Johannes Sixtinus was a Frieslander in London; see Ep 112 introduction.
43 wife] Cornelia Sandrien married Gillis in 1514; see Ep 312:93n.

to all its greatest men and above the rest; while he leaves posterity with 15
scarcely a hope, so that they hardly dare promise themselves that they will
ever see the like.

As heaven is my witness, it is remarkable how the sound of Erasmus'
name revives and cheers me. And this happens fairly often; for even in these
parts you have several admirers of your genius and distinguished heralds of 20
your famous name. Among them are Johannes Piso, whom you knew long
ago in Rome, the tutor of King Louis of Hungary, and Caspar Ursinus
Velius, author of that published poem in hendecasyllables on your birthday.
Besides which, my ears are never sated with the reading of Erasmus' works;
indeed I doubt if any man exists, of all those who have once looked into your 25
books, who has not laid them down under compulsion rather than of his
own free will. So it is: in reading books of the kind that you produce
everyone finds any interruption disagreeable; to go on reading is a pure
delight, and unbroken labour is a pleasure. For in all your writings,
numerous and richly furnished as they are, lies Homer's lotus, which 30
bewitches the minds of your readers so that they can by no means be
distracted from that desire that can never be satisfied. With him you share
this special property, that the reader of your works never feels satiety creep
over him; and if perchance a man should feel that he has had enough, it takes
longer for this to happen to your devotee, inasmuch as your work is a more 35
sacred thing than his poetry.

And so, when I reflect upon you as such a perfect work of nature
satisfied at last, complete on every count, I am wonderfully fired with a
desire to meet you. With this in mind, if I were ever to discover that you are in
some place within reach of a week's journey, I would promptly uproot 40
myself and hasten to you, and would indeed go farther – to Belgium even – if
business permitted. Surely if many visitors from Cadiz came to Rome to set
eyes on Livy, why should not the man who has heard Erasmus' name and
sipped the cup of his more than human learning, come to him wherever he

* * * * *

850

21 Johannes] Really Jacobus Piso. Erasmus had met him in Italy, 1508–9 (cf Ep
216). By 1515 he had returned home and become the tutor of Louis II (1506–26),
king of Hungary since 1516.

22 Ursinus] For Ursinus and his poem see Epp 548, 851.

24 sated] Reading *obsaturari*, a word used by Thurzo in Ep 1047, for *obturari* of the
manuscript copy.

30 Homer's lotus] *Odyssey* 9.94–9; *Adagia* II vii 62

32 satisfied] Translating *inexplebili*, which is probably what Thurzo meant,
although the manuscript has *inexplicabili*, 'that cannot be explained'

43 Livy] Pliny *Letters* 2.3.8

44 sipped the cup] *Adagia* I ix 92

may be, from the uttermost parts of the earth, to contemplate him and admire   45
him? Indeed when I consider how much of both profit and pleasure I derive
from the reading of your books, I cannot set forth how much I feel I owe you –
more at any rate than I can ever repay. And yet to give some concrete
evidence of my respect for you, I had it in mind to send you a present, far less
than you deserve, but perhaps acceptable to a man of your exceptional   50
modesty. And so I will – quite soon, when I have access to a reliable courier
and know where you are to be found. In the mean time, I propose to regale
myself with the delightful thought of you, in company with Caspar Ursinus,
my protégé and your most devoted follower. Let me end with the sincere
wish that immortal God may preserve you in health and wealth for his   55
service and the benefit of us all, as long and happily as may be. Farewell.
    Johannes Thurzo, bishop of Wrocław, with my own hand

851 / From Caspar Ursinus Velius   Wrocław, 20 June 1518

> Ursinus had gone to Italy in 1510 with Matthäus Lang, bishop of Gurk, co-
> adjutor of Salzburg, and soon thereafter cardinal. In 1518 he went to Wrocław,
> where Johannes Thurzo (cf Ep 850), an old patron from his student days, had
> nominated him to a canonry. Ursinus' modesty is artificial; he was already poet
> laureate and highly regarded in Germany. This letter was answered by Ep 944
> and published in the *Farrago*.

CASPAR URSINUS VELIUS TO ERASMUS OF ROTTERDAM, GREETING
Last year I was living a retired life in a small town in Bavaria, being blessed
with leisure (but the leisure of a courtier, not a man of letters, and entirely cut
off from liberal studies), the cardinal of Gurk, in whose service I then was,
having gone to Belgium with the emperor; and being deprived of all support   5
in the literary way I made bold, at great hazard and risk to my name and
reputation, to revive the ancient custom I used to follow in Rome, I mean of
trying to write, and began very boldly and rashly to set down my foolish
ideas. Hence came that birthday poem addressed to you, as a man hardly to
be matched at this time in the whole of Europe for high standing and high   10
character, and at any rate by common consent our greatest scholar, which
had a more successful outcome than its style deserved. Plunged as I was at

* * * * *

49 a present] His presents were sent with Ep 1047.

851
2 small town] Probably Mühldorf am Inn, the seat of Lang's government; cf
    Konrad Peutingers Briefwechsel (Munich 1923) Ep 177.
9 birthday poem] Cf Ep 548:5n, 6n.

that time in the troubles of court life, the necessary peace of mind had been
denied me. My critical judgment and such power of invention as I might once
have possessed had sunk to a low ebb, my studies having been interrupted   15
for ... and more. I lacked the critical eye of good scholars, and there was no
supply of books to help me as I tried prematurely to swim without the aid of
cork. What else could you expect? Before one could cook a dish of greens,
the poem I had written lay before me, my bantling was born before I was
ready to give birth; whence everyone may infer that I did all I could to   20
procure a miscarriage. In any case, I did not compose it with the idea that
such a worthless and inchoate piece of verse should be hurried into print
and come into the hands of the public, for it had been sent to be read by
Riccardo Bartolini, to whom I had the habit of showing all my odd pieces in
confidence, and to no one else; and he went beyond his brief in this respect   25
and was not afraid to pass it on to you. Your poor friend Ursinus is ashamed,
heartily ashamed, that his production should have got out; he ought to have
exercised his modest wits on some theme of no importance and not on such a
great man. O the rashness and folly of my behaviour! I set out to praise
Aeneas when I was not yet capable of extolling a gnat.   30

I have made two mistakes, both of them serious and intolerable: I see
this clearly, and I am very sorry. For one thing, so far are you (as I now
perceive) from being honoured by such youthful efforts that I feel I have
actually damaged your reputation, and my blockhead Muse is responsible.
And then, what is much worse, when I tried my hand at this unfamiliar kind   35
of composition, I was not yet sufficiently familiar with the distinguished
events of your pure and holy life, nor had I yet seen all the works – so various
and so invaluable – that bear the name of that most fertile author Erasmus.
Consequently I revive from time to time my plan to revise those ill-timed

* * * * *

16 for ... and more] Something seems to be missing from the Latin text.
17 without the aid of cork] *Adagia* I viii 42
18 dish of greens] *Adagia* III vii 5
22 into print] Ursinus' *Genethliacon* was first printed with a collection of Erasmus'
   correspondence, *Epistolae sanequam elegantes* (Louvain: Martens April 1517).
   Bartolini was in Antwerp at the time (cf Epp 547–8), and Pieter Gillis of
   Antwerp, the editor of the collection, did not act without Erasmus' approval;
   see CWE 3 349.
30 a gnat] The *Culex*, a poem by an unknown author on the death of a gnat, passed
   in Antiquity and later as an early work of Virgil, a practice-piece for his *Aeneid*.
34 blockhead Muse] *Adagia* I i 37
39 revise] In his *Poemata* (Basel: Froben 1522) ff i 1 verso–k 3 verso, Ursinus made
   a number of corrections which were adopted in the later editions of Erasmus'
   correspondence. The revised form (LB I (20)–(22)) mentions many of Erasmus'
   early publications.

hendecasyllables that they may be filled out and re-examined to the best of   40
my ability before appearing ultimately in a more elegant and fuller form,
especially as I am strongly recommended to undertake this task by that most
honourable prince Johannes Thurzo, lord bishop of Wrocław, a most
effective Maecenas of all men of learning and a man of no small achievements
himself. He has the highest opinion of your singular qualities and your out-   45
standing scholarship, coupled with special affection and sincere respect;
and I simply must do as he suggests, both to give the greatest possible
pleasure to his lordship, to whom I owe everything, and to give the impression that I have taken thought for my own reputation. In the mean time, most
learned Erasmus, I beg you, by the rich endowments of your genius and the   50
immortality that awaits your pious labours, to take in good part what has
been published in your honour without my knowledge or permission, and to
give the poem I now send, which is perhaps a worse poem and comes from a
humble press, a welcome that does not belie the kind and great man you are.
And pray consent to place the name of Ursinus, who loves and respects you   55
so much, in your list of friends, even if he must take very much a back seat,
and spare him some affection in return. Farewell.
    From Wrocław, 20 June 1518

852 / From Maarten van Dorp   Louvain, 14 July 1518

> This letter shows that Dorp, a Louvain professor, was now on terms of intimate
> friendship with Erasmus (cf Epp 304, 596 introductions) and, moreover,
> anxious to be known as Erasmus' friend in Basel and elsewhere. Unfortunately
> for him, this letter was not published right away in the *Auctarium* (cf Ep 861
> introduction). Contemporaries could read it for the first time in the *Farrago* of
> October 1519 (cf Ep 1009 introduction), and meanwhile some of them continued
> to remember Dorp's earlier criticisms of Erasmus' work (cf Epp 1000A, 1044).
> This letter answers one Erasmus has sent from Basel (line 3) and another sent
> earlier from Cologne (lines 91–2), both missing.

MAARTEN VAN DORP TO ERASMUS OF ROTTERDAM, THE
ACKNOWLEDGED LEADER IN THE FIELD OF LEARNING, GREETING
The receipt of your letter, dear Erasmus and most honoured friend, gave me
unspeakable satisfaction, and no less was the pleasure with which I heard of

    * * * * *

53 poem I now send] A hexameter poem (cf Ep 944:5–6) addressed to Johannes
    Thurzo. Erasmus printed it in the Martens edition of Helius Eobanus'
    Hodeoporicon (cf Ep 870 introduction); it is also in Ursinus' *Poemata*, f m 2
    recto–m 3 verso. LB I (20) reprints the last part.

the arrival of your man Jacobus; so much so that I promptly instructed our   5
friend Dirk, that devotee of Bacchus, on no account to let him depart until we
could have a talk, until we could dine together. My plan was to fill him with
food and myself with conversation and good news. So I asked him anxiously
how you were and how you have been all this time; how far you have
progressed with the great work; whether Froben was engaged on anything   10
by Erasmus or any other author – in short, I thought of everything. To all of
which Jacobus gave me quite satisfactory replies. While we were absorbed in
conversation, picture Dirk absorbed in drinking, and by no means slow to
play his part, for he too was not meanwhile left out of the conversation. He
spoke, or should I say interrupted, in almost all languages – German,   15
French, Italian, Latin – so that you might suppose he was some character
from the apostolic age reborn, and he bravely challenged Jerome, the great
linguist, not perhaps in elegance but in the number of the tongues he spoke.

Besides which, I asked him for news of the excellent Baer, the excellent
Fabricius Capito, the excellent Rhenanus (Beatus by name and beatitude   20
itself in fact); whose bare names, dear Erasmus, give a lift to my spirits.
Although I am quite unworthy of their affection, they themselves richly
deserve not only my affection but my respect as well. And I would indeed
that they knew of my feelings towards them. Rhenanus in particular, by the
zeal and vigilance with which he corrects the best authors, has made all   25
scholars ready to acknowledge his help. And Fabricius: think of the light he
has thrown by his most laborious Principles of elementary Hebrew on that
language they call sacred! Baer's gifts again are beyond all doubt, for was he
not unanimously placed first at Paris? To these outstanding people, this
triumvirate, as it were, pray, dear Erasmus, give my quite special greetings.   30
Tell them that there is one Dorp by name, who has a great enthusiasm for
them. How fortunate you are, Erasmus, to live in the daily society of such
splendid men on such close and friendly terms! And on the other side, how

* * * * *

852
5 Jacobus] Nepos (cf Ep 595:11n) had gone to Basel with Erasmus, but had now
    been sent back with letters. Subsequently he returned to Basel and stayed on
    after Erasmus' own departure to complete the proof-reading of the New
    Testament; see Ep 886:29–30.
6 Dirk] Martens, the Louvain printer; cf Ep 263:10n.
10 progessed] See Ep 864 introduction.
18 linguist] Cf 'Vita Hieronymi' Opuscula 141, 152–3.
19 Baer ... Capito] Ludwig Baer and Wolfgang Faber (or Fabricius) Capito were
    theologians at Basel; see Epp 488, 459 introductions.
27 Principles] The Hebraicarum institutionum libri duo; cf Ep 600:26n.
29 Paris] In his graduating class; see Ep 413:13–14.

nearly they approach the gods, enjoying your presence among them as they
do! My soul upon it, life has nothing to offer so delightful and so gay, so   35
frank and easy.

As for your ill health, I was sorry to hear it had troubled you, and am
equally glad it has departed. The honourable attentions which I hear were
paid you, quite rightly, by Pucci, the papal legate, gave me great satisfaction.
Everything in your letter was entirely satisfactory. Only one thing troubled   40
me, that this fire lit by the people in Cologne should not yet have been put
out, as it most certainly ought to be. I cannot think how such a stupid idea
ever entered their heads as either to compose or to publish those ridiculous,
foolish, and crazy *Lamentationes*. Besides, what was less called-for than with
this kind of doltish dialogue to secure the reopening of an old wound which   45
had almost completely healed over? Learning is indeed in a bad way, if
scholars must continue to be quite so foolish! Of Lefèvre's supporters I as
yet neither see nor hear anything. But what of yourself, my good friend? Can
the state of learning in the future ever be so unpleasant, with so little way of
escape as to make you abandon it? Your natural gifts, your upbringing, the   50
way you prepared yourself for life have made you the one person to face up
to any difficulty or unpleasantness or complication arising in the field of
scholarship, and to endure it and swallow it readily with your eyes on the
general benefit of learning. The pamphlet on Pope Julius and his exclusion
from heaven is read by everyone everywhere, and somehow few condemn it,   55
although you indeed have good reason to be indignant with the author, who
makes the humanities at this moment unpopular if they never were before.

But, dear Erasmus, what am I to make of this? Do you tell me not to
answer your letters, because, you say, you will soon be returning here,
unless business requires you to go off to Italy? Suppose business does   60
require this, what opportunity will there be, pray, to converse with you by
correspondence, when meeting will be impossible? Who will be such a
trustworthy courier? And suppose you do come straight back, what do I lose
by writing? For I know that, however busy you are, over your dinner
perhaps you will steal enough time to read this letter, foolish and unpolished   65

* * * * *

37 ill health] See Ep 847:7n.
39 Pucci] See Ep 860 introduction.
41 Cologne] Cf below lines 91–3; Epp 821:19n, 849:22n.
44 *Lamentationes*] The *Lamentationes obscurorum virorum*, an attack upon the
    Reuchlinists; see Ep 622 introduction.
45 dialogue] Probably Benigno's *Defensio Reuchlini*; see Ep 680:28.
47 Lefèvre's] See Ep 721 introduction.
54 Julius] Cf Ep 849:31–4.
60 Italy] See Ep 770 introduction.

as it is. As for the Englishmen, I promise that I will see to it. I gave your greetings with the greatest care to that venerable figure Doctor Atensis, as you told me to. Believe me, Erasmus, he jumped for joy at the sound of your name, and after a long speech about you which was also extremely complimentary, he told me to greet you in return with all possible warmth   70 and tell you you can rely on him for anything.

The death of our most honoured lord the chancellor of Burgundy has, I know, been reported to you by others, so that I need not arouse your grief once again. Public instruction in the ancient tongues would be making good progress here, if only stipends were paid and the teaching were free; but in   75 any case you know the temperament of the Louvain people, and how much they dislike paying. This vexes our Matthaeus, a man who has such a passionate aversion to money that he does not offer hospitality even for one night, although he busies himself very little with coin. Your friend (ours, rather) Borssele, who is a good sort, an honest open-hearted man, has   8o abandoned us, being nominated dean of Veere. The duty he had undertaken of teaching Latin has been committed to Baerland. There was in your part of the world not long ago a young man from Metz with a passion for sound learning, a candidate in civil and canon law and a very great friend of mine, whose name is Claudius Cantiuncula, who paid you his respects, I do not   85 doubt, if he was there at the same time that you were. I intended to write to him, but when I asked your man Jacobus whether he knew him, he said he did not. Should he happen to be with you, pray give him my warmest

* * * * *

67 Atensis] Jan Briart of Ath. A cautious approach was indicated; see Ep 843:538n.
72 death] Le Sauvage died at Saragossa, 7 June 1518.
74 ancient tongues] In the Collegium Trilingue (cf Ep 691 introduction). Regular courses, free of charge, began on 1 September 1518; cf de Vocht CTL I 294–5.
77 Matthaeus] Adrianus, the professor of Hebrew; cf Ep 686:7n.
80 Borssele] Cf Ep 849:7n.
82 Baerland] Adriaan Cornelissen van Baerland (cf Ep 492 introduction) was the first professor of Latin at the Collegium Trilingue, but he was not happy with his position (cf Ep 884) and amid increasing difficulties resigned after a year; cf Ep 1046.
85 Cantiuncula] Claude Chansonnette of Metz (1490–1549), known as Cantiuncula, had met Dorp during his years as a student in Louvain, 1512–17 (cf BRE Ep 121). In the latter year he matriculated at Basel. Since Dorp refers to him as a candidate he may have been requesting references or documents in support of his application to Basel. In the autumn of 1518 he was appointed to the Basel chair of civil law and in March 1519 he obtained a legal doctorate; cf G. Kisch *Claudius Cantiuncula* (Basel 1970) 26.

greetings, and tell him further that the whole matter about which he wrote to me over and over again is now safe in shallow water, as the saying goes, so that he need not worry any more. The thing you had written to me about from Cologne (for which I am most grateful) is slowly coming right, and indeed I hope that it will go as you wish. 90

There is nothing else known to me here that is worth writing about, for I do not doubt that your friends will have written to you fully about their own affairs and anything else that concerns us here. In any case, my dearest Erasmus, since I cannot apply the rule, which you stated with such perfect truth in your letter, that friendship is more enjoyable when it is also shared by many people, pray see to it, I beg you by your guardian genius, that I somehow become known to those eminent literary figures, not that I am keen on my own reputation, but to show them that by their own merit and scholarship they have deserved to be universally beloved. What is more, dearest Erasmus, while we all yield to you in everything, here is one thing I will never concede – that you should outrun me in the race of friendship. I realize from experience the perfect truth of what you said long ago, that men have much to gain from growth and time and knowledge of affairs. What I used to admire now fills me with regret and shame. Mind you take great care of your health, which is so subject to attacks of illness. And then make sure that the illness does not get worse or recur, so that you may long be fit for all your labours (I would compare them to a great rock or a treadmill, were not the labour so honourable and so glorious). If you set off for Italy, you must take greater care of your health there than anywhere, and please look after it, not merely for your own sake but for the whole of Christendom. If only you were to make an early return to us; it will indeed be a red-letter day that sees you back in Louvain. 95

100

105

110

115

Dear me, I had almost forgotten something by no means to be overlooked: please give my warmest greetings to Froben the prince of all printers (if our Dirk will not mind my saying so); for all we who are fond of books owe him no common debt. May the Lord God grant him many years of life and happiness, that he may be equal to his most honourable calling, in which to my thinking he has left Aldus himself far behind. What has he printed that is not distinguished for its scholarship, and so well finished too! Farewell, Erasmus, my phoenix among scholars! 120

Louvain, 14 July 1518

* * * * *

90 shallow water] Cf *Adagia* I i 45.
110 great rock] Cf *Adagia* II iv 40.
121 Aldus] The famous Venetian printer Aldo Manuzio; cf Ep 207 introduction.

853 / To Jean Le Sauvage Basel, 15 July 1518

This is an additional preface for a new edition of the *Institutio principis christiani* (Basel: Froben July 1518), originally written for the young Prince Charles and dedicated to him (cf lines 68–9, Ep 393). The text had been revised by Erasmus at Froben's request (cf Ep 801:16–19). Since it is unlikely that the news of the chancellor's death had not reached Basel by 15 July (cf Ep 852:72–3) one may assume that the letter was post-dated so as to agree with the expected date of publication. The date is given in Latin as 'Ides of July.' Such tentative dates as 'Calends' or 'Ides' occur frequently in contemporary prefaces (cf Epp 710, 799, 909, 1010). Indeed, the printing may have been well advanced when Erasmus and his friends learnt simultaneously about Le Sauvage's death and the arrival in the Netherlands of Prince Ferdinand. As it was too late to change the whole dedicatory epistle Erasmus hastened to add the last paragraph, suggesting that the edition was really undertaken for Ferdinand's benefit. On the printed page the corresponding lines are slightly indented. The first and third paragraphs are taken, almost without change, from Ep 793, the letter actually sent to Le Sauvage.

In 1524 Erasmus was evidently referring to this letter when he mentioned a 'preface to Ferdinand ... added to my book on the Prince,' which was often omitted in reprints of the *Institutio*; cf Allen I 39.

TO THE RIGHT HONOURABLE JEAN LE SAUVAGE, LORD HIGH
CHANCELLOR OF HIS CATHOLIC MAJESTY KING CHARLES, FROM
ERASMUS OF ROTTERDAM, LEAST AMONG THE SAME KING'S
COUNCILLORS, GREETING
From time to time your chaplain Pierre Barbier, who plays Pylades to my 5
Orestes, castigates me with the kind of letter that might pick a quarrel,
because after refusing to take part in your Spanish journey I do not at least
pay my respects to your Highness in the way of frequent letters. If I were
persuaded that a man of your wisdom either felt the need of a letter or
gauged the loyalty of your supporters by trivial tributes of the kind, I should 10
in this matter refuse to take refuge in any excuse, however just, although I
can say with perfect truth that hitherto I have been as heavily burdened by
my literary labours as you are by the business of so great a prince and of more
than one kingdom. That your burden is more glorious I would not deny, but
heavier I cannot think it, if for a moment I may compare the elephant and the 15

* * * * *

853
5 Pylades] Cf Ep 846:21n.
7 take part] Cf Ep 596 introduction.

gnat. As it is, I know you are cast in a heroic, superhuman mould, and yet there is but one of you, and you are assailed on every side by the great pressure of affairs; and so I think there could be no better way of showing myself truly dutiful than to forgo the duty of paying my respects. In fact, I should feel I was doing wrong in every way – both to his Catholic Majesty, to   20 whom you stand as Hercules did to Atlas, or (if you prefer) he is Hercules and you are his Theseus, and to the whole dominions of that mighty prince, the prosperity of which you seem sent by the kindness of heaven to promote – were I to interrupt you often with a letter, especially as it would convey no business but my humble duty. And this devotion I would gladly prove by   25 more solid evidence, were my powers of mind equal to my zeal; by Christ's help, prove it I will, some day, if the powers above graciously grant me a few more years of life and health.

But now I must grind on for some months more at the treadmill to which I have consigned myself; I made the bed, and I must lie on it; though all the   30 time I am employed much as your Highness is, with equal effort, though with unequal success and far from equal glory. You act with universal applause to a packed audience from the whole world; you guide the affairs of a prince on whose genius, more than on aught else, the sum of human affairs seems to depend and guide them in such a way that between you there might seem to   35 be a kind of noble competition: does he show more integrity as he holds supreme dominion all by himself over so many kingdoms, or you as you fulfil the highest office in the state, servant and master alike without parallel? I on the other hand, shut up and silent among my books, do all I can to promote the cause of the most liberal studies, doing the prince's business also, in a   40 way, as much as you; for I know that nothing is so near his heart as that, under his auspices, Christian piety and scholarship worthy of Christians should blossom more and more among us and be spread far and wide. And yet dominion may perhaps be spread by force of arms; the spreading of true religion needs other forces, other weapons. In this field, which I think even   45 more important than the other, I may be no general, but I do my duty as a private soldier and never shall I regret it, if I have to fight to the end. Only I pray that Christ almighty may give his blessing to the common efforts of us both. And so he will, if we in all sincerity promote his interests and not ours; and in no way shall we better promote our own than by promoting his.   50

* * * * *

16 gnat] Cf *Adagia* iii i 27.
21 Hercules] Cf Ep 793:14n.
30 made the bed] Literally 'I have pounded the herbs and must eat the results'; cf *Adagia* i i 85.

Buffeted as I am by ill health and by the onslaughts of malicious critics, I live in spirit more than body.

In any case, I count myself happy, and I render thanks to Christ our Saviour at the news which I learn in a letter from my friends, that amid the stormy seas of anxiety and peril which otherwise a heart of steel could 55 scarcely confront, your Highness has enjoyed unbroken good health, whether it is some rare felicity of nature that gives you this strength beyond your years, or you derive it from outstanding devotion to your great prince and to your country, or it is a gift made to you for the prince's sake, and through you to us all, by the kind providence of a heavenly power that 60 wishes to help the human race. As I look upon your active old age, equal to such a burden of affairs, I always seem to see a Massinissa or a Cato, except that you are their equal in endurance and surpass them in wisdom and toleration. If only we might be blessed with many such, we might hope soon to see the Christian world blossom with liberal studies, high standards of 65 conduct, and all the joys of peace.

I hear the illustrious Prince Ferdinand has arrived here safely. I have resumed work for his benefit on a book on the education of a prince, seeing that it has long been unnecessary for Charles, thanks partly to the natural gifts which anticipate in him all the qualities needed in a great monarch, and 70 partly to your intelligent and loyal counsels. Farewell.

Basel, 15 July 1518

854 / From Ambrogio Leoni   Venice, 19 July 1518

> This letter was answered by Ep 868 and published in the *Farrago*. Ambrogio Leoni of Nola (d c 1525) taught medicine at Naples before studying Greek. From 1507 he lived in Venice and belonged to Aldus' circle both as a physician and as a translator of Greek works.

AMBROGIO LEONI OF NOLA, PHYSICIAN, TO ERASMUS OF
ROTTERDAM, GREETING
Hitherto, dearest Erasmus, I have regarded as fabulous the ancient accounts of Pythagoras and Proteus, one of them returning often to this life-giving air

* * * * *

51 ill health] Cf Ep 847:7n.
62 Massinissa or a Cato] Cf Ep 793:29n.
67 Ferdinand] Younger brother of King Charles; see Ep 917 introduction.

854
4 Pythagoras] Of Samos, sixth century BC. He taught the transmigration of souls, and his own successive reincarnations (as a peacock, the Homeric hero

and each time dying afresh, the other changing himself into various shapes 5
whenever he pleased; for you know there was not much difference in the
behaviour of the two. But now I no longer smile at such tales as trumpery or
fables; I believe them to be history, for I know that we are blest with both of
them in your sole person. In such a short space of time you have often died
and returned to life, and no less often changed your shape for something 10
new and different. First I heard, actually from Aldus, that you had died in
France and a few years later come to life again in Germany. Then it was
reported that your loss was mourned in Germany, and soon afterwards you
reappeared in Italy. Lastly I was given to understand that you had met your
end in England and have now retraced your steps from Avernus and 15
appeared in France, whence you have written to me and to fellow-
countrymen of mine and made us all feel much better. So I thought I must be
seeing a second Pythagoras. Besides that, you not only changed from an
Italian to a Frenchman and from a Frenchman into a German (like the change
from a calf into a bird and from a bird into a kind of breadcorn, for which they 20
wrongly read *semen* in the text of Pliny) but you have turned from a poet
into a theologian and effected a transmigration from theologian to Cynic
philosopher, and then finally exchanged the Cynic for an orator – marvellous metamorphoses, which we thought the property of Proteus and no
one else. For I have seen numberless books of yours in print, in which you 25
have rung the changes on the different personalities or characters of which I
speak and have won praise and admiration from a large circle of readers,
who moreover all speak constantly of you and of what you say, not as

* * * * *

Euphorbus, Homer himself, etc) were celebrated (eg, Persius 6.11).

4 Proteus] The old man of the sea who can turn himself into any shape; cf *Adagia*
   II ii 74.
9 often died] For various rumours of Erasmus' death see Epp 194:11–15, 270
   introduction, 479:4–5, 948:63–4, 950:32–3, 1008, 1142.
15 Avernus] A volcanic lake in Campania, supposedly an entrance to the Nether
   regions; Virgil *Aeneid* 6.126 and 128
21 Pliny] The play on words cannot be translated. *Italus*, an Italian, was derived
   by Varro from a Greek word *italos* meaning 'calf' *(vitulus)* (Aulus Gellius 11.1.1);
   Gallus means a Gaul (Frenchman), *gallus* a cock; Pliny (*Historia naturalis* 18.82
   and 198) gives to a 'kind of grain' (spelt) the name 'seed' (*semen*), for which
   Leoni appears to write *germen* ('grain') in order to recall 'German.'
22 Cynic philosopher] The Cynics or 'dog' philosophers, so called after the
   nickname of Diogenes of Sinope (fifth century BC), were represented both in
   Greece and in ancient Rome, but they did not constitute a proper school of
   philosophy and were on the whole too individualistic to hold a common set of
   basic precepts. It is therefore difficult to know what Leoni wished to imply by
   using the term here.

though you were one individual who produced these important opinions, but as if they had three or four different authors.   3(

What is more, those transformations of yours have done something else for me. Long ago, I used to laugh at Pythagoras, who when born again used to recognize and refer to the fact that he had lived in another epoch; for Aristotle had proved that in death no memory remains of what had happened earlier during life. But now, when I see you have died so often   3!
and returned to the light of the sun without forgetting me and my friends and with your memory intact, I turn up my nose at Aristotle, whose diligence has led him astray. But though it may be like that, dear Erasmus, I have my fears, even though you may have enjoyed your changes, that they may turn out otherwise than what you intended and what happened in   4(
earlier transformations. I should like therefore to urge you to restrain your ambitions within the kind of life you lead at the moment, maintain the status quo by every means in your power, and incur no risk of further change for fear you may suffer what often happens to divers who, after frequently re-emerging from the water into which they have plunged so boldly,   4
sometimes swim confidently under the water and then are never seen to come up anywhere. Remember your own adage: Not without reason to Abydos sail; for I know no change more fraught with danger than the changes from life to death and from one shape to another.

Here however I have no news to send you that you might care to hear.   5
Apart from what goes on in the literary way there is nothing that seems appropriate to you; and literature itself is sadly neglected everywhere and shivering as though at death's door. For great rumblings of Turkish arms are heard in Italy, which take their rise in Egypt, Syria, and Persia; and this terrifies the poor Muses, who as you know are poor virgins and but ill clad;   5
they see death staring them in the face, and with them all literary activity must inevitably die out too. Still, I must think of something to say. You are to know that it has been resolved in the Venetian senate, and even published

* * * * *

34 Aristotle] Memory to him is an affection, in part at least physical, hence not separable from the body; therefore the essay De *memoria et reminiscentia* is included in the *Parva naturalia*.

47 adage] *Adagia* I vii 93. To sail up the Dardanelles against the current, past Abydos at their narrowest part, was proverbially hard work.

54 Egypt, Syria, and Persia] The Ottoman sultan Selim I conquered Syria and Egypt between August 1516 and April 1517. For frequent diplomatic contacts between Shah Ismail and Venice before and after the Turkish victory against Persia in August 1514 see E. von Palombini *Bündniswerben abendländischer Mächte um Persien* (Wiesbaden 1968) 45–60.

by the town crier, that a successor is to be chosen to Marcus Musurus, to give
public lectures in Greek; and the stipend has been fixed at one hundred gold   60
pieces. This has attracted a large field of competitors; for a two-month period
has been prescribed, in which candidates are to give in their names and to
demonstrate by publicly going through and expounding Greek authors
what manner of men they are, and whether tongue and brain are any good.
Should there be anyone therefore under those skies of yours who has a   65
reputation and some knowledge of Greek, pray inform him personally of this
decision, so that if it appeals to him to be a competitor and to expound Greek
texts, he may arrive here within the space of two months. You know
moreover that great crowd of listeners that used to cheep like chicks while
Musurus clucked over them. Not a few of these have now turned out good   70
big pullets; no more cheeping, they chirrup and cackle and have high hopes
of actually mounting their master's rostrum. Among the more polished
performers is one Pietro Alcionio, who has made a number of highly
polished translations from Greek into Latin. He has reproduced several
orations of Isocrates and Demosthenes in such pure Ciceronian style that   75
you might think you were reading our Arpinate himself, and has turned
many of Aristotle's pieces so lucidly that Latium could proudly say 'Lo
Aristotle now belongs to us.' This same young man, as a devoted student of
the best literature in both languages, is also very much attached to you and a
very great admirer of your researches.   80

    In conclusion you shall hear something of myself, who am now an old
man as well as an old friend. I have lived since you left us in the way in which
I lived while you were here, which you well know, steadily mumbling away
over books in both languages, with the idea of producing in my old age
something worthy of my Lion name; not like some woman who while only a   85
slip of a girl wants to find herself in a family way at the earliest moment and is
delighted to become a mother in no time at all, for the children of such are

* * * * *

59 successor ... to Marcus Musurus] Erasmus had already been encouraged to
    apply in June 1517 (cf Ep 589:18–31). For Musurus see Ep 574 introduction.
60 one hundred gold pieces] Undoubtedly Venetian ducats. If so, a stipend then
    worth £33 6s 6d gros Flemish = £207 10s 0d tournois = £22 18s 4d sterling. Cf
    CWE 1 314, 338. For the stipend cf Ep 836:8n. Leoni is referring to a motion
    passed by the Venetian senate in June 1518. In the end Vettore Fausto was
    appointed; cf J.B. Ross in *Renaissance Quarterly* 29 (1976) 544–5.
73 Alcionio] The only translations of his known to have been published were a
    collection of writings of Aristotle (Venice: B. de' Vitali April 1521), but his
    continued interest in rhetorical texts is attested to by his public lectures on
    Demosthenes in 1526–7; see Ep 450:29n; DBI.
76 Arpinate] Arpinum was the birthplace of Cicero.

MVSVRE Ó MANSVRE PARVM
PROPERATA TVLISTI PRÆMIA
NAMQVE CITO TRADITA RAPTA
CITO·

Marci Musuri Cretensis sepulchrum·

Petri Marsi·

QVÆ SOLA ELOQVII SVPERABAT GLORIA,ET ILLAM
PERDIDIMVS, TECVM VIXIT ET INTERIIT·

Roma·

Tomb of Marcus Musurus
Tobias Fendt *Monumenta sepulcrorum* (Breslau:
C. Scharffenberg 1574) fol 26
Reproduced by permission of the
Huntington Library, San Marino, California

weaklings from birth and cannot long survive. I have conceived several
books, some of which I bring to birth shortly; others are born now and
published. I have composed a modest work in three books on my native city   90
of Nola, which has been printed, and have also compiled a large work
divided into forty-six books, an attack on Averroes based on Peripatetic
principles, which is likewise in print; so you can see that I too have not been
wasting my nights on a pile of pillows.

Something in the way of a letter in reply to this, though it comes only   95
from me, would be most welcome; I long to hear from you, not only to know
that you are well, as I very greatly hope, but to be told by you some of the
things that go on among those who have said farewell to this life, and which
region makes the more agreeable place of residence. You really know both,
after exchanging life for death and death for life so often. Farewell, and keep   100
a kindness for me, as I know you do.

From Venice, 19 July 1518, from the grocer's at the sign of the Coral

855 / To Paolo Bombace   Basel, 26 July 1518

This letter is Erasmus' second answer to Ep 729. In a previous answer from
Louvain (Ep 800) he had still expressed the hope of meeting his old friend (Ep
210) in Switzerland, where Bombace was completing a mission as secretary to
the papal nuncio, Antonio Pucci. But by the time Erasmus arrived at Basel,
Bombace had evidently left for Rome. This second answer was published at
once in the *Auctarium* of August 1518. Its principal contents, the praise of Pucci
and of the English court and the declaration of peace with Lefèvre, are
inserted to gain immediate publicity.

DESIDERIUS ERASMUS OF ROTTERDAM TO HIS FRIEND
PAOLO BOMBACE, GREETING

I cannot agree: what more suitable destination for the warlike Bombace, that

* * * * *

88 weaklings from birth] Cf Aristotle *De generatione animalium* 767b.
89 shortly] In 1519 he published his translation of Actuarius *De urinis* (Venice: B.
   de' Vitali); cf also Ep 868:35n.
90 modest work] *De Nola patria* (Venice: J. Rubeus 4 September 1517)
91 large work] *Castigationes in Averroem* (Venice: B. and M. de' Vitali 25 September
   1517). Averroes (ibn-Rushd) of Cordoba was a highly controversial twelfth-
   century philosopher, particularly influential in the West.
102 Coral] Cf Ep 450:28.

855
3 warlike] Cf Ep 251:16–24.

doughty warrior, as Homer loves to say, than the Helvetii? Nor had you any
reason to fear the frostbite there, like poor Trebatius among the ancient   5
Britons, seeing how those ubiquitous stoves of theirs make one sweat even
in midwinter. I put off an answer to your letter, thinking I should be able to
greet you personally either at Rome or in Switzerland. I found the excellent
Antonio Pucci, the papal legate, here; he earns one's respect in any case as a
highly gifted man, but can have no higher title to my affection than his   10
sincere good will towards you. On arriving in Basel, he at once sent his
people to pay his respects, with a pressing invitation to dinner and
conversation. Not to put too fine a point on it, he had to entertain my
shadows, if I may so call the dear and familiar friends of mine whom he had
invited for my sake, especially Beatus and the Amerbachs, who are known to   15
you too. Great man as he is, he had to descend to this treadmill if he wished
to make the acquaintance of my noble self.

    And why, you may well ask, did that noble self show so much hauteur?
Dear Bombace, what made me so uncivil and so distant was not my feelings,
but the most accursed ill health. It afflicted me for over a month and after an 20
interval attacked me again so severely that I sent for the doctor, a thing I do
not normally do unless I am more or less tired of life; and so persistent is the
trouble that it seems destined to finish me off. Pace has returned to us and
has paid me his respects in a series of treatises rather than letters; but by bad
luck I had no speech with him, for he was soon summoned to England by the   25
king. That you found him congenial, I assure you, does not surprise me: you
are birds of a feather. I cannot tell you how popular he is with his own
people, especially that very civilized king, and that remarkable man, the
cardinal.

    You know, my excellent Bombace, how averse I have always been from   30

* * * * *

4 Helvetii] Erasmus is probably thinking not only of the warlike reputation of the
    Swiss but also of the campaigns of Julius Caesar in Gaul. For Erasmus'
    perception of the Swiss as warriors and mercenaries cf Epp 134, 360, 610:13n,
    809:30–2 and especially some highly critical remarks in the adage 'Ut fici' (II viii
    65; cf Ep 829:36n) in the 1517–18 edition. These were removed, however, from
    later editions; cf Ep 858:643n.
5 Trebatius] Cf Ep 800:7n.
9 Pucci] See Ep 860 introduction.
15 Amerbachs] For the brothers Bruno, Basilius, and Bonifacius Amerbach cf Epp
    331, 408 introductions.
20 ill health] Cf Ep 847:7n.
23 returned to us] After his embassy to the Swiss and Germans; cf Ep 619. For
    Richard Pace cf Ep 211:5n; for his letters cf Ep 742:1–2.
27 birds of a feather] Cf Adagia I ii 22.
29 cardinal] Thomas Wolsey

the courts of princes; it is a life which I can only regard as gilded misery under a mask of splendour; but I would gladly move to a court like that, if I could grow young again. The king is the most intelligent of the monarchs of our time and enjoys good literature. The queen is astonishingly well read, far beyond what would be surprising in a woman, and as admirable for piety as she is for learning. The men who have most influence with them are those who excel in the humanities and in integrity and wisdom. Thomas Linacre is the physician; it would be a waste of time to praise him to you, for he displays his quality in his published works. Cuthbert Tunstall is his 'Master of the Rolls,' an office which they regard as of the highest standing. You would hardly believe, my dear Paolo, what a world of all good things is embraced in the mention of that man's name. Thomas More is of the privy council, not only the Muses' darling but the pattern of all charm and of every grace, whose ability you have been able to discern to some extent in what he has written. Pace, almost a brother to him, is secretary. William Mountjoy is head of her majesty's household. John Colet is a select preacher. I have mentioned only the leaders. Among the chaplains is John Stokesley who, besides this scholastic theology, in which he is second to none, has a more than common skill in the three tongues. This is the kind of man of whom his palace is full, more like an academy than a king's court. What Athens or Stoa or Lyceum could one prefer to a court like that?

Your congratulations about Lefèvre are not more welcome than the confrontation itself was unpleasant. If only he had shown a little more moderation in his attack on me! But things are like that: no man is wise morning, noon, and night. If there is anything wrong in this, I like to think it is my destiny that is at fault. For what else could I do? Lefèvre is an upright

* * * * *

32 a mask] Seneca *Letters* 80.8
32 court like that] The following praise is a strong indication that Erasmus was seriously considering a move to England in the near future; cf Ep 834 introduction.
34 queen] Catherine of Aragon (1485–1536). For the remarkable humanistic education of Henry VIII's first queen cf G. Mattingly *Catherine of Aragon* (London 1942) 16–17.
37 Linacre] See Ep 118:27n.
42 of the privy council] See Ep 829:6n.
45 Mountjoy ... Colet] See Epp 79, 106 introductions.
47 Stokesley] John Stokesley (1475–1539). After extensive studies in Oxford and Italy, he became chaplain and almoner to Henry VIII and later bishop of London.
52 not more welcome] Reading *magis gratum* for the *magis ingratum* of the first edition
54 wise] Cf *Adagia* II iv 29.

35

40

45

50

55

Catherine of Aragon
Artist unknown
National Portrait Gallery, London

man, learned, kind-hearted, last but not least an old friend of mine. Some evil spirit, I suppose, grudged me that felicity; and now my attitude towards him is such that it will be extremely painful to me if anyone thinks worse of Lefèvre because of me. Certain people I could name, who enjoy this kind of 60 vendetta, spread rumours of a quarrel between us. But he and I are of one mind, and we shall give no grounds for thinking that a single shadow of disagreement has ended a true friendship of such long standing. If there was contention between Barnabas and Paul, what wonder if some human feeling of the kind arose between us? How important scholars in your part of the 65 world think my works are, I do not know; here they certainly attach to them an importance I cannot accept. And yet there are people who bark at them loudly, such people for the most part as either read nothing I write or would waste their time if they read it, good or bad. If the honest opinion of so many excellent men did not support me, I should long ago have repented of all the 70 midnight oil I have expended on promoting to the best of my ability the common cause of scholarship, and particularly of sacred study.

These widespread rumours about the Turks are suspected by most people, who have so often discovered before now that while the oarsmen face one way the boat goes the other, and that nowhere was there more truth 75 in the old saying 'In war what's new is mostly untrue.' But whatever is going on in those parts, I pray it may turn out for the general good; for a great change in human affairs is under way, and there must be danger in it. Your news of Marcus Musurus and Paleotti is distressing; and all the time the man by the entrance will outlive the whole tribe of crows. But all this is, as the 80 Greek says, on the knees of the gods. Fausto has died in France, and in England Andrea Ammonio, one of whom long held court in Paris, and the other would have reached the highest positions had he been granted a longer life. Mind that for your part you look after your health.

Basel, 26 July 1518 85

* * * * *

61 of one mind] Cf Ep 721 introduction.
64 contention] Cf Acts 15:39.
73 Turks] Cf Epp 729:56n, 854:53–5.
76 old saying] Cf *Adagia* II x 19.
79 Musurus and Paleotti] Bombace had reported the deaths of Musurus and Camillo Paleotti; see Ep 729:60n, 61n.
79 man by the entrance] Erasmus uses a Greek phrase, the meaning of which we do not know.
80 crows] The crow was famous for longevity; *Adagia* I vi 64.
81 Fausto] Andrelini; see Ep 810:489n.
82 Ammonio] See Ep 623.

856 / To Willibald Pirckheimer   Basel, [July–August] 1518

> This letter answers Ep 747, which dealt mostly with the controversy around
> Johann Reuchlin. It was not selected to appear in the *Auctarium* but was
> included in the *Farrago* (cf Ep 861 introduction). Pirckheimer, the Nürnberg
> patrician and scholar (cf Ep 318 introduction), did not see it until it was printed;
> cf Ep 1095.

ERASMUS OF ROTTERDAM TO HIS FRIEND WILLIBALD, GREETING
I do not know whose fault it was that that longish letter of yours took such a
time to reach me. It made clear to me that my friend Willibald, whom I knew
already for a civilized and upright man and a good scholar, is also endowed
with exceptional wisdom and a nobility of spirit proper to a man of no   5
plebeian sort. You speak of princes: my fortune would be made, did I not
find freedom too sweet. Anything that costs a loss of freedom seems to me
too dearly bought. Now that I have learnt to be content with my present
modest lot, I shall remain unmoved, whether they give me something or
nothing. I only wish I were not even less well endowed with the true wealth   10
you think me so rich in. Your account of what you have done I find entirely
convincing. It is typical of your courtesy that you seem actually to thank me
for my criticism, which was as bold as it was badly timed.
      When I think over the riots and the cabals that these men make, my dear
Willibald, I sometimes wonder what they are aiming at; sometimes I am   15
indignant, sometimes sorry for their blindness and their folly. Astrologers
tell us that some plagues both of mind and body are inflicted by the stars;
poets say, by the infernal powers; Homer puts the blame for turmoil of this
sort on Ate; some authors attribute something of the kind to the god Pan.
Whatever its source, this plague is a major disaster. I do not choose to think   20
of that circumcised fellow; even to mention him I regard as an evil omen.
What came into Gratius' head, that he should be willing to prostitute his
literary skill, such as it is, to the folly, or more truly the ambition, of certain
individuals, though he seems endowed with gifts which, coupled with
serious work and sound judgment, might have given him a place among   25
stylists and men of letters? As it is, the only feat he is known for is his abuse
of Reuchlin and his friends, and his having apparently lent the aid of a hack

* * * * *

856
18 Homer] *Iliad* 19.91
19 Pan] Cf *Adagia* III vii 3.
21 circumcised fellow] Johann Pfefferkorn; cf 485:22n, 694 introduction.
22 Gratius] For Ortwinus Gratius see Epp 622 introduction, 821:19n.

scribbler, writing for his bread, to spiteful men who cannot write. Many times it has entered my mind to warn the reverend father Jacob of Hoogstraten against putting the labour of so many years behind this quarrelsome business and doing himself so much harm in the eyes of the learned world by what he publishes. As I read his pamphlets, I often say to myself 'I wish you could see yourself with my eyes!' But he and I are not really intimate, so that neither knows the other very well. And I know from experience that a rather outspoken warning is not always successful even among friends. And so I was afraid that if I took too much thought for his reputation I might fall under the suspicion of doing Reuchlin's business for him; he and I are indeed friends, but from anything to do with his case I am as far as possible.

Some say that Hoogstraten's character is not wholly uncivilized; others tell a different story. Personally I always prefer to believe those who speak well of a man rather than ill. But to confess the truth quite frankly, when I skimmed through the man's pamphlets, I was forced to think less well of him than before – forced by the facts. He has some hangers-on to provide the applause, to cool his brow with cold water, to shout 'Bravo!' and their valuation, their adulation rather, gives him his clue to the whole world's opinion. He had supporters here too, but of the sort to act in secret and by trickery; though they have lately begun to put a bold front on it and betray the disease of the mind they have concealed so long. Nor am I yet on the scent of what disturbs them so, except that they are convinced, I feel, in their idiot way that if the humanities begin to flourish everywhere, as they now do, this will seriously weaken the authority of those who, beyond this modern teaching of theirs, have learnt nothing and have nothing to look forward to. We ourselves are in part the cause of this evil: we attack their work more bitterly than we should and cry up our own subjects to a pitch which they are bound to resent; we choose to imitate their bad points instead of surpassing them by our good ones, and we spend more time thinking how their chicanery deserves to be treated than how we ourselves ought to behave. I myself in several contexts touch on imperfect theologians who are unworthy of the name, but of a sort that I supposed not to exist among us. I have experienced behaviour in certain persons that I could not have credited

* * * * *

32 his pamphlets] Cf Epp 680:28n, 849:21–30. The following remarks provide an important clue to the existence of direct relations between Erasmus and Hoogstraten; cf Ep 1006 introduction; Allen Ep 1342:614–15.

47 here too] Erasmus is clearly thinking of Louvain and the opposition to the Collegium Trilingue; cf Epp 670, 691 introductions, and for Lee's criticism of Reuchlin Ep 898A introduction.

48 bold front] cf *Adagia* I viii 47.

Udalricus Zasius
Engraving by Théodore de Bry,
from J.J. Boissard *Icones virorum illustrium* (Frankfurt 1597)
Öffentliche Bibliothek, University of Basel

anywhere in the world in a brothel-keeper. As I hope for Christ's mercy, this
is the truth. In the virulent attacks of malice by which I am buffeted on all
sides, my first consolation is a good conscience; my second, the approval of
many men who are generally admitted to be of high character, outstanding   65
scholarship, and fine judgment.

My New Testament will shortly appear in a new edition, with a good
deal of revision, but somewhat less than I had hoped, owing to the state of
my health, by whose capacity we ought always to measure the tasks we take
on. That I have fallen into a controversy with Lefèvre grieves me as much as   70
it does you, and that for many reasons, but principally because I was sorry
that this business should give so much pleasure to men who from good
letters get nothing but pain. But steps are being taken, and there is good
hope that this surface wound will soon heal over. I am much attached to
Lefèvre and do not think he entirely dislikes me. As for paying you a visit,   75
my excellent Willibald, I only wish my ability to do so matched the warmth of
your welcome. Farewell.

Basel, 1518

857 / From Udalricus Zasius   Freiburg, 13 August 1518

The best source for this letter is a manuscript copy taken by Bonifacius
Amerbach (line 35), who was at this time Zasius' student in Freiburg but had
returned to Basel for the summer vacation (Öffentliche Bibliothek of the
University of Basel, MS C VIa 35 ii f19 recto). From a contemporary letter (AK II Ep
622) we learn that Amerbach was then collecting the correspondence between
Erasmus and Zasius. His collection includes copies of Epp 358 and 376 and the
original autographs of Epp 366, 379, and 859.

There is also a copy of this letter in the Deventer Letter-book, the first one to
be entered by Johannes Hovius (see Ep 867:189n; Allen I 605–6). Allen prints a
facsimile opposite Ep 857.

It appears that Zasius, a distinguished legal scholar (cf Ep 303 introduction),
had recently gone to Basel for his first personal visit with Erasmus; this letter
presents his reactions. It was answered by Ep 859, and both were printed in the
Auctarium.

* * * * *

67 New Testament] See Ep 864 introduction.
73 good hope] Cf Epp 721 introduction, 855:60–3.
75 visit] Pirckheimer apparently expected to see Erasmus on his return journey
   from Basel; cf P. Prachtbectius' letter to Pirckheimer, Freiburg, 5 August 1518,
   in *Documenta literaria varii argumenti* ed J. Heumann (Altorf 1758) 233.

Letter from Udalricus Zasius to Erasmus, Epistle 857
This is a copy made by Bonifacius Amerbach
Öffentliche Bibliothek, University of Basel, MS C VIA 35 ii fol 19 recto

UDALRICUS ZASIUS, TEACHER OF CIVIL LAW, TO ERASMUS OF
ROTTERDAM, GREETING

How right our Julianus is, great Erasmus, when he describes as impossible,
not to say merely difficult, questions which it will be impracticable to unravel
without the aid of the prince! I find this true in my own case: I forbear to ask   5
your help in the unravelling of literary questions because I see that this must
mean consulting the prince of humane studies, and to consort with him is, if
not impossible, at least very difficult. And so you must not dismiss me as
discourteous if I have not written to you so far. The prince is not to be
approached unadvisedly, although I both saw in you when I was with you   10
and have found by experience much that would provide matter for a letter.
At first sight the authority in your face and glance, and a certain look of the
great man, so frightened me that, though I had given much thought
beforehand to my reception of you, when I found myself in your presence I
could hardly open my mouth; like a man who totters unsteadily between   15
stops and starts, I could hardly bring out a few broken syllables. After the
failure of this first interview, nothing emerged in me later that could make me
look like the man you thought I was.

   I guessed that this would happen, but I wanted to see you at all costs,
even if my reputation must suffer for it. I set a higher value on meeting you in   20
person, even if it meant some loss of face, than on the misleading reports
which gave you a false idea of greater things in your Zasius when you were
at a distance. Your measured movements, your easy flow of words like some
delightful stream that runs from a fresh spring, your wonderful kindliness,
your air of authority graced with a beautiful courtesy – who would not wish   25
to see and wonder at and enjoy all this, even if it cost him something? Pass on
me then such judgment as you please, for I am only fit to be put in my place.
Yet I shall feel that I have made good use of the life I live, the air I breathe, for
I have seen Erasmus my great patron deity; and since the days of Cicero and
Quintilian no age has known a greater scholar or one who could surpass you   30
in divine and human learning and great gifts of style. Your disapproval, with
the verdict of your kindly nature, means more to me than praise from other
people, provided you do not abandon me, provided you suffer me to remain
among your dependents. Farewell, and do not abate your good will towards

       * * * * *

857
3 Julianus] Salvius Julianus, a leading Roman jurist of the second century AD
   and a quaestor under the emperor Hadrian, composed a digest in ninety books,
   which is often quoted in the *Digest* of Justinian. The specific reference has not
   been traced.
9 so far] Since their recent meeting

that true disciple of Erasmus, Bonifacius. My very best wishes to my kindest   35
of friends Beatus Rhenanus, and to the Amerbachs – heavens, what
excellent, what gifted characters!
    Freiburg, 13 August 1518
Forgive my unpolished writing; I was distracted by what I have in hand on
feudal uses, which as it happens breaks new ground, so that, my mind being   40
driven all astray, I was not my own master.
    Your sincere friend Zasius

858 / To Paul Volz   Basel, 14 August 1518

This is the preface to a new edition of the *Enchiridion militis christiani* (cf Ep 164),
printed by Froben in July (–August) 1518 (cf line 635n). Erasmus dispatched the
revised text in February or March 1518, and Froben promised to publish it at
once (cf Ep 801). The letter was reprinted in subsequent editions of the
Enchiridion and in the *Opus epistolarum* of 1529. While some passages may recall
Erasmus' own beginnings (lines 445–53, 476–88, 521–4), it is important as a
careful reflection on two matters of great concern at this time, Pope Leo x's
crusade (lines 85–165, 401–11) and Martin Luther's Ninety-five Theses (line
216n). More than that, it expresses with some coherence Erasmus' view of the
social and political order of Christendom (lines 244–394). For a recent and very
complete analysis of this letter see G. Chantraine *'Mystère' et 'Philosophie du
Christ' selon Erasme* (Namur-Gembloux 1971) 99–153.
    The new edition of the *Enchiridion* marks the beginning of a decade in which
the work achieved remarkable popularity as the manifesto of Christian
humanism, and this preface serves to underline the essential points. In 1523
Erasmus noted that adding this letter cost him the affection of certain
Dominicans who had previously praised the *Enchiridion* in public (Allen I 20).
Paul Volz (cf Ep 368 introduction) was a Benedictine abbot and member of the
Sélestat literary society.

TO THE REVEREND FATHER IN CHRIST DOCTOR PAUL VOLZ,
MOST RELIGIOUS ABBOT OF THE MONASTERY
COMMONLY CALLED HUGSHOFEN,
FROM DESIDERIUS ERASMUS OF ROTTERDAM, GREETING
It is true, most worthy Father, that I have begun to be less dissatisfied with   5
the small book entitled *The handy weapon of a Christian knight*, which I wrote

* * * * *

35 Bonifacius] Amerbach
40 feudal uses] *In usus feudorum epitome* was first published by H. Bebel, Basel
    1535.

long ago to please no one but myself and one quite uneducated private
friend, now that I see it approved by you and others like you; for being
yourselves endowed with pious learning and with learned piety, I know
that you would approve of nothing that is not equally pious and learned. But 10
now it almost begins to satisfy me, when I see it so often printed already and
still in demand as though it were a novelty – if what the printers tell me is not
entirely flattery. But then again I am often made uncomfortable by the
pointed comment of a learned friend some time ago, humorously uttered,
but I fear with as much truth as it had humour, that holiness of life is more 15
noticeable in the book than in its author. And I find this harder to bear,
because the same thing has happened in the man whose improvement was
the chief object of my labours: so far is he from tearing himself away from life
at court that he is plunged more deeply in it every day. How much piety this
shows I do not know, but in any case, as he himself admits, it is a very great 20
misfortune. Yet I am not wholly sorry for my friend, inasmuch as fortune
herself may teach him one day to repent, though he has been reluctant to
take my advice. But I myself, though I strive always to reach that goal, have
been assailed by my evil genius with so many mischances and so many
storms that compared with me Homer's Ulysses might be mistaken for 25
another Polycrates.

And yet I cannot altogether regret this work, if it encourages so many
people to the pursuit of true piety. Nor yet do I feel myself open to attack
from every quarter if I do not live up as I should to my own precepts. For one
thing, it is an element of goodness to have a sincere desire to be good, nor do 30
I think that one should reject a heart that is sincerely devoted to such
thoughts, although its efforts are sometimes unsuccessful. This must be
one's first purpose all one's life long, and repeated attempts will one day
succeed. A man who has really learnt the way has a good part of a
complicated journey already behind him. I am therefore unmoved by the 35
jeers of some men I could name who despise this small book as unlearned and
the kind of thing that any schoolmaster could write, because it handles no
Scotistic problems, as though nothing could show true learning without

* * * * *

858
7 private friend] Johann Poppenruyter; cf Epp 164, 698.
11 so often printed already] At least nine times
21 inasmuch] Reading *quoniam*
25 Ulysses] Ulysses symbolizes restlessness and countless misfortunes; Polycrates, tyrant of Samos, symbolizes unbroken felicity.
38 Scotistic problems] The Franciscan John Duns Scotus (d 1308) probably
represents here scholastic philosophy in general; cf Ep 798:24n.

them. Penetration I can do without, provided there is piety. It need not
equip men for the wrestling-schools of the Sorbonne if it equips them for the   40
tranquillity proper to a Christian. It need not contribute to theological
discussion provided it contributes to the life that befits a theologian. Why
deal with the questions that everyone deals with? On what else do our
swarms of students spend their time? There are almost as many commentaries on the *Sentences* as you can name theologians. Of makers of summaries   45
there is no end; one cannot count them – mixing this thing and that over and
over again, and like the men who sell drugs making old out of new, new out
of old, one out of many and many out of one all the time. How can a mass of
such volumes ever teach us how to live, when a whole lifetime would not
suffice to read them? It is as though a physician were to prescribe for a   50
patient who is acutely ill that he should read right through the works of
Jacques Desparts and all the books of others like him, in hopes of finding
what will restore him to health. Death will come upon him meanwhile, and
he will be past human aid.

Life flies so fast that we must have a present remedy within our reach.   55
Countless are the volumes they fill with their precepts on restitution,
confession, vows, scandalous behaviour, and endless other things! And
while they discuss everything in the smallest detail and define every point as
though they distrusted the intelligence of everyone except themselves and
indeed put no faith in Christ's mercy – they lay down precisely what he owes   60
in the way of reward or punishment for every action – yet they never agree
among themselves, and sometimes do not even explain the point clearly if
you consult them in more detail. So great is the variety in men's natures and
circumstances. Furthermore, suppose that they have defined everything
truly and correctly, not to mention the tedious and frigid style in which they   65
deal with these questions, how few men have the leisure to read through so
many tomes? Who can carry the *Secunda secundae* of Aquinas round with
him? And yet the good life is everybody's business, and Christ wished the
way to it to be accessible to all men, not beset with impenetrable labyrinths of
argument but open to sincere faith, to love unfeigned, and their companion,   70

* * * * *

45 *Sentences*] The *Sententiarum libri quattuor* of Peter Lombard, d 1164
45 makers of summaries] Cf Ep 575:34–7.
52 Desparts] Jacques Desparts (or Jacobus a Partibus) of Tournai (d 1458) was a
   physician, teacher, and canon of Notre Dame in Paris who left an enormous
   commentary on Avicenna, part of which was published in 1498; see DBF.
67 *Secunda secundae*] The second part of the second book of the *Summa theologiae* of
   Thomas Aquinas, often published separately as an authoritative manual of
   ethics

the hope that is not put to shame. Lastly, by all means let eminent rabbins, who must always be scarce, pore over these great tomes; but none the less we must take thought all the time for the unlettered multitude, for whom Christ died. He has already taught people the leading part of the Christian religion, who has fired them with the love of it. That wise king, bringing up his son to 75 true wisdom, takes not a little more pains in encouraging than in teaching him, as though to love wisdom were already close to having acquired it. It is a disgrace to do this in the eyes of lawyers and physicians, two kinds of men who have deliberately made their art as difficult as they can, that at the same time they may win richer profits and greater glory among the ignorant; but 80 how much more disgraceful thus to have treated the philosophy of Christ. On the contrary, it is right to strive for the opposite, to make it as easy and as open to all men as we possibly can; and our object should be not to show off our own attainments but to attract as many as we can to the Christian life.

At this moment war is preparing against the Turks; and whatever the 85 intentions of those who started it, we must pray that it may turn out well, not for a chosen few but for all in common. But what do we suppose will happen if, when we have beaten them (for I do not suppose we shall slaughter them to a man), to persuade them to embrace Christianity we set before them the works of Ockham and Durandus and their like, of Scotus and Gabriel and 90 Alvaro? What will they think, what will their feelings be (for though nothing else, they are at least human beings), when they hear these thorny and impenetrable thickets of argument – instances, formalities, quiddities, relativities – particularly when they see so little agreement on them among those eminent religious teachers that they often fight each other until they 95 are pale with fury and reduced to insults and spitting and sometimes even to fisticuffs? There are the Friars Preacher battling at short and long range for their precious Thomas; the Minorites on the other side defending their most Subtle and Seraphic Doctors, shield linked with shield, some speaking as nominalists and others as realists. What if they see it is such a difficult subject 100 that there can be no end to the discussion, what words we should use in

* * * * *

71 hope] Cf Rom 5:5.
71 rabbins] Cf below lines 484–7.
73 Christ died] Cf 1 Cor 8:11; Rom 14:15.
75 wise king] Prov 1:1, etc
85 Turks] Cf Ep 785:32–38.
90 Ockham ... Alvaro] A random assortment of scholastic theologians; cf Ep 844:199n. William of Ockham, d 1349; John Duns Scotus; Alvaro Pelayo, d 1352; cf Ep 575:37n.
99 Doctors] The Subtle Doctor is the Franciscan John Duns Scotus; the Seraphic is St Bonaventure.

speaking of Christ? Just as though you were concerned with some demon very difficult to please, whom you will have called up for your own damnation if you make any slip in the prescribed form of words, and not really with a most merciful Saviour, who demands nothing from us except a 105 pure and simple life. I ask you, in heaven's name; what good will such things do, especially if this self-confident doctrine finds its counterpart in our character and way of life? If our noise and bustle, worse than any tyrant's, give them a clear idea of our ambition, if from our rapacity and lechery and oppression they learn how greedy and profligate and cruel we are, how can 110 we find the effrontery to urge Christ's teaching on them, which is so infinitely different from all this? We shall have found the most effective way to defeat the Turks, once they have seen shining forth in us Christ's teaching and example, once they realize that we are not greedy for their empire, we have no thirst for their gold and no desire for their possessions, but seek 115 nothing at all beyond their salvation and the glory of Christ. This is the true and genuine and effective theology, which long ago made proud philosophers and unconquered monarchs bow the knee to Christ. If this and this alone could be our purpose, Christ himself will be at our side.

Nor does it make sense to prove ourselves truly Christians by killing as 120 many as we can, but by their salvation; not by sacrificing to Orcus many thousands of the infidel, but by turning as many as we can of those infidels into believers; not by cursing them with terrible execrations, but by praying religiously that heaven may send them salvation and a better state of mind. If we cannot put our hearts into something of the sort, we shall degenerate into 125 Turks long before we convert the Turks to our way of thinking. Suppose the chances of war, which are always doubtful, fall in our favour, the result may extend the kingdom of the pope and his cardinals; it will not extend the kingdom of Christ. His realm can never flourish until religion and charity and peace and innocence are in flower; as we are confident will happen 130 under the leadership of our excellent Leo the Tenth, if his zeal for what is best is not swept in another direction by the tide of human affairs. Christ declares himself the champion and prince of the kingdom of heaven; but there is nothing grand in this unless heaven is triumphant. For Christ did not die in order that the riches, the abundance, the armaments, and all the 135 fuss and fury of an earthly kingdom, which were once in the hands of pagans, or at least of lay princes not so very far from paganism, should now belong to a limited number of priests.

* * * * *

121 Orcus] The ruler of the realm of the dead, later identified with Pluto
133 prince] Cf John 18:36–7.

In my own opinion it will be found a good plan, long before we make the attempt by force of arms, to seek to win them by letters and by pamphlets.   140
What sort of letter, you ask? No threats, no bluster; they must breathe true fatherly affection and recall the spirit of Peter and Paul, they must not merely have the word 'apostolic' in the superscription, they must revive the activity of the apostles. I am not ignorant, of course, that all the springs and sources of the Christian philosophy are enshrined in the books of evangelists and   145
apostles; but the expression is alien and often confused, and the figures and turns of speech are out of the way, and this makes them so difficult that even we often have to toil quite hard before we understand them. It will be the best plan, therefore, in my opinion to entrust to a number of men both saintly and scholarly the task of reducing into brief compass the whole philosophy   150
of Christ, out of its purest sources in evangelists and apostles and its most generally accepted expositors, in a simple but none the less scholarly fashion, short but clear. What concerns the faith should be set out clause by clause, as few as possible; what relates to life should also be imparted in few words, and those words so chosen as to make them understand that Christ's   155
yoke is easy and comfortable and not harsh; to make them understand that they have acquired fathers and not despots, shepherds not robbers, and are invited to accept salvation and not dragged by force into slavery. They are human beings, as we are; there is neither steel nor adamant in their hearts. It is possible that they may be civilized, possible they may be won   160
over by kindness which tames even wild beasts. And the most effective thing of all is Christian truth. But those to whom the Roman pontiff chooses to delegate this task will be instructed at the same time not to diverge in any way from Christ our pattern, and at no point to consider the affections or desires of men.   165
        Something of this sort was taking shape in my mind after a fashion when I was working on this *Enchiridion*. I could see that the common body of Christians was corrupt not only in its affections but in its ideas. I pondered on the fact that those who profess themselves pastors and doctors for the most part misuse these titles, which belong to Christ, for their own   170
advantage; to say nothing for the moment of those whose fiat, yes or no, keeps all human affairs in perpetual flux, and at whose faults however obvious it is scarcely permitted to let fall a sigh. When all is dark, when the world is in tumult and men's opinions differ so widely, where can we take refuge, if not upon the sheet-anchor of the Gospel teaching? Is there any   175
religious man who does not see with sorrow that this generation is far the

* * * * *

167 *Enchiridion*] The title can mean either 'dagger' or 'handbook.'
171 yes or no] *Adagia* IV ix 39

most corrupt there has ever been? When did tyranny and greed lord it thus widely or go thus unpunished? When was so much importance ever attached to ceremonies? When did iniquity abound with so little to restrain it? When did charity wax colder? All we appeal to, all we read, all we hear, all our decisions – what do they taste of except of ambition and greed? Our plight would be sorry indeed, had not Christ left us some live coals of his teaching, some living unfailing rivulets from the spring of his mind. What we must do is this: abandon the cinders offered us by men and blow up those coals of his into flame (I gladly use Paul's word); follow up those rivulets until we find the living water that springs up to life eternal. We explore the bowels of this earth of ours to get the ores which feed our vices; are we never to mine the rich lodes of Christ, to win thence the salvation of souls? The winter of our wickedness never brings so low the fire of charity that it cannot be rekindled from the flint. Christ is our Rock; and this rock has in it the seeds of heavenly fire and veins of living water. Abraham long ago dug wells in every country, seeking veins of living water; and when the Philistines filled them with earth they were dug anew by Isaac and his sons, who, not content with restoring the old wells, dug new ones besides. Again the Philistines stir up strife and opposition; but he does not cease to dig.

Nor are we quite free of Philistines nowadays, who get more pleasure from earth than from fountains of living water – those people, I mean, who reek of earthly things and twist the Gospel teaching to serve earthly appetites, compelling it to be the slave of human ambition and to enhance their own discreditable gains and their despotic rule. And if some Isaac or one of his household should dig and find a pure source, at once they are all protests and objections because they know this source will be an obstacle to their gains and block their ambitions, even though it makes for Christ's glory. It is not long before they throw earth into it and stop up the source by some corrupt interpretation, driving away the man with the spade, or at the least so befoul the water with mud and filth that he who drinks from it gets more dirt and filth than liquid. They do not wish those who thirst after righteousness to drink from the crystal spring but take them to their trampled cisterns, which are full of rubble and contain no water. But the real sons of Isaac – Christ's true worshippers, that is – must not grow weary of this

* * * * *

185 Paul's word] 2 Tim 1:6; Rom 12:20
187 vices] Ovid *Metamorphoses* 2.769. Johann Poppenruyter owned a gun-foundry at Mechelen.
190 our Rock] 1 Cor 10:4
193 Isaac] Cf Gen 26:14–18.
209 cisterns] Jer 2:13

labour. For those who tip earth into the Gospel springs wish to be thought to be of their number, so that now it is by no means safe to teach the pure faith of Christ among Christians. So much have the Philistines grown in strength, fighting for earth, preaching earthly things and not the things of heaven, human things and not divine – those things, in fact, which tend not to 215 Christ's glory but to the profit of those who traffic in indulgences, in compositions, in dispensations, and suchlike merchandise. And this traffic is all the more perilous because they give their greed a façade of great names, eminent princes, the supreme pontiff, even Christ himself. And yet no man more truly forwards the business of the pontiff than he who publishes in its 220 pure form the heavenly philosophy of Christ, of which the pope is the principal teacher. No man does princes better service than he who sees to it that the condition of the people is as prosperous as possible and that they suffer as little as possible from tyranny.

But at this point someone from the serried ranks of our universities will 225 protest: 'It is easy to lay down in general what we should aim at and what we should avoid; but how in the mean time are we to answer those who need advice about what has happened and may happen?' In the first place, human affairs take so many shapes that definite answers cannot be provided for them all. Secondly, circumstances vary so widely that, unless we know what 230 they are, any definite answer is impossible. Last but not least, I rather doubt whether those who deal in principles can give a definite answer; they differ about so many points among themselves. And the more intelligent ones of that sort do not usually reply 'This you must do; do not do that' but 'This is in my view the safer course; this I regard as tolerable.' If only we have the single 235 eye filled with light of which the Gospel speaks, if our minds are like a house with the lamp of true faith set on a lampstand, these minor points will easily be scattered like a mist. If we have Christian charity like a carpenter's rule, everything will easily be set straight by that. But what will you do if this rule disagrees with the accepted tradition of centuries and the conduct laid down 240 by princes in their laws? For even that not seldom happens. Do not condemn what is done by princes in the execution of their duty; but conversely do not sully that heavenly philosophy of Christ by confusing it with the decrees of man. Let Christ remain what he is, the centre, with several circles running

* * * * *

216 indulgences] For Erasmus' recent acquaintance with Luther's Ninety-five Theses on indulgences see below lines 430–8, and Ep 785:39n. For Luther's reaction to this preface cf Ep 933:22–7.
236 Gospel] Matt 6:22
244 several circles] Cf J.K. McConica 'Erasmus and the Grammar of Consent' *Scrinium* II 82–4; Bietenholz *History and Biography* 85–6.

round him. Do not move that central mark from its place. Those who are   2.
nearest Christ – priests, bishops, cardinals, popes, and those whose
business it is to follow the Lamb wherever he may lead them – should
embrace the intense purity of the centre and pass on as much as they can to
those next to them. Let the second circle be for the lay princes, who with
their armies and their laws serve Christ after their fashion, whether in a just   2!
war they defeat the enemy and preserve the public peace or by lawful
punishments keep crime in check. And yet, since of necessity they deal with
business which involves the dregs of society and worldly affairs, there is a
risk that they may let things go too far: that they may fight a war not for the
public good but for their own advantage, that in the name of justice they may   2!
use severity even against men who might have been cured by mercy, that
under the pretext of absolute power they may pillage the people whose
interests it was their duty to protect.

Moreover, just as Christ like a source of eternal fire draws the order of
priests close to him and as it were kindles them and purifies them from all   2(
earthly contagion, so it is the duty of priests, and especially of those in the
highest stations, to summon princes, as far as they can, to themselves. If a
war threatens, popes must use all their efforts, either to secure a settlement
without bloodshed or, if the tempests in human affairs make that impossible,
to urge that the war is fought with less cruelty and does not last long. In the   2(
old days, even when criminals were justly condemned, bishops used their
authority to appeal for them, and sometimes rescued a criminal from the
hands of his judges, as Augustine openly records in his letters. For there are
some things very necessary to the ordering of a state which, even so, Christ
either accepted in silence or rejected, or neither approved nor disapproved   2
but as it were connives at them. He does not recognize the coin of Caesar and
his superscription; he orders tribute to be paid if it is due, as though the
question did not much concern him, provided that what is owed to God is
paid to him. The woman taken in adultery he neither condemns nor openly
excuses, only tells her to go and sin no more. On those condemned by Pilate   2
whose blood he mingled with their sacrifices Christ expresses no opinion,
whether they suffered this fate rightly or no; he only threatens a similar fate
to all men if they do not repent. Moreover, when asked to arbitrate in the

* * * * *

247 Lamb] Rev 14:4
268 Augustine] Cf Augustine's Epp 100, 133–4, 139, 204.
271 coin of Caesar] Cf Matt 22:17–22.
274 adultery] Cf John 8:7.
275 by Pilate] Cf Luke 13:1–3.
278 arbitrate] Cf Luke 12:13–15.

division of an inheritance, he openly refuses the task, as though to decide
about such mundane things were unworthy of himself, who must teach   280
heavenly things. On the other hand, there are some things which he openly
abhors. On the Pharisees for their greed, on hypocrites, on rich men in their
pride he calls down woe. Never does he rebuke his apostles more sharply
than when they are assailed by a desire for revenge or by a feeling of
ambition. When they asked whether they should call down fire from heaven   285
to burn up the city from which they were shut out, 'Ye know not,' he said,
'what spirit ye are of.' When Peter tried to turn him back from the cross into
the world again, he calls him Satan. When they were disputing about which
of them should be first, think in how many ways and how often he recalled
them to the opposite point of view! There are some things also which he   290
openly teaches and prescribes: not to resist evil, to do good to our enemies,
to be gentle at heart, and more of the same kind.

    We must make distinctions in these things and set them each in its
proper place. Let us not therefore without more ado make Christ responsible
for the actions of princes or lay magistrates, or ascribe them, as they say   295
nowadays, to a divine right. They handle a certain amount of worldly
business that has no part at all in Christian purity; and yet this must not be
criticized, because it is necessary for the conservation of society. It is not
their business to see that we are good, but to make us less bad and to reduce
the amount of harm that bad men can do to the common weal. We therefore   300
owe them their due honour, because as far as they can they promote divine
justice and the public peace, without which even the province of piety is
sometimes thrown into confusion. They must be honoured where they
perform their duty and put up with perhaps where they use their power for
their own advantage, lest something worse arise in their place. For even in   305
these there is a subdued image, a shadow rather, of divine justice; which
ought however to shine forth much more distinctly and visibly and in
greater purity in the character and the legislation of priests. A reflection is
one thing in polished steel and another in the glass of a mirror.

    In a third circle let us place the common people all together, as the most   310
earthy portion of this world, but not so earthy that they are not members of
Christ's body just the same. Not only the eyes are members of the body, but
shins too and feet and privy parts. These must be given more indulgence, but

* * * * *

283 woe] Matt 22:13–29
286 'Ye know not'] Luke 9:55
288 Satan] Matt 16:23
288 disputing] Mark 9:33–49
291 teaches] Matt 5:5, 39, 44, etc

in such a way as to invite them, as far as possible, to follow the things that
Christ approves. For in this body what was once a foot may become an eye. 3▪
And yet, just as princes, if they are wicked, should not be aroused by savage
attacks, for fear that if provoked they may cause more grievous trouble, as
Augustine remarks, so the people in their weakness must be tolerated and
fostered with paternal indulgence, following the example of Christ, who so
gently tolerated and fostered his disciples, until by degrees they grow to 3²
maturity in Christ. For piety like other things has its infancy, it has its
periods of growth, it has its full and vigorous adult strength. But every man
according to the measure that is given him must strive upwards towards
Christ. Of the four elements each has its appointed place. But fire, which has
the highest station, gradually sweeps all things into itself and transforms 3²
them so far as it may to its own nature. Water it evaporates and turns into air,
and air it rarefies and transforms into itself. Paul makes many concessions to
the Corinthians, distinguishing for the time being what ideal he would set
before those who are perfect in the Lord's name and what indulgences he
would allow to the weaker brethren in his own name; but always in the hope 3_
that they may make progress. Over the Galatians he broods a second time
until Christ take shape in them.

If now someone thinks that this circle is more suitable for princes, there
will be no serious difference of opinion between us. For if we observe their
characters, we shall hardly find Christians more rudimentary than they; I 3⁻
speak of the majority, but not of all.

Whatever is outside the third circle is abominable, whenever and
wherever it appears. In this class are ambition, love of money, lechery,
anger, revenge, jealousy, slander, and the other plagues. These however do
not become incurable until they make themselves respectable under a mask 3▪
of religion and duty and worm their way into higher circles: when, for
example, we exercise tyrannical power under a pretext of justice and right,
when we make religion an excuse for personal gain, when we seek worldly
rule in the name of defending the church, when laws are laid down which
purport to serve Christ's cause and in fact are poles apart from the teaching 3▪
of Christ. And so it must be impressed upon all men that there is a goal
towards which they must strive. And there is only one goal: Christ, and his
teaching in all its purity. If in place of this heavenly goal you set up an earthly
one, the man who strives to make progress will have nothing to which he can
rightly direct his efforts. The highest must be set before everyone, that at 3
least we may achieve something halfway.

* * * * *

318 Augustine] Cf *De civitate Dei* 5.21.
331 Galatians] Gal 4:19

And there is no reason to excuse any walk of life from pursuit of this
goal. The perfection of Christ lies in our desires, not in our walk of life; it is to
be found in the spirit, not in clothing or in choice of food. Among monks
there are some who are barely included in the outermost circle; and yet I   355
speak of good men – but of weaker brethren. Among those who have
married twice there are some whom Christ thinks worthy of the first circle.
Nor is it at the same time an insult to any calling in life if that which is best and
most perfect is held up to all alike. Do we suppose that Plato insulted all
existing city-states when in his *Republic* he put forward as a pattern such a   360
polity as had never yet been seen? Did Quintilian show contempt for the
entire profession of orators when he composed the pattern of such an orator
as had never yet existed? Are you far from your exemplar? This does not
mean rejection; it is a stimulus to progress. Are you fairly close? This tells you
to come even nearer. For no one has ever gone so far that there is no room for   365
further improvement.

Every single walk of life has certain special risks of degeneration
related to it. The man who points these out casts no slur on that class of men;
he does them a service. The prosperity of princes runs a risk of tyranny, of
folly, of flattery, of moral decay. He who points out that these must be   370
avoided is a benefactor to princes as a class. He means no reflection on that
majesty of which they are so proud if he shows them wherein the true
majesty of princes is to be found, if he reminds them of the oath they swore at
their accession, of their duty to their people and to its magistrates. The
princes of the church are exposed as a rule to two plagues in particular,   375
avarice and ambition. As though he foresaw this, that first shepherd after
Christ warns bishops to feed their flocks and not rob them or shear them
close; not to feed them with an eye to improper gain, but with a free and
willing heart; not to play the tyrant over those under them, and to urge them
on the path to piety by setting an example, not by threats and orders. Will a   380
man who points out how bishops become truly great and powerful and rich
therefore be thought to reflect on the clergy? The monastic profession,
moreover, is often dogged, besides other distempers, by superstition, pride,
hypocrisy, and slander. And so he does not immediately condemn their way
of life who tells them where true religion is to be found; how far from pride is   385
true Christian piety; how far from pretence is real charity; what strife there is
between genuine religion and a poisonous tongue – particularly if he shows
what must be avoided with the moderation which blames no individual and
criticizes no Order. Is anything in human affairs so prosperous that its

* * * * *

357 married twice] Such as Thomas More
377 feed their flocks] Cf 1 Pet 5:2–3.

particular pests have never been attached to it? And so, just as a man who   3·
points out the things by which true health is damaged or preserved promotes
and does not hinder the health of the body, so he who demonstrates the
corruptions of true religion and their remedies does not discourage the
religious life but rather spurs on others to adopt it.

For I hear that certain people so interpret the principles of this small   3
book, since they give less weight to ceremonies than those would wish who
give them too much, and not much to human regulations, as turning men's
minds away from the monastic life. So true is it that one can express nothing
cautiously enough to prevent bad men from seizing on it as a base for
calumny or a handle for sin, so that it is scarcely safe to give good advice any   4
more. If one discourages the wars which we have been fighting for some
centuries now for worthless objects in a worse than gentile spirit, one is
blackened with false accusations of sympathy with those who say that
Christians must never go to war. For we have made the authors of this view
heretical because some pope appears to approve of war. But there is no black   4
mark for him who disregards the teaching of Christ and his apostles and
sounds the trumpet for a war, regardless of the reasons. Should a man point
out that it would be in the true spirit of the apostles to bring the Turks over to
religion by the resources of Christ rather than by force of arms, he finds
himself at once suspected of teaching that when Turks attack Christians they   4
must by no means be restrained. If a man praises the frugal life of the apostles
and makes some criticism of the luxury of our times, there is no shortage of
people to accuse him of favouring the Ebionites. Should he urge on married
couples with some emphasis that piety and mutual understanding are a
better cement for their union than the physical relationship and that the   4
purity of wedlock should approach as near as possible to virginity, he is
suspected of thinking with the Marcionites that all sex must be foul. Should
he maintain that in disputes, and in theological disputes especially, there
should be no desire merely to win, no obstinate defence of one's position, no
theatrical desire to show off one's powers, he is wrongly traduced as   4
opposed to universities altogether. When St Augustine says that students of
dialectic must avoid a passion for disputation, he is not condemning
dialectic; he points out its besetting sin, that we may avoid it.

Again, suppose one were to criticize the topsy-turvy judgment of the

* * * * *

413 Ebionites] Name used since the second century for some independent sects of
    Judaeo-Christians
417 Marcionites] The sect of bishop Marcion in the second century, noted for
    severe asceticism and the rejection of marriage
421 Augustine] Cf De doctrina christiana 2.31.48 (CC 22:65–6).

public, who give first place among the virtues to those of least importance,   425
and conversely among the vices condemn most strongly those which are
most venial as though they were the worst, and the reverse; one is taken to
task at once as though one were in favour of the vices which one
subordinates to something worse and condemned virtuous actions to which
one prefers others as nearer to sanctity. If one said, for example, that it   430
would be safer to trust to good works than to papal dispensations, one is not
condemning his dispensations in any case, but preferring what according to
Christ's teaching is more reliable. In the same way, if one said that those who
stay at home and look after their wives and children do a better thing than
those who go off to inspect Rome, Jerusalem, or Compostella, and that   435
money spent on these long and dangerous journeys would more piously be
distributed to the deserving poor, one does not condemn their pious
ambition but puts it second to something nearer to true piety.

Again it is not confined to our own times to condemn certain vices as
though no others existed, while flattering others as though they were not   440
vices, when in fact they are the more outrageous class of the two. Augustine
complains in his letters that lechery is the one offence imputed to the clergy
in Africa, while the vices of avarice and drunkenness are almost counted to
their credit. One offence we exaggerate in tragic fashion as the last degree of
horror – to handle the Lord's body with the same hands that have touched   445
the body of a whore. There are even people who dare assert in public in
dramatic tones that it is a lesser fault for a woman to have connection with a
brute beast than with a priest. The man who refutes their impudence is not
thereby instantly in favour of unchaste priests, but he points out that factors
have been neglected which should be given greater weight. A priest may be   450
a gambler, a warrior or a swordsman, quite illiterate, wholly immersed in
secular business, devoted to carrying out criminal orders from criminal
princes: they do not protest so loudly against him, although as he handles
the holy mysteries he is entirely profane. A priest may be a scandalmonger
who with poisonous tongue and contrived scurrilities attacks the reputation   455
of a man who has done nothing to deserve it and has in fact done him a
service: why do we not greet this with cries of 'Outrage! How dare you with
that hellish poison on your tongue, with that mouth with which you butcher
an innocent man, both consecrate and eat the body of him who died for the

* * * * *

435 Compostella] Santiago de Compostela in Galicia, the third of the great centres
of pilgrimage
441 Augustine] Cf Augustine's Ep 22.1.3.
458 hellish poison] Cf Ep 908:11–18, Allen Ep 1053:421–40 and corresponding
note in CWE.

ungodly too?' But this is an evil of which we think so little that men who   460
profess religion in its purest form almost get credit for it. Those men who set
a shocking example to the public by openly keeping loose women in their
homes ought to be rebuked. Of course: but this other sin is not a little more
hateful in the eyes of Christ. One does not condemn butter if one would
rather eat honey; one does not approve of fever if one opines that frenzy is   465
more to be avoided. Nor is it easy to express what a decay in moral standards
stems from topsy-turvy judgments like this.

Again, there are things enrolled among the virtues which wear even so
the mask of piety without its genuine force; so much so that, unless you look
where you are going, they extinguish true piety altogether. If only a   470
moderate danger to religion lurked in ceremonies, Paul would not vent his
indignation upon them so vigorously in all his Epistles. And yet nowhere do
I condemn a moderate degree of ceremony; but I cannot endure that holiness
from stem to stern, as they say, should be thought to lie in them. St
Augustine even forbade the clerks who were members of his household to   475
wear any peculiar garb; if they wished to win public respect, he said, they
should win it by character and not costume. But nowadays what strange
prodigious dress we see! Not that I am against this; but I am greatly surprised
that too much importance should be given to things which might perhaps
rightly be criticized and so little to the only things that really are worth   480
notice. I have no wish to upbraid the Franciscans for being devoted to their
own rule and the Benedictines for devotion to theirs; I object that some of
them think their rule more important than the Gospel. I only hope that this
objection does not apply to the majority. I do not attack them because some
live on fish, some on vegetables and salads, and some on eggs; but I do point   485
out that those men make a grievous mistake who, in a Jewish spirit, flatter
themselves in things like this that they are just, and take such trifles invented
by mere men to be a reason to look down on others, while those same men
count it no fault at all to make lying attacks on another man's fair fame. On
discrimination in food Christ nowhere lays down any rule, nor do the   490
apostles; Paul often speaks against it. Virulent evil-speaking is execrated by
Christ and abhorred in the writings of the apostles. And yet on questions of
food we wish to give an impression of petty piety; in evil-speaking we are
bold and fearless. If a man calls attention to this, in loving language and in
general terms, must he, I ask you, be thought to harm the cause of religion? Is   495

* * * * *

474 stem to stern] Cf *Adagia* 1 i 8.
475 Augustine] Cf Ep 447:515–18 and PL 32:1380.
486 Jewish spirit] Cf Epp 541:149–70n, 694 introduction, 891:33.

anyone mad enough to seek a reputation for eloquence by bringing the faults
of monks out into the day? But these men are afraid that their subordinates
will be less docile, and also that fewer people will wish to be admitted to their
society. In fact, no one is more obedient, more *peitharches* to use Paul's
expression, than the man who has drunk deep of the spirit of Christ and now   500
begins to be free. True charity takes all things in good part, endures all
things, refuses nothing, obeys those who are set over it, not only if they are
kind and accommodating but even if they are difficult and harsh.

None the less this is a point that those set in authority must watch all
the time: they must not convert the obedience of others into tyranny for   505
themselves, and therefore prefer to have them superstitious rather than
godly, that they may observe their masters' lightest whim. They love to hear
themselves called fathers; and yet what father is there in real life who wishes
that his children may remain infants always, that he may rule them more
easily at his own sweet will? On the other hand, those who make progress   510
towards liberty in Christ must be on their guard particularly not to use their
liberty as a cloak for the flesh, as Paul points out, and not, as Peter teaches, to
make their liberty a covering for wickedness. And if two or three of them
have misused this liberty, it is not right for this reason to keep them all
without more ado in perpetual Judaism. This will be understood by anyone   515
who has observed that none of them tie the knot of ceremonies tighter than
those who use this as a pretext for their rule and live for their own stomachs,
not for Christ.

So they need not fear that the sect of Essenes may not spread, in all this
great variety of men and minds, which means that nothing is too absurd to   520
seem attractive to many. Not but what these men will find it more desirable
that recruits to the religious life should be honourable and genuine rather
than numerous. And would that it had been provided by law that no one
under the age of thirty should put his head into that kind of noose, before he
has learnt to know himself and has discovered the force of true religion! In   525
any case those who take the Pharisees as the model in their business, and
course over land and sea that they may make one proselyte, will never be
short of inexperienced young men whom they can get into their net and try
to persuade. Everywhere the number of fools and simple people is

* * * * *

499 Paul's expression] In Titus 3:1, meaning 'submissive'
512 Paul] Gal 5:13
512 Peter] 1 Pet 2:16
517 stomachs] Cf Rom 16:18.
519 Essenes] A brotherhood of ascetic Jews at the time of Christ
524 thirty] Note Erasmus' personal experience; Ep 447:714–15, 734–5.
527 proselyte] Cf Matt 23:15; Ep 447:26–37.

enormous. I at least would hope, and so I doubt not do all truly religious   53
men, that the religion of the Gospel might be so deeply loved by all that they
would be content with this, and no one go off in search of a Benedictine or
Franciscan rule; and Benedict himself and Francis would, I am sure, hope the
same thing. Moses rejoices to find himself obscured by the glory of Christ;
and they would rejoice likewise, if our love for the law of the Gospel made us   53
despise all human codes. How I wish all Christians lived in such a way that
those who are now called religious might seem hardly religious at all! Even
today this is true in not a few cases; for why need I conceal what is well
known? And yet in ancient days the first origin of the monastic life was a
retreat from the cruelty of those who worshipped idols. The codes of the   54
monks who soon followed them were nothing but a summons back to Christ.
The courts of princes were in old days more Christian in name than in their
manner of life. Bishops were soon attacked by the diseases of ambition and
greed. The primitive fervour of the common people cooled. Hence the retreat
aimed at by Benedict and Bernard after him, and then by many more. It was   54
the banding together of a few men aimed at nothing but a pure and simple
Christianity.

If anyone were to study with attention the life and rules of Benedict or
Francis or Augustine, he will find that they had no other ambition than to
live with friends who joined them willingly a life according to the teaching of   55
the Gospel in liberty of spirit; and that they were compelled to lay down
some rules for dress and food and other external things, for they were afraid
that, as often happens, more importance might be ascribed to the constitutions of human origin than to the Gospel. They had a horror of riches; they
avoided honours, even in the church. They laboured with their hands, in   55
order not only to be a burden to no man, but to have to give to others in need;
they occupied mountain-tops, they made their nests in marshy places, they
lived in sandy wastes and deserts. And then they ruled this great concourse
of men without violent language and whipping and prisons, but solely by
teaching and exhorting, by mutual service and by examples of godly life.   56
Such were the monks so loved and praised by Basil and defended by
Chrysostom; to them was appropriate, in any case, what St Jerome writes to
Marcella – that choirs of monks and virgins are a blossom and most precious
stone among the adornments of the church. On this tribute monks of all
kinds pride themselves astonishingly today; they shall be welcome to claim   56

* * * * *

544 cooled] Rev 5:12
548 If anyone ... 581 patriarchs] Added by Erasmus in 1529; see introduction.
561 Basil] St Basil the Great (fourth century), who formulated the rules of monastic
    life
562 Jerome] Cf Jerome's Ep 46.10 (CSEL 54:339).

the praise if at the same time they follow the example. For thereafter that
wisest of men subjoins a pattern for those monks whom he thought worthy
of the name. 'Their language differs,' he says, 'but their religion is one. There
are almost as many ways of chanting the psalter as there are different
nationalities. In spite of this – what is perhaps the first virtue among   570
Christians – they make no proud claims for their own ascetic life. There is a
contest of humility between them all. Whoever was last is thought by them to
be first. In clothing there is no distinction, no attempt to impress. The way
they may choose to walk is no subject for criticism or for praise. Fasting wins
no one promotion; refusal to eat earns no particular respect; moderate eating 575
carries no stigma. Everyone stands or falls by the judgment of his Lord. No
man judges another, that he may not be judged by the Lord; and what is
common in so many places, the use of their teeth to gnaw at one another,
simply does not exist.' Such is the picture of an ideal monk which he set
forth; let him that pleases compare it with the customs of the present day.   580
　　Such were the first beginnings of monasticism, and such its patriarchs.
Then gradually, with the passage of time, wealth grew, and with wealth
ceremonies; and the genuine piety and simplicity grew cool. And though we
see monasteries everywhere whose ways have sunk lower than the laity,
even so the world is burdened with fresh foundations, as though they   585
likewise were not likely to fall in the same way. Once, as I said, the monastic
life was a refuge from the world. Now men are called monks who spend all
their time in the very heart of worldly business and exercise a kind of
despotism in human affairs. And yet because of their dress, or because of
some name they bear, they claim so much sanctity for themselves that   590
compared with them they think other people hardly Christians. Why do we
so closely confine the professed service of Christ, which he wished to be as
wide open as possible? If we are moved by splendid names, what else, I ask
you, is a city than a great monastery? Monks obey their abbot or those who
are set over them; citizens are obedient to their bishop and their pastors,   595
whom Christ himself, not human authority, set over them. Monks live in
leisure and are fed by the liberality of other people, possessing in common
what has come to them without effort on their part (of wicked monks I say
nothing for the present); citizens, each according to his means, share what
they have won by their own industry with those in need. Then as concerns   600
the vow of chastity, I would not dare to unfold how little difference there is
between celibacy of the ordinary kind and chastity in wedlock. Last but not
least, we shall not greatly feel the lack of those three vows which are man's

*　*　*　*　*

603 three vows] The vows of poverty, chastity, and obedience were basic to
　　Christian monasticism.

invention in someone who has kept in sincerity and purity that one great
vow, which we took in our baptism not to man but to Christ. Then if you   60
compare the wicked men in both classes, there is no question that laymen are
preferable. Compare the good, and there is very little difference, if there is
any at all, except perhaps that they who live a religious life under less
compulsion seem more truly religious. The result is therefore that no one
should be foolishly self-satisfied because his way of life is not that of other   6
people, nor should he despise or condemn the way of life of others. But in
every walk of life let this be the common aim of us all, that to the best of our
power we should struggle towards the goal that is set before us all, even
Christ, exhorting and even helping one another, with no envy of those who
are ahead of us in the race and no scorn for the weak who cannot yet keep up   6
with us. And then, when every man has done his best, he must not become
like the Pharisee in the Gospel, who boasts of his good deeds before God: 'I
fast twice on the sabbath day,' and so on, but follow Christ's advice and say
sincerely, say to himself and not to others only, 'I am an unprofitable servant;
all I have done was what I had to do.' No one shows more true confidence   62
than he who shows this kind of diffidence. No one is further from true
religion than the man who thinks himself truly religious. And never does
true Christian piety come off worse than when what belongs to the world is
misrepresented as Christ's and man's authority is set above God's. We have
one head, and in him we must all agree if we wish to be truly Christians.   62
Moreover, he who obeys a man who summons him to follow Christ obeys
Christ and not man. And he who endures men who are all sham – cruel
domineering men who teach not what makes for religion but what bolsters
their own tyranny – displays the patience of a Christian only as long as the
commands they issue make him only unhappy and not ungodly too.   6
Otherwise, he will do better to meet them with the Apostle's answer on his
lips: 'We ought to obey God rather than men.'

But I long ago passed the bounds of a letter, so little count does one
take of time when gossiping most agreeably with a very dear friend. The
book, virtually reborn in Froben's types, is much more elegant and correct   6
than it was before and wings its way now to your arms. I have added some

* * * * *

617 Pharisee] Luke 18:12
619 servant] Luke 17:10
631 Apostle's] Acts 5:29
635 elegant] The bulk of the *Enchiridion* text was probably already set in type when
    this letter was added. The date of July is given in the colophon of Froben's
    edition, but a brief advertisement in the name of the printer on the second-last
    leaf is dated 19 August 1518.

fragments from early works of mine. And I decided to attach this new edition to you, such as it is, rather than anyone else, that he who draws principles of holy living from Erasmus may find an example, in the shape of Volz, immediately at hand. Farewell, most worthy Father and peculiar glory of the true religious life.   640

Tell Sapidus from me to keep his true wits about him, which means, to be always his true self. Tell Wimpfeling to get his shining armour ready, to do battle shortly with the Turks, now that he has waged war long enough with priests who live in sin. I hope that one day we shall see him a bishop, glorious in mitre with two horns and crozier, riding high on his mule.   645
Seriously though, I do ask you to give them and Ruser and my other friends my very warmest greetings. And remember sometimes to commend the salvation of your friend Erasmus in pure vows and pious prayers to Christ the almighty God.   650
Basel, eve of the Assumption, 1518

859 / To Udalricus Zasius   Basel, 22 August 1518

This is the answer to Ep 857. The autograph (Öffentliche Bibliothek of the University of Basel MS C VIa 35 no 105; cf Ep 857 introduction) was taken to Freiburg by Bonifacius Amerbach when he returned from his summer vacation. In AK II Ep 623 he describes Zasius' joy over it. The letter was printed at once, with amplifications, in the *Auctarium*.

* * * * *

637 fragments] Since the first edition some minor texts had been published jointly with the *Enchiridion* (cf Ep 93). Two more were freshly added in Froben's edition: Ep 110 (from Colet) and a translation from Basil (cf Ep 229).
642 Sapidus] Johannes Sapidus (Witz), master of the school at Sélestat; see Ep 323 introduction.
643 Wimpfeling] Just before Erasmus arrived in Basel, on 11 May 1518 Jakob Wimpfeling (cf Ep 224 introduction) wrote a letter to Bruno and Basilius Amerbach and Johann Froben (AK II Ep 615), stating his reasons for not coming to Basel and offering them for publication an oration on the character of the Swiss addressed to Maximilian I. He hoped the Swiss would not be offended, seeing that Erasmus had treated them much more harshly in his *Adagia* II viii 65 (see Ep 855:4n). Wimpfeling's oration was apparently declined. Its gist was, according to his letter, that the Swiss should come to terms with the Empire and that both should join with the other European powers for a crusade against the Turks; cf Ep 891:26n.
645 priests who live in sin] The topic was treated in Wimpfeling's *De integritate libellus* (Strasbourg: J. Knobloch 1505), which caused lengthy controversies; cf Charles Schmidt *Histoire littéraire de l'Alsace* (Paris 1879) I 49–54.
647 Ruser] For Johann Ruser and other members of the Sélestat literary society see Ep 302.

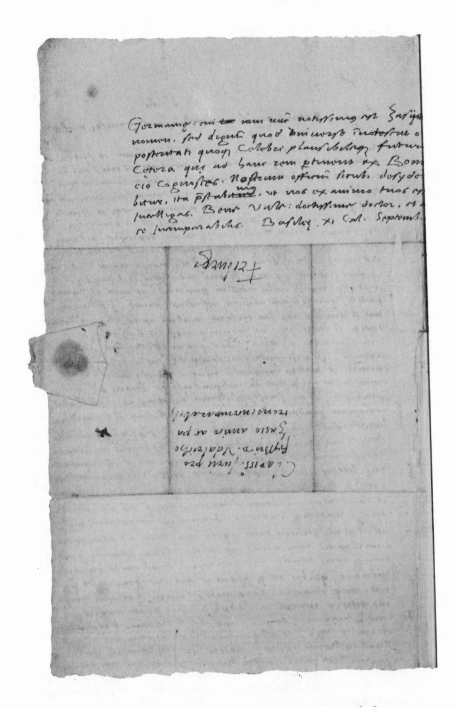

Autograph letter, Erasmus to Udalricus Zasius, Epistle 859
Öffentliche Bibliothek, University of Basel, MS C VIa 35 no 105

a Zasio

Erasmus Roterodamus Incomparabili suo vtriusque professori
S D

Non possum obtinere vir inter bonos optime, et inter
doctos doctissime: quin i tuis ad me litteris tui similis
sis, mi mox difficilem faciens, ex humilimo magnum
ex infortunatissimo felicem, ex rex reinscialiter litterato ut
tius q erudito, omnis doctrine principem: atque ut simul
finiam ex musca elephantem, vt quod est in prouerbio
Et tamen fauco similares, quo me depingis, plane
magis q apte, neq quicq est tamen, quod ex eo mihi
possim agnoscere. Verum quando Zasi inotus no Casu vt
La fuit supitus, patiar te tuo indulgere vel amori vel
ingenio: modo mihi veniam puritas, vt meo obsequor
pudori, qui soleam amicos offusus amare, q priores
aut si quando res ita tulerit, malim apud alios q cora
Deniq si viddeas, vt rerum quoque sit faciendum, mox
tum aliquanto partius. Sed quam obsecro mihi lartum
naueus! Cum antehac semp de Zasi prelare sensissi
tamen ex nostro congressu tantum accessit meq de te
opinioni, vt mihi videar magnitudine tuam prorsus
ignorasse. Ego Iureconsultum duntaxat expectabam
insignem quidem illum et admirabilem sed tantum
Iureconsultum. Cum autem es in Theologorum mys
terys aut etiam pastoris, quod tibi no venturam,
exrussum ac meditatum est videatur? Eloquentia
tue litteue. Literas neglectum et plusq extempore scripta
satis p se ferebant: at non expectabam diues ytud
et exuberans orationis flumen, nusq no paratum,
quirq vndique Iridiuet. Semoro no accersitus. no
affectatus, stilum tuu equabat. Quis no admiretur
Cam Caput tam vicens ingenium.? Tam presentem para
tamq rerum omnium memoriam.? Nihil eni dicam de
moribus, quibus neq gracius aut integrius esse po
test, neq suavius. Adeo mire totum Zasium tempe
uit artifex optime philosophia. Sed parce imprudens
laudi tuarum Campu ingredi. Coopare. etiam atq
etiam te rogo, vt aliquando lucubrationes tuas
sinas in lucem exire. patere hoc vtilitatis studiosi
bonaru litterarum, patere hoc decori nostro adiungi

ERASMUS OF ROTTERDAM TO HIS INCOMPARABLE FRIEND ZASIUS,
DOCTOR OF CANON AND CIVIL LAW, GREETING

I cannot prevent it, best of good men and most scholarly of scholars: in your
letters to me you are always like yourself, making me most unlike my own
self, great instead of lowly, prosperous instead of most unfortunate, a leader 5
in every branch of knowlege when I am not so much learned as barely
instructed in the rudiments – to put it in a nutshell, you make me, as the
Greek proverb has it, not a fly but an elephant. And yet I like your picture of
me, though it is more brilliant than lifelike, as if some Apelles were to
produce a splendid portrait finished with the greatest art and bearing no 10
relation to the sitter. Yet there is in fact nothing in it that I can accept for
myself. Only, as no shadow of deceit can fall on my Zasius' character, I must
give you leave to indulge your affection or your creative gifts, provided you
allow me in my turn to follow my natural modesty; for it is my way to let
myself go in affection for my friends and not in panegyric. If the moment for 15
that ever comes, I prefer to praise them in front of other men and not in their
presence; and if in the end it must be done when they are present, I like to be
somewhat more sparing.

But what pray is this loss of which you speak? I have always thought
very well of you, but since our meeting my opinion has risen so much that I 20
seem hitherto to have been quite ignorant of your quality. I was expecting a
lawyer and no more – distinguished, admirable, but still a lawyer. Yet in all
the mysteries (or may I say the wrestling schools?) of theology you have
unearthed, valued, and pondered everything. In every branch of philosophy you are so much at home that it might seem to be your only study. Is 25
there any book, ancient or modern, which you have not read, looked deeply
into, and absorbed? And the more intimate observances that make a truly
religious man are, I am told, yours in no common degree. Then you can write:
your letters, careless as they are and written on the spur of the moment, gave
proof of that; but I was not expecting that rich and copious flow of language, 30
always at your service, whatever subject might have arisen from any quarter.
In heaven's name, what brilliant conversation, fluent, apt, welling up
naturally, never far-fetched, never artificial! Your casual conversation was
as good as what you write. Who could fail to admire such intellectual vigour
in a man of your grey hairs, and such a well-stocked and ready memory for 35
everything? I will say nothing of your personality, with its unsurpassed

* * * * *

859
8 proverb] Cf *Adagia* I ix 69.
19 loss] Cf Ep 857:21.

authority and integrity, and its charm as well. With such admirable cunning was our Zasius formed by that supreme craftsman, philosophy.

But almost unawares I was beginning to embark upon the subject of your merits. I do most sincerely beg you to allow your exquisite *Lucubrationes*   40 someday to see the light. Do not refuse to confer this advantage on all lovers of humane letters, do not refuse to shed this new lustre on our native Germany; where the name of Zasius is already famous, but it deserves to become known to the whole world, and to be familiar and glorious among posterity. Anything else relative to this you will learn from Bonifacius   45 Amerbach, a truly gifted young man in every way. If there is anything I can do for you, it shall be done in such a way as to show that I am entirely yours. Farewell, most learned doctor and most treasured friend.

Basel, 22 August 1518

To the distinguished doctor of laws Udalricus Zasius, his incomparable   50 friend and benefactor. At Freiburg

860 / To Antonio Pucci   Basel, 26 August 1518

This letter, printed in the *Farrago*, is primarily intended to secure a papal brief for the revised New Testament; see Ep 864 introduction.

Antonio Pucci (1484–1544) was a Florentine like Leo x, who had conferred the cardinal's hat upon his uncle, Lorenzo Pucci. Antonio succeeded Lorenzo as bishop of Pistoia in 1519 and was later himself created cardinal. He was repeatedly sent to Switzerland as a papal legate. His business was primarily the recruitment of Swiss troops, allegedly for the pope's crusade against the Turks. On his first mission he left Rome c 11 November 1517 (cf Ep 729:15–17). In a document dated from Zürich, 6 December 1517, he summarized the pope's instructions (cf Hutten *Opera* v 143–6; Ep 785:40n). In the summer of 1518 he visited Basel. He wished to honour Erasmus by inviting him to dinner, but Erasmus was prevented by ill health from accepting the invitation. As a result Pucci had to call upon him at Froben's workshop (cf Epp 852:38–9, 855:8–20; J. Gertophius *Recriminatio ... adversus ... Leum*, Basel: A. Cratander June 1520, 13). Erasmus later described Pucci as 'amazingly choleric and uncontrollable' (cf Ep 1188); he must have thought that an apology was in order and addressed this letter to Zürich (cf Ep 905:30–2), but on 1 October Pucci was expected in Rome (cf Ep 865:69–71). He returned to Switzerland late in 1519, bestowed the degree of MA upon the Basel printers Hieronymus Froben and Nicolaus Episcopius (cf BRE Epp 149, 152), and urged the Swiss governments to suppress Luther's

* * * * *

40 *Lucubrationes*] Cf Ep 862.

writings. In April 1521 he took Swiss soldiers with him to Italy; cf Zwingli *Werke*
VII Epp 41, 161.

ERASMUS OF ROTTERDAM TO THE REVEREND DR ANTONIO PUCCI,
APOSTOLIC LEGATE IN SWITZERLAND

Respectful greetings, very reverend Father. I fear that your Highness must
have accused my humble self some time ago of discourtesy and perhaps
of gross ingratitude, seeing that, though the recipient of your most ready   5
generosity, I have not acknowledged your kindness so much as by a letter.
Yet if you knew the danger to which I have been exposed by attacks of
phlegm over more than a month issuing in cruel diarrhoea accompanied by
abdominal pain, while all the while I was obliged to find strength for the
work I had in hand, I know that with your habitual goodness you would   10
actually regret that I should have such a good excuse. Things came to such a
pass that I considered making my will. And now the plague spreading
everywhere drives me away from here, with the work not yet finished in the
zealous pursuit of which I have hitherto despised not money alone but even
life; such was my zeal to render a work which I had once dedicated to our   15
Holy Father Leo x worthy of his holiness. For the first edition did not satisfy
me at all points, though even that wins approval from all the most learned
and most expert critics; there was to begin with a certain amount of barking
from a few trouble-making curs; but they were men of no attainments, they
had never read the book, and their comments were reserved for my absence –   20
in front of me no one said anything. It will now reappear, if I mistake not, in
such a polished shape that I hope it will be thought not unworthy of Pope
Leo or of posterity. It would be vain to tell what labour it has cost me –
nobody would believe it; I only hope it may bring equivalent profit to the
common welfare of Christians, for that has been my only purpose.   25

And so your excellency in your turn will be able to make a substantial
contribution, if you will be so kind as to secure from his holiness some brief to
the effect that he welcomes this work of mine; this will stop the mouths of
those few trouble-makers. Two cardinals, through whom I had offered a
copy of the first edition to the Holy Father, had replied: Andrea Ammonio   30
sent one letter to me here and it was lost; he kept the other and now I have
lost both it and him. I wrote on this subject a few days ago to Cardinal
Grimani and to Paolo Bombace.

* * * * *
860
12 will] Erasmus' first known will dates from 1527 (see Allen VI 503–6). For his
illness cf Ep 847:7n.
12 plague] Cf Ep 861:7n.
29 cardinals] See Ep 835 introduction.

And to relieve your mind of any possible misgivings, I will briefly explain the principles on which I have been working. After comparing many 35 copies of the Greek and following the one which seemed the most accurate, I have made a Latin version and added my translation to the Greek to make it easy for the reader to compare the two; and in translating, my rule has been to try first of all to maintain as far as I could a pure Latin style, while respecting the simplicity of the Apostle's language. Secondly, I have 40 endeavoured to see that passages which previously puzzled the reader by their ambiguity or the obscurity of their expression or by faults and awkwardness of language should now be rendered smooth and lucid, diverging most sparingly from the form of words and never from the sense; and the sense I have not dreamed up for myself, but gone to seek in Origen, 45 Basil, Chrysostom, Cyril, Jerome, Cyprian, Ambrose, and Augustine. I have added annotations, which are now enlarged, in which I inform the reader what line I have followed and why, resting always on the opinion of ancient authorities. The common or Vulgate edition I do not pull down from its place (though whose it is is uncertain; it is known not to come from Cyprian or 50 Ambrose or Hilary or Augustine or Jerome), but I indicate where it is corrupt, issuing a warning where the translator nodded very badly and explaining anything complicated and crabbed.

If it is desirable that we should possess the Scriptures in as correct a form as possible, this labour of mine not only removes blemishes from Holy 55 Writ but provides an obstacle to similar corruption in the future. If it is desirable that they should be rightly understood, I have opened more than six hundred passages which had not been understood before even by eminent divines. They confess this themselves, deny it they cannot. If it is desirable that the argumentative species of theology, which is almost 60 over-dominant in our universities, should be joined with a knowledge of the sources, my work is specially conducive to this end. Thus no form of study suffers from these labours of mine, and all forms find them helpful. The reading of the Greek is the basis of my version everywhere, but I do not everywhere accept it; in other places I prefer our own, always pointing out 65 where the orthodox Latin authorities and the Greeks agree or differ. Besides which, variant readings are not merely no obstacle to the study of Holy Scripture, they are a great help, as St Augustine himself avers. But nowhere is the degree of variation great enough to imperil the orthodox faith. In short, either I am simply blinded by love for my own work or it will contribute no 70

* * * * *

33 Bombace] Cf Ep 865:2.
50 uncertain] Cf Ep 843:23n.
68 Augustine] Cf Ep 843:51n.

small advantage to sacred studies and no small glory to our Holy Father Leo in the future, when jealousy has subsided and men appreciate its value. This value will bear richer fruit and ripen earlier if it is blessed with the approval of the chief shepherd. Nor do I wish for his approval in any other terms than these, that he should declare my work acceptable to him on account of its 75 value for sacred studies.

In return for my dedication I ask for no other reward. One man might expect a present, another might demand a benefice; for me, whose sole aim it was to be of use, it will seem recompense rich enough if I achieve the object for which I have undertaken all these nightly vigils. Your excellency will 80 secure what I need with a couple of words, and thus will do what is pleasing to Christ himself and popular with all who wish to learn, especially welcome also to Froben, a man to whose printing-house the study of Holy Scriptures owes more than to any other. My book will be printed within the next three months; if the brief can be sent within that space of time, it can be printed at 85 the beginning of the volume. I beg your Highness urgently to give me in this matter practical experience of your generosity, and I will ensure in return that the serried ranks of scholarship understand their debt to the name of Pucci. I send all my best wishes to his eminence my lord of Sion, whose greatness and good deeds will soon, I hope, be rewarded by Almighty God. 90

Farewell, and be indulgent, for I write this with my loins girded, being just about to go on board.

Basel, 26 August 1518

861 / To Osvaldus Myconius   Basel, 26 August 1518

This is the last letter to be included in the *Auctarium* (cf Ep 886:57n). Oswald Geisshüsler, called Myconius, of Lucerne (1488–1552), graduated from the University of Basel and was at this time master of the Grossmünster school at Zürich. Subsequently he joined the reformers and in 1532 succeeded Johannes Oecolampadius (Ep 224:30n) as chief pastor (antistes) and professor of theology in Basel. At that time Erasmus thought poorly of him; cf Allen Ep 2778:24–8.

ERASMUS OF ROTTERDAM TO HIS FRIEND OSWALD, GREETING
Dearest friend, I was quite delighted to get your letter, and though I send a very brief answer, I am devoted to my dear Oswald, partly because he is so

* * * * *

89 Sion] Cardinal Matthäus Schiner, who had for long been engaged in the business that brought Pucci to Switzerland; cf Ep 447:66on.
92 on board] See Ep 867 introduction.

fond of me, and partly because he is as close to Glareanus, who is already my
friend on more than one count, as any Theseus or whatever closer there may   5
be. Stick to it, my dear Oswald, and win glory in the field of literature for
that Switzerland of yours, already so glorious in arms. The plague drives me
hence – plague take it! Farewell.

Basel, 26 August 1518

862 / To Bonifacius Amerbach   Basel, 31 August 1518

This is a letter of commendation for the *Lucubrationes* of Udalricus Zasius, a legal
work to be published by Froben. Its main component was a treatise, 'De origine
iuris,' in which Erasmus had taken an interest (cf Epp 376, 379, 632). On 8
September a specimen page was sent to Zasius together with the news about
this preface by Erasmus (AK II Ep 625). In December the work was hastily
printed (cf Ep 904:17–18; AK II Ep 642) and published. As a result there were
many misprints, which Beatus Rhenanus blamed on the corrector, Lambertus
Hollonius (cf Ep 904 introduction), and a sheet of errata had to be prepared (cf
a letter from Beatus Rhenanus to Francesco Giulio Calvo in *Marquardi Gudii ...
epistolae* ed P. Burman, Utrecht 1697, Ep 62). Following the *Lucubrationes* of
Zasius, this letter was reprinted in the *Epistolae ad diversos*.

DESIDERIUS ERASMUS OF ROTTERDAM TO BONIFACIUS AMERBACH
OF BASEL, A YOUNG MAN OF UNCOMMON LEARNING IN ALL
BRANCHES OF STUDY, GREETING

How great a part it is of happiness, and the greatest part of gratitude, to
recognize one's blessings! And so we must continually count our generation   5
fortunate and thank the powers above, over and over again, through whose

* * * * *

861
4 Glareanus] Henricus Glareanus and Myconius both attended the school in
   Rottweil (Swabia) under Michael Rubellus. They met again at Basel where
   Glareanus addressed an elegy to Myconius; cf E.F. Fritzsche *Glarean* (Frauenfeld 1890) 3, 11, 89.
5 any Theseus] The friendship of Theseus and Pirithous was proverbial in
   Antiquity.
7 plague] Justifying Erasmus' apprehensions (cf Epp 770 introduction, 803:9–
   11), there is evidence of sporadic outbreaks of the bubonic plague in the Rhine
   valley and adjacent regions during the second half of 1518. Still it would appear
   that the plague was no worse than in other years (cf Epp 860:12, 866:32,
   867:67–72, 210–74, 881:8–9, 904:18–19). Myconius quoted this sentence when
   explaining that as a result of his hasty departure from Basel Erasmus had left a
   letter from Joachim Vadianus unanswered; cf W. Näf *Vadian* (St Gallen
   1944–57) I 215.

Galen *De sanitate tuenda* title page
This is the edition of Paris: Guillaume Le Rouge 1517;
representations of Galen and Linacre, the translator,
appear at top left and right respectively;
the shield between them is that of Cardinal Wolsey,
for whom this particular copy was so lavishly decorated
Reproduced by courtesy of the British Library Board

bounty those humane studies, which for so many centuries had been almost buried, now flourish once more the whole world over and are so prosper-ously multiplied. Eighty years ago, more or less, it was not only the professors of what Virgil (even in his own age, the high summer of learning   10 and eloquence combined) calls the voiceless arts, that were inarticulate and tongue-tied; grammar itself, mistress of correctness in language, and rhetoric, the guide to abundance and brilliance of expression, lisped with a wretched, sorry sound, and the arts which had in old days been so well equipped with languages then spoke Latin only, and bad Latin at that.   15 Thereafter, as noble studies slowly increased, Italy alone had the gift of self-expression, and even there no science used it except rhetoric. But now, in every nation in Christendom, all branches of study (under the favour of the Muses) marry useful learning with splendour of expression.

Medicine first learnt to speak in Italy through the efforts of Niccolò   20 Leoniceno, an old man deserving of immortal fame; in France through Guillaume Cop of Basel. In Britain the efforts of Thomas Linacre have made Galen lately write such good Latin that he might be thought to write rather badly in his native Greek. He has made Aristotle too speak Latin, so well that, for all that he hails from Attica , he hardly seems to reach the same   25 elegance in his own language; though of course before Linacre's time Argyropoulos among the Italians with George of Trebizond, Theodorus Gaza, Marsilio, and Pico, and in France Lefèvre d'Etaples, had made it clear that philosophy was by no means speechless. Then the laws of the empire have been restored successfully to their original elegance, and indeed to   30 distinction in both Greek and Latin, by Guillaume Budé in France, and in Germany by a man without peer in every way, Udalricus Zasius, who has such rich fertility in the Roman tongue at his command that you would think the writer a second Ulpian, not a legal light of our own age.

Yet somehow, I know not how, equal success in this department still   35

* * * * *

862
10 Virgil] *Aeneid* 12.397, referring to the medical arts
20 the efforts of] Cf Ep 541:60–2; for Leoniceno cf Ep 216A:21n; for Cop cf Ep 523; and for Linacre cf Ep 118:27n.
23 Galen] Cf Ep 755:32n.
24 Aristotle] Cf Ep 868:79n.
27 Argyropoulos ... Trebizond ... Gaza] Cf Epp 456:117n, 36:3n, 233:12n.
28 Marsilio ... Pico] Marsilio Ficino (1433–99), was the leading member of Cosimo de' Medici's Platonic academy at Careggi near Florence. Apart from his own works he translated Plato, Plotinus, and other philosophical texts. Giovanni Pico della Mirandola (cf Ep 126:150n) was his pupil and friend.
34 Ulpian] Roman jurist, d 228; a major contributor to the Pandects

Marsilio Ficino
Portrait medal in the manner of Niccolò Fiorentino,
made shortly before 1499
Reproduced by courtesy of the Trustees of
the British Museum

eludes the theologians, although there may be some with a keen desire to write well. I hope however that we shall soon see this profession, like the others, shake off the dust and reassert its ancient brilliance. Hitherto, those who wrote with some attempt at polish were excluded from the ranks of the learned, nor would the professionals deign to admit to their order anyone   40
who had not mumbled the shameful stuff they talk themselves, without risking the infection of good literature at any point. It came so easy to say 'He's a grammarian, he's no philosopher' or 'He's a rhetorician, not a lawyer' or 'Style is his strong point and not theology.' But soon, if I am not mistaken, things will be very different: none will be admitted to the roll who   45
do not reproduce these ancient fountain-heads of learning in language still more elegant than their own, nor will it be thought right for any man to lay claim to wisdom unless it is accompanied by eloquence, its handmaid whom St Augustine wishes never to leave her mistress' side.

Zasius' commentary I have run through rather than read, for it reached   50
me just as I was ready for a journey. A taste of it gave me great satisfaction, and I do not doubt that I shall like the whole work still more when I have the opportunity to take my fill of such excellent fare. Pray encourage the author, my dear Bonifacius, not to keep us selfishly waiting for such glory, such profit, such enjoyment; unless you too are selfish, seeing that you have the   55
advantage of enjoying Zasius' familiar society. Farewell.

Basel, 31 August 1518

863 / From Jakob Spiegel   Augsburg, 31 August 1518

This preface was printed in Erasmus Vitellius *Oratio in Augusten. conventu ... habita* (Augsburg: J. Miller 1518).

Vitellius was the name taken by Erazm Ciołek of Cracow (d 1522), who was bishop of Płock from 1503, represented Sigismund I of Poland at the Diet of Augsburg (cf Ep 891), and on 20 August 1518 made the speech recommending the crusade on behalf of his king which was afterwards edited by Spiegel. Later in the year Maximilian I sent him to Rome, where he spent the rest of his life as Polish envoy.

The imperial secretary Jakob Spiegel (see Ep 323:13n) was perhaps anxious to secure Vitellius' support of Maximilian's diplomacy. Vitellius' speech is reprinted in Hutten *Opera* v 237–45. It is not easy to believe Spiegel's claim that he moved the audience to tears.

* * * * *

49 Augustine] Cf *De doctrina christiana* 4.5.7 (CC 32:120–1), quoting Cicero's *De inventione* 1.1.   `

50 Zasius' commentary] The *Lucubrationes*

51 journey] See Ep 867 introduction.

Sigismund I of Poland
From a fragment of the Sigismund Chapel in the cathedral at Cracow;
made in Nürnberg by Melchior Baier after the design of Peter Flötner, c 1531–8
Panstowe Zbiory Sztuki na Wawelu, Krakow

TO THE CELEBRATED DOCTOR ERASMUS OF ROTTERDAM,
LEADING SCHOLAR IN THE TWO ANCIENT TONGUES AND
EMINENT THEOLOGIAN, FROM JAKOB SPIEGEL OF SÉLESTAT,
SECRETARY TO HIS IMPERIAL MAJESTY, GREETING

His invincible majesty Sigismund king of Poland, who not many years and   5
months ago won a signal victory over the wagon-dwellers who call
themselves Muscovites and the Scythians known as Tartars, having
appointed as his envoy the right reverend Erasmus Vitellius, bishop of Płock
(a man of the highest character, rare learning, and true Roman eloquence,
who has a special claim on my attachment because he has the same name as   10
yourself and frequently speaks of you with great respect), the bishop had his
first audience (if I as a court official may use the courtier's word) before the
emperor, all the electors of the Holy Roman Empire, and the other princes
and magnates of Germany. He there spoke so eloquently and to such effect
that the force of what he said pierced his auditors to the very heart and   15
moved many of them to tears. In fact, as scholar and speaker alike all men of
learning and eloquence yield him the palm. For there were present not a few
elegant scholars and sensitive critics, the bishop of Trieste, Peutinger,
Hutten, Bartolini, Spalatinus, and Stabius that all-round scholar, Heinrich
Stromer the physician, and Lorenz Zoch the lawyer, chancellor of that most   20
prosperous prince the cardinal of Mainz. And so, having obtained a copy of
this most elegant speech in advance of everyone else, and knowing that
learned men consider that it deserves a wide circulation and that everyone
wishes to read it, I have had it printed and set your distinguished name at the
head of it, to which all offerings of respect are rightly due. Pray give it a   25
kindly reception; for I do not doubt that, if it moved its original audience to
tears, those who read it will be still more deeply moved, and their hearts will
be made the more ready to promote the good of Christendom.

My best wishes not only to you but to Beatus Rhenanus, who so well

* * * * *

863
6 victory] The Polish-Lithuanian victory over the Russians in the battle of Orsza,
8 September 1514, led to an understanding with Maximilian I on the questions
of the Teutonic order and the Hungarian succession.
18 Trieste] Pietro Bonomo (d 1546), bishop of Trieste since 1502, was a faithful and
honoured servant to the Hapsburg crown; see DBI.
18 Peutinger, Hutten] See Epp 318:3n, 365 introduction.
19 Bartolini] Cf Ep 547.
19 Spalatinus ... Stabius ... Stromer] See Epp 501 introduction, 409:28n, 578
introduction.
20 Zoch] Lorenz Zoch (b 1477) was chancellor of Magdeburg under Albert of
Brandenburg (cf Ep 661 introduction) until his conversion to Lutheranism.

deserves his name, and whom I bear in my heart. I wish for you both the　30
longest possible thread of life, that good literature, and sacred literature
especially, may flourish once again with prospects daily more and more
auspicious. Hutten, being accounted nothing by the blear-eyed admirers of
our popular productions, has produced a nothing, the work of Nobody,
which I should be happy to see you pass to our friend Froben for a reprint, if　35
you agree. I will send you his dialogue on life at court, as soon as it appears.
Once more best wishes.

From Augsburg, 31 August in the year of the Incarnation 1518

864 / From Leo x　　　　　　　　　　　　　　Rome, 10 September 1518

For some time Erasmus had wished for some formal expression of papal
approval for his New Testament (cf Epp 832:2–3; 835 introduction). As work on
the new edition advanced he made a concerted effort to obtain a brief, approaching the legate Antonio Pucci (Ep 860), cardinals Raffaele Riario and
Domenico Grimani (cf Epp 860:33, 865:22), and his friend Paolo Bombace. The
result was this brief, composed and given a putative date by Bombace, and
approved by Leo x late in September (cf Ep 865). The importance Erasmus attached to it can be gathered from the profuse thanks he sent Bombace (Ep 905).
It was printed on the reverse of the title page of Froben's text volume (cf LB IX
751D–E; Ep 885:5–6).

　From the publication of the *Novum instrumentum* (February 1516) Erasmus
had expressed dissatisfaction with his work, and he lost little time in gathering
notes in preparation for a revision (cf Ep 809:70n). He added steadily to these
during many trips and moves in 1516 and early 1517 (cf *Opuscula* 238–41), and
after he settled in Louvain (July 1517), in a congenial atmosphere, the New
Testament absorbed the major part of his energies (cf the indexes of CWE 5 and
6). He consulted additional manuscripts and endeavoured to enlist the help of
many scholar friends such as Fisher (cf Ep 784), Colet (cf Ep 825), Latimer (cf Ep

* * * * *

34 Nobody] Using the ironical twist on which the poem itself is based, Spiegel
　refers to Hutten's *Nemo* (cf Ep 365:30n) which proved extremely popular. One
　of the prefaces to the revised second version is dated from Augsburg, 24 August
　1518. At least five editions of 1518 are known; with the colophon date of
　September 1518 Froben twice reprinted the earlier edition of J. Miller,
　Augsburg, and a third Froben edition is dated January 1519. Martens printed it
　in October 1518 (NK 1149). There are passing references to Erasmus in both
　prefaces; cf Hutten *Opera* I 21*–23*, Ep 85, III 107–18, and for Erasmus' negative
　reaction Ep 961:32–4.
36 dialogue] *Aula, dialogus* ([Augsburg]: S. Grimm and M. Wirsung 17 September
　1518)

886:9n), Tunstall (cf Ep 597:18–20), Grocyn, Wentford (cf Epp 772, 833), and Glareanus (cf Ep 707:20–3). Most of them did make suggestions, while Budé saw his offer of assistance rejected (cf Epp 493 postscript, 531:596–617). Amid much approval and encouragement, there was also considerable criticism, much of it unsolicited. The objections of Jacques Lefèvre (cf Ep 597:37n, 44n), Edward Lee (cf Ep 765 introduction), and Johann Eck (cf Ep 769), in particular, caused Erasmus great anxiety. The need to answer his critics did not, however, cause him to abandon the revolutionary principles on which the first edition had been based. On the contrary, of the five editions published in his lifetime, the second was probably the most provocative (cf Ep 809:73–6).

At Basel Erasmus personally watched over the composition of the revised *Annotationes*. This second volume of Froben's edition was ready for printing when he left Basel to return to Louvain (the date in the colophon, p 548, is 23 August 1518). The first volume, containing the text of the New Testament, was undertaken next. To help with the proof-reading in his absence, Erasmus left his *famulus* Jacobus Nepos in Basel, and, lacking confidence in him, subsequently sent another young scholar from Louvain (cf Epp 885:2n, 886:28–30). In Louvain Erasmus continued to revise the text and on 22 October he sent Froben the last parts (cf Epp 867:82–3, 253–4, 885:2–3). In December the Epistles of Paul were being printed (cf Ep 904:15–16), and the date of 1518 appears in the first colophon, p 564, although distribution did not begin before the middle of March (cf Epp 950:45n, 955, 961:74–5; Luther w *Briefwechsel* I Ep 146). According to Erasmus the 1516 edition had exceeded 1200 copies (cf *Opuscula* 238–9), and after the new edition was published he wrote of a total of 3300 copies in print (cf LB IX 280D). Whether he included the first edition in this figure is not clear, but even if he did, an impression of close to 2000 copies of an expensive work partly in Greek, running to over 1250 pages in folio divided into two volumes, is remarkable by the standards of the time. See further Epp 373, 384 introductions; A. Bludau *Die beiden ersten Erasmus-Ausgaben des Neuen Testaments und ihre Gegner* (Freiburg 1902); B.M. Metzger *The Text of the New Testament* 2nd ed (Oxford 1968) 98–103.

TO OUR BELOVED SON ERASMUS OF ROTTERDAM, DOCTOR OF
DIVINITY, FROM POPE LEO X

Our beloved son, greeting and apostolic benediction. We derived great pleasure from the studies on the New Testament which you published some time ago, not so much because they were dedicated to us as for the new and exceptional learning by which they were distinguished and which earned them a chorus of praise from the world of scholars. The news that you had lately revised them, and enriched and clarified them by the addition of numerous annotations, gave us no little satisfaction; for we inferred from the

first edition, which used to seem a most finished performance, what this new   10
one would be, and how much it would benefit all who have at heart the
progress of theology and of our orthodox faith. Go forward then in this same
spirit: work for the public good, and do all you can to bring so religious an
undertaking into the light of day, for you will receive from God himself a
worthy reward for all your labours, from us the commendation you deserve,   15
and from all Christ's faithful people lasting renown.

    Given at Rome at St Peter's under the ring of the Fisherman, on the
tenth day of September 1518, being the sixth year of our Pontificate.

    Evangelista

865 / From Paolo Bombace   Rome, 1 October 1518

    This letter was answered by Ep 905 and first printed in the *Farrago*.

PAOLO BOMBACE TO ERASMUS, GREETING
Your letter dated 18 August reached me at last on 12 September and gave me
such pleasure that I could have enjoyed nothing more, being so bound to
you by some sort of fate that even the mention of your familiar name is a
refreshment, much more the appearance of something drawn from your   5
heart and mind. This I often desire but would always be too shy to ask for, in
fear that I might waste your time and 'sin against the public good,' as Horace
puts it. And how much you have done, in my opinion, for the public good,
not merely with untiring energy but hitherto with success, I would rather
praise before other men than recount to you. But you know me inside out   10
and in the buff; let me not give the impression of trying to convince you at
length of something you believe already and even know well to be true; so I
turn to your letter.

    So, with invitations from kings and princes on every hand, you have
rejected and thought nothing of them all and chosen to betake yourself to   15
Basel for the reprinting of the New Testament? This does not surprise me, for
I know my Erasmus, and you have never set a high value on anything
compared with your duty to the cause of learning. How I wish you had

        * * * * *

864
19 Evangelista] Evangelista Tarasconio of Parma, papal secretary under Leo x and
    Clement VII; see Pastor VIII 155n.

865
 2 letter] See Epp 860:32–3, 864 introduction.
 7 Horace] *Epistles* 2.1.3
11 in the buff] Persius 3.30; *Adagia* I ix 89

done this while I was still in your part of the world! I should have been the
happiest man alive, and Rome itself could not have called me back so easily.   20
To secure a brief that might serve as a helpful endorsement of your work, the
person to ask was not San Giorgio or San Marco, one of whom has been away
from the city for some time and the other went away a few days ago for his
autumn holiday, while my master, the cardinal of the Santi Quattro, an
outstanding patron of all men of letters and a decisive voice in all such   25
things, is more well disposed to you than to anyone. When I told him what
you wanted, he approved a draft brief composed by me and had it copied on
parchment and sent to Pope Leo, who had left the city two days before, to be
examined and, unless he did not like it, sealed.

But here see how your fate intervened, unless you would rather say   30
mine. A young classical scholar called Silvius, a Frenchman, much devoted
to you and he made no secret of it, was going to have an audience of the pope
in person, with a letter of introduction from my cardinal, and said he would
be coming back next day. Not expecting to find anyone more suitable to be
entrusted with such business, I committed the brief to him and gave him a   35
letter to his holiness' secretary, in which I asked him in the cardinal's name to
seal the brief and send it back at once by this Silvius aforesaid. Silvius in any
case had a touch of fever and was in poor health and, being prevented by
some mishap, I suspect, when actually on his way, he sent the brief and the
letter on ahead to the secretary. He in his turn wasted no time but gave the   40
brief and the letter of recommendation to his holiness forthwith. When he
had looked at the brief and signed it and had read through the letter, he gave
instructions for the man it recommended to be sent for; and when he was
nowhere to be found, they were to look for him most carefully. But so far
they have been unable to find him anywhere. I had expected the whole   45
business to be finished in a very few days, and when several had elapsed

* * * * *

22 San Giorgio or San Marco] Cardinals Riario (cf Ep 607:17n) and Grimani; cf Epp
   860:32–3, 864 introduction.
24 cardinal of the Santi Quattro] Lorenzo Pucci
28 left the city] He left Rome which was infested with malaria on 11 September,
   according to M. Sanudo *Diarii* (Venice 1879–1903) xxvi 38.
31 Silvius] He is unidentified. In Ep 905 Erasmus wondered whether he might
   have been Christophe de Longueil. Before this letter was available in print,
   Longueil visited Erasmus in 1519 and apparently tried to clear his name.
   Longueil's story was suddenly recalled by Erasmus in 1533 and retold with
   distortions. Silvius had then become the assumed name of a fugitive monk, an
   impostor exhibiting faked letters from Erasmus; cf Allen Epp 2798:49–58,
   2874:157–87.
36 secretary] Cf Ep 864:19n.

and I saw nothing happen, I wrote to the secretary again, accusing him of negligence and even of deliberate malice for sending countless briefs to the city almost hour by hour and holding up Erasmus' brief for so long. He replied at length, saying that the place of concealment of my messenger, of which I spoke, is still uncertain, and assuring me that the brief had been returned by some unspecified courier; and when after long search it could not be found anywhere, I arranged to send him another like it. Unless this is intercepted by some fresh evil spirit, it will reach you eventually.

Such is the somewhat long and tedious history of your brief; and do not be surprised at the date, for I chose to date it from Rome rather than anywhere else to make it more impressive. I am delighted that the letter in which you answered mine should have been printed, so that my reputation will have gone up, provided my letter is not printed with it, for, as I can well remember, it hardly deserved to be read once by a friend and compared with any common piece, let alone with an excellent letter from you. Lascaris is now in France, and so I could not arrange a meeting. If I have any opportunity to see such a learned man as you describe, I shall carry out your wishes and do him a good turn at the same time. I was turned away from a career in scholarship not so much by my own inclination or the prospects of a better position in life, as you suspect; it was the vagaries of chance carried me off, to which we owe most things both good and bad. The two Boerios are in Rome and return your greetings. Bernardo contracted a quartan fever, but not a very severe one; he was threatening to depart for Genoa. Pucci the legate has left your part of the world by now, I do not doubt, and is making his way to Rome; and I am therefore sending the brief itself not to him but to the protonotary Caracciolo, the pope's envoy to the emperor, whom I expect to find neither uncivil nor inefficient in sending it straight on to you. Farewell, dear Erasmus, and give my greetings to Beatus and the Amerbachs and the other good scholars in those parts.

Rome, from the apostolic palace, 1 October 1518

* * * * *

57 the letter] Ep 855. Bombace had not yet seen the *Auctarium*, which also contained his own letter, Ep 729.
61 Lascaris] In Ep 836 Erasmus had written to Johannes Lascaris in search of a Greek professor for the Collegium Trilingue at Louvain. Clearly he had done the same in his letter to Bombace.
67 Boerios] Giovanni and Bernardo, the sons of Giovanni Battista Boerio, physician to Henry VIII; cf Ep 267 introduction.
69 Pucci] See Ep 860 introduction.
72 Caracciolo] Marino Caracciolo of Naples (1469–1538), named protonotary and nuncio to the imperial court in 1517, afterwards cardinal and governor of Milan. He left for Germany in March 1518 and there attended the Diet of Augsburg together with Cajetanus; see Ep 891:26n.

866 / From Adolf Eichholz   Cologne, 6 October 1518

The autograph of this letter is in the University Library in Wrocław, MS
Rehdiger 254, f 56 (Ep 61).

Adolf Eichholz of Cologne (d 1563) went to Orléans to study law in 1515
under Jean Pyrrhus d'Angleberme and in 1517 presided over the German
'nation.' Returning to Cologne in April or May 1518, he had hoped to visit
Erasmus in Louvain but learnt from Pieter Gillis in Antwerp that he had left for
Basel. So Eichholz had to put his business down in writing. At Cologne he was
canon of St Mariengraden and in 1521 received a legal doctorate and c 1535 was
named professor of canon law; cf Epp 810 introduction, 819; AK III Ep 1136.

Greeting. Pray, dear Erasmus, most gifted of all men of letters, do not be
surprised or (as I fear you may be) indignant if I address a letter to you at
what is perhaps such an inconvenient moment. I have to do it for the sake of
one of your pupils, Jean Pyrrhus d'Angleberme, a professor in Orléans,
where he was lately for three years my teacher and a good teacher. I have set   5
out his business more fully for your kind attention in another letter attached
to this one. I have already written three letters on this subject, but so far, I
regret to say, in vain. The first went with Pieter Gillis, secretary of the city of
Antwerp, an excellent scholar, together with letters from Budé and others,
and that was in the month of May last past; then the letter which you see   10
enclosed in this one, sent last September to the Frankfurt fair, to which I
greatly hoped you would be coming; and now for the third and last time in
this month of October. So like the kind and honourable man you are, much
respected Erasmus, please not only to receive this in your usual straightforward way but read it through for the sake of the contents; and reply in a very   15
short note, if you please (but I do very strongly urge you to), not that I have
done anything to deserve it, I am sorry to say, but because the need to correct
the work and the delay in doing so necessitate it. If you are willing to do this,
as I am sure you are, I will send the short work in question, if this is possible
for you, to that same Pieter Gillis; for he, I am quite sure, will send it to you at   20

* * * * *

866
4 Angleberme] In 1500 Erasmus had tutored him in Paris; cf Ep 140:37–8.
6 business] From lines 17–19 it appears that Erasmus was asked to revise one of
    Angleberme's writings. Several were published between 1518 and 1520, among
    them *Militia Francorum regum* (Paris: J. Bade 21 February 1518 = 1519 new
    style?). In the title of an enlarged and revised edition of his works (Milan: A.
    Minutianus 1520) earlier French editions were accused of negligence; cf *Index
    Aureliensis* (Baden-Baden 1965–) I no 105.815.

Louvain as soon as he can. I beg you, dear Erasmus, in answer to this and all my other foolish letters do let me have, as I say, some kind of brief note when you conveniently can, addressed to me in Cologne, either at the Fat Hen bookshop or at the Coney. You will do me, I solemnly assure you, a very great service, although it is far beyond any claim I may have on you.   25

I hear you made a rapid survey of Cologne from the White Horse inn in the Haymarket. I was bitterly disappointed not to be able to speak to you about all this in person. I had also made plans long ago that the city council of Cologne should have given a public reception in your honour, as your high standing and your great eminence deserve, though I quite agree that far   30 more distinguished offerings would properly be your due.

I am convinced it was only the virulence of the plague that made you leave so soon. I hope you will one day come back by way of Cologne; and then I shall try with all my might to have a little speech with you, particularly in company with Hermann, count of Neuenahr, and Hermannus Buschius,   35 and Johannes Caesarius, who is now living at Münster, all my special friends. Until then, I remain entirely devoted to you, my supreme Maecenas and patron deity, and ask for your continuing good will. Farewell O greatest and most illustrious ornament of the whole world of letters, and above all the leading light and glory of the whole of Germany.   40

Cologne, 6 October 1518

Sincerely yours, Adolf Eichholz of Cologne licentiate in canon law

To the right excellent and learned Doctor Erasmus of Rotterdam, the leading theologian in the field of Scripture, his most honoured master. In Louvain   45

867 / To Beatus Rhenanus   Louvain, [first half of October] 1518

This letter gives an elaborate account of Erasmus' journey from Basel to Louvain and of the serious illness he contracted while approaching the

* * * * *

23 Fat Hen] 'Unter Fettenhennen,' the bookstore of the Birckmann brothers, which served as a name for the whole street. The house 'zum Hasen' ('the Coney') was adjacent; cf J. Benzing *Die Buchdrucker des 16. und 17. Jahrhunderts im deutschen Sprachgebiet* (Wiesbaden 1963) 224–5; H. Keussen *Topographie der Stadt Köln im Mittelalter* (Bonn 1910) I 312.
26 White Horse] No doubt the inn 'zum Ross' on the Rheingasse, just off the Heumarkt; cf Keussen I 70.
32 plague] Cf Ep 861:7n.
35 Neuenahr] See Epp 442 introduction, 867:79–88.
35 Buschius] See Ep 830 introduction.
36 Caesarius] See Ep 374 introduction.

Netherlands. It was composed in part as he lay recovering in the house of his friend, the printer Dirk Martens. After some four weeks (line 266) he returned to the College of the Lily by 15 October and resumed his normal correspondence with the pressing Ep 869. A week later the last pages of the revised *New Testament* were ready for dispatch (cf lines 83, 254, Ep 885). The young men who took them to Basel were also given Epp 877–85 for delivery to various friends along their way and an unsealed copy of this letter to be shown at each stop (cf Epp 877:36–7, 878:9–11). Thereafter the letter was printed in the *Farrago*.

With the usual reservations about the precision of such statements, the chronology of Erasmus' journey can be reconstructed as follows:
September

c 3–4	by boat from Basel to Strasbourg; dinner at Breisach; supper and night quarters in a miserable village
c 4	arrival in Strasbourg before dinner; the day spent there and probably also the night
c 5–6	on horseback to Speyer (line 162)
c 7–8	at Speyer
c 9	by carriage to Worms and Mainz
c 10	by boat to Boppard and Koblenz
c 11–12	by boat to Bonn and Cologne; after some hours in Cologne on horseback to Bedburg
12–c 17	at Bedburg with Neuenahr
c 17	by carriage to Aachen
c 18–19	at Aachen
c 19	on horseback to Maastricht and Tongeren
c 20	to St Truiden, partly by carriage and partly on horseback
c 21	by carriage to Tienen and Louvain

ERASMUS TO HIS DEAR RHENANUS, GREETING

Here, my dear Beatus, is the whole tragicomedy of my travels. I was still feeble and rather listless, as you know, when I was leaving Basel – for I had not yet made my peace with the climate after lying low for so long indoors – and distracted by continuous toil as well. The boat was not unpleasant, 5 except that around midday the sun was hot and somewhat trying. We dined at Breisach, and never have I had a more unpleasant dinner. The stench was terrible, the flies worse than the stench. We sat more than half an hour at table waiting idly while (if you please) they got their own dinner ready.

* * * * *

867

7 Breisach] On the Rhine, between Freiburg and Colmar

Eventually nothing was set on the table that one could possibly eat: dirty   1(
pease porridge, lumps of meat, sausage réchauffé more than once – it was
simply revolting. I did not go and see Gallinarius. Someone told me he had a
fever and added a charming story: that that Minorite theologian with whom I
had had an argument over echeities had pawned communion vessels in his
own name. There's a nice Scotist refinement for you! At nightfall we were   1!
cast ashore at some dreary village whose name I did not choose to inquire,
nor would I willingly write it if I knew. That place was nearly the death of
me. We had supper in a parlour of no great size with a stove, more than sixty
of us I should think, the dregs of the human race, and that at ten o'clock. The
smell! The noise! Especially when they were already heated with wine. But I   2(
had to sit there and take my timing from them.

    In the morning while it was still quite dark we were roused from our
blankets by the shouts of the shipmen. Supperless and sleepless I went on
board. Strasbourg we reached before dinner, about nine o'clock, and there I
was more agreeably entertained, especially as Schürer supplied the wine.   2!
Some part of the society were already there, and soon they all came to greet
me, but no one taking more trouble than Gerbel. Gebwiler and Rudolfinger
would not let me pay anything, a kindness which in them was nothing new.
From there we went on to Speyer on horseback, nor did we espy the ghost of
a soldier anywhere, though atrocious rumours were abroad. My English   3(
horse simply gave up and hardly got as far as Speyer; that miscreant of a
smith had done him so badly that both his ears are singed with hot metal. At
Speyer I slipped away from the inn and took refuge with my friend
Maternus, who lived nearby. There I was put up for two days very
pleasantly and courteously by the dean, who is a learned and civilized man.   3!
There by a happy chance I found Hermannus Buschius.

    From there I went by carriage to Worms and on again to Mainz. In the

    * * * * *

12 Gallinarius] Johannes Gallinarius (cf Ep 305:213n) was then parish priest at
    Breisach.
14 echeities] Cf *Moria* (ASD IV–3 144, 148) speaking of 'quidditates,' 'ecceitates' –
    'verbal portents dreamed up by recent theologians.' No more is known about
    the Minorite, but cf for a similar opponent Epp 557, 561.
21 take my timing] Erasmus refers, as he frequently does elsewhere, to the
    clepsydra or water-clock used in Athenian law courts; cf the colloquy
    'Diversoria' (first published in August 1523; ASD I–3 337), which may well
    embody reminiscences of this journey; *Adagia* I iv 73.
25 Schürer] Matthias Schürer, the Strasbourg printer; see Epp 224:49n, 883:8. For
    other members of the Strasbourg literary society cf Ep 302.
30 English horse] See Ep 785:51n.
34 Maternus] Hatten, the vicar of Speyer cathedral. The dean of the cathedral
    since 1517 was Thomas Truchsess. For both cf Ep 355.

same conveyance there happened to be by chance one of the emperor's
secretaries, by name Ulrich Varnbüler (as who should say Brackenbury). He
was incredibly kind – did things for me throughout the journey, and 40
furthermore at Mainz would not let me go to the inn but carried me off to the
house of one of the canons and gave me his company to the ship when I left.
The boat-journey was not unpleasant, thanks to the good weather, except
that it took rather a long time; the sailors saw to that. Besides which the
stench of the horses was offensive. The first day I had out of mere kindness 45
the company of Johannes Longicampianus, who lectured some time ago at
Louvain, and of some lawyer who was a friend of his. There was also a man
from Westphalia, a Father Johann, canon of St Victor's outside Mainz,
a most agreeable and cheerful person.

When we put in at Boppard and while the boat was being examined we 50
were stretching our legs on the bank when someone recognized me and
pointed me out to the customs officer: 'Behold the man,' he said. The
officer's name is Christopher (I suppose) Cinicampius, commonly called
Eschenfelder. I cannot tell you how delighted the man was. He carried me off
to his house. On his desk all among the customs forms lay the works of 55
Erasmus! He cried out on his good fortune, called for his children, his wife,
and all his friends. Meanwhile, as the shipmen were loudly protesting, he
sent them two flagons of wine, and when there were more protests replied
with two more, promising that the man who had brought him such a
distinguished guest should be excused the toll on his return. From here we 60
were accompanied out of kindness as far as Koblenz by Dr Johann
Flaming, the warden of a house of nuns there, a man of angelic innocence,

* * * * *

39 Varnbüler] Ulrich Varnbüler of St Gallen (1474–1545) was head of the chancery
of the imperial court (Reichskammergericht) at Speyer.
42 one of the canons] See Ep 880 introduction.
46 Longicampianus] For him and his lawyer friend see Ep 881.
48 Johann] According to information kindly provided by Professor A. Ph. Brück,
diocesan archivist at Mainz, there were eighteen prebends at St Victor's. In
1518 five were held by canons named Johann (J. Reuss senior, 1505–41; J.
Terlang, 1504–25; J. Vincenz von Bicken, 1514–51; J. Vonhoff, 1510–43; J.
Beuren, 1509–24) . Unfortunately none has so far been identified as a member
of a Westphalian family.
50 Boppard] On the Rhine, at the border of the principality of Trier, eight miles
south of Koblenz.
54 Eschenfelder] See Ep 879.
62 Flaming] Johann Flaming was a poet and a friend of Helius Eobanus, who
visited him in Boppard on his way to see Erasmus (cf Ep 870 introduction).
Apparently Flaming was still living there in 1528; cf Ep 2071.

Ulrich Varnbüler
Drawing in chalk by Albrecht Dürer,
for the woodcut dated 1522
Albertina, Vienna

sound and sober judgment, and uncommon learning. At Koblenz Dr
Matthias, the bishop's official, took me to his house – a young man but
mature in his ways, a careful and experienced Latin scholar and a first-class 65
lawyer. There I had a cheerful supper.

At Bonn the canon left us, to avoid the city of Cologne, which I would
gladly have avoided myself, but my servant had gone on ahead there with
the horses, and there was no one reliable in the boat to whom I could have
entrusted the task of recalling my man, nor did I trust the sailors. In the 70
morning therefore before six o'clock we reached Cologne, on Sunday, the
weather being now most oppressive. I entered an inn and requested the
host's servants to hire a carriage and pair, ordering food to be ready by ten
o'clock. Then I heard mass. Dinner was late. I had no luck with the carriage.
I attempted to hire a horse, for my own were useless. No luck. I perceived 75
what it was: they were determined I should stay there. I gave orders at once
to harness my own horses and put one of my valises on one of them; the other
I entrusted to mine host, and so on my lame horse I made the best of my way
towards the count of Neuenahr. It is about five hours' journey. He was at
Bedburg. 80

With him I spent five delightful days, in such tranquillity and comfort
that I finished a good part of my revision while I was there, for I had brought
that part of the New Testament with me. My dear Beatus, I wish you knew
that man! He is quite young, but of rare wisdom, more than you would find
in an old man; says little, but, as Homer remarks of Menelaus, speaks right 85
fluently, or rather right intelligently; learned without ostentation in more
than one field of study; a most open-hearted character and made for
friendship. I was already recovered and getting a little strength; I was by
now well pleased with my progress and looking forward to being in good

* * * * *

64 Matthias] Matthias von Saarburg (d 1539) was the official of the archbishop of
Trier at Koblenz in 1518 and from 1527 at Trier. He also became dean of St
Simeon at Trier and was Erasmus' eager host again in November 1521; cf Ep 880.

67 canon] Johann (of line 48) avoided Cologne because of the plague (cf Ep
861:7n), it seems. A month later so did Eobanus, according to his *Hodoeporicon;*
cf Krause *Eobanus* 1 292.

68 servant] Probably Hovius; cf line 189.

71 Sunday] Only 12 September is possible, since Erasmus was still at Basel on 31
August (cf Ep 862) and probably on 1 September too; cf Epp 869:3–4, 886:42–3.

72 inn] Cf Ep 866:26.

77 the other] For shipment by water via Antwerp; cf Epp 877:41–2, 878:6.

80 Bedburg] Sixteen miles west of Cologne; the large castle owned by Neuenahr is
still a landmark.

83 New Testament] See Ep 867 introduction.

85 Homer] *Iliad* 3.214

case for a visit to the bishop of Liège and a lively return to my friends in   9·
Brabant. The dinners, the parties of welcome, the long talks I was promising
myself! I had decided, if we should have a mild autumn, to go to England
and take up the offers the king had so often made me. But how deceptive are
the hopes of mortal men! How sudden and unforeseen the changes in human
affairs! From all these dreams of felicity I was plunged headlong into utter   9·
disaster.

A carriage and pair had already been hired for next day. The count,
reluctant to bid me farewell the night before, announced that he would come
and see me in the morning before I left. That night a kind of violent storm of
wind arose, which had preceded likewise the day before. None the less I got   1·
up after midnight to scribble something for the count, and when seven
o'clock came and he still did not appear, I told them to wake him. He came
and in his usual shy way asked whether I was determined to leave in such
unsuitable weather; he did not think I should be safe. Then, my dear Beatus,
some Jupiter, some evil genius robbed me not of half my wits, as Hesiod has   1·
it, but of my entire senses, for half my senses he had removed already when I
entrusted myself to Cologne. I only wish he had warned his friend more
emphatically or I had been more receptive of his shy but most friendly
warnings. Fate rapt me away; for how else can I put it? I climbed into an open
carriage, with a wind blowing 'such as upon the lofty mountain-tops /   1·
Splinters the swaying oaks.' It was a south wind but breathed pure
pestilence. I thought myself well protected by my wrappings, but the force of
that wind went through everything. Towards nightfall it was succeeded by a
fine rain more pestilent than the wind that brought it. I reached Aachen
exhausted by the shaking of the carriage, which was such a burden to me on   1·
the rocky pavement of the road that a badly foundered horse would have
been a softer ride. Here one of the canons, to whom I had an introduction

* * * * *

90 Liège] In response to an invitation from the bishop, Erard de la Marck,
   conveyed in Ep 746. By the time Ep 916 was written they had finally met.
92 England] Cf Ep 855:32n.
105 Hesiod] A mingled memory of Hesiod *Scutum* 149 and Homer *Odyssey* 17.322;
   cf Allen's note.
110 'such as ... swaying oaks'] Horace *Epodes* 10.7–8
117 one of the canons] Perhaps Johann Schoenraid (or Schoenrode etc, d 1541),
   who was canon and before 1529 dean (cf below lines 130–1; Ep 972:33; J.
   Strange *Genealogie der Herren und Freiherren von Bongart*, Cologne 1866, 18).
   Schoenraid may conceivably have been the canon in whose house Erasmus
   forgot his sword and who was said to have gone to Rome shortly thereafter (cf
   Ep 904:7–10). His family had connections with the German college of Santa
   Maria dell'Anima, where he had himself been registered in 1512; cf *Liber*

from the count, swept me away from the inn to the precentor's house. There I
found some of the canons at their usual potations. A very slender dinner had
made me hungry, but in their company at that hour there was nothing but   120
carp, and that cold. I ate my fill, and we sat drinking till late; but I made my
excuses and went off to bed, having slept very little the night before.

Next day I was carried off to the vice-provost's house, for it was his
turn in the rotation. There was no fish there except eels (the weather being at
fault, for otherwise he keeps a splendid table), so I ate my fill of a sort of fish   125
they hang up to harden in the wind, which, from the wooden batten with
which it is pounded, the Germans call stockfisch; for normally I rather like it,
but I soon discovered that some of this was still raw. After dinner, as the
weather was still perfectly pestilential, I retired to the inn and ordered them
to get the fire going properly. That same canon, a man of much courtesy,   130
talked with me for about an hour and a half. Meanwhile my stomach began to
give trouble; and as it persisted, I sent him away and retired to the latrine for
a good riddance. And before I had taken all the load off my stomach I put my
finger down my throat once or twice and up came that raw fish, nor did I
throw up anything else but that. Once I had been sick I lay down, not so   135
much sleeping as lying quiet with no headache and no pain anywhere.
After that, having made an agreement with the driver about my baggage I
was again invited to their evening potations. I begged to be excused,
without success. I knew my stomach would take nothing except a little warm
gruel, for the same thing had happened at Basel: one night, when I had an   140
attack of the phlegm coming on and could not bear the pain in my stomach, I
had relieved it in the same way, and it was a month before my digestion could
come to terms again with any food. This time we were very splendidly done
by, but it was no use to me. When I had comforted my stomach with a little
soup, I set off home; for I was sleeping at the precentor's. I went out, and my   145
frame with my empty stomach was shaken to its very core by the weather that
night. A dreadful night it was.

* * * * *

confraternitatis B. Marie de Anima Teutonicorum de Urbe ed C. Jänig (Rome 1875)
124. The eager conveyor is called 'dean' in Ep 1170. The same letter shows that
the canons of Aachen were far from pleased with the publicity they had
received through the publication of these lines in the Farrago of 1519. Erasmus
changed them when the letter reappeared in the Epistolae ad diversos of 1521.
Schoenraid, however, remained a good friend; see Ep 2130.
118 precentor] Johann Sudermann, d c 1537
123 vice-provost] Werner Huyn van Amstenrade was vice-provost of St Mary's at
    Aachen from 1517 and died in 1534; see O. R. Redlich in Zeitschrift des Bergischen
    Geschichtsvereins 41 (1908) 170, 177.
124 rotation] Cf Allen Ep 1170:33–7.

Next morning again I took a little mulled ale with a few scraps of bread
and mounted my horse, which was sickly and lame, and so all the more
uncomfortable to ride. I had already been reduced to such a state that it was a   1
better plan to keep warm in bed than to sit on a horse. But nothing is more
uncivilized or dreary or barren than that country, such is the fecklessness of
the inhabitants; so I was the more glad to get away. The danger of robbers –
which was very great in those parts – or at least the fear of them was driven
out by the distress of my illness.   1

Already, while I was still in Basel, in the course of scratching the parts
adjacent to my groin (as my custom is) to provoke a movement of the bowels,
I had scratched rather too hard and broken the surface of the skin under my
left hip with my finger-nail. The same happened in my right groin, but from
that there was no pain and no soreness. The lesion under my left hip was   1
made a little sore by the two days' riding that took me from Strasbourg to
Speyer, but to the extent that I only felt it if I pressed on it with too much
force. This trouble was so much aggravated by this last ride of mine, since I
was resting on the horse in just that spot, that the whole area became
inflamed. Besides which the place in my left groin swelled slightly, but with a   1
swelling that could be moved easily under the skin, and not enough to hurt
much. Besides this, at the top of my left groin a sort of hard lump came up and
gradually increased, but there was no pain and no soreness. And as I rode,
those parts of my body were not properly protected from the wind.

On this lap I completed four miles and reached Maastricht. There I   1
comforted my stomach as best as I could with a little broth, mounted again,
and set off for Tongeren, a town about three miles away. This last ride was
far the most painful of the lot. The horse went very awkwardly and tortured
me in the kidneys. It would have been more bearable to walk, but I was afraid
of getting into a sweat, and there was a risk that night might have overtaken   1
us in the open country; and so with incredible torment of my whole body, the
kidneys and liver especially, I reached Tongeren. By this time lack of food,
and physical effort on top of that, had sapped all my bodily strength, so that I
could neither stand nor walk properly. My tongue retained its powers, and
I used it to conceal the severity of my condition. There I warmed my stomach   1
with a little mulled ale and went to bed.

In the morning I gave orders to hire a covered carriage and pair. The
road was so rocky that I thought it wiser to stay on horseback until we came
to softer ground. I therefore mounted the taller of the horses in hopes that it
would move more comfortably over the stones and be more sure-footed. I   1

* * * * *

170 four] The distance from Aachen to Maastricht is c nineteen modern miles.
177 Tongeren] Eleven miles south-west of Maastricht

had scarcely mounted when I felt a film coming over my eyes on exposure to
the cold weather and asked for a cloak. But a fainting-fit soon took its place.
It needed no more than a touch on the hand to arouse me. At that point my
man Johannes and the other bystanders left me to come to in my own time as I
sat on the horse. Once I had come to, I climbed into the carriage. Shortly   190
afterwards I felt my bowels working; I got out and relieved them, and my
colour and a certain amount of cheerfulness returned. We were now close to
the town of St Truiden. I mounted my horse again, for fear that if I arrived in
the carriage I should be seen to be ill. Again I was affected by the evening air
and felt sick, but not enough to faint. I offered my driver double money if he   195
would drive me next day as far as Tienen, a town six miles beyond Tongeren.
He accepted the offer. Here mine host, whom I knew, told me how much the
bishop of Liège had been offended by my departing for Basel without
saying goodbye to him. I comforted my stomach with some broth and went to
bed. It was a most dreadful night, especially through the agony I was in from   200
the sore on my left hip; such was the piercing pain of the blood that
corrupted and grew hard round the place. At this point I found by chance a
four-horse carriage bound for Louvain (which was six miles away), and
flung myself into it. The discomfort of the going was beyond belief and
almost more than I could bear; all the same, at seven o'clock that evening we   205
reached Louvain.

It was not my intention to make for my rooms, partly because I
suspected that everything there would be deadly cold, partly because I
wanted to do nothing that might in any way embarrass the college, if any
rumour of plague should arise on my account. So I took refuge with Dirk the   210
printer, such a good friend that I could be happy with him alone if things
went as I could wish. That night unknown to me the largest boil had burst,
and the pain had now settled down. Next day I sent for a surgeon, and he
applied a soothing dressing. By now I had acquired a third sore place on my

* * * * *

189 Johannes] Johannes Hovius was already an MA when he joined Erasmus at
   Basel. At Louvain he remained in his service perhaps until Erasmus' departure
   in 1521 (cf Ep 1222). In 1524 he went on to Italy; see Ep 857 introduction and
   Bierlaire 54–5.
197 Here] At St Truiden, where Erasmus spent the night, twenty-one miles east of
   Louvain
198 Liège] Cf above line 90n and for the journey to Basel cf Ep 843 introduction.
202 At this point] Apparently at Tienen, although this is only eleven miles east of
   Louvain. For the relation between Erasmus' miles and modern miles see above
   line 170n.
207 rooms] In the College of the Lily
210 Dirk] Martens

View of Speyer
Woodcut from Sebastian Münster *Cosmographei*
Basel: Henricus Petri 1550
Historisches Museum der Pfalz, Speyer

back, which my servant had caused at Tongeren while massaging me with   21
attar of rose for the pain in my kidneys by rubbing too hard with his horny
finger on one of my ribs. This afterwards turned sore. A lump also swelled
up under my right pap of a loose kind, but this was not sore and gradually
disappeared of its own accord. As the surgeon went away he told Dirk and
my servant in confidence that it was the plague; he would send the emollient   22
dressings, he said, but he would not come and see me himself. I sent my
water to the physicians, who said there was no sign of disease; again I
consulted others, who gave me the same assurance. I sent for the Jew. 'To
judge by your urine,' he said, 'I wish I was as fit as you.' The surgeon not
reappearing next day or the day after, I asked Dirk the reason. He made some   22
excuse or other, and I guessed what was in the wind. 'What?' I said; 'does
he think it's the plague?' 'That's exactly what he says,' was the reply; 'he
swears there are three buboes.' I laughed heartily, and no idea of plague
entered my head for one moment.

Some days later the surgeon's father came and examined me; he was   2
of the same opinion and assured me to my face that it was a genuine case of
plague. Even so he could not convince me. I sent secretly for a second
surgeon of great reputation. He examined me. 'I shouldn't be frightened to
share a bed with you,' he said, being a rather boorish fellow; 'have
intercourse with you too, if you were a woman.' My Hebrew friend thought   2
the same. I sent for a physician of whom they think very highly in Louvain,
for good physicians in these parts are a very rare thing. I asked him whether
there were any sinister signs in my water, and he said 'No.' I told him the
story of my sore places, adding the reasons why I inferred it was not the
plague. The sores were not new and did not arise spontaneously; the   2
swellings to begin with were movable, and the one in my left groin always so;
there was no fever, no particular headache except from the roughness of the
journey, no drowsiness, the roof of my mouth permanently clean; when I
was sick, it was deliberate and not natural, and I brought up nothing but the
fish; once quit of that, my stomach settled down, and the subsequent loss of   2
appetite was a personal peculiarity; there was no sign of plague in my water.
He listened to the rest of it with some confidence, but the moment I
mentioned the sores I saw his nerve was shaken. I gave the doctor a gold

* * * * *

217 massaging] Cf Ulrich von Hutten *De guaiaci medicina* (Mainz: J. Schöffer April
    1519) f K 3 verso–4 recto. Hutten reports Erasmus' faith in such a daily
    massage, especially on getting up in the morning. Hutten, like other young
    friends, was advised to try it, and was pleased with the result.
223 Jew] Matthaeus Adrianus, who was a physician as well as a professor of
    Hebrew; his name is added in the margin of the *Farrago* of 1519.

crown and he promised to see me again after dinner. Terrified by what I said, he sent his servant. I refused to see him, lost patience with physicians, and   250 commended my fate to Christ the great physician.

My stomach recovered itself in a couple of days on minced chicken and a bottle of Beaune, and I went back to work too without delay and finished the missing parts of the New Testament. Seventeen days later black dead flesh came away from my sores, which was just what the surgeons had said   255 would happen. The swelling in my left groin had now come up, but not so as to hurt, and that frightened me seriously. An absurd suspicion entered my mind, and I only hope a mistaken one, that this trouble might have arisen out of contact with my horse. For two or three times I drove off flies sitting on the sore with my bare hand, and then I handled those parts of my body casually   260 while making water or putting on my under-shirt. But on this point the surgeon told me without hesitation that there was no cause for anxiety whatever. By now the swelling is softer and has gone down somewhat, but even so it makes no move at all as yet. The sores are now out of danger, the lump on my right chest is disappearing of its own accord.   265

My recovery in Dirk's house lasted some four weeks, and I went back to my own rooms. Only once did I get out to mass in the nearest church, for my strength was not really up to it yet. If it was indeed plague, I drove the plague away at the cost of great effort and discomfort and determination; for often a great part of any disease is our fancy that we have it. From the   270 moment of my arrival I had given out that no one should come and see me unless personally invited, for fear that I might make anyone terrified for his own safety or that anyone's kind attentions should be insupportable to me; all the same Dorp made his way in, before anybody else, and soon afterwards Atensis. Marcus Laurinus and Paschasius Berselius, who came   275 every day, did away a good part of my illness by their most charming company.

My dear Beatus, who would suppose that my emaciated frame, which was always delicate and is now even more feeble from advancing years, would after such laborious journeys and exhausting researches still support   280 so many bouts of sickness? You know yourself how gravely ill I was not long ago in Basel, and that too more than once. A certain suspicion had entered my mind that the year might prove fatal to me: so relentlessly did one disaster

* * * * *

274 Dorp ... Atensis] See Ep 852 introduction and 67n.
275 Berselius] See Ep 674 introduction.
281 ill ... in Basel] Cf Ep 847:7n.
283 fatal] Erasmus had paid some attention to the astrological predictions for 1518; see Epp 755:32n, 803:10n.

succeed another, each worse than the last. Yet even at the moment when
sickness lay most heavy upon me, my frame of mind was such that I was   28
neither tormented by the desire to live nor terrified by fear of death. In Christ
alone was all my hope, and all I asked of him was that he should give me what
he might think best for me. When I was a young man, I remember how I used
to tremble even at the mere name of death. In this at least I have profited as I
grew older: I fear death very little, nor do I measure man's felicity by length   29
of days. I have passed my fiftieth year; and seeing how few out of so many
reach it, I cannot fairly complain that my life has been too short. And then, if
this has anything to do with it, I have already built a monument to bear
witness to posterity that I existed. It may be that from the pyre, as poets put
it, not only will envy retire in silence but glory will shine out with more   29
distinction – though it is not right for a Christian's heart to be touched by
human glory. O that I might but win the glory of being acceptable to Christ!
My dearest Beatus, farewell. You will find the rest of my news in my letter to
Capito.

Louvain, 1518   30

868 / To Ambrogio Leoni   Louvain, 15 October [1518]

The source of this letter is the *Farrago* of October 1519, which gives the year date
as 1519 but does not otherwise include letters dated after 15 August 1519.
Moreover, this letter answers Ep 854, and if more than a year had elapsed
between the writing of Epp 854 and 868, Erasmus would probably have offered
an explanation or an apology.

ERASMUS OF ROTTERDAM TO THE DISTINGUISHED PHYSICIAN
AMBROGIO LEONI, GREETING
Your letter, my learned Ambrogio, gave me all the more pleasure for being
quite unexpected. It refreshed my whole memory of the days when we lived
together: as I read it, I seemed to be back in Venice, to see my old friends   5
around me and warm to their society – Aldus, Battista Egnazio, Girolamo
Aleandro, Marcus Musurus, and you above others, the dearest friend of all.

* * * * *

291 fiftieth] Cf Ep 868:101n.
294 from the pyre] Perhaps an allusion to Ovid *Amores* 1.15.39, quoted in *Adagia*
    II vii 11: 'Envy feeds on the living, and is silent after death.'
298 letter] Ep 877

868
  6 society] See Ep 269:54–7; for Aldo Manuzio cf also Ep 207 and for Aleandro Ep
    256.

I felt again the same habitual charm in your letter, full as it is of humour and
wit. How I envy you, growing old in the most honourable pursuits in what is
easily the grandest city of them all among patricians and men of learning,   10
while my own destiny has inflicted on me more mishaps and more
wanderings than ever Neptune in Homer gave Ulysses! You must not think
any of this is due to my own inconstancy; in all the changes and chances of
my fate I have always been the same Erasmus who never changes. Nor have I
ever been different from what I am now; but the plot of the play took charge,   15
and at different times I have had different parts to play. Yet it is really not
until you know all the scenes in which I have had to play my part that you
could accuse me of being a Pythagoras or a Proteus. The number of times,
after all that has happened, that those men have buried me, the number of
times I have survived my own decease! The enemies of humane letters kill me   20
off nearly every year and report me dead and buried. How often have I made
my way to Basel through the thick of robbery and plague! The monsters I
have had to contend with, the labours I have had to get through! You might
well think your old friend Erasmus, who used to be made of glass, was now
pure adamant. What would you? So runs my destiny. How much happier   25
you are, who can argue quietly about philosophy in honourable and tranquil
ease, nor does any storm assail you and drive you off course out of the even
tenor of your life.

The productions of which you write are eagerly awaited, offspring
worthy not merely of a Lion, as you call them, but of an Ambrose, which   30
means they must be as charming as they are forceful and make us think of
Homer's Nestor with his 'honeyed gift of speech.' It is right and proper that
you should write of your native Nola, for all that Virgil once grudged it any
renown. How I wish your great book against Averroes, that thrice-accursed
atheist, had come out! What of your problems of natural history, a work you   35
had in hand long ago? I wonder you do not mention it; nor do you say
anything of Greek, which you took up when already grey-haired and yet

* * * * *

14 never changes] Although men were called to play changing roles, in Erasmus'
   view their character was static; see Bietenholz *History and Biography* 69–87.
32 Nestor] Homer *Iliad* 1.249
33 Virgil] Aulus Gellius 6.20.1 recounts how Virgil cut the name of Nola in
   Campania out of his *Georgics* because the inhabitants had annoyed him.
34 Averroes] The book was in print, as Leoni had said (Ep 854:91–3). Erasmus'
   expression of abhorrence is conventional, as it was generally believed that the
   twelfth-century Muslim philosopher had maintained the mortality of the soul.
35 problems] Leoni's *Novum opus quaestionum seu problematum ... utilissimorum ...
   in philosophia et medicinae scientia* (Venice: B. and M. de' Vitali 1523). Ten years
   earlier during his sojourn in Venice Erasmus had seen a manuscript of it; cf
   Adagia III vii 66.

with such success – an important precedent: hereafter let no young learner ever despair. You remind me that one should 'not without reason to Abydos sail,' and I wish you had issued the warning earlier. As it is, once I have 40 entrusted myself to winds and waves, I am inevitably borne away as they may please. All the same, in the great upheavals aroused nearly every day by the rascals who are in league against the humanities, I trim my ship with reason and philosophy for my ballast and fight the storm with such skill as I can muster.   45

The movements on the part of the Turks need give us no cause for fear, if only the Christian princes would be of one mind. I see you have the heart of a true philosopher: you fear the effect not on landed property and private fortunes but on culture – and culture may perish without calling in the Turks! This is the objective pursued with the greatest energy by certain monks and 50 theologians I could name. For how small a part of culture does a man leave untouched who will do away with all knowledge except sophistical theology and a distorted acquaintance with the law, who shows the door to the learned tongues, and at one blow condemns the humanities in any form! But these people, who have more brass than brains, get nowhere. The whole of 55 France, all Germany, and Britain itself welcome good literature with open arms, with the warm approval and even assistance of their rulers.

Marcus Musurus chose to be a bishop rather than a professor, but as he was hastening to his goal he was sucked in by Rome. I doubt if anyone among us here has the effrontery to expose himself willingly on such a stage 60 as yours; no Frenchman or German would enter the lists against the Italians, indeed against Musurus' own progeny, with the certainty of getting nothing but mockery and catcalls for his pains. I was very glad to learn from you the name of Pietro Alcionio, and I wish I could also see what he has written, especially his versions from Aristotle. I should like to know the whole man 65 more intimately, especially since he does not despise my own work, which would not be the case unless he were a singularly fair-minded person. I will approach him by letter on some other occasion; for the moment, please give him my best wishes.

In Britain there is a man of all-round erudition, Thomas Linacre, who 70 will have been known to you long ago from the glowing reports of Aldus and myself – a man of the same calling as you and, if I mistake not, the same age.

* * * * *

39 Abydos] See Ep 854:47n.
58 Musurus] Cf Ep 729:60–2.
68 approach him] No exchange of letters between Erasmus and Alcionio is known to exist.

He is engaged on the same task as yourself, the publication of a series of works which he has been polishing for many years. His Galen *On the Preservation of Health* is out – a version so faithful, so clear, in such stylish 75 Latin, that the reader who knows Latin only loses nothing; in fact, he will find everything better done than in the Greek. This was followed by his *Therapeutice*; and you know what a state our text was in before. We hope his next production will be the *Meteorologica* of Aristotle, first corrected with incredible labour and then most felicitiously translated. He has a great many 80 things among his papers which will be very valuable to those who wish to learn. With these publications he secures himself an immortal name, adds glory to his native England, and sheds lustre on the king's court, and above all on the king, to whom he is physician in ordinary. In France too that great man Guillaume Cop with a new book from time to time is establishing our 85 right to be heard in medicine. Budé works his way through the legal authorities, cleansing the Augean stables as he goes. All receive advice with pleasure; we theologians alone are unwilling to learn a more excellent way.

Mind you take great care of your health, my learned Ambrogio, so that you may long be a pillar of the humanities and that, now we are both getting 90 old, I may enjoy your friendship for many years. You have a lead over me, but I am not far behind, being now almost entirely white-headed. Aldus when the conversation was running free used to be rather amusing, imitating the broken accents of a decrepit old man which he thought we should use in time to come in addressing one another.'And how goes it then, Master 95 Erasmus?' he would say; and then in just such a snuffling voice, but rather weaker (representing me) he would reply 'If you're all right, I'm all right.' Such was the merry picture he would draw, especially if we went on to discuss the foundation of a new academy; but he did not play his promised part. Before he had reached that toothless age, he left us; though Aldus was much 100

* * * * *

74 Galen] For the publication of the two translations by Linacre cf Ep 755:32n.
79 *Meteorologica*] Never published. Writing to Dorp on 21 October 1515, More reported that Linacre had completed the translation of two books before he became absorbed with Galen; cf Rogers Ep 15:1299–1310.
97 reply] 'Si vales, ego valeo' is a pedestrian commonplace in humanistic epistolography, though it has a distinguished ancestry in Cicero.
99 new academy] A statute for such an association was printed by Aldus, probably in 1502, and mentioned in his colophons over the next few years, but as patronage was not forthcoming it gradually became, as this passage shows, a subject for nostalgic jokes; see M.J.C. Lowry 'The "New Academy" of Aldus Manutius – Renaissance Dream' *Bulletin of the John Rylands Library of Manchester* 58 (1975–6) 378–420.

older than me, more or less twenty years, I should think. For I am now in my
fifty-second or fifty-third year.

I should love to go on chattering to you, dear Leoni, but business calls
me away. Your name will last for ever in my proverbs, provided only that
they last themselves; nor will you be unwilling in your turn to mention the   10⁵
name of Erasmus in your own work. Be sure to give my greetings to the
excellent Battista Egnazio, and also to Asolano and his household, especially
little Manuzio who used to play round us as a child, when I was with you.
Farewell.

From Louvain, 15 October [1519]   110

869 / To Guillaume Budé   Louvain, 15 October 1518

This letter, which was published in the *Farrago*, continues Erasmus' flamboyant
correspondence with the leading humanist of France (cf the preface to this
volume). It is a preliminary reply to Budé's long and ambiguous Ep 810, which
had gone astray and only reached Erasmus when he was about to leave Basel at
the beginning of September (cf lines 3-4; Ep 886:41-3). When he wrote this,
Erasmus was recovering from his severe illness (cf Ep 867) and was not yet well
enough to compose a full answer. This letter reached Budé on 30 October (Ep
896:116); he lost no time in giving vent to his displeasure in Ep 896.

ERASMUS OF ROTTERDAM TO HIS FRIEND GUILLAUME BUDÉ,
GREETING

That prolix letter which you wrote about the 13th April reached me about the
first of September, having been sent back from Genoa; and such a letter it
was as made me think it might be better for your reputation and mine too if it   5
were suppressed. I fancy I have come to know your characteristic way of
thinking, and I am sure you were sincere in what you wrote, but I have my

* * * * *

101 more or less twenty] Aldo Manuzio was born in 1451. The following remark
about Erasmus' own age, particularly if compared with the even vaguer
statement in Ep 867:291, is typical of the difficulties involved in clarifying the
date of his birth; cf Ep 940.
104 proverbs] Cf *Adagia* I ii 63 and above line 35n; for the publication of the *Adagia*
see Epp 269 introduction, 609:5n.
107 Egnazio ... Asolano] Cf Epp 588-9. Andrea Torresani of Asola was the
father-in-law of Aldo Manuzio and his partner and successor in the printing
firm.
108 little Manuzio] Paolo Manuzio, Aldus' youngest son; cf Epp 589:58, 61:47.

869
4 Genoa] Cf Ep 896:113.

doubts whether I could] persuade others of that. And then, suppose what
you say reaches the eyes of posterity. Beatus Rhenanus read your letter to
me, as it was then after dinner and my eyes were troublesome, and he is an   10
educated man and wonderfully fair minded and (what is the chief thing in
scholarship) of sound judgment. I would rather not repeat his comments,
and that although I had warned him that you are by nature rather outspoken
in humorous intercourse between friends. Competition in abuse is unworthy of an honourable man, and to match one quibble with another is a   15
dreary business. In solid arguments I could defeat you as easily as you out-
class me in the resources of style, as even Deloynes or Ruzé would agree or
any even more devoted partisan of yours. But I would rather have the friendship of one Budé than ten victories of that kind. One defence is more than
enough.   20
      In Basel I was ill almost all the time. On the journey I had recovered, but
once past Cologne I was at death's door again. So I am still sitting idle at
home. The surgeon inspected three sore places, and pronounced that it was
plague, wrongly, in my opinion. I will write to the bishop when I have time,
and to you too at greater length. Give my greetings to Glareanus, if you   25
happen to see the man. His last letter has also reached me. Farewell.
      Louvain, 15 October 1518

870 / To Conradus Mutianus Rufus   Louvain, 17 October 1518

Epp 870–6 were written as a result of the visit of Helius Eobanus (see Epp 874
introduction, 877:9–11), who delivered letters and gifts from several of his
fellow humanists in the circle gathered around the University of Erfurt. At
nearby Gotha, Konrad Mut, called Mutianus Rufus (see Ep 501:9–10n), had
been the teacher of most of them and continued in the role of fatherly friend and
adviser. Epp 870–1, 873–4, 876 were published by Eobanus with his *Ad Des.
Erasmum Roterodamum Hodoeporicon* (Erfurt: M. Maler [January 1519]), which is
an account in hexameters of his journey.
      Eobanus and his companion, Johann Werter (see Ep 875), reached Louvain

* * * * *

17 Deloynes or Ruzé] François Deloynes and Louis Ruzé, close friends and
   relations of Budé (see Epp 493:62, 494). From later remarks it would seem that
   each had sent a letter to Erasmus enclosed with Budé's Ep 810; see Epp 906:227,
   611–12, 915:139–41.
19 defence] The *Apologia ad Fabrum*; cf Ep 597:37n.
21 ill] Cf Ep 847:7n.
24 bishop] Etienne Poncher, bishop of Paris; see Ep 529.
25 greater length] Ep 906
26 last letter] Missing; cf Ep 866:9–10.

on 16 October (or 17, as stated in the *Hodoeporicon*). On the following morning they visited their idol, but as Erasmus was still recovering and anxious to resume the revision of the New Testament (cf Ep 864 introduction) they had to rely on their own enthusiasm to compensate for his impatience, which is reflected in some of the letters he felt compelled to give them (Epp 873, 875; cf Ep 942:31–3; Allen Ep 2495:16–21). This is why Erasmus would have preferred to amplify them before publication (cf Ep 982) and never included them in his collected correspondence. In fact, Erasmus was not indifferent to the admiration shown to him by his visitors (cf Epp 877:9–11, 883:15–17); he had the *Hodoeporicon* reprinted by Martens in 1519 (NK 764; cf Ep 982) and he did publish Ep 875, which was not included in it. Eobanus' visit led to new homages from the Erfurt circle, which Erasmus received with a similar mixture of gratification and impatience; see Ep 963:6n, and for the *Hodoeporicon* see Krause *Eobanus* I 288–99.

TO THE HONOURABLE MUTIANUS RUFUS, PARAGON OF ALL
LEARNING, FROM ERASMUS OF ROTTERDAM, GREETING
Unfortunately Eobanus found me ill and very busy; otherwise his visit would have given the greatest pleasure. In the Muses' name, what fluency his verses show, what an original vein of talent, what happy phrasing! You   5
would think him a poet born, not made by practice. He has the same gifts in prose, and a character such as would grace even our theologians, if my prayers were answered. Happy indeed is Germany, and Erfurt especially, did she but know her good fortune. I was delighted by your letter too, with its fairness of mind, the mirror of its fair-minded writer. As for the gift, for a   10
long time I would not accept it, till I learnt that it came from you. I have composed a list of all the things I ever wrote, though I myself can hardly recall the lightweight pieces. Farewell.

Louvain, 17 October 1518

* * * * *

870
9 but know] An oblique allusion to Virgil *Georgics* 2.458. Eobanus may have complained about his salary at Erfurt; cf Ep 874:17n.
9 your letter] Starting out from Erfurt, the travellers had spent the first night with Mutianus at Gotha; Mutianus gave them a letter for Erasmus, but it is now missing.
12 list] Evidently an early draft for *Lucubrationum Erasmi Roterodami index* (Louvain: Martens 1 January 1519); cf Allen I 1 (not in NK); Ep 492 introduction.

871 / To Johannes Draconites   Louvain, 17 October 1518

For the source of this letter see Ep 870 introduction. Johannes Draconites
(Drach or Trach) of Karlstadt on the Main (1494–1566) was a canon and
professor at Erfurt. Subsequently Luther attracted him to Wittenberg, where
he received a theological doctorate in 1523.

ERASMUS OF ROTTERDAM TO HIS FRIEND
JOHANNES DRACO OF KARLSTADT, GREETING
I send a brief answer to your most friendly letter, dear Draco. After a
prolonged illness in Basel, I had suffered a most dangerous relapse and was
also more burdened with the pressure of business than anyone would   5
believe possible; and so it was not only a great pleasure but profitable too,
when our friend Eobanus, who in himself deserves admiration and affection,
introduced you to me as a new friend, though in friendship I was well
supplied already; and Helius by himself would suffice to protect my native
Germany from a charge of barbarism. In heaven's name, what ease and   10
fluency in his verse! I think of him as Ovid reincarnate. And he is the same in
prose; for he produced a sample of his work in both, and that on the spur of
the moment. And then how fair-minded he is, how charming and how
natural – immune at all points from the faults so common among lovers of
poetry, especially Italians! How pure and truly religious is the vein in which 15
he sings of the heroines of Christianity! Germany would be thrice blessed if
more poets like him would come forward; and some do so already. But I perceive that far more will appear once princes and prelates begin to do honour
to men of talent; though this is already the practice of the noble Duke
Frederick of Saxony and the archbishop of Mainz, a great and famous figure   20

* * * * *

871
 4 illness] Cf Ep 847:7n.
 9 Helius] Also Hessus (line 22), names of Eobanus; see Ep 874 introduction.
16 heroines] Cf *Heroidum christianarum epistolae* (Leipzig: M. Lotter, preface dated
    13 June 1514), letters of holy love in elegiac form addressed to God, Christ, and
    others by Mary, Mary Magdalen, and other saintly women. A Christian
    imitation of Ovid, from whom the title *Heroides* is borrowed, the work
    established Eobanus' reputation as a poet. But Eobanus was not entirely free of
    what Erasmus considered the faults of Italy's neo-Latin poets: his earlier
    Bucolicon included passionate verses of bucolic love.
20 Frederick ... archbishop of Mainz] Erasmus set great hopes on their patronage
    of learning and thought that it was befitting to commend them for it in one
    breath (cf Ep 919:48–50). Frederick the Wise had founded the University of
    Wittenberg and was collecting a substantial library (cf Ep 711:17–18), while
    Albert of Brandenburg was the chancellor of the University of Erfurt apart

even if we overlook his cardinal's hat. One thing grieves me, that our friend Hessus should have endured so long a journey to no purpose; for what could he profit by it? Could it be worth while, just to see Erasmus full-length? The better part of me, if there is any good in me at all, he had already perused in my published work. As for the rest, what could there be in it worth a visit? 25 Your present was welcome as a token of your feelings towards me.

Farewell.

Louvain, 17 October 1518

872 / To Johann Lang   Louvain, 17 October [1518]

From a manuscript copy in the Forschungsbibliothek Gotha, MS chart. A 399 f 222. The copy was probably made around 1553, but the authenticity of the text is generally accepted (cf line 20n), although J. Beumer (*Scrinium* II 319) has recently questioned Erasmus' authorship of some harsh expressions both here and in Ep 983.

Johann Lang of Erfurt (c 1485–1548) became prior of the house of Augustinian Eremites in his native city in 1516 and also taught in the university. He and Luther had lived under the same roof both at Erfurt and at Wittenberg, where both were under the direction of Staupitz (cf line 5n). Lang was a close friend of Eobanus (Ep 874) and like him favoured the Reformation, for which he won Erfurt in 1525. But at his request Eobanus did not publish this extraordinary letter with his *Hodoeporicon*, evidently because at this time Lang still judged the contents incompatible with his position as a member of a religious order. Erasmus ought to have been grateful. See Eobanus' dedicatory epistle to Justus Jonas, reprinted in *Jonas Briefwechsel* I Ep 21.

TO THE WORTHY FATHER JOHANN LANG,
A DISTINGUISHED THEOLOGIAN

You must be content, most fairminded of theologians, if you are my creditor in point of letters, provided I keep level with you in affection. Hessus, that most gifted of men, found me both ill and very busy. Staupitz is a great figure 5

* * * * *

from surrounding himself with humanist councillors such as Hutten; cf the preface to this volume and for Albert's cardinalate Ep 891:27n.

872
5 Staupitz] Johann von Staupitz, 1469(?)–1524, of Saxon nobility. An Augustinian Eremite, he was called to Wittenberg in 1503 to become the first dean of the theological faculty. Notwithstanding his personal affection for and considerable influence on the young Luther, he remained a Catholic and died in Salzburg as court preacher to the archbishop, Cardinal Matthäus Lang.

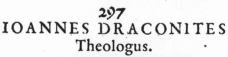

IOANNES DRACONITES
Theologus.

Tam benè tot linguis apto dum Biblia sancta,
Heu morior. morior? nunc quoque viuo Deo.

M. D. LXVI.

T 5

Johannes Draconites
Woodcut from Nikolaus Reusner *Icones sive imagines* (Strasbourg 1590)
Centre for Reformation and Renaissance Studies,
Victoria University, Toronto

Johann von Staupitz
Contemporary portrait in the Erzabtei St Peter, Salzburg
Photo: Oskar Anrather, Salzburg

and I like him very much; those malignant opponents of yours I long ago dismissed; for what else could I do? As though I were obliged to give them chapter and verse for what my conscience tells me! Enough for me if I satisfy all the bishops and the first and best of the divines. If I saw any way of life wherein I could think myself more likely to be pleasing to Christ, I would   10 follow it forthwith; for my spirit is no longer attracted by reputation or money or pleasure or love of life.

Your present shall be placed among my treasures, with those I value most. On the quotation of Cleopas, Egranus has already published a learned reply. Eleutherius, I hear, is approved of by all the leading people; but they   15 say that his writings are not what they were. I imagine that his Conclusions satisfied everyone, except for a few of them on purgatory, which that school of thought are loth to lose because of its effect on their daily bread. I have seen Silvestro's very ill-judged reply. I perceive that the absolute rule of a certain high-priest you know of, as that See is now run, is the curse of   20

* * * * *

14 Egranus] Johannes Wildenauer of Cheb (Eger) in Bohemia (d 1535), called Egranus. He was at this time a preacher at Zwickau and frequently corresponded with Luther. In 1517 he rejected the traditional opinion that St Anne had married Cleopas (cf Luke 24:18; John 19:25) after the death of Joachim, and soon had to defend his view in two publications. The one referred to here is most likely the *Apologetica responsio* (Wittenberg: [J. Grünenberg, early April] 1518). On 4 September 1518 Capito wrote to Luther that Erasmus had read it with approval in Basel and encouraged a reprint. The latter is *Apologetica responsio* (Basel: P. Gengenbach August 1518); see Luther w I 315 and *Briefwechsel* I Epp 55, 65, 68, 91.

15 Eleutherius] The form often used at this time by Luther for signing his letters.

16 Conclusions] The Ninety-five Theses; cf Ep 785:39n. The controversial issue of purgatory was raised primarily in theses 10–25; subsequently Luther had to defend and expand the stand here taken in his *Resolutiones*; cf Ep 904:20n.

19 Silvestro] Silvestro Mazzolini of Priero, Piedmont (1456–1523), commonly called Prierias. A Dominican since 1471, he was a professor in Rome and the pope's master of the sacred palace. In this capacity he had to examine books for heresy and published his objections to Luther's Ninety-five Theses in a dialogue *In presumptuosas Martini Lutheri conclusiones de potestate papae* [June 1518] repr in Luther *Opera latina varii argumenti* ed H. Schmidt (Frankfurt-Erlangen 1865–) I 341–72. Prierias maintained emphatically that the papal teachings were infallible and Luther's theses heretical; cf Boehmer *Luther* 218–20; F. Lauchert *Die italienischen literarischen Gegner Luthers* (Freiburg 1912) 7–30.

20 high–priest] The manuscript text (cf introduction) has in Greek 'the monarchy of the Roman archpriest' – certainly an unguarded statement at a time when Erasmus was eagerly soliciting papal protection for the New Testament (cf Ep 864). Had it been published, it would no doubt have caused him embarrassment and could have forced him to alter his public stance towards the

Silver Klappmütztaler, c 1500–10,
with portraits of Elector Frederick III (obverse)
and dukes George and John of Saxony (reverse)
American Numismatic Society, New York

Christianity, and the Preachers bow down before it at every point and are quite shameless. All the same, I doubt whether it is wise to tackle this sore place openly. This should be the business of the princes; but I fear they are in collusion with his holiness, hoping for a share in the spoils. I cannot think what has come into Eck's head, that he should take up the cudgels against   25
Eleutherius; but 'What canst thou not drive mortal hearts to do, / Accursed thirst of fame?' To the noble duke whose new coin you sent me I have dedicated my revision of Suetonius. Farewell, my excellent friend, and commend me to Christ in your prayers.

Louvain, 17 October
Erasmus of Rotterdam   30

* * * * *

Reformation sooner. He did, however, insert an uncompromising attack on the abuse of papal powers in the *Annotationes* of the 1518–19 edition of the New Testament (LB VI 64D–E; cf Ep 864 introduction), and as late as 1532 he wrote of the 'tyranny' of the pope, which, when it occurs, must be broken (Allen Ep 2615:257–8). For other critical assessments of the use popes sometimes made of their powers see Epp 891:27–34, 983:13–17, Allen Ep 1039:110–17, 262–4.

21 Preachers] Dominicans, such as Prierias
25 Eck] Eck had put down his objections to the Ninety-five Theses in a series of 'Obeliscs,' to which Luther replied in the spring of 1518 with his 'Asteriscs.' Both pamphlets circulated in manuscript; cf Luther w I 278–314; *Briefwechsel* I Epp 76, 77.
26 'What canst ... fame?'] Virgil *Aeneid* 3.56, 57, with 'fame' substituted for 'gold'
27 coin] 'Nomisma': probably Lang's gift of line 13, mentioned here again on an afterthought. There were many coins and medals with the portrait of Frederick the Wise. The gift may have been one of several 'Klappmütztaler' struck by Frederick in conjunction with his relatives (see, eg, F. von Schrötter *Wörterbuch der Münzkunde*, Berlin 1930, table 15 no 257).
    A similar 'nomisma' is mentioned in Ep 978, but this was probably one of the special commemorative medals which were produced with much personal involvement on the part of Frederick and were probably based on a design by Lucas Cranach (see G. Habich *Die deutschen Schaumünzen des 16. Jahrhunderts,* Munich 1929–34, 1-2 p lvii–lix, plates p 5). The second gift coin bore 'a truly lifelike portrait' of the elector and was delivered by Justus Jonas and Kaspar Schalbe together with a letter now missing (cf Ep 963:6n), both in recognition of the dedication of Suetonius to dukes Frederick and George of Saxony (cf Ep 586). Since Lang had contacts with Frederick's court, the second gift coin may have been sent in view of the pleasure Erasmus here expressed with the first. That the two are not one and the same is indicated by the fact that when Erasmus wrote Epp 939:7–18, 947:43–5, the dedication of Suetonius had not yet been acknowledged, since Erasmus had failed to send the book.

Helius Eobanus Hessus
Woodcut portrait after Albrecht Dürer, 1526
Reproduced by courtesy of the Trustees
of the British Museum

873 / To Heinrich Beyming   Louvain, 17 October [1518]

For the source of this letter see Ep 870 introduction. Heinrich Beyming of Butzbach, south of Giessen, matriculated at Erfurt University in 1502 and later returned there to take his MA in 1515. He was subsequently a schoolmaster in Butzbach and died as a village priest; see G. Bauch *Die Universität Erfurt* (Wrocław 1904) 162–3; E. Kleineidam *Universitas Studii Erffordensis* (Leipzig 1964–80) I 395, II 236, 309.

ERASMUS OF ROTTERDAM TO HIS FRIEND HEINRICH BEYMING, GREETING

To return the affection of all my friends, excellent Beyming – that I can do, but to write to them all is too much; how am I to keep up single-handed with such a crowd of Germans, Italians, Frenchmen, Englishmen, Hungarians 5 even? Our mutual friend Eobanus I found charming in every way, more than anything I have yet seen in Germany. As for Jodocus Winsheim the theologian, please return his greeting on my behalf. I know already that you will dub me uncivilized for not writing to him; but if I were at this moment to try and satisfy everyone, ten secretaries would not be enough, assuming I 10 did nothing else. While actually writing this, I have refused to see several tedious Spaniards who were pressing obstinately for an interview, though I know this will give offence, their national character being what it is. Thus am I compelled in pursuit of the civilized life to be uncivil. Farewell, my dear Heinrich.

Louvain, 17 October

15

874 / To Helius Eobanus Hessus   Louvain, 19 October 1518

For the source of this letter see Ep 870 introduction. Eobanus (properly Eoban Koch, 1488–1540) was a peasant's son from Halgehausen near the Cistercian abbey of Haina in Hesse. He adopted the first name Helius in honour of the sun god because he was born on a Sunday. From 1518 he held a Latin chair at Erfurt and became the head of a circle of humanists and poets, establishing his

* * * * *

873
7 Winsheim] Jodocus Textoris (Eckart) of Winsheim near Würzburg, d 1520 in Erfurt. He matriculated, like Beyming, in 1502 and became vicar of the church of St Severus. In 1520 he was offered a lectureship at the University of Leipzig and obtained a theological doctorate at Erfurt, but he died two weeks after his promotion; see Kleineidam (cf introduction) II 220–1, 308–9.
12 Spaniards] Cf Ep 545:16–19.

reputation as one of Germany's leading Latin poets. He offered his talent in the service of Reuchlin, Luther, and German patriotism; see NDB; Krause *Eobanus*.

ERASMUS OF ROTTERDAM TO HIS FRIEND EOBANUS HESSUS, GREETING

I thought I knew my Germany well and had sought out all its distinguished minds. I was devoted to the abilities of Beatus Rhenanus, found Philippus Melanchthon's character delightful, admired Reuchlin's dignity, and was   5
much taken with Hutten's charming conversation. And here is Hessus all of a sudden, uniting in himself all I had previously loved or admired in others separately. What does one think of in your *Heroides* but a Christian Ovid? Who is so happy in plain prose as you are in verse of every kind? Your learning balances your gifts of expression, and your Christian piety   10
enhances both. In prose you are already so successful that one would think you had no poetry in you. Yours is a truly golden vein of talent. And your character matches your style: nothing could be more frank, more simple, more unspoilt. A rare bird indeed is learning untouched by arrogance. What more can one hope for, my learned Hessus, except that your great gifts,   15
which you owe partly to hard work and partly to heaven, should be answered by good fortune? And this will come to pass if the princes of Germany begin to pay honour to men of talent and add this, the better part of glory, to the fame they have won in battle. I might well have sought you out over land and sea; and of your own accord you make a long and dangerous   20
journey to see my humble self, a creature of small reputation, and even that much he does not deserve. I congratulate myself on a great acquisition, the friendship not only of Hessus, but of other outstanding men; it is you who have my sympathy, who have undertaken so much to gain so little. Farewell, chief ornament of our native Germany.   25
    Louvain, 19 October 1518

* * * * *

874
5 Melanchthon] See Ep 910 introduction.
8 *Heroides*] See Ep 871:16n.
17 fortune] Eobanus had recently been appointed professor of poety in Erfurt, but with a growing family to support he was continually troubled by poverty and may have complained to Erasmus about the inadequacy of his salary. In 1523 he began to study medicine but never managed to join the wealthy medical profession.

875 / To Johann Werter   Louvain, 19 October 1518

Johann Werter, a young nobleman, not otherwise known, matriculated at
Erfurt in 1511. He received an MA in 1517; a year later he accompanied Eobanus
on his visit to Erasmus (cf Ep 870 introduction) and lived for a while in Eobanus'
house after their return to Erfurt. This letter was not published with the
Hodoeporicon, either because it was felt to be tactless or because Werter had
already left Eobanus and taken it with him. Erasmus did not hesitate to publish
it in the *Farrago*; see Krause *Eobanus* I 289–97.

ERASMUS TO HIS FRIEND JOHANN WERTER, GREETING
I already supposed the Germans invincible in arms, at any rate, and now I
see that nothing defeats them, since you have succeeded in extracting a
letter, a letter without a purpose, from Erasmus, when he is in poor health
and almost done for by the endless toil of writing. I cannot express how   5
much I am pleased by your devotion; I wish I could respond in the same vein.
But I think it more worthy of a philosopher to pursue his friends with more
controlled affection and to stand by them with help when they need it, not to
burden them with it when they do not. When your friend's reputation is
attacked, when he is laid low by disease, when he is short of money or   10
oppressed by trouble of some other kind, then is the moment to prove your
friendship, to mend the situation if you can; if not, to relieve his distress with
the spoken or the written word. Otherwise, what sort of kindness is it that
hurts the giver and is no help to the recipient? Why expect your friend to be
grateful, under the heading of benefits received, for something from which   15
he has felt no advantage? In the same way, some people expect credit from St
James for any great loss they have suffered on their pilgrimage, or think that
Christ owes them something in return for a visit to Jerusalem paid at great
personal risk, when they could have earned the blessing of either had they
stayed at home and done something of real service. Long ago you had seen a   20
better picture of Erasmus in his writings, if any can be called good; indeed, if
Plato is right, you had seen Erasmus entire. What then was left to be
achieved by such long journeys? True affection exists between two spirits,
and often it is diminished or dissolved by personal contact. But I should be
less than human if I were really annoyed with you; you deserve affection in   25
return, for this very reason that you do not seek to moderate yours. Farewell.
    Louvain, 19 October 1518

        * * * * *

875
 4 poor health] Cf Ep 867 introduction.
16 St James] Cf Ep 858:435n.

Justus Jonas
Engraved portrait by R. Boissard
in J.J. Boissard *Icones virorum illustrium* (Frankfurt 1597)
Rijksmuseum, Amsterdam

876 / To Justus Jonas   Louvain, 19 October [1518]

For the source of this letter see Ep 870 introduction. Justus Jonas (really Jobst
Koch) of Nordhausen in Thuringia (1493–1535) studied at Erfurt, where he
received a legal doctorate in 1518. As a priest he received in the same year the
chair of canon law and for his support a canonry at St Severus church. In 1521
he became an influential colleague of Luther and Melanchthon at Wittenberg.
His letter must have impressed Erasmus, for the warmth of this reply is
noticeable in comparison with the tone of Epp 873, 875. It encouraged Jonas to
visit Erasmus in the spring of 1519 (cf Ep 963:6n) and led to a regular
correspondence that lasted until 1521, when the gulf between Luther and
Erasmus became unbridgeable. But Jonas' admiration for Erasmus continued
well beyond that date.

TO THE RIGHT WORTHY AND LEARNED JODOCUS JONAS, HIS RIGHT
GOOD FRIEND, FROM ERASMUS OF ROTTERDAM, GREETING
Really, my learned Jonas, you have sent me not so much a letter as affection
undiluted, all the warmth of a very loving heart. In heaven's name, what
breathing life, what power it has to move one and touch the heart in many   5
ways! You try in it to draw a picture of me, but all you produced is a reflection
of yourself, and while exalting my eloquence you exhibit your own. For
praise of my learning or my literary skill I care nothing; one thing seriously
gives me pleasure, if what I write makes anyone better, if my productions
contribute to the glory of Christ. My *Enchiridion* has been printed in these   10
last few days by Froben. I added among other things a long preface
addressed to Abbot Volz. But, my dear Jonas, which side should I be on? You
find gold in what I write; there are others who roundly declare that I can
neither think nor write, that out of what I publish can be sucked things that
will poison the faith. What storms of obloquy, as friars and divines stoned   15
my New Testament – but all of it so far behind my back; to my face no one says
a word! The praise you give me I cannot accept; what they accuse me of, I
abhor. I am resolved to credit neither party, and with spirit unbowed
through honour and dishonour, through evil report and good report, to
fight on with all my might towards the goal of Christ. You must forgive my   20
brevity. As I write, I am in poor health and more than overcome by the labour
of writing. Farewell.
       Louvain, 19 October

       * * * * *

876
11 preface] Ep 858
19 through honour ... Christ] Cf 2 Cor 6:8.

Wolfgang Faber Capito
Engraving by Peter Aubry, c 1660, after an original now lost
Cabinet des Estampes, Musées de la ville, Strasbourg

877 / To Wolfgang Faber Capito   Louvain, 19 October [1518]

This letter from the Deventer Letter-book complements the account of Erasmus' journey given in Ep 867. It was actually sent to Basel but was not published with Ep 867, possibly because it contains some news and views unsuitable for public consumption.

ERASMUS TO HIS FRIEND CAPITO, GREETING

At Speyer I happened upon Irenicus with his dull childish book. I grow weary of scholarship when I see such raw youths handling the sacred vessels of the Muses. He carries round with him a page which he has altered, which he had also shown in Mainz, as though the object of the change had 5 not been to conceal what he had written earlier. Gnostopolitanus has written me a very dull and astonishingly ignorant letter. Melanchthon has uttered a characteristic remark: that he would criticize many points in my New Testament had I not been friendly to Reuchlin. At Louvain I had a visit from Helius Eobanus the poet, a pleasant man, who had come all the way 10 from Erfurt only to set eyes on your humble servant. Someone writes to me that Martin Luther is in danger. The *Julius* now enjoys widespread

* * * * *

877
2 Irenicus] Franz Friedlieb, called Irenicus, of Ettlingen near Karlsruhe (1495–1559 or 1565). A student of Melanchthon, he received an MA at the University of Heidelberg in 1517 and subsequently taught there. He joined the Reformation after hearing Luther at the Heidelberg disputation and later combined school-teaching with the Lutheran ministry. At about this time he published his *Germaniae exegesis* (Haguenau: T. Anshelm for J. Koberger August 1518). A section in praise of German scholars is headed by a naive eulogy of Erasmus (f xlii). The work had been written earlier (cf *Scheurl's Briefbuch* Epp 136–7, 140) and was given a mixed reception (cf *Der Briefwechsel des Mutianus Rufus*, Kassel 1885, Ep 636). Allen thought that the page mentioned here was connected with this publication.
6 Gnostopolitanus] Most likely Johannes Cellarius of Burgkundstadt on the Main east of Bamberg (c 1496–1542), who may have been in Liège and Louvain in 1517 (cf Ep 674:30n). In the summer of 1518 he published a Hebrew grammar and subsequently taught the language at Heidelberg and Leipzig. Like Erasmus Melanchthon was not impressed by him; cf Luther w *Briefwechsel* I Ep 179; Melanchthon *Werke* VII–1 Ep 22; de Vocht CTL I 496.
8 he would criticize] Cf Ep 910.
10 Eobanus] See Ep 870 introduction.
12 in danger] On 7 October Luther arrived in Augsburg to face the papal legate Cardinal Cajetanus (cf Ep 891:26n). He wrote to his friends about the hearings, alternating between courageous determination and feelings of despair and doom; Luther w *Briefwechsel* I Epp 96–102.
12 *Julius*] Cf Epp 821:19n, 849:32n.

circulation and has often been printed. What times we live in! I have been
visited by the author of an eightfold psalter, the bishop of Nebbio, who has
read the passage in my *Apologia* where I mention him favourably. There is
more vanity than venom in him. He has eight hundred francs a year from the
French king.

Buschius, whom I found at Speyer, told me a nice story about
Hoogstraten. When tempers were already running high in print, there
appeared at his monastery a knight with a fearful great beard, who glowered
at them and demanded to speak with Hoogstraten. The brethren said he was
not at home. The knight insisted. They said, no, he was not there, and
promised they would give him any message. 'This gallows-bird,' says he,
'has attacked in print my noble kinsman, the count of Neuenahr, and he
shall pay for it. I give you solemn warning not to set foot on the estates of any
of my family to collect your cheeses. You will get only a good thrashing.'
Here they broke in with excuses: it was not done to please them, it was most
disagreeable that for the sake of one man they should become universally
unpopular. They pressed this on him at great length, and at last the knight
said, 'Very well; I will believe you are speaking the truth if you throw this
rascal out of your society. Otherwise, we shall assume it was done with your
agreement.' So Hoogstraten is now in hiding, and he is to leave the house.
He tried for a place at Koblenz, so the bishop's official told me, but was rejected. He has also been in Louvain, where I suppose he is looking for a
place.

You will learn how things are with me from my letter to Beatus; please
pass it around among my friends, if he does not happen to be present. Our
Hebrew is a triumphant success, and all goes well with him. He is much
annoyed with you; says he has been severely censured by you and even

* * * * *

14 Nebbio] Agostino Giustiniani (cf Ep 810:397n); for Erasmus' *Apologia ad Fabrum*
   cf Ep 597:37n and for the reference to Giustiniani cf Ep 906:529n.
16 eight hundred francs] Undoubtedly French livres tournois are meant here. If
   so, a stipend then worth (in silver content) about £17 4s 5d gros Flemish =
   £11 16s 10d sterling. Cf CWE 1 318.
18 Buschius] See Ep 884 introduction.
19 Hoogstraten] Cf Ep 849:22n. Erasmus loved the story and kept repeating it; cf
   Epp 889:42–6, Allen Epp 1173:140–4, 1892:56–62, 2126:117–28; *Adagia* IV vii 64.
33 official] Matthias von Saarburg, see Ep 867:64n. Nothing is known about
   Hoogstraten's aspirations at Koblenz.
36 Beatus] Ep 867
38 Hebrew] Matthaeus Adrianus, Capito's former teacher of Hebrew. No more is
   known about Capito's criticism.

accused of impiety. I should be sorry if you did so, supposing you really   40
did. Silvestro's book has been stolen out of my bag; so please send me
another copy. The news of your dancing made me laugh. Farewell, and
continue to be my sincere friend.

Louvain, 19 October

Give my cordial greetings to my gracious lord, and to Doctor Baer, if he   45
is with you.

878 / To [Hermann von Neuenahr]   Louvain, 19 October 1518

Cf Ep 867 introduction and lines 79–88. That this letter is addressed to
Neuenahr, in reply to a letter now missing, follows from the allusions in
lines 5, 12.

Greeting. That bitter dispute between two theologians made me laugh. I
have had a visit from the bishop of Nebbio, author of an eightfold psalter,
whom I mentioned with credit in my *Apologia* against Lefèvre. There is more
vanity than venom in the man. He gets a salary of eight hundred francs from
the king of France. What you write about the prince's return from Spain is   5
quite incredible. A book has been stolen from my bag, at Antwerp if I am not
mistaken, which grieves me very much. I have written to Basel to get another
copy from there.

The sad story of my misfortunes you will learn from my letter to Beatus;
when you have read it, please give it back to the young man who brings you   10
this, and he will show it likewise to my other friends. How I wish I had
followed your advice! This is the source of all my calamities. Dorp was the
first person to visit me when there was a rumour that I was suffering from the
plague, and next came Atensis. Hoogstraten has been here and had much

* * * * *

41 out of my bag] See Epp 867:77–8, 872:19n.
45 gracious lord] probably Christoph von Utenheim, bishop of Basel; see Ep 598
   introduction.

878
1 dispute] Cf Ep 821:19n.
2 Nebbio] Agostino Giustiniani; see Ep 906:529n, cf Ep 877:13–17.
5 you write] Cf Ep 893:39–43.
6 book] Cf Ep 877:41; the word 'Silvestro's' may inadvertently have been omitted
   in the Deventer Letter-book.
10 young man] Menard of Hoorn; see Ep 885:2n.
12 your advice] See Ep 867:100–110.
14 Hoogstraten] See Ep 849:22n.

talk with the Carmelite, Egmondanus. 'Thief knoweth thief, and wolf to wolf   15
is known.' Farewell, most honourable count.

I am still keeping the house, my scars not being healed yet.

Louvain, 19 October 1518

879 / To Christoph Eschenfelder   Louvain, 19 October 1518

Cf Ep 867 introduction and lines 50–60. Christoph Eschenfelder, the customs
official at Boppard (territory of Trier), would be almost unknown but for
Erasmus. After the first encounter on Erasmus' return from Basel their
friendship continued until Erasmus' death. This letter was published in the
Farrago.

TO CHRISTOPH ESCHENFELDER, CUSTOMS OFFICER AT BOPPARD
Greeting. What could be more unexpected than for an admirer of mine,
Cinicampianus by name, to be found at Boppard? And moreover a customs
officer devoted to the Muses and to liberal studies! Christ set it to the
discredit of the Pharisees that harlots and publicans would enter before they   5
did into the kingdom of heaven. Is it not equally discreditable that priests
and monks should live for their stomachs' sake in luxury and ease, while
customs officers pursue good literature? They devote themselves entirely to
their appetites, while Cinicampianus divides his time between Caesar and
book-learning. You made it clear enough what opinion you had formed of   10
me; I shall do very well if it has lost nothing from a personal meeting.

But, my word, that red wine of yours went down wondrous well with
the shipman's wife, 'great bosom and great boozer she,' as the poet sings; in
spite of frequent appeals, she would let no one else have a turn. She drank
plenty, but it was not long before she was up in arms. She nearly killed the   15
cook-maid with her great basting-spoons; we could scarcely separate the

* * * * *

15 Egmondanus] Nicolaas Baechem of Egmond near Alkmaar (d 1526) matriculated in Louvain in 1487 and received a DD in 1505. He entered the Carmelite
   order in 1507 and from 1510 he directed the Carmelite study house at Louvain
   while also teaching theology at the university. He was a prominent opponent
   of the Collegium Trilingue (see Ep 934 introduction) and of Erasmus himself,
   who detested him and ridiculed him in many places as the 'camel'; de Vocht
   CTL I 460–1.

15 'Thief ... known'] Cf *Adagia* II iii 63.

879
 3 Cinicampianus] 'Cinderfield,' a Latinization of Eschenfelder's name
 4 Christ] Cf Matt 21:31.
13 the poet] Laberius, cited by Aulus Gellius 3.12

combatants. Soon she emerged onto the upper deck and went for her husband; there was some risk that she would send him headlong out of the boat into the Rhine. You see how powerful your liquor is.

The sad story of my misfortunes you will learn from my letter to Beatus,   20
if you have leisure to read it. Farewell, dear friend. Give my greetings to Johann Flaming, a good scholar and a man of true Christian integrity.

Louvain, 19 October 1518

880 / To [Matthias von Saarburg?]   Louvain, 19 October 1518

Cf Ep 867 introduction and lines 47–9, 63–7. The greetings in line 12 are probably addressed to Johann of Westphalia. If so, this letter might be addressed to a resident of Mainz, like Johann. Perhaps he was the unnamed canon who was Erasmus' host on his return from Basel. Erasmus might have forgotten his name but expected the messenger to find out on arrival at Mainz. Allen tentatively identified the unknown canon as Theoderich Zobel (cf Epp 881:7n, 919:51–5). Zobel was a canon, but as Erasmus makes clear in Ep 919, he was more than that. He was scholaster of his chapter and vicar-general of the archbishop. Had he been Erasmus' host, one might have expected this fact to be mentioned in Ep 867 even though Erasmus might have forgotten his name.

From Ep 867 it appears likely that the canon at Mainz had not previously been known to Erasmus, but the beginning of this letter suggests a friend of longer standing. Since his Latin conversation is paid a special compliment he may well be Matthias von Saarburg (cf Epp 867:64n, 877:33). Erasmus stayed with him again in November 1521 (cf Ep 1342), and there are traces of a continuing correspondence (cf Epp 1799, 1946). Johann of Westphalia was evidently in Erasmus' company during the stay with Saarburg at Koblenz in September 1518.

Greeting. I am grateful, excellent sir, for your good will towards me; you have so often honoured me with your kind offices and encouraged me by your generosity. What could have been more enjoyable than that dinner, or better served? And the character of the company, so free-spoken, so full of learning without arrogance! The charm, the elegance of your own conver-   5
sation! It might have been an ancient Roman speaking. Now let the Italians go and accuse the Germans of barbarism! You will learn the sad story of my misfortunes from my letter to Beatus; when you have read it, please give it back to the young man who brings you this, so that he can show it to other people too. There is not a word in it that is not true. This was all I lacked,   10

* * * * *

22 Flaming] See Ep 867:62n.

after so many sufferings. This year really does deserve a black mark in my
annals, if any year ever did. Farewell. Greet my friend Westphal.

Louvain, 19 October 1518

Your sincere friend Erasmus

881 / To Johannes Longicampianus   Louvain, 20 October [1518]

Cf Ep 867 introduction and lines 45–7. Johann Gusebel, called Longicampianus
(d 10 March 1529), was a Bavarian. He had visited Erasmus at Brussels in 1516
(cf Ep 496). He was then at Mainz and may have hoped for a position at
Louvain. With the help of Melanchthon he was appointed to teach mathemat-
ics at the University of Wittenberg in 1525. He also ran a private school there,
but died in poverty; see Melanchthon *Werke* vii-1 Epp 99, 112; Luther w
Briefwechsel v Ep 1396; H. Volz in *Festschrift für Josef Benzing* (Wiesbaden 1964)
456–75.

Greeting. The learned Eobanus gave me your letter, with two speeches,
though they were very carelessly copied. I arranged for your letter to be
delivered to Dorp. You will learn how things stand with me from my letter to
Rhenanus, if you have time to read it. This year has not gone well for me; may
Almighty God grant that better may be in store. I was most grateful for your   5
sympathy and for your kind help. Please give my greetings to Wolfgang
Angst and those civilized Franconians with whom I supped on my last day,
and everyone else who wishes me well. There are sparks of plague here too,
but only moderate and brought in from elsewhere; there is no mischief in the
atmosphere. Farewell, my most learned and civilized friend. My greetings to   10
the lawyer who regaled us with those speeches in the boat.

Louvain, 20 October

Your sincere friend Erasmus

* * * * *

881
1 Eobanus] He and his friend left Mainz on 8 October for Louvain after they had
   learned that Erasmus had returned there; cf Krause *Eobanus* i 290–1.
7 Angst] He had recently arrived in Mainz from Basel and worked as a corrector
   for Johann Schöffer; his Franconian friends may have been Theoderich Zobel
   and Nikolaus Carbach; cf Ep 919.
8 plague] Cf Ep 847:7n.
11 lawyer] He has not been identified; cf Ep 867:47.

882 / To Maternus Hatten
Louvain, 20 October 1518

Cf Ep 867 introduction and lines 32–4.

ERASMUS TO HIS FRIEND MATERNUS, GREETING

This year, my dear Maternus, my evil genius has led me a proper dance. It would take too much time to describe it to everyone, so you must learn the story from my letter to Rhenanus. Give my cordial greetings to the dean, who can be so learned without ostentation and so civilized without insincerity; also to that charming Eucharius and the excellent Kierher and all the other canons whose conversation cheered me so much while I was with you. The young man who brings this is being sent to Basel at my own expense for the sake of the copy for the New Testament. Farewell, dear Maternus, most faithful of friends.

Louvain, 20 October 1518

Please let me have the Christian name and surname of the dean.

883 / To Nikolaus Gerbel
Louvain, 20 October 1518

This letter was first printed in the *Farrago*; for the contents cf Ep 867 introduction and lines 23–8. Nikolaus Gerbel lived at Strasbourg as legal adviser and secretary to the cathedral chapter. He also frequently assisted Matthias Schürer, the printer; cf Epp 224:49n, 342 introduction.

ERASMUS TO NIKOLAUS GERBEL, DOCTOR OF CANON LAW, GREETING

What a dance my evil genius has led me this year just as he pleased, my learned Gerbel! You will learn the sad story of my misfortunes from my letter to Beatus Rhenanus. I am still in the surgeon's hands and confined to the

* * * * *

882

4 dean] Thomas Truchsess

6 Eucharius] Eucharius Gallinarius (Henner) of Bretten in the Palatinate. He studied in Heidelberg from 1475 and received his MA in 1479. In 1500 he was at Strasbourg, but in 1502 he moved to Speyer, where he subsequently became a canon. He contributed a letter in support of Erasmus to *Epistolae aliquot eruditorum virorum, ex quibus perspicuum quanta sit Eduardi Lei virulentia* (Basel: Froben August 1520; cf Ep 1083 introduction). In the title of Hermannus Buschius' reply, in the same collection, he is described as professor of canon law and pastor of the Holy Cross (at St Germanus' church) in Speyer.

6 Kierher] Johann Kierher, another canon at Speyer; see Ep 355.

8 young man] Menard of Hoorn; see Ep 885:2n.

Johann Rudolfinger
Woodcut by Hans Baldung Grien, 1534
Staatliche Graphische Sammlung, Munich

house. Christ will grant better things when we deserve them, or rather in his own good time. In all these troubles I have kept my spirit unbroken. I wish I could hear that my friend Schürer had recovered. Please greet the whole society, especially Sturm and then Gebwiler and Rudolfinger, who with their habitual generosity wished me to have nothing to pay in the inn, as   10 though they had not done enough by honouring and amusing me with their company. You know already, I expect, that Bruno Amerbach too has found a bedfellow. I hope the affair you have begun with such promise will have a most promising outcome. Be sure to give my greetings to my new friend Pathodius; in this respect I grow richer day by day. I have had a visit from   15 Helius Eobanus, a pleasant man, in verse recalling the fluency of Ovid and much the same in prose. He had come all the way from Erfurt merely to set eyes on my humble self. I approve his motive; his kind action I do not approve, the sort that is a burden to the doer without benefit to the recipient. The air here is still clear; there have been a few sufferers, but the infection   20 has come in from elsewhere. Farewell, my beloved Gerbel, and keep Erasmus' name among your friends; believe me, this will be repaid.

Louvain, 20 October 1518

884 / To Hermannus Buschius   Louvain, 21 October [1518]

Buschius had returned to Cologne in 1518 (cf Ep 866:35). When Erasmus returned from Basel Buschius met him at Speyer (cf Ep 877:18) and was probably then in search of a teaching position. Back in Louvain, Erasmus heard rumours that Baerland might resign from the Latin professorship at the Collegium Trilingue (cf Ep 852:82n). When his resignation actually took place a year later, Buschius apparently came to Louvain but found that the position had been given to another candidate; (cf Ep 1050; de Vocht CTL I 448–9, 482–3;

* * * * *

883
8 recovered] See Ep 801:23n.
9 society] For the members of the Strasbourg literary society see Ep 302.
12 Amerbach] He married Anna Schabler in September 1518; see Ep 604:12n.
13 affair] When Erasmus passed through Strasbourg in September, Gerbel had announced his marriage, or at least his engagement; cf AK II Ep 628.
15 Pathodius] Lukas Hackfurt, called Bathodius (d 1554). At Strasbourg he was for some time vicar at the cathedral. Later he directed a private school and in 1523 became almoner to the Reformed city (cf AK II Ep 775 n1). As his chosen name, Bathodius, is apparently derived from the greek βάτος, the spelling is awkward. Erasmus preferred 'Pathodius,' which is more compatible with the Greek language but implies another meaning.
20 infection] Cf Ep 881:8–10.

Buschius' interest in this position may also be reflected in Epp 722, 1050–1). The year must be 1518 because the letter is copied into the Deventer Letter-book; cf the preface.

ERASMUS TO HIS FRIEND BUSCHIUS, GREETING

I had heard hints privately that Baerland, who holds the Latin chair, was thinking of resigning, because he was tired of the work and dissatisfied with the exiguous salary. I raised the question with him and found this was not the case. I had already written to the executors of the will to say that, if they   5 had not deputed this task to Baerland, I had found a man well able to carry that department. So I was disappointed. Yet I should like to have you living here; but the pay here is mean. However, Fortune may smile on you elsewhere. The bishop of Liège has a special love of scholars. So has the abbot of St Hubert's, a man of wonderful generosity. Hoogstraten was here   1 before my return; some suspect that he means to settle here. Farewell, dearest Buschius, and love your Erasmus in return, as he loves you.
        Louvain, 21 October

885 / To Johann Froben   Louvain, 22 October [1518]

The original of this letter in Erasmus' own hand is in the Öffentliche Bibliothek of the University of Basel, MS G II 13a f 52. A copy in the Deventer Letter-book ends with line 23, the rest being afterthoughts to some of the topics mentioned in the first part.
    Erasmus appears somewhat angry and impatient (cf Ep 886:30), but his frankness attests to the strengthening of friendly ties during the summer months spent in Froben's house. There was first of all the old problem of how Erasmus should be compensated for his collaboration with the Basel press (see Ep 629:7n). One of his requests had been agreed to: apparently a sum had been specified to pay him for the revised New Testament (cf Ep 864). In considera- tion of this sum (cf Ep 886:25–7) Erasmus was to receive expensive Greek books

* * * * *

884
5 executors of the will] For the will of Jérôme de Busleyden, which provided for the Collegium Trilingue, cf Ep 691 introduction. The executors named in the will included Jan Robyns (Ep 178:9n), Jan Stercke (Ep 1322), and Bartholomeus van Vessem (Ep 1046). Antoon Sucket (Ep 1331) was added to these subsequently, while Gilles de Busleyden represented the family; see de Vocht CTL I 44, 50–62.
9 Liège] Erard de la Marck (cf Ep 738); for his esteem for scholars cf Ep 746.
10 abbot] Nicolas de Malaise; see Ep 894.
10 Hoogstraten] See Ep 849:22n.

from Italy and other books as requested. He had given Froben a list. Franz Birckmann, who regularly did business with Froben, was to supply the books in Louvain, but what he produced did not satisfy Erasmus. In the second place this letter comments on the internal problems of Froben's firm. Froben's partner, Wolfgang Lachner, had recently died (cf Ep 781:8n) and was survived by his wife, Ursula, a son not in the book trade, and six daughters, three of whom were to die from the plague in September 1519. The oldest, Gertrud, was the wife of Johann Froben. Lachner's heirs must have owned something like a controlling interest in Froben's business; hence Erasmus' fear of petticoat government (line 18; cf AK II Ep 643). Finally his reference to the donkeys (line 33; Ep 902A:7) requires an explanation. After Lachner's death Johann Schabler, called Wattenschnee, (cf Epp 330:15n, 1508) acquired a stake in the Froben firm and subsequently also acquired Lachner's bookstore. He was the head of a closely knit group of book-sellers who distributed Froben's products in France much in the same way as the Birckmann brothers did in the Netherlands and probably in England. Schabler's daughter had recently married Bruno Amerbach, Froben's assistant (cf Ep 883:12–13). In the opinion of Beatus Rhenanus, Erasmus' trusted friend, Schabler resembled Lachner in that both were more interested in profit than in scholarship. As Beatus had quarrelled with Lachner (see Ep 594 introduction), so he was to quarrel with Schabler; cf Ep 1014; Bietenholz *Basle and France* 28–30; Grimm *Buchführer* 1366–7.

ERASMUS TO HIS FRIEND JOHANN FROBEN, GREETING

I send by the bearer of this, Menard of Hoorn, the whole remaining text of the New Testament. I also send arguments to be put one at the head of each Epistle, and shall soon send the rest. It is for you to see that the work comes out successfully. Let me know if any answer has come from Rome to what I wrote by Pucci. I have had your letter. As to the books, not a word from Franz; it was a mistake to entrust him with the valuation, and you have bought few Greek books. I think you must have lost the list of those which I had ordered to be purchased. You send me back the bill I had told you to give

5

* * * * *

885

2 Menard of Hoorn] A young man sent to Basel with printer's copy and letters (cf Ep 867 introduction). Following a previous agreement and Erasmus' recommendation (lines 26–30), Froben employed him on the New Testament (cf Ep 864 introduction), but he died of the plague before 5 December; cf Ep 904:18–20; AK II Ep 642:13–14; Bierlaire *La familia* 54.

3 arguments] See Ep 894 introduction.

4 the rest] Cf lines 25–6; perhaps sent at the time of Ep 902A.

6 by Pucci] See Epp 860, 864 introductions.

8 few Greek books] Among them probably the Herodotus mentioned in Ep 841:3n

to Arnold, having I suppose forgotten what I asked you to do. This is no way   10
to treat a friend and fellow-godfather.

If you want anything done about the lexicon, get the things copied out
that were added by Cono, I think in Bruno's old lexicon. Then send me the
manuscript lexicon of rhetorical terms, and also Mazzocchi's lexicon printed
at Ferrara, which is not to be found here anywhere. I will do my best for your   15
benefit. See to it that you collaborate for your share. You have the
reputation; it can be very profitable for you if you take the necessary care on
your side. But I do not like that petticoat government in your household.
How can a dancer of hornpipes pull his weight in the boat? As for those Paris
people, there is no risk if you show yourself a man. Here is a piece of news,   20
so have your reward for the bearer of it ready. Your friend Cavillotus alias
Dissutus is a Franciscan in Bruges, a great luminary of the church. Write a
line to him if there is anything you want.

This trouble and expense was quite unnecessary, if you had tackled the
business in good time. I will soon send the rest; that is, the prefaces and the   25
appendices. The young man who brings this seems to be able, with a fair
knowledge of Latin and Greek, and lastly he is a Hollander. He comes to you
in hopes of a place in your printing works with a reasonable salary. Make
him feel that even a recommendation from me has done some good. Though
what I did was done at your request.   30

I urge you most emphatically in the name of our friendship not to
neglect the reputation enjoyed by your press, and not to take advice from

* * * * *

10 Arnold] Probably Arnold Birckmann (d 1541/2 in Cologne), the brother,
partner, and successor of Franz; cf Grimm *Buchführer* 1528–30. For his bill see
Ep 829:2n.

12 lexicon] No Greek lexicon had been published in Basel so far, and Froben was
apparently considering such an edition. Erasmus reminds him of Johannes
Cono or Conon (Ep 318:21n), the Greek teacher of the Amerbach sons, who had
provided them with manuscript translations of Greek authors (cf AK II Ep 571)
and evidently written notes into Bruno's Greek lexicon. Erasmus further
mentions G.M. Tricaglio's *Dictionum Graecarum thesaurus* (Ferrara: G. Mazzocchi del Bondino or Maciochius 27 September 1510). The latter did in fact
serve as a basis for the first Greek lexicon to be published in Basel: *Dictio-
narium Graecum, ultra' Ferrariensem aeditionem locupletatum*, ed V. Curio
(Basel: A. Cratander 1519).

19 dancer] Cf *Adagia* III ii 55.

19 Paris people] Probably a reference to Jean Petit's intention to reprint the Jerome
edition; see Ep 802.

21 Cavillotus alias Dissutus] He is not identified; *dissutus* means 'with his
mouth wide open.'

donkeys. Listen to Beatus; he is the only man of any sense. I gave this young
Menard four gold florins and one franc; please give instructions for me to be
reimbursed by Franz. I have had enough to do at my own expense and at my   35
own risk, as you will learn from my letter to Beatus. Farewell, dearest
fellow-godfather, you and your wife and all the family.

    Louvain, 22 October

    To Master Johann Froben the celebrated printer. In Basel

    Get Beatus to read this with you, or someone else who understands   40
Latin.

886 / To Cuthbert Tunstall   Louvain, 22 October 1518

> After completing a bundle of letters to friends along the Rhine route (cf Ep 867
> introduction), Erasmus now turned to his English friends (Epp 886–93, 895).
> His letters to them are often repetitive, so that complete annotation is
> unnecessary. Erasmus' main concern was his own future. Early in the year he
> had planned to go to England in the autumn, possibly to stay (cf Ep 834
> introduction), but his health, uncertainty about the terms offered to him by
> Wolsey and the king (lines 49–52), and the renewal of the French offer in the
> recently received Ep 810 made it advisable to postpone the journey. Thus he
> owed his English friends an explanation. See further Ep 964 introduction.

ERASMUS TO HIS FRIEND TUNSTALL, GREETING

This year my evil genius has led me a proper dance. I made a most difficult
journey to Basel, both from unsuitable companions (for by some fate I had
fallen in with a party of Hollanders) and from the heat, which was
oppressive for the time of year. In Basel I was ill almost all the time, first with   5
a most pestilent phlegm, of which many people in those parts died, and then
with stomach trouble and a dangerous looseness of the bowels. I would have
given a great deal at that moment for reliable health, which would have

* * * * *

34 four gold florins and one franc] The four gold coins are undoubtedly
   Burgundian philippus florins, which then would have been worth 16s 8d gros
   Flemish = 12s 0d sterling = £5 5s 0d tournois. The 'franc' was probably not the
   old French gold coin nor a French livre tournois, but the Burgundian livre
   d'Artois = 40d or 3s 4d gros Flemish, in silver coins. Cf CWE 1 318, 320,
   347; Ep 608:8n.
36 my letter to Beatus] Ep 867

   886
2 difficult journey] See Epp 829:9–21, 843 introduction.
5 ill] See Ep 847:7n.

allowed me to finish my task properly. Latimer's notes were very late in
reaching me; otherwise they would have been most welcome, but my own   10
notes were finished, and some part of Mark. I wish he had done the same in
the Epistles of the apostles. When I left Basel, I was still rather weak; but the
rest of the sad story of my misfortunes you will learn from my letter to Beatus,
of which I have sent a copy to your part of the world. I had decided to visit
England before the winter, and for that reason was in a hurry to leave Basel;   15
but Fate thought otherwise. I am still in the surgeon's hands on account of
two sore places, but the third is almost healed over.

Today I have sent a man at my own expense to Basel with the rest of the
copy and my arguments to the apostolic Epistles, which you advised me to
add; and I shall soon send the prefaces and tail-pieces. The work comes to   20
more than a hundred six-leaf quires, though, as the paper is larger, each
page contains ten lines more than in the previous edition. I had ordered one
to be printed on vellum, and he has struck off three. One will reach you at the
earliest possible moment, for the whole thing will be finished by January.
When Froben wanted to make an agreement with me, I told him to spend the   25
money he had intended to give me on seeing that the work was properly
done. The Amerbachs are extremely skilled in this art, and I persuaded them
by urgent entreaties to help with the corrections; for I felt that my servant
Jacobus, whom I had taken to Basel with this in mind, would not in fact be
much use, and as for Froben, nothing more stupid can be imagined.   30

From the bankers I received sixty francs against your bill on my return
to Louvain. Now that I am disentangled from that task, I mean to finish the
paraphrases, if Christ so please. I have had a visit in Louvain from a
Dominican who has edited an eightfold psalter; I mentioned him to his credit

* * * * *

9 Latimer's notes] At long last (cf Epp 520:21–2, 540:9–25) Latimer had produced
   some notes for the New Testament, but apparently only on the Gospels, and
   when they reached Erasmus the printing had progressed too far for them to be
   used; cf Ep 864 introduction.
13 letter to Beatus] Ep 867
18 a man] Menard; cf Ep 885:2n.
19 arguments] See Ep 894 introduction.
21 hundred] The text volume has fifty-eight quires of six leaves, the annotations
   forty-nine.
23 on vellum] See Ep 848:10n.
25 agreement] It seems that one was made but did not involve a cash payment,
   only the provision of books; thus Erasmus could state that he had travelled to
   Basel at his own expense; cf Ep 885 introduction and line 35.
29 Jacobus] Nepos; cf Ep 864 introduction.
31 sixty francs] A gift from Tunstall; see Ep 832:8n.
33 paraphrases] See Ep 916 introduction.
34 Dominican] Agostino Giustiniani; see Ep 906:529n.

in my *Apologia*, a fact which did not escape him. His work being quite   35
unsaleable, he goes to and fro presenting it to men in great position, and so
makes more by it than he ever could across the counter. He has a salary of
eight hundred francs from the king of France. My chancellor has died in
Spain, on whom the main of my hopes was pinned. His chaplain writes that,
had he lived another three months, your friend Erasmus would have been   40
amply provided for. I have another invitation from France, as you will learn
from Budé's letter, of which I send you a copy; it was written about 13 April
and reached me about 1 September. In it I sense a lack of ordinary human
feeling, but this offends me less than it might, because I know his nature
intimately. I send you also a copy of the letter which annoyed him so much.   45
Lefèvre begins to grow milder, and I hope that we shall make it up. There
were people in Germany who were starting to grumble; but they laid off,
terrified by the example of Lefèvre, when they saw that their Erasmus was
not wholly toothless. I do not see myself as a newly fledged guest in France
and would gladly know what I may hope for from England. I am getting   50
older, and my energy grows less. If I could have the further hundred marks
which the king offered me long ago, I should not seek for any more. Here I
have nothing to hope for. Nowhere in the world are liberal studies more
despised or worse looked-after. My Suetonius has appeared, a rather
majestic book, and so has Quintus Curtius. The *Institutio principis christiani*   55
has been reprinted, so has the *Enchiridion* with some additions, and a
supplement to my correspondence, selected by Beatus. My *Apologia* has been

* * * * *

38 chancellor] Jean Le Sauvage; cf Epp 608:19n, 852:72n. His chaplain was Pierre
Barbier, whose letter is not preserved.
42 Budé's letter] Ep 810
45 letter which annoyed him] Ep 778
46 make it up] Cf Ep 721 introduction.
51 the further hundred marks] Cf Ep 694:11n.
54 Suetonius] See Epp 648 introduction, 801:15.
55 Quintus Curtius] See Ep 704.
55 *Institutio*] See Ep 853.
56 *Enchiridion*] See Ep 858.
57 supplement] The *Auctarium selectarum aliquot epistolarum Erasmi* (Basel: J.
Froben August 1518), a small collection of 63 letters not formerly printed. In a
prefatory letter addressed to Michael Hummelberg (CWE 3 352–3), Beatus
Rhenanus took full responsibility for the selection of letters to be released to the
printer, but made it clear that the selection was made while Erasmus was
present in Basel; thus few readers would assume that he had not approved
Beatus' choice. In fact, Erasmus had long planned a new edition of his
correspondence (Epp 634, 783:32–4) and took the Deventer Letter-book with
him to Basel when he went there to see the New Testament through the press
(cf the preface to this volume). In Basel letters were included in the *Auctarium*

published afresh, with some additions; I am sending you a copy. Farewell, most learned Tunstall, and think kindly of your Erasmus, as you always do.

Louvain, 22 October 1518

A little before I left Louvain, Lee, with whom I had been on friendly terms, ceased, I know not on whose instigation, to be my friend. He began to make some notes on my New Testament, which he thought of great importance, while to me they seemed just the opposite, except in one or two places. Yet I took this as kindly meant, though I understood that he had 60 boldly declared to some regular canon or other, an ignorant man who had nothing to do with the question, that I had written something extremely risky in saying that Christ could not be called a first principle absolutely, my view of this being that it was possible to name something of which Christ is not the first principle. He is not the first principle of the Father, while the 65 Father is the first principle of all things absolutely. And now he is beginning to mix little spurts of indignation in with his notes, in the most stupid way, where he had not understood what I wrote. I made myself clear on these points and told him to remember that the man he was correcting was only a human being, and that he was such another. Next he ceased to correct me 70 any more, but after we parted he spread the story that he had marked a couple of hundred places; and he is planning some move against me, I know not what. He has not come to see me, nor does he send greetings. He is a good enough fellow, but very fond of his own opinions, irritable by nature and a careless talker. He thought he knew all the answers about the 75 genealogy of Christ in St Luke, as if he had found a flagrant blunder,

* * * * *

until the very end of Erasmus' stay, the latest, Ep 861, bearing a slightly later date than Beatus' letter to Hummelberg, which, incidentally, makes a friendly reference to Tunstall (cf also cwe 3 349). In marked contrast to the next following selection, the *Farrago* of October 1519 (cf Ep 1009 introduction), the *Auctarium* on the whole avoided controversial issues; see P.G. Bietenholz in *The Sixteenth Century Journal* 8 Supplement (1977) 61–78.

57 *Apologia*] The *Apologia ad Fabrum*; cf Ep 778 introduction.
61 Lee] The name is in Greek; cf the preface to this volume and Ep 843 introduction.
67 I had written] In the first edition of the New Testament, 1516. In the second edition, 1518–19, Erasmus' translation and annotation of John 8:25 in conjunction with the beginning of John were still more uncompromising. They take up much space in his future controversies with Lee; cf LB VI 335–9, 375–6, IX especially 173–4. See further Ep 1072 introduction.
81 genealogy of Christ] Cf Luke 3:23–38. In this sentence Erasmus meant to refer to Pseudo-Philo (see Ep 784:54n) rather than Josephus. Joseph is the name in Luke 3:23 around which the controversy hinged. The text edited by Giovanni Nanni ('Annius') is termed unsatisfactory rather than spurious; see LB VI 243D,

whereas in my discussion I am careful to leave the responsibility with Josephus and Annius, his authority. On my return to Basel I went into the thing at leisure and found Lee was completely wrong. Farewell once more.

887 / To Richard Pace   Louvain, 22 October 1518

For this letter cf Ep 886 introduction. It was published in the *Farrago*.

TO RICHARD PACE, FIRST SECRETARY OF HIS SERENE MAJESTY THE
KING OF ENGLAND, FROM ERASMUS OF ROTTERDAM, GREETING
For me this whole year has been very black; may Christ of his goodness send brighter successors. The long Iliad of my misfortunes you will learn in part from my letter to Beatus, of which I have sent a copy to Tunstall. I am now   5
waiting with my mouth open for the return of your library and am pitifully afraid that those things of mine will have disappeared. Your book is being read eagerly in Germany, though it offends some of the good people of Constance, because you seem to strip them of their education and credit them with drunkenness instead. I had decided to visit you this autumn, to   10
take up the offer made of his own accord by your generous king. The chancellor being dead, there is nothing to be hoped for from my own people. In France I have no wish to find myself a newly arrived guest. If I could add what the king offers me, I should look for nothing further. Linacre's translation of Galen at last begins to be on sale here, and I like it exceedingly.   15

* * * * *

IX 154–5, and 'Apologia invectivis Lei' *Opuscula* 243–5 (with additional details about the events mentioned here).

887
4 Iliad] Cf *Adagia* I iii 26.
5 Tunstall] See Ep 886:13–14.
6 return] Apparently lost between Italy and England, it had included a manuscript with the beginning of Erasmus' *Antibarbari:* see Epp 706:38n, 787:21–3.
7 Your book] *De fructu* (see Ep 776:4n). In his three prefaces Pace stated that *De fructu* was composed in an inn at Constance where there were neither scholars nor books, a circumstance he begged his readers to remember in case they found shortcomings (cf Richard Pace *De Fructu* ed Francis Manley and Richard S. Sylvester, New York 1967, 11, 25). For the predictable reaction in Constance cf Ep 1103; *Briefwechsel der Brüder A. und Th. Blaurer* ed T. Schiess (Freiburg 1908–12) Ep 26; and a letter by Michael Hummelberg to Urbanus Rhegius, 5 April 1519, in A. Horawitz *Analecten zur Geschichte der Reformation ... in Schwaben* (Vienna 1878) Ep 19.
12 chancellor] Jean Le Sauvage
15 Galen] Cf Epp 755:32n, 868:74–8.

After this I may even be ready to become a physician. I do not like this design for a tenth from Germany. Our crafty Midases are turning the screw to some purpose. Farewell, most learned Pace. Give my greetings to Linacre and encourage him to publish the rest of his work.

Louvain, 22 October 1518 20

888 / To [William Blount, Lord Mountjoy]   Louvain, 23 October [1518]

For this letter cf Ep 886 introduction. That Mountjoy is being addressed is inferred from a comparison between the last lines and the beginning of Ep 829.

Greeting, most generous of patrons. Who would think that this feeble body of mine could support so many trials – the difficult journeys, the intense heat (which in Basel was really intolerable), the effort and the ill health? For in Basel I was ill almost the whole time, first with a prolonged and pestilent phlegm, which in fact carried off quite a number of people, and then with 5 stomach trouble and a dangerous looseness of the bowels. Once I was past Cologne, things went very well, and I was promising myself a happy return to such friends as I had left behind in Louvain. And lo and behold I suddenly found myself at death's door, so far robbed of all my forces that I nearly died. Only my determination never left me. I was carried to Louvain with three 10 sore places, one under my left hip, one on my groin on the right side, and the third on my back. There was also a very hard swelling on my left groin, which has not entirely gone even now. Two surgeons assured me it was the plague. The physicians said there was no sign of sickness in my water. After a fortnight black flesh, quite dead, came away from the sores. This is now the 15 sixth week that I am confined to the house, and I am not yet free of the surgeons. If it was plague, this at least was on my side, that I did not believe it.

If I am very late in thanking you for your generosity, the fault lies with my servant John, who gave me the impression that he remembered the 20 money as coming from some other source. I should be glad to have news of your lordship and your lady and your son. Farewell.

Louvain, 23 October

* * * * *

17 a tenth] Cf Ep 891:26n.
17 screw] Literally 'tightening the cord'; cf *Adagia* 1 v 67.
888
19 Very late] Cf Epp 829:2n, 895.

889 / To [John Fisher]   Louvain, 23 October [1518]

For this letter cf Ep 886 introduction. Evidently an English bishop is being addressed, most likely Fisher (cf Ep 653 introduction). The bishop of Rochester was a patron of long standing (cf Ep 229 introduction) who had shown great interest in the Reuchlin controversies (see Ep 824). The letter repeats much information from Ep 867.

Greeting, my Lord Bishop. This year has led your old friend Erasmus a proper dance. I had a very difficult journey in both directions, partly because of the heat, which in Germany was intolerable, and partly through the most pestilent winds. I was still very weak when I left Basel; but I had gradually improved, so that I was in fairly good shape when I arrived to stay with the   5
count of Neuenahr. I found him in his castle at Bedburg, four miles this side of Cologne. He is a young man of ancient family, very silent, abstemious, with a very modest and almost saintly character, and a good scholar in more than one field. What a disgraceful exchange it is, if priests and monks live devoted to their stomachs, while knights are men of high character pursuing   10
humane studies! I also found at Boppard a customs officer who jumped for joy, exclaiming that he was a happy man because he had had the good fortune to see Erasmus. There was nothing he would not do for me. All among the documents of the customs-house he showed me the works of Erasmus. I get letters from Nürnberg, from Bohemia, from Hungary, from   15
Poland breathing the spirit of Christ; but they are nearly all from laymen. Only monks and certain theologians like them carry on this campaign of slander.

But to speak of business: I was hoping it would be possible to revisit you this autumn, with satisfaction on both sides; but you know the sudden   20
changes in human affairs. The moment I left the count, I was suddenly at death's door. Apart from the determination to live, there was no life in me. They carried me half-dead to Louvain, deprived of all my forces. I had three sore places, a large one under my left hip, which was made worse by riding, another in my left groin, and the third on my back. I also had a very hard   25
lump in my left groin, and another under my right pap, which has gradually disappeared after four weeks. From the three sores there came away a black,

* * * * *

889
15 letters] None such seem to be preserved.
26 left groin] This should be 'right,' as in Epp 888 and 893. Erasmus would not have made this mistake; it may be a confusion due to the transcriber of the Deventer text.

dead flesh. Both my surgeons maintained it was the plague, and still do. I
refused to believe them. I have now been six weeks in the surgeons' hands –
a most perilous class of men – and I sit idle at home. This was a trouble I had   30
never experienced. Who would have thought that my feeble body could
have endured all these journeys, all this sickness, this toil and care? Christ
our Saviour will one day grant that things may go better. Although whatever
he wishes me to bear, I will bear with fortitude, provided only – and this I
hope for, relying on his goodness – that he does not allow this member,   35
feeble though it is, to be parted from his body. It is he who is our life, if we
die, and our stronghold, if we live.

The New Testament, which was quite successfully completed, will
appear at the next fair. You will see my other things, or have already seen
them, when they reached England. My arguments to all the Epistles of the   40
apostles are now printing, which I wrote while I was ill. I am girding up my
loins to attack the paraphrases. Hoogstraten has been driven out of Cologne
and is looking for a home somewhere else. The affair developed from
argument into blows. In his dialogue he attacks the count of Neuenahr. This
has stirred up many military characters, his relatives and kinsmen in the   45
neighbourhood. I think he will move to Louvain. Farewell, most saintly of
bishops, and remember your humble servant Erasmus, as I know you do.

Louvain, 23 October
Erasmus etc.

890 / To Henry Bullock   [Louvain, c 23 October 1518]

Cf Ep 886 introduction. This letter and Ep 891 survive only as fragments in the
Deventer Letter-book since an intermediate leaf containing the end of the first
and the beginning of the second is lost. For details see Allen's headnote.
Bullock was a fellow of Queen's College, Cambridge; cf Ep 225:5n.

ERASMUS TO HIS FRIEND BULLOCK, GREETING
What news of my friend Bullock? Are you still waging war with the
supporters of Lefèvre? I have had one or two letters, in which you said you
had written something against that spiteful crew, but what you wrote has
not reached me yet ...   5
* * * * *
39 other things] See Ep 886:54–8.
42 Hoogstraten] See Epp 849:22n, 877:19n.
44 dialogue] Hoogstraten's *Apologia* (cf Ep 680:28n) took the form of a dialogue.
890
3 supporters of Lefèvre] Cf Ep 826:12–13. No records of such controversies in
Cambridge seem to have survived.

891 / To John Colet   Louvain, 23 October 1518

> For the fragmentary character of this letter see Ep 890 introduction. Like Ep 889
> it evidently began with a summary from Ep 867.

... and lo and behold at Aachen I suddenly found myself at death's door.
Partly on horseback and partly on wheels I was carried to Louvain, more
dead than alive, with three sore places and two severe swellings, one of
which has disappeared, but the other is still there, in my left groin, and does
not yet come to a head. From the three sores there came away a kind of black   5
dead flesh. The biggest was under my left hip. The one in my right groin is
almost healed over; the other two are still open. Both my surgeons assured
me it was the plague; but that thanks to the troubles of my journey I was now
in no danger. The physicians said there was no sign of disease in my urine. I
sent for the chief among them; he repeatedly declared there were no   10
untoward signs in the urine, but when I told him about the sores, he made off
and has not reappeared. I have now been sitting idle at home for six weeks,
troubled with surgeons, physicians, and druggists, which is not how I like
it. You often say Erasmus is unlucky. What would you say if you could see
him now, or still more, could have seen him? This was one trouble I had   15
never experienced. Who would believe that this feeble body of mine could
support such efforts, such journeys, and such sickness? Not to mention the
slanderous theologians and begging monks, none of whom bark to my face
but many from behind. May it be Christ's will that better times may some day
come, or that my bodily ills may be brought to an end.   20
    The New Testament will soon be out; it has gone quite well. My
arguments to all the Epistles of the apostles are now in process of
publication. After that I shall attack the paraphrases of the remainder. Tell
me what you did not like in the seventh chapter of the Epistle to the Romans.
I send you a copy of the speech delivered by the general of the Friars   25
Preacher, Cardinal Cajetanus, in the council of princes at Augsburg, where

* * * * *

891
20 brought to an end] Supplying *finiantur* for the missing verb
22 arguments] See Ep 894 introduction.
23 paraphrases] See Ep 916 introduction.
24 Romans] See Ep 825:13n.
26 Cajetanus] Tommaso de Vio of Gaeta, 1469–1534 (cf Ep 256:49n). He became
   general of the Dominicans in 1508, cardinal in 1517, and archbishop of Palermo
   in 1518. Appointed legate to the emperor, he left Rome on 5 May and on 7 July
   entered Augsburg, where Maximilian's last diet was gathering (cf the preface to
   this volume). Cajetanus' immediate task was to win the princes over to the
   papal crusade against the Turks (cf Epp 729:56n, 785:40n), but the confronta-

the emperor is staging a very pretty play. And he persuaded the archbishop
of Mainz so far to demean his own dignity as to accept the hat from him – for
he is only a young man – making himself one of the Roman pontiff's monks.
My dear Colet, what a topsy-turvy world we live in! Out of men we make
gods and turn priesthood into tyranny. The princes, together with the pope,
and I dare say the Grand Turk as well, are in league against the well-being of
the common people. Christ is out of date; it is Moses we follow now.
Farewell.

Louvain, 23 October 1518

892 / To Thomas Bedyll   Louvain, 23 October [1518]

For this letter cf Ep 886 introduction. Thomas Bedyll (cf Ep 387) was the
secretary of Archbishop Warham (see Ep 893). The financial transactions
mentioned in this letter are explained in Ep 823 introduction.

ERASMUS TO HIS FRIEND BEDYLL GREETING
Well, I am restored to you somehow, after so many perils, ending almost with
shipwreck as I entered harbour. Both my surgeons steadily maintained it
was the genuine plague. I have my doubts. I at least found it bad enough. I

* * * * *

tion with Luther soon took precedence (cf Ep 877:12n). Cajetanus' oration to
the diet proposing the levy of a tithe in Germany (cf Ep 887:16–17) to be used
exclusively for the German crusaders was delivered on 5 August. In the face of
fierce opposition from the estates, the emperor Maximilian made counter-
proposals which amounted to a voluntary tax on everybody receiving
communion, but in the end was content to see the matter stalled. Ulrich von
Hutten had prepared a speech to promote the crusade as a German national
enterprise and as an expression of independence from Roman tyranny. It was
not given before the diet but soon appeared in print; cf Ep 951:29n; Ulmann
Maximilian I II 713–22; Pastor VII 244–6; Holborn *Hutten* 103–6. The relevant
texts are assembled in Hutten *Opera* V.
27 archbishop] The cardinal's hat was bestowed on Albert of Brandenburg by
Cajetanus in the cathedral of Augsburg on 1 August, but before the ceremony
the two men had quarrelled over protocol and precedent (cf Hutten *Opera* V
265–6). This quarrel between the primate of Germany and the pope's
cardinal-legate may have inspired the highly nationalistic reaction of Erasmus'
informant; cf Ep 904:28–9, where Albert is likewise seen as a potential check to
papal interference in Germany.
31 tyranny] Cf Ep 872:20n.
33 Moses] Cf Ep 858:486n.

892
3 harbour] Cf *Adagia* I v 76.

can't think what Potkyn is up to. After my bill had been refused so many   5
times, at length I sent my own servant over to England on purpose, with a
bill which Sixtinus himself says was better written than Potkyn's. I expected
the money to be forthcoming. Franz, thinking the thing a certainty, wrote me
a bill against which I could draw money on his credit in Germany, having
received part of the sum forthwith. When he arrived in England, Potkyn   10
made difficulties about the bill and produced no money. He sent me a copy of
an idiotic bill mentioning the year '19, whereas this annuity is for the year
'18. I ask you, what makes him so difficult? Suppose no bill came into it at all:
is he afraid I shall demand money twice that is only due once? I undertook
such a dangerous journey and suffered from all that illness, and thanks to   15
that bill I should have been destitute had I not found men in Germany more
disposed to believe me than that Potkyn of yours. For Franz, when the
money was refused, altered his bill, reasonably enough.

Please pass this on to your master, for such things go better by word of
mouth than in writing; and do your best to see that the money is not   20
deposited with Arnold. Here I shall draw it from Franz, and in future I hope
his grace will prefer to act through Maruffo. Please let me know whether his
grace has received the volumes of Jerome, for they often hold on to my books.
If he has not had it, I will see that he gets it. Farewell, most faithful of friends.

Louvain, 23 October   25

893 / To [William Warham]   Louvain, 24 October 1518

For this letter cf Ep 886 introduction. In accordance with Ep 892:19–20, only a
passing reference is made here (lines 34–6) to the concern of that letter. For
William Warham, archbishop of Canterbury, who had given Erasmus the
benefice at Aldington, see Ep 188 introduction.

* * * * *

5 Potkyn] William Potkyn, a notary public serving Warham; see Ep 782:4n.
7 Sixtinus] Johannes Sixtinus, priest and notary in London, cf Ep 112 introduction.
8 Franz] Franz Birckmann, bookseller and banker; cf Ep 258:14n.
21 Arnold] Probably Arnold Birckmann (cf Epp 885:10, 895:3 and the plural used
by Erasmus in line 24). He was at this time dissatisfied with the Birckmann
brothers (cf Ep 885:6–7) and preferred that Raffaele Maruffo (cf Ep 387:3n)
should be used in future for the transfer of the Aldington annuity.
23 Jerome] Erasmus' edition was dedicated to Warham (cf Ep 396), and he was
among the first to receive a copy, although he did not receive all nine volumes
at the same time (cf Epp 413:36–9, 474 postscript, 475:35–7, 543 postscript).
Warham's set may still have been incomplete at this time, or he may have been
ordering another.

View of Aachen cathedral
Drawing by Albrecht Dürer, 1520
Reproduced by courtesy of the Trustees of the British Museum

Greeting, most reverend Prelate and most generous of patrons. Though few
things as a rule turn out well for me, no year has ever been as bad as this. My
journey was most difficult on account of the intolerable heat. In Basel I
suffered first from a prolonged and most pestilent rheum; then from stomach
trouble and a most dangerous looseness of the bowels, the trouble attacking   5
me so often that I was almost perpetually ill. If I had had no sickness, the heat
was so great that the most robust constitutions could hardly endure it. On
my way back I had begun to recover, and once past Cologne I was quite
pleased with my progress. I was hoping for a joyful reunion with you before
the winter and promised myself many different pleasures. But O the ups and   10
downs in human affairs! Around Aachen I suddenly found myself at death's
door. I was carried on a lame horse as far as Tongeren, but in such torment
that I sometimes thought of throwing myself on the ground and just dying
there under the open sky. From Tongeren I was taken home to Louvain in a
carriage and pair more dead than alive, with three sores, one under my left   15
hip, another in my right groin, and a third on my back. I sent for two
surgeons; both said it was the plague. The physicians said there was no sign
of disease in my water. There was also a very hard swollen lump in my left
groin, but short of an open sore. Under my left hip it was an immense sore.
Flesh that was black and dead came away from them all, but not till about   20
three weeks had passed. I have now been in the surgeons' hands for more
than six weeks, confined to the house with two sore places still open. This
was one trouble I had never experienced. Who would have thought that this
fragile body could have supported such troubles, so many and such difficult
journeys, such laborious researches, so many diseases renewing their   25
attacks so often with unimpaired severity? To say nothing meanwhile of
certain cursed monks and several numbskull theologians, who bark like
cowardly dogs when I am not there and are silent to my face.

Such is the sad history of my calamities, to which yet another was
added by the death in Spain of our prince's chancellor, on whom all my   30
hopes in this country depended, for he was my one convinced supporter. I
have no spirit for a move to France, though I am often invited already. I shall
be either an Englishman or a mixture of England and Brabant. I will not fail, if
I have your Grace's favour. Potkyn leads me a fine dance, rejecting all bills.
As far as he was concerned I might have died of hunger, for nothing could be 35
extracted from him. In the diet at Augsburg nothing of any note has

* * * * *

893
  8 way back] The following is a summary of Ep 867.
30 chancellor] Jean Le Sauvage; cf Ep 852:72n.

Reuerendo patri ac domino D. Nicolao
a Malefiis, Abbati apud diuum
Hubertum, Erafmus Rote
rodamus S. D.

QVod hactenus nufq̃ gentium, quã apud nos,
contemptiores fuerint bonæ literæ pater am
pliffime, magis morum integritate, q̃ dignitatis fa
ftigio venerabilis, illud in primis arbitror in cau-
fa fuiffe, q̃ apud noftrates principes, nullus fuerit
egregiis igeniis honos, cũ iã pridẽ & apud Germa
nos, & apud Vngaros, ac Bohœmos, deniq̃ apud
Anglos, & Scotos, honeftis ftudiis & præmiũ fit, &
dignitas. Et tamẽ bona quẽdã fpes affulget, hanc
quoq̃ laudis portionẽ regioni noftræ propediem
acceffuram, Pofteaquam video D. Erardum cla-
riffimum principem, & fanctiffimũ præfulem Le-
odienfem, nullos arctius complecti, q̃ viros doctri
na, vitæq̃ integritate cõmendatos . Quo quidem
in genere laudis, tui quoq̃ nominis præconiũ, ve-
luti bonus quifpiam odor Chrifti, reficit ac recre-
at animos omnium, qui veræ pietati, fanctifq̃ ftu
diis fauent. Quamuis enim nulla in re non fplen-
didus fis ac magnificus, tamen longe ab iftorum
quorũdam moribus diffidens, qui luxu duntaxat,
& caballis Abbates agunt, nihil prius habes, quã
modis

Erasmus *Argumenta in omneis epistolas apostolicas nova* preface
The first page, as it is found in *Ratio sive methodus ...*
(Louvain: Martens November 1518)
Courtesy of the University Library, Amsterdam

happened yet, except that the young archbishop of Mainz has been given a
cardinal's hat. A speech on the levying of special tithes was not very well
received; I have sent Tunstall a copy. The count of Neuenahr writes to me
that the diet is to be transferred to Frankfurt, and that there will be   40
discussions there about the coronation of Ferdinand. He is rather wasting
his time here. The count adds 'You will soon see the king returning from
Spain.' There is a rumour that he will come to Naples, which is nearer the
truth. There are flashes of plague everywhere; it has shown little virulence in
Louvain, much in Cologne. My respectful best wishes to your Grace, to   45
whom I sincerely devote myself as your humble dependant.

Louvain, 24 October 1518

894 / To Nicolas de Malaise   Louvain, 24 October 1518

> This letter is a dedicatory preface for *Argumenta in omneis epistolas apostolicas
> nova* (Louvain: Martens November 1518; NK 2973), published together with the
> *Ratio verae theologiae* (cf Ep 745), but also bound and sold separately. These
> arguments for each Epistle had been composed together with Erasmus' original
> translations of the apostolic letters before September 1506 (cf Ep 384 introduc-
> tion; Allen II 182). During his illness (lines 32–4; cf Ep 867) Erasmus revised the
> arguments for inclusion in the new edition of the New Testament (cf Ep 864).
> They were sent to Froben (cf Epp 885:3–4, 886:18–19) and printed in all his
> subsequent editions of the New Testament (also in LB VI and VII). At the same
> time, however, Erasmus gave them to Martens for a separate edition, which is
> the only source for this letter. He probably wished to show some consideration
> to Martens, who had nursed him in his sickness (Ep 867:211–67) at the time
> when he seemed to work exclusively for Froben. In adding this preface, he

* * * * *

37 Mainz] See Ep 891:27n.
38 speech] See Ep 891:26n. A copy was sent to Colet. Since Tunstall was sent other
   enclosures (see Ep 886:42–5), a confusion of names is not impossible.
39 Neuenahr writes] Cf Ep 878 introduction. The rumours here reported reflect –
   apparently with some confusion as to the respective roles of Ferdinand and
   Charles – speculations following a pact signed at Augsburg on 27 August 1518
   in which five of the seven electors had pledged themselves to elect Charles of
   Spain to be the Roman king, a step designed to facilitate his succeeding
   Maximilian as the emperor. It was hoped to hold the election in Frankfurt in the
   spring of 1519. Meanwhile the pope was expected to finally grant Maximilian I
   his long-awaited formal coronation as the Roman emperor, and Maximilian
   himself seems to have dreamt of his retirement to the kingdom of Naples,
   perhaps as administrator in the name of Prince Ferdinand, who was to be made
   king of Naples; cf Ulmann *Maximilian I* II 703–7.
44 plague] Cf Ep 847:7n.

wished to gratify a new patron (cf Ep 884:10), Nicolas de Malaise, who from
1503 to his death in 1538 was abbot of the Benedictines of St Hubert in the
Ardennes near the frontier of Belgium and Luxembourg.

TO THE REVEREND FATHER NICOLAS DE MALAISE, LORD ABBOT
OF ST HUBERT'S, FROM ERASMUS OF ROTTERDAM, GREETING
In no country in the world have liberal studies hitherto been rated lower
than our own, and the chief cause, my honoured Lord Abbot (who for all the
eminence of your position are yet more to be respected for your upright life),   5
I believe to be that among our princes no respect is paid to intellectual
eminence, while in Germany, in Hungary and Bohemia, and even in
England and Scotland, the humanities have long enjoyed reward and
honour. And yet a bright hope dawns that in this field as well our country
will soon be adding to its laurels, now that I see that noble prince and saintly   10
bishop Erard of Liège seeking to have none about him so much as those who
have learning and purity of life to recommend them. And in this field of
honour the sound of your name equally, like some excellent savour of Christ,
revives and refreshes the spirits of all who are devoted to true piety and
sacred studies. For though in every other field you use a splendid   15
munificence, yet (O how different from some who show themselves abbots
only in their soft living and their palfries!) you think nothing more important
than in every way to restore the ruined discipline of the religious life and
then to consolidate and to advance it. And this you do, not so much by the
exercise of your authority as by the example of your life, the most effective   20
way there is to improve the character of those who are set under one. You
pass your time, not in games of hazard but in sacred study, and not in
hunting but in prayer, and by your daily sacrifices make the day, however
long, seem short. But next to this is your interest in encouraging or arousing
the study of Holy Scripture, since this is the spring from which all holiness of   25
life must flow. And that these outstanding gifts in you are no pretence but
true and genuine is shown by, among other things, your complete freedom
from arrogance of every kind, for, with all your merits, not the least is that
you seem to be the only person who is unaware of them. That is the true mark
of a really Christian spirit, one that measures the stem and stern (as they   30
say) of all its actions by the glory of Christ, to whom alone all honour is due.
    Such thoughts as these, reverend Father, were the brands that kindled

* * * * *

894
11 Erard] Erard de la Marck; cf Epp 746, 884:9.
13 savour of Christ] Cf 2 Cor 2:15.
30 stem and stern] Cf Ep 858:474n.

the fire of my affection for you, the more so as Paschasius Berselius had
painted me an enthusiastic word-picture of you; and so I wished that the
little book containing arguments to all the apostolic Epistles, which I have   35
made these last few days while detained at home by illness, should go forth
into the world under your auspices; not that I thought you had any need of
this work of mine, but because it seemed appropriate to dedicate to a
champion of true religion a work that has the encouragement of true religion
as its goal. After the majesty of the Gospels, what should we treasure more   40
than the Epistles of the apostles, which show us marvellous flashes of the
fresh and primitive spirit of the early church? There are indeed arguments
made by the Greeks, but these seemed to me to have been not so much
written as thrown together by some ignoramus, and so the versions I made
long ago of these have been allowed to lapse; those of uncertain authorship   45
which circulate in some manuscripts in Latin are thin and barren. I have
made versions of the Epistles of the apostles, somewhat more lucid, I think,
and in fact more faithful than their predecessors. I have added notes in
which not a few difficulties are cleared up. I have tried also to throw light by
a paraphrase, and this work, which I began recently, will soon with Christ's   50
help be finished and published. After which, if the favour of Heaven will
second my desires, I hope to finish the commentary which I started long ago,
and so to kindle many people to the study of these life-giving texts, who are
now deterred, many by the unfamiliar language, some by the corruption of
the copies, and others by the obscurity of the subject-matter. Farewell,   55
excellent Father, and henceforth write the name of Erasmus in the list of
those devoted to you.

  Louvain, from the College of the Lily, 24 October 1518

* * * * *

34 word-picture] During his recent visit to Louvain (cf Ep 867:275). It was most
 likely Berselius, a Benedictine in the confidence of Erard de la Marck, who had
 brought about the connection between Erasmus and Malaise.

42 arguments] A traditional set of introductions in Greek to each of the Pauline
 Epistles. No more is known about Erasmus' translation of them. Another set of
 very short and elementary prefaces is found in many printed editions of the
 Latin vulgate. It also appeared in the New Testament of 1516 but was
 subsequently replaced by Erasmus' own arguments.

50 paraphrase] See Epp 710, 916. The paraphrases took the place of the earlier
 planned commentary on Romans and other Epistles, but as late as 1524 Erasmus
 was still expressing the hope that this latter project would be realized, perhaps
 partly because it must have been among his earliest; cf Epp 164:39–46,
 301:20–2, 685:25; Allen I 42:8–10.

895 / To John Smith   Louvain, 25 October [1518]

For this letter cf Ep 886 introduction. John Smith was formerly in Erasmus'
service; for his return to England see Ep 820 introduction. This is the last of
the letters preserved in the Deventer Letter-book; cf the preface to this volume.

ERASMUS TO JOHN SMITH, GREETING
I wonder very much why you told me that twelve angels had been paid over
by More and committed to Arnold. Relying on what you said I accepted a bill
from him, which afterwards I was obliged to change. Let me know how you
are. I have been more than once in great danger of death. Mind you serve
your master faithfully and avoid bad company. Above all, never run the risk
of catching the French pox by contact with anyone. Never forget Christ, but
pay your duty to him sincerely every day. If there is anything I can do for you
here, I will do it gladly. Farewell, dearest John.
    Louvain, 25 October

896 / From Guillaume Budé   Paris, 31 October [1518]

This melodramatic letter may seem an unjustified reaction to Erasmus' Ep 869,
which was certainly not friendly but sounds no more offensive than many other
remarks exchanged earlier in the correspondence with Budé. Towards the end
of Ep 810 Budé had made a considerable effort to restate in cordial terms the
king's invitation to Paris, and he may have resented the fact that Erasmus'
answer made no reference to it, although Erasmus had promised a further letter
in the near future. At any rate, lines 102–4, 114–15, and the postscript show
clearly that Budé did not seriously intend to sever his relations with Erasmus.
Fortunately Erasmus saw this at once (cf Epp 906:269–71, 931:21–2), but less
happily he still insisted on examining Budé's arguments one by one in Ep 906.
This letter was published in the *Farrago*.

FROM GUILLAUME BUDÉ, HIS ERSTWHILE FRIEND, TO ERASMUS
WITH BEST WISHES, AND NEVER AGAIN
I remember once when writing to you I said something like 'I know you as
well as you know me.' How very wide of the mark I was I now understand
for the first time, after reading right through that ill-tempered letter you

* * * * *

895
3 by More] The confusion is explained in Ep 829:2n.

896
3 I said] Ep 493:241–2

wrote me from Louvain, when you were, I imagine, not yet restored to your true self after the troubles of that illness, or at least not restored to *me*. I used to hope that the Graces had given it their blessing when I struck up my friendship with you – you who were in any case a great lover of wit and humour, and not only a master of courtesy but one who fully understands a joke and knows how to take one, with whom I could let my pen run on just as I pleased with no risk to the smooth course of the friendship contracted and by now established between us. One more disappointment! I now see that I am clumsy, absurd, preposterous, obtuse, hard to get on with as a companion, and a proper blunderer, one who must be avoided and kept away with jests that are barbed and double-edged and full of menace, like a bull with hay tied round his horns. For so I am resolved to believe, since you and your friends, good men and true, have so decided, whose judgment I rate of course far above my own. Nor do I see any future in defending myself, for I cannot attempt to deny a charge of which you for your part have so often suspected me before now, while to your friends I am clearly guilty; or in begging to be excused from these malevolent suspicions, for I have no hope of dislodging the opinion fixed in the hearts of either yourself or your friends. Suppose I tried to do this, when you have already prejudged the case: I should perhaps incur another charge, of impudence this time, especially as, if I tried to plead my case with you on the bench, my empty verbiage (you make this abundantly clear) would win little credit and carry no weight, for the time of the court, as the phrase goes, is reserved for solid arguments, with which on your own showing I am very ill supplied.

Up to this point I have a clear grasp of the sense of your letter and have decided not to appeal against the interpretation you and your friends put upon the case, however unfair it may be to me, either to the friends we share or to my own friends to whom you refer me; though their opinion on this subject is as wrong-headed as mine, which means it is quite opposed to the view of those friends of yours. When however you say that competition in abuse is beneath you and you take no pleasure in quibbling, what that has to do with me I do not see; for I cannot think you so indignant that you mean this to refer to me. And yet, for fear that this sore place may spread, since as far as I can see there is no dispersing it, my view is that we must use the knife, which means that we must be satisfied with mutual silence for the future: you are to suppress my prolix letter (as you call it, meaning needlessly verbose

* * * * *

17 bull] Cf *Adagia* 1 i 81; a bad-tempered animal had a warning wisp of hay tied on his horns.
28 time of the court] Cf *Adagia* 1 iv 73; Epp 810:356, 867:21n.
41 prolix letter] Ep 810, described as prolix in Ep 869:3.

and tedious), and indeed tear it up if you like or bury it in live coals among the ashes, and in reply to yours (which is already published, as I saw today for the first time) I will hold my tongue and cause you no further trouble. But why you went for me like that I do not see, if you wished me not to answer. You have prescribed silence: very well, I accept, and will keep silence, if you allow me to do so. I must be a marvellously foolish and stupid listener; but though I have often read that ill-starred and accursed letter of mine since I got yours, even after all this length of time, as I go over it again and hear myself reading it, I cannot detect that poison of malevolence – call it what you please – which offends you so much. Which makes me realize how absurd is my judgment and how keen is yours.

But in heaven's name, was it the first part of my letter that gave you such offence, where I speak of your difference with Lefèvre, or the second part, in which I put the king's offer to you? If it was the former, why write me such a long letter, provoking me with such powerful arguments to reply? When I replied to that letter, I supposed that I should make you find the business satisfactory. What is there about it, for pity's sake, which to an experienced and acute observer would not redound to your credit? Could I of all people wish to criticize you or give my support to anyone except Erasmus? Away with such an unpleasant suggestion! All the more so since Lefèvre has never mentioned the subject to me, although he has often spoken with me in the mean while. But when I saw that the victory in that dispute was awarded to Erasmus by every fairminded person, but with the proviso that they were saying you wished to press your victory to excessive lengths and had not sufficiently taken account of your own position and your opponent's, I wished to give you a picture of the position in my letter; I wished to offer you both consolation and excuse on this account, that you would have suffered a common human experience if (as does happen) you had grown unduly warm in the course of a dispute – a fault from which even your hero Jerome was not free. I wanted also to wean you from the opinion you appeared to hold and to turn you away from thoughts of opening a campaign from which the humanities and sacred studies could only suffer.

At the same time I do not deny one thing: your letters give me such pleasure that I enjoy sharpening your pen even against myself and provoking you to write. So that even in that letter which has caused so much mischief my object was to turn the force of your attack against myself,

* * * * *

43 published] Ep 778, published recently in the *Auctarium*
48 accursed letter of mine] Ep 810
56 a long letter] Ep 778
71 Jerome] Cf Epp 778:266–71, 810:123–8.

although in fact I have found your indignation very hard to bear, for you were in a bad temper when you wrote me a mere note. Nor have I ever taken offence at anything you have said in your other letters to me, though there are passages in them which certain of my friends felt to carry more innuendo than our friendship or your natural caution would seem to warrant. I am so far from agreeing with them that I do not suppose, even in the future, I have to fear anything too outrageous. In fact I sometimes enjoy being chastised by a man as dear to me as you, with a lash so skilful and well directed that my friends make fun of my weals for many days afterwards. I am quite willing to accept pardon for any offence I may have given you, on this condition, that you enjoy yourself to the top of your bent in trouncing your friend, provided the punishment is worthy of us both; for I do not think all scholars taken together have such high standards as you and your friends.

If however what distresses you is what I said in my letter about the king's proposal, on the ground that in a serious matter I seem to be making a fool of you, I at least, as far as that goes, seem to be making a fool not of you but of myself. I want you to be clear about this: such was your reputation at the time in the inner circle of the court that, when it was suspected that you were rejecting the royal offer with much hesitation because you feared the most illustrious Prince Charles might be offended, the king of France in his eagerness to have you was prepared to write to the prince on this subject, had you said anything of the sort by way of excuse.

Then there are other things which it would take too long to set down – nor should they perhaps be entrusted to a letter – but which impelled me all the same to write a letter like this, so far at least as this subject is concerned. If however you have had the idea of renouncing your friendship with me for several months, until your feelings against me have cooled down, this is not a sufficient reason why you should not write to the bishop of Paris, for I am quite ready for this business to be put through without my presence as arbiter or go-between. And please understand that my criticisms stem from a certain lack of tact and not from malice (which I fancy you will do quite willingly, if your friends would permit it), and do not love me any the less than you have all this long time; for I can see that it goes against the grain to take this hostile line with me. As I hope for the favour of heaven, I wish all

* * * * *

79 a mere note] Ep 869
92 king's proposal] In Ep 810:400–89 Budé had made it clear that Erasmus was still welcome at Paris and could expect attractive conditions if he chose to come, but at the same time he had cast some doubt both on Erasmus' motives for delaying a decision and on his own determination to act as an honest broker in this matter; cf Ep 906:100n.
105 bishop of Paris] Etienne Poncher

may go well with you and rejoice at your safe return to Louvain. There was a constant rumour here that you had moved to Rome or Milan. I greeted Glareanus for you, who came to see me today. Farewell; and when you think you have hated me long enough, resume your affection for me.

Paris, 31 October, having received your letter yesterday, bad luck to it!

A further reason for consigning that accursed epistle to the flames (though I leave the decision to you, for it was written for your benefit rather than mine, if you have had your fill of rereading it) – in any case a reason for my disliking it – is that when I was reading it today I found a mistake in the draft of it which had been kept by me. It comes on the second page, where it says 'Id quod tu inficiando non eris,' and if it is the same in your text, I expect you have made proper game of me. What I meant was 'cui tu rei inficiandae.' Yet I do not see why that letter is any less worthy to see the light than the one written on Midwinter day, in which you published private remarks made as between you and me, which I hoped would remain secret, so much so that I did not keep a single word of the draft. I had written you another letter half in Greek which does not I think deserve to be suppressed any more than that one. If in two or three lines, or more, there are things put that you do not like, you have my permission to change them or strike them out as you think best.

897 / To Maarten Lips   [Louvain, c October] 1518

Epp 987–902 are all preserved in one or both of Lips' copy books, which contain many letters from Erasmus (cf Ep 750 introduction); only Ep 897 was published by Erasmus (in the *Epistolae ad diversos* of August 1521). A probable sequence can be established, although precise dates cannot. The first letters probably date from October 1518; Ep 901 very likely dates from November or early December. The main concern is always Edward Lee (cf Ep 865 introduction). Lips evidently managed to remain friendly with both sides. He showed Lee Erasmus' answers to his critical notes on the New Testament. Lee probably felt tricked, seeing Erasmus' public rejoinder to his unpublished notes. Quite naturally he now planned a publication of his own, trying to keep his further notes concealed from Erasmus until it was ready. But thanks to Lips Erasmus

* * * * *

113 Rome or Milan] Cf Epp 869:4 and 770, 831 introductions.
117 the flames] Instead Erasmus published Ep 810 in 1519, just as Budé wished him to.
122 'Id quod tu inficiando non eris'] 'as you will not deny' (Ep 810:55). Erasmus printed the amended version, which means the same; cf Ep 906:603–5.
125 Midwinter day] Ep 744, recently published in the *Auctarium*
127 half in Greek] Ep 568, published only in LB, from the Deventer Letter-book

saw some of them. For the subsequent developments cf Epp 936:34n, 960 introduction.

   In the Brussels manuscript (cf Ep 750 introduction) Lips introduced this letter with a short argument, referring to Erasmus' return from Basel, to his recovery from illness (cf Ep 867), and to Johannes Hovius' (cf Ep 867:189n) visit to Lips with a copy of the *Auctarium*, evidently accompanied by this note.

TO THE WORTHY MASTER MAARTEN
Greeting. My most worthy friend, I send you a copy of my correspondence, among which there is a letter in reply to a very foolish pamphlet which you had sent me. You will find it on page 99; though afterwards I was sorry I had spent so much time on a thing of so little merit. I suppressed your name, for 5 fear of stirring up trouble for you; and his too – or else he will protest that I have made a public exhibition of him, though publicity is just what he craves. Farewell, and bear me in mind, especially in your prayers.
   1518

898 / To Maarten Lips   [Louvain, c October 1518]

   For this letter cf Ep 897 introduction. Lips' argument in the Brussels manscript refers to the gift of a copy of Froben's enlarged *Enchiridion*. It also states that before showing Erasmus' reply (Ep 843 in the *Auctarium*) to that 'theological caviller' (Lee), 'Brother Maarten [Lips] had consulted with Erasmus. He had also put Augustine ahead of Origen and equal to Jerome [in reference to Ep 843 and especially Ep 844:132–41, 271–4, also published in the *Auctarium*]; but as usual Erasmus vehemently took the side of the Greeks.'

Greeting. You speak of stirring up the logic-chopper; steady, steady! Peace and concord must come first. My answer was not addressed to him, but to others who talk the same sort of nonsense. Read your Jerome and you will think I let him off very lightly. Augustine is one of the great doctors, but not to be compared with any of the Greeks. If you want a demonstration, read 5

* * * * *

897
3 letter] Ep 843, which in the first edition of the *Auctarium* (cf Ep 886:57n) begins on page 99, although it does not in the reprint of March 1519. For the suppression of names see Ep 843 introduction.
6 his too] Edward Lee's

898
1 logic-chopper] Edward Lee, who is not mentioned by name in Ep 843
3 Jerome] See Epp 778:266–71, 896:70–1.

Chrysostom's commentary on John, and then Augustine's on him. Ambrose
was more learned than he; so were Hilary, and even Cyprian, but they wrote
less. Comparisons are odious; they were all great men, but there is an order
of greatness.

I send you my *Enchiridion*; I expect you have it, but in this copy you will   1
find some new stuff, preface etc. Farewell, and keep some affection for me, as
I have much for you. I will visit you, when my health permits.

Your sincere friend Erasmus

898A / To Maarten Lips   [Louvain, c November 1518?]

For this letter which is Ep 912 in Allen's edition, cf Ep 897 introduction. The
date is uncertain. Allen preferred January 1519 because of the resemblance
between lines 9–11 and Ep 906:494–8, but Lips himself apparently thought that
this letter was prior to Ep 899, which it precedes in both his copy books. Lips'
argument is very full and offers a proper identification of Lee, who had not
been mentioned by name in Erasmus' earlier letters. By contrast, Lips'
argument for Ep 899 is short and refers to Lee as having often been mentioned
before. Finally, Erasmus' remark in Ep 899:3–4 would seem to be a suitable
sequence to lines 6–7 of this letter.

Lips' argument begins with the identification of Edward Lee, as an
Englishman of noble birth, from the circle or family of the bishop of Winchester
(Richard Foxe; cf Ep 187). According to Lips, Lee produced – initially in a
friendly spirit – many notes to the first edition of Erasmus' New Testament,
which he began to communicate to the author one by one. When Erasmus
brushed them aside as misleading and petty rubbish (cf Ep 750), Lee became
stubborn and irritated and took to agitating against him during his absence at
Basel. Lee had his notes recopied, imparting them first to Jan Briart and then
also to a friend in England (cf Ep 1026). On learning this, Erasmus tried, not
very successfully, to get hold of them with the aid of others as well as Lips, who
kept in close contact with Lee. Lips ends his argument by adding that Lee also
began to criticize Reuchlin (cf Epp 849:21–30, 856:47n).

ERASMUS OF ROTTERDAM TO MAARTEN LIPS OF BRUSSELS,
GREETING

You have not been very clever in your dealings with Lee, by changing the
line I had laid down for you. The complaint about the friars made your case

* * * * *

6 Chrysostom's commentary] Erasmus' preference is clearly reflected in many of
   his notes on John in the New Testament.
10 *Enchiridion*] Republished in August 1518; cf Ep 858 introduction.

more difficult; you must take care by all means to avoid any suspicion of the   5
kind. How like himself he always is – always the censor, always the prince of
critics! But it is lèse-majesté even if I had suggested that his notes are lightweight. What pompous stuff it is to say 'If I were seeking reputation, I could
achieve it on the facts without help from the friars.' And then it was only last
week that he started Hebrew, yet he has these extraordinary delusions of   10
being Reuchlin or even Jerome, no less. But you, my dear Maarten, must
keep on good terms with him.

I am sending you the New Testament. It is Marcus Laurinus' copy; you
will not be asked by me to return it unless he demands it back, so you can
keep it, and welcome. Farewell.   15

899 / To Maarten Lips   [Louvain, c November 1518]

For this letter cf Ep 897 introduction. In his argument Lips explained that he
had managed to obtain for Erasmus another of Lee's notes but since the end
was missing (in the transcript) he had summarized it on a small sheet of paper
(*schedula*) that was composed of formulations of his own as well as quotations
from Lee's note; Erasmus had overlooked this fact and thought the criticism
came from Lips. The sheet here mentioned may be the *scheda* that Erasmus had
rashly destroyed (cf Ep 901:18–20). The answer to this letter is Ep 900.

ERASMUS OF ROTTERDAM TO MAARTEN LIPS OF BRUSSELS,
GREETING
I suppose it had to happen, that you too of all people should turn censor of
my life and my researches and summon me to a solemn recantation. The time
is not ripe, my dear Maarten: at your age you should be learning still, not   5
passing judgment, especially with such authority. As though you think
better of Augustine than I do, or follow him more closely than I do! That rule
under which you live comes from anywhere rather than Augustine. He was
never a monk, he invented no monks, he did not shut men up in pens like

* * * * *

898A
  6 prince of critics] Erasmus uses the name of the greatest of ancient grammarians,
    Aristarchus (see *Adagia* I v 57), just as for 'pompous' he writes 'Thrasonical,'
    thinking of the proverbial braggart in Terence's *Eunuchus*.
 13 New Testament] Since Lips received a copy of the new edition (cf Ep 864
    introduction) with Ep 955, the one mentioned here was probably the edition of
    1516.

899
  7 rule] See line 31n.

dangerous animals. If I bound myself to your rule of life, it was never from   10
conviction, but trapped by a thousand stratagems; not that I am against the
life, but it could not possibly be right for me. And yet it was never my
intention to abandon it, if for no other reason, to avoid scandal, for men will
never believe there is no cause for it.

If Lee does not approve my leaving that most religious way of life, I owe   15
this to England, which compelled me to do it; this you would easily credit if
you knew the whole story as it happened. I have no reason for more disliking
Britain, though I have always found it a very unhealthy place. And yet I have
done more good since I was alienated, as he calls it, than many who stay at
home drinking or criticizing me. I have lived among men of higher character,   20
and still do, than if I were living among your colleagues, tippling. Is it not
good enough if I satisfy my conscience, the bishop, the Holy Father, and my
other spiritual superiors, unless I also win approval from the censor, Lee?
The wiser he thinks himself, the more fool he is. If I were to tell you the whole
story, you would agree that I could not do otherwise than I did. But it's a   25
long history. It is not for you, or for anyone, to lay down the law for another
man's conscience. Lee thinks my change of status a grave sin; I think it a far
more grave one to cast aspersions on another man's life, as he does with a
will, when it is nothing to do with him. And yet as he does this, he sees
himself in something of a halo. Take my word for it, there is not much   30
Augustine in a man who has nothing of him except the rule (which is not his,
anyway). When it says in the rule 'You shall not attempt to please by raiment
but by good behaviour,' it is clear that this monstrous and most extraordinary way of life could never have had his approval. Tell me: if a man has
signed away himself to Augustine, must it be wrong ever to dissent from   35
him, even in places where he dissents from the truth? In some passages,
undoubtedly, there are such lapses that no one can deny them. And yet I

* * * * *

11 trapped] Cf Ep 447.
16 England] Cf Ep 296:202–11.
17 disliking] A surprising statement, especially at this time (cf Epp 886, 964
   introductions), but Erasmus tended to react very emotionally to personal
   attacks upon his past. Allen noted several unpleasant recollections of England
   in Epp 105, 119, 145, 190, 282, 597.
31 rule] Large portions of a *Regula ad servos Dei* (PL 32:1377–84), traditionally
   included in the works of St Augustine, are also found in his letter 211,
   addressed to certain nuns. Modern scholarship does not follow Erasmus, who
   thought that only the letter was genuine; cf his edition of Augustine (Basel:
   Froben 1528–9) I 591–2; *Lexikon für Theologie und Kirche* ed M. Buchberger et al,
   2nd ed (Freiburg 1957–68) sv Augustinusregel.
32 'You … behaviour'] PL 32:1380

never fail to speak with reverence of Augustine. What people think who are
both more learned and more saintly than Lee, I need not mention here. But of
course it is no surprise if he has a passion for Augustine, for he supposes that   40
he alone understands him.

Consider, pray, the arrogance with which you say 'Recant, I tell you,
where you have sung out of tune; remove the errors from your book; and you
will find you had much better submit to criticism than seek to dispense it.'
There's folly and arrogance for you! As though I needed your assistance to   45
correct my work! There are others whose judgment I follow, nor am I so short
of judgment myself as to need correction by you. If you wish to be taken for a
real Augustinian, imitate his zeal and his way of life. If Augustine were alive
today, he would be much more ready to own me as his disciple than many of
those who foolishly boast his name.   50

I write freely to you, but in a friendly spirit. Tear up this letter. If you
want to keep it, make a copy of it; destroy what I have written. In future, if
you write, seal your letter because of the servants. Farewell.

900 / From Maarten Lips   Louvain, [c November 1518]

For this letter cf Ep 897 introduction. It answers Ep 899 and is answered by Ep
901.

MAARTEN LIPS OF BRUSSELS TO THAT EMINENT DOCTOR OF
DIVINITY ERASMUS OF ROTTERDAM
I read your letter of reproof, my dear and most learned friend, and could
hardly keep a straight face: you seemed to be living in some quite different
world. When and where did I ever set up as a judge of your life and your   5
researches? It is true, I have sometimes pointed out politely some passages
where I did not think you had entirely satisfied the attentive reader. But I
know that hitherto, while you have always resented severe and supercilious
criticism, you have always regarded polite and friendly advice as something
to be grateful for. Have you changed your mind? Not a bit of it. Then how   10
has it come about that you write to me like this? Shall I guess what has
happened to you? I wrote for you a small sheet of paper, and that on the spur
of the moment, for I was busy with other things. In this I quoted some words

* * * * *

38 with reverence] Cf Ep 844.
43 your book] The New Testament
53 because of the servants] Cf Epp 901:19–21, 902.

900
12 paper] Cf Ep 899 introduction.

from one of Lee's notes, indicating that the writer's name was not Lips but
Lee. You therefore were either half-asleep or in a trance when you read what   1
I wrote, for you did not distinguish between Lee and Lips, and in your letter
you openly attribute to me words which are really Lee's. 'Pray consider,' you
say, 'the arrogance with which you say "Recant, I tell you, where you have
sung out of tune,"' and so forth. Pray reread my note, and see under whose
name these words are repeated; and you will soon realize that you were   2
under a surprising delusion as you read.

But why need I defend myself any longer when I am clearly right?
Apart from that, I see at the end of your letter 'Tear up this' and what
follows. I do not usually destroy letters from famous men. I much prefer to
lay them up in a casket of cedar-wood.   2

Farewell, dear Erasmus, and pray convince yourself that the man Lips
is not a hostile critic of your work, but much more a devoted reader.

From the College of Canons of St Martin's

901 / To Maarten Lips   Louvain, [c November 1518]

> This letter answers in part Ep 900; however lines 10–17 and 21–8 respond to
> further reactions to Ep 899, which Lee may have chosen not to record. Erasmus'
> remarks in lines 10, 21 are perhaps in response to the paper mentioned in line 19
> (cf Ep 899 introduction). In his argument Lips stated that he accepted this letter
> as a token of true friendship and added: 'and to prevent any difficulty arising
> from this use of *gemitus* ['regrets' (line 21)] let me explain that I had dropped a
> hint to Erasmus about the taking of vows of perpetual celibacy; but I did this
> more to disarm his suspicions than out of deliberate policy. For I was afraid that
> he would think I made light of him if I had appeared quite satisfied with my
> vows' (see further Ep 1070). The approximate date is indicated by the publica-
> tion mentioned at the end.

ERASMUS OF ROTTERDAM TO MAARTEN LIPS OF BRUSSELS,
GREETING

I am delighted that what otherwise astonished me was all a dream. Some of it
I knew was Lee's, but you had mixed in some words of your own about his
scandalous references in front of you to my change of status. And then came   5
what I quoted in my letter, which I likewise thought was yours. Now I have
no cause for astonishment, in fact I am surprised his language was not more

* * * * *

17 you say] Cf Ep 899:42–3.
25 cedar-wood] Cf *Adagia* iv i 54.

arrogant. I suspected that this was precisely the reason why he would not let me see his book. Thank you for your present.

The passage you want in Augustine is in volume xi, in the *De haeresibus ad Quodvultdeum*, on the second leaf of the book; the chapter begins 'Apostolici qui se' etc. Read Augustine's letter to Aurelius, which is number 76. It is clear enough from that that Augustine was not a monk. In two of the sermons which he delivered to the people about his clergy (they are among the spurious sermons *Ad fratres in eremo*, numbers 52 and 53), he mentions religious profession and vows, but he refers to the vow as a resolution. Monasticism he does not mention.

Please send me again the conclusion of Lee's annotations; for after reading your paper two or three times I threw it in the fire, in case it might fall into the hands of my servant. In things like this it is not safe to trust the young. Furthermore, I do not approve your regrets; so far are they from doing good that they may double your grievances. Though I should have no misgivings in dissuading a young man of promise from putting his neck into your noose, I would not dare persuade anyone who was once in the net to break out, unless some chance of freedom should present itself, so that it might seem heaven's doing. So many are the traps and barricades with which those Pharisees of yours have fenced in their despotic rule. In the mean time, seek relief in reading holy books. I send you two small things, one my system of theological study, and the other my arguments to the Epistles of the apostles. Farewell, dearest Maarten. From the College of the Lily.

902 / From Johannes Hovius to Maarten Lips   Louvain, [1518?]

Cf Ep 897 introduction. Allen added this letter to the preceding exchanges between Lips and Erasmus at about this time because it affords a valuable

* * * * *

901

9 present] For an earlier gift see Ep 807 introduction.
10 *De haeresibus*] Chapter 40, stating that it is heresy to reject categorically marriage and individual property (cc 46:307). Erasmus' reference is to Augustine's works (Basel: Amerbach, Petri, and Froben 1506).
12 number 76] Now Ep 60
14 sermons] Nos 555–6 in PL 39:1568–81. Erasmus recognized that they were authentic but inexplicably placed among spurious pieces; see his edition of 1528–9, x 994 and *Dictionnaire de théologie catholique* ed A. Vacant et al (Paris repr 1923–67) I-2 2310.
18 conclusion] Cf Epp 765, 898A, 899 introductions.
20 servant] Cf Ep 902.
21 regrets] See introduction and Ep 1070.
28 system ... arguments] See Ep 894 introduction.

insight into Erasmus' relations with his amanuenses. In addition it may perhaps reveal the specific cause of Erasmus' suspicions in Epp 899:51–3, 901:18–21. Lips probably wished to check a paper which he had sent to Erasmus, perhaps without keeping a proper record. So he tried to borrow it from Erasmus' files, addressing himself to the secretary because he did not dare to bother the master himself. For Hovius see Ep 867:189n; for Erasmus' subsequent recollections of him cf Allen Ep 1437:192–5.

Greetings. I send you the small book of Greek prayers not bound yet, as you wished. Thank you for the present you sent me, though there would have been no need of it; you know I am devoted to you. As to the note that you sent me back, let me tell you what happened. Your brother comes to our house, knocks at the door; I appear promptly and ask him what he wants, 5 and he gives me what you sent. My master, as luck would have it, while I was opening the door, caught sight of this brother of yours, and asked me whether I had taken in a letter for him. I replied that I had not received anything like that. He asks me again what my business is with your brother. After some hesitation I gave him the worst possible answer, poor fool, that I 1 had had back a note which I had sent for you to see. He flared up at once and would have almost extinguished poor me with his thunderbolts, I mean that irony of his, had I not known my man. It was not that he did not want it shown to you, but he was sure I had done the same with other things. Had I not been a perfect dolt, something else would have come into my head, either 1 about the Greek prayer-book, or I might have thrown in something else that was gospel truth. So I beg you, dear Master Maarten, keep it to yourself; it is a thing of no importance, but because this is what my master wants, I thought it not unreasonable to fall in with his wishes. Make sure however that no one discovers that I have written you this, and when you have read 2 it, please consign it to the flames. If my master ever comes to see you, mind you say nothing about it. Farewell. From the College of the Lily.

Johannes Hovius, Erasmus' servant

902A / To Bruno Amerbach   Louvain, 4 November [1518?]

This letter, which is Ep 705 in Allen's edition, is known only from a nineteenth-century manuscript copy: Öffentliche Bibliothek of the University

* * * * *

902
17 gospel truth] To speak 'from the tripod' like the priestess of the Delphic oracle is to speak the solemn truth (cf *Adagia* I vii 90).

of Basel, MS G II 13a f 54. The date must fall in between Erasmus' arrival at
Louvain and Bruno's death, therefore in 1517 or 1518. With some hesitation
Allen chose 1517; Alfred Hartmann (AK II Ep 637) preferred 1518, and the
connection with other letters of recent date bears this out; see lines 5n and
especially 7n.

ERASMUS TO HIS DEAR BRUNO, GREETING
I recall that some time ago a mistake of some sort was made in the critical
notes on the letters which I rejected as ignorant. Please either send my
original to me here or tell me where the mistake lies, so that it can be put right
in the next edition. I am grateful to you for your help in seeing my things   5
through; you are what you always were. For Froben by some unhappy fate
always likes donkeys. Best wishes; also to your excellent brothers Basilius
and Bonifacius.
    There is an old Greek proverb, 'Nothing worse than three c's.' Now we
can adapt it to you: Nothing better than three B's, Bruno, Basilius,   10
Bonifacius. Give my greetings to Doctor Zasius.
    Louvain, 4 November
    To that excellent scholar Bruno Amerbach of Basel, gifted in the three
tongues. In Basel

903 / To Henricus Glareanus   Louvain, [December?] 1518

From the first sentence it appears likely that Glareanus had sent a letter to Basel
in the autumn (after the one mentioned in Ep 869:26), believing Erasmus still to
be there. This is the answer, which may perhaps have been sent to Paris
together with Ep 906. It was published in the *Epistolae ad diversos*.

ERASMUS TO HENRICUS GLAREANUS, GREETING
Your letter was brought here from Basel and delivered to me by Hieronymus

* * * * *

902A
 2 mistake] The reference apparently is to the critical essays *(censurae)* inserted in
    Erasmus' edition of Jerome's letters *(Hieronymi opera,* Basel 1516, III; cf Ep
    396:315–20) to question the authenticity of a specific text; cf Allen Ep
    1000:27–31.
 5 help] With the proofs of the New Testament. Erasmus had made a plea to the
    Amerbach brothers for help; cf Epp 886:27–8, 904:42n.
 7 donkeys] Cf Ep 885 introduction and line 33.
 9 proverb] Cf *Adagia* III vi 82, referring to the Cappadocians, the Cretans, and the
    Cilicians.

Froben. My affection for you remains quite unimpaired, although my bodily
vigour loses something every day, partly from age and partly from the
constantly increasing burden of my work; most of all from the weariness   5
engendered by those noisy ruffians and their conspiracy against humane
studies and genuine piety. On the society of Johannes Lascaris I warmly
congratulate you; he is always the same, always frank and open in his
encouragement of young men of promise. God grant him a very long life, for
the advancement of the humanities. Do not fail, my dear Glareanus, to equip 1●
yourself in every way you can, that when I have to hand the torch on to you,
you may take my place and throw the name of Erasmus in the shade.
Farewell. Give my greetings to Cyprianus Taleus, to Nicolas Bérault, to
Herman of Friesland, and all my other well-wishers in your part of the world.
       Louvain, 1518   1●

904 / From Lambertus Hollonius   Basel, 5 December 1518

The autograph manuscript of this letter is in the University Library, Wrocław,
MS Rehdiger 254 f 99 (Ep 92).
    Lambert de Hollogne or Hollonius, a young scholar from Liège, was sent to
Basel by Erasmus together with Menard of Hoorn (cf Ep 885:2n). According to
Johann Froben (cf AK II Ep 642) he was an MA and a jurist. Froben was satisfied

* * * * *

903
 3 Froben] Hieronymus Froben (1501–63), the eldest son of Johann Froben and
   subsequently his successor in the Basel press. In 1515 he registered in the
   University of Basel. His visit to Louvain at this time may have lasted for six
   months, or he may have repeated his trip in 1519. In early July 1519 he returned
   from Louvain to Basel with a letter from Johannes Hovius to Beatus Rhenanus (cf
   BRE Ep 416). In it Hovius politely declined a suggestion that he go to Basel and
   work for the Froben press, pointing out that Erasmus could not do without him
   since Hieronymus Froben was unable to take his place in Louvain; cf AK II Ep
   631.
 7 Lascaris] See Epp 865:61, 905:25–7.
11 hand the torch on] Cf Adagia I ii 38.
12 name of Erasmus] Cf Epp 905:24, 906:52–4.
13 Taleus] Taleus lectured on Pliny; cf Ep 768:5n.
13 Bérault] See Ep 925.
14 Herman] Haio Herman of Friesland, of Emden (d 1539/40), was the son of
   Haio Ubbena and Eiske Hompen and a kinsman of the famous Rodolphus
   Agricola. At this time he was a student in Paris. In the summer of 1519 he came
   to stay at the College of the Lily in Louvain and thereafter remained in contact
   with Erasmus. He continued his studies in Paris and Italy and in 1532 became a
   member of the Council of Utrecht; see de Vocht CTL I 393–4, II 13–15; Luther w
   Briefwechsel II Ep 265.

with his work, but Zasius and Beatus Rhenanus were not (cf Ep 862 introduction), although the latter had called him a learned young man (cf BRE Ep 80) and collaborated with him on the ill-advised first edition of Erasmus' *Colloquia* (cf Ep 909 introduction). Hollonius later went to Italy and died in Rome before 25 May 1522; cf Ep 1284. See de Vocht CTL II 24.

TO ERASMUS OF ROTTERDAM, PRINCE OF SCHOLARS, FROM
LAMBERTUS HOLLONIUS, GREETING

On 30 November I wrote you a letter, honoured sir, by a carrier I know from Liège, and so it would be needless to repeat what I said, to avoid a second helping of cabbage. But not being sure whether you have had that letter or 5 no, I thought it best to retell the whole story briefly. And so let me tell you that I have not found the canon of Aachen with whom you had left your sword, because he was said to have gone to Rome, and his servant was not there. All the same, while I was there Dr Leonardus, one of the canons, said he would see that you got it back. At Bedburg, as the count was away, I gave 10 the letter to his steward. Other news you will be able to learn from my letter to Baerland.

I have taken a post with Froben the printer, who at the instance (as the common phrase is) of Rhenanus was glad to take me on. Your man Jacobus is in charge of the revised Testament; it has got as far as the Pauline Epistles, 15 which are printing now. More's *Utopia* approaches the end. It will be followed by a work by Zasius, of which I think Bonifacius Amerbach gave you a taste when you were about to leave here. The plague is rife here; it has carried off my friend and indeed colleague Menard, on which I have written at length to my friend Rutgerus. Froben is sending you a book by 20 Luther, a truly Christian theologian, but unpopular with our strict, not to

* * * * *

904
5 cabbage] Cf *Adagia* I v 38.
7 canon of Aachen] Perhaps Johann Sudermann or Johann Schoenraid; cf Ep 867 introduction and lines 117n, 118n.
9 Leonardus] Priccardus; cf Ep 972 introduction.
10 Bedburg] Hermann von Neuenahr's castle; cf Ep 867:80n.
12 Baerland] See Ep 852:82n.
14 Jacobus] Nepos; cf Ep 864 introduction.
16 *Utopia*] Froben's second edition, with the date of November 1518 in the colophon; cf AK II Ep 642.
17 work by Zasius] See Ep 862 introduction.
18 plague] Cf Ep 861:7n.
20 Rutgerus] Rescius, recently appointed professor of Greek at the Collegium Trilingue in Louvain; cf Epp 546, 691:19n.
20 by Luther] At least two had been printed by Froben by this date. The one he

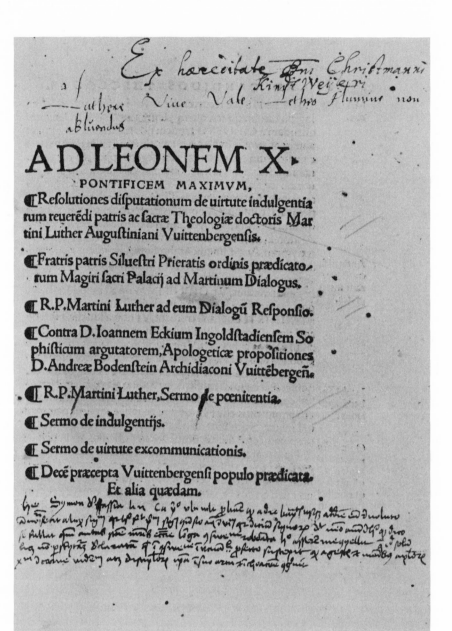

AD LEONEM X·

PONTIFICEM MAXIMVM,

¶ Resolutiones disputationum de uirtute indulgentia
rum reuerédi patris ac sacræ Theologiæ doctoris Mar
tini Luther Augustiniani Vuittenbergensis.

¶ Fratris patris Siluestri Prieratis ordinis prædicato-
rum Magiri sacri Palacij ad Martinum Dialogus.

¶ R.P.Martini Luther ad eum Dialogũ Responsio.

¶ Contra D. Ioannem Eckium Ingoldstadiensem So
phisticum argutatorem, Apologeticæ propositiones
D. Andreæ Bodenstein Archidiaconi Vuittébergeñ.

¶ R.P.Martini Luther, Sermo de pœnitentia.

¶ Sermo de indulgentijs.

¶ Sermo de uirtute excommunicationis.

¶ Decé præcepta Vuittenbergensi populo prædicata.
Et alia quædam.

Martin Luther *Ad Leonem X* title page
Basel: Froben October 1518
By permission of the Houghton Library, Harvard University

say superstitious, characters who dress up as theologians. I cannot tell you how well it has been received by those who are keen on the subject; I at least, who am a mere nobody, have felt my mind set free from its former enslavement to all the most frigid details of ceremonial. How blessed we are 25 to live in an age like this, in which with you to guide and lead us and bring us to perfection both literature and true Christianity are being born again!

The archbishop of Mainz, after two months as a cardinal, has died. What a prey for the Lion!

Well, there is a short, unscholarly, and barely coherent letter for you! 30 You must take it in good part and forgive me if my nonsense offends you. With many, many assurances of my devotion, farewell, O foster-father of good literature.

Basel, 5 December 1518

Greetings from Beatus and Basilius too, and Froben and his wife; all 35 send their best wishes. Johannes Oecolampadius took his degree in theology last week and departed soon after for Augsburg, where he has a post as public preacher. Farewell once more.

* * * * *

enclosed here was most likely the first – the earliest collection of Luther's Latin writings, *Ad Leonem X ... resolutiones disputationum de virtute indulgentiarum ...* (October 1518). By February 1519 Froben had sent six hundred copies to France and Spain alone and other consignments to the Netherlands and England (cf Luther w *Briefwechsel* I Ep 146). Froben only obtained the copy for this collection at the Frankfurt autumn fair of 1518, so Erasmus had left Basel when the edition was undertaken. Froben clearly had no misgivings about sending Luther's book to Erasmus as a gift, and Hollonius had none about expressing his own enthusiasm for it, so evidently Erasmus was not expected to react adversely to it; in fact he may well have expressed himself in Basel much the same way as he did in Ep 872 (cf Ep 967:107n). However, Erasmus' reaction was unequivocal. In letters to correspondents opposed to Luther he claimed that he had not even read the book (cf Epp 961:36–9, 967:110–14), and soon, probably in February or March, when he was under attack in Louvain and accused of connivance with Luther (cf Ep 930:12n), he threatened to end his own co-operation with the Froben press if it continued to publish Luther's writings (cf Epp 938, Allen Epp 1143:20–2, 1526:34–7). The threat worked. It seems that after this only one minor Luther edition was undertaken by the press, allegedly when Froben himself was away to attend the Frankfurt autumn fair of 1519. Froben's collective volume, however, was eagerly picked up by Matthias Schürer in Strasbourg, who published reprints in February and August 1519; see Benzing *Lutherbibliographie* nos 3–5; Volz *Die ersten Sammelausgaben*.

28 has died] A false rumour; for the following allusion to Leo x ('the Lion') cf Ep 891:27n.
35 his wife] Cf Ep 885 introduction.
36 Oecolampadius] He became a DD on 28 November 1518.

When I was about to seal my letter, your Jacobus asked me to add at the same time something he would have written himself if he had had time, that 40 the lives of the Evangelists have been printed in the Testament but only in Greek. Also that Bruno alone is helping him with the proof-correction, and Basilius is doing none of it; and so he is surprised that you have not written to them. Farewell once more.

From your same devoted Lambertus Hollonius of Liège, with his own 45 hand

To the glory of letters and of all literary men, Erasmus of Rotterdam, his most beloved teacher. In Louvain

905 / To Paolo Bombace   Louvain, 13 December 1518

This letter answers the points raised in Bombace's Ep 865. It was published in the *Farrago*.

ERASMUS TO HIS FRIEND PAOLO BOMBACE, GREETING

Truly the Muses and the Graces presided at your cradle! You overwhelm me with so much kindness that I am ashamed of offering you gratitude so often that never gets beyond words, and indeed I cannot always think of fresh ways to express it. His eminence the cardinal of the Santi Quattro Coronati 5 has put me the more in his debt, inasmuch as I had no claims whatever on him. Monsignor Marino Caracciolo, the papal nuncio to the emperor, took great trouble over the business, besides writing me a most kind letter. As to that first copy, I wonder who intercepted it; for I do not see that a letter of this kind can be any use to anyone except the person to whom it is 10 addressed; it would be different if some wealthy bishopric or a splendid benefice were concerned. It grieves me to think of all the extra trouble I have caused you when you were already so busy; but I appreciate these opportunities of seeing your nobility of character more clearly day by day. I only wish this country of ours had even a few people like you. Who ever 15

* * * * *

41 lives] The new edition had both the Latin lives by Jerome and the Greek by Sophronius.

42 Bruno] Cf Ep 902A. His brother, Basilius Amerbach, apparently left Basel for some time because of the plague. Thus he was likewise unable to help with Zasius' book (above line 17; AK II Ep 638). In a final letter at the end of the New Testament dated 5 February 1519, Johann Froben acknowledged the assistance of the brothers but made clear that the bulk of the correction was done by Nepos.

905
5 cardinal] Lorenzo Pucci

displayed more sincere or constant affection for his most distinguished
friend than you have done without recompense for a man of lowly station
like myself, from whom you could hope for no service in return, and all this
when you have so much greater learning and greater fortune than my own?

I cannot guess who the Frenchman was who, you say, disappeared,   20
unless perhaps it is Christophe de Longueil, a young man with a natural gift,
to judge from what he has published, for all liberal disciplines and especially
for writing. He is one of those, if I mistake not, who will one day put the
name of Erasmus in the shade. But this gives me nothing but pleasure, if the
loss of my reputation is a gain to the republic of letters. I cannot think what   25
could drag Johannes Lascaris away from Rome, particularly with Pope Leo at
the head of affairs and of the revival of learning. Please greet the Boerio
brothers most warmly on my behalf.

Your letter did not find me in Basel, nor was Monsignor Antonio Pucci,
the papal nuncio, there at that moment. I had however written to him on this   30
subject while he was at Zürich; for to pay him a visit, which he greatly
desired and I had almost promised, was ruled out by my state of health,
which could not yet allow me to mount a horse, and by my literary labours.
Travelling by water, though it had its drawbacks, gradually allowed me to
recover strength. With the honourable Count Hermann of Neuenahr I spent   35
about five days in great comfort and enjoyed myself so much that I thought I
was almost a new man. But I was soon precipitated into imminent danger, so
that I had to be carried to Louvain more dead than alive, whether I owe this
trouble to the violent and pestilential winds that were then blowing or to my
own folly in risking a journey through the middle of Cologne, when the city   40
was full of death everywhere. Two surgeons successively confirmed that it
was the plague; that three scabs came away I cannot deny. I was in no mood
to be ill, and I did not think it was the plague, and this belief did me good. But
by the mercy of heaven I am now getting better – a great disappointment in
the mean time to those who hate to see the resurgence of a better sort of   45
studies. Farewell.

Louvain, 13 December 1518

* * * * *

21 Longueil] Cf Epp 865:31n, 914 introduction. For Erasmus' acquaintance with an
early piece of work by him cf Ep 935:6, but in the absence of any personal
contacts prior to March 1519 (cf Ep 914:100–2), Erasmus' praise here may seem
exaggerated and out of context; perhaps it is the result of amplification at the
time of printing.
30 written to him] Ep 860
32 health] Cf Ep 847:7n.
34 water] See Ep 867 with the details of Erasmus' journey to Louvain and his
sickness.

906 / To Guillaume Budé   Louvain, 22 December 1518

This letter offers a second and fuller answer to Ep 810 and also answers Ep 896. Budé in turn answered with Ep 915. All were published in the *Farrago*. For the uneasy relationship reflected in this profuse letter cf the preface to this volume.

ERASMUS OF ROTTERDAM, PERPETUAL FRIEND OF GUILLAUME BUDÉ WHETHER HE WILL OR NO, WISHETH HIM ALL PROSPERITY, NOT FOR THE LAST TIME, AND MAY IT LAST FOR EVER AND EVER
On top of that scolding epistle that reached me in Basel here comes a fresh one like some official missive carried by an envoy extraordinary, formally 5 and openly denouncing our ancient treaty of friendship and declaring war to the death for the future. Let me start, my dear Budé, by wishing you joy of that state of blessedness which leaves you with time and spirits for these pleasantries; for this is proof enough that a friend whose prosperity I have much at heart is not only flourishing but gay and happy. Consequently, 10 though I myself this whole year and a half have been immersed in researches of such a kind that neither body nor spirit is equal to the burden (especially since my tedious load was made heavier by the knowledge that I was labouring mainly for an ungrateful public and prejudiced critics); though my evil genius has tormented me with so many cruel attacks of illness and other 15 cares and disappointments which I need not now go into (for, though you congratulate me on returning to Louvain safe and sound, I was in fact deposited there more dead than alive) – in spite of all this, I say, even in the midst of a storm of troubles your lively letter cheered me or at least made me feel better, although to return your pleasantries and give you some sort of tit 20 for tat, which I would greatly have enjoyed, I certainly had neither liberty nor leisure. Not but what even now I am not sufficiently recovered to satisfy myself or my friends, such was the severity of my illness; unless you prefer to ascribe the trouble to excessive overwork. So after all I will send a single answer to both your letters –treatises rather – but before doing so I must get 25 one solemn undertaking out of you on oath: you must believe me when I say I

* * * * *

906
4 epistle] Ep 810
5 official missive] Erasmus is referring to the *fetiales*, the three envoys, accompanied by another delegate, the *pater patratus*, who were sent out by ancient Rome to demand satisfaction and declare war if they did not get it. Cf the salutation of Ep 896.
11 year and a half] That is, since he settled in Louvain; cf Ep 864 introduction.
17 congratulate me] Ep 896:111–12; for Erasmus' sickness on arrival see Ep 867.

am absolutely convinced that whatever you write, be it grave or gay, is the fruit of friendship deep and sincere, and you must believe the same of me and credit me when I swear by the god of friendship if you will not accept my unsupported word.   30

Your complete sincerity was the first thing I emphasized to Beatus Rhenanus. I make the same point quite clear in my last letter, which in your usual playful way you call indignant. There is no one whose letters I enjoy as much as yours, and I get profit of all sorts out of them as well as enjoyment. To begin with, whether you are disputing with me or joking or attacking me,   35 I end up having learnt something, for nothing comes from you in your most careless moments that others can equal when they write with the greatest care. And then your copious flow of language rouses me in my lethargy, your warmth puts an edge on me when I am cold, your ever-flowing abundance criticizes and corrects my thin, dry style. Finally, since the chief   40 pleasure in life, in my opinion, is to pass one's idle hours in the company of loyal friends, what more delightful thing could come one's way than to converse by exchange of letters with such a special friend? Indeed, when I read your letters, written with such a high degree of literary skill, I seem somehow to have a more lively impression than if I were listening to you face   45 to face, for all that you are such an entertaining companion in the flesh.

This pleasure I renew from time to time by rereading your letters after an interval; and again when I show them to friends my enjoyment is as fresh as if they had only just reached me for the first time. Even supposing that the gain in reputation I thus acquire were not brought to account in the mean   50 while, a man with his eye on posterity will find it in my view far from negligible. Let my own works die with their author or (more likely) before he does; yet our descendants will speak of a certain Erasmus as one whom the great Budé did not dislike or think wholly of no account. This is an ambition (to speak frankly) of which I am not ashamed, nor would I unsay it. And so   55 when I saw that long elaborate letter of yours all ready to be published, I was afraid of losing some of this reputation, afraid that posterity might judge that between Budé and Erasmus there was not the same affectionate relationship that I had hoped might appear, and that I believe there is. I had reason to fear

* * * * *

31 Beatus] Cf Ep 869:9–14.
33 indignant] Ep 896:5
45 face to face] Budé and Erasmus may have met in Paris, but nowhere else, it seems, is there any evidence of personal contact.
52 die] Cf Ep 903:11–12.
56 letter] Ep 810; down to line 69 below Erasmus is responding to Budé's postscript to Ep 896.

the same loss of face among friends of mine who do not know and   60
understand your nature intimately at first hand. This seemed to affect you
almost more than me, for I should be more or less protected, I thought, from
any such suspicion by my writings, if any should chance to survive. But
there remained a risk that someone might form a wrong idea of Budé's heart,
though nothing can be more sincere. So I foresaw two possible results: if I   65
showed my friends the letter, some loss of reputation was inevitable, and if I
did not show it, I must be deprived of part of my enjoyment. This fear at the
time possessed my mind; but I will dismiss it gladly, such as it is, on your
advice, if you seriously tell me to do so.

The point here is not how skilled I am at taking humour and pleasantry,   70
but what men are likely to think of us who form their opinion on our
published books alone. I know there is a kind of Gallic wit which is quite
unbridled, which lets itself go almost too freely and by severe and sober
critics might be thought very close to insolence. I thought I had noticed at
close quarters that you by nature very much delight in this kind of   75
pleasantry, especially at the expense of people you particularly like, so that
you can enjoy yourself at will, almost as the great ones of the earth habitually
keep some humble friend as a favourite at the lower table, not far above their
own household, at whose expense they can say and do what they like for
their own amusement. Nor should I grudge you this entertainment, if what   80
passed had no spectators except such as know us both well and are likely to
put as favourable an interpretation on our humour as I do myself. As it is,
you can see how even the most straightforward remarks are twisted by most
people into accusations; and in these days every place is full of people like
that, on the lookout for mischief. What do you suppose they will say when   85
they read joking remarks of yours which look exactly like serious abuse –
remarks which scarcely any besides myself can appreciate or interpret as not
serious?

Next, I admit readily enough that I rank below you no less in literary
gifts than in worldly position, and (this I know you will not deny) it was your   90
scholarship and not your money-bags, it was the Muse and not our lady of
Rhamnus that brought us together or, rather, bound me so closely to you. I
wish you well of your prosperity, but it is your intelligence I love and admire.
I have no doubt whatever that you hold your worldly fortunes for the benefit
of all your friends and not for yourself alone; but it is out of what you write   95

* * * * *

72 Gallic wit] Cf Epp 636:15–16, 961:42–8, 967:175–6, suggesting French origins
  for the *Julius exclusus*.
92 Rhamnus] A shrine of Nemesis, whom Erasmus does not distinguish from
  Fortune; cf *Adagia* II vi 38.

that I so much enjoy enriching myself, and this source is no whit diminished
by your generosity towards everyone. Against your purse I have never yet
harboured any designs, nor taken anything from it. Nor should a man be
considered as in modest circumstances if he is contented with his lot. I rather
think that between scholars some other subject for pleasantry would be   100
appropriate, especially if they are close friends. Cicero jokes at the expense
of his friend Trebatius, Ausonius plays with his Symmachus, Pliny enjoys a
pleasantry with two or three of his acquaintance. This kind of humour I
doubt if you will find anywhere in the works of the learned. These lighter
passages are commonly added here and there, as though to season serious   105
discourse. But what sort of a style are we to call it when the whole discourse
from head to foot, as they say, contains nothing but flouts and japes and
innuendoes?

Be that as it may, the exchange of pleasantries between friends should
certainly be mutual. Otherwise the effect will be, not of friends exchanging   110
jokes with one another, but of some great man letting fly at a professional
butt whom he has hired with a place at his table. As it is, if I say anything at
all unguarded or outspoken, you treat it as monstrous abuse; if I soften down
something which might have seemed too outspoken so as not to give offence,
I am a flatterer and a toady; if I happen to say anything in jest, you take me up 115
as though it contained some hidden meaning. These are the most unfair
conditions within which I am confined: if I answer your jokes seriously, I am
thought to infringe the dignity of a powerful friend; if I repay one joke with
another, I am accused of a concealed attack; if I answer you mildly, I am said
to be humble and grovelling; and if I say nothing, this is fear of a man more   120
influential than myself. Tell me, my dear Budé, in the name of all the Muses,
what was there even in that earlier letter, the publication of which you
regret, that let fly at you so wantonly, indeed that was not friendly and
respectful? I had heard that some people were indignant merely with the fact
that I had dared to answer Lefèvre; others, that I had answered him with   125
some freedom. I wished to placate this latter class, once you had given me an
opening by your letter of protest. So I put forward my dilemma, and this is

* * * * *

100 subject for pleasantry] Erasmus prefers to assume that Budé was joking when
he relayed the royal offer; see Epp 810:453–4, 896:91–4.
102 Trebatius] In the seventh book of his *Epistolae ad familiares*
102 Ausonius] A professor in Bordeaux in the fourth century AD; he and Pliny the
Younger were obvious names to choose as having left behind some correspondence with their friends.
123 regret] Ep 778; cf Ep 896:43–5.
127 letter of protest] Ep 744

my argument: if you give me advice you are too late, and if you are rebuking me you do it without cause.

But I having rashly added to the first part a mention of Epimetheus, because on that subject you had issued a belated warning, what a turmoil you proceed to raise! 'Now, dear brother Prometheus,' you say, 'have you forgotten saying in your letter?' as though you were fastening some monstrous charge upon me, so that I cannot deny it. And a little later 'Pray, dear Erasmus,' you say, 'bite your lip and let me borrow your patience for a little while, while I upbraid you in my turn.' And then again 'For from time to time you slap me or box my ears.' Will not anyone who believes this take me for an abusive fellow, as much of a stranger as can be to the Graces – though with my temperament I would rather not hurt a friend even in fun? I think it happens to you sometimes that you have some good remarks stored up and are afraid of their being lost, so you use them for no better reason than to avoid wasting them. These are pretty remarks all right, I agree, if they were uttered in the right place. And in order to find a place for them, you put words into my mouth which are quite alien to my own character and feelings. 'So what is the object of speaking out now? Unless you wish to give the impression of giving a black mark, or a black-and-white one, to my *Apologia*; for you nearly always under-value my work on some preconceived principles, misusing (some people think) your confidence in our long-standing friendship.' This is the remark you attribute to me, then turn round and contradict it, changing character all of a sudden, defendant one minute and prosecutor the next. Your victory is assured if the judges give you so much freedom that, when it suits you, you can answer for me as well as for yourself. And yet you were answering my letter, in which nothing of the sort is to be found. But at this point it will appear, I know, that you were simply joking. All the same, were you joking then too, when you said 'I simply must reply to your letter, which was elegantly written and successful in point of style, but in fairness and sympathy left something to be desired'? Pray consider whether that looks like another of your jests: 'At that point you should give advance warning that you are planning a defence, and I perhaps

130
132
139
145
155

* * * * *

130 Epimetheus] Cf Ep 778:116n.
132 you say] Ep 810:37–57
139 hurt a friend] Cf Ep 39:84–5.
145 'So what is the object] In the original of this letter, as it was sent to Budé, Erasmus must have written 'you say' (*inquis*) after 'object,' whereas Budé's text (Ep 810:47–51), which he was quoting, had the hypothetical 'you will say' (*inquies*). In Ep 915:149–56 Budé protested against this change, and when publishing this letter Erasmus omitted the word altogether.
155 'I simply must] Ep 810:52–4, and the following citation, lines 42–6

should have performed my function. It was you made me an Epimetheus; for 160
all you cared, I was not to discover that the play was to be produced until you
had already sent someone on the stage to speak the prologue.'

Those were your words, all very elegant and scholarly, no doubt. I
might perhaps have done what you tell me to do, had I then had my Budé at
my elbow. The wounds which Lefèvre had dealt me I did not feel for some 165
time, and in Louvain there was no one at that moment (for I was a new
arrival) on whose advice I could set much store or trust it. You perhaps
would have told me to reply in a more temperate spirit and with more
restraint, and that is what I was the first to tell myself at the time. I am not so
undisciplined by nature as you make me out to be, nor was I at that time so 170
deeply moved as you imagine. It was in sorrow that I wrote that *Apologia*, not
in anger or resentment. You are welcome to disbelieve me, if any mortal ever
heard me, when the pain of that wound was still fresh, using angry words
about Lefèvre, even over the wine. I therefore thought at the time that I was
in my sound senses; and some people I could name thought so too, who are 175
Lefèvre's keenest supporters and proud of being his pupils. Their opinion
seems to me, on this point at any rate, to carry ever so slightly more weight
than yours and your friends', whose judgment I value most highly in other
respects. I might take the point that the French naturally support a
Frenchman and exercise my right to reject jurors for partiality. You were, as I 180
said, a long way away, and the case called for immediate action. I might, I
suppose, have consulted you; you would have summoned a committee of
your friends; and a year later the pronouncement of the oracle might have
reached me. But why was I expected to consult you rather than all my other
friends? Were you the only one who descried the proper course? Have the 185
rest no eyes? Assuming that you do not let me be judge in my own case.

Now, suppose I had consulted several friends: it may be they would all
have advised me to moderate my *Apologia*. I should have undertaken to do
so. At this point again, what might have seemed very mild to me might have
appeared to one or other of them not nearly mild enough; or was it your idea 190
that my *Apologia* should be reproduced in several copies by the scriveners
and circulated to Germany, Spain, England, and France before being set up
in type? If only we could do that with all the books we publish! Yet even if
one takes no count of expense, it is difficult, for one thing, to have many
ideas on someone else's work; and for another, I can scarcely find a single 195
friend with the leisure to attend to what other people have written, for it
needs a good deal of attention. It is easier to find people to read a published
work in order to pick it to pieces than those who will go through something

* * * * *

165 for some time] Cf Ep 597:37n.

before publication and correct it. In the end, since my friends' opinions would have varied here too, surely the question, what do we mean by 'mild,' would come back to me for decision? Granted that a man could be found with time to spare, where is there a flute-player so reliable that he could stand by me, and I sing soft or loud to match his accompaniment? This whole business of writing and printing was polished off within about a fortnight. There were many witnesses, so do not suspect me of embroidery. And do not think I have devoted so much time or energy to this controversy that I needed advice from you to recall me to sacred study and restore me to my true self from some sort of exile: consider what I have written in the mean time, and you will see that your advice was not required.

But suppose that I lost my temper and did pay too little attention to the way I ought to behave: does this mean that I made an Epimetheus of you? If a man had fallen into a well and your advice was 'You ought to have gone the other way; you would not have fallen in if you had listened to good advice,' would not the man be justified in replying 'I wish you had warned me in time; what I need now is not advice but help'? Though your answer to this latter point is to say you were thinking of my future. Can you find anything to that effect in your letter? Had you said 'You made an intemperate answer to Lefèvre; in future kindly do not be so stupid,' it was possible to understand what you meant. As it is, I am Erasmus and no Oedipus. For I could not even guess that you would put this interpretation on what you call your advice. If you fill such a long letter with criticism of a friend, who has made a mistake if you like, and all the time do nothing for him, what has become of my fairminded old friend Budé? All you do is to distort and exaggerate a friend's mistake and reopen a wound that was already beginning to heal over. There remained one way of being really helpful, if you had made up the quarrel between him and me. This kind office you obstinately refused to perform, though Ruzé was insisting on it, and yet in the beginning of your letter you call yourself a peacemaker, against whom 'I have taken offence passionately, and have suddenly turned my horns.' If you are jesting in both places, I think your jests ought at least to be consistent. Which was it you were afraid of, that I should attack Lefèvre again after being so reluctant to defend myself against him (a thing that you too seem to understand) or that he would make a fresh attack on me? When I

* * * * *

204 fortnight] Cf Ep 597:37n.
207 advice from you] Cf Ep 810:332–4.
216 my future] Cf Ep 810:221–34, referring to Ep 744.
219 Oedipus] Cf *Adagia* I iii 36.
227 Ruzé] See Ep 869:17n.
228 peacemaker] Ep 810:16, 21

assure you that I have no fear of this, you declare there is absolutely no
danger and make fun of the suspicions of my friends; although none of my   235
friends in fact suspected it – it was a rumour set on foot by certain people
who side with Lefèvre, or at least wish me no good. For I myself have always
thought too well of Lefèvre and also of his learned friends and disciples to
be afraid of anything of the sort from them. I was more afraid of ignorant and
noisy wretches, with whom it is discreditable even to engage in controversy.   240

Meanwhile you open up again this question of my 'trivialities.' On this
subject I have never felt any resentment and never expressed any, and yet
you describe me as returning to the subject because I cannot 'control my
indignation'; and this you infer pretty brazenly from the passage where I
assure you that I was not moved in the very least, so much so that when   245
certain German friends gave this a very impatient reception, I made fun of
them instead of trying to pacify them. What then is the point of those fierce
and formidable words: 'Is this necessary? If I say something to you as an old
acquaintance, relying on the privilege of friendship, must you unsheath the
flashing blade of your eloquence against me? In order to oblige your rather   250
passionate spirit, must you have the law on me until it is satisfied?' and much
that follows to the same effect? If you are serious when you write this, where
in anything of mine do you find this uncontrolled bad temper? Where is this
wrangling? Where do I rely on my patroness Minerva and supported by the
resources of eloquence fight against justice? If you are jesting, by what signs   255
can a reader who knows neither of us detect that it is only a jest, when you
give such a lifelike performance as an angry man that anyone genuinely
indignant could not express himself better than your counterfeit of him? If
you wish to engage your friend in that Spartan game that normally ends in
weals and bruises, to teach me endurance I suppose, mind you do not   260
provoke the criticism that it is not exactly well timed to do this to a man rather
older than you are, while Lycurgus' matches with their bloody outcome were
exercise only for young men. There is now a danger that it will occur to
someone to say something about you like Plato's famous retort to Diogenes.
Diogenes had trodden on Plato's luxurious cushions and said he was   265
treading on Plato's vainglory. 'So you do,' said Plato, 'but with vainglory of

* * * * *

235 suspicions] Epp 810:186–8; cf 721 introduction.
241 'trivialities'] Cf Ep 810:62–3.
244 the passage] Ep 778:218–20
248 'Is this necessary?'] Ep 810:68–72
259 Spartan game] Perhaps a reminiscence of Plutarch *Lycurgus* 16.9
261 rather older] Budé was born in 1468 and was thus hardly younger than
    Erasmus.
264 Plato's … retort] Diogenes Laertius 6.26

another sort.' It is to be feared therefore that someone, when he sees the
indignant letters in which you castigate my indignation, may say to you
likewise 'You scold him for being indignant, but yours is indignation of
another sort.' In any case you act the indignant man; you are not angry.   27
Granted that it is an act, it is certainly a very clever one, like that of the actor
in Lucian playing Ajax who broke two or three people's heads in the process
and frightened plenty more. But he was wearing an actor's mask; you are not
in character, and you are dealing with a friend. Surely, if anyone could see
your face as you speak or write like this, he might understand that your   27
savage words are merely a jest. But as it is, a reader cannot see a writer's face;
he must judge what he means from what he writes.

More of this elsewhere; now I will take your letter in order. You say
that if I had still been free to choose, you would have advised me to overlook
what Lefèvre has written against me, though in the same letter you admit   28
that, if the case were being heard in your court, you would not deprive me of
the right to defend myself but would limit the time allowed me. How this
plan would work out, I make for the moment no estimate. Of one thing I am
absolutely certain – that some scholars I could name, men of by no means
negligible reputation, when they read that attack by Lefèvre were anxious   28
on my behalf; and that when my defence came out, they laid aside all their
fears and expressed their satisfaction at my innocence. How many people do
you suppose there would have been among those who read Lefèvre's attack
on me with some attention, who would balance what we wrote one against
the other, seeing that most men would have thought me sufficiently   29
condemned by the fact that I had been attacked by Lefèvre, and attacked to
such a tune that I was unable to reply?

And on this point you use arguments of which (if you don't mind my
saying so) you ought to be ashamed. First, when you say that I have reached
a level of reputation which makes it needless for me to depend in future on   29
eulogies from other men; then you go on to say that Lefèvre touched on me
in the course of defending his own writings, when at that point there was no
call for him to mention me at all; besides which, you call my *Apologia*, which is
short considering the size of the issues involved and the speed with which it
is known to have been put together, a 'long and carefully thought-out   30

* * * * *

270 act] Cf Ep 896 introduction.
272 Lucian] *De saltatione* 83
278 You say] Ep 810:79–83
280 you admit] Ep 810:352–6
282 limit the time] Erasmus is thinking of the waterclock; cf Ep 867:21n.
294 you say] Ep 810:87–99

defence'; lastly, you assume that I should have run no risk in the world of scholars, even had I not replied to Lefèvre or had replied carelessly. I have never sought for reputation or aimed my labours at any target of the kind – a charge, my dear Budé, which you bring against me rather often. I have not reached such a pitch of reputation that it is safe for me to hold my peace when   305
someone brings charges against me such as Lefèvre brought, nor is my reply to him biting or savage, but friendly and fairminded. It moves me not at all that your language makes so little of something in reality so outrageous – 'one who somehow or other casts some reflection on you' and 'at some point thinks differently, as often happens, about what you have written' and 'if   310
any author passes some wrong judgment on you.' These astonishing understatements, when the facts are known, are not much less outrageous than if, in consoling a man who has had an elephant stolen from him, one were to call it the mark of a dismal spirit to be cast down by the loss of some mere paltry quadruped, or if one told the loser of an enormous emerald that it   315
is unmanly to let oneself be tormented by the loss of a single coloured stone.

But suppose we attribute all I have mentioned hitherto to your sense of humour, I still find in you a lack of consistency. Though in a later letter you declare me the winner, you call my defence at this point 'wrong' and 'disputatious.' Then in the Greek that comes after that you have softened a   320
little and allow me eloquence, but with the proviso that I have no system or method of using it, exactly as if you were trusting a madman with a sword. Then you expect me to produce the entire works of Jerome, as though I have justified an error of my own by his example. Quite the contrary: I maintain that I did not return a ferocious answer, as he did, though I was under   325
greater provocation than he was. So that it is no longer relevant when you maintain so loudly that Jerome and Augustine were only human; for it is abundantly clear that you are only jesting when you say you half wonder whether it was because of what he wrote against Rufinus that Jerome was brought before the judgment-seat of Christ and whipped. For that famous   330
dream, as he tells us himself, came to him when he was a youth, and he was

* * * * *

318 a later letter] Ep 896:63–7
319 at this point] Ep 810:107–33: Erasmus continues his scrutiny of Budé's letter line by line.
330 that famous dream] A vision, taken seriously at first, in which Jerome had beheld himself being accused before God's tribunal of excessive love for the pagan classics. Later in his life he believed that the experience was a dream of no consequence (cf 'Vita Hieronymi' *Opuscula* 153–4, 176–7). Jerome's dream had symbolic importance for Renaissance humanists and for Erasmus in particular. In reply, Budé admitted his lack of familiarity with Jerome; see Ep 915:86–90.

an old man when he wrote against Rufinus, and he was writing to Augustine later still.

I pass over deliberately much that you invent at your own sweet will: when you say, for example, that I gave you a rough passage in my long letter as though you had betrayed our friendship and sided with my opponent or reduced the current value of my works by the excessive freedom of your letters. Anyone who reads this will at once look for this quarrelsome letter of mine; while in the letters which survive I have not so far given this topic a single word. After that, you mock me in your most ironical vein for having added in passing that all orthodox writers ancient and modern are in the same position in which Lefèvre puts me; for I myself was negligible, as far as that topic is concerned. Granted that those distinguished characters need no defence from me, I shall certainly be seen to have had more excuse for defending against Lefèvre a view which I share with so many eminent men. Besides which, let them be never so eminent, no one is ever blamed for defending even the greatest from false accusations; are there not people who write books to defend Christ himself against impious calumnies? Nor is it sufficient compensation for me to make common cause with men of the greatest distinction, if they are excused for their antiquity while I am called to account.

What follows in your letter is much the same. I had written that had I met Lefèvre's attack by attacking him myself, I could plead the familiar and universal principle that the use of force is justified in repelling force, though I maintain that I did not take advantage of my rights; and yet you argue against me as though I had admitted using them. He attacks me with innuendoes, and I reply with arguments: is this using force to repel force? You say that this clause was not incorporated by the Supreme Judge in his law or code of practice; and yet rank upon rank of theologians recognize the principle, which they would hardly do, I suppose, if it conflicted with Christ's prohibition. How can you find that I have failed to respect the limits of justifiable self-defence, when in return for being attacked with unpleasant insults I discharge no insult in reply? Unless you judge it equivalent to an insult if I reject a malignant attack and the resulting unpopularity falls of its own accord on the man who spread the lie. What am I to do if you find my *Apologia* rather too long and too outspoken? I adjusted the length to suit my own feelings, not having access to yours as a standard. Nor is there any reason to cast the blame for this mistake on friends who spurred me on. I took

* * * * *

334 much] Cf Ep 810:134–42.
352 What follows] Ep 810:159–65; cf Ep 778:197–202.
362 justifiable self-defence] Cf *Codex Justinianus* 8.4.1.

no one's advice except my own. It was printed almost before anyone knew
that it had gone to press. I made haste all the more to avoid being held up for   370
long by a business as unpleasant as it was necessary. What I had to do was
dictated by the facts. I am sorry that I was attacked by the last man I would
wish; but so far am I from repenting of my *Apologia* that if anyone were to
attack me today like that, and attack me without my deserving it, I should
prepare a similar *Apologia* tomorrow, whether milder or less mild I cannot   375
say. This is the one form of dispute in which gentleness does not appeal to
me; and yet in that *Apologia* of mine, whatever its length, you will find less
bad temper than in your friendly and humorous and witty letter, in which
you divert yourself at your friend's expense.

Here is another of your highly witty observations: 'Who would be   380
surprised if you were to make him unhappy on a point where you are not
happy yourself?' Just as if an innocent man on trial before the Areopagus for
burglary or sacrilege were to abandon his defence simply because he
disapproved of being compelled to defend himself. The dissatisfaction felt by
Lefèvre is very different from what I feel myself; my own discomfort is like   385
that of a man bitten by a scorpion, while he applies the antidote. So this
remark is not so eminently witty as it seems at first sight. Then you go on to
add that I have made an attack on you, when I accuse you falsely of reducing
the value of my work and making light of my *Copia*. You shameless talker!
What you wrote about my poor books still exists. So far is it from giving me   390
offence that I make excuses for it and put the best sense on it that I can. And
you make me out to be a scandalmonger; you find me lacking in fairminded-
ness because I try to blacken your name among my friends – all of whom you
represent as raging like wild animals because two or three of them were not
entirely satisfied with your attack on my *Copia*. I have not forgotten, you see,   395
what you wrote to Tunstall about my pieces; but since you say everything in
jest, where are you more likely to be only jesting than in the place where you
speak so highly of my work?

But, after joking all this time, you say that you propose to be serious in
what follows. You repeat that in my letter I do not hesitate to treat you as a   400
hostile witness, though nothing of the sort can be found anywhere. But
what you say seriously now, you said not long ago in jest. Then you remark
that even if both of us asked you to arbitrate, you would not willingly

* * * * *

380 witty observations] Ep 810:191–3
382 Areopagus] Cf Ep 915:91n.
387 you go on] Ep 810:206–9; for *De copia* see Ep 260 introduction.
396 to Tunstall] Ep 583
399 you say] Ep 810:212–18, also for the following comments
402 in jest] Ep 810:196–205

undertake it. Where has that peacemaker vanished to, whom I was scaring away with lowered horns? After that, you urge me to resume our original friendship. Get Lefèvre to accept your idea if you can, for I have been urging him to do this myself in ever so many letters, not the least deterred by the malice of those who keep saying that I do this from fear, not from a true Christian spirit. I undertook that I would alter all the passages in which I had differed from him, if he would either alter or defend the points I had noted. I promised that I would do my best to extinguish my *Apologia*, provided he would call off his attack. Finally I advised him, besought him even, to publish something that would make it clear that we were agreed in spirit and thus deprive those who wish good or ill – some to him, some to me – of their excuse for fighting our battle for us. He never paid me the courtesy of a reply, even by way of a third party; and yet I still do not cease to be friends with Lefèvre. After all which, you make me out to be violent and savage. You express the hope that this minor damage to my reputation will somehow heal over. Yet what else is the result of that letter of yours, which deplores the fate of both of us at such length and exaggerates the whole business in the most tragic tones, except to rub off the scab which had somehow begun to close the wound?

On top of that you urge me to follow your example and never hereafter, however much I am attacked, to descend into the fray – as though your affair and mine had anything in common! In your discussions, maybe, someone objected that you had explained some passage in a way that he himself could not approve. Let him be ever so successful, no penalty awaits the defeated party except that you may be thought to have been careless at that point, or to have overlooked something which did not occur to you or even which you might not have read. In my case the rules of the contest are very different – if indeed contest is the word, when an attempt is made on my life and all I do is to defend myself. And yet you too wish one exception to be reserved for you, in a cause by no means parallel: 'if you see your silence being turned to your discredit or likely to do you serious harm.' But why are you unwilling for me to enjoy this exception too? For when you say it would have done no harm to my reputation to have held my tongue, you are not, in

* * * * *

409 I undertook] The promise was repeated in the *Apologia ad Fabrum* (LB IX 20A), where Erasmus claimed that it was originally made in two letters to Lefèvre. They are now missing but were evidently prior to the *Apologia*.
410 I promised] Ep 778:184–6
412 advised him] Ep 814:27–9
418 express the hope] Ep 810:226–7
423 you urge] Ep 810:294–301
433 'if you see] Ep 810:300–1

my view, sufficiently convinced of this yourself, however much you attempt
to convince me. I only wish I had plenty of friends like that, people of
all-round intelligence and insight, who could give me definite instructions
when and how far to answer my opponent. Friends of this kind are perhaps
not to be had in our barbarous country; no, they are all as short-sighted as I
am myself. Nor will I concede, my dear Budé, that you hate and abominate a
venomous dispute any more strongly than I do. Nor do I think myself in
danger of any such accusation, seeing that it was under compulsion and
after such provocation that I replied to Lefèvre.

Then again when, in the middle of all this, you set me on a pinnacle of
glory and declare the name Erasmus world-famous, and more of the same
sort, I think you are simply jesting, however much you may declare you are
serious; for there are other places too where you dress me in the lion's skin
and make me out to be some great prophet of piety and literary high-priest,
secure of immortality already and famous beyond any peradventure. And
yet you talk to this reverend divine in the accents a mother would use to a
small child; or rather, you are a brutal schoolmaster, frightening me and
punishing me now with the cane and now the birch. In fact, whatever this
glory is that you hope to share with me, when you say 'we who have long
been slaves in the dreary and toilsome service of ambition,' I do not accept it,
and recommend that you transfer my share to some other recipient. I should
be a most unhappy creature had I sacrificed all those nightly vigils to
ambition.

At this point you again make many somewhat rash assumptions: I
indulged, you say, in mutual recriminations with Lefèvre, while it is
characteristic of a good man that his 'innocence should rely on its own force
and its own merits and not try to win acceptance by defending itself against
other men's calumnies.' In my view, the good man is not he who takes no
thought for his reputation, especially when it is attacked in this way and
(what is more) in print. I need not go into details: what you say has been
often humorous, often serious, often simply to be taken at its face value; you
have been full of arguments, full of generalizations; but it all comes down to
this, that you have no wish to see me suffer for having defended myself
hitherto, but you warn me of danger if I add one word more. On the question
at issue between us you make no pronouncement; you consider that it

* * * * *

446 set me] Ep 810:314–16, 337–8
449 lion's skin] Cf Adagia I iii 66.
455 you say] Ep 810:308–9
461 while] Reading quum; Ep 810:348–50
470 warn me] Ep 810:330

should be adjourned. One point there is in which you find me deficient: my defence should be somewhat shorter, and more moderate in tone. My first point is that since, as I said before, I could not adjust the level of my style to suit everybody's feelings, I adjusted it to suit my own, especially as I was hurt rather than angry. If you bring into the account how much more time on the clock used to be allowed to the defendant than to the prosecutor, and at the same time compare my *Apologia* with Lefèvre's attack, you will understand that here too I have not been very grasping – all the more so if you consider the kind of accusation, and how much easier it is to throw mud than to wipe it off. That is why in certain types of case it is the custom to give defending counsel several spells of the clock above the traditional number. Again, I can only congratulate you on your happy temper, that citadel from which you cannot be lured down into the battlefield. Even so, you loose off long-range missiles from your citadel to such a tune that it is not hard to guess what you would be like, if you were to be shaken by a tenth part of the siege-train concentrated on me. You do not even feel all the battering-rams with which I am assailed on every side. The more happy you for not knowing what it is like! And I hope it may never come your way, this experience of being in conflict with such a tribe of monsters rather than men, who call themselves theologians and are merely purveyors of falsehood. I have no quarrel with theologians as a class, only with some I could name who are unworthy of that rank and title.

Just lately, if you please, there arose a little creature, pale and skinny – which might surprise you, for no man ever had a better conceit of himself – childishly crazed by a thirst for glory, turned Grecian overnight and two days ago Hebraist as well, so effectively that he allows no merit even to Jerome or to Reuchlin. With a natural gift for innuendo, he stops at nothing, tries his hand at everything to make himself a name; and this he thinks is the short cut. He does not deserve a reply, unless one should wish to return good for evil, and yet the little serpent is too venomous to be endured. No place is free from his falsehoods, as he rambles round street-corners, crossroads, markets, churches, monasteries. Everyone gets his letters, full of outrageous calumnies. Yet this mountebank has his followers, with their enthusiastic applause and cries of 'Bravo'; it is always so, every thistle finds its donkey. And while behaving like this he even thinks himself halfway to a halo, as though one qualified for perfect sanctity merely by abstention from

* * * * *

472 adjourned] Ep 810:328–9
483 citadel] Ep 810:318–19
494 little creature] Edward Lee; cf Epp 898A, 998, Allen 1061:420–4.
505 every thistle] Cf *Adagia* I x 71.

adultery or gambling. I have not yet made up my mind how to deal with him. If he proves too much for my patience, I shall see to it that others are not as well pleased with him as he is with himself. I make no other promise for the 510 moment, though he promises mountains of gold and more on his own account; and I shall ensure that out of me he gets more notoriety than glory.

But to return to your letter. You say the decision on the whole case is still within your power. Far from it: I never gave you power to decide. All I gave you was an invitation, if you so wished, to pronounce whether I did 515 wrong in replying to Lefèvre, or in replying as I did; and so that you might do this with greater certainty, I asked you at your leisure to run through what we have both written. Yet on this point you clearly decide against me, first, for answering when I should have done better to have held my tongue; secondly, for answering too carefully and at too great length; and finally, for 520 answering with some feeling. For whether the reading should be *ab angelis* (than the angels) or *a Deo* (than God) is not for me to decide; it is other people's business. Besides which, that the abuse Lefèvre heaps on me is nothing to do with me is clear on the facts; no judge need do the sum. Nor has anyone any call to protest that he was overborne by my powerful 525 eloquence; I have no powerful eloquence and make no claim to have. He had only himself to blame; it was he who made an unfortunate choice of ground on which to challenge me.

Bishop Giustiniani has visited us at Louvain. He seemed to me a friendly person with no animosity in him; so I am sorry that I spoke 530 slightingly of him in my *Apologia*. I had put a special mark on that page and

* * * * *

511 mountains of gold] Cf *Adagia* i ix 15.
513 You say] Ep 810:213–14
522 *a Deo*] Cf Ep 778:203n.
524 clear on the facts] 'res ipsa loquitur'; *Adagia* iii iv 49
529 Giustiniani] His visit took place during Erasmus' convalescence, shortly before 19 October. In Epp 877:13–17, 878:2–5 Erasmus said he had more 'vanity than venom' but also mentioned that he was holding an appointment from the French king. Thus a letter to Budé, destined for publication, offered a suitable context for the apology which was due to Giustiniani. In the *Apologia ad Fabrum* (LB IX 25C–E) Erasmus had called Giustiniani's psalter (cf Ep 810:397n) 'divine' and 'straight down from heaven,' but the praise was evidently ironical and followed by some openly critical remarks. Although Giustiniani was not named in the text, his identity was evident from the appended section of Lefèvre's commentary to which Erasmus replied. Giustiniani's name was added on the margin of Froben's edition of the *Apologia ad Fabrum* (February 1518), and despite Erasmus' promise to amend the passage the text was not changed in Martens' reprint of 1518 (f 9 recto, kindly checked for me by Dr R. Dogaer in the Bibliothèque Royale de Belgique) or in subsequent editions.

given strict instructions to the printer that absolutely nothing was to be printed off unless revised by me; and that was the one page they printed without my knowing. When I found out, I made him reprint it with my revisions, for that was why I had marked it. If I have written nothing hitherto either to the king or to the bishop, this is your fault, because your letter cut short my hopes of concluding that business as I wished, although the question did not affect me very seriously. There was no definite offer from the bishop. Those who wrote in the king's name only held out hopes. Here, though a recent recruit to the prince's retinue, I was soon given a substantial benefice; an annual salary was earmarked for me, to which I had no definite right before. You Frenchmen were at that time on bad terms with the English, and I was entirely absorbed in the labour of revising my New Testament. My affairs being in this position, would you have advised me to show ingratitude to my friends, hazard my position in England, abandon the work for the sake of which I was neglecting everything else, and run off to France in pursuit of some hope, I know not what, chasing birds that never settle? Especially since my present position is by no means to be regretted. Finally, you know at what moment your last letter but one reached me. Why is it necessary for me to bind myself to this prince or that prince, on such conditions that I must cut myself off from all the others? I would rather be the servant of none and do good service, if I can, to them all.

But on this subject I have written to the bishop, as you told me to. I am delighted to hear you think well of Glareanus; I like him so much that I shall be quite content to have anything you can do for him regarded as a service to myself.

And now for a few hurried words in reply to your last letter. My dear Budé, how unreasonably you do exaggerate or diminish everything! I said in my letter that I was afraid our friends or our successors would take your mockery in a different way from what you intended; though I knew that, whatever it might read like, it sprang from a most friendly spirit. And here

* * * * *

536 the bishop] Etienne Poncher
536 your letter] Cf Ep 744:21–5.
538 definite offer] A surprising statement; see Epp 778:33n, Allen Ep 1434:3–7.
539 Those who wrote] Apart from Budé, Guillaume Cop; see Ep 523.
539 Here ... I was ... given] See Epp 370:18n, 436.
542 on bad terms] prior to the treaty of London; see Ep 964:39n.
545 position in England] See Ep 694:11n.
547 birds] Cf *Adagia* III iii 44.
553 I have written] The letter is missing; cf Ep 915:158–9.
558 in my letter] Ep 869:6–9.

you go, stirring up a great commotion: 'the Graces were against you when you made friends with me, and I now regard you as clumsy, absurd, preposterous, obtuse, hard to get on with as a companion, and a proper blunderer, one who must be avoided and kept away with jests that are 565 barbed and double-edged and full of menace, like a bull with hay tied round its horns.' None of these remarks of yours was prompted by my letter. Not that I forbid you to reply to a letter which you see in print; but pray consider what suits the standing of us both. For that letter of mine was written not so much with you in mind as other people whom I needed to pacify. Nor do I go 570 for you with all these arguments to provoke you to reply, but to make reply impossible. I wished my dispute with Lefèvre to be plunged in oblivion, if that could somehow happen. Lastly, make no mistake: do not forget that that letter was printed some time before yours reached me. Nor was this my doing. There was a sudden danger that all Froben's presses might stand idle 575 because the paper-maker was not up to date with his deliveries, and so I very reluctantly allowed Beatus Rhenanus to choose whatever he could find in my bundle of papers, for at the time I had not a free moment. The thing was done in a hurry, and he was not satisfied with his own choice. Even so I cut a good deal out of the letter of yours to which I was replying, where there 580 were things I thought it better not to publish.

Again, I having described your letter as prolix, you take this to mean 'needlessly verbose and tedious,' and when I allow you credit for eloquence but state that in this dispute I may perhaps have a stronger case than you, you take it that I allow you only an empty plethora of words; and after that 585 you call me in more than one place unduly suspicious. And yet this I can truly affirm about myself, that you will find few people who are less suspicious in their friendships than I am. Further, when you say that there is nothing in your letter that will not redound to my credit, it being always far from clear whether you are jesting or being serious, you will more quickly be 590 taken to be jesting when you praise me than when you castigate me. Will that too redound to my credit, that you should make me out to be insolent to such

* * * * *

562 'the Graces] Ep 896:7–17
568 in print] Ep 778
574 reached me] See Epp 810, 869 introductions.
577 to choose] Cf Ep 886:57n.
580 letter of yours] See Ep 744 introduction.
582 take this to mean] Ep 896:40–2
585 take it] Ep 896:26–7, related by Erasmus to his statement in Ep 869:16–17
586 suspicious] Ep 896:21–2
588 you say] Ep 896:58–9

an old friend, at one minute biting my lip in uncontrollable anger, at another stamping my foot or calling heaven and earth to witness, and in such a storm of rage that, like a modern Pythagoras, you were compelled to play solemn 5 music to restore me to my senses? All which, to be sure, I can read with a smile, because I know very well that you were joking. My only fear is that other people may not give it the same meaning. But if you tell me to lay aside this fear, and your friends are of the same opinion, very well: mock me to your heart's content, give your pen some exercise, tear me in pieces, turn me 6 upside down. You will never ruffle my feelings because I think I am certain of yours. If you agree, your letter shall be added to the next edition.

I took no exception to the passage you comment on, so well satisfied am I with everything you write; nor have I any hesitation in following blindfold anything you have ever written. So you must keep a look out, when you 6 write to me, and have a care for the reputation of us both. But there is another place on the first page which made me pause a little; for two or three lines seemed to have been somehow inserted which did not quite fit the rest of the context: it begins 'Lefèvre who is given … so often' and ends 'I regret the opening thus afforded' and so on. You might have a look at it. 6

Please greet your friends and my benefactors, Deloynes and Ruzé, for at the moment I have no leisure to write to more people.

Farewell, from Louvain, 22 December 1518

What I feel towards you Glareanus, if you like, can testify, and he is the most sincere of men. If this letter annoys you, remember that I have purged 6 myself of my bad temper, which is what you told me to do. Anyhow, when you have read it, throw it in the fire, if you like, and I will do the same with my draft, though it is so heavily altered that I cannot read it myself. Get your own back on me in any way you please, provided you do not cease to be my friend and do not hold your peace. Though we have had more than enough 6 of Lefèvre; we will find some more attractive subject. Farewell once more.

* * * * *

593 biting my lip … stamping my foot] Ep 810:51, 134
595 Pythagoras] A familiar anecdote of the early Greek sage; Boethius *Institutio musica* 1.1.
602 shall be added] In response to Ep 896:124–5
603 the passage] Cf Ep 896:120–3.
607 another place] Cf Ep 810:37n.
611 Deloynes and Ruzé] See Ep 869:17n.

907 / From Thomas More   [London? 1518?]

This fragment, from the same source as Ep 845, was probably written not long
after John Clement's arrival in Oxford, where his presence is documented for
the autumn of 1518. He had been a tutor in More's house until he entered the
service of Wolsey, who appointed him to his newly founded lectureship (cf Ep
967) in rhetoric in the University of Oxford; cf Epp 388:185n; LP II Appendix 56.

My Clement lectures in Oxford to a larger audience than anyone has ever
had before. It is remarkable how popular he is; he is a general favourite. Even
those who almost hate the humanities love him none the less; they attend his
lectures and are gradually softening. Linacre, who, as you know, is not easy
to please, praises and admires his letters so much that even I, who love the   5
man more than anyone, am almost jealous of the massive eulogies he piles on
him.

908 / To Thomas More   [Louvain], 1 January [1519]

The date must be 1519 because of the meeting with Pucci at Basel (lines 16–18)
and the state of Erasmus' health (line 25). This letter was first printed in the
Farrago. The *Opus epistolarum* of 1529 adds a marginal note identifying the
pamphlet in line 5 and a year date which is clearly wrong.

ERASMUS OF ROTTERDAM TO HIS FRIEND THOMAS MORE,
GREETING
Really the malice of my enemies knows no rest anywhere! They leave no
stone unturned that may make mischief for Erasmus. In Cologne they had
convinced two or three people that that scandalous pamphlet, fit only to be   5
burnt repeatedly, was written by me, and many more would have believed
them had I not been there in person to rebut such a shameless calumny. In
case any suspicion of this kind has raised its head in your part of the world –
and in such business guesswork as a rule is highly infectious – I send you a
copy of my letter to Paolo Bombace; for it would take an age to write the same   10
thing separately to more than one person. Those rascals with their false
accusations are perfectly shameless, and somehow it is the crudest false-

* * * * *

908
3 no stone unturned] Cf *Adagia* I iv 30.
5 pamphlet] The *Julius exclusus*; cf Epp 821:19n, 961:40–55.
7 in person] On his way to and from Basel; cf Epp 843, 867 introductions.
10 letter] Now missing; cf Ep 865:2.

hoods that are more willingly swallowed by the public. I had the idea some
time ago of suggesting to the pope that he should put a stop to this form of
lawlessness, which spreads wider every day; but the opportunity has not   15
yet arisen. I did however speak to Antonio Pucci, the nuncio, at Basel, and
he promised to do something about it; for he too felt the thing could not be
overlooked.

When you send twelve angels in place of nine, I do not see what you
get out of it. I foresee that the favouring wind of fortune will bear you away 20
from me; but this I endure with the more resignation, because you at least are
prosperous, whatever may be in store for me. There is an ancient custom of
sending good-will presents to friends when they get better; but from your
part of the world no one sends me so much as a letter, though I have
recovered from so many illnesses.   25

As for certain theologians and their well-disguised trickery, it would
make too long a tale to write. My letter to the bishop of Rochester will tell you
part of the story, and I enclose a copy. Farewell.

1 January [Basel 1515]

909 / To the Reader   Louvain, 1 January 1519

This letter is a preface for the first authorized edition of Erasmus' *Colloquia*. A
glance at the texts from successive editions in ASD I-3 is sufficient to show that
the *Colloquia* as the modern reader knows them did not even begin to take shape
before the enlarged edition of March 1522 (cf Ep 1262). The character and
purpose of the earliest editions is described in this preface, and so are some of
the circumstances leading to their publication.

Between 1497 and 1500 formulae for polite conversation and letter-writing in

* * * * *

16 Basel] Cf Ep 860 introduction and lines 27-9. For Erasmus' later protests
against libel and slander see Allen Ep 1053:421 and corresponding note in CWE.
19 twelve angels] As the result of an embarrassing confusion More had recently
been asked to pay for a gift of twelve angels which had really been pledged by
Mountjoy (cf Epp 829:2n, 895:2-3). It appears that he reacted with typical
generosity by sending twelve angels of his own, perhaps as a new year gift.
The reference to nine angels could conceivably be another coy joke acknowl-
edging a gift from More (cf Ep 829:2-3). After Pseudo-Dionysius and Gregory
the Great it was commonly assumed that there were nine orders of heavenly
angels; thus More's gift of twelve coins was in excess of the standard number.
20 favouring wind] Cf Ep 829:6n, cf *Adagia* II v 16.
25 illnesses] Cf Epp 847:7n, 867.
27 Rochester] Apparently an appeal to John Fisher for support against Lee and his
friends in Louvain (cf Epp 886 postscript, 898A introduction). Fisher's reaction
induced Erasmus to reiterate his complaints; cf Epp 936:34n, 937:4-13.

good Latin were being assembled by Erasmus for the benefit of his pupils in
Paris. He lost sight of this text, but a manuscript survived in the hands of
Augustinus Vincentius Caminadus (cf Ep 130:108–9n), who also had access to
other early compositions by Erasmus (cf Ep 131:16–17). According to Erasmus
Caminadus used these as well as his own questionable learning to produce a
text which was finally sold to Froben through an intermediary, Lambertus
Hollonius (cf Epp 904 introduction). Froben published it in November 1518,
and several reprints followed promptly. This first edition was clearly unauthorized, yet in this letter Erasmus' displeasure is directed primarily against
Caminadus, who had been dead for a decade or so, while Froben and his associates are spared any blame. In 1536, in contrast, Hollonius was made out to
be the main culprit (cf Ep 3100). There is no clear evidence that any one had
played false. Before going to Basel in 1518 Erasmus had tried to recover another
manuscript of the *Colloquia* from Roger Wentford (cf Epp 772, 833), so in Basel
he must have mentioned that he planned to publish such a work. Moreover,
Hollonius, who took the manuscript to Basel, had been recommended to
Froben by Erasmus himself, and Beatus Rhenanus, who acted as an editor, had
repeatedly been given a fairly free hand with the publishing of Erasmus' texts.
In his preface to the unauthorized edition (BRE Ep 80; ASD I-3 29–30) Beatus
stated clearly that Erasmus had not seen the text and would very likely wish to
make further changes in addition to his own corrections. In fact Erasmus
quickly resolved to publish an amended version of the unauthorized publication – *Familiarum colloquiorum formulae* (Louvain: Martens 1 March 1519; NK
2866). This authorized edition too was followed by several reprints in quick
succession, all including this letter to the reader. To obtain the text here translated, Allen used both the version that was published with the first authorized
edition and some of the variants found in a shorter version included in Froben's
reprint of May 1519.

ERASMUS OF ROTTERDAM TO THE YOUNG
WHO DESIRE TO LEARN, GREETING

It is not hid from me, gentle reader, that what I say is out of place; but as no
more suitable moment presents itself, I thought it right to issue this brief
warning. There has recently appeared a book of everyday conversations,   5
Colloquia familiaria, which is commonly fathered on me, and the school-
children are getting it by heart, I am told, with my name to it. Even were it the
ideal book out of which to learn good classical Latin, I should still not wish to
see ascribed to me what is not mine. But as it is, since there is so much in it
that reeks of pure barbarism, I will explain in brief the state of the case.   10
    Once upon a time, I freely admit, when I was in Paris more than twenty
years ago, I did set down some lightweight material, when I had a mind to

gossip after supper by the fireside, and take my slippered ease, as Horace has it, on phrases useful in daily intercourse and on conversation over the dinner-table. Besides that, I had written a very crude paraphrase on the 15 *Elegantiae* of Lorenzo Valla, not surprisingly, as I wrote it for a numbskull rather than a human being; though this was likewise fruitless, as he was an ageing parrot with a headpiece full of lead. In addition, I had already produced some sort of outline of my *Copia* and had started my *De conscribendis epistolis* on the art of letter-writing, and another book against barbarians, 20 which by the help of certain persons I lost sight of. Above all, I gave my pen daily practice in writing letters to my acquaintance, throwing off any kind of nonsense to one or two dear friends and rattling on in the way one man talks to another in the intimacy of a glass of wine between friends and cronies. There was an inexhaustible snapper-up of these trifles in the person of 25 Augustinus Caminadus, with whom I was intimate at that time for several months. It was he who put together this book, like Aesop's crow, or rather, like a ballad-seller he strung together his mish-mash as a cook pours his many galley-pots into one, adding names and headings and other bits of his own invention, to make sure that like the ass at Cumae he would give himself 30 away. For even to say nothing worth saying in Latin is not as easy as some people think.

I am still able to state definitely, in respect of each part, where he took it from. And there are people who still have in their possession rough papers of the kind I speak of, who confess this and recognize that I speak the truth. 35 With this sad stuff he imposed on certain stupid people without my knowledge, with a view to scraping together some coin, the poor starveling creature. Nor can I allow Beatus Rhenanus, a fairminded man and a good

* * * * *

909
13 Horace] *Satires* 2.1.73
16 *Elegantiae*] Cf Ep 23:108n.
16 numbskull] Apparently Robert Fisher; cf Epp 62, 71 introductions.
19 *Copia*] Cf Ep 260.
19 *De conscribendis epistolis*] Cf Ep 71.
20 barbarians] The *Antibarbari;* for the loss of Erasmus' manuscript cf Ep 706:38n.
25 snapper-up] Literally Laverna, the goddess of theft; cf *Adagia* IV i 3.
26 Caminadus] Cf Ep 131.
27 Aesop's crow] Fable 200 (Halm); in Babrius' collection 72
30 ass] Wrapped in the skin of a lion, the ass managed to elude his masters, who had never seen a lion, until a visitor arrived at Cumae who knew better: *Adagia* I iii 66.
34 rough papers] Of the texts mentioned above only *De conscribendis epistolis* was published at the time, edited by Ulrich Hugwald (Basel 1519).

friend, to defend me on the ground that I wrote this book twenty years ago.
Whether in the intervening years I have gained anything in knowledge or   40
judgment, I leave to others to determine; but undoubtedly Latin, and what
they call classical literature, was far more at my finger-tips then than it is
now, though even then my holding in these subjects was below the average.

And now, dear reader, a few examples, from which you may guess the
remainder. Who ever said *dare salutem* for *dicere salutem*, which he puts on   45
page a.iii? Or, as on page a.vi, *Me in derisum habes*? Again, on the same page
he has added *Occupationes tuae excusationis locum habent* out of his own head.
On page a.vii *Ago tibi gratias qui litterarum fasciculis nos onerasti*, he has not
noticed that causal *qui* demands the subjunctive, *qui nos oneraris*. On page
a.viii, *Ad clunes mundandos*, he has put *clunes* for another part of the body.   50
Again, in the same place, *Laudo te virum praestitisse*: did any Geta ever speak
like that?

But I refrain from further instances, for fear my reader will find me
tedious; and these are in the first few pages! Yet in these there are other
things too which I cannot approve; among them *qua valetudine es praeditus*?   55
Perhaps a doctor might properly so express himself if he were enquiring
about a patient's permanent state of health, and not about his condition at
the moment.

You have been warned; I have done my duty. Henceforward whoever
voluntarily deceives himself has only himself to thank. As for Hollonius, if   60
he scraped together a little coin out of this, I do not grudge it him. But I do not
propose to thank the man, unless he does something else to earn my
gratitude; and if he continues, I shall reckon him not so much Hollonius as
wholly felonious. I know it is no trifling injury to publish under my name
something that is not mine, particularly while I am still alive; but like Balaam   65
of old, who hardly flinched when his ass spoke to him because he was so
used to marvels, I am so hardened to more serious affronts that these light
ones rouse me less. Otherwise the whole thing would be not far short of
outrageous, even had I really written the book; unless we are to give to any
casual person the right to print and publish to the world whatever we may   70
scribble when testing a pen, or in our childhood, in our off-moments, in our

* * * * *

39 defend me] In the preface Beatus had written for the unauthorized edition; cf
   introduction.
42 is now] Cf Ep 704.
44 a few examples] From the unauthorized edition; in the authorized all were
   emended by Erasmus; see ASD I–3 32–8, 76–82.
51 Geta] A rough character in Terence's *Phormio*
65 Balaam] Cf Num 22:28–32; the statement here is repeated with slight changes
   from the *Apologia ad Fabrum* (LB IX 47E).

cups, in love, or in anger. What impertinence, to ascribe to me in my own lifetime whatever anyone thinks fit and play fast and loose with another man's reputation! And yet, since I saw that the book was being eagerly snatched up everywhere, I have read it through and corrected it, for fear that 7 the young might be taken in by this specious use of my name and be contaminated with bad Latin. Gentle reader, farewell.

Louvain, 1 January 1519

910 / From Philippus Melanchthon   Leipzig, 5 January 1519

This is the earliest known letter in the exchange between Erasmus and Philippus Melanchthon, who had been professor of Greek in Wittenberg since the autumn of 1518 but had gone to Leipzig to attend the New Year's fair. Although they may not have exchanged formal letters before, Melanchthon had already given ample proof of his admiration for Erasmus (cf Epp 454, 563:56–60). This letter, which evidently accompanied Ep 911, was published in the *Farrago*. Erasmus replied with Ep 947.

PHILIPPUS MELANCHTHON TO
DESIDERIUS ERASMUS OF ROTTERDAM
Greeting in Christ Jesus. It gives me great pain, my dear Erasmus, that the false accusations of a worthless wretch should make a man of your distinction suspect me of wishing to criticize and act as censor of your noble 5 commentaries on the Scriptures. It would be absurd for any man of straw to make trouble for a master mind, and ungrateful too to do a disservice to one who has done so much for us. On this point I appeal to your own feelings: can you think that a man knows so little how to behave and has such a cursed passion for finding fault, who was previously recommended to you by the 1

* * * * *

910
4 wretch] Cf Ep 947:3n.
5 suspect me] Cf Ep 877:7–9. The charge was repeated by Johann Maier von Eck in an *Excusatio ... ad ea quae falso sibi Philippus Melanchthon ... adscripsit*, 25 July 1519. Melanchthon replied with a sincere tribute to Erasmus in his *Defensio* against Eck; cf Melanchthon *Werke* I 16–17.
6 man of straw] This seems to be the meaning, but it is a mere paraphrase; literally 'for a chickpea Dionysus to interrupt with his clamour the supreme Jove himself.' Melanchthon seems to take 'a Dionysus not worth a pea' to mean a man of no account (the phrase comes in the Greek proverb-collections); in *Adagia* II vi 47 Erasmus, supposing it to mean a *thing* of no account, explains it as a reference to the worthless drinks brewed from other vegetable substances by nations which cannot grow the grapevine, of which Dionysus was patron.

approval of men you can trust, and not without good success? I beg you, for
pity's sake, please realize how that slanderous villain (I can guess pretty well
who it is) has taken unfair advantage of my innocence, and please believe
that I reckon all my work, if it comes to anything, to be indebted to you as its
only begetter.   15
    I know you must think the question too trivial to be worth pursuing;
otherwise I might perhaps cite witnesses of my good intentions who would
carry weight with you. Though one thing, to be sure, I do not entirely deny,
that at first some points in your paraphrase struck me as a little far-fetched;
but when I thought them over more deeply, I changed my mind. It was here, I   20
well know, that the man found his chance to make trouble. But while the
opinions of scholars ought to be correct, they ought also to be unfettered. In
all other respects my conscience is clear; if I have gone wrong on this one
point, forgive me for Jesus Christ's sake. I do not yet read my Erasmus with so
little attention that I have yet to learn from the man himself what I owe to my   25
teacher and to a brother in Christ.
    I write briefly because I write in great distress of mind and on the spur
of the moment, and at a difficult time too. Martin Luther, who is a keen
supporter of your reputation, desires your good opinion at all points.
Farewell, my eminent friend.   30
    Leipzig, 5 January 1519

911 / From Petrus Mosellanus   Leipzig, 6 January 1519

Peter Schade (cf Ep 560), called Mosellanus as a native of the Moselle valley (cf
line 23), had taught Greek at the University of Leipzig since 1517. He had
close contacts with Melanchthon, his colleague at Wittenberg, and this letter
was written during Melanchthon's visit to Leipzig (see Ep 910 introduction). It
was answered by Ep 948 and published in the *Farrago*.

TO DESIDERIUS ERASMUS OF ROTTERDAM, THE THEOLOGIAN,
FROM PETRUS MOSELLANUS, GREETING
As I hope for Christ's blessing on my studies, Erasmus, dearest to me by far
of mortal men, I have often smiled before now at the effrontery of men who
interrupt with their foolish letters those labours of yours which are a   5
blessing to the whole world; and here am I doing just that, under pressure
    * * * * *
11 men you can trust] Cf Epp 560:27–31, 563:56–60, and for the success Ep
    605:35–7, and Erasmus' tribute to young Melanchthon in the 1516 edition of the
    New Testament, notes on 1 Thessalonians 2 (later removed).
19 paraphrase] The *Paraphrasis in Romanos*; cf Ep 710.
28 Luther] See Ep 933.

from other people. There is here an immense crowd of sophisters and what you call with no less justice than elegance windy word-spinners, with whom I and a few other defenders of the public respect for literature wage continual war. In this contest those who have attracted the majority of the 10 young men to their own party are the winners. Great efforts are deployed by both camps, in brave deeds on our side, in ambushes and trickery on theirs. 'Cunning or valour? In the foe, who cares?' Yet Mars, who in battles of this kind is in no hurry to change sides, inclines to favour us. Nor do I doubt that if you, like some patron Minerva, stand at our right hand propitious, we 15 shall soon be singing our song of triumph.

The worthless fellows on the other side, who are sworn foes to all liberal studies and especially to Greek (which I teach here publicly by the liberality of George, the prince of our Mysia, not as it deserves, but as best I can and with all my heart), are always telling the crowd of inexperienced 20 young men that, however much one ought to learn Greek (a concession I have won with difficulty after all these conflicts), yet it cannot be learnt from a German or (such is their notion of Trier) a semi-Frenchman like myself; for, say they, if you were any better at this language than the common herd, you would surely long ago have made friends somehow, at least by a mutual 25 interchange of letters, with Erasmus, the father of this time-wasting subject (as they think it) in Germany. And then, if a man has time and money to waste in any case, he ought to seek his knowledge of Greek from Italians and Greeks. In this strain these clever fellows go on croaking and try to dissuade the young from attending lectures on Greek. As though a man like you 30 honoured with his friendship only men like Budé, Lascaris, Musurus, Bembo, Leoniceno, Aleandro, Reuchlin, Birchemer, and did not also, approachable and kindly as you are, do what you can to meet the selfish

* * * * *

911
8 word-spinners] Mosellanus uses the Greek word *mataeologus* in Titus 1.10 translated 'vain talkers,' which is not so very far from *theologus*, a theologian.
13 'Cunning ... cares?'] Virgil *Aeneid* 2.390
13 Mars] an allusion to Homer *Iliad* 5.831 and 899; it recurs in Ep 951:39 and more than once in the *Adagia*.
19 Mysia] The province of Meissen, which is dignified with the classical name of Mysia in Asia Minor, was the main territory of the Albertine duchy of Saxony, and the city was one of Duke George's residences.
32 Bembo] Pietro Bembo of Venice (1470–1547), papal secretary and from 1538 cardinal, was an outstanding figure among Italian humanists and writers. Erasmus knew him by reputation from his own stay in Venice and corresponded with him from 1529 to his death; cf Allen Ep 2106 introduction.
32 Birchemer] Mosellanus used the same form of Willibald Pirckheimer's name in Ep 560:30.

requests of many ordinary people (how could you do otherwise?), besides
revealing clearly enough to a sensible reader in various places in your works, 35
though it is not your immediate subject, what your opinion is of Italian
teachers.

Not that this sophistry would draw very many away from me, if we
were not all by nature averse from hard work, and if this conviction about
Italian scholarship, from which Germany is not the only sufferer, was not 40
supported also by the votes of those whom I find to be enemies when they
should be allies, and who, I rather think, do much more harm than the
barbarian blockheads themselves. I mean the people who, having picked up
three or four Latin figures of speech, advertise themselves, some as poets
and some as orators, finding (happy men!) an audience worthy of them, in 45
front of whom they declaim with great temerity against Greek studies as
having (if you please) little or nothing to contribute to Latin. One impious
wretch of this kidney has been carried by some accursed northern gale into
the heart of our university all the way from Dalmatia. In a word, you will give
me great pleasure and will also delight the students of our liberal subjects 50
here if you will write me even one letter to show your feelings towards
us. Do this in return for the affection I bear you, having followed you
scrupulously as my guide in literary matters since my boyhood; do this in
pity for those poor imbeciles who do not wish well to all men of good will.
Must I be the only person towards whom you are not your true self? Surely 55
not; for elsewhere, like your favourite Paul, you are all things to all men, in
order that (so far as in you lies) you may bring them all to a sound mind.

Johann Eck, our champion sky-walker and master head-in-air – like
Socrates in Aristophanes, he looks down on the gods out of a basket – is
about to descend into the cockpit of disputation to fight for his life (his fees, 60
that is) against Andreas Karlstadt, the archdeacon of Wittenberg. The arena
will be the thinking-shop of our theologians, and the judges too will be the

* * * * *

48 wretch] Tranquillus Andronicus Parthenius of Dalmatia. He had arrived in
Leipzig in the early summer of 1518 and had given some lectures; see Ep 991
introduction and Allen IV 617.
56 Paul] 1 Cor 9:22
59 Aristophanes] *Clouds* 225, 226
61 Karlstadt] Andreas Rudolf Bodenstein (c 1480–1541), called after Karlstadt on
the Main, his native town. He came to Wittenberg in 1505 and there received a
theological doctorate in 1510 and a chair of theology. Since the Ninety-five
Theses he had become a fervent supporter of Luther, and his attack on Eck's
'Obeliscs' (cf Ep 872:25n) provoked the Leipzig disputation (cf Ep 948
introduction). But his unimpressive performance at the debate was an ominous
beginning for his radical role in the Reformation, which forced him to lead an
erratic, unhappy life.

Andreas Rudolf Bodenstein of Karlstadt
Contemporary woodcut by unknown artist
Stadt- und Universitätsbibliothek Bern

local word-spinners. Our great chief himself is invited by Eck to attend – the
donkey listening to the lyre, with a vengeance. The day has not yet been
fixed, but great preparations for the contest are going forward on both sides.   65
One of them will bring a claque of Augustinians; the other will produce a
proper party of Preachers, for they never fail to turn up when their daily
porridge is called in question. People will flock from all quarters to watch the
great fight, for 'tis a right noble pair of Scotists that we shall see matched.
Shall I foretell what will happen? Uproar, followed by violence; and more   70
blood shed in the fight, I fear, than you so entertainingly sketched for us in
your chapter about Esernius and Pacidianus. Such will be the dénouement
of the whole piece, for I know well what tempers are like on both sides.
Democritus ten times over will find plenty to keep him laughing. The
outcome, if worth hearing, shall be reported to you in full. I meanwhile shall   75
play martial music to our paladins, to the tune of 'Be wise, bethink you of
fierce valour now,' and as I watch them, I shall turn epic poet: 'Then leathern
shields and glaives did clash, I wis.'

But whither do I wander? I have forgotten myself, rattling on to a
doctor of divinity like you as though you were some familiar crony. Farewell,   80
Erasmus dearer to me than life itself, and mind you live a long and happy life
for the benefit of all men of good will.

Leipzig, feast of the Three Kings 1519

One thing I ask of you specially, in the name of Christ himself: do not
let yourself be persuaded by those who speak ill to you of Philippus   85
Melanchthon. Do not suspect anything to his discredit. He is an excellent
young man, born for distinguished scholarship and piety no less.

912 / To Maarten Lips

This letter has been assigned a new date and is Ep 898A in this edition.

* * * * *

63 great chief] Obviously not Luther, as was suggested in a marginal note in the
   Farrago, but perhaps Duke George of Saxony (the compromising words are in
   Greek). The disputation was under his patronage and took place in his castle,
   part of it in his presence. When Mosellanus saw the *Farrago* he complained
   (cf Ep 1123). As a result this passage was omitted from the subsequent editions.
64 donkey] Cf *Adagia* I iv 35.
72 Esernius] Cf *Adagia* II v 98; cf Ep 829:36n.
74 Democritus] Democritus of Abdera, a contemporary of Socrates, was known as
   the 'laughing philosopher' (cf Ep 618:65) because of his supposed distrust of
   reason and rejection of conventional theology and ethics: by contrast,
   Heraclitus was the 'weeping philosopher.'
76 'Be wise ... now'] Homer *Iliad* 6.112
77 'Then ... I wis'] *Iliad* 4.447, 8.61

913 / To Jan de Hondt   Louvain, 22 January 1519

Erasmus' autograph of this letter is in the British Library, MS Harl. 4935 f 26.

Jan de Hondt was the canon of Courtrai responsible for the payment of Erasmus' annuity; cf Ep 751 introduction.

Cordial greetings, my honoured Lord and more than ordinary friend. Hitherto you have sent the money for my annuity before the due date, and this time I hope it will not be inconvenient to send it now the date is past, which, if I remember right, is Christmas day. Pierre Barbier wrote to me from Spain that he had written to your Reverence on the subject; and I know you 5 will gladly comply with his wishes. He has been nominated bishop of Paria. So I beg you to pay the money to the bearer of this letter. For I have been ill more than once and at death's door, which has meant great expense, and my journey to Basel cost a good deal of money. I would have sent you a receipt but could not lay hands on your form of words. Pray send me a second copy 10 by this messenger; I will duly give it him in my own handwriting before he pays over the money. He is returning shortly and will bring you the document.

I send your Worship my best wishes. If there is any business in which I can be useful to you, you will find me ready to do all I can. 15

Louvain, 22 January 1519

Sincerely yours, Erasmus of Rotterdam

To the honourable Jan de Hondt, canon of Courtrai, my honoured and respected friend. In Courtrai

914 / From Christophe de Longueil to Jacques Lucas

Rome, 29 January [1519?]

Erasmus himself chose to publish this letter in the *Farrago*. It reappeared in the

* * * * *

913

2 before the due date] Cf Ep 794:5n.

6 Paria] A coastal stretch of South America opposite Trinidad. It was discovered by Columbus on his third voyage and is mentioned under the name of Garcia in his report to Ferdinand and Isabella dispatched from Hispaniola. Nothing seems to be known about the erection of a bishopric there. For decades Barbier had been a humble chaplain, although the favour of Chancellor Le Sauvage may have improved his fortunes of late. In Erasmus' correspondence references to his rich benefice in the Indies always occur in a humorous context (cf Ep 476:15–17, Allen Ep 1225:348–52, 365–9), and in Ep 532 it is equated with Utopia.

7 ill] Cf Epp 847:7n, 867.

later collections of his correspondence and also in the numerous editions of Longueil's letters (at the end of the fourth book). Large sections were also included in Louis Le Roy's biography of Budé, first published in 1540 (cf Budé *Opera omnia* I, preliminary pieces). It received much attention in Erasmus' correspondence (see Epp 935, 1209, 1347) and in that of his friends (see AK II Ep 674, IV Ep 1490). It has often been examined by modern scholars (see, for example, Marie-Madeleine de la Garanderie and Margaret Mann Phillips in *Scrinium* I 42, 49–52, 349–50).

Christophe de Longueil (b Mechelen 1485 or 1488, d Padua 1522) came from a distinguished Norman family. He studied law and in 1515 was elected to the Parlement of Paris. In 1516 he went to Rome, supported, it seems, by the patronage of Louis Ruzé. He was already considered the Ciceronian par excellence and received much favourable attention. But he also aroused resentment by allegedly extolling the glories of France at the expense of Italy and had to leave Rome in May 1519. Meanwhile Ruzé obtained a copy of this letter and passed it on to Erasmus in March 1519 (cf Ep 935:8). Erasmus reacted with Ep 935, and in his dialogue *Ciceronianus* (1528) one of the speakers, Nosoponus, shows some resemblance to Longueil.

The letter is addressed to Jacques Lucas, dean of Orléans since 1510, who was in Rome between February and May 1519 to promote the canonization of St Francis of Paola. The year date is not indicated. P.A. Becker (*Christophle de Longueil*, Bonn and Leipzig 1924, 72) preferred 1518. But although the letter could well present Longueil's reaction to the *Epistolae sanequam elegantes* of April 1517 (containing Epp 522–3, 531, 533), Lucas' visit to Rome and the publicity suddenly gained by this letter in the spring of 1519 make the later date somewhat preferable. It may be noted, however, that this letter became a focus of attention at a time of heightened political tension when the two monarchs served respectively by Erasmus and Budé were competing for the imperial crown.

CHRISTOPHE DE LONGUEIL TO JACQUES LUCAS,
DEAN OF ORLÉANS, GREETING

We shall never lack for topics if, as I said to you long ago, we stimulate ourselves to write by asking one another questions; and with this in mind I wrote to you not long ago and said I should be most grateful for a fuller 5 explanation from you why your prince preferred Erasmus to Budé – a German not a Frenchman, a foreigner not a native citizen, a stranger not a

* * * * *

914
6 preferred Erasmus] A reference to the generous terms by which Francis I had attempted to attract Erasmus to Paris; cf Epp 522:42–58, 926:37n.

man he had long known. As far as learning goes, I see no point at which
Budé falls short of Erasmus, whether you choose to consider liberal studies
or those proper to a Christian. As for their power as writers, in my opinion   10
they deserve equal praise in such very different styles. Both are greatly
blessed with abundance of ideas and language, but with a difference: one
flows more broadly, the other in a narrower but deeper channel rolls down a
great mass of waters. The one a fuller stream, the other clearer. In Budé I
think I detect more muscle, more blood, more energy; in Erasmus rounded   15
flesh, smooth skin, fresh colouring. One is more thorough, the other more
ready; one fertile in epigram, the other in wit; one all intent on practical ends,
the other above all on pleasing. Budé's weapons are industry, natural
fertility, a serious impressive style; Erasmus fights his way to victory by skill
and subtlety, he is so smooth and so readable. You can love Erasmus and   20
wonder at Budé; you give Erasmus your allegiance and do as Budé tells you.
In fact, the latter carries one forcibly along, the former wins one over by
delight. One attracts by his charm, the other sweeps one away by force, strict
in his choice of words and lucid in his exact use of them; if the subject calls for
illustration, he is happy in metaphor, telling in epigram, versatile in figures   25
of speech, in the overall air of what he writes noble, exalted, severe and
splendid. Erasmus, on the other hand, all charm and modesty, takes his
reader with him; eloquent, richly endowed with language, in arrangement
workmanlike and elegant at the same time, full of examples and close-knit
arguments and agreeable sallies. Budé is always wholly committed to what   30
he writes but keeps his thunder and lightning chiefly for passages where the
subject admits an attack on present-day society; Erasmus, even when
attacking public morals, gives more the impression of defending his
principles more in sorrow than in anger, and attempting a cure with
poultices and salves and plasters and treatment with other bland applica-   35
tions of the kind, while the other man applies remedies which are painful but
for the moment necessary, strong medicines and the knife and cautery, to
attack deep down the advancing force of the disease.

In a word, if they set out to be historians, Budé would be more like
Thucydides than Sallust, Erasmus more Livy than Herodotus. If they are to   40
write poetry, the former will give us the deep thunder of some tragic or
heroic piece, weighty in word and thought; the latter's inspiration will be
more polished in comedy, in lyrics more exquisite, in elegy more tender. Yet
he too can be lofty with another man's native force to support him; but in his
own, he finds it difficult, just as the other would never lower his style even   45
if he wanted to. In other ways, those higher qualities, though present in
both, are more obvious in one, more hidden in the other; the result is the
same, the manner different, so that a man would not go far wrong who said

that one was born for oratory and one for the courts, one inspired by Pallas
and one escorted by a party of the Graces.   50

In any case, to show you that 'nought is at all points blest,' as the poet
says, or at least is capable of satisfying all tastes, let me tell you the shortcomings noticed in them by men who feel themselves to have made some
progress in the literary way. Budé's fault they think to be that he is faultless;
Erasmus', that to his own faults he is too kind. Budé, they say, is so careful to   55
measure everything by the standard of the Ancients that he often forgets for
whom he writes and makes music only for himself and the Muses; Erasmus
gives his own genius so much rein, thinking nothing so current that it cannot
honourably claim a place in his style sooner or later, that sometimes he
muddies the waters. The former hints at his meaning rather than expresses   60
it, the latter with his excessive flow of language chokes the crop with a rich
growth of weeds. The former now uses an indirect approach and eddies
round the point, now soars into rhetoric and thus he often overdoes it; the
latter on a lower plane, bare and straightforward, is more prone to crawl
along the ground. Erasmus to them is softer and more effeminate, Budé is   65
harder and more austere. In short, one, they think, could be wonderfully
popular with highly educated readers, the other with ordinary men as well,
if when swept away by their own eloquence (to use their critics' words) they
knew how to hold the balance and, while relying always on their own gifts,
sometimes owed their style to the judgment and advice of other men. For   70
since they are able to produce what results they wish, it is right, men say,
that they should wish only for the best and not make a show and try to
impress us; things have come to such a pass that we need help in good time,
not entertainment out of season. Whatever the declared purpose of a book,
we need to be scrupulously instructed in accordance with it, not held in   75
suspense in a roundabout way by frequent and quite undisciplined
digressions. Seneca and Pliny did indeed digress, but one of them sparingly,
the other hardly ever; and even then it was never deliberately, but because
the theme so presented itself.

So say the critics, whose opinion I do not accept forthwith for many   80
other reasons, but especially because there have been eminent orators who
established as the arbiter of eloquence not the professors but the public. But
be it so: let us give a vote to no one but the learned; let our jury in this case be
drawn solely from leaders of the literary world: who, I ask, in our own day is

* * * * *

51 the poet] Horace *Odes* 2.16.27, 28
57 makes music] Cf *Adagia* III v 80.
62 weeds] Quintilian *Institutio oratoria* 8. pr 23
64 crawl] Horace *Ars poetica* 28

good enough to be rightly entrusted with so exalted a jurisdiction? Both   85
parties will support their case not merely with weighty precedents but with
arguments of the greatest force. They will say it is not they that write amiss
but their critics whose judgment is distorted; the points objected to in what
they write are not native weeds, but imported by unskilful readers; Erasmus
will say that he had all men in mind, Budé that he is content with an audience   90
of the few. So I myself make no decision, either because the cobbler (as they
say) must stick to his last, or else because to me they come out even,
balancing their faults, if they have any, by their virtues, or even outweighing
them; for there is in them more to praise than to forgive. One thing I wonder
at, which I mentioned at the start: why your prince, given Budé's great   95
integrity and learning and eloquence, has preferred a German not a
Frenchman, a foreigner not a native citizen, a stranger not a man he had long
known.

Nor do I say this as one who looks askance at Erasmus' good fortune. I
think as highly of him as any man alive, although I have never seen him   100
face to face; and this because we share a common country, for we were born,
as you know, to speak the same language and under the same government. I
venerate him for his great intellectual gifts, for which I look up to him so
much that it would be the sum of my ambition in the next twenty-two years
(for he is that much older than I am) to reach, if not the literary eminence he   105
now enjoys, at least the next thing to it. A selfish wish, you say; selfish, if
you like, but one he would not wholly disapprove of. So I do not look
askance at the reputation or the advantages of so great a man, whose
eloquence I value more than all the wealth of France. But my reason for
writing this is to ask you to tell me forthwith, if you can, why, having always   110
neglected able Frenchmen, you are now beginning to despise Italians and
pursuing Germans with such determination.

Farewell, from Rome, 29 January.

915 / From Guillaume Budé   Paris, 1 February [1519]

This letter answers Ep 906 and is answered in turn by Ep 930 and more fully by
Ep 1004. It was printed in the *Farrago*.

GUILLAUME BUDÉ TO ERASMUS OF ROTTERDAM, GREETING
I have seen the comments you wrote on my letter, and full of kindness they

* * * * *

91 cobbler] Cf *Adagia* I vi 16.

915
2 comments] Ep 906

were – kindness of a sort unfamiliar in you; everything in it made me very happy, but even so I suppose I should not have answered just now, being immersed in every kind of business, had you not forbidden me in your   5
postscript to remain silent. You must not think me a man who sits back and does nothing: I have long been the father of a family and have now been blessed with a seventh son; I have lately bought a house and moved into it, arranging at the same time in a great hurry for the workmen to come in and do it up, while my books and papers lie in heaps meanwhile. During this   10
transfer I went through my possessions, about which I was ill informed hitherto, so you must not think I did not take seriously your casual remarks about my being so rich. But how such an idea came into your head I do not understand, for it is in books and children that I have invested a great part of my worldly goods; this has always been my principle, and I have even made   15
a point of it.

But how witty do you suppose I thought it when, in speaking of Epimetheus, you describe me as rattling on with a show of learning as though I had it all out of a notebook? So that I have a small store of the things you call good remarks put by as it were in ready money; and even those I ran   20
the risk of losing, you thought, unless I had found a friend like you against whom I could discharge them. I remember you accused me of something of the sort on another occasion, though now I cannot find the passage. My good sir, you who have religious scruples against criticizing a friend even in fun, did you think that when I read you I am so hard of hearing that I would   25
not have taken in properly what you said only once? Before your time we know the legal position of collectors of proverbs was this, that every man sufficiently interested was entitled to the use and enjoyment of the discoveries of Antiquity, on condition that he was seen not to usurp other men's property, but to use them as a man might pick flowers that had grown   30
on land in common ownership and were available to the first comer. But now, since the publication of your volumes of proverbs, I suppose it will be lawful to use only such as you have ranged in their centuries and assigned as it were to their proper stations, as though a man who erects a fence round a

* * * * *

8 seventh son] His name is not known; for Budé's family cf Epp 403:165–7, 989:25.
8 a house] In the rue Saint-Martin, now number 203. Elsewhere Budé described the amenities of the house and the nature of the repairs; cf M.-M. de la Garanderie *La Correspondance* 185 n 2, 277.
12 casual remarks] Cf Ep 906:89–97.
18 Epimetheus] Cf Ep 906:130–62.
22 I remember] Cf perhaps Ep 480:257–62.

piece of common pasture so as to shut out his neighbours could then lawfully   35
maintain that he had acquired a prescriptive right and made it his own
property. Which might be even more inequitable if you were to decide that
the word 'proverb' has such a wide extension as would bring all witty,
graceful, and humorous utterances within your jurisdiction.

But let it be granted that you had a right to do this, the regulation and   40
determination of every part of the whole field of literature having by common
consent been entrusted or relinquished to you: let it at least be permitted to
use your proverbs on sufferance, as you observed of Epimetheus, and to ask
your leave to make use of them, especially for those who are familiar with the
conduct of business and know how to secure the title even to other men's   45
property. But what an example of selfishness you offer us, that in that great
sea, that ocean of Antiquity which by natural law is common to all (if we may
believe the lawyers), one individual should give himself leave to pull out all
the finest fish and debar all men from enjoyment of the fishing! Were you not
satisfied with increasing your volumes of adages, repeated annually with so   50
much labour until the flood of them spills over, and scooping up in your
dragnet with its jealous meshes all the elegance and charm of ancient
literature, but you must also look askance at others who follow in your
footsteps? But if you are a good man, a man such as I have always supposed
you to be, after reaping the wide fields of Greek and Latin until you have got   55
yourself a great harvest of reputation, you will not be annoyed with me if I
follow up, to glean what you either overlooked when faced with such plenty
or neglected, good husbandman (close-fisted, even) that you are. But as it is,
you are a little jealous and make trouble for the gleaners, though you have
mown all the meadows of the Muses and reaped all the cornfields of the   60
Ancients.

Now here's another thing I should much like to know, if I do not seem
inquisitive. When you say that I am unwilling to lose the phrases I have put
on one side, what about you? As you put out all these great tomes every day,
until the supply of presses almost runs out and the printers can hardly spare   65
a moment for anyone but you, do you pour these out on the spur of the
moment under the influence of some prophetic frenzy without having the
yarn of which they are to be woven laid up beforehand and I dare say all put

* * * * *

38 the word 'proverb'] Down to line 85 Budé is responding to Erasmus' casual
   remark in Ep 906:139–43. Budé was extremely sensitive to accusations of
   plagiarism (cf Ep 648:58n). Apparently he feared, no doubt unnecessarily, that
   Erasmus' paragraph charged him with plunder of the *Adagia*.
65 printers] Budé was no doubt thinking of Martens and Froben. His statement is
   truer of Martens.

in boxes and labelled? Some say the things which now stream in procession
from the press were all got ready seven years before. If I knew that to be true,   70
I should welcome your generous spirit and your benevolence towards the
public with every vote that I could muster; for what more admirable than to
refuse to take with you to the grave the treasures you collected in your
youth? To me it seems just as if some citizen of Rome richly endowed by all
the Muses made up his mind to earn public applause by yearly and monthly   75
largesse to the people and to distribute all his goods, deserving well of the
community by sending tickets for his distributions even to the grandees and
the upper classes. If only all those who are too fond of money had learnt to
do the same and would distribute the fortunes they have made so greedily in
charity before they die! We should not see so much wealth everywhere   80
removed from circulation, condemned to life imprisonment and buried in
dust. For as far as I am concerned, I do not deny that I have much stored up in
my notebooks for the benefit of my friends, out of which I might one day
have composed tomes not to be despised, had I been blessed with happier
fortune and leisure for a literary life.   85

    To pass on to the rest: you rightly make fun of me for not stopping to
think when I wrote that about Jerome carried before Christ's judgment-seat,
for I cannot plead that I was trying to be funny, as you unkindly suggest. I
remembered hearing the story told and had not made a proper note of the
Jerome passage. But you will grant me an amnesty, as this is not a capital   90
offence – we might perhaps class it with your slip about the Areopagites,
when you bring persons accused of theft before their tribunal. But while I do
not deny that I have said many things in jest, I will never confess to such
self-confidence as not to be a little ashamed if I am called a jester, even in
jest. Nor did I make your friends, who are (I doubt not) good men and mild   95
men, since they are your friends, rage like wild animals in my letter. Let it be
admitted that some things I said were out of place, since so it seems to you,
who are the arbiter of all times and places and things said; and to you I
entrust myself and all I do, as I have in what I wrote to you about Tunstall,
bidding you move anything that was out of place or badly arranged. Not   100
only that, but I also authorize you to bring yourself down, gently or forcibly,

                        * * * * *

69 Some say] An unfair charge; the many reprints of Erasmus' earlier works were
    due to demand. Throughout 1517 and 1518 he had laboured to revise the New
    Testament, yet he had also managed to complete a number of fresh publica-
    tions, of which only some minor ones had been composed in his youth.
86 make fun of me] Ep 906:326–30.
91 your slip] Ep 906:382–3. The Areopagus dealt primarily with religious offences
    and major crimes such as murder and arson.
96 in my letter] Ep 906:394, followed by the reference to Tunstall

from the pinnacle of glory and reputation to which you say that I have
elevated you in such unwelcome fashion; for you make so many difficulties
about accepting the tributes offered to you that it might perhaps have shown
more true modesty to reject them openly. Consider which of us is more   10
entitled to his grievance: you complain that I have undervalued what you
write; I take it hard that you should think what I say so important.

Yet what a fairminded man you are, and grateful by nature, when you
call me the person responsible for your not writing either to the king or to the
bishop, your great supporter! This is the reward for good news which I   11
maintained you owed me. And on the other hand, how sharp you are – not
to understand me even in that part of my letter in which I tried to bring to
fruition for your benefit what we had decided on, so that all that was left for
you to do was to hum and haw and make difficulties about the offers made to
you from here! But like the shrew in the fable, you yourself have given the   11
show away.

I rejoice to see you have purged yourself of your bad temper, so that
when at length you come to us you will be Erasmus pure and simple.
Certainly you have tried with all your might to sweat off that attack of spleen
derived from a misunderstanding, the miasma of which has never upset me   12
to the same extent; so do not be too jubilant in your victory over me, so that
you find me harder to pacify. And so, if any dregs remain in the bottom of
your heart, clean them out and purge yourself properly, now that you have,
I hope, swallowed the pill contained in my letter. Though if Homer found
nothing more outrageous than to be accused of impudence – a charge you   12
rain on me like stones, no doubt to get practice in exchanging jokes with me –
I do not see what you have left for yourself with which you can deal me a yet
more splendid blow. Though if you have anything, I shall be a willing target:
anything to give you satisfaction. I would however gladly persuade you of
one thing: if that evil genius of yours is still tormenting you with tempests of   13
this kind, you should turn your sword, or rather your pen, against that
dried-up monosyllabic theologian who plans so much trouble for you, poor
halfpenny creature that he is. For I seem to have given your indignation
quite enough exercise already. For the time being I will lie low, in hopes of

* * * * *

102 you say] Ep 906:446–7
109 call me] Ep 906:535–9
110 good news] Cf Ep 810:482.
112 my letter] Ep 810:441–79
115 like the shrew] Cf *Adagia* I iii 65.
117 purged yourself of] Ep 906:615–16
124 Homer] *Iliad* 22.414–15
132 theologian] Edward Lee; cf Ep 906:494–512.

watching more closely the confrontation between yourself and him if ever he   135
pops up out of the hiding-place where he lurks; and I shall consider ways to
beguile your indignation somehow or other, for as a friend you are nice and
difficult to please and prefer your friends to butter you up. And so, if you
please, write to Deloynes, not as my friend any longer but your own, who
will keep you in play with letters sweet as honey; though he on his side   140
complains already that two letters of his have had no answer. Ruzé hardly
dared trust me to send you greetings on his behalf; I thought he was very
reasonably indignant with you, for I showed him your letter which was so
pleasant and charming on the surface and so bitter underneath. My advice to
you therefore is to entrust yourself entirely to these friends, who know how   145
to handle friendship with kid gloves. I meanwhile shall resume contact with
serious things and bid a long farewell to the pleasantries that have failed to
keep me on good terms with that eloquent pen of yours.

Another most unfair attack I had almost forgotten to mention: in
quoting the words of my letter, you make out that I put 'you say' in the   150
present tense instead of 'you will say,' as though I had actually invented
words from some earlier letter of yours. This is what you complain of,
although in fact I was using the figure anthypophora, maintaining not that
you did but that you might have said so; for everywhere in my draft it has the
future tense 'you will say.' So you have begun to attack me not merely with   155
rhetorical subtleties, as your custom was, but with fabrications!

I have not yet spoken to the bishop since you wrote to him, though I
have seen your letter. Farewell, and if this exchange of letters gives you any
pleasure, start up some different topic. I leave that entirely to you.

Paris, 1 February   160

The passage which troubles you in my letter reads as follows in the
draft, which I still have: 'Lefèvre, whom I have so often mentioned in
honourable terms, is repaying me thanks of a kind; inadequate thanks at
least in the opinion of many men. To me also it seems that he is acting more
harshly towards me than agrees with his usual courtesy. I am sorry that this   165
opportunity has been given, etc. Were you to announce at that stage' – this
last phrase of mine means 'You ought to have added to your earlier remarks

* * * * *

139 Deloynes ... Ruzé] For letters from Deloynes and Ruzé, now missing, see Ep
869:17n. For Louis Ruzé see also Ep 926.
150 quoting] Cf Ep 906:145n.
153 anthypophora] This rhetorical term is used for a rejoinder to the arguments of a
hypothetical opponent.
157 wrote to him] Cf Ep 906:553n.
161 my letter] Cf Ep 810:37n.

the news of your proposed *Apologia*; for then perhaps my warnings would
not have been quite so belated.' From which letter of yours I took this, I do
not know; for at the time of writing I have not got my books arranged nor my   170
papers sorted in this house into which I have now moved.

There's a letter for you; good Latin, beautifully written, and in my own
hand. But it is only fair that you should let me do just as I please, especially
as I have no friend who can act as my amanuensis and no leisure to look for
one elsewhere; and it is disagreeable to write you a prim and proper letter.   175
We are beginning to do everything here in a high imperious spirit since the
death of Maximilian, so don't think you will find me any longer so very mild
and fairminded. Farewell once more, and pray do not cease to be my dear
friend: it was you told me not to remain silent.

916 / To Erard de la Marck   Louvain, 5 February 1519

With the last texts for his critical edition of the New Testament finally
dispatched (cf Ep 864 introduction), Erasmus resumed his work on the
paraphrases (cf Ep 710). This letter is a dedicatory preface to the *Paraphrasis in
duas epistolas Pauli ad Corinthios*, first published in Louvain by Martens with the
colophon date of 30 January 1519 (NK 844). Some copies of the *Paraphrasis in
Corinthios* were joined together with Erasmus' *Apologia pro declamatione de laude
matrimonii* (cf Ep 946), which was published by Martens with the date of 1
March 1519 (cf Allen's headnote). The date of this letter (Nones of February)
was probably chosen to coincide with the anticipated publication of the
paraphrase. Distribution had begun by 19 February (cf Ep 918), and Erasmus
went straight on to compose the paraphrase on Galatians (cf Ep 956
introduction). Froben reprinted the *Paraphrasis in Corinthios* in March 1519.

Erasmus composed this preface after he had finally met the bishop of Liège
(cf Ep 738); it may contain faint echoes of a legal presentation on behalf of Erard
before the Diet of Augsburg (cf the preface to this volume), which was noticed
by Luther and his friends because of a fierce attack upon the Roman curia; cf Ep
980; Harsin *Erard de la Marck* 241–52, 267.

TO THE RIGHT HONOURABLE PRINCE AND RIGHT REVEREND
PRELATE ERARD DE LA MARCK, BISHOP OF LIÈGE, FROM
ERASMUS OF ROTTERDAM, GREETING
Often had I heard your Highness' praises sung, both in letters from many

* * * * *

172 beautifully written] Budé's handwriting was hopeless. Reading Ep 906:617–18,
    he recalled Ep 480:27–44.
177 Maximilian] He died on 12 January 1519 at Wels in Austria.

correspondents and in conversation, as of a person richly endowed with   5
every quality and every gift that could be thought worthy of a prince; but
while enjoying a few days of your society I found you such that my friends
seemed to have given a niggardly and stinted – I would almost call it a jealous
– account of your felicity or (it would be truer to say) ours. And so the
situation was reversed. You, who had long been fired by the kind words of   10
several friends with an excessive wish to meet me, must (I think) once we had
met have begun to modify your high opinion and will take the first
opportunity of protesting to those who had tried to sell you a small fly like
myself as a great elephant; I on the other hand, who felt already a
considerable desire to see you, once given the opportunity to observe you at   15
close quarters was quite carried away by love and admiration for your great
qualities and was soon making my protest to those who had given me such a
niggardly picture of you.

This is not the place to tell of the historic eminence of your family and
your pedigree of illustrious ancestors, of the wide extent of your territories,   20
or of the heroic aspect of your physical presence, which bespeaks a splendid
prince even from afar, although I know full well that things like these help to
set off your gifts of personality. I would more gladly dwell on the qualities
which are more essentially yours: the incredible charm of your character; the
courtesy so readily open to all comers, which makes everything more   25
cheerful whichever way you turn; that wonderfully supple and wholly
versatile intelligence, which is always certain of itself and always ready; that
exceptional judgment in affairs of every kind which, unerring in its own
nature, is rendered more so by wide experience of business; that unparalleled vigour in counsel, on account of which I reckon our prince too and our   30
court so fortunate; besides these, your uncommon propensity towards piety
and sound learning, in both of which you are yourself pre-eminent; above
all, your unbroken pursuit of peace, for after all those warlike prelates you
have shown such incredible wisdom in ruling a people in other respects
ready to rush headlong into war that they have never fallen a prey to anyone   35
and never taken the offensive. Difficult and exceptional as it is to be a good
prince, it is even more exceptional to be an upright and untainted prelate.

* * * * *

916
7 your society] This meeting had been planned for some time; see Epp 748,
867:89–91, 198–9.
14 elephant] Cf *Adagia* I ix 69.
30 reckon ... fortunate] The Hapsburg diplomacy had recently succeeded in
winning the De la Marck family over from their alliance with France (cf Epp
748:29n, 956 introduction). The realignment marked the beginning of an era of
peace and prosperity for the territory of Liège.

You alone fill both positions with a completeness which any other man could scarcely achieve in one alone and are no less a religious leader than you are a head of state.   40

But there will perhaps be a more appropriate occasion to dwell on this elsewhere, and it will be better done, I think, in other ears than yours. Meanwhile, that I may not a second time meet such a prince, who has laid me under so many obligations, empty-handed and without a gift, and that you may not think this most flourishing university of yours has nothing to offer   45 you except spiced wine, in the last few weeks I have made ready this modest present in the literary way, a paraphrase on the two Epistles to the Corinthians, so that having Paul, the supreme interpreter of our religion, in this form, you can carry him round with you wherever you please and have him speak to you in future in clear and familiar language without a lengthy   50 commentary. Nor do I doubt that you will gain as much profit as pleasure from what he says. For in the first place much is revealed in these two Epistles about the beginnings of the infant church, on which I am surprised to find almost nothing recorded by serious historians and such as one can safely trust. Luke alone touches on a few points relating to a few of the   55 apostles in the course of conducting Paul as far as Rome. Dionysius, who in his second Hierarchy gives a fairly full description of the early rites of the church, is thought by the learned to be someone more recent than the celebrated member of the Areopagus who was a disciple of Paul. I have read a liturgy of the Greeks attributed by them to Chrysostom, to whom they are   60 willing to attribute almost anything; that does not make it seem likely to me.

If only the liturgical matters which Paul touches on here and shows us

* * * * *

45 university of yours] A hint at the litigation over the right of nomination to certain benefices in the diocese of Liège which continued to trouble the relations between the University of Louvain and Prince-Bishop Erard; cf Harsin *Erard de la Marck* 230–3, 248. For a comparable dispute see Ep 762 introduction.

50 without a lengthy commentary] See Ep 710 introduction.

56 Dionysius] The *Hierarchies* attributed to Dionysius, Paul's convert on the Areopagus at Athens (Acts 17:34), are Neoplatonic treatises of the early fifth century. The first explains the ranks of angels, while the second deals, as here mentioned, with the rites of the church. Before Erasmus there had been little questioning of the traditional attribution; as a result he was more than once attacked because of this statement. In the *Declarationes ad censuras Lutetiae* he pointed out that his view was shared by Lorenzo Valla and William Grocyn; see LB IX 916–17.

60 liturgy] A mass which Erasmus himself had translated into Latin (cf Ep 227:2n; PG 63:901–22; 64:1061–8). Erasmus' doubts about the authorship are justified.

as it were through a lattice had been handed down by him somewhat more fully and more clearly! How concise is his mention of the eucharist or synaxis, as though he were afraid of saying something that he ought not to say about that great mystery, on which certain moderns hold forth at length and issue pronouncements without pausing, as the saying goes, to wipe their feet! If only he had told us one thing at least: the persons, the time, the vestments, the rite, the wording customarily employed to consecrate the mystic bread and the cup that contains the Lord's most holy blood, from the unworthy handling of which, Paul tells us, spring frequently disease and death – words that should make us too consider with more circumspection whether this could be the source of the pox that has been spreading everywhere for some years. And it is handled unworthily, not only by the man who approaches it when polluted by lust, but much more by him who is befouled with envy hatred and malice, with scandalmongering and a passion for revenge, and other faults of the kind which by their own nature are diametrically opposed to the Christian charity which in this mystery we set forth. He speaks rather more fully of the gift of tongues, of interpretation, of prophecy, and other gifts the place of which was later taken by church music, the reading of Scripture, and preaching. For the gifts of healing and apocalyptic vision have long since left us, since charity grew cold, faith languished, and we learnt to depend on human resources rather than on the help of heaven.

     He has something too to say about ecclesiastical jurisdiction, when he forbids recourse to gentile judges and gives instructions that financial disputes must be settled by Christian arbitrators. He even claims some right of judicial enquiry for himself when he says 'When I come, in the mouth of two or three witnesses shall every word be established.' And again in the execution of judgment he leaves his authority as an apostle in no doubt when he delivers unto Satan the man who has associated with his father's wife, the place of which is now filled by excommunication – a weapon which in these days is to my mind used rather too readily: this terrifying thunderbolt is aimed indiscriminately and for the most frivolous reasons, and never with more energy than when some contemptible sum of money is at risk, while Paul (if I mistake not) besides Hymenaeus and Alexander delivered unto Satan one person only. Those two he condemns for their

65

70

75

80

85

90

95

* * * * *

63 through a lattice] Cf *Adagia* III i 49.
64 eucharist] 1 Cor 11:23–31
65 saying] Cf *Adagia* I ix 54.
88 he says] 2 Cor 13:1
91 unto Satan] 1 Cor 5:1–5
96 Paul] 1 Tim 1:20, 1 Cor 5:5

obstinate opposition to the Gospel though they passed for Christians – and though we read of their condemnation, we do not read that they were ever reinstated; the other man for his open and notorious abomination. And yet even against him he did not pronounce sentence except in accordance with a unanimous vote, nor did he ever give the man's name. When condemning him, he was satisfied with denouncing his offence; in readmitting him, he does not even mention the offence, whence one can perceive it was the sin and not the sinner that was the target for his severity. Nor did being delivered unto Satan in those days mean more than being shunned for a time by everyone, so that shame might bring one to repentance. For Paul adds to his sentence 'for the affliction of the flesh, that the spirit may obtain salvation in the day of the Lord'; so that even the severity with which he cures the evil breathes the charity of the Apostle. But not long after, see with what zeal he recommends the man to the Corinthians, telling them to receive him kindly into their society after correction, for fear lest he be overwhelmed by grief too heavy for him. This penalty was at that time enough to satisfy the merciful Apostle.

Besides which, though there were many who had sinned, he preferred to take steps against one alone as a warning to the others, but with a mild penalty which should be not so much a punishment as a remedy. The rest he menaces in his letters with repeated threats, to make them repent, as though he would have no right to be severe against those who had repented of their own free will. But now look at the ferocity with which we rage against the common folk, although we have more grievous crimes on our own consciences! But at the same time the case of this man guilty of abomination, who is condemned and then received back again, makes nonsense of the doctrine of Montanus and Novatianus, who refuse to receive into Christ's flock anyone who has lapsed seriously after baptism. Not but what in the days of Augustine only a single opportunity for public penance was allowed, that the remedy might not lose its value by frequent use; though he does not deny to those who have relapsed into the same offence the hope of forgiveness in the presence of God, in his long discussion of the point in the letter to Macedonius, which now bears the number 54. The same precedent gave rise to the retributions authorized by canon law, which were once very

* * * * *

111 recommends] Cf 2 Cor 2:5–11.
124 Montanus and Novatianus] Founders in the second and third centuries of sectarian movements characterized by eschatology and severe asceticism
130 letter] Augustine's Ep 153.3.7
131 very severe] The early churches required public penance and other forms of chastisement; cf *Dictionnaire de théologie catholique* ed A. Vacant et al (Paris repr 1923–67) XIV-1 1136–48, 1152.

severe, as appears from the decrees of the early popes. From these again arose, it is clear, what are now commonly called indulgences, out of which I only wish it were as much our good fortune to grow rich in religion as it is certain other persons' to fill their coffers with coin. First of all, some   135
relaxation was allowed in the regular penalties inflicted by the bishop, but sparingly, and only for weighty and religious reasons; but nowadays the remission of the torments of purgatory is openly hawked up and down, and not merely sold for money but forced upon those who do not want it, for reasons which in these days I will not mention. You remember the false   140
apostles whom Paul knew to be a grievous plague, but none the less he lets them be for a time, for fear that severity directed against a few men may bring the general state of the church into jeopardy; for he does not dissent from Augustine's view that some men should be set right in secret and not openly, for fear of rousing them to greater madness and turning mere criminals   145
into tyrants or leaders of heresy.

Besides which, he lays down the law as befits his apostolic office, on marriage lawful and unlawful, equal and unequal, on remarriage, and on divorce, recommending some things as being valuable and requiring others as being necessary. Of these precepts we retain some quite inflexibly enough   150
in my opinion, not to say too much so – for example, on divorce; some have been abandoned entirely, for instance, Paul's advice that a Christian wife should continue to live with a gentile husband if he does not seek a divorce. He lays down rules also about meat sacrificed to idols, on which decisions are given in the Acts as well by James and Peter; and this perhaps has no   155
relevance now, for no one sacrifices to demons nowadays. Though this decree too has now lost its force, inasmuch as it is not now thought an abomination to eat an animal that has been strangled or an animal's blood. But Ambrose interprets the prohibition of the blood as forbidding us to eat all living creatures that have blood in their veins and thinks for this reason that   160
the 'things strangled' are a superfluous addition by the Greeks, because he who expressly forbids the eating of animals forbids us at the same time to eat anything strangled. But whether one should subscribe to Ambrose's opinion

* * * * *

140 false apostles] Cf 2 Cor 11:13–19.
144 Augustine's view] See, for example, Sermons, attributed to him, no 268 (PL 39:2229–30).
152 Paul's advice] 1 Cor 7:13–15
154 rules ... about meat] 1 Cor 8:4–13, Acts 15:20, 29, 21:25
159 Ambrose] This startling claim is repeated in the 1518–19 edition of the New Testament, notes to Gal 2 (p 396), with a reference to [Pseudo]-Ambrose's commentary on Gal 2. Later Erasmus recognized that [Pseudo]-Ambrose did not make such a claim. Consequently he amended his note.

is for others to decide. It seems to me more like pure Christianity and more in
keeping with the teaching of the Gospels and the apostles to lay down for no   1
man any specific form of food, but to instruct all men to eat in accordance
with their habit of body, whatever is most conducive to each man's good
health, with a view to moderation and not self-indulgence, with thanksgiv-
ing and a lively desire to think aright.

But, to let my pen run on, the Apostle teaches us here in passing how   1
far we ought to condescend to weaker brethren and how far to avoid any
cause of stumbling: whenever, that is, there is an immediate threat to their
faith and the occasion of stumbling is scarcely to be overcome, being newly
identified and a survival from a former way of life, not originating in us and
deliberately introduced. For whether we should agree with Augustine, who   1
in a letter to Publicola in which he treats of various questions in this field
expresses the simple view that it is better to starve to death than to eat
sacrificial meat discovered by accident, if you know it to be sacrificial, I leave
for others to determine; Paul finds nothing wrong in this, unless it is a cause
of stumbling to the weak, and openly protests that neither idols nor meat   1
offered to idols are anything, indignant that he should be criticized in
respect of something for which he himself gives God thanks. Once that
scruple has been removed, why need a Christian starve to death? For there is
no similarity in the things which Augustine compares in his *De bono coniugii,*
parenthood and death by starvation. Nor does Paul confuse the issue like   1
this; on the contrary, he instructs us to refrain for the time being, since there
are other sources on which you can draw in order to silence your ravening
stomach. If I am allowed to steal food in order to preserve life, why am I told
to die rather than arouse another man's misgivings? And all this was at that
time the mere rudiments of ecclesiastical legislation, when as yet dignities   1
and prebends, the pallium and the wearing of the pallium, and tithes predial
and personal and annual dues were not yet the central questions.

Besides this, he opens to some extent the question of the property and
pay of priests when he plainly lays it down as right that those who are
servants of the Gospel should live of the Gospel; but his word is 'live' –   1
nothing about growing rich and faring like a prince, and no living either
unless they serve and attend constantly upon the altar. Not but what, while
maintaining this right for others, he does not take it up himself, although
labouring more than them all in the cause of the Gospel. Such is Paul's noble

* * * * *

176 letter] Augustine's Ep 47.6
184 *De bono coniugii*] 16 (PL 40:385–6)
187 ravening stomach] Literally 'barking' – a reminiscence of Horace *Satires* 2.2.18
195 should live] 1 Cor 9:14

and truly generous spirit, and in all the centuries since then I see no one keen   200
to emulate him. Nothing is done free; on the contrary, a price is asked for
everything, and no one does it as his bounden duty and service, while the
apostles used what was freely offered to them and Paul would not use even
that. They collect money too, but it was the freewill offerings of those who
have more than they need, and not exactions; moreover they collect for the   205
benefit of the faithful who are in want and not to give the rich more luxury,
and the terms of the collection are such that neither Paul nor Titus, who were
in charge of the business, got anything whatever out of it. Hence, it is clear,
it came about afterwards that many men entrusted their wealth to the
church, to be expended on the needs of widows and the aged amongst   210
others; from which the selfishness of certain people later diverted it to
support their own personal rule. Representatives are sent this way and that,
and they are given due honour both on arrival and on departure; but I
fancy less was spent on ceremony than we see now. About the business
entrusted to them I raise no questions. One can but rejoice at this great   215
increase in the church's wealth, if religion has grown in proportion to the
grandeur and the turmoil. Not that in those early times the apostles lacked
their proper dignity and standing, nor did they lack resources. Paul boasts
that his forces are not carnal but spiritual, owing their power not to troops
clad in iron but to the protection of God, and intended not for the   220
destruction of cities, for the plundering of common people and the slaughter
of human beings, but for the overthrow of every thought that raises its head
against the providence of God. The nature of those forces is explained even
more clearly by Ambrose in his *De viduis*. 'It is not by the weapons of this
world,' he says, 'that the church overcomes hostile powers, but by the   225
spiritual weapons which owe their strength to God.' And a little further on,
'The church's weapon,' he says, 'is faith; her weapon is prayer, which
overcomes the adversary.' This opinion finds support in Pope Nicholas,
whose words are recorded in the *Sentences* book IV, distinction 37, in the
paragraph beginning 'His adiiciendum.'   230
    These were the weapons and these the forces, such was the equipment
of the troops with which Paul, that invincible warrior, conquered Greece
and a great part of Asia Minor and proceeded to attack and take possession
of the Roman empire, which at that time was more than the weapons of any
monarch could defeat. But all the territory that he subdued, he subdued for   235

* * * * *

224 *De viduis*] 8.49 (PL 16:262–3)
228 Nicholas] Corpus iuris canonici, *Decretum*, part 2, causa 33, quaestio 2, chs 5–6,
    quoting Nicholas the Great, 858–67
229 *Sentences*] Of Peter Lombard: PL 192:931–2

Christ and not himself; with Christ to support him he proved himself invincible by the very fact that he depended on no support from men. He maintained the rights of the kingdom of heaven with heavenly weapons and fought the battles of the Gospel with the resources which the Gospel supplies. Tentmaker and pontiff, offscouring of the world and chosen instrument of Christ, who picked this sublime humility, this tongue-tied eloquence and stammering flow of words to spread the glory of his name through superstitious Jewry, clever Greece, and Rome, the queen of earthly kingdoms. Of him it is true, as was once said of Pericles, if I mistake not, that with thunder and lightning he confounded, not Greece alone like Pericles, but the whole round world.

There is another thing which it occurs to me to marvel at from time to time: the danger that faced the Gospel teaching at the start in its early stages, had not Paul put his best foot forward, as they say, to withstand it, much as the life of some unborn babies is in danger before they have ever come forth into life. Such a mass of weeds sprang up, which almost overwhelmed Christ's sowing while it was young and still in the blade; nor was it long before worldly philosophy and Jewish superstition, as though they had deliberately joined forces, were conspiring against Christ. Philosophy threw doubt on the resurrection and began to some extent to spoil the simplicity of the Gospel with quibbles of men's making. Judaism would have imposed on us the whole of Moses and even the crowning indignity of circumcision and would have reduced that heavenly philosophy to a matter of coarse and lifeless ritual, had not this valiant Isaac of ours opened so many wells of the authentic Gospel, so many springs of living water against the Philistines that would fill all with dirt. Philosophy at that time, led by sage fools with tongue and pen and even by tyrants with the sword, was advancing against Christ's small and innocent flock and has left traces which remain to this day. Judaism, acting through men disguised as apostles, was creeping in still more perilously under a false mask of piety and occupied Christ's whole cornfield to such an extent that even now it cannot be weeded out. Saint Augustine at any rate, in a letter to Januarius which now bears the number 119, witnesses that in Africa vessels used for washing the feet, which Juvenal also mentions, used to be kept with such superstitious respect that a graver rebuke was in store for the man who had touched the earth with his

* * * * *

244 Pericles] The greatest of Athenian statesmen; Erasmus adapts the description of his oratory in Aristophanes *Acharnians* 531.
249 as they say] Cf *Adagia* III i 34, from Quintilian 12.9.18.
259 Isaac] Paul, following Isaac's example; cf Gen 24:62, 26:12–22.
267 Augustine] Ep 55.19.35
269 Juvenal] It is not clear what Erasmus had in mind.

bare foot during their octaves than for one who had drowned his wits in
drink; for he was most indignant that the church of Christ, which God in his
mercy willed should be free and have very few sacramental rites, should be
loaded with the slavery of so many burdens that the state of the Jews might
seem preferable in that, though they had not recognized their day of   275
freedom, yet they were subjected to the burdens of the Law and not to
human innovations.

Tares of this kind among the wheat he somehow tolerates, although
reluctantly; what he finds quite unbearable, as openly contrary to the faith
and wholly inconsistent with sound doctrine, is the way some people carry   280
abstention from meat-eating to the length of regarding those who do eat it as
unclean. Of this superstition likewise clear traces survive to our own day, for
most people think that a good part of religion lies in the choice of foods,
which God created of equal value that we might eat and give him thanks.
Their judgment on this point is no less preposterous than the view of those   285
Africans on the washing of feet, nearly everyone regarding it as a more
serious crime to eat meat on a Saturday than to attack their brother's
reputation with virulent falsehoods or even to cut a fellow-creature's throat.
As Paul foretold, some were found to forbid marriage entirely. It seems to be
a relic of this superstition when even St Gregory lays down as the practice of   290
the Roman church and proper to be observed that a man who has had
commerce with his own wife should abstain for some time from entering a
church and should not enter until he has had a bath and, as the poet puts it,
has 'washed off the night in running water'; and for this piece of superstition
he produces a reason on which I will express no opinion: to wit that, though   295
matrimony is an honourable estate, yet pleasure, without which there can be
no intercourse between man and woman, cannot possibly exist without
guilt. What I say will be found in the *Sentences* book IV, distinction 31, in the
paragraph beginning 'Si forte aliquis.' And the defence excogitated at that
point by the Master of Sentences, that we should understand this to refer to   300
copulation provoked by incontinence, is a broken reed; the man who says
'cannot possibly' allows no room for exceptions.

There are other heresies too, the names of which have disappeared, but

* * * * *

289 Paul] Cf 1 Cor 7:8–9, 25–40.
290 Gregory] Corpus iuris canonici, *Decretum*, part 2, causa 33, quaestio 4, ch 7
293 poet] Persius 2.16
298 *Sentences*] Of Peter Lombard: PL 192:921–2 (quoting Pope Gregory)
301 broken reed] Literally 'a prop of figwood,' which was proverbially weak and
useless (*Adagia* I vii 85)
303 other heresies] The following names of heretical sects of early Christianity,
including the Jewish sect of the Essenes and the perpetrators of the sin of

their vestiges and, so to say, the scars of them can be detected even now –
those, for example, of the so-called Essenes, Ebionites, Apostolics, Psallians, 3(
or Euchites, to say nothing of the Simoniacs, a word that has long been
classed as obsolete. But disputes between sects of this sort, which later set
almost the whole world on fire (especially under the leadership of Arius,
when things were so uncertain that it was not clear which way the world
would go), multiplied even during Paul's lifetime – disputes not about 3:
indulgences or applications or other questions of the kind, which we now
drag by the scruff of the neck into the substance of the faith, but about the
resurrection of the dead, which is the foundation and the crown of our
belief. Against this plague Paul fights with all his might, but even so I fear
that this viper still lives in some men's hearts; for in Italy every year in 3:
sermons before the people they try to defend the resurrection, thinking that
they will be home and dry on this question, once they can show that
Aristotle did not entirely abolish the immortality of the soul. I say nothing for
the moment about their conversation at table. In any case, what other men
believe it is not my business to conjecture; one thing at any rate is obvious, 3.
that there are men, and particularly men in high worldly station, who live as
if they have no belief whatever in a future life.

And would that here too Paul had given us somewhat more light –
whether souls exist separate from the body and where they exist; whether
they enjoy the glory of immortality; whether the souls of the wicked are in 3:
torment even now, whether our prayers or other good actions are of any
service to them, whether an indulgence from the pope frees them all of a
sudden from punishment; for I observe that many men are in doubt on these
points, or at any rate dispute about them, which would have been needless
had Paul left us clear definitions. Besides which, although those who are 3:
born again in Christ ought to put off the old man with his deeds and his
affections, we see nevertheless that while the Gospel was still fresh, under
Paul's leadership, lust, avarice, strife, ambition, discord, and other pests of

* * * * *

simony, may have been chosen at random and from memory. Simoniacs apart,
a connection with the problems of the church of Erasmus' own day is not
immediately apparent. See, eg, Augustine *De haeresibus* 1, 40, 57 (CC 46:290,
307, 326); cf Ep 901:10n.
304 even now] Reading *hodieque*, altered by Allen in error
314 Paul fights] 1 Cor 15
315 for in Italy] Reading *quandoquidem*; the position here outlined is reminiscent of
Paduan philosophers such as Pietro Pomponazzi; see E. Garin *Italian Humanism, Philosophy and Civic Life in the Renaissance* (Oxford 1965) 136–150.
317 home and dry] Literally 'in harbour'; cf *Adagia* I i 46.
327 Indulgence] Cf the doubts raised by Luther's Ninety-five Theses, Ep 785:39n.

religion and morality had crept in among the people, while certain vices left
over from their former life it had not been possible altogether to root out. Let   335
no one therefore be surprised if in our own day some men abound in iniquity
because their love has grown cold. Even in Paul's lifetime false apostles had
made their way in, ready to turn the Gospel enterprise to their own profit, to
divert the glory of Christ into their own personal rule, and to preach
themselves rather than God; to teach the world in place of Christ and the   340
flesh in place of the Spirit; to gloss over heavenly teaching with the teachings
of men and build on Christ our foundation a structure unworthy of him. And
they were made more dangerous enemies of the church because they did all
this under the pretext of Christ's name and recommended by the title of
apostles, whose mask they wore.   345
      If only the church of Christ had no false apostles today! If only all those
who have succeeded to the office of preaching the Gospel would follow
Paul's example and preach Jesus Christ not for profit, not for advancement,
not for the favour of the great, not to wreak hatred or earn favour among
men, but in sincerity and truth! Paul himself when in chains boasts that the   350
Lord's word is not chained. But now – and a sorry sight it is! – we can see men
who have been virtually hired by salaries from the great for that very
purpose and preach what tends not so much to Christ's glory and to true
religion as towards the hunt for benefices, the setting of snares to entrap
preferment, and the spreading of nets to catch bishoprics; vigorous and   355
vocal when flattery is not only safe but profitable, and where truth would
mean loss, more dumb than fish. If salt has lost its savour, what else is there
with which ordinary folk that taste of nothing can be salted? If the light be
turned to darkness, what can dispel the shadows of the uneducated public?
If shepherds become wolves, what hope for the flock? If the leaders on the   360
path are blind, who will call them back from a wrong turning? If men are
buying and selling who ought to be the fathers of their people, where else
can we look for honesty?
      Has terror of men so much more power over us than the fear of God?
Are we more moved by men's rewards than God's? Can it be that we first   365
indulge our own self-love in order with more disastrous results to flatter the
self-love of others? Paul does not allow any mortal man to be acclaimed, he
does not suffer the praise due to the Gospel to be transferred to men. But
some men nowadays, as though Christ were outmoded, introduce a new
species of idolatry, making gods, if I may so put it, out of men. And all the time   370
humble folk are misled, all the time the multitude lie under a tyranny of more
than one description. This most of us can see; and we hold our peace. We not

* * * * *

350 Paul] Cf Col 4:18, 1 Cor 9:12.

merely hold our peace; we help the other side. 'I admit,' we say, 'that this is right, but it is not safe.' If among Christians it is not safe to preach the Gospel unadulterated freely, where then will it be safe? Had this fear always equally prevailed, who would have passed the Gospel down to us? Perhaps the ears of princes do not take kindly to sincere advice because we have made them too familiar with smooth words.

I do not say this to find fault with anyone. Would God there were no one at whom it might be fairly aimed! I shall not give them away; but by the books they publish and the sermons they deliver they daily give themselves away, with such shameless compliance that their very apes hold them in scorn. The voice which should be dedicated to religion is the slave of gain; it ought to teach the kingdom of heaven and it is enslaved to the kingdom of the world; it should expound the mysteries of Christ and it recounts the dreams of men. The trumpet of the Gospel, which Isaiah bids sound to publish forth the glory of God, is turned into a lyre to tickle the ears of men. As for the tongue, while Isaiah boasts that he has been given the tongue of the learned to root out the nurseries of vice and plant the seeds of religion, it is adapted to a very different purpose, teaching what it ought not to teach and attacking what it ought to praise. The dog's tongue, which ought gently to lick the wounds of those who have done wrong, often attacks the reputation of the innocent and, what is more disgraceful, of those who have done it a service. We use it as a weapon with which we attack anyone who offends us or even, without offending us, has done us a service unasked. The tongue of healing, one might think, has changed into the tongue of a viper. Why can we not imitate instead a tongue like Paul's, which can utter nothing except the Lord Jesus? Why can we not bear in mind that a preacher is an angel of the Lord, from whose mouth the people expect to hear the law of God, and not abuse of fellow-members of the body of Christ; and that there is a world of difference between hierophant and sycophant, between godliness and gossip, between teaching and treachery? At this point we need the bishops to play their part; for it is their business to see that opportunity to preach to the people is not given casually to the first comer. And let us not suppose it sufficient for performing this apostolic office that a man wears a cowl. Not all who have a tongue have heart and brains.

But to speak of these questions there may be a more convenient opportunity elsewhere; let me now return to my subject. This Paul of ours is

* * * * *

388 Isaiah] Isa 58:1, 50:4
408 Paul of ours] For the following comparisons see Bietenholz *History and Biography* 86–7. Vertumnus is the old Roman god of the seasons, constantly changing his shape.

always skilful and slippery, but in these two Epistles he is such a squid, such
a chameleon – he plays the part of Proteus or Vertumnus to such a tune that   410
in dealing with the Corinthians, who are more than Greeks, he seems
somehow to exemplify the old proverb 'Cretan with Cretan stand,' turning
himself into every shape that he may shape them anew for Christ; with
such freedom does he himself twist and turn like a man who threads the
windings of a maze, and appearing to us in a fresh guise every time. How   415
humble and ingratiating he sometimes is, as he beseeches them by the mercy
of Christ and begs them to bear with his foolishness for a space! Then again
he cries in harsh and threatening accents 'Do ye seek a proof of Christ
speaking in me?' Elsewhere he abases himself and calls himself an offscouring, misbegotten and unworthy of the name of Apostle; and then becomes   420
grand and exalted and sets himself even above the greatest of the apostles,
crawling upon the ground at one moment, and the next appearing to us out
of the third heaven. Now he praises the piety of the Corinthians, now
thunders against their faults. Some things he demands openly; others he
suggests by a kind of underground approach. Sometimes he is an unready   425
speaker who knows nothing save Jesus, and him crucified; sometimes he
speaks wisdom among them that are perfect. In one place he acts the part of
an intelligent and sober man; in another he dons the mask of one who is
foolish and beside himself. Now he boldly claims his own rights, now
courteously resigns them. In one place he speaks from the heart, sometimes   430
resorts to irony, with a 'Forgive me this wrong.' You may find that he gives
an appearance of inconsistency; but he is most like himself when he seems
unlike, and most consistent when he seems the reverse. Always Christ's
business is his main concern; always he thinks of the well-being of his flock,
like a true physician leaving no remedy untried which may restore his   435
patients to perfect health.

The greatest scholars labour to explain the intentions of poets and
orators; but in this orator far more toil is required if you are to understand
what he has in mind, what he aims at and what he is avoiding; so full of tricks
is he everywhere, if I may so express it. Such is his versatility, you would   440
hardly think it is the same man speaking. At one time he bubbles up gently
like a crystal spring, at another pours roaring down like a great torrent,
carrying many things before him; now flows peacefully and gently, now
spreads himself as though into a spacious lake. Again, he sometimes plunges

* * * * *

412 'Cretan with Cretan stand'] The Cretans were proverbial for quarrelling
amongst themselves yet standing by each other when assailed by misfortune or
by other people; cf *Adagia* I i 11
419 calls himself] 1 Cor 4:13, 15:9

underground and reappears suddenly in another place; then, when it suits   445
him, meanders unexpectedly, caressing now this bank and now that;
sometimes fetches a long digression and turns back again upon himself. I am
the more amazed at some people who, though they have hardly a smattering
of grammar and no idea what it is to write, yet suppose an understanding of
Paul's language to be an easy and almost childish thing. What I have   450
achieved it will be for others to decide. Ambrose and Theophylact the
Bulgarian bishop have been my chief guides; and though the latter is more
recent, he read commentaries of the early Greek Fathers which are now lost
to us. But though I have always had these two as my advisers, I have always
adopted the solution that seemed closest to Paul's meaning. That I have tried   455
to be faithful, I call Paul himself to witness.

My preface, I perceive, is longer than it should be, nor have I any
excuse except that I share this fault with many other writers in our own age
especially, and that my affection for you has made me run on. May your
Highness be preserved for us as long as possible in health and wealth by our   46c
Prince and Master, Jesus Christ.

5 February 1519. Louvain

917 / To [Juan de la Parra]   Louvain, 13 February 1519

This letter was published in the *Opus epistolarum*.

Juan de la Parra was Prince Ferdinand's personal physician, who accompanied him to the Netherlands. He was bishop-elect of Almeria in 1520 and was
still with his young master when Ferdinand attended the Diet of Worms
(January–May 1521), but he died during the diet on c 15 May (cf *Deutsche
Reichstagsakten* Jüngere Reihe, Gotha 1893– , II 911). In one of the prefaces of
his *Declamationes Syllanae* (Antwerp: M. Hillen 1520) Juan Luis Vives addressed
Prince Ferdinand and mentioned that his physician was to read with him daily
in Erasmus' *Institutio principis christiani* (cf Epp 853 introduction, 943:26–7,
970:27–8). Like Erasmus, however, Vives failed to mention the physician's
name. Apparently he was not well known in Louvain.

Prince Ferdinand (1503–64), the younger brother of Charles v, was born and
raised in Spain. He had arrived in the Netherlands between 24 May and 19 June
1518 (cf Epp 846, 849). There was soon speculation as to what parts of the
Hapsburg empire he should rule (cf Ep 893:39n), and at the time this letter was
written Princess Margaret had recommended that he should succeed her

* * * * *

451 Theophylact] Archbishop of Okhrida in the early eleventh century. His
commentaries on Scripture are often quoted in Erasmus' annotations to the
New Testament.

father, the emperor Maximilian (cf K. Brandi *Kaiser Karl V.* new ed, Darmstadt 1959–67, II 103–4). But after the death of Maximilian (cf Ep 915:177n) Charles was determined to secure the imperial crown for himself. In 1521 Ferdinand was appointed to rule the Austrian lands.

This letter was evidently brought about by suggestions that Erasmus himself should play an active role in the education of young Ferdinand. It shows that from the outset he was determined to decline, but to his embarrassment negotiations continued for some time; see Ep 927 introduction.

ERASMUS OF ROTTERDAM TO N, PHYSICIAN AND TUTOR TO
PRINCE FERDINAND, GREETING
A state owes no small debt to the fidelity and vigilance of the physician who has its ruler in his care, his body being the dwelling-place or instrument of the spirit whereby he rules. How great then is the debt this country owes to   5
you, and not this country only; for whatever may befall, Ferdinand cannot be other than an outstanding prince, as the brother of so great a king. For you not only watch with all your medical skill to ensure that the young man enjoys good bodily health; you mould him according to a Christian philosophy and shape his mind with its sacred ideas, filling a heart that is   10
still unspoilt and teachable with principles worthy of a true prince. Though what makes him teachable, it seems to me, is not so much his youth as the goodness of his disposition. I only wish more men were to hand like yourself, that our court might imitate the English court, which is filled with men learned in every branch of knowledge. Scholars attend the royal table;   15
literary questions are discussed, such as concern the education of princes or in other ways promote high moral standards; in a word, the company in that court is such that you would rate any learned academy below it. May it please Almighty God to effect such a revolution in human affairs that while ambition, pleasure, and avarice have invaded our universities, the courts of   20
princes may welcome honourable studies.

We have amongst us Luis Vives of Valencia, a man not yet past his twenty-sixth year, I think, but of much more than common learning in every branch of philosophy, and in humane studies and the arts of writing and speaking so far advanced that in this generation I know scarcely another   25
man I would dare set against him. There is no subject on which he has not a practised pen. When he writes he reproduces in our own time the example of

* * * * *

917
14 English court] Cf Epp 834, 855.
16 questions] For an example see Ep 964:132–6.
22 Vives] See Epp 927, 1082 introductions.

the Ancients, and that with such skill (believe me) that if you took away the author's name you would suppose the thing had arisen, not in our country and our age so much as in those fertile periods of Cicero and Seneca, when 3 cooks and scullions commanded a somewhat better style than men do now who are ready to instruct the world. He is most scrupulous in observing the technicalities but conceals his use of them so skilfully that you would hardly think he was following a preconceived plan. It seems to me that he is the ideal person to assist you in the education of Ferdinand and to ensure that 3 no one shall despise your court as tongue-tied and illiterate. Besides his other gifts he has perfect Spanish, as a native Spaniard, and very good French, having lived some little time in Paris. My own native tongue he understands rather than speaks. But I rather wonder whether the Cardinal de Croy, whose tutor he now is, will be willing to lose him (for he loves him, 4 as he deserves, most cordially), and then whether it would be right to deprive a young man of great fortune and exceptional gifts of such a tutor. I am sincerely devoted to Prince Ferdinand; but I owe so much to the cardinal that I would not dare set on foot anything that might inconvenience him. Finally, I do not yet know whether Vives himself could bear to be torn from 4 such a patron, who he knows is very fond of him. If on this point you in your wisdom feel as I do, I will suggest another name in my next letter. Farewell, honoured sir.

Louvain, 13 February 1519

918 / To Erard de la Marck   Louvain, 19 February 1519

This letter was sent with a presentation copy of the *Paraphrasis in Corinthios*; see Ep 916 introduction. It was printed in the *Farrago*.

TO THE RIGHT REVEREND ERARD DE LA MARCK, BISHOP OF
LIÈGE, FROM ERASMUS OF ROTTERDAM, GREETING
My Lord Bishop, I send your Highness herewith a small token of my feelings towards you, in the shape of a paraphrase on the two Epistles to the Corinthians. The work is a new departure in every way, even if it deserves 5 no commendation for any other reason. There was a competition between the printer and myself, whether he could print off with his types every day more than I could write out with my pen. I think the work will live, whether

* * * * *

31 scullions] Erasmus uses *apicius*, the name of a famous Roman gourmet (which is attached to a cook-book that survives from late Antiquity), having learnt from Tertullian *Apologeticum* 3.6 that it could be used to mean 'cook.'
40 Croy] Guillaume de Croy; cf Ep 945 introduction.

the enemies of the ancient tongues dislike it or not. You, I know, with your
wonted generosity will take it in good part. The young man who brings you   10
this volume is a good scholar and a very attractive person, secretary of the
town of Antwerp, whom I love as the better half of my own soul. Give him, I
beg you, a generous reception. And so farewell.

Louvain, 19 February 1519

919 / To the Reader   [Louvain], 23 February 1519

This letter is a commendatory preface for an important new edition of Livy
(Mainz: J. Schöffer, colophon date of November 1518, but published only after
the death of Maximilian; some copies also with an appendix of critical notes by
Nikolaus Carbach dated 15 March 1519). The edition was based on a newly
discovered manuscript in the library of the Mainz cathedral chapter, which is
now missing. It offered the text of books 33–40 with many variants and
included two sections of books 33 and 40 which had formerly been unknown.
Erasmus probably wrote this preface at the request of Wolfgang Angst (cf Ep
951:10), while Carbach, who had made the actual discovery and prepared the
text, asked his friend Ulrich von Hutten to write a dedicatory epistle; cf Hutten
Opera I 39* and Ep 110.

TO ALL ANTIBARBARIANS AND LOVERS OF GOOD LITERATURE
FROM ERASMUS OF ROTTERDAM, GREETING
Those who in ancient times provided scribes and parchment for the use of
Origen and Jerome won credit of no common kind; think then what credit is
due to those printing-houses which publish daily for our benefit such a flood   5
of valuable books, and that too at very reasonable prices. If Ptolemy
Philadelphus earned an undying name among posterity by his foundation of
the library at Alexandria – a famous place indeed and well endowed but yet
only one among its kind – what recompense do we not owe to those who
daily offer us whole libraries, a whole world so to say of books, in every   10
language and every branch of literature? And of that credit a great part is
owing to the inventors of this almost superhuman art; among whom the chief

* * * * *

918
10 young man] Pieter Gillis (cf Epp 312 salutation, 531:585), who was in his early
   thirties.

919
6 Ptolemy] Ptolemy II 'Philadelphus' (308–246 BC) expanded and systematically
   arranged the famous library founded by his father, Ptolemy I 'Soter.'

ERASMVS ROTERODAMVS MISO-
BARBARIS ATQVE IISDEM PHI
LOMVSIS OMNIBVS, S.D.

I LAVDEM HAVD QVAQVAM
uulgarem meruerunt olim qui Origeni & Hieronymo no
tarios ac membranas suppeditarunt, quantum uero laudis debetur Typographorum officinis, quæ nobis cotidie bonorum uoluminum effundunt examina , idق̃ mi-
nimo pretio. Si Ptolemæus ille Philadelphus memoriam
apud posteros sibi parauit immortalem , ob bibliothecam
Alexandriæ comparatã, insignem quidem illam ac locu-
pletem, sed tamen unã, quid præmij debetur ijs, qui nobis
cotidie totas bibliothecas, totosque , ut ita dixerim, libro-
rum mundos in omni genere linguarum ac literarum sub-
ministrant? Atque huius quidem laudis præcipua portio debetur huius pœnè diui-
ni opisicij repertoribus, quorum princeps fuisse fertur , totius æui memoria
celebrandus, IOANNES FAVST, auus eius, cui Liuium hunc. tum auctum
duobus uoluminibus, tum innumeris locis ex codice uetustissimo castigatum debe-
mus, ut hoc egregium decus partim ad IOANNEM SCHEFFER, uelut
hæreditario iure deuoluatur, partim ad Moguntiaci ciuitatis, & aliãs multis nc mini-
bus inclytæ, gloriã pertineat. Etenim si de laude reperti tormẽti, quod nouo uocabulo
Bombardã uocant, non pauci certant, quanto iustius laudibus uehendi sunt, quorũ in
dustria, pulcherrimum hoc eruditionis ac ueræ felicitatis instrumentum contigit? At
que utinam ut inuentum est eximium, ita non nisi libris , ac disciplinis egregijs excu-
dendis dedicetur. Atque hic rursum malim ueterum monumentis restituendis, quàm
nouis adglomerandis operam dari. Tametsi non desunt his quoque temporibus fa-
teor, qui scribant haud indigna posteris. In huius igitur pulcherrimæ laudis studium
incumbat nostra Germania, cui multos bonos authores ab inferis in lucem reuocatos
cum olim debet orbis, tum nuper Cornelij Taciti libros aliquot, pergat ex tam uasto li
brorum ac disciplinarum omniũ incendio, ex inaudito naufragio, ex miserabili ruina,
fragmenta , quæ licet, rapere , rumpãtur ut ilia Codris istis, qui cum rursus in hoc con
spirarunt, ut sub prætextu tuendæ religionis quicquid est elegantioris eruditionis cõ
spurcent atque extinguant, nihil aliud assequentur, quàm ut quod oppugnant red-
dant illustrius, & suum liuorẽ stoliditati parem magis ac magis denobilitent. Hanc
laudem expetant Germani principes, hactenus ornamẽtis rei bellicæ abũde clari. Fuit hoc olim regum studium, aut extructis pontibus, aut communitis fluminum ripis ,
aut alio deductis amnibus , tum thermis, porticibus , basilicis , aquæductibus, stratis
uijs, oppidis erectis , alioue quopiam insigni monumento sui memoriã posteris relin
quere, nunc fere ex miserandis urbium ac uicorum ruinis , ex uastatis atque incensis
agris nobiles sunt. Belli gloria tum uerũ habet decus , cum ad id coẽgit necessitas, aut
patriæ pietas, huius laudis semper parata seges est, nec̃ desunt exempla. Huc prouocat
insignis ille nobilitatis pariter ac religionis antistes ALBERTVS Cardinalis &
Archiepiscopus Moguntinensis. Huc clarissimus Saxoniæ dux FIDERICVS,
nequid interim dicã de notæ inferioris proceribus. Porro tametsi ex hac editione non
ita multum accessit Tito Liuio, tamen habenda non mediocris gratia primũ incompa
rabili uiro THEODORICO TZOBEL ædis Moguntinæ summæ Scho
lastico, & Reuerẽdiss. domini Moguntiñ. Vicario, qui singulari studio curauit hoc lau
dis suæ ciuitati asserere , deinde non uulgariter erudito uiro Nicolao Carbachio, quin
quennium iam Titum Liuiũ publico salario summa cum laude profitenti, tum Vol-
phango Angusto, à quibus quantum laboris exhaustum sit , dum ex codice non scri-
pto, sed picto coguntur addiuinare quid sit legendum, difficile fuerit æstimare. Nul-
lum autem tam deprauatum exemplar , unde solers confectator non multa queat resti
tuere. Proinde iuuenes optimi Liuiũ illum olim orbis delitium , ueluti renatum emi-
te, complectimini, legite , ediscite, præter uberrimam rerum gestarum cognitionem,
haud mediocrem eloquentiæ fructũ lucrifacturi. Bene ualete.   VII.   CAL.
MART.   AN.   M.D.XIX.

a ij

T. Livius … historicus duobus libris auctus title page
The first page of Erasmus' preface
in the edition of Mainz: J. Schöffer November 1518
Reproduced by courtesy of the British Library Board

was Johann Faust of immortal memory, grandfather of the man to whom we owe this Livy, not only enlarged with two new books but revised in countless passages with the aid of a manuscript of great antiquity. So that   15 this honour in one way descends to Johann Schöffer as it were by right of inheritance, and in another is part of the glory of the city of Mainz, which has so many titles to distinction.

For if there is such competition for the honour of inventing that engine which they call by the new-fangled name of bombard, how much more justly   20 do those men deserve honour through whose efforts this admirable instrument of scholarship and true prosperity came into being! Though, brilliant as the invention was, we may wish that its use could be confined to the printing of books and subjects that deserve it. And here again I would rather see effort devoted to restoring the great works of Antiquity instead of   25 adding modern works to the pile; although even in our own day, I agree, there is no lack of persons whose writings will deserve the attention of posterity. So let our native Germany devote herself to the pursuit of this glorious end; the world already owes to her the recall from the shades into the light of day of many excellent authors, and most recently of several books   30 of Cornelius Tacitus. Let her continue to rescue all the fragments she can from that vast conflagration, that unparalleled shipwreck and pitiful collapse of literature and learning, and so cause Codrus and his like to burst with spleen. Though they renew their machinations, plotting under the guise of defenders of the faith to vilify and do away all trace of enlightened   35 scholarship, they will achieve nothing except to make their target shine more brightly and bring increasing discredit on men who are as envious as they are stupid. Here is glory to be pursued by the princes of Germany, who have hitherto won fame in plenty in the form of battle-honours. In olden days it

* * * * *

13 Faust] Johann Fust (c 1400–66), a citizen of Mainz. He became the partner of Johann Gutenberg and financed the commercial use of his inventions. From 1457 he published books in partnership with Peter Schöffer, who married Fust's daughter, Christine, in 1467 and was succeeded by his son, Johann Schöffer (c 1470–c 1531); see NDB.

20 bombard] Cannon or cannon-ball. Crude weapons using as a propellant gun powder, invented in China, first appeared in Europe in the early fourteenth century and were probably developed independently in different places. National pride soon led to disputes over priority; cf J.R. Partington A History of Greek Fire and Gunpowder (Cambridge 1960) ch 3.

31 Tacitus] Books 1–4 of Tacitus' Annals were rediscovered in the abbey of Korvei in Westphalia and sent to Italy about 1508; the manuscript entered the library of Pope Leo x and was first edited by Filippo Beroaldo the Younger (Rome: S. Guilleret 1 March 1515).

33 Codrus] A personification of jealousy from Virgil Eclogues 7.26

was the ambition of kings to leave a name among posterity by building   40
bridges or embanking rivers or diverting streams, or again by the erection of
public baths, porticoes, basilicas, aqueducts, highways, towns, or some
other such distinguished monument; now, as a rule, they owe their fame to
the pitiful ruin of cities and villages and to the burning and devastation of
the countryside. Glory in war is true renown for those alone who are   45
compelled to fight by necessity or devotion to their mother-country. Fame of
this kind is a crop always ready for harvest, and examples are not hard to
find. In this field we have the challenge of that paragon of noble birth and
godly life Albert cardinal-archbishop of Mainz, or of Frederick the famous
duke of Saxony, to say nothing of princes of a lesser sort.   50
      Furthermore, although our Livy is not much increased by this edition,
we must be exceptionally grateful, in the first place, to that remarkable man
Theoderich Zobel, master of the cathedral school at Mainz and vicar-general
of the most reverend the archbishop, whose enthusiasm secured this
additional glory for his city; secondly to that exceptionally learned scholar   55
Nikolaus Carbach, who has now held for five years with great distinction a
lectureship on Livy provided out of public funds; and, with him, to
Wolfgang Angst. How much labour these men have expended – for they
were compelled to guess what should be read in a manuscript that is
sketched in with a brush rather than written – it is difficult to assess. But no   60
copy is so badly corrupted that skilful divination cannot restore a great deal.
      And so, my excellent young friends, now that Livy, once one of the
world's favourite authors, has been virtually born anew, buy him, enjoy
him, read him, and learn him by heart, and your reward will be not only a
fruitful knowledge of history but also no ordinary improvement in your   65
powers of expression. And so farewell.
      25 February 1519

            * * * * *

53 Zobel] Theoderich Zobel von Giebelstadt, south of Würzburg, (d 6 October
   1531) was a canon first in Strasbourg and subsequently in Mainz. In 1506 he
   became vicar-general to the archbishop and in 1518 scholaster of the cathedral
   chapter. He maintained friendly contacts with Hutten and other humanists and
   was probably personally known to Erasmus; cf Ep 880 introduction; AK II Ep
   655.
56 Carbach] Nikolaus Fabri, called Carbach (c 1485–c 1534), of Karbach, Lower
   Franconia. From c 1512 he occupied the oldest chair of history in Germany, at
   Mainz, and was a friend of Hutten and Reuchlin. He frequently assisted the
   printer Johann Schöffer as an editor and adviser; see NDB.
58 Angst] Wolfgang Angst (cf Ep 363) was Schöffer's corrector. In September 1518
   Erasmus had met him in Mainz and perhaps dined with him and with Zobel and
   Carbach (cf Ep 881:7). For an echo of their conversation see AK II Ep 628.

920 / To Ludovicus Carinus   Louvain, 27 February 1519

This letter was published in the *Farrago*.

Ludovicus Carinus (Kiel), c 1496–1569, was descended from a leading family of Lucerne. In 1513 he took possession of a canonry at Beromünster, north of Lucerne, which had been reserved for him since his childhood, and then returned to his studies at the University of Basel, where he graduated as an MA in 1514. He made friends with the Basel humanists associated with the Froben press and became acquainted with Erasmus. As a schoolteacher and tutor of wealthy students he was later to live in many places before settling down first in Strasbourg and finally in Basel. Despite his Protestant faith he was in the end reconciled with his family in Catholic Lucerne; see W. Brändli in *Inner-schweizerisches Jahrbuch für Heimatkunde* 19–20 (1959–60) 45–100.

In August 1517 Erasmus had greeted Carinus in a letter to Wilhelm Nesen (Ep 630:10–11); shortly thereafter Carinus went to Paris to continue his studies under Nesen's supervision. In a reprint of the unauthorized edition (cf Ep 909 introduction) of Erasmus' *Colloquiorum formulae* (Paris: H. Estienne for K. Resch February 1519) Carinus was permitted to add on the last page a short letter to an English fellow student, dated 4 February [1519] (reprinted in Allen's introduction to Ep 920). Erasmus may be responding to this letter or to one addressed to him directly and perhaps accompanied by a copy of Estienne's publication. For some time after Carinus had arrived in Louvain to continue his studies Erasmus went on treating him as a budding scholar of great promise (see Epp 1034, 1091), but in later years their relationship seems to have ended in mutual suspicion and anger.

DESIDERIUS ERASMUS OF ROTTERDAM TO HIS FRIEND
LUDOVICUS CARINUS, GREETING

For the friendly sentiments in your letter, my dear Carinus, many thanks, and on its scholarship, many congratulations. Nesen had some difficulty in persuading me that it was, as they say, all home-made; but persuade me he 5 did, partly because he is a man absolutely devoid of vanity, and partly because I have long known that you show great promise. Keep it up, dear friend; earn for yourself true happiness. The way to do this is to combine genuine scholarship and high standards of conduct. Heaven will provide the rest without your asking. Farewell.   10

Louvain, 27 February 1519

* * * * *

920

4 Nesen] Perhaps in a letter accompanying the present Ep 920. However, since Wilhelm Nesen (cf Ep 329 introduction) visited Louvain in the early months of 1519 he could have met Erasmus personally; but cf Ep 925 introduction.

921 / To Maarten Lips   [Louvain, c second half of February 1519]

This letter was answered by Ep 922. The text of both letters is preserved in the two copy books which Lips kept (see Ep 750 introduction). The book sent to him is identified in his argument in the Brussels manuscript as the *Paraphrasis in Corinthios*, presumably in Martens' edition (cf Ep 916 introduction) since it came fresh from the press. Lips' reply was probably prompt and prior to Ep 934; cf Ep 922:50–1.

DESIDERIUS ERASMUS TO MASTER MAARTEN LIPS OF BRUSSELS
Greetings, my dearest Maarten. I was too busy to come and see you, but that I may not seem to have forgotten you, I send you a pamphlet still warm from the press. Farewell.

922 / From Maarten Lips   Louvain, [c second half of February] 1519

See Ep 921 introduction.

TO THE HONOURABLE DESIDERIUS ERASMUS OF ROTTERDAM, DD,
FROM MAARTEN LIPS OF BRUSSELS, GREETING
I could well believe, my dear Erasmus, that you were prevented by your countless occupations from visiting a friend so humble and useless as myself. But what friend of Erasmus, however devoted, would not patiently endure 5
to be deprived of his society, if he fairly balanced up in his own mind how fruitful, how honourable, in a word how truly Christian those avocations are which divide you from him? As for me, it is not merely my own view, it is an article of faith that you are expending not only all you have but all you are for the benefit of the Catholic church. True, many people not merely fail to see 10
this; they actively dislike you, though your whole purpose is to deserve well of all men; and the reason for this (to say nothing of their blindness) is that they see this subject mastered by a man who is, in their view, a poet and a practised writer, but of small stature as a theologian. Heaven forbid that my own heart should accept their opinion! 15
You say you have sent me a pamphlet (I should call it a book) simply to show that you have not forgotten me; and this, I admit, covered me with shame. Never mind. All the same, my dear Erasmus, there is no danger of my forgetting you, who on countless points and in so many ways have led the way and followed up our friendship, which you cannot value. No, no: it 20
is for me to say things like this; it is my business humbly to beg such things from you – I who am of no benefit to our friendship and contribute nothing to the relationship between us. But this is part of your great reputation and is

rightly counted among your virtues, that, heavy as is the burden of business
that weighs upon you without recompense, you acknowledge even the least   25
among your friends, not only with your delightful letters but even with the
tangible evidence of your works. Why, what more could you have done for
Atensis or Dorp or Delft (to say nothing of others) than you have done for
me? Besides which, you modestly call a pamphlet what I think worthy of the
name of book, as though whatever you generously give your friends were a   30
mere trifle; and you gave it me with the smell of the press still on it, as though
the warmth of your affection could brook no delay.

I received protests from Edward Lee, having answered him once
openly and with some force. Now I suppose we have parted, for he has not
answered my letter, though up to now he has been most ready to answer.   35
But it was rather foolish of me to hope that he and I could maintain our
relationship unshaken when he could not keep the peace for a short time
even with you.

But enough of that. There are a number of people, dearest Erasmus,
who share my confidence and hope that you will one day think our beloved   40
Augustine (for we call him 'ours') a worthy object for your skill as a critic. If
only you were able to do that (for that you are willing I have no doubt), you
would see many men, my most generous friend, who have not been brought
closer to you by your restoration of Jerome (for Jerome's style is not to
everyone's taste) – you would see them, I say, your devoted supporters in   45
return for your work on Augustine, whose intelligence they admire so much.
There are others who think it quite wrong that you should not have done
this for so great a doctor of Holy Church, when you have shown so much
respect to many gentile authors – all the more so, since on your own
admission you have made a start. But the second edition of your New   50
Testament I long for as eagerly as its most ardent admirers. This one work is
the key to everything; on this, it is my belief, depends our victory, the

* * * * *

922
28 Atensis ... Delft] Luminaries of the theological faculty, such as Jan Briart of Ath,
   the 'vice-chancellor,' and Gillis van Delft, a Paris doctor of theology who was
   then in Louvain. On 31 May 1519 Delft dated from the College of the Lily the
   preface to his *Conclusiones in sententias* (Louvain: Martens June 1519; NK 2238);
   cf Ep 946 introduction.
33 Lee] See Epp 765, 898A introductions.
41 Augustine] See Ep 844:275n.
41 'ours'] See Ep 899:7–8.
44 Jerome] See Ep 396 introduction.
50 second edition] Cf Epp 864 introduction, 898A:13n.

reward of so much controversy and the triumphal welcome due to all that
toil.

Finally, there is one thing I would like to add at the end of my letter. On 55
account of the friendship between you and me, which I have done so little to
deserve, several of our community (but men to whose opinion in such things
I attach some weight) beg and beseech me to help them in the theoretical part
of their system of studies, and especially (what will surprise you still more) in
the acquisition of a good style, in which they say I have had some moderate 60
success. I am however well aware of my own shortcomings and 'how scant
the gear I have at home,' and I am almost ashamed at what they say about me;
I freely admit that I possess no style, though I would be most ready to meet
their admirable wishes if I had the power, but they are wasting their time in
asking me for something in which, for all my wish to do so, I cannot satisfy 65
myself. Besides which, they enquire what rules or principles you gave me in
the beginning. I tell them that you advised me to read Jerome and any other
ancient and genuine authors; but they are not content with this and do not
cease to pester me. Such poverty, such meagre resources have to be endured
by the most promising talents amongst us that they do not despise the 70
instruction even of someone like myself. How sad it is! We ought to be
ashamed to boast of Augustine as the father of our Order, when in spite of
that we have, I will not say no use, but extremely little use for the humanities.
For every single thing a time is laid down; but for the study of good
literature, just as though it had nothing to contribute, one single short hour 75
is provided. We live in sorry times indeed.

But I must not go too far, or I shall rouse the passions of the partisans of
ancient ignorance. I had these handkerchiefs ready some days ago, with no
purpose except to send them to you; but I was too shy to do so, partly
because I knew my small offering was of no importance and partly because I 80
had found by experience more than once that you always respond with
something more worth the having. But now that you have forestalled me
with a quite uncalled-for present, I know not why I should delay any longer.
Farewell and best wishes, my most generous friend and best of patrons.

In haste, from my cell in our house of Canons at St Martin's, in the year 85
of our Lord 1519

* * * * *

61 'how scant ... home'] Persius 4.52, a phrase which Erasmus himself often uses
67 Jerome] See Ep 750:5.

923 / From Ulrich von Hutten   Mainz, 6 March [1519]

This letter was published in the *Farrago* together with Erasmus' answer, Ep 951.

ULRICH VON HUTTEN, KNIGHT, TO ERASMUS OF ROTTERDAM,
GREETING

Silent though you are, I shall continue to bombard you with letters, and I
shall remain devoted to you, if you despise me even. His eminence is
impatient for a sight of you. The other day, on his way back from Thuringia, I   5
had gone to meet him, and we had hardly shaken hands when he said
'Where is our friend Erasmus?' As for your book, he asked about it again and
again and was surprised that I should not know what it is that you are
dedicating to him. He thinks I know all your news, and I wish you would
provide some basis for that opinion. He is wonderfully devoted to you;   10
which your virtues richly deserve, but it is outside the normal practice of
German princes.

So much for the prince and for your obstinate silence; now about
myself. I have had more than enough of court life, having nothing in common
with these gentlemen in silk and satin. I think I have secured from his   15
eminence that wherever I am he will send my salary after me; you will think
well of him for this, and it is very convenient for me. You have much
encouraged him to favour the humanities by your *Annotationes*, in which you
praised him for his support of me. This was a great stimulus and now,
whenever he welcomes a good scholar, he expects an immediate mention   20
from you. You may be surprised to hear that I have been very merry on the
subject of court life for the whole of this year; and other little things of mine
will have reached you lately. I now send you my *Febris*, which has just

* * * * *

923
3 letters] Only his Ep 611 is known today; a letter from Erasmus to Hutten was
   now on its way; cf Ep 986.
4 eminence] Albert of Brandenburg, archbishop of Mainz; cf Ep 661.
5 way back] Albert had spent the winter in his Saxon dioceses. Hutten may have
   met him at his castle at Steinheim near Mainz, since he did not enter the city
   until 17 March; cf Allen's note.
7 your book] The *Ratio verae theologiae*; cf Ep 745.
18 *Annotationes*] To the New Testament of 1516 (see Ep 611:59n). The praise of
   Albert was even more elaborate than that of Hutten.
22 court life] In his dialogue *Aula*; see Ep 863:36n.
23 *Febris … Phalarismus*] *Febris, dialogus Huttenicus* ([Mainz: J. Schöffer] February
   1519), later to be followed by a second dialogue, and *Phalarismus, dialogus
   Huttenicus* (March 1517). Both were quickly reprinted several times, for
   example together with *Aula* (Paris: P. Vidoue for K. Resch 1519), probably the

Ulrich, duke of Württemberg and Teck
Woodcut by Hans Brosamer (d 1552), undated
Reproduced by courtesy of the Trustees of the British Museum

appeared, and my *Phalarismus*, on which I know that you will criticize my
rashness rather than praise my courage.   25

Meanwhile there is a great expedition preparing here, both horse and
foot, in which I shall take part; so far am I from being frightened of that
brigand. Before long you will see the whole of Germany in turmoil. If I am
swallowed up on the field of battle (for the other side are not without
resources, and they have their supporters), please ensure that posterity is at   30
any rate aware of my devotion to you, and let your immortal writings bear
witness at least to the fact that I once existed. Farewell.

From Mainz, 6 March, in haste and not read through

Reuchlin's Triumph is now published to the great confusion of the
theologues.   35

924 / From Guillaume Budé   Paris, 6 March [1519]

This letter had not reached Erasmus by the time he wrote Ep 930 to Budé, but Ep
936 may betray a knowledge of Ep 924. Only in Ep 954 did Erasmus
acknowledge with obvious relief the receipt of Epp 924 and 929, also from
Budé, noting the similarity between them, which seems to preclude the
possibility that both were carried by the same messenger (cf Ep 925 introduction). This letter was published in the *Farrago*.

BUDÉ TO ERASMUS, GREETING

You say you have written me a rather tiresome letter, which I have your

* * * * *

edition to which Erasmus refers in Ep 951 (see Hutten *Opera* I 16*–38*). The
Febris was in part a personal attack on Cardinal Cajetanus (cf Ep 891:26n); the
Phalarismus, an attack on Duke Ulrich (cf line 27n), was based on a plot
reminiscent of the *Julius exclusus*.

27 that brigand] Ulrich (b 1487), duke of Württemberg (1498–1550), who had
conquered the free city of Reutlingen on 28 January 1518, hoping to act with
impunity because of the interregnum following the death of the emperor
Maximilian two weeks earlier. The move, designed to end years of political
instability, turned out to be disastrous. Under the leadership of Bavaria and
Austria, the Swabian League gathered an army and expelled Ulrich from his
German territories (March–April 1519) after he had failed to gain the expected
support of the Swiss. Ulrich von Hutten joined the league's army as part of his
family's campaign against the duke, who in 1515 had murdered Hans von
Hutten, Ulrich's cousin. Hans had served Duke Ulrich faithfully, but the
beauty of his wife attracted his master's attention; cf Ep 986.

34 *Reuchlin's Triumph*] For this anonymous poem, probably by Hutten, see Ep
636:29n. It was published in 1518.

924

2 tiresome letter] Ep 906; see its postscript.

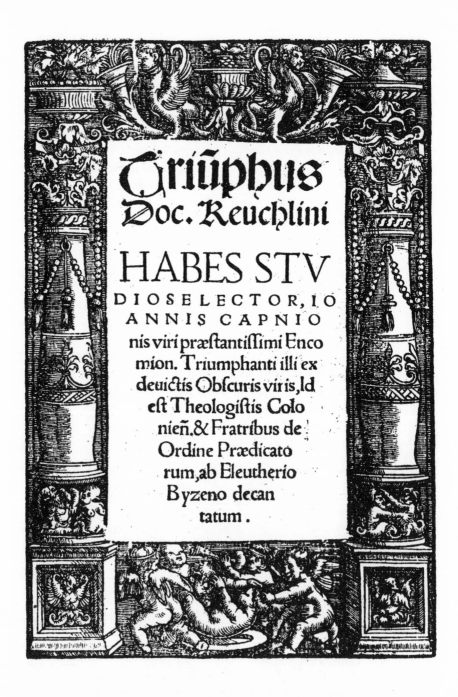

Triũphus
Doc. Reuchlini

HABES STV

DIOSELECTOR, IO
ANNIS CAPNIO
nis viri præstantiſſimi Enco
mion. Triumphanti illi ex
deuictis Obſcuris viris, Id
eſt Theologiſtis Colo
nien̄.& Fratribus de
Ordine Prædicato
rum,ab Eleutherio
Byzeno decan
tatum .

Ulrich von Hutten *Triumphus Doc. Reuchlini* title page
Hagenau: Thomas Anshelm 1518
The Joseph Regenstein Library, University of Chicago

permission to consign to the necessary house. On this point I shall certainly differ from you, even if as a result you are annoyed with me; I shall follow the example of Augustus, who refused to carry out Virgil's dying wishes. I   5
suspect that when you went over your letter again, you disliked things which seemed to you rather good sense in the heat of composition. That often happens to me too. But what is one to do when one considers the state of human affairs and human actions? 'For e'en what men think wise is foolishness.' But I would have you believe that to a sympathetic person like   10
myself these light-hearted things give pleasure, even when serious things are mingled with them; so far are they from seeming cheap. I have replied with my usual freedom; you must not expect that a man like myself, who am now nearly fifty, can be made to do better by correction.

The bishop of Paris has now been made archbishop of Sens by the royal   15
bounty, though the business has not gone through yet. He is now absorbed by the court, and I have no opportunity to speak with him. All the same, one day when he was in his majesty's privy chamber, he told me that he had decided to write to you. He will shortly be going off towards Narbonne on a mission with the grand master of the household; and the king has instructed   20
me to go with him too, to be a mere cypher rather than to perform any definite task in that province, or so I suppose. Still, I have been to the bishop's house twice and sat at his table; only there were so many guests that intimate conversation with him was impossible. So what he has done or decided to do, I do not know. And in any case, he has no leisure himself and does not   25
tell me much about his intentions. As for you, I learnt on what friendly terms you are with him from the letter you sent him recently. You are thus in a

* * * * *

5 dying wishes] That the manuscript of his *Aeneid* be destroyed; the story is told in the ancient life of Virgil attributed to Donatus.

9 'For ... foolishness'] The source of this, if it is a quotation, has not been identified.

14 nearly fifty] He was fifty-one on 26 January; cf Ep 493:401n.

15 archbishop] Poncher's appointment is dated 14 March 1519.

19 write to you] Cf Ep 929:5n.

20 mission] Negotiations between France and the Hapsburgs, represented by Chièvres, took place at Montpellier amid heightened tension as Francis I and King Charles both pursued their candidacy for the imperial title with single-minded determination. The negotiations dealt with the outstanding provisions of the treaty of Noyon (cf Ep 532:30n) and the imperial election. Despite the good will of the participants they were bound to fail, even if they had not been terminated prematurely by the death of Artus Gouffier, seigneur de Boisy, grand master of the household, on 13 May 1519.

21 cypher] Cf *Adagia* II iii 23.

27 letter] Cf Epp 906:553n, 915:150.

Le Roy demande,
Quant vous heuſteʒ dõne char
ge a Quintus Pedius vouſtre legat
& bon ſeruiteur des deux legions

Artus Gouffier
Miniature by Jean Clouet in volume II of
Les Commentaires de la guerre gallique, 1519
Bibliothèque Nationale MS Fr 13429 25 verso

position to sound his opinion once again. The king seems wonderfully well
disposed towards encouraging and inspiring good literature. But this
business of the election now occupies the whole court, so that they seem to   30
have hardly any time for everything else. As it is, I do not know where I
stand myself, and so am the less able to keep you posted about other things. I
am now beginning by some stroke of fate to make a fool of myself, though I
had not the least intention of doing so. But what was I to do? One must abide
by the web the Fates have spun. Lord, what fools we mortals are! Adieu.   35
Paris, Sunday last before Lent

925 / From Nicolas Bérault   Paris, 16 March [1519]

This letter was sent to Louvain with Wilhelm Nesen (cf Ep 994). Perhaps
Erasmus was in Mechelen (cf Ep 927 introduction) at the time and thus unaware
of Nesen's visit, which is not mentioned in Epp 928, 931 and Allen 1002:20–1.
On the other hand Ep 994 rather seems to suggest that they had actually met.
Perhaps Nesen carried Ep 929 too, or conceivably Ep 924. Presumably after his
return from Louvain – his presence at Paris is documented in April and June –
Nesen approached Jacques Lefèvre d'Etaples in search of texts by Cyprian
(cf BRE Ep 105), of whom Erasmus was then preparing an edition; see Ep 1000.
    The year date of 1518 added in the *Opus epistolarum* of 1529 and in LB to the
sequence of Epp 925, 989, 994, 1002–3 (all first published in the *Farrago*) is
obviously wrong, since Poncher is archbishop of Sens in Epp 994 and 1002; for
his appointment see Ep 924:15n. This letter was finally answered by Ep 1002.
    Nicolas Bérault (c 1470–c 1550) taught the humanities, first in his native
Orléans, where Erasmus met him in 1506, and subsequently in Paris. He was a
member of Budé's circle and became royal historiographer in 1529. At this time
he was preparing to accompany his patron, Poncher, to Montpellier; cf Epp
924:20n, 929:10–14.

TO THAT MOST ELOQUENT THEOLOGIAN ERASMUS OF
ROTTERDAM FROM NICOLAS BÉRAULT, GREETING
It has often distressed me, my dear and learned Erasmus, that two letters
from me in these last two years should have been lost; for I reckon a letter lost
to which you have sent no reply. Francesco Calvo had promised to take them   5
to Basel and deliver them to you; and I would rather think him careless than

* * * * *

925
3 two letters] Both are missing; the second may have been contemporary with Ep
819. In Ep 1002, Erasmus cannot remember exactly what Calvo gave him. For
the bookseller Francesco Giulio Calvo, see Epp 581:33n, 831 introduction.

dishonest, for after only three days in his company I seemed to myself to have made a very pretty assessment of his honour and integrity. In the mean while I thought it foolish to bombard you with another letter, the more so as you were busy on more serious subjects; for you have been devoted for several years now to the renewal of the study of theology, and occupied heart and soul (so the story goes) with great expenditure of lamp-oil and of labour on the elucidation of the Pauline Epistles. That you have made a second edition of your New Covenant (as they call it) I do not doubt, especially since this is confirmed by our friend Nesen, who has also seen a full explanation by you of the Epistle to the Romans, as he reported more than once to Louis de Berquin and myself (he is a good scholar and very zealous for your reputation), when he was with me the other day in Paris. I only hope I may soon have the good fortune to see all this really well printed; I mean, of course, in Froben's types, which are the clearest and most elegant and agreeable that one can imagine. And this precisely is the hope of everyone here of more than common attainments – Budé, I mean, and Du Ruel and Ruzé and Deloynes and the bishop of Paris himself, the greatest and almost unequalled Maecenas of our times – so much so that I cannot think any other work by any author was ever awaited more eagerly.

I foresee, my dear Erasmus, yes for my own part I foresee that the object of my most fervent prayers will be fulfilled: I mean that these divinity professors of ours, who have far too long been devoted to their prickly, futile sophistries and useless logic-chopping, will abandon the party politics of Scotist, Ockhamist, yes, even Thomist, and turn back, most of them, to the historic true theology, if only you will continue to assert the true importance

* * * * *

9 bombard] Perhaps an echo of Cicero *Letters to Atticus* 8.1.4
13 Pauline Epistles] See Epp 710, 916.
14 second edition] See Ep 864.
14 New Covenant] *Novum instrumentum,* the title of the first edition of the New Testament
16 explanation] Erasmus never published a proper commentary on Romans (cf Epp 710 introduction, 894:50n). Nesen may have seen the draft of some annotations at Basel in 1516.
17 Berquin] Louis de Berquin (1490–1529) was a nobleman and councillor of Francis I. He was a friend of Bérault and a great admirer of Erasmus, but increasingly of Luther too. He translated works of both into French and was finally executed as a heretic.
20 Froben's types] For the admiration Froben's books had won in Budé's circle cf Bietenholz *Basle and France* 40.
22 Du Ruel] Jean Du Ruel, royal physician and a member of Budé's circle; see Ep 346:13n.
23 bishop] Etienne Poncher

of the heavenly mysteries of Scripture. I consider you to have done this
hitherto with such success that I really do not see which of the divines of
ancient times anyone could rightly set above you, whether one chooses to
consider and weigh up your skill in languages, your various and universal 35
learning, or your incomparable energy and that industry which I would call
almost inexhaustible. A bold claim, someone will say, and bold it is, I admit;
but I believe it as true a word as ever was spoken. I know you have no lack of
admirers to assail you continually with panegyrics and victory odes and pay
you tributes which, even if you were to accept them, you would never ask 40
for. For my part, I write nothing to please Erasmus; I write what I think, and
nothing else. I know not how to curry favour, nor would I wish to if I could,
with Erasmus above all, who is such a modest man. But how can I not hold
the same opinion of you that I hear expressed by the best scholars everywhere? That man must be ignorant and mulish and a stranger to the Muses 45
and the Graces who does not praise your gifts, your scholarship, your style,
above all your religious wisdom and rule of life. On then, Erasmus, great
glory of our age! Onward to compete with and surpass yourself, especially
in that arena of Christian devotion and the religion of the Gospels in which
you have hitherto competed against us with such glorious results that 50
nothing remains but to excel your own self. Farewell.
Paris, 16 March [1518]

926 / From Louis Ruzé   Liège, 16 March 1519

Ep 926 is answered by Ep 928. Both were published in the *Farrago*, where the
date of Ep 928 is given in a very unusual fashion as XVIII Cal. April. (15 March).
The conflict with the date of this letter is best resolved by changing that of
Ep 928.

After the death of the emperor Maximilian (cf Ep 915:177n) Francis I
increased his diplomatic efforts to secure his election as emperor. Ruzé, a royal
official in Paris and a friend of Budé's, was sent to the Estates of Liège (rather
than to the prince-bishop, Erard de la Marck, who had recently broken with
France; cf Epp 738 introduction, 748:29n) with proposals for political and
military co-operation. But the mission failed (see Harsin *Erard de la Marck*
351–2). At the time Ruzé was writing this letter, Erard had gone to Mechelen,
where he met Margaret of Austria and Prince Ferdinand, himself a candidate
for the imperial throne (cf Ep 917 introduction), and leading noblemen. The
political situation was bound to be discussed. Erasmus too happened to be at
Mechelen (cf Epp 927:2–3, 951:12–13), but Ruzé probably did not know this (cf
line 24n), and although he may have been aware of Erard's patronage of
Erasmus (cf Epp 916, 918) there was apparently no immediate connection

between his political overtures at Liège and his hopes of seeing Erasmus in the French capital.

LOUIS RUZÉ, SUB-PREFECT OF THE CITY, TO HIS FRIEND
ERASMUS OF ROTTERDAM, GREETING
Whenever I tried, while I was in Paris, to express in writing my warm admiration for the great scholar that you are, my dear Erasmus – and I tried often enough – every time my efforts were foiled, partly by a kind of   5
shyness, and partly by an unbroken series of labours in the public service, with the result that all my attempts came to nothing beyond a single sheet at most. If I hear that you would care to read this, such as it is, I will gladly see that it reaches you promptly, as soon as I return to Paris, on one condition however: you must take off the mask of friendship, and either it must be   10
punished for its temerity by the critic's – that is, by your – blue pencil, or (and this I should prefer) it must fall bodily upon the sponge, so that I do not become what they call a minnow among the Tritons. I shall be sufficiently repaid, and more, if it makes you see clearly why I have kept silence so far. But at the moment, since I am on a mission for the most Christian King in   15
Belgium, I should rightly be accused of idleness and of letting my friendships go to seed if I left this place without sending you a greeting, encouraged as I am to write by your being so near, and as I have a little more leisure for the purpose; above all because I am blessed with a messenger whose peremptory demands I neither can nor ought to refuse. I mean your – I should say, our –   20
friend Paschasius, a young man (if my judgment has any value) of great promise, a very good scholar already in Latin and devoted to Greek; in fact, it was because of his burning passion to learn Greek that he told me he was just leaving for your part of the world and would take my letter. If only the king's business would brook a little delay with no loss of honour on my part, I   25

* * * * *

926
6 unbroken series] An echo of Martial 1.15.7
11 blue pencil] Cf Adagia I v 57.
12 sponge] The emperor Augustus wrote a tragedy about Ajax, who took his life by falling on his sword; dissatisfied with his effort, Augustus rubbed it out on the slate which he used for the rough draft and said that his tragedy had fallen on its sponge; cf Suetonius Augustus 85.2; Adagia I v 58.
13 minnow] Literally 'pimpernel [a worthless bitter herb] in the salad'; Adagia I vii 21
16 Belgium] The Latin form here and in the heading of Ep 928 is 'apud Eburones,' which suggests the country between Liège and Aachen.
21 Paschasius] Berselius; cf Ep 674 introduction.
24 your part of the world] Evidently Louvain is intended, since he wanted to study and Erasmus is thought to be 'so near' to Liège.

would snatch up my winged boots and be off with him 'on greetings and embraces all intent.' There I should drink from your words to my heart's content all that Venus and the Graces have to offer.

As it is, I must forgo such a pleasure for the present, which I endure with the more resignation in the hope that you will soon be shedding 30 brightness on my native Gaul like a second sun. And as its light increases every moment, wonderful to relate, you may see the very hills nod their heads and rejoice in company, while such of the darkness as yet remains gradually disappears and takes refuge so deep in the nether regions that the land far and wide will take on an aspect entirely new. A kindly and blessed 35 mother she will be, if she sees herself bathed in the equal radiance of her two great sons; for that you are a true Gaul and one of us, you will not deny. Indeed she expects to gain from you and Budé, both brilliant lights of the ancient tongues, to say nothing of the rest, no less glory than Italy won of old from Livy and Sallust or Greece from Herodotus and Thucydides. Rise 40 therefore, rise (I say) without delay, and at long last give the pleasure of your society to the mother-country and the friends who are devoted to you. Farewell.

From Liège, 16 March 1519

927 / To Juan Luis Vives   Mechelen, 17 March 1519

This letter was published in the *Farrago*.

Erasmus' presence at Mechelen (cf Ep 926 introduction) was connected with the efforts to find a suitable tutor for Prince Ferdinand. In Ep 917 he had suggested Vives, adding however that Vives' present employer, Cardinal Guillaume de Croy, might not wish to let him go. Erasmus' presence at Mechelen is documented until 21 March (cf Ep 931). From the present letter it may be surmised that he had gone there in the first half of March and then been sent back to Louvain to approach Vives and the cardinal. He had been given a letter for Croy but preferred not to hand it to him and thus came back to Mechelen without his answer. Perhaps the letter referred to both Vives and Erasmus as possible tutors. Thus if Croy wished to retain Vives, he would merely have had to add his voice to those who were urging Erasmus to accept; cf Epp 932:62–4, 943:22–7, 952:66–9.

Juan Luis Vives (1492–1540), the famous Spanish humanist, had come to the

* * * * *

37 true Gaul] Erasmus himself had once written to Budé in such a vein (cf Ep 534:28–32), but Ruzé may be alluding to Ep 914:4–6, a letter he had recently shown to Erasmus; cf Ep 935:51–5. Like Budé, Ruzé makes it clear that the king's offer to Erasmus is still valid; cf Epp 896:92n, 932:59–61, 952:61–5, 961:8–9, 994.

Netherlands from the Collège de Montaigu in Paris, where Erasmus had lived and suffered in 1495–6. He continued his studies in Louvain, becoming the tutor of Guillaume de Croy (cf Ep 628:70n) and making the acquaintance of Erasmus. In 1519–20 he published a collection of short writings (*Opuscula varia*, Louvain: Martens; NK 2172) dedicated to Croy and frequently inspired by his familiarity with Erasmus and his works (cf Ep 957 introduction). It included a violent attack on Paris scholasticism (*In pseudo-dialecticos*; cf Ep 1108). His friendship with Erasmus was to be crowned by their collaboration on St Augustine but in the end was seriously threatened by it. In 1523 Vives went to England and was appointed to one of Wolsey's lectureships at Oxford; cf Ep 967:40n.

ERASMUS OF ROTTERDAM TO HIS FRIEND LUIS VIVES, GREETING
At Prince Ferdinand's in the course of conversation the bishop of Liège complained that I had not brought a reply from his eminence the cardinal. I had some difficulty in thinking of an excuse, for I suspect that the letter never reached him. My own fault for not giving it him myself. The letter you   5
handed to me had clearly been opened. The more opportunity I have of conversation with Prince Ferdinand, the more attractive a person I find him. If only this part of the world could be allowed a hundred years of prosperity under a prince like that! As things are, he seems likely to be banished to Germany, and their dilatory methods will cost us dear.   1

But we must leave this to fate. Remind his eminence, in case he wishes to reply to the bishop, who will be here I think another three or four days. Farewell.

Mechelen, St Gertrude's day 1519

928 / To Louis Ruzé   Mechelen, [c 19–25] March 1519

This is the answer to Ep 926; it was published in the *Farrago*. For the date see Ep 926 introduction.

ERASMUS OF ROTTERDAM TO THE HONOURABLE LOUIS RUZÉ,
SUB-PREFECT OF PARIS AND ENVOY OF HIS MOST CHRISTIAN
MAJESTY TO THE BELGIANS, GREETING
Your letter was all the more welcome for being quite unexpected, though

* * * * *
927
2 Liège] Erard de la Marck; cf Ep 926 introduction.
10 dear] The unashamed bargaining of German electors and other princes with the rival candidates for the imperial title was bound to be costly to the subjects of the house of Hapsburg; cf Ep 1009.

more than once I had eagerly wished that you would write, especially as I   5
never receive a letter from Budé in which you are not mentioned. He is of
course a most reliable witness and a most skilful and stylish artist with the
pen; but even so your letter gave me a picture of you that was somehow more
vivid and more lifelike. I am most grateful to you both, to Paschasius whose
prompting overcame your reluctance, and to you for allowing your natural   10
modesty to be thus over-ruled. As you hope for the favour of the Muses,
mind you do not disappoint me of the sheet which you say you had intended
to send me from Paris. If you write such highly finished letters on the spur of
the moment and on a journey, it is easy to guess how good something must
be that you have polished at leisure and at home. What you have dedicated   15
to me in intention begins already to be mine, and I shall not cease to press
you for it until I get it out of you, should you by any chance be unwilling to
let me see it.

It is most kind of you to invite me to come to France. I have always been
much devoted to your country, but it is the society of Deloynes and Ruzé and   20
Budé that would attract me more than any offers from his majesty, generous
though he is. But I 'while this wind blows can neither go nor stay.' I have
such portentous people to deal with, that I really do hold the wolf by the ears
if ever man did. Happy the state of France, and happy the cause of humane
learning, to the pursuit of which you offer both opportunity and honour,   25
under the favour, of course, of him 'whose is the power supreme'! In
England also these studies flourish under the patronage of princes. Germany everywhere is rousing herself. Only in my own country are we still
backward, and barbarism, defeated elsewhere, seems to have fled to us as its
last refuge. The reason is partly that the court here has not yet learnt to treat 30
good literature with respect; partly the personal pretensions of a few men,
who are convinced that humane studies will interfere with the distinction
they have hitherto enjoyed among the common herd. Personally I have here
no axe to grind; I do not wish to make my fortune, being content with my lot

* * * * *

928
9 Paschasius] Cf 926:21.
22 'while this wind ... stay'] From the lost *Philoctetes* of Aeschylus (fragment 250).
In *Adagia* II v 21 (composed in 1508) Erasmus had already joined it with the
proverbial phrase 'I hold the wolf by the ears' (*Adagia* I v 25), said by the man
who can neither hold on nor let go.
26 'whose ... supreme'] Homer *Odyssey* 1.70
27 England] Cf Ep 917:14-21.
28 my own country] Cf Ep 930:12n.
34 no axe to grind] Cf *Adagia* I vi 82; literally 'the sowing and the reaping is none of
mine,' an expression which Erasmus often finds convenient

such as it is, nor am I in the market for reputation, of which I already have   3
enough to surfeit me. All the same, humane studies and their practitioners
have my hearty good wishes, though I get nothing out of it. Not but what I
think it unfair to blame the generality of men for what is caused by the ill
nature of a few.

But what is this you say, my excellent Ruzé? Can I contribute   4
distinction to that France of yours – adorned as she is already by such jewels
and such stars? For besides you three she has Lefèvre and Cop and Paolo
Emilio and Germain de Brie and Jean de Pins and Nicolas Bérault ... The more
fool I, for setting out to count the sand. Among such brilliant lights I must
inevitably be overshadowed; and yet it would be a pleasure to be   4
overshadowed like that, provided I were allowed to enjoy the society of the
men who seemed to put me in the shade. That I am a Frenchman I neither
affirm nor deny, born as I was in such a place that it might be considered an
open question whether I am French or German. Not but what among the
devotees of good literature it is right that the differences between country   5
and country should be held of very small account. Anyone who has taken
the same vows to the Muses as myself I reckon as my fellow-countryman.

From my friends' letters I gather that I am in Budé's bad books on
account of a letter in which I expressed myself, for his taste, rather too freely.
Personally, I judge him far too sensible to be much put out even if a friend of   5
no importance writes something ill timed or out of order and think him too
good a friend to abandon a friendship for such trivial errors. My own view is
that the man who for any reasons whatever has ceased to be a friend never
was one. Nor do I really see what there was in my letter so petulant or
outspoken as could reasonably rouse the resentment of a scholar, a wise   6
man, and above all a friend – and a friend who can claim the credit for his
mildness and moderation while laying the blame for bad temper on me.

But I leave the letter for you to judge of; unquestionably, so far as my

* * * * *

42 Cop] For the physician Guillaume Cop cf Ep 124:18n.
43 Emilio] For the historian Paolo Emilio cf Ep 136:2n.
43 Brie] For Germain de Brie, cleric, poet, and secretary to the queen, cf Epp
   212:2n, 620.
43 Pins] Jean de Pins (c 1470–1537), of Toulouse, a priest who went to Italy to
   study the humanities and met Erasmus in Bologna. Subsequently he was
   councillor in the Parlement of Toulouse, ambassador in Venice and Rome, and
   from 1523 bishop of Rieux. He corresponded with Erasmus between 1532 and
   1535.
54 letter] Ep 906; cf Ep 930.
58 ceased to be a friend] Echoed from Aristotle; cf Adagia II i 72. For Budé's threat
   to end the friendship see Epp 896, 906 salutations.

own feelings are concerned, I believe there can hardly be anyone even in
France whose sentiments towards Budé are more generous than mine or   65
whose praise of him is more outspoken. In this Henricus Glareanus will bear
me out, and Wilhelm Nesen and Beatus Rhenanus, men in whose company I
normally blurt out what I really think. Farewell, most excellent Ruzé.

From Mechelen, in haste. March 1519

929 / From Guillaume Budé   Paris, 19 March [1519]

Cf Ep 924 introduction. This letter covers in part the same topics as Ep 924. It
was published in the *Farrago*.

BUDÉ TO ERASMUS, GREETING

The day before yesterday I dined with Etienne Poncher, the new archbishop
of Sens. After dinner your name came up. I took it on myself to ask whether
he had written to you, and he said no, but assured me that he would be
writing shortly. It is true that for these two months he has hardly had a free   5
moment to think of you and me; partly because of public business and the
king's, and partly because of his own private affairs. What he intends to
write, and what he has done where you are concerned, I do not yet fully
know; and I would rather you learnt the whole story from him than from me,
for I do not visit him very often. Nicolas Bérault was present at our interview;   10
he is well read in both Greek and Latin and a good friend of yours, and he is
already very close to the archbishop, who will set off with him in two days'
time for the province of Narbonne, and I shall be of the company, unless
something happens either to me or to those who are the principal actors.

I wrote to you earlier this month to say that I do not regard your letter in   15
the light in which you thought I should regard it, and that I had not obeyed
your instructions to suppress it and did not intend to. I have suffered no
inconvenience as yet from your displeasure, real or assumed. As one who
makes free use of pleasantries myself, I do not easily take offence at the
pleasantries of others without very good reason, and I would rather have my   20
own feelings hurt than other people's. This is the principle I have decided to
apply in the maintenance of my friendships with other men; and if with
others, how much more with you, to whom, of all my friends and all
distinguished persons, I would most readily yield second place, taking no

* * * * *

929
5 writing shortly] It is doubtful whether Poncher did write; cf Epp 994, 1016.
10 Bérault] See Ep 925 introduction
15 wrote] Ep 924

offence at any pleasantries you might use against me nor putting a low
interpretation on what might seem to be such! Nor can you think to
persuade me that you were so well intentioned yourself; you had not much
use for such things yourself until you experienced my own powers in that
regard; wherein I may in the end of all have said much or little that seemed
foolish, but nothing, I do assure you, that was ill intentioned or spiteful, I
swear it by my patroness Philology or any oath you may think more sacred. If
I deliberately mislead either you or any other man who may read this letter, I
enter no defence if for that reason it please God to curse me. But how foolish
of me! For you now begin to believe me, even though I were not on oath,
unless I have convinced myself of this without reason. Farewell and best
wishes. Go on as you are, doing good work in the most important fields.

Paris, 19 March

By the way 'bear and forbear' until it begins to be certain what there
will be for you from us here. We hardly yet know ourselves what our
intentions are. All planning is bankrupt, thanks to the emperor's death, and
it is barely possible to decide anything.

930 / To Guillaume Budé   Mechelen, 21 March 1519

This letter was published in the *Farrago*. It answers Ep 915 and is answered by
Ep 987. Epp 930–1 were probably sent to Ruzé together with Ep 928 so that he
might take them back with him to Paris.

ERASMUS TO HIS FRIEND BUDÉ, GREETING

To your last letter, my learned friend, I shall send no reply whatever, for
discussions of this kind have gone on long enough. I have no desire to
display my eloquence on such a subject and have no use for victory when it is
paid for by the loss of friendship. What you think of me in your own heart, I
do not know. But this I would not hesitate to swear by all that is sacred, that
there is no one here who has a more favourable notion of your gifts, your
style, and your scholarship or speaks of them in public with more admiration
than I do, although you do not attach much weight to my opinion, I well

* * * * *

38 'bear and forbear'] Do nothing which might preclude the acceptance of the
French offer (cf Ep 926:37n). Budé cites in Greek a famous Stoic precept,
ascribed by Gellius 17.19.6 to the philosopher Epictetus; cf Ep 958:45n; *Adagia*
II vii 13.
40 emperor's death] See Ep 915:177n.

930
2 last letter] Ep 915; cf Ep 924 introduction.

know, nor do you need me to advertise your worth. It is incredible how the   10
Philistines of the whole world 'Cretan with Cretan stand' and add to their
forces whatever they can pick up. This makes it all the more necessary that
you and I should be of one mind. As for the letter which seems to have hurt
your feelings, I will do whatever you please and am ready to cut out or water
down what you do not like; or, if you prefer, I will hand it over for execution,   15
so that it may pay the penalty as you think best. Farewell.

Mechelen, 21 March 1519

931 / To Wilhelm Nesen   Mechelen, 21 March 1519

Cf Epp 925, 930 introductions. This letter was published in the *Farrago*.

ERASMUS TO HIS FRIEND WILHELM NESEN, GREETING
I understand from my friends' letters that in your part of the world Don
Agostino, the bishop of Nebbio, is vigorously declaiming against me by
name, though I am not yet persuaded to believe this. If it is the truth, he
and I have been employed on very different business: I praise him here as a   5
fairminded man while he is making mischief against me in Paris. I know for
an absolute certainty that the Philistines everywhere have put their heads
together, meaning to leave no stone unturned that they may suppress
humane studies. Take care not to put anything risky when you write to me,
for letters are frequently intercepted, especially those coming from Paris,   10
and this last letter of yours found its way back to me from Zeeland. I also hear
from other people that Budé is annoyed with me about something, nor can I

* * * * *

11 'Cretan with Cretan stand'] Cf Ep 916:412n.
12 can pick up] Despite many analogies in letters of other periods, Erasmus'
   complaint is relevant; even the astrologers agreed (cf Ep 948:19–20) that this
   was a time of particular trouble. He faced major personal problems in the wake
   of the Louvain controversies over the Collegium Trilingue (cf Epp 934; 938:5n,
   946, 961:37n, 991). In turn these added new momentum to Lee's agitation,
   which was spreading into Germany (cf Epp 936:34n, 972). Another cause for
   continuing concern was the *Julius exclusus* (cf Ep 961:42n), and the news
   reaching Erasmus from Paris was also troublesome (cf Epp 928:53–4, 931 :2–10).
   Eventually, however, there was a turn for the better; cf Ep 968:21n, CWE 7
   preface.
13 letter] Ep 906; cf Ep 928:53–4.

931
3 Agostino] Giustiniani; cf Ep 906:529n.
7 Philistines everywhere] Cf Ep 930:12n.
9 anything risky] Cf CWE 7 appendix.
11 letter of yours] No letter from Nesen subsequent to Ep 473 is extant.

see any reason why he should be. I have no doubt that he is very highly thought of in your city, as is right and proper, but I can hardly believe there is anyone who has a more favourable notion of him or speaks of him with more respect than I do; although he is too great a man to need any advertisement from me. He had challenged me to a literary contest, and he seemed to me to take excessive delight in unlimited pleasantry; but he took offence at my last letter and answered in truly French style, to put it no higher – or rather he did not answer, for it was quite off the point. Of course I have no desire to display my eloquence on such a subject, although I cannot yet be persuaded that he is seriously indignant. He thought this offered a way of testing my good nature, or at least of letting himself go; for, take my word for it, the man who ceases to be your friend for some trivial reason never really was a friend at all. Farewell, dearest Nesen.

Mechelen, 21 March 1519

932 / From Jan Becker of Borssele   Veere, 28 March 1519

This letter was answered by Ep 952 and published in the *Farrago*. For Jan's recent move to Veere see Ep 849:7n.

JAN OF BORSSELE, DEAN OF VEERE, TO ERASMUS OF ROTTERDAM, GREETING

I have been longing for some time to hear – and to hear in a letter from yourself, my kindest and most learned teacher – what is your state of health and what you are putting out day by day that will contribute to raising the standard of public morality to a truly Christian level and will be a stand-by to students of Holy Scripture. Since you finished the second edition of your New Covenant, I see that you have published summaries on all the Pauline Epistles and a brilliantly clear paraphrase on Paul's two Epistles to the Corinthians. I also peruse with great pleasure and (I trust) with no less profit the enlarged edition of your system and method of theological study. But though these rightly seem to others to be very great works, as indeed they

* * * * *

19 last letter] Ep 906, answered by Budé's Ep 915
22 seriously] Cf Ep 896 introduction.
24 ceases to be your friend] Cf Ep 928:58n.

932
7 second edition] Cf Ep 864.
8 published] For the following publications see Epp 894, 916.
11 system and method] The *Ratio verae theologiae*; cf Ep 745.

are, yet I know that you completed them in a few days. I know the indefatigable energy with which you work; I know you are incapable of being idle or taking time off from your literary pursuits. So I have no doubt   15
that there are other things which you either have already written or have in hand, which will greatly assist and promote the general state of learning as a whole, and especially of sacred study.

But there is one request I wish to make of you: that when you get a little time to spare from your more serious researches, you should devote a few   20
days to writing a book on the theory of preaching for those who wish to preach the Gospel. Long ago you laid down the principle of a Christian knight, and then of a Christian prince, besides which you have provided a theory for those who wish both to learn and to teach, in the exquisite books you have written with this subject and title. It remains for you to lay down   25
the right principles for a preacher of the Gospel, which will in fact be a benefit to a far larger public, not only to those who have imbibed your instruction and thereafter will preach better and with better results, but also to the public who in this way will listen to preachers more effectively and with much greater profit. Such a thing will be the greatest joy to me on behalf   30
of us all and privately for my own use. Not long ago I was enrolled, as you know, among the shepherds of the Lord's flock, and what food can I find for my Lord's flock committed to my charge more nourishing and better for them than that provided by evangelists and apostles, if only I had been trained under your guidance and knew how to feed it to them with wisdom and   35
skill? Say yes, I beg you, for two reasons: the very great and widespread benefits that will accrue and your own passionate devotion to the religion of Christ. On promoting that religion you have spent so much energy and toil, with enormous expense and to the unquestioned prejudice of your health, despising too the hostility and open attacks of all those jealous enemies; do   40
not refuse it this small amount of further effort. Allow some influence in this regard to my own perpetual devotion to you, ever since the day when I first knew you and admired you. If all this does not suffice to move you,

* * * * *

21 preaching] The suggestion may have stayed in Erasmus' mind. Although his *Ecclesiastes sive de ratione concionandi* was not published until 1535, an outline for it existed in 1523 (cf Allen I 34:19–22). A more immediate echo can perhaps be found in Ep 967A.
23 knight] See Epp 164, 858.
23 prince] See Epp 393, 853.
24 to learn and to teach] For Erasmus' educational writings cf Epp 66, 71, 260, 298, 341, 428, 771, 909.

remember that you promised me you would do it, in the winter of last year, when I was constantly, perhaps even tiresomely, at your side.   4

News of my state of health you will obtain in plenty from the bearer of this letter, who met you in Basel last summer. But if I may tell you something myself, my circumstances here are somewhat easier and to all appearance more comfortable, though there is less freedom than I could wish, especially to pursue my studies; for I am at court. You know that my patroness, the   5 Lady Anna van Borssele, died three months ago and was succeeded by her son Adolph, of whom you used to express such a high opinion. Those who know him well say much the same of him or even more. Having no ambitions, I have not yet made my way into closer knowledge and familiarity with him; nor has there been a suitable opportunity. Farewell.   5

Please give my greetings to our common host Master Jan de Neve, that civilized and learned man, to Master Joost of Gavere, to Jacob the physician, and my other messmates. From the town of Veere, 28 March 1519

I had almost forgotten to say that a man coming lately from Paris said he had heard the chancellor of France say that you had received an invitation   6 from the king of France on very generous terms and would be moving there, a thing I cannot believe will really happen. Others assert that an annual salary, a fairly substantial one, is being paid you by Ferdinand, the brother of his Catholic Majesty; this I should much prefer. Farewell, great teacher to whom all lovers of the humanities and the Christian religion owe more than   6 anyone.

* * * * *

44 winter] 1517–18, when Jan was living in the College of the Lily at Louvain; cf Ep
   687:18–19.
48 circumstances] Cf Ep 849:7n.
51 Anna] This former patroness of Erasmus died on 8 December 1518; cf Ep 80
   introduction.
52 Adolph] Of Burgundy, heer van Veere; cf Ep 93.
56 common host] Cf Epp 717:20–1, 737:7–8.
57 Gavere] Joost Vroye of Gavere; cf Ep 717:22n.
57 Jacob] Jacob van Castere, of Hazebrouck. He taught philosophy in the College
   of the Lily from 1511 to 1519 and was presumably studying for a medical degree.
   His whereabouts after 1519 are not known; see de Vocht CTL II 82–3.
60 chancellor] Antoine Duprat (1463–1535), later archbishop of Sens and cardinal
   (see DBF); for the French offer cf Ep 926:37n.
63 Ferdinand] Cf Ep 917 introduction.

933 / From Martin Luther   Wittenberg, 28 March 1519

This is the first of the six surviving letters exchanged between Erasmus and Martin Luther (1483–1546), the German reformer. Before their correspondence ended in 1526, their relations had entered a new phase. In place of the basic agreement over many issues still being freely expressed in the period of this letter, the fundamental gulf between Christian humanism and the Protestant Reformation was being emphasized and analysed in the apologies which they published against one another.

This letter and Erasmus' answer (Ep 980) were published in the *Farrago*.

MARTIN LUTHER TO ERASMUS OF ROTTERDAM. JESUS
Greeting. Often though I converse with you, and you with me, Erasmus my glory and my hope, we do not yet know one another. Is not this monstrous odd? And yet not odd at all, but a daily experience. For who is there in whose heart Erasmus does not occupy a central place, to whom Erasmus is not the 5 teacher who holds him in thrall? I speak of those who love learning as it should be loved. For I am not sorry if among Christ's other gifts this too finds its place, that many disapprove of you; this is the test by which I commonly distinguish the gifts of God in his mercy from his gifts in anger. And so I give you joy of this, that while you are so highly approved by all men of good will, 10 you are no less disapproved of by those who wish to secure the highest places and highest approval for themselves alone.

But what a dolt am I to approach such a man as you with unwashed hands like this – no opening words of reverence and respect, as though you were a most familiar friend, when I do not know you nor you me! But with 15 your habitual courtesy you will put this down to strength of feeling or lack of experience; for having spent my life among scholastic philosophers, I have not even learnt enough to be able to write a letter of greeting to a learned man. Had it not been so, think of the great letters I should have plagued you with long since! Nor should I have allowed you alone to do all the talking as I 20 sit here in my study.

* * * * *

933
2 Often though I converse] Luther is referring to his reading of Erasmus' works. For Erasmus' acquaintance with Luther's ideas cf below lines 22–5.
9 gifts in anger] Manifested in God's silence and withdrawal; see H. Strohl *L'Epanouissement de la pensée religieuse de Luther de 1515 à 1520* (Strasbourg 1924) 50.
13 unwashed hands] Cf *Adagia* I ix 55.

As it is, having heard from my worthy friend Fabritius Capito that my
name is known to you through the slight piece I wrote about indulgences,
and learning very recently from the preface to your *Enchiridion* that you have
not only seen but approved the stuff I have written, I feel bound to
acknowledge, even in a very barbarous letter, that wonderful spirit of yours
which has so much enriched me and all of us; although I know that it can
mean absolutely nothing to you if I show myself affectionate and grateful in a
letter for you are quite content with the gratitude and Christian love, secret
and laid up in God's keeping, that burn within my heart when I think of you,
just as I too am satisfied because, though you know it not, I possess your
spirit and all that you do for us in your books, without exchange of letters or
converse with you in person. Yet shame and my sense of duty insist on being
expressed in words, especially since my name too has begun to emerge from
obscurity, for I would not have anyone think, if I keep silence, that this is
due to jealousy, and of the wrong kind. And so, dear Erasmus kindest of
men, if you see no objection, accept this younger brother of yours in Christ,
who is at least much devoted to you and full of affection, though in his
ignorance he has deserved nothing better than to bury himself in a corner
and remain unknown even to the sky and sun that we all share. Which is a
state I have always wished for with the liveliest emotion, as knowing well
enough how curt are my resources. But by some fate or other things have
turned out very differently, so that I am compelled, to my great shame, to
expose my disgraceful shortcomings and my unhappy ignorance to be
discussed and pulled to pieces even by the learned.

Philippus Melanchthon flourishes, except that all of us together have
scarcely strength enough to stop him from hastening the ruin of his health by
an insane devotion to learning. He burns with the ardour of youth both to be
and to do all things for all men. You will do a good deed if you write to him
and tell him to preserve himself for our benefit and for the cause of liberal
studies; for so long as that man is safe and sound, I promise myself almost

* * * * *

22 having heard] This letter from Wolfgang Faber Capito is lost, but his next letter
    to Luther (Basel, 4 September 1518) opens with the words: 'Your last letter,
    dear friend, I answered from Strasbourg and I also mentioned Erasmus' opinion
    of you, namely how sincerely and frankly he admires your Theses on
    indulgences' (Luther w *Briefwechsel* 1 Ep 91; cf above Ep 785:39n). Capito
    continued his efforts to promote friendship between Erasmus and Luther with
    Ep 938.
24 preface] See Ep 858:216n.
49 all men] 1 Cor 9:22
50 tell him] Erasmus did so in the postscript of Ep 947.

more than I dare hope for. Greetings from Andreas Karlstadt, who is wholly devoted to Christ as he sees him in you. The Lord Jesus preserve you, most worthy Erasmus, for ever and ever. Amen.

I have written at length. But you will bear in mind that it is not always 55 the scholarly letters that deserve to be read; sometimes you must be weak with those that are weak.

Wittenberg, 28 March 1519
Brother Martin Luther

934 / To Maarten Lips   Louvain, 30 March 1519

This letter was published in the *Epistolae ad diversos*. In the Brussels manuscript (cf Ep 750 introduction) Lips added to it an argument which identifies the book mentioned in line 2 and ironically congratulates Latomus (see line 4n) on his achievement in writing the pamphlet that accompanied this letter.

Latomus' pamphlet appeared amid mounting conflict between the theologians and the humanists of Louvain, in which Erasmus was soon personally involved. When he returned from Basel in September 1518 the Collegium Trilingue (cf Ep 691 introduction) had introduced regular courses in all three languages, and his relations with leading theologians remained at first polite, if not cordial (cf Ep 867:274–5). But the latent hostilities surfaced when Petrus Mosellanus' (cf Ep 911 introduction) inaugural lecture at Leipzig, *Oratio de variarum linguarum cognitione paranda* (Leipzig: V. Schumann August 1518), began to circulate in Louvain. It contended that a sound knowledge of classical languages was indispensable even for theologians, in much the same way that Erasmus had done in his recently published *Ratio verae theologiae* (cf Ep 745 introduction). It was this contention which Latomus attacked in his two dialogues *De trium linguarum et studii theologici ratione* (Antwerp: M. Hillen 1519; NK 1326). The pamphlet was apparently rushed to the printer. It exhibited conflicting tendencies which could have left a reader with the impression that additional authors might be hiding behind Latomus' name. In February 1519 Erasmus had been publicly criticized in Louvain for views expressed in another recent book of his (see Ep 946 introduction); and in early March Alaard of Amsterdam (see Ep 676 introduction) had been prevented from giving a course of lectures on Erasmus' *Ratio* under the auspices of the Collegium Trilingue. With some justification Erasmus thought that Latomus was attacking him as well as Mosellanus, who was easily identified as a speaker in the dialogue (cf

* * * * *

52 Karlstadt] See Ep 911:61n.
57 are weak] 1 Cor 9:22

IACOBVS LATOMVS

Ædificat Latomus multa & præclara difertus
Difponenséque manu conftruit artifici.
Qui loca quæfierit fidei bene commoda noftræ
Flla petat, doctus quæ pofuit Latomus.   Cz

Jacobus Latomus (Jacques Masson)
Engraved portrait by Philip Galle in *Illustrium ... scriptorum icones*
Antwerp: T. Galle 1608
Rijksmuseum, Amsterdam

Ep 936:39–65, 970:14–15). Rejoinders were inevitable. On 21 March, when Erasmus was at Mechelen (cf Ep 927 introduction), Matthaeus Adrianus answered in public on behalf of the Collegium Trilingue, and in July 1519 Wilhelm Nesen continued the dispute by publishing a vitriolic *Dialogus bilinguium ac trilinguium* (cf CWE 7 appendix). Erasmus' own contribution was an *Apologia contra Latomi dialogum* (Antwerp: J. Thibault, n d; NK 2850; and, with corrections, Basel: J. Froben May 1519; cf LB IX 79–106). He took issue merely with those who saw in Latomus' dialogues an attack upon himself, and his courtesy and moderation helped to bring about a gradual détente; cf Ep 968:21n; de Vocht CTL I 298–346.

ERASMUS OF ROTTERDAM TO MAARTEN OF BRUSSELS, GREETING
As soon as the book reaches me, you shall have a copy. None the less, what you sent enclosed in your letter shall be kept safe for your own use. I send a pamphlet by Jacobus Latomus, a scholarly and elegant performance which many people suspect to be not his own unaided work but put together by the   5
theologians in conclave, and aimed at me. My own view is that it is good enough for Latomus but not good enough to look as though it had been passed by a majority vote of the theologians; nor do I deserve, I think, to be the target for such things. Other questions when we meet; I am summoned suddenly to Antwerp but shall return shortly. Farewell, dearest Maarten.   10
    Louvain, 30 March 1519

* * * * *

934
 2 book] The second edition of the New Testament (cf Ep 922:50–1). It appears
    that enclosed in Lips' letter was a sum of money to pay for his copy, but that
    Erasmus intended to give it to him as a present; cf Ep 955.
 4 Latomus] Jacques Masson called Latomus (d 1544), of Cambron near Mons. He
    studied at the Collège de Montaigu in Paris and was already an MA in 1502
    when he became the head of a residence for poor students in Louvain. He took
    his theological doctorate on 16 August 1519 and for the major part of his life
    continued to teach theology in Louvain, later becoming an outspoken defender
    of orthodoxy and critic of Erasmus; cf de Vocht CTL I 324–7.
 4 scholarly] Lips noted on the margin of the Brussels manuscript: 'ironically.'
10 Antwerp] The dates of Epp 936, 939 seem to indicate that Erasmus was in
    Antwerp on 2 and 14 April, whether continually is not clear. In Ep 952:12–13 he
    spoke of a purely recreational visit, but Lips suggested (cf Ep 955 introduction)
    one connected with the publication of his *Apologia contra Latomi dialogum* (see
    introduction.) The printing is so careless, however, that Erasmus could not
    have supervised it personally; see de Vocht CTL I 344.

935 / To Christophe de Longueil   Louvain, 1 April 1519

This letter presents Erasmus' carefully measured reaction to Ep 914 but curiously was not published at the same time. It did not appear in print until the *Epistolae ad diversos* of August 1521.

ERASMUS OF ROTTERDAM TO CHRISTOPHE DE LONGUEIL, GREETING
Your letter gave me pleasure for many reasons, dear Longueil, my learned friend – a letter written not to me but about me; and specially because it revived my long-standing impression of your natural gifts and the hope of something more than common in the way of style which I had formed some 5 years ago from the festival oration you pronounced when you were quite a young man in honour, if I remember right, of Saint Louis, king of France. Your letter was shown to me by Ruzé, the sub-prefect of the city of Paris, a good scholar himself and a most generous judge of scholarship in others. So far am I from resenting your preference for Budé as against me that I think 10 you were almost too chary of his praises and too lavish with mine. In your fairminded way you paid him a very high tribute; but whenever I contemplate his almost more than human gifts, I think I see something more there than eloquence can express. Of me on the other hand you speak more highly than I can either accept or expect; for me it is glory and triumph enough to be 15 compared with a man who is in all respects incomparable. You could not in my humble opinion do more for the fame of Erasmus than by making him second indeed to Budé, but second by a short head. But I read Budé's praises with greater pleasure than my own, partly because I am more jealous for his reputation than for that of any man alive, partly because whatever he 20 possesses in the way of honour I reckon to be also mine, not only by that general principle of the Pythagoreans that friends have all things in common, but also under the terms of a private agreement between us, formally signed, sealed, and delivered long ago, so that no one can deny it.

You paint me a pretty picture of myself, but I doubt whether it is alto- 25 gether in my true colours. And yet in front of this portrait I rather fancy myself; not that I believe it at all, but because it is a pleasure to be done by the

* * * * *

935
6 festival oration] *Oratio de laudibus divi Ludovici* (Paris: H. Estienne, n d). It was delivered at Poitiers in 1510 and published with a preface dated from Poitiers, 5 September 1510.
8 shown to me] The expression could suggest a personal meeting following the exchange of Epp 926, 928.
22 in common] Cf *Adagia* I i 1; cf Phillips 1–13.
26 true colours] Cf *Adagia* I iv 6.

hand of an Apelles. What is more, when you point out the shortcomings found in me by the critics I get no less profit than I do pleasure, though I could somehow wriggle out of some of them did I not set so high a value on   30
your judgment. When you say that I am too kind to my own faults, believe me, this is not so much kindness as either ignorance or more probably idleness. I am like that; I cannot conquer nature. I really do not so much write everything as let it pour out, and the work of revision is more troublesome than composition. In the choice of words, it is true, I should be sorry to seem   35
altogether careless; but I do not think it proper for one who seeks to convince on serious subjects to be careful and meticulous in adopting an ornate style. Nor will anyone wonder that the river of my style should sometimes run turbid and muddy who remembers the authors through whom it has to flow, mean as they are and debased in language, so that it   40
must inevitably pick up some dirt from them. It happened not seldom even to those great leaders of the art of writing that from their familiarity with Greek texts they often spoke Greek unawares. One point should perhaps be attributed to the copyist, where you allow me an excessive flow of language, a gift which is particularly Budé's. For a bare and straightforward style suits   45
an uncomplicated nature, nor is it odd that a man's writing should be on a lower plane who is lower in every way, in body, mind, and estate. Moreover the frequent and excessive digressions ascribed by the critics to us both alike (and the critics are a mask, if I mistake not, under which you have chosen to present your own opinion) each of us had complained of already in letters to   50
the other.

Above all however I wonder how it occurred to you to wonder that Francis king of France should have 'preferred a German not a Frenchman, a foreigner not a native citizen, a stranger not a man he had long known.' The king preferred neither of us but was keen to unite us in any way he could. No   55

* * * * *

28 Apelles] The most famous painter of ancient Greece
31 you say] Ep 914:55
39 authors] A hint at Erasmus' 'night watches' devoted to the New Testament. The evangelists and apostles neither possessed nor needed the accomplishments of rhetorical style; cf Ep 844:63–108.
44 allow me] Ep 914:61–2
50 letters] Cf Epp 493 and 531, an exchange which seems to suggest the approach taken in Longueil's letter.
53 'preferred ... known'] Ep 914:6–8, 95–8. The statement may have expressed openly what some of Budé's friends thought in secret and was bound to be received with sympathy among the Paris humanists. But Budé himself, although perhaps jealous of Erasmus' international reputation, had always worked loyally to bring him to Paris, and some of his friends had written to Erasmus with the same sincere intent.

one would have had to give place had I moved to France, so untrue is it that I should have stood in Budé's way. When you say that you and I were born under the same government, in the same country, speaking the same language, I am happy not so much for my own sake as for that whole region, which I rejoice to see daily grow in honour from such distinctions, which are 60 genuine and lasting. Nothing in fact more hoped-for could happen to me than that many men should arise like you, not merely to take over from me in this race we run for fame, but properly to overtake me and to throw into the shade by their own brilliance the little reputation that my work has earned me. Yet posterity, I feel, will recognize, and will confess it owes me 65 something for it, that in an unpromising age, and in a part of the world where liberal studies had been quite extinct and were resented, I have fought a long and unpopular fight against the most obstinate opponents of the humanities. But whatever view may be taken of me in the days to come, I rejoice that at the moment the best subjects are coming into flower everywhere to good 70 effect. Farewell, Longueil, my learned friend; devote yourself unsparingly to these studies, as you have already begun to do, and may success attend you.

Louvain, 1 April 1519

936 / To John Fisher   Antwerp, 2 April 1519

This letter was published in the *Farrago*. For Erasmus' presence in Antwerp see Ep 934:10n.

TO THE RIGHT REVEREND JOHN, LORD BISHOP OF ROCHESTER
FROM ERASMUS OF ROTTERDAM, GREETING
It is a long time since I enjoyed anything more than your Lordship's letter. Repeatedly I raised to my lips that well known and friendly hand. You increased my delight by not only writing but writing a long letter; for kind 5 your letters always are. You accuse me of prolonged silence, but I do not deserve this. However busy I may have been, I have interrupted you with a letter from time to time; but I think that some things one starts on their way never arrive. The book in which you maintain against Lefèvre that there was never more than one Magdalen I have only dipped into; but of those who 10

* * * * *

57 When you say] Ep 914:101–2

936
3 letter] Perhaps a reply to Erasmus' letter mentioned in Ep 908:27–8
9 book] *De unica Magdalena libri tres* (Paris: J. Bade 22 February 1519), the first of Fisher's three interventions in the steadily widening discussion on the Magdalens (cf Epp 766:26n, 1030). Fisher took issue with Lefèvre d'Etaples,

have read it everyone thinks you have easily the best of it. Only, some of
them are sorry to see you sometimes treating rather harshly (as they think) an
old man and a good man like Lefèvre, who has also done well by these
subjects; nothing could give more satisfaction to those who like to see
nothing added to the traditional disciplines in which they were brought up.   15
On this score Lefèvre has a bad name with them too. But it is almost bound
to happen that in discussions of this sort which involve a clash of views,
one's pen may sometimes get out of hand unintentionally. I certainly
sometimes find that when I suppose myself to have written nothing but pure
endearments, there are people all the same who think I have shown my   20
teeth. However that may be, I envy Lefèvre such an opponent, by whom he
may be laid absolutely low, but he will have the consolation that 'tis great
Aeneas' hand that fells him. But the scum with which I have to contend! And
the malignant libels! They cannot earn honour for themselves anyhow else
by doing good, so they hunt for a little notoriety by befouling other men's   25
good name.

The man of whom you write will never be other than himself; in fact at
* * * * *

who had rejected the traditional view that several passages in the New
Testament all referred to one woman, Mary Magdalen. Erasmus later claimed
that he was accused of being the author of Fisher's book; cf Ep 967:168–71.
23 Aeneas' hand] Virgil *Aeneid* 10.830
27 Poncher] Fisher states at the beginning of books 1 and 2 of his *De unica
Magdalena* that the work was undertaken at Poncher's specific request; see J.
Fisher *Opera omnia* (Würzburg 1697; reprint 1967) 1395, 1425. Poncher's
interest in the matter is understandable, since it divided the scholars of Paris.
When Josse Clichtove intervened in support of Lefèvre, he too addressed his
preface to Poncher; cf *Disceptationis de Magdalena defensio* (Paris: H. Estienne 19
April 1519). Poncher could have asked Fisher to examine the question during
his embassies to England late in 1517 (cf Ep 744:40n) and in September 1518; cf
Ep 964:39n. The news concerning Poncher may have been derived from Ep 924.
29 profit for the Holy See] Such as the fee for conferring the pallium and perhaps
the annates
34 The man] Edward Lee, likewise in line 99 (cf Epp 908:27n, 1026, Allen Ep
1061:434–8). Erasmus was clearly in no mood for the mediation attempted by
Fisher (cf lines 99–106). Rather Lee was attacked afresh in Erasmus' *Apologia
contra Latomi dialogum* (cf Ep 934 introduction; LB IX 106A). There Erasmus

this moment he is exceptionally active in this purveying of slanders for which   35
he seems to me to have a natural gift; and yet he seems to himself to have a
touch of sanctity. If I had on my conscience even the least portion of his
malignant libels, I would not dare approach Christ's table.

There has appeared a dialogue by Jacobus Latomus, a theologian at
Louvain, in which he does not entirely condemn the study of the ancient   40
languages, but so handles them as to reduce their importance as far as he
can. He then opposes different principles to my *System of Study*, but for the
time being without mentioning names; though in this way he puts me in a
more invidious position, for the strictures that he passes on this man or that,
and specially his strictures on Luther, may be supposed by the uninstructed   45
reader to be meant for me. This kind of restraint without restriction is a new
invention of our theologians. I myself certainly liked the book on many
counts, and I only wish they would write until they have had enough, and
stop scandalmongering. As it is, I am falsely accused by many people in such
a roundabout way that I have no one against whom I can draw my sword   50
with any certainty. I had entirely decided not to answer his pamphlet, but
my friends' opinion won the day; though my answer is such that it might be
thought no answer at all. I had said in my *System* that a good part of theology
is to have a pious mind and the right spirit. Latomus rejects this, showing at
some length that to be a theologian and a pious man is not the same thing.   55
But I fear that, if this goes farther, there will be people later on who say that it
is not the same thing to be a theologian and a man of sense. I perceive clearly
that the plague is deadly and almost believe the astrologers who not only
ascribe to the influence of the heavenly bodies the physical ills from which

* * * * *

repeated the charge made here, added more insults, and promised to identify
his critic as soon as he would make his charges in public. Lee, of course,
realized that the anonymous attack was directed against him and prepared to
answer the challenge. More than once Erasmus tried unconvincingly to deny,
not that Lee was meant, but that the readers had reason to believe that he was
(cf Allen Ep 993:34–8; *Apologia invectivis Lei* in *Opuscula* 268–9). Finally there
was an equally transparent and even cruder attack on Lee in Nesen's *Dialogus
bilinguium ac trilinguium*; see *Opuscula* 219, 229, 269; cf CWE 7 appendix.

39 dialogue] See Ep 934 introduction.
42 *System*] The *Ratio verae theologiae*
44 strictures ... on Luther] Cf Ep 938:5n.
48 they would write] Written charges can be answered; verbal innuendo cannot;
   cf above lines 34–7 and Allen Ep 1053:388–400, 429–40.
53 I had said] Literally in the last sentence of the revised *Ratio verae theologiae* (cf Ep
   745; LB V 138), but the formulation merely repeated one of Erasmus' fundamental views.

men now suffer everywhere but also think they give rise to plagues of the   60
mind. But O the madness of it! We waste our own valuable time and other
men's leisure on malignant falsehoods of this kind, and in our own eyes we
are saintly, we are theologians, we are Christians! And where all this time is
the Christian's tranquillity, his simplicity of mind, his blissful holiday in the
fields of Scripture?   65

What penalty can I pray for that is bad enough for those evil tongues
who have tried to persuade you that Erasmus does not approve of you? I do
not reckon you among those of whom I ought to approve, but for whom I
ought to feel entire respect and veneration – and you more than any other,
for I have always regarded you as my special teacher and unflagging   70
benefactor. If you are seldom mentioned in my letters, the reason is only my
respect for your high position; for there are so many ways in which your
greatness comes upon me – your eminence as a bishop, your admirable brand
of learning, but above all the saintly life in which you recall to our
generation, as few others do, the famous bishops of Antiquity. Towards   75
others I allow myself more freedom; but you I have always thought should
never be named by me without due thought, especially in a published book.
And yet I have dared to mention you in some other places, and especially in
the last edition of my *Enchiridion*, in which I have added a fragment of Basil
translated by me some time ago. But for the time being I look round for some 80
work which I can suppose likely to endure and which must seem not
unworthy of your eminence and your personal authority; and this shall be
dedicated to you, by which I mean that your name shall recommend it to the
world.

As to the proceedings in your part of the world for the reform, as the   85
story goes, of the clergy, I fear your reformers may be following too closely
the example of the physicians, who first reduce to a shadow the patient they
have undertaken to cure. O that Christ would at long last arise and liberate
his people from tyrants of so many kinds! For the end seems likely to be,
unless steps are taken, that it would be more tolerable to live under the   90
tyranny of the Turks.

* * * * *

60 plagues of the mind] Cf Ep 930:10–12, and for Erasmus' half-hearted belief in
   astrology cf Epp 755:32n, 948:19–28.
67 does not approve] Cf Ep 1068.
77 named] Many past letters to Fisher were not published by Erasmus. His name
   was even omitted in the heading when they were copied into the Deventer
   Letter-book; see Epp 653, 889 introductions.
79 fragment of Basil] *Basilii in Esaiam commentariolus* (cf Ep 229), printed in the
   recent edition of the *Enchiridion;* cf Ep 858.
85 reform] Cf Ep 967:29–31.

But to return to your book: I wish it had been more elegantly printed. If there is anything I can do in this respect, you will not find me unwilling. I could wish also that your pains had been devoted to some other subject; though this too has both piety and elegance. But those short notes by which   95 you establish the succession and significance of the Gospels, of which I had a taste some time ago much to my liking, would in my judgment have added something more worth having to your reputation.

As I was about to seal up this letter, the man I mentioned just now, transformed, I suppose, by the magic of a letter from you, sent an envoy to   100 me in Antwerp to treat of the re-establishment of friendship between us. I replied that if he could re-establish the damage he had done to my reputation, I should be most ready to return to our previous relationship. In the spirit of a Christian, I have no wish to injure any man, even when injured myself; but I am not so easily swayed that I can put my trust all at once in a   105 man whose nature I know from experience to be like that. In fact he never was a friend whose friendship ended as his did. On Luther I will write at more length another day. My very best wishes to your Lordship, to whom I tender my respectful devotion.

Antwerp, 2 April 1519   110

937 / From Richard Pace   Richmond, 5 April [1519]

The date must be 1519 because of the *Paraphrasis in Corinthios*. This letter was answered by Ep 962; both were published in the *Farrago*.

RICHARD PACE TO HIS FRIEND ERASMUS, GREETING
I could do nothing for Pieter the One-eyed, whom you recommended to me in your last letter, because the king has never thought of having a fair copy made of the book you mention. I have read the copy of that tragi-comic story which you sent to our friend More, and what you say about the case is quite   5 right: men of that sort are being swept away by a kind of fatal insanity, so

        * * * * *

92 your book] See line 9n. In keeping with Erasmus' offer here, a sequel to *De unica Magdalena* was in fact published at Louvain; see Ep 1030.
95 notes] Cf Ep 667:4n.
99 just now] See line 34n.

        937
2 Pieter] Meghen (cf Epp 231:5n, 653 introduction). Erasmus had apparently recommended him in a missing letter subsequent to Ep 887.
4 the book] Possibly the manuscript mentioned again in Ep 964:132–41
4 story] Probably the appeal for support against Lee mentioned at the end of Ep 908

fatal that in my view only the shears of Fate can cut it short. Even if some
sovereign remedy were at hand, and the physician at their bedside urging
and begging them to take care of their own health, they are reluctant to spew
up the poison they have swallowed. If you listen to me, you will continue on   10
your admirable course and earn the gratitude not only of sound learning but
of the whole church of Christ; let those men and their incurable insanity go to
perdition.

I have read your paraphrase on the two Epistles to the Corinthians
with the greatest care and wish to say that from this labour of yours I have   15
gained so much that at long last (for such a thing never happened to me
before) I dare affirm that up to a point (not to rate my own wits too highly) I
understand both what St Paul says and what he means. At last that divine
spirit in Paul, which used to seem stilted and intermittent, has its full force.
At last those divine precepts, which before tasted to me of bitter aloes, are   20
turned to honey. As it is, your paraphrase has made all so clear to me that I
shall bid farewell to all the commentaries by modern interpreters of the
Apostle, seeing how in so many places they have merely spread darkness
over an author who had enough obscurity and to spare of his own already.
There is another point of which I strongly approve: you have pitched your   25
style low enough so that the enemies of good writing cannot possibly accuse
you of affected language, but have to recognize the simple utterance proper
to the church, whose smooth flow exerts a powerful charm over the reader
and holds his attention however long he reads. As a result, for all the
simplicity of the style, to my taste no element of eloquence is wanting. Were   30
Paul himself alive today, what could he do except prefer his new self to his
old?

Keep it up then, my dear Erasmus, I do beg you, and explain the other
Pauline Epistles too in the same way. It is a task fully worthy of your genius,
your learning, and not least your cloth, and the completion of it will win you   35
great glory not only among men but in the eyes of God himself. I for my part
am impelled to urge you to do so by the fact that the reading of what I have
seen was so enjoyable and so profitable as to make me wait eagerly for what
is yet to come.

This reminds me of something you said in another letter, that you had   40
resolved to spend your declining years in England and thought of coming
over next summer. It is a great joy to me to know that you are planning this. A

* * * * *

12 to perdition] Pace uses the Greek expression 'to the crows,' *Adagia* II i 96.
14 paraphrase] See Ep 916.
40 another letter] Perhaps Pace's recollection of Ep 887:10–14 or a missing letter
   resuming the same argument; cf Ep 886 introduction.

very warm welcome will await you from us all; only have a care of your health above all in taking such a step – 'think twice ere for Abydos you set sail.' Meantime you may be sure that the king's good will towards you increases 45 daily and that he is continually singing your praises; he has men round him too who do not forget you.

Farewell. From Richmond, 5 April

938 / From Wolfgang Faber Capito [Basel], 8 April 1519

> This text comes from a collection of Capito's letters in the possession of his grandson, Dr Wolfgang Meyer zum Hirzen (1577–1653), published by A. Scultetus in his *Annalium Evangelii ... renovati decas prima* (Heidelberg 1618) 45. The date was recorded by Scultetus in his introduction. The letter illustrates Capito's efforts to bring about contacts between Erasmus and Luther (cf Ep 933:22n). It also forecasts the future disagreement between Capito and Erasmus, since they evidently differed sharply in their advice to Froben as to whether or not he should continue to publish Luther's writings; see lines 1–2, Ep 904:20n.

Do not, I beg you, exaggerate this business of Martin into a public issue. You know how much your vote matters. I really mean this. It is important that Luther's reputation should not suffer. This will encourage the rest of the younger generation to risk something in the cause of liberty in Christ; though there is much in him I do not like. Do not let Louvain prove an 5 obstacle. We will maintain Germany and Saxony in a proper respect for you, where the prince is a powerful supporter of Luther and so is the flourishing university of Wittenberg, and there are so many persons of distinction who wish equally well to both Erasmus and Luther. There is nothing his enemies wish more than to see you indignant with him. He himself and his party are 10

* * * * *

44 Abydos] Cf *Adagia* I vii 93.
46 men round him] Among them More and Pace himself. His letter is dated from Richmond, south-west of London, where the court was at this time; see LP III 76, 165, 197.

938
5 Louvain] In Ep 936:44–6 and especially at the end of his *Apologia contra Latomi dialogum* (see Ep 934 introduction; LB IX 106) Erasmus expressed concern that some of Latomus' general criticisms, perhaps intended for Luther and Hutten, might be taken to refer to himself. On 22 February 1519 the Louvain faculty of theology had written to their colleagues in Cologne questioning the orthodoxy of certain statements made by Luther and asking for their opinion; cf Ep 930:12n, CWE 7 preface.
7 supporter] Cf Ep 939:48n.

devoted to you. Better make enemies of all the theologians than of his supporters; they include several princes, cardinals, bishops, and all the leading churchmen, who have the business much at heart.

939 / To the Elector Frederick of Saxony   Antwerp, 14 April 1519

The original letter, autograph throughout, is in Thüringisches Landeshauptar-chiv Weimar, MS Reg. N 156 ff 2–6; cf Ep 979 introduction. It was printed in a pamphlet containing the questions which Eck and Karlstadt were to dispute at Leipzig (cf Ep 948 introduction, *Contenta in hoc libello, Erasmi Roterodami epistola* ... [Leipzig: M. Lotter c May 1519], and again in *Tomus primus omnium operum ... Lutheri* (Wittenberg 1545), together with the elector's answer, Ep 963 (cf Benzing *Lutherbibliographie* nos. 356–7). It may be noted that Erasmus never published Epp 939 and 963, although the exchange with Luther, Epp 933 and 980, appeared in his collected correspondence. He may have felt that this letter recommended Luther more warmly than was compatible with the reserved position he was attempting to maintain in public. By contrast Frederick's secretary, Spalatinus, used Erasmus' letter to strengthen his master's support for Luther and also sent a manuscript copy to Wittenberg, which Melanchthon (on 21 May; cf *Werke* VII-1 Ep 22) and Luther (on 22 May; cf W *Briefwechsel* I Ep 179) acknowledged with understandable satisfaction. They gave it to Mosellanus and Lotter for printing, and on 30 July Martin Bucer had seen a copy at Heidelberg. Noting that the letter was dated from Antwerp (cf Ep 934:10n), he thought that Erasmus had turned his back on the scheming theologians of Louvain (BRE Ep 119). Cf Höss *Spalatin* 161–2.

Greetings and all good wishes, most illustrious Prince. Although it has never been my good fortune to see or to speak with your serene Highness face to face, a fact which I count not the least among my misfortunes, I took fire from the remarkable unanimity with which everyone extols your distinguished gifts, worthy even of the highest rank, and the wonderful spirit in which you   5 encourage good literature and have even shown very special favour to myself, and made bold to dedicate to you my revision of the *Lives of the Caesars*, seeking nothing from your Highness in return, and with no ulterior motive except to deepen your approval of liberal studies and give some indication of a kind of mutual esteem answering in me to the favour so great a   10 prince has freely bestowed upon me.

* * * * *

939
5 highest rank] The imperial crown is intended; cf Ep 1030.
7 *Lives of the Caesars*] By Suetonius; see Epp 586, 947:43–5.

If, moreover, I did not send you the volume from Basel, where the work was printed, the reason was the length of the journey (for at that time you were in Wittenberg) and the lack of any reliable person to whom it might safely be entrusted; and soon it came to seem superfluous to send you a book   1
which was in circulation everywhere. I chose however to send this letter in the meantime as it were to spy out the land, to discover thereby whether my labours were welcome or no. If my boldness was ill timed, I will take care to remedy my mistake on another occasion. Nor do I doubt that, with the singular mildness of disposition of which all men speak, you will easily   2
pardon the fault of one whose spirit at least is zealous and well meaning. Good judgment may have been lacking, but there was no lack of the desire to earn your Highness' gratitude.

If on the other hand my boldness has met with success, I ask no reward for my service except that your Highness should continue your patronage of   2
those more liberal studies which are now coming into flower everywhere even in this Germany of ours and add a reputation in this field also to your other glories. Who knows if this will not bring at least as much credit to our country and to our princes personally as they have reaped hitherto from glory in war? This felicity will be ours if the liberality of princes will   3
encourage those who profess humane studies and the younger men whose gifts hold out no ordinary promise, and if their authority were to be our defence against those enemies of the Muses who obstinately assert the tyranny of ancient ignorance with every weapon they can command. Is there anything that these devoted adversaries of liberal subjects do not attempt?   3
Any tricks and calumnies and deceits they do not invent? Any saps and mines they do not use as they creep up on us? How they advance their artillery, how they rain missiles on us steeped in deadly poison! O the conspiring, O the tight-knit plots among them for the destruction of humane letters! They did not learn these in their youth and are too proud to learn   4
them in old age, though they could acquire them with less effort than they put into attacking them. What unity they show in this field, these men who never agree except when they are bent on mischief! How clever they are now, who would be blockheads for any better purpose! How they keep watch, who would be half asleep in a good cause!   4

There have recently appeared some pieces by Martin Luther, and at the same time rumour has reached us that he is persecuted beyond all reason by

* * * * *

12 not send] For a similar omission cf Ep 835. For Frederick's acknowledgments of the dedication cf Ep 963:5–8.
46 some pieces] See Ep 904:20n.

the authority of his eminence the cardinal of San Sisto, who is now as papal legate in Swabia. What instant rejoicing at this, what triumphant glee, as they think they see a perfect opportunity offered them to do harm to the 50 humanities! For, as the Greek proverb has it, rascals have all they need save opportunity, which gives scope for wrongdoing to those who have an ever-present desire to do wrong. Immediately the pulpits, the lectures and committees, and the dinner-tables were loud with nothing but cries of Heresy! and Anti-Christ! And in with this business, charged as it is with 55 prejudice, especially among foolish women and the ignorant multitude, these cunning fellows mix allusions to the ancient tongues and good writing and humane culture, as though Luther trusted to these for his defence, or these were the sources whence heresies were born. This worse than libellous effrontery did not find favour with men of principle but none the 60 less was hailed as a pretty invention by some persons who suppose themselves the standard-bearers of theology and pillars of the Christian religion. See how in the blindness of enthusiasm we pander to our own faults! We count it a monstrous calumny, almost as gross an offence as heresy, if anyone calls a brawling theologian, of whom we have not a few, 65 not a theologian but a vain talker; and we forgive ourselves if before a large audience we use words like heretic and Anti-Christ of anyone who rouses our disapproval.

I know as little of Luther as I do of any man, so that I cannot be suspected of bias towards a friend. His works it is not for me to defend or 70 criticize, as hitherto I have not read them except in snatches. His life, at least, is highly spoken of by all who know him; and not only is this very far above all suggestion of greed or ambition, but his integrity wins approval even among the gentiles. How unsuitable to the mildness proper to a divine when instantly, and without even reading his book right through, they break out 75 with such ferocity against the character and reputation of an excellent man, and do so moreover in front of the ignorant multitude, who are quite without judgment! All the more so, seeing that he put forward points for discussion and submitted himself for criticism by everyone qualified and unqualified. No one has given him advice or corrected him or proved him wrong; they 80

* * * * *

48 San Sisto] Cajetanus (cf Ep 877:12n). After much hesitation, Frederick wrote to the papal legate on 8 December 1518 rejecting his request that Luther be sent to Rome or at least expelled from Saxony. It was a crucial step; see Höss *Spalatin* 141–2; Boehmer *Luther* 245–9.
51 Greek proverb] Cf *Adagia* II i 68.
66 vain talker] Erasmus uses a Greek term from Titus 1:10; cf Ep 911:8n.
69 know as little] Cf Epp 961:37–8, 967:86–7, 980:19, Allen Epp 993:45–7, 1033:39, 1143.

merely cry heresy, and with disorderly uproar encourage people to start
throwing stones. One would think they thirsted for human blood rather
than for the salvation of souls. The more the word heresy is repugnant to
Christian ears, the less should men be permitted to attach it wantonly to
anyone. All error is not heresy without more ado, nor does something   85
instantly become heretical if this man or that disapproves of it. They do not
always advance the cause of the faith who attach grand labels of this kind;
many of them, in fact, are advancing their own cause, with an eye to their
own advantage or their own despotic rule. Indeed, a headstrong passion for
causing mischief often leads men to attack in others what they equally   90
approve at home.

Finally, there being so many authors ancient and modern, and none of
them having yet been discovered in whose books they do not agree that
there are dangerous errors, why do we read the remainder in silence with
our minds at rest and let fly so ferociously against one or two? If we uphold   95
the cause of truth, why are we not aroused equally whenever something is
found that is contrary to the truth? To defend the purity of religion and the
faith is a most pious thing; but it is a most pernicious thing under pretext of
defending the faith to serve one's own appetites. If they wish anything that
is accepted in the universities to be regarded as an oracle, why do   10
universities disagree among themselves? Why do our professors continually
do battle one with another? If it comes to that, why does one theologian
differ from another inside the very walls of the Sorbonne? On the contrary,
you will find very few who agree, unless they are in some conspiracy.
Besides which, they are not seldom detected condemning in the books of   10
modern scholars what they do not condemn in Augustine or Gerson, as
though truth altered between one authority and another. The authors they
approve of they read in a spirit that is ready to twist everything and stick at
nothing; those they do not like, in a spirit that will find fault everywhere.

The best part of Christianity is a life worthy of Christ. If this is   11
forthcoming, the suspicion of heresy ought not to arise too easily. As it is,
some men I could name are inventing new foundations (so they call them) –

* * * * *

100 in the universities] Cf Ep 938:5n.
103 Sorbonne] Cf Ep 936:27n.
105 of modern scholars] The reference is evidently to Luther. The controversial
views of Augustine on justification and of Jean Charlier de Gerson (1363–1429)
on Conciliarism had been invoked to a degree in his early Latin writings (cf Ep
1033). On both counts he had been sharply criticized by Cardinal Cajetanus;
see Boehmer *Luther* 236.

in other words they lay down new laws under which they can declare anything heretical which they do not like. Whoever accuses another man of heresy ought himself to display a character worthy of a Christian – charity 115 in correction, mildness in finding fault, a fair and open mind in passing judgment, and no haste in coming to a decision. As none of us is free from error, why are we so merciless in pursuing other men's faults? Why would we rather conquer than cure, why rather suppress a man than put him right? Why, he who alone of all men was wholly free from error did not break the 120 bruised reed nor quench the smoking flax. Augustine, dealing with the Donatists, who were worse than heretics, does not wish to apply force alone without instruction and tries to protect from the sword of justice the necks of men whose daggers were drawn to smite him every day. We who have teaching as our special duty prefer to use force because it takes less trouble. 125

I write this to you very freely, most illustrious Duke, because Luther's case has very little to do with me. Be that as it may, it is your Highness' privilege to protect the Christian faith by your personal religion; and it is no less your business as a wise ruler not to allow any innocent man, while you are the source of justice, to be delivered under the pretext of religion into the 130 hands of the irreligious. This is no less the policy of Pope Leo, who has nothing more at heart than the protection of the innocent. He rejoices in the name of father and has no love for those who under his shadow exercise despotic rule; nor does anyone more fully carry out the pope's wishes than he who dispenses perfect justice. What is thought of Luther in your part of 135 the world, I do not know; here, at any rate, I perceive that his books are read eagerly by all men of judgment, though I have not yet had leisure to read them through. My best wishes to your Highness, and may Christ the Almighty long preserve you for our benefit in health, wealth, and happiness. 140

From Antwerp, 14 April, in the year of our Lord 1519

Your Highness' most devoted servant Erasmus

To the most illustrious prince, Frederick, duke of Saxony, elector of the Holy Empire, etc

* * * * *

121 flax] Cf Isa 42:3, quoted in Matt 12:20
121 Augustine] For Erasmus' reactions to Augustine's views on heresy and tolerance cf Ep 858:268n; Wallace K. Ferguson 'The attitude of Erasmus toward toleration' in his *Renaissance Studies* 2nd ed (New York 1970); P.G. Bietenholz in *Bibliothèque d'Humanisme et Renaissance* 34 (1972) 35–7.

940 / To Jacobus Theodorici of Hoorn   Louvain, 17 April 1519

Epp 940–2 are addressed to residents of Erfurt and were published in the *Farrago*.

Jacobus Theodorici (Jacob Dierckx) of Hoorn matriculated at Erfurt in 1500. He was rector of the university for the winter term 1519–20, doctor and professor of theology in 1520, and dean of the theological faculty in 1523; see E. Kleineidam *Universitas Studii Erffordensis* (Leipzig 1964–80) II 310 and passim.

ERASMUS OF ROTTERDAM TO HIS FRIEND JACOBUS OF HOORN, GREETING

I welcome your kindness most warmly, for this reason among others, that you take the lead in making overtures of friendship, though in addition the fact that we come from the same country and share a love for similar studies 5 would have no small weight with me. You say that you think you once saw me at Deventer, but from this fact if no other you will easily perceive that you are the victim of a delusion: when I left Deventer, the bridge over the river that flows past the town was not yet built. Nor did I go to England when I left Deventer, for it is only nineteen years since I first set eyes on Britain. I left 10 Deventer when I was fourteen, and I am now in my fifty-third year. The problem which you discussed has not yet been demonstrated by anybody. Farewell, dear Jacobus.

Louvain, 17 April 1519

941 / To Euricius Cordus   Louvain, 17 April 1519

This letter was published in the *Farrago*; cf Ep 940 introduction. Euricius Cordus was the name taken by Heinrich Ritze Solden (1484–1535) of Simtshausen near Marburg. He obtained an MA at Erfurt in 1516 and became the head of the school at St Mary's and a lecturer in the faculty of arts. In 1519 he took up the study of medicine to improve his income, just as his fellow-poet and friend Eobanus (cf Ep 874) would do a few years later. In 1534 he was town physician and a teacher in Lutheran Bremen (see NDB). The original of this

* * * * *

940
8 bridge] Across the Ijssel. The accounts of the building contractor are preserved and run from 15 June 1482 to 1487, but the bridge was open to traffic from early March 1483. Thus it appears that Erasmus believed he had turned fourteen (line 11) on 28 October not later than 1482; cf A.C.F. Koch *The Year of Erasmus' Birth* (Utrecht 1969) 31–6.
10 nineteen] Close to twenty, in fact; cf Ep 103 introduction.

letter was probably signed 'Erasmus Roterdamus ex animo tuus'; its arrival prompted Cordus to compose an ecstatic poem; cf Ep 1008 introduction; Allen IV xxix; Krause *Eobanus* I 103.

ERASMUS OF ROTTERDAM TO EURICIUS CORDUS, HEADMASTER, GREETING

I only wish it were as easy to reply to all one's friends by answering their letters as it is by returning their affection: I would not then allow myself to appear second to anyone in the performance of my duty. As it is, being by   5
myself and at the mercy of so many people, I have to give up one or the other, all the more so since, besides the exchange of correspondence which takes up no small share of my time, I am burdened in addition with such a load of learned work – not to claim any credit on the side for the labour that is devoted to refuting the malicious inventions of my critics. Whether I have   10
gained any men for Christ, as you suggest in your letter, I do not know, although many express gratitude to me on this account; certainly I have done what I could, and I wish that I might have gained Christ for myself in the process. Over and over again I bless the good fortune of our country of Germany as I see her daily warming to the influence of humane studies and   15
putting off the spirit of her native forests.

You say you are opening a school in Erfurt. I pray for a blessing on your enterprise. The university is already famous on many counts, and your labours will add to its lustre. To make you more zealous in the duties of your office, never forget that after princes and bishops no one can possibly   20
perform more distinguished service to the community than a schoolmaster, if he can instil into minds that are still unformed and ready to take any shape a spirit worthy of Christ and those studies that have appealed to the best men in every age. If you take my advice, you will devote more effort to the encouragement of humane studies than to the refutation of their   25
enemies. In the light of day the monsters of the dark disappear of their own accord. Be sure to give my greetings to Eobanus, the Ovid of our times, but a pure and godly Ovid. Farewell, most cordial Cordus.

Louvain, 17 April 1519

* * * * *

941
3 easy] Erasmus expressed anxiety about the volume of his correspondence in Epp 944:28–32, 948:241–6, 951:2–3; 952:16–18.
10 critics] Cf Ep 930:12n.
27 Ovid of our times] Cf Ep 871:16n.

942 / To Johannes Draconites   Louvain, 18 April 1519

This letter was published in the *Farrago*; cf Ep 940 introduction, and for Draconites see Ep 871.

ERASMUS OF ROTTERDAM TO JOHANNES DRACO, GREETING

In setting out to sing my praises, you ask pardon for your style and reject any suggestion that you flatter me. For my part, I was delighted with the ease of your writing, which is both clear and natural, particularly for a young man; and from this I promise myself that you will develop a style of rare 5 distinction. Apart from that, I see no reason why anybody should either be jealous of me or try to flatter me. What advantage could be gained by any such adulation? It may be that praise of this kind, which I owe to some people's partiality or readiness to think the best of others, gives me a heavy load of jealousy to bear; and yet the affection which gives rise to it is 1(something I cannot entirely refuse. I only wish there might be some truth in what you say about the benefits which the Christian world has derived from what I write. Who am I that I should be able to do the world any great service? Though I have tried to lay out my talent, small as it is, so as to make a profit for my Lord. Success may have failed me, but my good will has never 1! failed. Some people protest, with undue spite; others praise me beyond reason. I do not deserve the virulent attacks of the one party, nor do I accept the panegyrics of the other. Till further notice, I measure myself by my own standards; I am not inflated by the enthusiastic praise of my supporters, nor am I at all cast down by the perversity of my detractors, consoling myself for 2(the time being by a clear conscience and looking to receive the reward of my unsleeping labours from Christ, if men are not as grateful as they might be. Though I perceive that all good men welcome my efforts; but bad men are in the majority.

Speaking in the name of Erfurt University, you assure me of their 2! enthusiastic support at present and promise it for the future. The approval of so famous an institution was extremely welcome to me; for they would not show me such friendship unless they approved of me. I only hope that Eobanus does not regret his journey here as much as I rejoice in my own

* * * * *

942
14 talent] Cf Matt 25:14–30.
16 with undue spite] Cf Ep 930:12n.
18 measure myself] cf *Adagia* I vi 89.
29 journey] See Ep 870 introduction.

good fortune in getting to know such a good scholar, such an excellent 30
writer, and a man of such integrity and high character. Though I myself
gave him a rather uncivil reception, being at the time excessively busy – not
that I am otherwise than busy ever. Farewell, my dear Draco.

Louvain, 18 April 1519

943 / To Johannes Thurzo   Louvain, 20 April 1519

> This letter answers Ep 850 and in turn is answered by Ep 1047. It was published
> in the *Farrago*. Two contemporary manuscript copies survive and were used by
> Allen in establishing his text; one is in the Bayerische Staatsbibliothek,
> Munich, Clm 965 pp 349–53, which is also the source for Ep 850; the other is in
> the Library of the University of Bremen, MS a 8 no 5.

TO THE RIGHT REVEREND FATHER IN CHRIST JOHANNES THURZO,
LORD BISHOP OF WROCŁAW

Greeting. Your letter, my Lord Bishop, was full of kindness no less than of
scholarship and eloquence and polished grace, and I should have thought it
richly deserved to be published to the credit of your reputation, if it did not 5
rate my own reputation much too high. Its brilliance very nearly deterred me
from replying, but I thought it better to lose face than to seem ungracious.
And I should be very ungracious indeed if, in response to such a letter from
so eminent a prelate, I had simply kept silence. So far am I however from
thinking it a disgrace when I am outdone by younger men that it is my 10
particular pride and delight to see our age outgrow its old unlettered
lethargy and put forth the fresh and fruitful blossoms of good literature. Nor
do I claim any share in the credit of this for myself, except in so far as my own
writings have aroused some men to more humane studies; so you must not
think that I accept the praise which you offer me with more charity than 15
truth.

Of course it is no new thing for distinguished abilities to be found in
Hungary, since the celebrated Janus Pannonius made such a name in poetry
that Italy readily yielded him the palm. Then Piso – you refresh my memory

* * * * *

943
18 Pannonius] Janus Pannonius (Ivan Česmički), a famous Hungarian humanist.
   After studies in Italy he returned to his country and was bishop of Pécs from
   1459 to his death in 1474. In July 1518, when Erasmus was in Basel, Froben
   published a selection of his poems edited by Beatus Rhenanus; cf BRE Ep 76.
19 palm] Literally, 'gave him the tuft of grass,' which in some ancient athletic
   contests was a sign that the loser admitted defeat; cf *Adagia* I ix 78.
19 Piso] The tutor of Louis II; cf Ep 850:21n.

of him, and the recollection is as delightful as was his company long ago in
Rome: who more learned, who more gay than he? I think his majesty your
king is to be envied even more for his tutor than for his crown. Here too there
was a move to make me tutor to Prince Ferdinand. He is indeed a young man
divinely gifted, wonderfully teachable, the natural seat of honour and
virtue, and with a charmingly serious demeanour; only there were good
reasons for my reluctance to commit myself to court life. Yet, as he told me
himself, he has my book on the education of a prince constantly in his hands.

As I read Velius' poem, which reached me recently, I seem to hear the
trumpet-tones of Lucan; he should be writing of famous monarchs, not of an
Erasmus. I shall never encourage you to undertake an eight days' journey, as
you suggest, for the purpose of seeing a poor creature like myself; I know
very well that you would regret your journey, and I should suffer some loss
in your good opinion of me. If there is anything worth a visit in your humble
servant, you have had a view of it in what I write. Nor, for that matter, am I a
Livy, and you some unlettered tourist from Gades. Furthermore, what
present can you be preparing for me? Is not this letter of yours, in which you
offer me your heart, the most generous of all presents? To me, at least, no
more precious memento of you could be offered, especially as your Lordship
condescended to write a long letter in your own hand. Farewell.

Louvain, 1519, 20 April
Erasmus of Rotterdam in his own hand

944 / To Caspar Ursinus Velius   Louvain, [c 20 April 1519]

This letter answers Ep 851. It is clearly contemporary with Ep 943 and was
published in the *Farrago*.

ERASMUS OF ROTTERDAM TO CASPAR VELIUS, GREETING
You were not satisfied apparently, my learned friend Velius, with a most
eloquent but most mendacious poem in my praise, but you must needs add a
letter too, which might be mistaken for a panegyric. Even that was not
enough; for you add a heroic poem so sublime and in such splendour of

* * * * *

23 Ferdinand] See Ep 917 introduction, and for Erasmus' personal acquaintance
   with him at Mechelen see Ep 927.
28 poem] See Ep 851:53n.
35 Livy] A man came all the way from Gades (Cadiz) to set eyes on the historian
   Livy; Pliny *Letters* 2.3.8.

944
5 heroic poem] Cf Ep 851:53n.

language that compared with it Lucan's trumpet might seem a twanging lyre. The publication of the first poem might make me blush, but it need cause you no regrets, and I cannot allow you to take Bartolini to task for this. I have the highest opinion of his judgment, and he has paid you in my hearing such a tribute as he has to no one else in this world of ours. He thought it his duty to   10 see that such a successful poem was not lost to sight. I too, I admit, was in favour of publication; but modesty restrained me, and a sort of fear that I might seem to take pleasure not so much in your brilliance as in my own praises. Yet it was by no means unwelcome when someone appeared to blow these scruples to the winds. Your letter makes it clear that experience has   15 given you almost equal felicity in both prose and verse, a thing which has fallen to the lot of few mortals hitherto. Moreover, as I read your heroic poem, I was reminded of Homer's *Battle of the Frogs and the Mice*, which recounts in tragic language the most ridiculous subject. And I admired your gifts all the more, because you had such barren material.   20

All the same, after being lauded by you in this fashion, I must not let it be said that I have made you absolutely no return, and so, my dear Velius, here is a piece of advice: in future, please exercise that most fertile vein of poetry that you possess on more promising subjects. I am delighted to hear that you have such a patron, and congratulate him in his turn on having you   25 as his friend or his teacher. I have replied to his most polished letter with a very ordinary note. It does not escape my notice that this is discourteous and shameless. But what would you do? I am so much overwhelmed with work and am expected to deal with letters from such an immense number of people everywhere that I cannot reply to each one singly; perhaps I might even the   30 score if I had fewer to deal with, though Hercules himself was not ashamed to yield to two adversaries at once. Farewell, dearest Velius.

Louvain, [1518]

945 / To Guillaume de Croy   Louvain, 20 April 1519

This letter, published in the *Farrago*, is a flattering reply to a short note from the young cardinal, who was continuing his studies in Louvain (cf Ep 628:70n) and was unwilling to release his tutor, Vives, whom Erasmus had proposed as preceptor for Prince Ferdinand (cf Ep 927 introduction). Erasmus now faced a second embarrassment in that Latomus' dialogues *De trium linguarum … ratione*

* * * * *

7 first poem] The *Genethliacon;* for Bartolini's involvement cf Ep 851:22n.
25 patron] Thurzo; cf Ep 943.
29 letters] Cf Ep 941:3n.
31 Hercules] Cf *Adagia* i v 39.

(cf Ep 934 introduction) were dedicated to the cardinal. As soon as his *Apologia contra Latomi dialogum* was ready Erasmus must have sent Croy a copy together with an explanatory letter (cf Ep 959:41–3). The cardinal probably replied with a short acknowledgment, perhaps saying politely that he hoped to read the *Apologia* soon and that he expected it to resemble the other pamphlets, that is, those by Mosellanus and Latomus. For Croy's subsequent support of the Collegium Trilingue cf de Vocht CTL I 413, 526–8.

TO THE MOST REVEREND GUILLAUME, CARDINAL DE CROY,
ARCHBISHOP OF TOLEDO ETC FROM ERASMUS OF ROTTERDAM,
GREETING

Most reverend Lord and right honourable Prince, your note, laconic in its brevity but vividly expressed, gave me a sample of a keen and lively mind; for   5
on this point, I think, you will allow your humble servant to gauge the lion by his claw. Literature is indeed happy if it is to find such well-wishers, and happier still if it finds not wishes only but active support. Your Lordship guesses rightly that this pamphlet will be like the others; it is very like – in other words, sad stuff. But I was unwilling to lay out serious work on such   10
rubbish and thought it not unreasonable that the lid should fit the dish. If your Eminence will be so good as to add the name of Erasmus to the list of your admirers, I will give you good reason not to think you have an idle or ungrateful recruit. Christ keep you long in health and wealth, to the restoration of true religion and the promotion of good literature.   15

Louvain, 20 April 1519

946 / To [Jan Briart of Ath]   Louvain, [c 22 April 1519]

This letter reflects another of Erasmus' current troubles at Louvain (cf Ep 930:12n). Speaking at the graduation ceremony of a new licentiate in theology, the Carmelite Jan Robyns (cf line 4n), on 21 February 1519, 'Vice-Chancellor' Briart chose to attack Erasmus' newly published *Encomium matrimonii* (cf Ep 604:12n) for what seemed to him an impious challenge to the ideal of celibacy. He did not name the piece or the author, but his audience knew what to think. A meeting between the two men followed (line 7), attended by Dorp, who supported Erasmus, and by Gillis van Delft (cf LB IX 107D; Ep 922:28n). Briart conceded that his charges were ill founded. Since they had been made in public, Erasmus would be entitled to make a public reply. He wrote a short,

* * * * *

945
6 gauge the lion by his claw] Cf *Adagia* I ix 34.
11 the lid should fit the dish] Cf *Adagia* I x 72.

respectful *Apologia pro declamatione de laude matrimonii* (LB IX 105–12). It is dated
1 March 1519 and was published by Martens, no doubt without delay (cf Ep 916
introduction) and reprinted by Froben in May. Unfortunately Briart's disciples
renewed the attack in the wake of Erasmus' controversy with Latomus (cf Ep
934 introduction), who was one of their number. In order to stop them,
Erasmus sent Briart this appeal (see de Vocht CTL I 313–14). An approximate
date is suggested by a comparison with Ep 948:167–71 – very likely another
reference to the detractor N.

This letter was published by Erasmus in the *Farrago* of October 1519. That he
preferred to suppress N's name is not surprising, but that he did not wish to
name Briart is noteworthy. In Erasmus' *Apologia de laude matrimonii* Briart's
name is mentioned in a most respectful, even friendly manner; and the tone of
this letter is no different. But there is little doubt that Erasmus was privately
more and more incensed against the 'vice-chancellor' (cf Epp 843:538n, 2045);
yet had he known about the unfortunate publication of the *Dialogus bilinguium
ac trilinguium* at the time the *Farrago* letters were being prepared for print, he
might well have been anxious to forestall any suspicions by identifying Briart as
the recipient of this respectful letter; see Ep 948:27n.

ERASMUS TO A CERTAIN THEOLOGIAN, GREETING
Most learned teacher, I perceive that this poisonous habit of detraction
spreads more widely and grows more deadly day by day: so barefaced are
the lies about myself spread shamelessly by a certain N, a licentiate, as they
call him, first in Louvain, then in Mechelen, and now in Antwerp. I see no   5
remedy, unless you with your wisdom and your authority will put an end to
this plague. I had agreed on a method of doing so with yourself and Dorp.
My own conscience does not rebuke me for ever having written a word that
might do hurt to religion and piety. To disagree I hope we have no cause and
will do all I can to ensure that we have no opportunity. Latomus had invited   10
me to a confrontation of our arguments, and this I carried out with perfect
courtesy, so that, unless he is wondrous hard to please, he should have no
cause for offence. But it would be better to speak of all this, if you will be so
kind as to name a time. May Christ's wrath be upon me if I wish for anything
which I know to be displeasing to him. I will endure any misrepresentation,   15

* * * * *
946
4 N] Henry de Vocht suggests that he was the Carmelite Jan Robyns (not to be
confused with Erasmus' friend, Jan Robbyns, dean of Mechelen), at whose
graduation ceremony Briart had spoken (cf introduction). The Carmelites had
houses in Mechelen and Antwerp, and some of them, like Robyns' friend
Nicolaas Baechem Egmondanus, prior of Louvain (cf Ep 948:141n), were
notorious critics of Erasmus; see Ep 1072, de Vocht CTL I 349.

however false, provided I am not falsely maligned as a heretic – a task some people are now engaged on, as I will show you when we meet. Farewell.

[1515]

947 / To Philippus Melanchthon   Louvain, 22 April 1519

This letter answers Ep 910 and was published in the *Farrago*.

ERASMUS OF ROTTERDAM TO PHILIPPUS MELANCHTHON,
GREETING

The man who gave me a hint of your opinion is neither wretch nor rascal but a particularly open-hearted friend and well disposed to us both. Nor have you any reason to be so much annoyed with him, for you yourself admit the truth of something he said to me, not with any desire of making mischief between us but because the topic happened to come up in conversation. Though the man did not say you disapproved of anything in my paraphrase; he said the New Testament, on which I would sooner accept your opinion than on the paraphrase, for no one will easily pronounce on that who has not been through all the ancient commentators with his eyes well and truly open. But do not think me such an inconstant friend that for any slight difference of opinion I might be a friend no longer, or so unfamiliar with criticism as to be much moved by a free expression of opinion from this man or that.

Nor have I any wish to prevent the opinions of scholars from being unfettered, provided they are correct. I think your remark to me would have been more correct if you had put it the other way round: while the opinions of scholars ought to be unfettered, they ought also to be correct. But you yourself withdraw that first opinion of yours and move your man back again. Besides which it is desirable that the opinions of scholars, and especially of those who are devotees of the literary Muses, should be not only correct but honest and fair. You can see the venom with which certain persons conspire

* * * * *

947
3 The man] Somebody Erasmus had met during his travels in the summer of 1518 or a visitor to Louvain soon after his return, perhaps Eobanus Hessus (cf Ep 877:9–11). He was not necessarily the person criticized by Melanchthon in Ep 910:4. The often noted similarity between that passage and Mosellanus' reference to Tranquillus Andronicus in Ep 911:47–9 may well be accidental. It rather seems that the defence of Melanchthon in the postscript of Ep 911 was added only as an after-thought. At any rate, Ep 991 seems to preclude the possibility that Erasmus here refers to Andronicus.
20 move your man] A metaphor from an ancient board-game; Cf *Adagia* I v 55.

against the humanities. It is only fair that we too should 'Cretan with Cretan stand against the foe.' It is a mighty bulwark, is harmony. In any case, there 25 is one thing I want you to be sure of, that I love my friend Philippus with all my heart and take no common interest in the success of his most promising talents.

I can hardly say how delighted I am with the hymn in which, like old Orpheus reborn, you sing the praises of the angels. I have also read that 30 inaugural lecture of yours, in which you preach classical learning, boldly too and with great spirit as a young man and a German should. But, if you will take advice from your friend Erasmus, I could wish that you put more energy into staking out the claim of liberal studies than into attacking their opponents. They deserve, it is true, to be torn in pieces by the concerted 35 attacks of the learned, but the other method, if I mistake not, will be found more profitable. Besides which we must try very hard to show ourselves superior to them not only in eloquence but in modesty and civilized behaviour.

Martin Luther's way of life wins all men's approval here, but opinions 40 vary about his teaching. I myself have not yet read his books. He has made some justified criticisms, but I wish they had been as happily expressed as they were outspoken. I have written to Duke Frederick about him, and also because I long to know in what spirit he received the *Lives of the Caesars* which I dedicated to him. Farewell, most learned Melanchthon, and strive 45 with all your might to equal and even surpass the high hopes which Germany entertains of your gifts and your character.

Louvain, 22 April 1519

Mind you do not overwork, that you may have strength as long as

* * * * *

24 'Cretan with Cretan ... foe'] Cf Ep 916:412n.

29 hymn] It was never printed and is apparently lost today. On 24 September 1518 in a letter to Spalatinus Melanchthon listed a Greek hymn to the angels among the writings he expected to publish in the near future; cf Melanchthon *Werke* VII-1 Ep 6. In February 1519 Bonifacius Amerbach was looking for a copy and learnt that an autograph fragment, with annotations, existed in Pforzheim; see AK II Ep 646.

31 inaugural lecture] Erasmus' expression 'praedicas' suggests that he meant the text of Melanchthon's inaugural lecture at Wittenberg. It was first published under the title *Sermo ... de corrigendis adolescentiae studiis* (Wittenberg: J. Grunenberg [autumn] 1518) and soon reprinted several times. It contained spirited attacks on Rome and the leading theologians of Germany and Paris; see Melanchthon *Werke* III 29–42.

44 to know] Ep 939:7–18; the dedicatory preface for Suetonius' *Lives of the Caesars* is Ep 586.

49 overwork] Cf Ep 933:46–51.

possible for the promotion of the humanities; for I hear that your health is not   5
absolutely impregnable. In the end there is another reason for looking after
yourself – to disappoint these barbarians. Farewell once more.

948 / To Petrus Mosellanus   Louvain, 22 April 1519

Allen's text for this letter is based on: 1/ a volume published by Mosellanus
himself, which also contained Ep 980 and Mosellanus' oration at the opening
ceremony of the Leipzig disputation between Eck, Karlstadt, and Luther, 27
June–16 July 1519, *Petri Mosellani oratio de ratione disputandi* (Leipzig: M. Lotter,
n d, and Augsburg: S. Grimm and M. Wirsung 1519); 2/ Erasmus' *Farrago* of
October 1519 (where the text was evidently edited from his rough draft);
3/ Erasmus' *Epistolae ad diversos*, August 1521, where Erasmus made some
additions, in particular lines 150–61.

This letter is clearly intended as the public expression of support which
Mosellanus had requested in Ep 911:49–52. In that letter he had also treated the
planned Leipzig disputation as a ridiculous exercise in scholastic theology. His
inaugural oration shows that by the time the disputation took place he was
aware of its significance and tried to take an impartial attitude. Although he
was accused of hostility towards Eck, his views remained closer to those of
Erasmus than to Luther's.

ERASMUS OF ROTTERDAM TO PETRUS MOSELLANUS, GREETING
Some time ago, my dear Petrus, from your first letter I conceived an affection
for your mind, which seemed to me in those days to be sensible and lively –
for gifts of this sort have always been my favourites; I do not like the element
of excess, tending to enthusiasm rather than judgment, in some of our   5
countrymen – and this affection was increased by your second letter, which
was both more scholarly and more elegant than the other. As soon, however,
as I had read your oration in defence of the study of classical languages
against those who, where the art of writing is concerned, are tongue-tied
and in denigrating the humanities are as fluent as you please, I thought your   1
gifts so full of promise that I had hardly ever seen their like – your style is so
lively, it flows along carrying the reader with it, yet is soundly based on

* * * * *

948
2 first letter] Ep 560
6 second letter] Ep 911
8 oration] *Oratio de variarum linguarum cognitione paranda* (Leipzig: V. Schumann
   August 1518), also mentioned in lines 42, 77. For the echo in Louvain cf Ep 934
   introduction.

reason; you are acute in detecting a good argument and show yourself the
skilled craftsman in presenting it. Your language testifies to wide and varied
reading, which in a young man is all the more admirable.   15

You tell me in your part of the world the battle rages between the
champions of good literature and the defenders of ignorance outworn, and
this does not surprise me, for it rages everywhere; one might think it the
result of a conspiracy or of destiny in some form. I have consulted several
eminent astrologers, and they ascribe this evil to the eclipse last year. It   20
happened, if I am not mistaken, in Aries, and Aries belongs to the head;
besides which, Mercury was blighted by the influence of Saturn. Consequently, they say, this evil afflicts particularly those who are under Mercury,
among whom they specify the inhabitants of Louvain. For this university,
the peaceful home of literary studies, has been racked by extraordinary   25
turmoil, the like of which I have never seen in all my life. You would have
thought some Ate was confounding the whole business of learning.

But what the astrologers foretell is their own business. My opinion, if I
have any eyes in my head, is that the whole thing is deliberately organized
by a sworn conspiracy, so universal is this outburst, as though at a given   30
signal, against the classical languages and the liberal arts. The clans are
gathering to defend themselves by numbers if nothing else against a mere
handful. They have made a division of labour among themselves, some of
them talking nonsense at the dinner-table or in the council-chamber, others
ranting to the ignorant mob which is so easily imposed upon; some arguing   35
in the lecture-room, some dropping their poison in the ears of princes. Some
of them write books, especially in Cologne, where the university has always
had its stubborn defenders of bad literature. There has lately come before

* * * * *

20 astrologers] Cf Epp 930:12n, 936:60n.
20 eclipse] See Allen's note: there was no eclipse in Aries in 1518, but on 8 June the
   sun was eclipsed in Gemini; cf J.F. Schroeder *Spezieller Kanon der zentralen
   Sonnen- und Mondfinsternisse* (Kristiania 1923) 57 and map 111b. On 6 June
   Mercury and Saturn had been in direct opposition to one another. The relation
   of Aries to the head and the evil power of Saturn as opposed to the neutral
   influence of Mercury are traditional elements of astrological belief; cf eg *Eyn
   nyge Kalender, recht holdende; und eyn nutte, künstlick ... bock* (Lübeck 1519) ff H iv
   verso, K iii–iv.
27 Ate] The Greek personification of harm, fate, guilt (cf Ep 856:19). There is little
   doubt that Erasmus is alluding to 'Atensis,' that is, Jan Briart of Ath (cf Ep
   843:538n, 946 introduction). The same allusion occurs in Ep 991:66, and in Ep
   1029 Briart is called 'Noxus' (from the Latin *noxa*, harm). In the *Dialogus
   bilinguium ac trilinguium* (cf Ep 934 introduction) Briart is grossly and
   transparently abused under the name of Ate.
37 Cologne] Cf Ep 821:19n.

the public here too a dialogue by the theologian Jacobus Latomus, a man who in old days was not particularly against the humanities, and my good friend, nor can I guess what has suddenly changed his whole nature. Some suspect that a good part of his first book is directed against the oration in which you preach the classical languages, but that much the greatest part is a veiled attack on me. I have rebutted this suggestion in a pamphlet thrown off rather than written in a couple of days, for it galled me to have to devote much labour to this sort of nonsense. Nor shall I recommend you to answer the man; or if you do answer him, pray use argument rather than invective, especially as he has refrained from mentioning names and writes with very little venom. Even were he really venomous, I should advise you to keep your pen under control, to make clear to posterity that we have not only the better cause but better manners.

Frenzy in the old days was attributed to poets; now it seems to have gone to live with the very people who most ought to keep a wise passiveness. Not but what there is a great gulf between the poets' frenzy and theirs. One gave us so many notable works, on history, on manners, on the emotions, on the starry heavens, on the nature of plants, trees, gems, and living creatures, and on geography. The frenzy of these other men has no offspring except venomous but tedious and pointless innuendoes, in which lies all their hope of victory. In this affair first place is taken by certain troupes of monks; and as there are enough of them to put the Grand Turk himself to flight, they have seconded numerous emissaries to this noble enterprise: they wander up and down sowing foul libels or preach sermons encouraging the mob to throw stones. They have killed off their Erasmus so many times and attacked me with baseless rumours! Behaving like this, they see themselves as pillars of the Christian religion, and worthy of course to be kept in idleness by the rest of the world at its own expense. Though I should be sorry to see the resulting unpopularity laid at the door of the monastic orders, whose better members all disapprove of this behaviour. But everywhere it is the most outrageous who rule the roost, and they do everything as though all the rest were behind them. And thus a few reprobates give a bad name to the whole body.

On this point I find not merely an absence of Christian feeling in those who claim the glory of religion as their special province; I find a lack of ordinary modesty and common sense. As they spread abroad the most tangible falsehoods, they can easily guess that the time will come when they

* * * * *

39 dialogue] See Ep 934 introduction.
45 couple of days] Cf Epp 934:10n, 952:23.
63 killed] Cf Ep 854:9n.

are shown up by the facts. What could be more shameless than the monk of
whom you speak in your oration – the one who, I having said in my note that
συλλαλοῦντες is more correctly translated *confabulantes*, had the face to declare
in public that I regard the text of Scripture as no better than old wives' fables,
whereas everywhere I give the text so much authority that some people I   80
know can hardly stomach it? There's a herald of heavenly doctrine for you,
with a tongue sanctified to the preaching of Christ's glory! They think fit to
behave like this and then are furious and confound heaven and earth if
anyone lets fall a word of criticism of the ceremonies of certain monks, even if
he does not drag their name into it; and though their malice is so open and   85
uncontrolled that you would think them mad, it is their exquisite reason,
they think, that must determine whether we are Christians or the reverse.
Here too there was a theologian of the same kidney, who used to be thought
a sensible man; but after making Luther's cause as unpleasant as he could
before public audiences, ranting away about heresies and Antichrists and   90
'The faith is in danger,' he mixed in with his affair the whole business of
classical languages and the humanities, repeating that these are the springs
from which heresies flow. As though in old days eloquence had been a mark
of heretics rather than orthodox, or the begetters of recent heresies had not
been quite unable to speak or write – in a word, much like our present   95
opponents; or as though Luther had been equipped with these weapons,
and not rather with scholastic authorities – as the word 'scholastic' is now
understood.

* * * * *

76 monk] Mosellanus describes him as a Dominican of Leipzig. He took issue with
the treatment of Matt 17:3 in Erasmus' New Testament. Erasmus translated
'colloquentes' but explained in his note that the Greek term really meant
'confabulantes.' In subsequent editions he merely added a polemical sentence
with reference to the Dominican, who, he said, was a bachelor of theology (cf
LB VI 91–2). Allen discovered in a copy of a reprint of Mosellanus' *Oratio* (Basel:
Froben May 1519, p 38; Oxford, Bodleian Library Tract. Luth. 4.50) an
identification of the detractor, added on the margin by a contemporary hand:
'Ogssenfardium Paulensem intelligit.' This reference is no doubt to Johann
Löblein, often called Ochsenfurt after his native town. He matriculated at
Leipzig in 1496 and was a Dominican by 1498. In 1517 and 1519 he was regent
of the Dominican monastery of St Paul's and in the latter year was also
appointed preacher at its church. Having graduated MA, from 1518 he lectured
on the *Sentences* of Peter Lombard in preparation for the theological doctorate,
but he died prematurely in 1523; see Gabriel M. Löhr *Die Dominikaner an der
Leipziger Universität* (Vechta-Leipzig 1934) 92–3.
83 confound] Cf *Adagia* I iii 81.
88 theologian] He is not identified.
97 'scholastic'] Cf Ep 933:17.

When the emperor was in Antwerp lately, his eminence the cardinal of
Sion, a man of learning and unfettered judgment, had invited me to dinner.   100
He had been persuaded, as I learnt from his conversation, by some
theologians, I know not who, to believe the most monstrous falsehood, that
in the song of the Virgin Mary, the Magnificat, I had changed 'to Abraham
and his seed' into 'and his seeds,' at grave risk to the Christian faith, because
Paul wrote 'not in seeds, but in thy seed, which is Christ.' When I got home, I   105
went to the book and realized how impudent and crazy the man must have
been who invented this out of his own head.

There was another man, a Preacher, who complained to his congregation in a tearful voice that all the midnight watches he had devoted to
defending the faith of Christ were fruitless and wasted. 'What is left for us,'   110
he said, 'except to throw our books into the fire, now that men have arisen
who write new books to put right the Paternoster and the Magnificat?' For
my notes on the New Testament had just come out.

I myself heard a Carmelite I know, a man with powerful lungs and the
title and violet bonnet of a doctor of divinity: when he knew I was there (for I   115
was standing opposite him), he proceeded to lay to my charge two out of the
three sins against the Holy Spirit. I was guilty of presumption, because I
wrote new books to do down all the old ones and actually had not hesitated
to emend the Lord's prayer and the song of Mary; and of attacking received
truth, because having heard two preachers in one day, I had said at supper   120
that neither of them really understood his text. The text was from 1 Peter
chapter 4: 'Be ye therefore prudent and watch unto prayer, and above all
things have continual charity in yourselves.' Here a good part of the sermon
was spent in analysing the elements of prudence, though the Greek has
σωφρονήσατε 'be sober,' and a good part in discussing 'in yourselves' and   125
the process of charity, though 'in ἑαυτοῖς' means 'among yourselves.' Yet I
did not follow up their mistakes; I praised both sermons, and added 'What a

* * * * *

99 cardinal] Matthäus Schiner (cf Ep 584). This incident, in May 1517, and the one
   which follows next were recalled again in Ep 1967.
103 changed] In Luke 1:55 (LB VI 228A). The charge is baseless.
105 Paul] Gal 3:16, abbreviated
108 Preacher] For members of the Dominican order who had criticized Erasmus cf
   the indexes of CWE 5–8.
114 Carmelite] The same incident is related in a note on 1 Pet 4:7–8 (LB VI 1052E)
   which first appeared in the New Testament of 1519, and in Ep 2045. The latter
   account permits the identification of the Carmelite: he was the prior of the
   Antwerp house, Sebastiaan Craeys (d 1523), who preached a sermon in
   Erasmus' presence at Pentecost (31 March) 1517. For Erasmus' hostility towards
   the Carmelites cf the indexes of CWE 4–8.

pity this was lacking!' for five words from my commentary would have saved
them from this mistake. Nor is it a trivial misdemeanour for a man who
teaches in public with such authority not to understand the basis of his   130
whole sermon. When the doctor I speak of had heard from somebody or
other what I said, his reply was: 'I have often preached before you, and by
the grace of Christ I shall do so again. But if anyone says that a preacher does
not understand the text of his sermon, especially when he has taken it from
Holy Scripture, that man sins against the Holy Ghost.' Pieter Gillis, a very   135
faithful friend, was standing beside me, and he was so angry I thought he
would explode; I could not refrain from laughing – who would not laugh at
such ridiculous stuff? Yet these men think it fair that for the sake of one
ranter such as that an immense crowd of monks should be kept at the public
expense.
                                                                                   140
    When the New Testament restored by me first appeared, a Carmelite
divine, who is in his own opinion a wonderful scholar and a holy man,
started clamouring that a great crisis threatened the Christian religion and
that the coming of Antichrist was at hand; for they use this dramatic
language to rouse the superstitious multitude. When it came to a discussion   145
between us and I asked him with some urgency to produce what offended
him in my New Testament, he replied in a simple-minded way that he had
never read the book or even set eyes on it. This is what I usually find: none
raise a more offensive clamour than those who do not read what I write.
    The New Testament had scarcely come out when some Preacher or   150
other in Strasbourg (for that order, which once produced so many men of
learning, now has a great many who expect somehow to rule the roost) was
thundering against the book full blast, as they say, before a crowd of
students. Jakob Sturm, a young man of excellent wit and good judgment,
unusually learned and a very great supporter of mine, happened to be there.   155
He let the man spout on until he had had his fill. When he had said
everything he could think of, and in his own opinion to very good effect,
Sturm asked him if he had seen the book; and he said no. 'How then,' said
Sturm, 'can you say so much about a book you have not read nor even seen?'
The laughter was general; and even so he was not ashamed of his imper-   160
tinence. If I told you all the stories of this kind, there would be no end to it.

* * * * *

128 commentary] Cf LB VI 1052.
141 Carmelite] Nicolaas Baechem, called Egmondanus, who had apparently begun
    his attacks upon Erasmus in Brussels in the autumn of 1516 (cf Ep 483:29n,
    Allen Ep 1162:88–90). The incident reported here seems to have occurred soon
    after Erasmus' move to Louvain in the summer of 1517; cf Allen Ep 1196:115–22.
153 full blast] Cf Adagia I v 96.
154 Sturm] See Ep 302:14n.

The other day one of these scandalmongers, who thinks himself not only a theologian (which is the last thing he is) but even a little bit of a saint, writing to a friend called me, who have tried with so much effort to restore and explain the text of Holy Writ, a perverter of Holy Writ and himself its defender.

And in these last few days another man, a loquacious fool who does not know how to speak and yet cannot hold his tongue, had been enthusiastically declaiming against my reputation in various towns as though he had been hired to do it, attacking my character as well as my teaching with the most slanderous falsehoods. It so happened that we found ourselves at the same dinner-party the day after one of my friends had written to tell me part of the story. I protested openly, in the hearing of several scholars and produced the lies he had used to blacken me. The man made it clear enough that the material for his sermons had not been his own reading but hearsay from other people. And just as though it were a trivial offence to attack another man's character with fabrications, these men have the effrontery with all this on their heads to approach Christ's holy table without seeking reconciliation with the man whom they have wronged. So true is that remark of Tychonius that what we wish is holy to us. And this is quite a new form of scandalous attack. First they condemn anyone they do not like; then they hunt for holes they can pick in the man they have condemned. If a man resists their malice or protests against it, there is a cry that peace and tranquillity are being overset, precisely as though you boxed a man's ears and told him to keep quiet for fear he might commit a breach of the peace. They are so grand and so touchy – a single word can upset them – that we have to show a patience worthy of Socrates. And they hold other mens' reputation so cheap, while expecting their own to be held so dear!

But how foolish of me, my dear Petrus, to waste so much time on this! I will add one more story and then stop. England possesses two universities by no means obscure, Cambridge and Oxford. Greek is taught in both, and in Cambridge without disturbance, because the head of the institution is Father John Fisher, the bishop of Rochester, whose learning and life are alike worthy of a divine. But at Oxford, where a young man of more than common

* * * * *

162 scandalmongers] Lee, in his correspondence with Lips; cf Ep 922:33–5.
167 another man] Probably N of Ep 946
180 Tychonius] Quoted in Augustine's Ep 93:43; cf *Adagia* IV vii 16.
187 patience worthy of Socrates] Cf *Adagia* v i 56
194 at Oxford] The incident may have occurred in the spring of 1518, when the court was at Abingdon near Oxford and was attended by Pace and More, who then wrote his famous letter to the university against the opponents of Greek studies (cf Ep 829:6n). The two detractors of Greek studies in this incident and

learning was publicly teaching Greek with some success, some barbarian or   195
other in a public sermon began to inveigh against Greek studies with
monstrous great falsehoods. The king, who being quite a scholar himself is a
supporter of the humanities, happened to be in the neighbourhood, and
hearing about this from More and Pace, he declared that those who wished
should be welcome to follow Greek. And so those rascals were put to silence.   200
I only wish we had some such prince or viceroy, for ours is far away. You are
more fortunate, if what I heard some years ago about Duke George is true.

Here is another story like the last. A theologian I could name, when he
was preaching at court before the same king, began to declaim against Greek
studies and modern interpreters in a style as brazen as it was stupid. Pace   205
glanced at the king to see how he was taking this, and the king soon gave
Pace a friendly smile. When the sermon was done, the theologian was sent
for, and More was given the task of defending Greek studies against him.
The king was pleased to be present at the disputation; and when More had
spoken fluently and at length and the preacher's reply was awaited, he fell   210
on his knees and contented himself with begging for forgiveness, extenuat-
ing what he had done with the plea that as he was preaching he was carried
away by some spirit to make this attack on Greek. 'Well,' said the king, 'that
was not the spirit of Christ; it must have been folly.' Then he asked the man
whether he had read anything by Erasmus; for it had not escaped the king's   215
notice that he had directed some shafts at me. He said no. 'That shows,' said
the king, 'what a fool you are, if you condemn what you have not read.' 'I
have read something,' the theologian said; 'it was called the Folly.' Here
Pace interrupted with 'And a very suitable subject too, may it please your
Majesty.' Then the divine thought up another argument to palliate his   220
offence: 'I am not all that much against Greek,' he said, 'only because Greek
is derived from Hebrew.' The king was amazed at the man's extraordinary
stupidity and told him to go, but on condition that he never appeared again
to preach at court.

I cannot refrain fom adding one other very ridiculous thing. A certain   225
bishop of the order of Preachers who is confessor to the queen, a woman of

* * * * *

the following one are not identified; cf E.E. Reynolds *St Thomas More* (New
York 1957) 104–5.
201 for ours is far away] This remark was suppressed by Erasmus in the *Farrago*,
perhaps an indication that it was meant to convey criticism, but cf Epp
969:19–20, 970:16–17.
202 Duke George] For the sources of his favourable impression of Duke George of
Saxony cf Epp 586:292–5, 1122.
226 bishop] Jorge de Ateca (d 1545), confessor to Queen Catherine and bishop of
Llandaff (Wales) from 1517 to his resignation in 1537, after her death. In 1538 he

great sense and saintliness and not unlearned, had persuaded her that I had perpetrated something inexcusable by correcting the works of Jerome, a very learned man and more than that, a saint. In this belief she protested as follows to one of the courtiers, who is a friend of mine: 'Was not Jerome a very great scholar?' 'Yes, ma'am.' 'Is he not now in heaven?' 'Yes, ma'am; he is.' 'Very well then: how will you defend your friend Erasmus, who has corrected his books? Is he cleverer than Jerome?' And people here too seriously preach this who regard themselves as pillars of the church. Such are my opponents, such are the champions of Christ's religion. Nothing could be more stupid, more absurd. And yet it is with malicious falsehoods like these that I am vilified in front of the uneducated multitude and poor foolish women.

But enough of this nonsense. If I have been rather slow in answering your letter, pray imagine anything to be the reason rather than that I undervalue you. I am overwhelmed by the daily bundles of letters. If I do not answer, I am thought discourteous; if I do, I suffer in three ways. First, I do not even give satisfaction to the people to whom I must perforce reply the first thing that comes into my head; secondly, by writing like this in a hurry I make my style, which is bad enough in itself, still worse; and lastly, I endure some loss of reputation. How absurd to prefer to apply to an Italian for what one has at home! This is like the common herd, who think the best doctor the man who pretends to be an Arab or an Indian, seeking reputation among fools from the distance they think he has travelled. Educated men ought to be as far from this prejudice as can be. Whoever is familiar with good literature should in our eyes count as an Italian. It is not my plan in future to join battle with this class of men. I have now reached the age-limit and earned my release; I am tired with running and hand on the torch to you younger men. Even without me you will win, if you keep on as you have begun.

Philippus Melanchthon needs no support with me and no apologist. That young man is a great favourite of mine. It would need to be a very grievous wrong to sever my friendship for him. Farewell.

Louvain, 22 April 1519

* * * * *

had returned to Spain and was named bishop of the joint see of Ampurias in Catalonia and Tempio in Sardinia.
241 overwhelmed] Cf Ep 941:3n.
246 an Italian] Cf Ep 911:36–49.
253 hand on the torch] Cf *Adagia* i ii 38.

949 / From Lodovico Ricchieri Milan, 22 April 1519

The original autograph is in the Herzog August Bibliothek, Wolfenbüttel: MS
Gudianus latinus 2° 25, f 128. This letter was printed by Allen after *Gudii
epistolae* ed Pieter Burman (Utrecht 1697) and LB, without knowledge of the
original. As a result the address is omitted in his edition and replaced by a
salutation, which is not in the original letter.

For Ricchieri and his *Antiquae lectiones* see Ep 469:10n. He wrote this letter
upon learning that Erasmus had launched a serious charge against him in his
Adagia of 1517–18; see line 11n.

Francesco Calvo who is devoted both to you and to myself, after his recent
departure from your native Germany paid me a visit, as nearly all men of
letters do, and I asked him particularly what new things he brought back
from such long wanderings which might help the cause of learning. 'Not
much, really,' he said, 'but there will be a few more things quite soon.' 'And   5
how is my friend Erasmus?' said I. 'Is he still producing? He is a very fertile
field, like that famous land at Byzantium that used to bear a hundredfold;
there is always a crop growing that will soon be ready to be cut.' He smiled:
'What would you say if you knew what he thinks of you? It's not very
friendly.' 'Pray how can that be? What reason can he have for any   10
estrangement?' 'He says that in your *Antiquae lectiones* you have dissented
from his opinion, with the air of a man who wants to put him right.' I was
astonished, absolutely astonished; no graver or more unexpected blow
could have befallen me. My conscience was crystal clear; I had been perfectly
open without a trace of hypocrisy, and I knew well I had used no expression   15
in which a man with a nose like a bloodhound could have scented anything
coming from me which he might consider a slur on his reputation. This has
been my bearing even towards simple folk and those from whom little was to

* * * * *

949
1 Calvo] Cf Epp 831 introduction, 925:5–8.
7 Byzantium] Pliny *Historia naturalis* 5.24 and 17.41 mentions the exceptional
   fertility of Byzacium in North Africa; in both places in the text the name was
   corrupted commonly to Byzantium.
11 dissented from his opinion] On Plutarch's understanding of the adage
   'Choenici ne insideas' (*Adagia* I i 2). In his *Antiquae lectiones* (Venice 1516, 441–3;
   Basel 1542, 610–12) Ricchieri had proposed a new interpretation of Plutarch's
   text. He criticized earlier commentators but did not mention any names.
   Erasmus retaliated in the *Adagia* edition of 1517–18 with a charge that Ricchieri
   had extensively borrowed from him. After Ricchieri's death he added a short
   eulogy without withdrawing the earlier charge. Ep 602 proves that he did not
   mind recommending Ricchieri's work; cf Phillips 123.

be expected; how much more towards you who are in my eyes (do not suspect me of trying to curry favour) a man of the first rank. If I seem to differ   20
from you, need you promptly have the law on me, as if I had rubbed off some
contagion on you or tried to box your ears? Such an idea is unworthy of a
scholar, for it always has been permissible and always will be to add to what
has been discovered and to think of fresh solutions if men's intelligence
allows, provided this is done without venom, without the gnawing malice of   25
some pretended supporter, and we do not descend to foolish and vulgar
abuse. In fact, if you care to look more closely, you will find yourself singled
out for praise, clearly enough though not by name. In this straightforward
way the greatest men have always competed with their predecessors; and in
your own works you are not without experience of this kind of contest. Do   30
not therefore judge me unfairly, for unless one side gives the provocation
there can be no dispute.

    But there is another point. I have lately read, on a hint from Francesco
Sacchetti of Pavia, a good scholar and a member of the council, your
complaints in the last edition of your *Proverbs* that in my books I never   35
mention you by name, although it is probable that your works have given me
some assistance. My learned friend, around the time when my own things
came before the public, I had read absolutely nothing that came from your
workshop apart from the *Proverbs*. When they appeared, I felt myself struck
to the heart. My own collection of proverbs was on the stocks at the same   40
time, and I know for a fact that you were told this in Padua. When you
forestalled me, what you did nearly reduced me to suicide. All my nights of
toil went for nothing; my lungs so often filled with smoke from the lamp, my
clothes soaked in honest sweat were a dead loss. Imagine what I felt then! I
had to set up a new web, to enter a fresh field of battle, unless I should be   45
willing to let my endurance be crushed and plunge myself in more than
Cimmerian gloom.

    This then is the origin of my *Antiquae lectiones*, and when they have
been further digested and enriched as well – for things worth knowing to the
number of five thousand more or less will be added – they will be published   50

* * * * *

26 vulgar abuse] Ricchieri employs another proverb (cf *Adagia* I vii 73) referring to
    the wagon which could serve the ancient comedians as a stage for freely
    criticizing public figures and even gods.
34 Sacchetti] Francesco Sacchetti is not identified.
40 my own collection of proverbs] It was never published.
41 Padua] Late in 1508, Erasmus visited Padua and Ferrara, and it seems that he
    met Ricchieri; cf Ep 556:32 and *Adagia* I i 2 in the 1517–18 edition.
42 suicide] Cf *Adagia* I v 21.
47 Cimmerian gloom] Cf *Adagia* II vi 34.

without delay; whereupon, to earn your good will by some more substantial offering, I shall inscribe one book to you by name with a formal dedication, with the special object of putting on record how much your labours have contributed to life. You may say if you please that I am 'untwining other men's garlands to make new chaplets of my own,' but I shall shortly give you and everyone else satisfaction. Till then, farewell. 55

Milan, 22 April 1519

Your sincere friend Lodovico Celio

To the right learned doctor of divinity Erasmus of Rotterdam. In Basel, or wherever he may be 60

950 / To Jan Šlechta   Louvain, 23 April 1519

This letter was published in the *Farrago*. Šlechta says in his answer, Ep 1021, that this letter did not reach him until 11 September because it had remained in the hands of Justus Jonas (cf Ep 963:6n) for four months for want of a safe messenger. The lost letter which Erasmus here answers had evidently been Šlechta's first approach to him and had invited him to visit Bohemia.

Jan Šlechta (1466–1525), of Všehrdry in western Bohemia, received his BA at Prague in 1484 and later (cf lines 7–8) became the secretary of Vladislav II. About 1507 he retired from the court to his estates at Kostelec on the Elbe, north-east of Prague; see P.S. Allen *The Age of Erasmus* (Oxford 1914) 281–4.

ERASMUS OF ROTTERDAM TO THE HONOURABLE
JAN ŠLECHTA OF KOSTELEC, GREETING

I must thank you for your panegyric (for it was that rather than a letter), which sings my praises with such ability and eloquence that it does more credit to the author of the encomium than to me, its object. I am delighted to 5 think that there is no country without men to support higher studies and, what is more, to pursue them. Those sixteen years that you expended at the court of Vladislav, king of Hungary and Bohemia, were not wholly lost; of

* * * * *

52 one book] Each book of the *Antiquae lectiones* had an individual dedicatory epistle. But the enlarged and newly arranged edition did not appear until 1542. By then the author and Erasmus were dead, and the promise was not carried out.

54 may say] In the *Adagia* of 1517–18; cf above 11n.

950
8 Vladislav] Vladislav II Jagiello (c 1456–1516), King of Bohemia in 1471. Supported by the Hungarian barons who knew him to be weak, he gained recognition as king of Hungary in 1491, after the death of Matthias Corvinus.

that, this letter of yours is sufficient evidence. In any case, of all the praises
that you pile upon me, I can accept nothing except that of a mind that longs to   10
encourage Christian conduct and liberal studies. It is a great pleasure to me if
anyone finds help in the fruit of my nightly vigils. I cannot sufficiently
wonder at my unpopularity with some people I could name, seeing that
hitherto my labours have made no one blacker by a single hair. I perceived
that this prickly and dreary sort of theology gets daily worse, while the   15
sources and the classical writers of orthodoxy are virtually regarded as
obsolete. And so I have tried to recall all men to that genuine theology, not
wholly condemning the studies that are accepted in the universities, but
partly seeking to hold them in check and partly pointing out the additions I
should wish to make. For I cannot accept those who have no use for liberal   20
studies; but equally I disapprove of those who condemn the studies of
modern theologians altogether.

I marvel at the impudence of that canon of Prague, whoever he may be,
who has spun such a remarkable tissue of lies, like a he-spider, out of his
own entrails. The people at Cologne once had a dispute with that excellent   25
man Johann Reuchlin, but with me they have never quarrelled either in print
or face to face, so far are they from burning my books and their author with
them. On the contrary, whenever I have passed that way, the leading men
have given me a distinguished welcome and sent me on my way most
courteously. Not but what I could readily believe that there also may be there   30
men who snarl at Erasmus in the company of their own sort; for instance, a
certain member of the order of Preachers who recently related among his
brethren as an ascertained fact that I had died at Louvain, and the lying
fellow added a jesting comment fully worthy of him, 'With no light, no cross,
no God.' His narrative evoked frequent applause from the monks who are   35
his boon-companions. Well, if they are not afraid to invent such tales about

* * * * *

14 single hair] Cf *Adagia* I viii 4.
21 condemn] Cf Epp 622 introduction, 947:42–3. For Erasmus' advocacy of a
modus vivendi permitting the universities to combine traditional theology
and the new learning see also Epp 952:49–51, 967A:16–18, 980:43–5, CWE 7 preface.
23 canon of Prague] We have no information on this episode related in Šlechta's
lost letter.
26 never quarrelled] But cf lines 30–6, Ep 821:19–21.
29 welcome] Cf Epp 440:16n, 842 introduction, 866:26–31.
33 died] Probably in view of his severe illness in the autumn of 1518 (see Ep 867;
cf Ep 854:9n). Luther had heard the rumour by 13 April (cf w *Briefwechsel* I
Ep 167). For feuds with Dominicans cf the indexes of CWE 5–8.
34 no light] The defective grammar of this remark cannot be reproduced in an
uninflected language (*sine lux* for *sine luce*).

me when I am not far away, it is less surprising if they lie like this in Prague. But from actions like this, which they perpetrate freely every day, one can guess what a Fury now dwells in them. As I hope for the love of Christ, I swear I am more sorry for their case than for my own. For I find support in a good conscience and in the favourable judgment of men of good will; for no mortal man has yet had the good fortune to please everyone all the time.

The New Testament has come out again in its new form, revised by me at the price of such sleepless nights as you would hardly credit, and enriched with a considerable amount of new material. Prefixed is an official letter from Leo the Tenth, in which he approves the old edition and encourages me to make this new one.

What business I can have in Prague I do not see. You promise that there will be no lack of people to convey me in safety wherever I wish, but I do not care for countries in which convoy of this kind is necessary. Here I am free to go where I please, even by myself. Not that I have any doubt of finding in your part of the world, as you say in your letter, plenty of good scholars and religious men, not polluted by the vices of schism. But it surprises me that none can be found to bring this whole division to an end. It is better to have concord on conditions that are not wholly fair than perfect fairness and divisions. For my part I fear it is the love of money – that universal enemy of high standards of behaviour – that does not allow concord to come into existence. Paul refuses no loss by which he may win Christ. There are in the world so many cardinals, so many bishops, so many princes: would that Christ might inspire some of them to take up this task in a truly Christian spirit! If Paul were supreme in Rome, I know very well he would not only submit to some reduction in his income, he would even accept some cut in his authority, if for this price he could purchase concord.

If we are never so fortunate as to meet face to face, the interchange of letters will make me feel that sometimes I am talking with you as I walk on the banks of your Elbe or you are living with me in Brabant. How small a part of friendship is the physical presence of our friends! Farewell, my honoured friend.

Louvain, 23 April 1519

* * * * *

45 letter] Ep 864. A copy of the New Testament reached Šlechta on 14 May 1519; cf Ep 1021.
53 schism] The large majority of Bohemians, both clergy and laity, were Hussites. The archbishopric of Prague remained vacant until 1561. Conceivably Šlechta in his letter to Erasmus had taken issue with a generalizing reference to Bohemian schismatics in Ep 549:14 now published.
58 Paul] Cf Phil 3:8.

951 / To Ulrich von Hutten   Louvain, 23 April 1519

This letter answers various points raised by Hutten in Ep 923. It was published in the *Farrago*.

ERASMUS TO HIS FRIEND HUTTEN, GREETING

Plunged as I am in so much work that it is a marvel if I answer anyone at all, I have sent you more answers than you have sent me letters, assuming that what I send gets through to you; and yet you accuse me of being obstinately silent and pick a quarrel with me as though I were short of men to disagree 5 with me. It was a great joy to hear from you that the archbishop of Mainz feels towards me as he does, and I never cease to think how happy you are in possessing such a patron. In any case, the book I have dedicated to him I sent long ago at my expense by the hands of a certain young man, and with it a letter for you and a preface for Wolfgang Angst. I understand from a letter 10 from Rhenanus that he got as far as Basel; what he did in Mainz I do not know. I am surprised if he did not do everything I told him, since I added a list to remind him. I have prefixed to the book the archbishop's learned and elegant letter, not so much to put on record his kindness towards me as to fire others with zeal for the humanities by the example of so great a prince. And I 15 think I have done some good; for that distinguished young man Guillaume de Croy, duke and bishop of Cambrai, archbishop of Toledo, and finally cardinal, though he seemed for other reasons properly devoted to liberal studies, seems even so to have felt a powerful stimulus when he read the archbishop's letter. 20

Your *Aula* has often been in my hands, but hitherto I have always been forced to drop it by some piece of business which interrupted me when I was longing to read it. What I have read, I like very much; for what is there of yours that I do not like? Your *Febris* and *Phalarismus* have been reprinted by someone or other. But the *Febris* is forbidden to be sold in Louvain, because it 25 was thought to attack certain demigods by name; otherwise it is very much liked everywhere. The *Phalarismus*, because it was attached to the *Febris*, is

* * * * *

951
2 anyone at all] Cf Ep 941:3n.
10 letter for you] Now missing, but apparently received by Hutten; cf Ep 986 introduction. Beatus Rhenanus' letter is also missing.
10 preface] Ep 919
14 letter] Ep 661; cf Ep 745 introduction.
17 Croy] For Erasmus' recent contacts with him see Epp 927, 945 introductions.
21 *Aula*] Cf Epp 863:36n, 923:22.

outlawed with it, but only in Louvain; for the despotic rule of this university extends no further. They had also undertaken to print your oration, nor do I know the reason why they postpone it.   30

But what is this I hear? Will my friend Hutten fight armed cap-à-pie in the battle line? I can see you were born for battle, when you fight not only with the written and the spoken word, but even with the arms of Mars. Though there is nothing heroic in your now daring to fight against a single adversary with so many on your side, seeing how you once routed so many   35 foes all by yourself at Bologna. I praise your valiant spirit; but if you take my advice, you will keep your precious self safe for the Muses. Where shall we look for another man with your gifts, if anything happens to you, which heaven forfend? You know how Mars changes sides, and is not as well disposed as he should be to choicer spirits, being the biggest blockhead   40 among all the gods. I hope all may go well; at least, if anything happens, you have built for yourself in your writings a monument more enduring than bronze. Even so, I shall not fail to do my part; if my own works have any power, 'from Time's long memory the circling years / Shall ne'er delete us.'

Your *Triumph* I have not yet seen. I was glad that they kept it dark so   45 long on my advice, and no doubt they have toned down the whole argument. Of quarrelling there is no end. If I were better in everything else, in innuendo, lying, and abuse I am left far behind. I must frankly confess this, for it is the absolute truth. But in this field it is better to yield the palm than to fight to a dishonourable finish; for we ought to consider not only what suits the men   50 against whom we write but also what is suitable for us, the writers. Moderation is sometimes more creditable than a victorious cause; and I have other things to do. I would rather spend a whole month expounding Paul or the Gospel than one day in squabbles like this. Farewell, dearest of mortals.

Louvain, 23 April 1519   55

* * * * *

29 oration] *Ad principes Germaniae, ut bellum Turcis invehant, exhortatoria* 1st ed (Augsburg: Grimm and Wyrsung 1518); cf Ep 891:26n.
36 Bologna] A slight confusion; cf Ep 611:14n, 20n.
39 Mars] See Ep 911:13n.
42 monument] Horace *Odes* 3.30.1
43 if my own works] Virgil *Aeneid* 9.446–7
46 on my advice] Cf Ep 636:29n.
47 quarrelling] Cf Ep 930:12n.
49 palm] See Ep 943:19n.
53 Paul] Cf Ep 956.

952 / To Jan Becker of Borssele   Louvain, 24 April 1519

This answer to Ep 932 was published in the *Farrago*.

ERASMUS TO HIS FRIEND JAN OF BORSSELE, GREETING

I do not call that a letter; it was an incantation – you beg and pray and
beseech me on so many grounds, even threatening me with an action for
specific performance if I refuse to write something on the theory of
preaching, just as though I were made of iron or adamant. Is there anywhere   5
a field so fertile that it cannot be exhausted by over-cropping? I have been
toiling at this barren and sterile plot of mine with continuous crops now for
so many years, and do not make this good with any manure in the way of
reading, except of a desultory kind. After such severe illness I must make
some provision for re-establishing my health. Here, so far have I been from   10
giving myself any indulgence that I have not even had leisure to be ill; and
this Lent would nearly have been the death of me, had I not gone to Antwerp
for a change of climate and of food. Moreover, while I was obliged to play
the courtier at Mechelen, and to pay my respects to my patrons the bishop of
Liège, the bishop of Utrecht, and the other magnates, your Adolph among   15
them, I wasted several days. Finally, I am assailed by so many letters from all
directions that in answering them a large part is wasted of the time that might
have been spent on study.

    After finishing the paraphrase on the two Epistles to the Corinthians, I
had begun one on Galatians; but while intent on this, I was interrupted by   20
troubles of a new and heretofore unheard-of kind which must have been
aroused by some avenging Fury. The *Apologia* in which I reply to Latomus'
dialogue hardly cost me three days, for I was not prepared to spend much
effort on such worthless stuff. If he has leisure to publish several books of
the kind, there will be no lack of people to reply; like Veianius, I retire from   25

* * * * *

952
3 action for specific performance] To oblige a man who has broken his contract to
    meet his obligations. The Latin is *actio ex pacto*.
9 illness] Cf Epp 847:7n, 867.
12 to Antwerp] Cf Ep 934:10n.
14 Mechelen] Cf Epp 926, 927 introductions.
14 patrons] Erard de la Marck (cf Ep 783); Philip of Burgundy (cf Ep 603); Adolph
    of Burgundy, heer van Veere (cf Ep 93).
16 assailed] Cf Ep 941:3n.
20 Galatians] Cf Ep 956.
21 troubles] Cf Ep 930:12n.
22 *Apologia*] Cf Ep 934 introduction.
25 Veianius] A retired gladiator in Horace *Epistles* 1.1.4

the arena. I perceive that this serpent cannot be overcome by fighting back; and so I have said farewell to warfare and am taking shelter in the harbour of Christian gentleness, consoling myself in face of hostile critics with the opinions formed of me by men of good will and with a good conscience, at least as far as this business is concerned. Desire for money has never 30 possessed my mind; the burden of reputation I will gladly lay down if I can. I am not tired of life, nor do I desire it; whenever Christ, my commanding officer, calls me hence, I shall willingly and promptly leave my allotted post in the body, in reliance on him. So tedious is the malignant ingratitude of certain persons I could name, and so strong the poison of malicious gossip 35 that, had I not fully learnt it from the facts, I would never have believed that such mischief could arise, I will not say, among educated men, but even among human beings, although I have lived among nations and men of so many kinds.

Your letter, I suspect, was delivered to Louvain and sent on from there 40 to Antwerp, where I was at the time; with the result that I did not see the man who brought it. My plan is to devote this month of spring weather to restoring what little strength I have of body and mind, if only I am allowed to. After that, if Christ so please, I shall attack my paraphrase, and the subject about which you are so anxious – though I shall write of it with others in 45 mind and not my friend Borssele: I know that heart of yours and that intelligence, that zeal. You have such a spring of your own that you need not draw water from another man's cistern. There will be plenty of people to extol the authority of the pope, which I admit ought to be sacrosanct; plenty to extol the precepts of Scotus and of Thomas, of which I do not wholly 50 disapprove either. Make it your business to instil Christ pure and simple into the minds of your flock, for that we see done by very few. I rejoice that a position has fallen to your lot in which you have a certain standing, and that at the same time you are offered material and a field in which you can do good service to Christ's flock. Blessed indeed is leisure for the pursuit of 55 knowledge; but Plato's philosopher ought to come down to earth, for he is born for others besides himself.

Your excellent Prince Adolph seems to retain the same feelings for me still that he had when a youth. You will most easily get to know him better if you use the good offices of Pieter Zuutpene of Cassel, one of the most sincere 60 and friendly men I have ever met. You suggest that Francis, king of France, has tried to get me to move to France on pretty generous terms; and the story is not wholly false. He did try once and again in letters from people I could

* * * * *

60 Zuutpene] An official of Adolph van Veere; see Ep 1005.

Johannes Fabri (Heigerlin)
Tomb sculpture in the church of St Stephen, Vienna, possibly by Loy Hering
Bildarchiv, Österreichische Nationalbibliothek, Vienna

name; but as yet I have heard nothing definite in my waking moments, nor
am I so inexperienced in human affairs as to be moved by mere promises. 65
Strenuous efforts were made to get me to be tutor to Ferdinand, especially by
my lord of Bergen among many others; and a better and more teachable
prince one could not wish to find. But I am warned off it by certain things
which cannot safely be entrusted to a letter. Farewell.

Louvain, Easter day 1519   70

953 / From Johannes Fabri   Constance, 26 April 1519

This letter was published in the *Farrago* and answered by Ep 976. Johannes
Fabri (cf Ep 386 introduction) had moved to Constance in 1517 as vicar-general
to the bishop.

TO ERASMUS OF ROTTERDAM THE EMINENT THEOLOGIAN
FROM JOHANNES FABRI, SPIRITUAL VICAR OF THE BISHOP OF
CONSTANCE, GREETING

If I have failed to write as I should for so many months, most learned
Erasmus, I do not plead business as my excuse, as lazy men often do, though 5
I could do so with perfect truth, for I really am always very busy. Nor for that
matter have I forgotten my friend Erasmus, for such forgetfulness is
unknown in true friendship, and I am scarcely more likely to remember my
own existence than yours. Separated we may be by so many mountains and
the immense stretch of travel that lies between us, yet my eyes can always 10
rest with pleasure on your beloved offspring, the products of your more than
human genius; and when I look into them, as I often do, I look upon their
author, and that in a truer sense than they who greet you face to face and
grasp your hand in theirs. They see the face, the physical presence, behind
which the real Erasmus dwells whom all the world respects; but all those 15
books of his give a truer account of him and a clearer picture to the eye than
the continual sight of his person.

You see how zealously I strive to preserve myself from even the
semblance of forgetting my friend. What then can excuse my long-continued
silence? Why, the facts: you live a long way away, so that couriers were hard 20
to come by, and your address was so uncertain. At one moment you were
said to have taken wing to England; then there was a sudden rumour that

* * * * *

66 tutor] See Ep 917 introduction.
67 Bergen] Jan van Bergen; cf Ep 969;7n.

953
22 England] Cf Epp 886, 964 introductions.

you had gone to Holland. As a result I thought my writing would be a waste
of time, and in the mean while several friends told me to wait hopefully for
your return to Basel; and so I waited, in a fever of longing for you. At length   25
by good luck I met a man at Constance who stands high in the court of
Charles your king and soon, I hope, to be ours too, a noble and well read
man, who kindly promised to find messengers and to do all he could – such is
his wonderful courtesy towards everybody – to get a letter to you. I was
delighted, and promptly set myself to write.   30

Do you wonder then how your friends are getting on? By the grace of
God we are all flourishing, and we all wish you the very best of health, that
you may enrich our low estate with more productions of that fertile genius of
yours; for everything you write is of such a quality that it deserves not merely
to be compared to the learning of Antiquity but to be esteemed above it.   35
Countless are the people in Germany who meditate upon the outcome of
your nightly vigils and the reflections of your genius and read them, who
have made such progress in knowledge of languages, in scholarship, and in
religion that now they will do great credit to you as the teacher to whom they
owe it all. Countless people under your guidance have rubbed off the rust of   40
traditional ignorance and are now making great strides towards bearing
fruit, and that not only the younger ones, which I find less surprising, but
the seniors too. Under such a commander-in-chief the forces of learning, as .
though they heard the trumpet, open war on the whole host of barbarism
and hope even now for victory. Such is the irresistible force of your eloquence   45
that you win over to your way of thinking barbarians who were given up for
lost; late starters they may be, like the Phrygians, but they are exerting
themselves all the same, and the valuable time they once invested in untimely frivolities they now devote to true literature and true philosophy.

* * * * *

27 ours too] Cf Ep 893:39n.
27 well read man] Perhaps Maximiliaan van Bergen, heer van Zevenbergen (d
    1544), whose cousin Antoon was studying in Louvain (cf Ep 969 introduction).
    Maximiliaan was the statesman who masterminded the election of Charles v (cf
    Epp 968 introduction, 986:67n) and he was at this time engaged in negotiations
    with the Swiss, primarily about the fate of Württemberg (cf Ep 923:27n). He was
    in Constance on 12 April 1519; cf A.J.G. Le Glay ed *Négociations diplomatiques
    entre la France et l'Autriche* (Paris 1845) II 415. See LF III 173; L.P. Gachard and C.
    Piot eds *Collections des voyages des souverains des Pays-Bas* (Brussels 1874–82) II
    57, 66; de Vocht CTL II 462; K. Brandi *Kaiser Karl V.* new ed (Darmstadt 1959–67)
    I 85–6, II 107, 111.
47 Phrygians] *Adagia* I i 28
48 all the same] Reading *moliuntur tamen*

Need I mention myself? In years gone by I enjoyed your delightful 50
society, and you so caught hold of me and transformed me that you almost
made me another person. In olden days I had devoted myself to an ill-chosen
course of study and adhered too strictly all my life to modern theology; but
you with irresistible persuasion soon made me enjoy reading real theology
more than anything else. So you will not take it amiss, for you are the mildest 55
of men, if Beatus Rhenanus, whose integrity of learning and of life are alike
conspicuous, lately dedicated your *Ratio verae theologiae* to me. True, the best
and most learned of men might well have used every means to secure so
distinguished a dedication; but you will be the less put to shame by his
decision because I, and many others with me, were fired by you to pursue 60
the study of ancient theology; so clearly does that short but perfect book
display your learning in the Scriptures and your great powers of mind that
many even among the barbarians, who used to be express opponents of a
more scholarly divinity, have been won over by this brief essay and become
your keen supporters. 65

    That the New Testament newly enriched by you is a magnificent work,
I do not doubt, and I look for its appearance more eagerly than ever mother
did for a beloved son returning from foreign parts; for such time as can ever
be spared from the tedious business of my very busy post is all devoted to
reading your books ten times over. As for our friend Pace, on whom nature 70
has lavished such gifts of body and mind, I should dearly like to know where
he is and what he is doing now; I found his society singularly delightful and
enjoyed it very much. So please, dear friend, forgive your old Fabri; I have
given in to my love and admiration for you and not been afraid to interrupt
you, burdened as you are. I welcome a letter from you as a most precious gift, 75
yet as far as I am concerned, provided you do not cease to love me, you are at
liberty not merely not to answer my letters but not to read them even, if that
suits you best. Farewell, O prince of theologians and of scholars everywhere.

    From Constance, 26 April AD 1519 80

* * * * *

51 society] In Basel, 1515–16, when Fabri was the bishop's official; cf Ep 541:175.
55 take it amiss] Cf Epp 745 introduction, 976:18n.
66 New Testament] Cf Ep 864 introduction.
72 society] At Constance in 1517; cf Epp 619 introduction, 776:4n.

954 / To Guillaume Budé   [Louvain, April] 1519

This letter, published in the *Farrago*, answers both Epp 924 and 929 and is answered by Ep 987.

ERASMUS TO HIS FRIEND BUDÉ, GREETING

I have to thank you for two letters on roughly the same subject, but such as to make it clear to me that our previous disagreement has been carried on so far without any breach of the friendship between us. I am dissatisfied with that long letter of mine for this reason more than any other, that it seemed to have   5
hurt your feelings; and you are obliged now to take a more kindly view of it, seeing that you are responsible for its survival, after I myself had condemned it to execution. I pray that your mission may be successful, and that you will at last find yourself in favour at court and be the better for it. When I consider these disturbances about electing an emperor, that line of Horace comes into   10
my mind about the unwisdom of princes and their people.
    Farewell. 1519

955 / To Maarten Lips   [Louvain, c end of April 1519]

This letter is known only from the Brussels manuscript (cf Ep 750 introduction), where Lips explains in his argument that Erasmus had gone to Antwerp (cf Ep 934:10n) to publish his *Apologia* against Latomus and called on Lips after his return. On this occasion he promised Lips a copy of the recently arrived second edition of the New Testament, which was promptly delivered, together with this note, by Erasmus' servant, Johannes Hovius. From Ep 961:12, 74–6 it appears that the first copies of the New Testament arrived in Louvain very shortly before 1 May.

Greetings. Examine the book and make sure it's complete. As for the money, whatever you think best. It shall either be sent back or kept at your disposal or spent on books of your own choice. Farewell, dearest Maarten.

* * * * *

954
4 breach of the friendship] Cf Epp 896, 906 salutations.
5 letter of mine] Ep 906
7 condemned it] Cf Ep 906 postscript.
10 electing an emperor] The words are in Greek; Erasmus adds, also in Greek, a phrase from Horace *Epistles* 1.2.8, where Homer is said to depict the folly of princes and peoples alike, with the common people paying the bill. For the flurry of diplomatic activity preceding the election cf the preface to this volume.

955
1 money] Cf Ep 934:2n.

956 / To Antoine de la Marck   [Louvain, c end of April 1519]

This is the preface to the *Paraphrasis in Galatas*, first published by Martens (Louvain May 1519; NK 845). Work on the new paraphrase began soon after that on Corinthians was published in February (cf Ep 916 introduction) with a dedication to Erard de la Marck, Antoine's uncle, but the troubles in Louvain caused delays (cf Epp 930:12n, 952:19–22; LB IX 112A). On 24 April work still remained to be done on the manuscript or the proofs (cf Ep 952:44), but on 25 May distribution had begun (cf Ep 974). The *Paraphrasis in Galatas* was reprinted by Froben (Basel August 1519), by V. Schumann (Leipzig 1519), and by Johann Prüss (Strasbourg March 1520). Thereafter it appeared regularly in conjunction with paraphrases on the other Epistles. Allen found this preface for the last time in two Froben editions of 1522. Erasmus' reason for dropping it afterwards was probably his embarrassment with Antoine's life and politics.

Antoine (c 1495–1528) was a son of the powerful Robert de la Marck. Among his benefices was the Cluniac abbey of Beaulieu-en-Argonne, south-west of Verdun (from 1507), which owned enough land to rank as a county. Antoine followed the political moves of his father, who sided in turns with France and with the government of Brussels (cf Ep 748:29n). But after the failure of attempts to put him in the place of his uncle, the bishop of Liège, he broke away again from the French alliance in 1525. In the name of Charles v he undertook a campaign into Champagne in 1527 and finally died in the fighting when the duke of Guise besieged and sacked his abbey; see P. Harsin *Recueil d'études* (Liège 1970) 163–7.

TO THE HONOURABLE COUNT ANTOINE DE LA MARCK FROM
ERASMUS OF ROTTERDAM, GREETING
After I had set my hand to a paraphrase on Paul's Epistle to the Galatians, I was looking round from time to time for some person to whom I could dedicate the work, since this practice has lasted from early times down to our   5
own day. At that moment your devoted admirer Paschasius Berselius brought me a letter from your Highness, which gave me a clear picture of an upright and lofty spirit, full worthy of your distinguished lineage, and of a fiery nature born for the study of that sublime philosophy which summons us to the contemplation of heavenly things and breeds contempt for those   10
inferior objects which catch the attention of the vulgar crowd.

This gave me great pleasure, though it was no surprise, especially when I recalled the gifts of your father, Robert, a warrior to be compared in

* * * * *
956
6 Berselius] Cf Ep 926:19–24.

Charles de Croy (d 1527)
Funeral monument at Chimay
Institut Royal du Patrimoine Artistique, Brussels
Copyright A.C.L. Bruxelles

military prowess with a Scipio or a Pyrrhus, and the character of your noble
mother, who so resembled her excellent brother the prince of Chimay that it   15
was not kinship so much as rivalry in all the virtues proved her his sister; and
then that incomparable prelate the prince bishop of Liège, your uncle, to
whom I dedicated the last volume of my paraphrase. Henceforward, surely,
priests and even monks will be ashamed to spend their days in luxury and
sloth, in games of chance and other sordid pleasures, when you with your   20
exalted birth and your great fortune, in the flower of youth (for you are
barely four and twenty), think nothing more important, more pleasant, or
more glorious than to devote your time to liberal studies and honourable
accomplishments, and recall the most famous of historic princes? Well done,
O noble youth: keep on your course, adding a glorious lustre by such   25
pursuits to a lineage already distinguished in its own right and spurring on
other young men of great family to pursue honourable studies, as some of
them are already inclined to do of their own accord.

Your Lordship would, I suppose, have been satisfied, had I repaid
your letter with a letter of my own; and now here is a book to keep my letter   30
company, which I will not recommend to your approval, but I hope to see all
men approve it for your sake. The subject may seem somewhat remote from
our own time; but in it you can see how far a wise man may praise himself
sometimes without offence; how much weight we should give to human
authority; how little to ceremonies, and how great the danger to true religion   35
if men trust in ceremonies overmuch. In this Epistle is to be found the famous
problem, never, I think, solved by any of the Ancients, out of which rose the
well-known dispute between Jerome and Augustine about lying. I have
pointed out this still unsolved problem rather than explained it. Here indeed
is a worthy subject for the exercise of all your mental force and power.   40

Farewell, noble young man. I shall count this a most fortunate omen for

* * * * *

15 mother] Catherine de Croy (cf Ep 748:29n); her brother was Charles de Croy (d
   1527), first prince of Chimay, knight of the Golden Fleece in 1491. Until 1509 he
   preceded Chièvres, his kinsman, as the first guardian in charge of Prince
   Charles.
39 problem] In Gal 2:11–14 a clash is reported between Paul and Cephas over the
   correct attitude of Judaeo-Christians towards their brethren recruited from the
   gentiles. Paul accused Cephas and his friends of timidly abandoning the truth
   of the Gospel. Erasmus, like Jerome in his commentary (PL 26:363–8) and
   Augustine (Ep 28), who criticized Jerome, followed a reading which put Peter's
   name in the place of Cephas'. In the New Testament (cf LB VI 807–10) Erasmus
   devoted to the problem a long note that was critical of Augustine. In the
   paraphrase (cf LB VII 949–50) he reported Paul's narrative with some amplification, explaining that Peter used deliberate dissimulation and that his purpose
   was pious but short-sighted; cf Epp 778:270n, 974:5–7.

our friendship if I find that you give this book a cheerful welcome and read it all through with alacrity.

957 / To Guillaume de Croy   Louvain, [c May 1519]

Epp 957–9 were published together in the *Farrago* of October 1519. Presumably they followed one another at short intervals, and from a comparison between Ep 945:11–14 and Ep 957:138–42 and between Ep 945:8–10 and Ep 959:41–3 it can be gathered that the present exchange of letters was somewhat later, but not much. The philosophical argument treated in these three letters is unusual given Erasmus' dominant preoccupations in this period, but it bears a close relation to the concerns of Croy's tutor, Juan Luis Vives, whose influence may be detected in the Stoic stance of his pupil's letter, especially in the heavy reliance on the concept of virtue (Ep 958; cf C.G. Noreña *Juan Luis Vives*, The Hague 1970, 203–4). Erasmus later perceived Vives to have outgrown this prevalent commitment to the problems and methods of classical philosophy and welcomed this development, which he may have helped to bring about; cf Ep 1082.

TO THE MOST REVEREND GUILLAUME DE CROY CARDINAL AND ARCHBISHOP OF TOLEDO FROM ERASMUS OF ROTTERDAM, GREETING

It is not very far from the truth, most reverend Prelate and most excellent Prince, to hold with the ancient Stoics that the sum of human felicity lies in 5 the regular practice of virtue; yet it seems to me that the ordinary opinions of men and their ordinary life are closer to the doctrine of the Peripatetics, who think that happiness is a circle which can only be complete if three orders of blessings concur among themselves and give each other mutual aid and support. Of these, what are called the blessings of the mind deserve, on the 1 one hand, more than any others to be called good things, and contribute most to the sum of felicity, yet on the other hand they are mostly to be obtained by our own industry and forethought; so that we owe the chief part of our happiness to no one after God except ourselves, in so far as we can be said to owe ourselves anything. As for the gifts of nature, since they befall 1 us, as it were, in our sleep without effort on our part, in my opinion we are not so much blessed in them as fortunate, although these too can be

* * * * *

957
7 Peripatetics] Cf Plato *Euthydemus* 279A–C, *Philebus* 48E, *Laws* 743E; Aristotle *Nicomachean Ethics* 1098b; Thomas Aquinas *Commentary on the Nicomachean Ethics* trans C.I. Litzinger (Chicago 1964) I 64–5.

preserved and even increased by forethought and taking pains. Demosthenes, for instance, though he had a weak voice and was short of breath, and besides that had an impediment in his speech and an unattractive appearance, which in a public speaker carries no little weight, yet by assiduous care and practice conquered all these difficulties. Cicero so built up his otherwise indifferent health by careful management of exercise and diet that he proved a match for great exertions, and that to an advanced age. As for worldly advantages, which are like tools for the achievement or exercise of virtue, they come to most men late in life. For in securing honours or wealth or fame and position many use up almost their whole lives, so that by great and long-continued cares they seem to achieve nothing, except to be rich or titled on their death-beds. As a result they get little good from their own blessings and are very little use to other people.

On this score your Eminence always seems to me to be exceptionally fortunate, since all the gifts of nature and the favours of fortune have come to you unasked, and plentiful, and early, so that you can enjoy your advantages for a very long time and be the greatest blessing to your fellow-men. Apart from your intellectual gifts, apart from a bodily frame excellently moulded and fashioned for the whole practice and pursuit of virtue, such is the authority, and such the dignity and wealth conferred upon you by the generous favour of the Holy See and the more than fatherly affection of your uncle the prince of Chièvres, that one would scarcely wish more, nor is any exalted dignity yet wanting, except what could be wished for one man alone. Others therefore have many struggles before them, if they would win their way to the summit of felicity; but you, who have all else in abundance, have but one object and one purpose still before you: to go on as you do now and win spiritual distinctions worthy of the greatness of your fortune. These alone are not lavished by kindly nature or indulgent fortune; they must be bought with toil and sweat. This is the only price at which the heavenly powers are willing that this commodity should be on sale to mortal men, and even kings and sultans have to pay it.

For he who crowns a king does not install in him a kingly mind. Nobility of birth and the plaudits of his people may make a man emperor; a spirit worthy of empire is not theirs to give, and yet, if this is lacking, they who conferred the honour imposed a burden, not a dignity. True dignity of an admirable and exalted kind arises when, and only when, the distinctions

* * * * *

18 Demosthenes] Cf Plutarch *Demosthenes* 6.3, 11–7.
22 Cicero] Cf Plutarch *Cicero* 3.4–5, 8.2–3.
39 Chièvres] Guillaume de Croy; cf Epp 532:30n, 628:69–72.
41 for one man alone] Presumably a tactful reference to the papacy

of nature and fortune add lustre to gifts of the mind in such a way that they
themselves receive light in their turn, or rather, if it be possible, are put in the   5
shade. That man alone is truly great, whose greatness remains even if his
crown is taken from him. Many are debarred by lowly birth or 'straitened
means at home' from the struggle to achieve those admirable virtues which
fall to the lot of none save the few 'welcomed by favouring Jove,' or if they
reach the goal, they do not possess the same power to improve the lot of   6
other men by doing good. And yet suppose there were a man dowered
beyond all others with all the gifts of all the gods, as once Pandora was, and
not unworthy of this galaxy of all good things; such a one seems to me to
have a colour of deity about him, for he is sent by the powers above on
purpose that he may diffuse his munificence over all men far and wide. This   6
duty he will perform if, first, he recognizes his endowments – for some there
are, as the great poet says, who know not their good fortune – and,
secondly, if he remembers that, whatever his endowments are, all is the
Lord's; all is entrusted to him that by being spent for the good of his fellow
men it may earn the Lord a plentiful return, who of this kind of profit can   7
never have enough. But the prime thing needful is a lofty spirit, which looks
down on those trifles which the common herd admire and can no more be
bent from the path of honour than a wall of bronze. Let such be the constant
rule he follows: let him devote the whole arsenal of his felicity to the common
good; for the Ancients rightly held it to be above all the peculiar function of   7
deity to aid mortal man.

   And needs must they approach most closely to this ideal who are
placed by the favour of the eternal deity on that pinnacle of society where
you find yourself. It will add spurs to his resolution if a man remembers that
he is placed as it were in a vast theatre, with the eyes of the whole world bent   8
on him alone; that it is expected of him that he should nothing common do or
mean; that whatever he says or does will be seized upon as an example. If an
actor considers anxiously how he can prove equal to the part he has
undertaken and the audience before which he plays, how much more must
the great ones of the earth feel it their responsibility to answer the world's   8
expectations and their own high place! The more honours Fortune has
bestowed upon you, the harder must you strive that the profit may be worthy
of the capital at stake. There is no concealing what is expected of an abbot, of

* * * * *

57 'straitened means at home'] Juvenal 3.165
59 'welcomed by favouring Jove'] Virgil *Aeneid* 6.129, 130
67 poet says] Cf Virgil *Georgics* 2.458
73 wall of bronze] Cf Horace *Epistles* 1.1.60; the notion of bending the wall,
   however, is new.

an archbishop, of a cardinal, of one whose ancestry and honours are so
brilliant – in short, of a true leader. It is not such a great thing to succeed to   90
very high station; when you have succeeded, to maintain and support it is
the most difficult thing in the world. It has been rightly said that it is sometimes better to deserve distinction than to be given it. Best of all, I believe, is
to achieve great place without ambition, and when you have reached it, to
meet all its demands in such a way that it does not so much shed lustre on   95
you, as you on it. A large part in the making of a great prince is certainly the
wish to be a good one. And if ever there was reason to hope for this from anyone, it is you who have shown yourself in many ways so full of splendid
promise, that all of us not without good reason are full of confidence in your
future.   100

Your Eminence has already given us in many indications a fair sample
of your qualities; still greater things are promised by your virtues and your
natural gifts, as yet so to speak in the blade, but daily growing up and
hastening to maturity. And another thing: although a nursery of virtue has
been implanted in you by Nature, a power (I must admit) of exceptional   105
force, yet it makes no small contribution to have always round one, in
council, in office, and in familiar conversation, men who are intelligent,
honourable, educated, and wise. Even more important is it to do as you do
and practise actively all through one's life the reading of the best authors,
especially such as can give encouragement or guidance in acting the part of a   110
virtuous prince; though we see some great princes gain an added distinction
from learning in subjects by no means their own, as Mithridates from his
skill in languages and medicine and Gaius Caesar from his knowledge of
astrology. Much help comes from one's friends, but from none more than
from good books, which Cato used to carry with him as his companions into   115
the actual Senate-house, and read something in the intervals while the
senate was assembling. No prince needs a complete knowledge of every
subject, and there are far too many books for him to find time to read them all.
In both fields he must learn in the first place what is most important and what
comes closest to his business as a prince. For it would be unwise in a man   120
born for public affairs to gather dust by constant meditation in the company
of what they call dumb teachers; on the contrary, just as Plato moulds the

* * * * *

112 Mithridates] This king of Pontus in the first century BC could speak twenty-two
    languages fluently and was an expert in the antidotes of poison: Gellius
    17.16–17; cf LB I 541F.
113 Caesar] Cf Plutarch Caesar 59.
115 Cato] Cf LB IV 731C; Plutarch Cato the Younger 19.
122 dumb teachers] Cf Adagia I ii 18.
122 Plato] Cf Republic 3, especially 411–12.

spirit of his citizens by a judicious mixture of music and gymnastics, so the lives of great men should be kept in balance by interchanging leisure for study and the business of public affairs.

But I am carried away, forgetting that I am writing a letter, and that to so excellent a prince, wise enough to need no advice from me, fortunate enough to deserve all my felicitations. But it was a pleasure to dwell upon the thought of your great qualities, who as a prelate are one of the chief ornaments of this generation, and I pray that they may continually increase, so that we may constantly have new reasons for rejoicing with you, while you daily become even greater and better than you were before. That you should practise speaking and writing alternately is, I think, an excellent plan; and so I have the more readily done as you asked, though in other ways much pressed with business, in order to provoke you to an answer. I send your Eminence a letter ill written on two counts and I fear tedious on a third, for it is as long as it is shapeless. But on this point you must not be hard on me, for you brought this Arabian piper on your own head. If you will do me the honour of adding the name of Erasmus to the list of your humble servants, I in return will ensure you a special place in my list of Williams, for I notice that some destiny associates this name in my experience with friendship and good omen. It would take too long to name them all; but you will, I think, not be sorry to find yourself classed with William, archbishop of Canterbury, with William Mountjoy, with William Budé. If there is anything in which your Eminence may find me of the slightest service, pray give your instructions to a man who greatly desires to please you. My respectful duty to your Lordship.

From Louvain

958 / From Guillaume de Croy   Louvain, [c May 1519]

For this letter, published in the *Farrago*, see Ep 957 introduction.

GUILLAUME DE CROY, CARDINAL, TO ERASMUS OF ROTTERDAM, GREETING

I have your letter, my dear Erasmus, but in what words to extol it I simply do not know, such are its elegance and its learning, so characteristic of you and of all your letters. If I am to answer it, you must please grant me one thing: you must not mind if, while my views are the same as yours, my expression is

* * * * *

138 Arabian piper] Cf *Adagia* I vii 32; the Arabian pipers did not know when to stop.
140 list of Williams] Cf Ep 534:33–54; Bietenholz *History and Biography* 60–1.

very different. I will do what Glaucon does in Plato, when he dispraises
justice in order to rouse all the eloquence of Socrates to praise it as one of the
great virtues. When you come as though by definite stages to speak of the
felicity of the soul, you seem to approve the Peripatetic doctrine of the good   10
life, rather than the Stoic view, and assert that it agrees better both with the
general feeling of mankind and with the facts of life. If however this criterion
has any force in establishing the theory of human happiness, Epicureanism
will easily vanquish all its rivals, having such popular appeal that the section
of mankind which thinks us born solely for pleasure is much the largest. Yet   15
you are not much moved, I notice, by the numbers of the cobblers, tailors,
cooks, butchers, and other tradesmen, but seek your evidence from the
oustanding men who, with their supreme endowments of intellect and
learning, are not carried aimlessly this way and that (I mean, wherever profit
and pleasure may drive them), but stand above the chances of human life,   20
beyond the reach of disturbing emotions, and see things clearly as they
really are, piercing, as they say, to the quick. How these men argue will
repay examination; and let us approach it, in Stoic fashion, with a little
more subtlety. Do not be surprised if I bring to this discussion absolutely
none of that popular and florid eloquence appropriate to the courts, which   25
would be beyond my reach even were I praising pleasure before a popular
audience; for we are not all like Erasmus, who can write of great things and
make them seem familiar, of small things and make them seem sublime, of
dark things and make them lucid, of paradoxes and make them perfectly
probable.   30
    But to return to my subject, if wealth and possessions and health and
strength and good looks and all other bodily and external good things, as
you call them, make some contribution to felicity itself, the greater these are,
the fuller and more eminent must be the state of happiness that they produce, so that a man who is handsome and rich is far happier than one who is   35
poor and ugly. If you add wealth, possessions, honours, influence, power,
friends, lineage, physical strength, fleetness of foot, how many parasangs
behind him in the race towards happiness he will leave the good man who is
without these things! It will be clear that Socrates, that deity of our philosophers, with all his famous virtue has advanced scarcely one step towards   40
happiness. To say this is almost impious: for if these things taken singly make
some contribution towards blessedness, all together they will have such

* * * * *

958
7 Plato] Cf *Republic* 2.358–62.
22 as they say] Cf *Adagia* ii iv 13.
37 parasangs] The Persian measure of distance; cf *Adagia* ii iii 82.

immediate effect that the man who possesses them will be more blessed than the good man deprived of them; and thus it may prove easy to call that brutal tyrant Nero more blessed than Epictetus, the Stoic slave who is such a favourite with gods and mortals. Pray relieve Socrates of his famous physical ugliness, his lowly birth, his railing wife, his poverty and lack of means; give him good looks and pedigree and a devoted helpmeet, and endow him with wealth and the highest honours; and what will you find in your new Socrates grander or more exalted or more admirable than was in your old one?

What say you, Erasmus my prince of scholars? Wealth is a blessing; so are beauty and physical strength; why then was no man ever made better by them? Cicero, who was as expert in the sense of Latin words as anyone in Rome, the Latin capital, itself, expresses surprise, as you know, that possessions were called 'goods' in early Rome, although nothing could be less so, nor is the word really suitable to that particular thing. Think you that some most worthless dross of gold or silver, that silken garments and tapestries and splendid mansions add much to happiness? So that if human luxury had never invented such things, no man would have been perfectly happy? Do you consider beauty – a complexion, say, blended of white and red – is part of blessedness? Then is no Ethiop ever blessed? Not one, in our view, if we judge blessedness by this, and none of us on their view, assuming that they judge by the same standards as we do, a vulgar standard suited to the coarse tastes of the mob. And to draw an example from the Scriptures, as befits both of us, me as a bishop and you as their most diligent and honest expositor, what thrones, what riches can you add to Christ to make him more blessed than he was in the world?

But let us say no more of this, for God himself is king of kings, as he always was, and lord of lords. Peter, at any rate, boasts that he has neither gold nor silver. Be careful, Peter! Why deprive yourself of no small part of felicity? Bestow on Paul the Roman empire – I mean that same Paul who says that he rejoices in adversity (so men call it) and in defeat: will you get a happier, greater, more admirable Paul? Are you prepared to adopt Quin-

* * * * *

45 Epictetus] Epictetus of Hierapolis (Phrygia), c 50–120, was a slave and one of the last important representatives of the Stoic school. Some of his teachings are perhaps influenced by and certainly compatible with Christian thought.
54 Cicero] *Paradoxa Stoicorum* 7
70 Peter] Acts 3:6
72 Paul] Rom 5:3
74 Quintilian's phrase] The quotation comes from Quintilian's second declamation, *Caecus in limine*, rather than from the first, *Paries palmatus;* the error was corrected in the *Epistolae ad diversos*, 1521.

tilian's phrase in the *Paries palmatus*, 'Those whom their virtues have made   75
unhappy'? Be in no hurry to call them unhappy whom Christ (who is truth
itself) declares to be blessed when the moment comes that men persecute
them for his sake. I wanted to have this discussion with you, if you do not
mind, to give myself some practice in this subject; but I have not ranged so
widely in this field as to forget that this is a letter I am writing. So please take   80
this practice effort of mine in good part.

I pass on to other sections of your truly delightful letter. In the second
place, you set my duty before me, Peripatetic as you are, in terms such as
could hardly be expected from Zeno of Citium himself. Please send me such
precepts often, so that under your tuition I may know how I am to behave.   85
For though I am not one of the highest and best class of men – those who
know everything themselves – I would much the most willingly belong to the
next class, those who follow good advice when they are given it. And I hope
to live my life in such a way as to maintain my own honour and my dearest
uncle's, whose affection for me you have rightly called greater than a   90
father's. He could not show such intimate feeling for me, though he were my
father twice over; and I confess I owe him more than I could to a most
generous uncle and father rolled into one. As for scholarship, what I should
like most of all, if it were possible, would be to complete the all-round
knowledge in Greek they speak so much of; if a heavy load of business makes   95
that impossible, at least, as you advise, I will devote myself to liberal subjects
and those to which I have a natural inclination of my own accord, to the more
humane Muses, to elegance in Latin and, up to a point, in Greek, and to
philosophy of the kind that Socrates brought into the cities and the homes of
men – ethics they call it – which has always seemed to me far the most useful   100
for the conduct of public affairs.

Now I wish to review a few words in your letter: 'But I am carried away,
forgetting that I am writing a letter, and that to so excellent a prince!' Of this
at least you are oblivious, dearest Erasmus, that you write to a man to whom
you could send a letter longer than the whole *Iliad*, and still not satisfy his   105
appetite for reading you or do away with the pleasure he finds in hearing your
news – in fact, you would continually increase it. As for what you say about
my humble servants, there is no call for you to use such words in addressing
me. Call yourself a fellow-worker in my studies, or rather, call yourself the

* * * * *

76 Christ] Matt 5:11
84 Zeno] C 334–263 BC, the founder of the Stoic school
86 class of men] Hesiod *Works and Days* 293–5, cited by Aristotle *Nicomachean Ethics*
    1.4.7; Allen detected that Croy is using the Latin version of the *Ethics* by
    Johannes Argyropoulos; cf Ep 456:106n.
94 all-round knowledge] Quintilian 1.10.1

teacher and me the pupil. And as regards your Williams, I like to think that I   11
am blessed with a name that is so congenial to you; nor shall I ever be sorry to
be joined in any way with a man of such eminence and so perfect in
excellence of every sort as William Warham, archbishop of Canterbury, or as
that distinguished and active nobleman Lord Mountjoy, of both of whom
you always speak so highly and about whose merits I have heard so much   11
from almost everyone that I could not be induced to suppose them other than
men of the very highest quality. What can I say of Guillaume Budé, the
chosen darling of the Muses both Greek and Latin? For my dear Vives never
tires of singing his praises; and his researches, his published work, his
natural gifts and learning and eloquence and character I respect, admire, and   12
venerate with reverence and wonder. I would much rather you enrolled me
in their company than among the wealthiest magnates of any other description.

Farewell, dearest Erasmus, and forgive my loquacity; and as soon as
you have the time, send me a reply. Since I thought you might find my   12
writing rather hard to read, I have employed a secretary.

Louvain, [1518]

959 / To Guillaume de Croy   Louvain, [c May 1519]

For this letter, published in the *Farrago*, see Ep 957 introduction.

TO HIS MOST REVEREND LORD GUILLAUME DE CROY, CARDINAL
AND ARCHBISHOP OF TOLEDO, FROM ERASMUS OF ROTTERDAM,
GREETING
Most reverend Lord Archbishop and most illustrious Prince, in my last letter
I said in jest that I was afraid you had set an Arabian piper on your trail. Now   5
it is the other way round, and the same thing seems to have happened to me,
so careful are you to answer every point in that letter, long as it was, and
moreover you drag me by the scruff of the neck into a very wide field of
philosophical discussion, starting a topic that might fill more than one
volume. Had I not convinced myself that your Eminence can turn your mind   10
to anything, I should wonder a little whether in writing as you do you had
some sophist at your elbow; such is the skill you show in distorting some
things and turning them to a purpose at which they were not aimed. For the
moment, I will not engage with you in a pitched battle but will touch on a few

* * * * *

959
5 Arabian piper] Cf Ep 957:138n.
8 by the scruff of the neck] Cf *Adagia* IV ix 50.

points in few words, not losing sight of the fact that I am writing a letter. 15
Furthermore, when you assert that, however you may have argued, you
think as I do, I likewise cannot fail to think as you do, however I may have
argued myself. In the same way, they say, the Peripatetics agree with the
Stoics as to the facts and differ only in their language and their system of
laying down the law. In fact, though their teaching is the same, I prefer 20
Peripatetics to Stoics for this reason, that the Stoics employ paradoxical
arguments so far removed from common life and experience, while the
Peripatetics bring themselves down more, as it were, to the level of popular
understanding, though they have the same object in view as the Stoics. In
the same way, Plato wishes his wise man to descend from the marvellous 25
light of those things which really exist into the shadows with the common
crowd, so that he may be of more use to them; and in the same way eternal
wisdom speaks to us nearly everywhere as children. It by no means follows
that whatever satisfies the lowest class of men must be the best; you distort
your argument in this direction, but with more force than fitness. Who 30
would be impressed if some Stoic were to proclaim that kingship, riches, and
good health are not blessings at all, and on the contrary that slavery,
poverty, sickness, old age, and death are no kind of ills, because perfect
felicity is to be found in some state of being he calls wisdom? These
arguments at least cut no ice even with educated men, and to the commonalty 35
they are just ridiculous. If however a man were to say that these things are by
no means to be anxiously pursued, but that, should they fall to one's lot,
they must be turned into opportunities and materials for virtue, his words
will fall more acceptably upon the ears and enter the minds, not of the
cobblers and tailors and cooks of whom you speak, but of magistrates and 40
princes and bishops and (I will add) even theologians; for on this point I do
not believe Latomus would differ from me, however much he is thought to
differ in the business of the ancient tongues. Not that the common people
necessarily approve what they follow in herds; everyone condemns dishonourable pleasures, no one has a good word for drunkenness. I am thinking of 45
their settled opinions, not of their appetites or their mental aberrations.

But (not to be long-winded) your first argument runs like this: if
physical and worldly advantages are blessings, then the more plentifully
they fall to one's lot, the happier they must make one. In the first place, your
Eminence must remember that this class of blessings, however much one 50
may pile one on another, does not bring happiness, but when added they
perfect the happiness that virtue alone can give, at least as concerns the

* * * * *

25 Plato] Cf *Republic* 7.519–20.
42 Latomus] Cf Epp 934, 945 introductions.

active exercise of virtue. Secondly, although the things you speak of contribute to felicity, it does not immediately follow that felicity increases in the same proportion as they do. Food and drink conduce to the maintenance 5 of man's life, but it does not follow that he has most life who eats most. Apart from wisdom alone, there is nothing in human affairs so advantageous that it does not become the opposite when present in excess. Moderate beauty has helped many people on their way; excessive beauty has been the ruin of many. Pythagoras, Scipio Africanus, the emperor Trajan derived not a little 6 of their authority from the nobility of their appearance. And then you think a man almost impious who would suppose Socrates happier even by a hair's breadth if some god had added to his gifts of mind good looks and wealth and noble birth. If nothing else, we shall find he can do good to more people. Now it is virtue's purpose to spread its blessings over many men; but the 6 virtue of Socrates benefited very few of his fellow-citizens and was disastrous to himself. To measure how many parasangs ahead the man is who is thus equipped is not for me; I am satisfied if he gets some increase in happiness. Again, it is proper to weigh these blessings and not count them, as you do when you make virtue deprived of these things scarcely one step 7 towards felicity. Virtue is the only thing of such importance that even by itself it can achieve felicity and stands so far above blessings of every other kind that they are not even admitted into the class of blessings except in so far as they are in the service of virtue. All this makes it sufficiently clear that in this context it is off the point to compare Nero, the most infamous of 7 tyrants, and Epictetus, the most upright of philosophers. It is true that Nero's power and riches were no help to save him from ill fortune; but had that excellent man Epictetus been given these advantages, he would have been not a little better equipped for the exercise of virtue.

On this you argue as follows: if they are blessings, why does their 8 support make no man better? In the first place, if a man has wealth that was left him by his forbears or honourably acquired in some other way and expends it on relieving the poor or some more pious use for riches, if there is one, does not that wealth support him in a process of daily self-improvement? Or are we not to suppose that an addition of virtuous acts 8 adds something also to a man's standing in virtue? Secondly, it has not escaped you as a man of intelligence that wealth, beauty, good health, and other blessings of the kind are called blessings in a different sense than virtue. We call these blessings much as we call royal heralds kings because kings are their masters. What the Stoics perhaps would call advantages, the 9

*****

89 heralds kings] Addressed with the name of the royal house whose colours they wear. In English the expression 'king-at-arms' has survived.

Peripatetics, using the word in a wider sense, call a sort of blessings. No one can make a bad use of virtue; but these gifts are misused by many people – the gifts are not to blame, the fault is theirs. Again there are some things called not disadvantages but evils by the Peripatetics, which all the same often provide materials for virtue; and perhaps more men are corrupted by poverty 95 than by wealth in moderation. Cicero, you say, expressed surprise that in early Latin the word blessings can be applied to property; but, if I mistake not, he said this while playing the part of a Stoic philosopher. God is called good in one sense; a virtuous man, a good horse, a good coin, in other senses. Why be surprised that bodily health and strength should be called 100 good things, when according to the philosophers the predicates of good and thing are completely applicable to both? Nor do I speak of things invented by luxury, though nothing prevents even discoveries bad in themselves from being put to good uses. It is more clever than convincing when you say that if no one is blessed unless he has a complexion blended of white and red, 105 therefore no Ethiop is ever blessed. A person of this complexion is not ipso facto handsome, nor is there any reason why an Ethiop among Ethiops should not be handsome just because of his colour. If nothing can be added to Christ, why is he so often asking something of his Father? Why does he exult that power should be given him in heaven and in earth? 110

But let us not bring Christ into this discussion, if you so prefer. The fact that he wished the apostles to be poor does not prove that riches are bad; he did not wish the glory of his gospel to be ascribed to worldly advantages. Nor do I deny that the moment often comes when such advantages must be abandoned, if religion so requires. 115

Now answer me in your turn. If these are not blessings, how can we ask for them even in public worship from him who neither will nor can give us anything that is not good? Heaven forbid that we should call unfortunate those who are endowed with virtue; of course we call them truly blessed but think their blessedness is more complete if they possess the things of which 120 we speak, whether freely given them or won by honourable means, unless circumstances demand something different.

I will give over my philosophizing if your Eminence will answer me one more small question. Imagine two men. One of them as ugly as Thersites and as poor as Irus, in pitiful health, defective in speech, with a useless memory 125 and wits of lead, of disreputable origin, universally unpopular, banished from his country, old, and decrepit. The other in the flower of his age, of

* * * * *

96 Cicero] Cf Ep 958:54.
124 Thersites ... Irus] Thersites is ugliness personified (cf *Adagia* IV iii 80); for the proverbial poverty of Irus cf *Adagia* I vi 76.

noble and impressive appearance, in perfect health, a clear and ready speaker, with a reliable memory and a nimble wit, rich, powerful, well born, and universally respected for his high station. Imagine that all this time you have a mind worthy of an honourable man, which above all loves what is best and after that desires to do as much good as he can to all men; and that there is beside you some deity who bids you choose which of these you prefer, for you will henceforth be what you have chosen. Tell me in honesty, which will you choose? And do you think the good man's choice unworthy of the name of good? I know you will retort 'If these are good things, why are we bidden to despise them?' That man despises them who thinks them nothing worth compared with virtue, who puts no trust in them, who does not hold them for his own enjoyment, who shares them generously, who does not grieve when they are taken from him, if Fortune one day asks for the return of what is really hers. The man is not blessed who thinks he owes his blessedness only to them. He is not blessed who ceases to be blessed when deprived of them.

But enough of philosophy; 'Acorns have had their day.' If your Highness is willing to take advice even from me, I am bound to admire your modesty of spirit, which even such a splendid position could not spoil – not but what I have spoken as I have not so much from a desire to put you right as to provoke you to practise your pen. The feeling that you show for the subjects worthy of a great prince gives you, I think, a better claim to felicity than your red hat itself, exalted as it is. If your modesty rejects the notion of me as your humble servant, I leave you free to call me by what name you will, as long as you count me among your devoted supporters. And as you with your accustomed courtesy do not despise the company of those three other Williams, so I do not doubt of their rejoicing when you join them and put them in the shade, if so it can be called, and not rather to make them more distinguished by the splendour that you bring with you. I have stolen a brief hour or two in order not to seem wholly unconscious of my duty. Shortly, I hope, it will be possible to bear witness on a larger scale to my feelings towards your Highness, for whose continual prosperity I tender my best wishes.

Louvain, [1518]

* * * * *

144 'Acorns ... day'] A Greek proverb, supposed to refer to the use of acorns in the early days as food, before cereal crops were developed; cf *Adagia* I iv 2.

960 / To Maarten Lips   [Louvain, c March–May 1519]

This letter is known only from Lips' two copy books (cf Ep 750 introduction). In the Brussels manuscript he added an argument to the text, telling how Edward Lee had asked him for numerous lettters he had written to Lips under the pretext that he needed a reference. Subsequently these letters were not returned at the stipulated time. The argument further mentions how Lee had told Lips that Briart (d 8 January 1520) was prohibiting the sale of Erasmus' *Apologia*, of which a copy accompanied this note. As so often in the correspondence between Erasmus and Lips the circumstances and the date must be inferred. From Ep 922:34–5 it was learnt that Lee was no longer writing to Lips. With the friendly message here mentioned he was apparently attempting to get back his letters to Lips, who was apt to show them to Erasmus. This desire is understandable, especially after the publication of Erasmus' *Apologia contra Latomi dialogum* (cf Ep 936:34n). Possibly this was the book sent by Erasmus; or it might have been Erasmus' *Apologia de laude matrimonii* which interested Briart directly; see Ep 946 introduction.

ERASMUS OF ROTTERDAM TO MASTER MAARTEN LIPS OF
BRUSSELS, GREETING

Lee treats you as the wolf treated the lamb. For some months I have not set eyes on him, so far am I from having had it out with him. I wish you had not given him the rest of the letters; you might have found some excuse not to.   5
Watch your step; he will learn nothing from me, for I trust him less than the devil in person. That friendly letter was written by him for the sole reason of deluding you still further. The story about my *Apologia* is false; it has been approved by Atensis and is now on sale. I send you a copy. It is safest in this season of storms to trust no one and keep one's mouth shut. Farewell.   10

961 / To Lorenzo Campeggi   Louvain, 1 May 1519

Lorenzo Campeggi (1474–1539), originally a professor of canon law at Bologna, entered the church as a widower and was created a bishop and in 1517 a cardinal. After other diplomatic missions he went to England as the papal legate (summer 1518–August 1519). Despite many obstacles he managed to win the confidence of Henry VIII, who made him one of his agents in Rome and in

* * * * *

960
3 wolf] Aesop fable 155
9 Atensis] Jan Briart
10 season of storms] Cf Ep 930:12n.

1524 bishop of Salisbury. Erasmus clearly believed that the legate was in a position to influence his own aspirations for preferment in England (cf Ep 964 introduction). He wrote this letter to establish direct relations and to win a sympathetic ear. He continued to praise Campeggi along with Wolsey (cf Epp 968:15, 970, 990), and he dedicated his *Paraphrasis in Ephesios* to him in February 1520 (cf Ep 1062). By that time the present letter, together with Campeggi's answer, Ep 995, was already published in Erasmus' *Farrago*.

TO THE MOST REVEREND CARDINAL LORENZO CAMPEGGI FROM
ERASMUS OF ROTTERDAM, GREETING

My most reverend Lord, the report of your distinguished qualities and exceptional learning has fired me with a desire, now of long standing, to enjoy a closer acquaintance with your Eminence and pay my humble duty in 5
person. Hitherto however I have been prevented, partly by my state of health, which, as a result of prolonged illness, is still too weak to be readily risked on an uncomfortable voyage; partly because some months ago I was summoned to France by a letter from his most Christian Majesty, to whom I could not excuse myself for very long. But I would not have my devotion to 1o
your Eminence pass in the mean time without some concrete evidence, and so I send you the New Testament newly revised with great labour by myself, which his holiness Pope Leo encouraged me to publish with a dedication to him, as his brief added at the beginning of the volume bears witness. This work met at the outset with some opposition, but only from people who did 15
not read it or did not understand what they read. By now it has received a general welcome, except from a very few who are ashamed to change their minds. These men leave no stone unturned to suppress the humanities, which are coming into fresh bloom everywhere. This campaign they conceal behind splendid maxims – Down with Heresy, The Church is in danger – 2o
while I assure you there is quite other game afoot. As far as I am concerned, my sole object, forgetting all else, has been to put my modest gifts and such

* * * * *

961
5 in person] In England
9 letter from his most Christian Majesty] Had Erasmus received such a letter, it would be most unlike him to leave it unanswered and unpublished. Nor is such a letter mentioned anywhere in his correspondence with Budé and others. Perhaps a word is missing in the printed text of this letter. Erasmus could originally have written: 'Christianissimi regis nomine literis evocatus sim' (by a letter (or letters) I was summoned to France in the name of his most Christian Majesty'), perhaps thinking of Epp 810:400–89, 926:30–42; cf Ep 896:92n.
14 brief] Ep 864
18 leave no stone unturned] Cf *Adagia* i iv 30.

small scholarship as I have at the service of Christ's glory and the good of the church. But I am a man; I may make mistakes. Yet, if my judgment has sometimes been at fault, my intentions at least have been anything but faulty. No one ever yet satisfied everybody; I am content that I give satisfaction to all critics of the highest standing.

But pray observe how perverse, I may say how ungrateful, some ill-natured persons are. Mistrusting the printed word and solid arguments, some of them attack me with malicious inventions. Any pamphlet that makes its appearance, and such things nowadays are given far too much licence, they ascribe to me. A book called *Nobody* appeared – that was its ridiculous title; they spread the tale that it was mine, and this calumny would have won the day, had not the indignant author laid claim to his bantling. Some absurd letters were published; people were found to say that I had a hand in the writing of them. Finally there appeared under somewhat dubious auspices a book by Martin Luther. I know as little of the author as I do of anyone; I have not yet read the book through, yet from the outset they were saying it was mine, though I did not write a line of it.

Since none of this makes any headway so far, their lies being refuted by the facts, they are trying to throw suspicion on me in connection with a certain dialogue. This, as the plot makes clear, was written to discredit the late Pope Julius at the time of the schism, but by whom is quite uncertain; some five years ago I dipped into it rather than read it. Afterwards I found copies of it in the hands of several people in Germany, but under various names. Some declared the author was a Spaniard but kept his name dark. Others gave it to Fausto the poet, others again to Girolamo Balbi. What to make of this I do not know. I followed the scent as far as I could, but have not yet arrived at any satisfactory conclusion. The man who wrote it was a fool; the man who published it deserves the heavier penalty. And I wonder

25

30

35

40

45

50

* * * * *

32 *Nobody*] Hutten's *Nemo*; cf Ep 863:34n. Hutten's authorship cannot have been seriously in doubt. His name is given in the title of the earliest printed editions; those of 1518 have an anonymous title, but the poem is attributed to him on the verso of the title page; cf Hutten *Opera* I 9*–11*, 21*–24*.

35 letters] Probably the *Epistolae obscurorum virorum*; cf Epp 363 introduction, 622:5–11.

37 book] Froben's collection (cf Ep 904:20n). It was published under Luther's name, but Erasmus' close association with the Froben press could be held against him, especially by his current critics in Louvain; cf Ep 980, CWE 7 preface.

42 dialogue] Evidently the *Julius exclusus*; for the following cf Epp 636, 849:32n, 967:173–215.

47 Fausto ... Balbi] Balbi was a Venetian humanist who lived in Paris (cf Ep 23:49n) like Fausto Andrelini.

anyone could be ready to father it on me on grounds of style alone, since it is not my writing, unless I am quite ignorant of my own self; nor would it be surprising if there were people whose style smacked of Erasmus, since my things are in everyone's hands, and we commonly reproduce the tricks of an author whom we are constantly reading. 55

There are even people here who assert that your Eminence has almost come to suspect the same thing. Of this I certainly shall never be convinced, as long as I retain my conviction that what is commonly said by persons of the highest standing about your learning and your wisdom cannot be untrue. Nor have I the least doubt that, if some sort of suspicion has taken 60 possession of your mind, I shall dissipate it without difficulty, given the opportunity of a conversation with you, which Christ in his goodness will one day permit. Until then I beg you of your kindness to believe that pieces of this kind written by others and ready for publication have actually been suppressed by me, so far am I from having published or being ever likely to 65 publish anything of the sort myself. Nor is it surprising if in your part of the world there are people prepared to tell lies like this about me, seeing that here some men who are quite close to me are not ashamed to invent the most outrageous falsehoods. All the slanders spread by all these men it is impossible for me to answer, but what I can do, that I will. If my brains, my 70 reading, and my industry have any value, it shall all be devoted to the purposes of Christ and his spouse. The truth of this will be clear to your Eminence if you will ever pay me the compliment of putting me to the test.

I send the book now in its native nakedness, for it has just come from the printer and there was no time to beautify it; but in a few days' time you 75 shall have another suitably dressed. Your Eminence will be so kind as to remember me, his humble dependant, to the most reverend cardinal of York; to whom I intended to write, did I not think that for the moment you would share both this letter and the book with him. My respectful best wishes to your Eminence, to whom my services are entirely devoted. 80

Louvain, May day 1519

* * * * *

65 suppressed by me] Cf Epp 636:29n, 904:20n.
74 nakedness] Probably unbound; from Campeggi's answer (Ep 995) it appears that this was one of the two parts of the New Testament, 1518–19, probably the text volume; cf Ep 864 introduction.
77 York] Wolsey

962 / To Richard Pace   Louvain, [first half of] May [1519]

This letter was first published in the *Farrago* of October 1519, together with Ep 937, to which it is the answer. Thus the year given in the *Farrago* must be corrected. Also the day indicated, 'Ides of May' (15 May), is not beyond doubt, since Erasmus dated Epp 964, 966 on the same day from Antwerp. It seems clear, however, that this letter was sent either with Ep 961 or with Epp 964–7. When he wrote it Erasmus was evidently not expecting to meet Pace as soon as he actually did; cf Ep 968 introduction.

ERASMUS OF ROTTERDAM TO THE HONOURABLE RICHARD PACE, FIRST SECRETARY OF HIS MOST SERENE MAJESTY THE KING OF ENGLAND, GREETING

If what you say about the paraphrase is true, I am glad, to be sure, that my labours are not wholly unsuccessful. Is it not pure bliss to win great grati- 5 tude for small pains? If I chose to compare one piece of work with another, writing the paraphrases is child's play compared with the efforts which the New Testament costs me. I only wish that everyone might experience the same result which you describe; for that they should find Paul at every opportunity more attractive will be quite sufficient return for all my labours. I 10 should be sorry, however, if my paraphrase carried so much weight that anyone in reliance on them should neglect the explanations of the commentators, and especially the older ones; on the contrary, I hope that my work will rouse people to read them with more care. There will, I dare say, be some inquisitive people who will wish to test where I agree or disagree with 15 the commentators, and perhaps there will be some who find fault. Paul takes it in good part, in whatever spirit the Gospel is preached, provided Christ is made known; nor does it make much difference to me in what spirit my paraphrase is read, provided that by this opportunity everyone is encour- aged to study Paul. For the style, I have followed Seneca's advice, not aiming 20 at elaborate language but using whatever came to hand unsought. The people who pride themselves on the precise fact that they are portentously barbarous and uncouth, ought not, I think, to be given so much importance that to please them we should aim at a hideous style, especially if it would

* * * * *

962
7 child's play] Cf Ep 710 introduction.
16 Paul] Cf Phil 1:15–18.
20 Seneca's advice] For Erasmus' view of Seneca's style cf Ep 325:89–114, Allen Ep 2091:275–97.

cost us as much effort to write in their fashion as it costs them if they ever try   25
to write well.

When you urge me to go on and finish what I have begun, you spur the
willing jade. I have never seen anything more determined than this
conspiracy against humane studies. Food and drink, sleep, music and
dancing – of all such pleasures one can have enough, as Homer says; but the   30
love of mischief-making in these men is never satisfied. And the lessons
taught by the leaders are practised with such energy by the younger men
that never was that saying (it is Euripides', if I mistake not) more in place:
'Many the pupils who outstrip their teachers.'

On the question of my crossing over, I will follow your advice: I will be   35
guided by my state of health. That the king's feelings towards me should be
unchanged gives me joy not only for my own sake but for the common cause
of learning; for his good will to me has no other cause except his belief that
Erasmus is something of a scholar. I have a poor appetite for praise; but, to
confess the truth openly, in praise from such a prince there is neither   40
discomfort nor disgrace. Farewell, my dear Pace, most scholarly of my
friends and my best friend among scholars.

Louvain, 15[?] May 151[8]

963 / From Frederick of Saxony   Grimma, 14 May 1519

This letter was composed in Frederick's name by his chancellor, Georgius
Spalatinus, and published in 1545 together with Ep 939, the letter that it
answered. Both evidently came from the same source, although no draft or final
copy of Ep 963 remains in Weimar; cf Höss *Spalatin* 162.

FREDERICK BY THE GRACE OF GOD DUKE OF SAXONY, MARSHAL,
PRINCE ELECTOR, AND VICAR OF THE HOLY ROMAN EMPIRE,
LANDGRAVE OF THURINGIA AND MARKGRAVE OF MEISSEN
SENDETH GREETING
Although we have no doubt, most learned Erasmus, that you will fully   5

* * * * *

28 jade] Homer *Iliad* 8.293–4; cf *Adagia* I ii 46.
30 Homer] *Iliad* 13.636, 637
32 younger men] Cf Ep 930:12n; Lee, Latomus, and the licentiate of Ep 946 were all
   younger friends of Briart.
33 Euripides] A Greek line of unknown authorship, quoted by Cicero in *Epistulae
   ad familiares* 9.7; cf *Adagia* III v 23. It is no 651 in the *Sententiae* ascribed to
   Menander, and adesp. 107 in Nauck's collection of the fragments of Greek
   tragedy.

understand from the letter we gave to Jodocus Jonas when he was lately
setting out to visit you how much we appreciate your exceptional good will
towards us, which so clearly appears more than anywhere else in the
dedication of Suetonius and the other historians, yet we thought we ought
to reply to the letter you wrote us from Antwerp on 14 April, for many other   10
reasons but in particular because it was at once so learned and so eloquent
and showed even more clearly your zealous feelings and religious affection
(of which we have long been well aware) towards us and towards sincere
and true Christian learning and the truth of the Gospel.

There is, as you say, an extraordinary conspiracy of those who hate   15
more liberal studies, which can have no result except to do harm to good,
pious, and educated men. That the Lutheran cause should not be condemned by the learned and that Dr Martin's works should be eagerly read
by all men of good will in your part of the world is a joy to us; all the more
because most men of good will and learning in our countries and principali-   20
ties, to say nothing of foreign parts, write in praise of his life and character
no less than of his scholarship. For his living hitherto among our people in
Saxony has been a tribute not so much to the man as to his cause, for the last
thing we would wish to achieve is to lay penalties upon those who deserve
rewards. Nor, with the help of Almighty God, shall we ever so act that   25
through our fault any innocent man is handed over to the impious keeping of
those who seek only their own advantage.

Besides which, if God so please, we intend to show favour in future no
less than in the past to the humanities and liberal studies and to those who
teach and strive to learn them; and of this, in view of our special feeling for   30

* * * * *

963
6 letter] It was delivered by Jonas (cf Ep 876) and answered by Ep 979 but is now
   lost, perhaps as a result of the circumstances mentioned in Epp 978, 1001.
   For a hint of its contents cf Allen Ep 1030:49–53. Following the example of
   Eobanus' pilgrimage (cf Epp 870 introduction, 982) two young teachers in the
   University of Erfurt, Justus Jonas and Kaspar Schalbe, set out at the end of term
   to visit Erasmus in Louvain. But they actually found him 'in Antwerp, on the
   sea shore' (Jonas Briefwechsel Ep 25) between c 20 and 26 May (cf Ep 964 introduction). Eobanus sent with them a copy of his Hodoeporicon (cf Ep 870 introduction), which was dedicated to Jonas. On 28 May the two travellers were in
   Brussels (cf Ep 977), and two days later they may have called on Erasmus at
   Louvain, eliciting from him Epp 981–3 to take home with them. Erasmus likewise entrusted them with Epp 950, 978–80. See Krause Eobanus I 300–2; cf also
   Ep 1157.
9 Suetonius] Ep 586; cf Ep 939:7–18
15 as you say] Ep 939:33–45
26 handed over] Cf Ep 939:48n.

you, we do not wish you to be unaware at this time. Farewell, most learned Erasmus.

From our castle of Grimma, 14 May 1519

964 / To Henry VIII Antwerp, 15 May 1519

Erasmus dated Epp 964–9 from Antwerp between 15 and 20 May, Ep 970 from Brussels on 21 May, and Epp 973–4 again from Antwerp on 25 May. In all likelihood he briefly interrupted his visit to Antwerp to accompany Richard Pace to Brussels (cf Ep 968 introduction). There are indications though, that he went to Antwerp repeatedly during the spring of 1519. The purpose of his visits was partly recreational (cf Epp 934:10n, 952:12–13, 963:6n) and partly serious and unpleasant (cf Ep 991:21–2) because of his conflict with Edward Lee; cf Allen Ep 1061:584–600.

A common purpose of Erasmus' recent and current letters to England (Epp 961–2, 964–7), all published in the *Farrago*, was to elicit a clear assurance of adequate financial provision to allow him to settle there. He had planned to revisit England after his return from Basel in the autumn of 1518 (cf Epp 834, 886 introductions), and the troubles he had experienced in recent months (cf Ep 930:12n) must have reinforced his desire to carry out the plan and find a haven for his remaining years. With the second edition of the New Testament out of his way (cf Ep 864 introduction), he had turned to the paraphrases, a far less controversial undertaking than the critical edition. The work progressed smoothly (cf Epp 916, 956 introductions) and did not require the same exigencies of research and close collaboration with the publisher. Despite his repeated praise of Oxford Erasmus' hopes were pinned primarily on the king and Wolsey, who alone could offer a position of complete independence in the form of a rich benefice (cf Ep 970:20–1 and the absence of any reference to the projected journey in Epp 973, 990). Erasmus' present initiative, however, met with little response (cf Ep 1025), and he was never again to cross the English Channel.

TO HIS MOST SERENE MAJESTY HENRY VIII, KING OF ENGLAND, FROM ERASMUS OF ROTTERDAM, GREETING
This lower world of ours, your Majesty, depends upon the heavenly bodies, upon those especially which hold first place among the stars; and in the same way the state of a commonwealth and people depends upon its princes, and 5 specially upon supreme rulers of wide dominions, whose temperament and policy and character and feelings, and whose alliances and disagreements,

* * * * *

33 Grimma] Town and residence, fifteen miles south-east of Leipzig

affect the multitude from time to time, just as the sea ebbs and flows as its changing tides follow the course of the moon or the earth obeys the movements of the sun, now all spring flowers, now parched with heat, now loaded with fruit, now hard with frost. And further, as the people's will and passions depend upon the king's lightest wish, even so (as the Hebrew sage's proverb puts it) 'The king's heart is in the hand of the Lord'; who, as often as he is angered by the crimes of mortal men, sometimes (in the words of Isaiah) gives them 'children to be their princes' and (in the words of Job, that holy man) 'alloweth the hypocrite to hold the reins of the kingdom,' where by the word 'hypocrite' he means one who is a king in name but in fact is a tyrant and a robber. Again, when he thinks fit to show the nations that his spirit is appeased and looks kindly upon them, then he gives princes a heart worthy of their kingly station.

Now here is an argument from which I think it possible to infer that at length, after so many tempests of misfortune, the eternal Godhead is reconciled to us once more – that he breathes such a spirit into the outstanding monarchs of our generation that they set the highest value of all on the things which belong to peace and piety and make for the well-being of the commonwealth. Though your Majesty, it is true, always showed this spirit; but the storms of fate have stood in the way hitherto. And now, now that the time is ripe and lends its aid, you do not so much plan what is best as carry out what was planned long ago by your mind, so worthy of a king.

To this glorious object many are the eminent princes who devote their efforts – Leo the Roman pontiff, Francis the king of France, his Catholic Majesty King Charles, the most serene king of Scots; yet in my view it is your Majesty who deserves the principal share of the credit, for this reason if no other, that it was your leadership, your encouragement, your wisdom that set this business on foot and controls it now. For when the Roman pontiff, who in other ways has shown his great desire for peace, was negotiating with a number of kings to secure peace at least for five years, it was your Highness who bound so many princes, the most powerful in the whole world, by the strictest undertakings to keep the peace, we hope, for ever. There was

* * * * *

964

12 Hebrew ... proverb] Prov 21:1
15 Isaiah] Isa 3:4
15 Job] Job 34:30
32 Scots] The Latin text adds 'N': Erasmus could not recall the name of James V – an indication that since the death of Alexander Stewart (cf Ep 604:4n) he had lost touch with developments in Scotland.
39 for ever] After negotiations reaching back to July a treaty of perpetual peace was signed in London between French and English representatives on 2

a spirit truly royal, there was a lofty mind worthy above all of a Christian   40
monarch! No king is better furnished with all the sinews of war; and yet you
devote all your zeal and all your resources to the restoration of the peace of
the world, wisely perceiving that nothing is more pernicious than the
engagement of Christian peoples in mutual pillage and warfare, and that
nothing renders Christ's people so formidable to the enemies of our religion   45
as concord between princes and between their peoples.

    That this same mind is certainly not adopted by you to suit the time but
is deeply rooted in you by nature is clear enough from this if nothing else,
that in the war with France, which you undertook against your will but yet
at the bidding of Christian piety, you behaved with such humanity and   50
moderation that it was clear enough how much peace was nearer to your
heart, had you not been summoned, say rather compelled, to take up arms by
the peril of the whole world and of the Christian church. Not content with
this, when peace has been restored by your wisdom and your influence, you
make it your object to adorn her with her proper arts, that she may not seem   55
either barren and idle or the mistress of luxury and pernicious pleasures. The
robberies, from which no part of England was safe hitherto, you put down
with admirable severity, you break the spirit of evil-doers, you free your
dominions from idle vagabonds, you give good laws their proper force
again, abolish those that have lost their value, and add valuable new ones.   60
You promote the pursuit of higher studies, you restore religion and
discipline in all men and especially in the monks and clergy, knowing that
it is from them above all that a high standard of morals, or else corruption,

* * * * *

October 1518 (cf LB II 4351, 4469); among the latter were More, Tunstall, and
Mountjoy. Public proclamation of the peace treaty, in the name of the Empire
and Spain as well, took place at St Paul's Cathedral on 3 October, and later on
many lesser powers acceded to the treaty. During the ceremony at St Paul's
Wolsey celebrated high mass, and Pace made a speech. Another oration in
praise of peace had been delivered by Etienne Poncher a few days earlier.
Ostensibly concluded in compliance with the pope's appeal for a crusade (cf Ep
891:26n), the peace in fact brought little more than agreement on the final
remaining differences between England and France (settled in subsidiary
treaties signed on 4 October), but it was a triumph for Wolsey and a diplomatic
defeat for Leo x and his legate, Campeggi, as Erasmus fully understood (cf Ep
967:21–4); see also Pastor VII 239–43; J.J. Scarisbrick *Henry VIII* (London 1968)
71–4.

49 war with France] Erasmus did not believe that Henry's wars against France in
    1512–13 had been undertaken from pious motives, but at least his praise for the
    king's moderation was sincere. In Allen Ep 1211:576–616 he described candidly
    how with an expert display of pious concern Henry had managed to silence
    Colet's protests and perhaps his own conscience.

spreads through the common people. Clearly it is your policy in every way to do especial honour to men especially distinguished, either by high character 65 or learning more than common or (what is both most admirable and most rare) by both. These are the ornaments which, as you believe, add to your realm far more lustre than any trophies or triumphal arches.

Nor are you only the cause and stimulus of these good things: you are their great example. Not content with precept, you are yourself the pattern; 70 say rather, you do more yourself than you demand of others. It is a powerful and effective force, a king's authority when he issues orders; but it is wonderful to tell of, how much greater the effect when he displays obedience to his own orders and holds the standard of his own laws before his eyes all his life long. For you the laws hold no penalties, and yet what 75 private person is more obedient to law than you? Who more incorruptible, who more strictly observant of his obligations, who more constant in friendship, who more devoted to what is right and just? What family of citizens offers so clear an example of strict and harmonious wedlock? Where could one find a wife more keen to equal her admirable spouse? What private 80 home, what religious house indeed or university anywhere better supplied with men outstanding for their integrity of life and eminent learning than your court? The poets of Antiquity have handed down to us among their inventions something called a golden age. And yet, while your Majesty pursues these ideals, surely you are restoring to us an age truly of gold, if 85 such a thing there ever was; and this difficult enterprise succeeds so well under your leadership that upon it beyond all doubt there rests the favour of heaven. What country is there in the world that does not rejoice with England, if she is your friend, or envy you if she does not wish you well? What kingdom in the whole world today more noble or illustrious? 90

Because, of course, it is the spirit of the king that makes kingdoms noble or obscure. Think of the books, the languages in which posterity one day will tell the story, how under her eighth Henry, a prince (as it might seem) sent forth by heaven for this express purpose, England blossomed with excellence of every kind until she seemed born anew! How he raised her 95 standards of morality so high that even ancient Massilia might take her as a pattern of civic virtue; gave her so strong a sense of duty that she might offer Rome itself a lesson in devotion; filled her with learned men in every branch of knowledge until Italy might envy her, were not a common devotion to

* * * * *

80 wife] Catherine of Aragon; cf Ep 855:34n.
85 truly of gold] Cf Epp 966:43, 967:19, 43; Bietenholz *History and Biography* 31–5.
96 Massilia] The city reputed for its high standard of public morals; cf *Adagia* II iii 98.

learning proof against envy; above all, how she enjoyed in him such a prince   10
as might be the lodestar of the art of government for all future princes. As
heaven is my witness, now at last we know what kingship means, what it is
to be a king, to have a court worthy of a prince. Time was when from a sort of
passion for literature and the delights of learned ease I felt some repugnance
to the courts of kings. But now, when I contemplate what a prince and   10
governor rules the English court, its queen, its nobles, counsellors, officials,
I am eager in spirit to betake myself to a court like that. Nor should I be
ashamed of such an ambition, did not the ill health, which grows upon me
even out of proportion to my years, discourage it; not that I need fear in this
the ugly reputation of an amibitious man; for I am encouraged to such   11
thoughts even today by offers that do not deserve to be rejected, and from
monarchs more than one. I am not, I confess, a native Englishman, only a
grafted shoot; and yet when I turn over in my mind the years I have spent
there, the benefactors that I owe to England, the eminent and trusty friends,
the part of my resources (such as they are), I rejoice at the thought of her   11
felicity no less than I should were she my mother-country.

All this time I have said nothing of your excellent gifts of body and
mind, the things we owe to God and nature rather than to our own industry;
yet these blessings tend no less to the felicity of a commonwealth if they fall
to the lot of an upright prince. What is more, although for some centuries   12
now a good education has not brought kings much praise, yet it will be your
Majesty's doing when in time to come, just as in old days it was the special
glory of kings to excel in knowledge, so it will be again a most excellent thing
for a prince to be well read. Your excellence will refute the old complaint of
some people, who maintain that an interest in learning saps the vigorous   12
spirit of a king. Among princes with no learning was there ever one more
skilled than you in every office of kingship? More zealous in the repression
of crime, more skilled in counsel, of keener foresight, more effective in action?
And yet in the subjects which your Majesty once took up with such happy
results you have now made such progress, perhaps without much study but   13
with unheard-of natural gifts, that even the most learned theologians are
astonished at your sane and piercing judgment. Why, in the disputation

* * * * *

112 monarchs more than one] Cf Ep 809:146–53.
132 disputation] A theological essay by the king on this topic is also mentioned in
    Allen Ep 1313:72–4, and perhaps in Ep 937:3–4 (cf also Ep 917:16), but is
    otherwise unknown. The question was much debated by the scholastics.
    Erasmus himself favoured private and personal prayer as an expression of
    heartfelt conviction rather than the mechanical repetition of traditional
    formulae. He was taken to task for his stand by the Sorbonne theologians; cf LB
    V 1128A–C, IX 895–7.

which your Majesty lately conducted for your own pleasure with a very
acute and learned divine, supporting the view that no prayers should be
expected from the laity except such as are addressed to God in the thoughts   135
of the heart, what an expert, in heaven's name, you showed yourself! Whose
invention could have been more piercing, whose inferences more vigorous,
whose exposition more elegant? And to crown all your gifts and accomplishments, no one was more courteous in conflict than yourself, no one
showed less pride or superiority; and yet all the time with no abatement of   140
your royal dignity when it was called for.

In days of old, Horace wrote that Olympic victories raised the lords of
the earth to join the gods; of old, the glorious rulers of an empire were
formally added to the roll of deities. These are the achievements which earn
true immortality; thus men rise to the stars. The genius of the men of letters   145
whom you support and cherish in so many ways will not allow the memory of
your virtues to fade as time grows old. In gratitude for what you have done,
equally Greek and Latin scholarship will never tire of telling how the
English once had an eighth Henry who in his sole person made the gifts and
glories of so many heroes live again for their benefit: a Ptolemy Philadelphus   150
for zealous support of good literature, an Alexander the Great for success,
a Philip for courtesy, a Caesar for invincible energy of spirit – wise as
Augustus, mild as Trajan, upright as Alexander Severus, learned as Antoninus
Pius, religious as Theodosius, an embodiment of all that is great in the
individual princes of Antiquity. We pray that God, the giver of all these   155
gifts, may will that they bring prosperity and happiness to you and yours,
and that he who set these impulses in you may advance them with his favour
and bring the same to good effect.

I knew that it might be tedious for me to interrupt your Majesty, so busy
as you already are, with such vain words as these. But the strong desire to   160
utter my felicitations was too much for me, for I had learnt from many sources
of the greatest worth what an age thanks to your virtue was to dawn upon us
all; and at the same time it seemed right to go on record that I have not
forgotten your favour towards me, which you have already shown in deeds
and not in words alone. Many are the distinguished men whose gifts are   165
illuminated and fostered by your noble self, and whose writings in return
shed lustre on their service with you. Suffer your Majesty's humble servant

* * * * *

142 Horace] *Odes* 1.1.3–6
145 rise to the stars] Virgil *Aeneid* 9.641
150 Ptolemy] Cf Ep 919:6n.
153 Trajan ... Theodosius] Roman emperors of the first to fourth centuries

Erasmus, for what he is worth, to be enrolled among their number. And may Christ the Almighty ever preserve you in health and prosperity.

Antwerp, 15 May 1519   170

965 / To William Blount, Lord Mountjoy   Antwerp, [15?] May 1519

Cf Ep 964 introduction. The date of this letter given in the *Farrago*, 'Calends of May,' was perhaps already questioned by the editors of the *Opus epistolarum* of 1529, who simply dropped it. It seems to conflict with that of Ep 961. One solution is to substitute 'Ides' for 'Calends,' since the letter could very well have been dated the same day as Epp 964, 966, although the more optimistic mood of Epp 967:59–61, 968:20–3 still appears to be absent from lines 30–3; cf Ep 930:12n.

TO THE RIGHT HONOURABLE WILLIAM, BARON MOUNTJOY FROM ERASMUS OF ROTTERDAM, GREETING
Best of patrons, up to now I have rejoiced in the good fortune of your native England, as the home of so many men of outstanding character and accomplishments to match; but now I am in a fair way to be jealous, when I   5
see her blossoming in liberal studies of every kind until she takes the lead over all other countries and puts them almost in the shade. Not but what this is no new feather in your island's cap, for it is well known you had great men in times past. Your universities, for instance, are a proof of this, rivals as they are in antiquity and distinction of the oldest and most famous that exist. I   10
have a great devotion to my lord the bishop of Winchester, who has founded a magnificent college at his own expense expressly for the humanities. Even more do I love the noble and heroic spirit of the most reverend the cardinal of York, whose wise provision will win fame for the schools of Oxford in the learned tongues and every other field of knowledge, and also for those gifts   15
of character which belong with liberal studies. As for Cambridge University, it has for some time now been adorned with every excellence under the rule

* * * * *

965
12 college] Corpus Christi College was founded by Richard Foxe, bishop of Winchester, at the time of his retirement from politics, 1516–17. It was the first in Oxford devoted to the new learning, and its foundation parallels that of Busleyden's Collegium Trilingue in Louvain; cf Epp 691 introduction, 990:7n, and T. Fowler *The History of Corpus Christi College* (Oxford 1893).
14 provision] Of public readerships; cf Ep 967:40n.

of the bishop of Rochester, a man fit from every point of view to play the part
of a distinguished prelate.

Even so, a large part of the credit for this belongs to your highly   20
intelligent king, who is the source of all these plans. You enjoy unbroken
and, we may reasonably hope, unending peace with all those monarchies
and princes; offenders are banished, wise laws enjoy full force, sound
learning is encouraged. Of all this the king himself is not only the originator
and promoter but the great example, being the first to practise what he has   25
ordained. There is no man living whose prosperity I desire more than yours;
and yet I am almost jealous of your Lordship when I see you enjoy such
blessings without me, your former partner in both weal and woe. And what
makes it worse is that, during this time that you are blessed on so many
counts, I have to do battle with certain frightful monsters rather than men,   30
against whom I assure you I would gladly try what eloquence could effect,
were I not restrained by Christian misgivings, or shall we say by some Pallas
out of Homer, who plucks me by the hair as I lay my hand on my sword-hilt.
Farewell.

Antwerp, [1] May 1519   35

966 / To Henry Guildford   Antwerp, 15 May 1519

> Cf Ep 964 introduction. The beginning of this letter suggests that Erasmus did
> not know the addressee personally, but he evidently knew that Sir Henry
> Guildford (1489–1532) had the king's ear. A congenial companion in sport and
> pastime, he was Henry's standard-bearer in the campaign of 1513 and
> continued to be a trusted and well-rewarded member of the royal household.
> When this letter was first published in the *Farrago* his name was given as
> Richard in the salutation and in line 48, but the slip was corrected in
> subsequent editions. Richard (d 1506) was Henry's father; see *Dictionary of
> National Biography* (Oxford and London 1885–   ).

TO SIR HENRY GUILDFORD, KNIGHT, MASTER OF THE HORSE TO
THE KING OF ENGLAND, FROM ERASMUS, GREETING
I know from talking with many people of your Excellency's kindly feelings
towards me, whether the first spark of this good will was kindled in you by

* * * * *

18 Rochester] John Fisher had become chancellor of Cambridge University in
  1504, the year of his appointment to the see of Rochester. For the beginnings of
  humanism in Cambridge cf McConica 78–80.
22 unending peace] Cf Ep 964:39n.
33 Homer] *Iliad* 1.194–7

something I had written or whether you derived it from conversation with Dr   5
John Colet and my other friends. You think well of me because you suppose
that I really am such a man as they have made me out to be. I in return am
devoted to you, because with your whole heart you esteem excellence – yes,
and humane studies, inasmuch as for their sake you esteem me too; not that I
possess any gifts of the kind, but because you believe that I am thus gifted.   10
At least I have always tried to promote sound learning, especially of the sort
that makes for true religion. Would that the effort had been matched by the
success! The world regains its senses, as a man wakes from the depths of
sleep; and even so some people obstinately still resist, defending their
ancient ignorance hand and foot, tooth and nail, they will be ashamed of   15
their folly when they see great kings and their officers of state offering
welcome and support and protection to studies of a better sort.

How astonishing are the revolutions in human affairs! In the old days,
zeal for literature was to be found among the religious orders; and now they
are devoted for the most part to good living and luxury and lucre, and the   20
love of learning is moving over to live with the princes of this world and the
great men of their courts. What university or monastery anywhere contains
so many men of outstanding integrity and learning as your court can show?
We should indeed be quite right to be ashamed of ourselves. The
dinner-tables of clergymen and divines are sodden with drink, they are   25
infected with scurrilous jests and loud with intemperate uproar or full of
poisonous backbiting; and it is at the tables of princes that one finds
moderate discussion of things that contribute to learning and piety.
Everyone, of course, is quick to follow the example of your admirable king.
To say nothing of his other gifts (which he shares with other monarchs, but   30
in such a way that he excels in most of them, and is not outdone in any),
where could one find greater keenness in argument, originality of thought,
sanity of judgment, elegance of expression?

Time was when I was captivated by the charms of leisure and good
letters and shunned the courts of kings; but to a court like yours I would   35
gladly transfer myself with all my belongings (which are nearly all papers), if
weak health and years which begin to tell on me did not dissuade me. What
has become of the people who are always telling us that if a prince has any
education, his energy must suffer? Look at Henry the Eighth. Who more
skilful in war, more intelligent in legislation, more far-seeing in counsel, in   40
the repression of crime more active, in the choice of magistrates and officers

* * * * *

966
15 hand and foot] Cf *Adagia* I iv 15 and 22.
28 discussion] Cf Epp 917:14–18, 964:132n.

more painstaking, more successful in concluding alliances with other kings? For my part, I perceive the dawn of a new golden age, which maybe I shall not live to enjoy, for the part I play on the world's stage has reached its climax; but I count the world fortunate, and fortunate the younger genera- 45 tion, in whose memories the name of Erasmus will somehow live, in return for what he has done for them.

But to conclude, my dear Sir Henry, I return your cordial feelings, and for your more than common kindness to me I am all the more grateful, because you showed it without waiting to be solicited by some service on my 50 own part. My warmest good wishes to the noble lady, your mother, whose acquaintance I owe to several conversations. May the Lord Jesus preserve this present mind in you, and preserve you for the common good. And I hope your Excellency will proceed to place the name of Erasmus on the list of your dependants, for you will certainly have none more zealous than myself. 55

Antwerp, 15 May 1519
Yours with all sincerity, Erasmus of Rotterdam

967 / To Thomas Wolsey   Antwerp, 18 May [1519]

Cf Ep 964 introduction. This letter shows many parallels with Ep 961, addressed to Campeggi, the other papal legate in England. Campeggi actually was a Legatus missus, or special envoy, whereas Wolsey was the Legatus natus, or perpetual legate (cf the salutation). This letter was published in the *Farrago*.

TO THE MOST REVEREND THOMAS ARCHBISHOP OF YORK, CARDINAL PRIEST OF ST CECILIA, PRIMATE OF ENGLAND, LEGATUS NATUS, AND THE MOST WORTHY CHANCELLOR OF THE WHOLE REALM, FROM ERASMUS OF ROTTERDAM
Respectful greetings, my most reverend Lord, who are not least among the 5 glories of the most eminent college of cardinals. If I have hitherto not paid a further visit to the distinguished benefactors whom England holds for me in such plenty, part of the reason is the burden of my labours, which almost overwhelm me when one task is piled on another, 'as wave succeeds to

* * * * *

42 alliances] Cf Ep 964:39n, and lines 83–5 for the 'golden age.'
47 what he has done] For Erasmus' school–books cf Ep 932:24n; for their popularity cf F. Vander Haeghen ed *Bibliotheca Erasmiana: Répertoire des œuvres d'Erasme* I: *Liste sommaire* (Ghent 1893, reprint 1961) and McConica 31–2 and passim.
51 mother] Joan (d 1538), sister of Sir Nicholas Vaux. After the death of her first husband, Sir Richard Guildford, she continued to attend the court.

wave,' if I may borrow Ovid's words; but principally it is the state of my   10
health, which from much serious and prolonged illness is still so feeble that I
dare not entrust myself to a trying sea-voyage. If furthermore I have not paid
my respects in a letter to your Eminence, this is partly because I was ashamed
that my worthless remarks should interrupt one so fully occupied with
important business of both realm and church, and partly that I was deterred   15
by your exalted station, whom the greatest in the land do not address
without misgiving. Since, however, those who visit us from your country
report with one accord how energetic and how successful your wisdom and
your piety have been in turning the bronze age of England into gold, I could
not refrain from sending my felicitations to you on your policy, and to my   20
beloved England on possessing you. For, as all the world avers, it is you who
have cemented with such close-knit treaties that peace which all the greatest
monarchs had long desired, while Pope Leo, who is in any case such a lover
of peace, was thinking only of a five-year truce.

The whole of England is purged, thanks to you, of robbers, brigands,   25
and idle vagabonds, so that there is no more danger from ruffians than from
poison or dangerous wild beasts. The tangles of the law you cut asunder as
successfully as ever great Alexander did the Gordian knot. Disputes among
the nobility are settled, monasteries everywhere restored to their old
religious discipline, the whole clergy recalled to a more praiseworthy form   30
of life – and all by you. The study of the humanities, hitherto somewhat
fallen, is rebuilt; the liberal arts, still struggling with the champions of
ancient ignorance, are supported by your encouragement, protected by your
power, gilded in your reflected glory, and nourished by your munificence,
as you offer princely salaries to attract outstanding scholars to come and   35
teach. In the getting-together of libraries richly furnished with good authors

* * * * *

967

10 Ovid's words] Horace *Epistles* 2.2.176, not Ovid; but Ovid *Metamorphoses*
   15.181 is close to it.
22 peace] Cf Ep 964:39n, and lines 83–5 for the 'golden age.'
25 purged] For Wolsey's vigorous administration of justice see J.D. Mackie *The
   Early Tudors* (Oxford 1952) 295–7; G.R. Elton *England under the Tudors* (London
   1962) 81–2.
28 Gordian knot] Cf *Adagia* i ix 48.
29 monasteries] In August 1518 Wolsey received papal authority to hold visitations of exempt monasteries (cf LP ii 780, 968, 4399, iii 693). In March 1519 he
   issued a set of reformatory constitutions for the non-exempt Austin friars. Up
   to 1529 he used his various powers to suppress some twenty-nine houses and
   attempted to improve others, perhaps combining personal gain with genuine
   reform and the promotion of scholarship; cf D. Knowles *The Religious Orders in
   England* (Cambridge 1948–59) iii 157–64.

of every kind, you rival Ptolemy Philadelphus himself, who owes his fame to
this even more than to his crown. The three ancient tongues, without which
all learning is handicapped, are revived among us by you; for I regard the
generous benefaction now offered to the famous university of Oxford as a   40
blessing to the whole of Britain. Indeed I am confident of this also, that the
splendid example you have set will one day rouse the ambition of our princes
likewise. I see, I see a kind of golden age arising, if once that spirit of yours
enters a certain number of princes. The due reward for these your pious
undertakings will be laid up for you by him under whose blessing we see   45
them go forward, but posterity will not be ungrateful: the new and blessed
state of things which you inaugurate for the world will be the theme of gifted
writers in the future. Your mind, designed by Nature to be a blessing to our
mortal state, will be recorded in everlasting works by the most gifted pens in
both Latin and Greek. Such are the columns and the pyramids which build   50
up and enshrine the undying memory of a noble name.

For myself meanwhile, rejoicing as I do in this general felicity, I am
delighted to find my own name eclipsed by the brilliance of younger men,
while talents now come into flower compared with which I am ignorant and
tongue-tied. Enough for me is the credit, if I may be thought to deserve it, of   55
being rated one of those who attempted to drive far from this quarter of the
world the inspissated barbarism and shameful lack of style for which we
used hitherto to be criticized by Italy. What success has been mine, I do not
know; I know the attempt has not been wholly popular, for unpopularity
must accompany great enterprises, as shadows keep company with light –   60
though the majority grow more well disposed. A few rebellious spirits still
resist, too grand to expect, too stupid to encompass, too arrogant to desire
the knowledge of better things. Such men cannot be induced to believe that
their authority need not utterly collapse if we read the Scriptures in a
corrected text and seek our understanding of them from the fountain-head.   65
Such is the value they set on their own high position that they would rather
see widespread ignorance, widespread error in the reading and citation of

* * * * *

37 Ptolemy] Cf Epp 919:6n, 964:150.
40 benefaction] In the spring of 1518 Wolsey had announced his intention to
found several public readerships at Oxford. Among the early appointees were
Erasmus' humanist friends Clement, Lupset, (cf Ep 270:69n), and Vives. The
first readers were lodged at the new Corpus Christi College (cf Ep 965:12n);
hence Erasmus on a later occasion mistakenly referred to Wolsey as the founder
of Corpus Christi (cf LB IX 781F). Actually in 1524–5 Wolsey created Cardinal
College to house his foundation; cf C.E. Mallett *History of the University of
Oxford* (London 1924–7) II 20–6.
61 more well disposed] Cf Ep 968:21n.

Holy Writ than have it thought that there is anything they did not know. So feeling themselves to have the worst of the argument and, if they compete in print, to achieve nothing except to advertise their own mixture of ignorance and folly and make themselves a laughing-stock to the learned, they lose confidence in open fight and take refuge in trickery, loading with slanders the humanities and their champions, above all myself, whom they suppose to have made a not wholly valueless contribution to the revival of these studies.

Any publication that is likely to cause trouble is laid at my door. You could fairly say that here even calumny has its ingenious side. They confound the cause of the humanities with the business of Reuchlin and Luther, though there is no connection between them. Personally I have never felt the attraction of Cabbala or Talmud. I have met Reuchlin once only, in Frankfurt, and there is nothing between us except friendship and courtesy such as exists between almost all scholars; nor for that matter would it embarrass me to be linked with him in some relationship. He has a letter from me, in which before we had ever met I told him to refrain from the open abuse with which in his *Defence* he lets fly at his opponents as Germans often do; so far am I from having ever approved of defamatory publications. I know as little of Luther as I do of anyone, nor have I yet found the time to leaf through his books except for a page here and there; not that I despise him, but the pressure of my own work has not yet allowed me the leisure. And yet some people, they tell me, have a trumped-up story that he has had help from me. If what he has written is right, none of the credit is mine; if not, I deserve no blame, for in all his work not a jot anywhere belongs to me. That this is perfectly true will be clear to anyone who is willing to look into it. The man's way of life is universally well spoken of; and this is already no small argument in his favour, if his character is so upright that even his enemies cannot invent a scandal to his discredit.

But even had I all the time in the world to read him, I do not rate myself so highly as to be willing to pronounce on the writings of a man of his stature, although mere boys nowadays often pronounce in the most irresponsible manner that one statement is erroneous and another heretical. In fact, I was at one time somewhat unfair to Luther, for fear that some of his

* * * * *

78 Reuchlin] Cf Epp 622, 694 introductions, 821:19n.
79 Luther] Cf Epp 933, 938:5n, 939 introduction.
80 Cabbala or Talmud] Cf Ep 798:21–3.
81 Frankfurt] In March or April 1515; cf Ep 332 introduction; Hutten *Opera* I Ep 26.
83 letter] Cf Ep 300:20–7.
90 help from me] Cf Ep 761:37n.
101 somewhat unfair] Cf Ep 904:20n.

unpopularity might rub off on the humanities, which already had, I thought, enough to carry; for I had not failed to notice what an unpopular thing it is to undermine whatever provides priests or monks with a rich harvest. There had appeared, to begin with, a number of propositions on the papal   105 remission of sins; then came two or three pamphlets on confession and on penance. When I sensed that some men I could name were anxious to publish these, I seriously dissuaded them from imposing this burden of unpopularity on the humanities. Luther's own supporters will bear witness to the truth of this. At length there appeared a swarm of pamphlets. No one   110 saw me reading them, no one heard me express approval or disapproval. I am not rash enough to approve what I have not read, nor malicious enough to condemn what I do not know; though nowadays this is a habit even in those to whom it is least becoming.

Germany possesses several young men who hold out great promise in   115 the way of both scholarship and style, and with their help I foresee that Germany can some day be as proud as England rightly is proud now. None of them are personally known to me except Eobanus, Hutten, and Beatus. These men employ every species of artillery in their battle with the enemies of the ancient languages and of those liberal studies which every man of   120 liberal outlook supports. The liberty they allow themselves I would myself agree to be insupportable, did I not know the outrageous provocation they have suffered in public and private alike. Their opponents seize the opportunity of sermons, lectures, and conversation at the dinner-table for ranting away to their hearts' content, no matter how full it all is of prejudice   125 and even of sedition, before the ignorant public; and then they call it an

* * * * *

105 propositions] The Ninety–five Theses; cf Ep 785:39n.
106 on confession] *Ein Sermon von Ablass und Gnade*, frequently published between 1518 and 1520 (cf Benzing *Lutherbibliographie* nos 90–114). A Latin translation was printed in Froben's collection; cf Ep 904:20n.
106 on penance] *Sermo de poenitentia*; for editions 1518–19 cf Benzing *Lutherbibliographie* nos 127–34.
107 some men I could name] Perhaps in Basel, where several books by Luther were published in 1518 and where Capito, together with Oecolampadius, Beatus Rhenanus, and Conradus Pellicanus (cf Allen Ep 1637 introduction), had encouraged Froben to launch his collection (cf Allen Ep 1526:34–7; Volz *Die ersten Sammelausgaben* 186, 192; but cf Ep 904:20n). The vagueness of the statement here may be deliberate. Martens in Louvain too, who had recently printed the *Julius exclusus*, never participated in the lucrative boom of Luther publications.
118 Beatus] Beatus Rhenanus. The following statements seem to refer to the younger German humanists in general, since Beatus Rhenanus could hardly be considered a typical example of unbridled language; but cf BRE Epp 75, 81.

outrage if one of these young men dares open his mouth, though even the
poor bee has a sting to strike back with when she is attacked and mice have
their tiny teeth for defence against assault. Whence comes this new race of
divine beings? They make heretics of anyone they please and then confound   1͘
heaven and earth if someone calls them mischief-makers; they are not afraid
to form crazy ideas which would be too much for Orestes himself; and yet
they demand that we should never utter their names without some honorific
prefix – so complete is their reliance on the folly of the multitude, not to say,
of princes.   1͘

For myself, though scholarship has never been within my grasp, it has
always been my first love. Its defenders have my support, and they are
supported by men in high place everywhere, except a few ass-eared Midases
whom someone some day will put in the pillory. And yet my support has this
limitation: it is their good qualities I love and not any faults that may be there   1͘
as well. If anyone considers the faults in which those men were steeped who
long ago in Italy and France brought aid and comfort to the rebirth of ancient
studies, he cannot fail to support these men of ours, whose characters are
such as to deserve imitation rather than rebuke from the theologians who
criticize them. Whatever is put out by these men is suspected of being mine;   14
and the same in your country too, if the merchants who visit us from your
parts speak the truth. I will make a candid confession: a gifted nature I
cannot help but love, an unbridled pen no matter whose I cannot approve of.

Long ago Hutten wrote a trifling thing which he called *Nobody*. Nobody
can fail to see that the subject is humorous; it was said to be mine by the   1͘
theologians of Louvain, who think they have sharper eyes than any
Lynceus. Next came his *Febris*; this too was mine, though the whole spirit
and the whole style are unlike mine. A speech appeared by Petrus
Mosellanus in support of the three tongues against our anti-linguists. They
thought this a stick to beat me with, though I was still unaware the thing   1͘
existed; as though, let anyone take it into his head to write no matter what, I

* * * * *

128 poor bee] Cf *Adagia* II v 31.
131 heaven and earth] Cf *Adagia* I iii 81.
132 Orestes] Struck with madness after killing his mother, Clytaemnestra, he
    presents the standard type of madness in the Greek tragic theatre.
138 Midases] Midas, king of Phrygia, was punished for his arrogance by being
    given the long ears of a donkey; cf *Adagia* I iii 67.
149 *Nobody*] Cf Ep 961:32n.
152 Lynceus] Cf *Adagia* II i 54.
152 *Febris*] Cf Ep 923:23n.
154 Mosellanus] Cf Ep 934 introduction.
155 a stick to beat] Literally 'these beans would be threshed'; *Adagia* I i 84.

must be ready with an answer on behalf of them all, or as though I had not
enough to do to defend at my own risk what I write myself. They are
Germans, they are young, they have pen in hand, they are not short of
brains; nor is there any shortage of men to provoke them by their hostility   160
and spur them on and brace them to the task. They have all had letters from
me telling them to restrain their licence, or at least to keep off the highest
figures in the church; not to arouse animosity against liberal studies in those
whose support enables our studies to withstand their enemies and to lay this
burden of unpopularity on the champions of the humanities. What am I to   165
do? Warn them I can, compel them I cannot. My own pen I am in a position to
control; to be responsible for what other people write is not my business. In
fact – and this is the most foolish thing of all – the book lately written by the
bishop of Rochester against Lefèvre was suspected of being mine, although
the style is so entirely unlike mine and though I fall so far short of that gifted   170
prelate as a scholar. There were even men ready to give me More's *Utopia*, so
universal is the rule that any new publication, willy nilly, must be mine.

    There appeared a few months ago – and ill-starred its appearance
was – a humorous pamphlet, clearly written during the recent schism, as
the subject proved, but who the author was is not clear, except that the text   175
shows him to have been, whoever he was, on the French side. Suspicion
knocks at many doors, especially in Germany, where the work circulates in
manuscript under various titles. This I discovered several years ago was to
be had here on the side, and I sampled the thing – for I ran through it rather
than read it – and many people can bear witness to the abhorrence I   180
expressed and the active steps I took to ensure that it should be buried in
eternal obscurity. Many too will agree that I have done the same in respect of
other pamphlets as well. There is more evidence of this in a letter of mine to
Johannes Caesarius, which certain persons copied secretly and have
published at Cologne. I hear too that there are some people in your part of   185
the world who try to fasten on me the suspicion of having written this
pamphlet also; so determined are they to try everything, those men who are
sorry to see this revival in the ancient tongues and in liberal studies. In so
doing they rely on no argument except the style; which however is not much
like my style, unless I have very little idea of it. Not but what it would be no   190
great surprise if in that piece or elsewhere there were some resemblance to

* * * * *

168 book] Cf Ep 936:9n.
174 pamphlet] The *Julius exclusus* (cf Ep 961:40–55). Among the most recent editions
     was that of Martens (Louvain September 1518; NK 3283–4); cf *Opuscula* 55–8.
183 other pamphlets as well] Cf Epp 636:29n, 904:20n.
183 letter] Ep 622

my way of writing, for hardly anyone writes nowadays without rousing some echoes of my style, simply because my books are in the hands of nearly everyone, so that even in the work of those who attack me in print I not seldom recognize my own phrases and feel I am transfixed with an arrow I myself have feathered.

I have never yet written any work, and never shall, to which I do not set my name. I indulged my humour some time ago in the *Moria*, but without drawing blood, though maybe I let myself go rather too freely. But one point I have always watched, that nothing should issue from me which could corrupt the young by impropriety or offend in any way against religion or provoke civil strife and faction or leave a black mark on any man's reputation. All my efforts hitherto have been devoted to the promotion of honourable studies and to the advancement of the Christian religion. All men everywhere express their gratitude to me, except for a handful of theologians and monks who have no wish to be better scholars or better men than they are now. May Christ's displeasure ever be my lot if I do not wish whatever I may possess of ability or literary skill to be entirely dedicated to Christ's glory, to the catholic church, and to sacred study. That this is true will be clear to anyone who is prepared to identify my purpose at first hand.

But enough of all this – more than enough. Yet I would not have written it at all had not a certain English merchant visiting us from your part of the world assured me with some emphasis that people exist who have tried to infect your Eminence with suspicion on this point, than which nothing could be more baseless. But your exceptional wisdom makes me quite confident that you will not lend your ears or your mind to such impudent inventions. In fact, if you will ever deign to test me at close quarters, you will find in your Erasmus a whole-hearted servant of the Roman See, and especially of our Holy Father Leo the Tenth (for of my debt to his generosity I am well aware), and whole-heartedly devoted to those outstanding men who promote the interests of the humanities and of the Christian religion among whom your Eminence holds first place. I send you the New Testament and shall consider it greatly honoured if you think it worthy of a place in your library. Respectful good wishes to your Eminence, to whom I profess myself entirely devoted.

Antwerp, 18 May [1518]

* * * * *

196 feathered] The eagle in Aesop 4 was shot by an arrow fledged with eagle feathers.
198 I indulged] Cf Ep 622:23–4.
202 black mark] Cf Horace *Ars poetica* 446, 447.
223 New Testament] See Ep 864 introduction.

967A / To Justus Jonas   Antwerp, [c 20–6 May?] 1519

This letter, which is Ep 985 in Allen, was published in the *Farrago* with the date of 1 June (Calends). This is questionable for several reasons. Erasmus' presence at Antwerp (cf Ep 964 introduction) does not seem to have extended beyond c 26 May, and in view of Epp 975, 984 it is unlikely that he would have returned there again on 1 June. We also have Jonas' own comments on the composition of this letter (*Jonas Briefwechsel* Ep 36). In March 1520 he recalled that Erasmus had written a short letter for him during his visit (cf Ep 963:6n). This text, Jonas stated, was amplified in the *Farrago* as a sign of friendly tribute and reached more than twice the length of the original letter. The assumption that this letter was originally composed when Jonas and Schalbe visited Erasmus in Antwerp would also explain the insistence of Schalbe in Ep 977 that he desired a letter no less ardently than Jonas (who actually got one; cf Ep 981:14–15). The date 'Calends of June' as in Epp 965, 975 may be an approximation only added at the time of printing, or the type-setter may have omitted a numeral before the abbreviated words 'Calends of June,' which would have moved the date back to the second half of May.

The main theme of this letter, preaching in accordance with the philosophy of Christ, is reminiscent of the request Erasmus received in Ep 932.

ERASMUS OF ROTTERDAM TO JODOCUS JONAS OF ERFURT,
GREETING

A long and scholarly letter from such a learned and most open-hearted friend as you are, my dear Jonas, must not go unrequited: let me submit to your better judgment the following thoughts. Although Almighty God had it in   5
his power to endow each individual man with every gift, yet to encourage concord between man and man, by which he set particular store, he thought it more appropriate to distribute his gifts, one to this man and another to that, in such a way that men were obliged to help one another; with the further intention that none should trust unduly in himself alone, knowing   10
that whatever faculties he possessed came entirely from divine goodness, nor should one man despise another as he bore in mind that God had wished men to receive a large part of his bounty from the unselfish action of their fellows. In this way too no man would claim as his own doing a benefit that he had conferred upon another or expect the man he had helped to feel   15
obligation, because he would know well that he was the servant and tool of

* * * * *

967A
1 Erfurt] Jonas was not a native of Erfurt. In his Ep 36 (cf the introduction) he
  noted the slip and expected that it would be corrected in a second edition.

another's bounty and not the originator, while the man who was conscious of a benefit received would feel gratitude to his fellow-man but express his thanks to God as the author and source of all good things, not only for the receipt of the benefit from him through another man but directly for the   20
benefit itself, because both the will and the power to do good to his neighbour had come to that man from the divine bounty.

It ought therefore to be the common purpose of us all to help one another in turn whenever we can, and not refuse help one from another when we are in need. Since however God's gifts are of many kinds and   25
differently distributed as though to divers members of the same body, each man should devote himself especially to the place where he feels he can be of especial use. For it is not sufficient if as a member of the body you are not wholly idle; you must do what you can for the body where you can do it best, especially because such faculties as each man may possess were given him by   30
God on purpose that he might contribute them to the common good. It is not enough to consider how many talents you have, you must consider the value and use of each talent separately. Thus it will come to pass that the lord who, rich as he is, is very eager for profits of this kind may rejoice to see his house grow more and more rich from the business activities of his faithful servants.   35
On this point I find some people lacking in wisdom or good fortune, who before they are really acquainted with themselves plunge into some way of life in which they can be of no use either to themselves or to others.

This train of thought, dearest Jonas, immediately entered my head as I conjured up an image of your mind from what you write and the manner of   40
man you are, and then from your expression and your person. Although I suppose you know something of yourself, yet I thought I should tell you this: God did not design you for the base activity of the law-courts, but he seems rather to have made you as a chosen instrument for the greater glory of Jesus his son and to kindle the souls of mortal men with zeal for him. You   45
must therefore devote all your powers to this most life-giving activity, and that too in good time, while your frame can endure hard work and your mind retains its vigour. Your efforts will be brought to good effect, believe me, by him who equipped you with so many excellent gifts for this very purpose. He who gave you a heart fervent with the love of true religion and a practised   50
tongue, to scatter, to root out, and to plant, will not fail you as you attempt

* * * * *

35 faithful servants] Cf Matt 25:14–30, Luke 19:12–27.
43 base ... law-courts] A recent licentiate in law (August 1518), Jonas began to study theology after his current journey to the Netherlands. In 1520 he lectured on Corinthians.
51 to scatter ... plant] Jer 1:10

these tasks, especially if you keep no end in view except that Christ may
gain. It may be splendid to move your hand in blessing over a multitude on
its knees, it may be a great thing to administer the sacraments of the church;
unquestionably the noblest office, the most truly worthy of apostle or of   55
bishop, is to offer the doctrine of salvation to the people and make their
thoughts and their life worthy of Christ.

Yet in that office, which is at once the fairest and the most difficult of all,
who are the men whom we see active everywhere today? Most of them lack
higher education, some of them have no heart, without which all Christian   60
eloquence must be lifeless, many of them no gifts of nature – they have no
tongue, the instrument of speech; their lungs and their physique in other
ways cannot support such efforts. Never mind: we must follow Paul and
make the best of what they are trying to do, provided Christ be proclaimed, if
proclaimed he really is! A good many preach not Christ but man, themselves   65
in fact. But to deplore this now is not my point. Some treat of Scotist
subtleties before the ignorant multitude, choosing for the purpose the most
complicated themes that they may be thought marvellous by their hearers, if
they do not understand a word. What could be more tedious? Or (what
matters more) more unfruitful? Other men bring nothing to their sermons but   70
the dogmas of the schools, some of which are the kind of thing that it does
not matter not to know and some, when treated outside the lecture-room, are
merely tedious. There are even people who, in the attempt to satisfy their
hearers' curiosity, collect from all sources (as though they were epic lays) a
kind of patchwork of civil law, canon law, and doctors in variety, for fear   75
there should seem to be any book they have not read. All human ambition
must be laid aside by the man who aspires to instil true religion into the
hearts of mortal men.

You are too sensible to need to be told by me that it does more to implant
in men's minds the philosophy of Christ if one presents the admirable and   80
lovely image of true religion in as lively colours as one can, rather than strain
voice and lungs in a denunciation of the forms and kinds of vice. The face of
virtue has a power of its own, and when she is displayed before uncorrupted
eyes, they are rapt straightway with love of her. It is an endless task to run
through all the ways in which men go astray from what is right. It is better to   85
exhibit the pattern and let each man silently examine himself against that;
except that there may be a fault of this special kind, that a man be deceived by
the appearance of piety that is not really there. It will also be appropriate to

* * * * *

62 instrument] Erasmus uses *plectrum,* with which the lyre was plucked; perhaps a
   reminiscence of Cicero *De natura deorum* 2.149.
63 Paul] Cf Phil 1:15–17.

mention faults by name in suitable contexts, so that no one may fall into error through ignorance. As things are now, you may see some preachers holding forth on the basis of men's secret confessions, describing monstrous vices in such detail as to teach how to commit them, and criticizing them in such a way that you would think they envied the sinner or enjoyed the sin. What does it profit, if a man catalogues all the ways in which one can sin from lust, or declaims that there are adulterers everywhere? It will prove more to the point to set before the mind's eye the honourable old ideal of purity, the mere sight of which made Augustine instantly reject with loathing all kinds of dishonourable lust. It is the same with the others: whoever has once conceived a passion for the lovely image of Christian piety begins at that moment to hate all that he sees to be incompatible with it.

Nor have I any use for those men who, in order to acquire a reputation for holiness among common people, rant like demagogues against the faults of bishops or princes; this kind of clamour only makes them still worse, while they are often put right by a rebuke tendered at the right moment and in tactful and courteous fashion. Religion has its right of free speech, but this should always be tempered with the honey of charity. So far as one can, one should go easily with those who exercise supreme authority in the state. If the facts call for severity, one should be severe not so much against the great ones themselves as against those who misuse the authority of pope, bishops, or princes to satisfy their own desires. Nor should one be severe at random against whole orders of men; it is better to protest against those who by their faults bring otherwise admirable orders into disrepute. It will be found more profitable to demonstrate how far from true religion are those who profess the rule of Benedict or Francis or Augustine and yet live for their bellies, for gluttony, lust, ambition, or avarice, than to attack the regular religious life itself. It would be more unprofitable to condemn the universities than to indicate what should properly be pruned away from them or might usefully be added. Human nature is like that – more easily drawn by courtesy than dragged by harsh treatment.

It will add not a little force to what you say if your teaching is drawn principally from Holy Writ, if your life answers to your teaching, if your work as a teacher is spoilt by no taint of ambition or desire for gain. Force and brilliance will be added if you are truly in love with what you teach, if you proceed to your pulpit not from profane conversation or the convivial glass but from concentrated prayer, that you may come forward to kindle the hearts of others with fire in your own heart.

* * * * *

97 Augustine] Cf *Confessions* 8.11, 26–7.

But how long-winded I am become – and to you, from whom I ought rather to have been anxious to learn. Farewell, my dear Jonas.

Antwerp, [1 June] 1519

968 / To Albert of Brandenburg   Antwerp, 20 May 1519

Published together in the *Farrago*, Epp 968–70 show many parallels. All three are letters of introduction for Richard Pace, who was on his way to Frankfurt, where the electors were assembling to choose the new emperor. Pace's mission was to promote the election of Henry VIII or at any rate to prevent that of Francis I. On 14 May he arrived in Calais and on 17 May he was in Bruges. It appears likely that he met Erasmus at Antwerp on 20 May (cf Epp 968–9) and they travelled together to Brussels (cf Epp 970–1), where Pace had an interview with Margaret of Austria on 21 May (cf Ep 976:40). Pace was still waiting for his credentials to follow from England, hence in part his desire to have Erasmus' introductions. While Erasmus returned to Antwerp, Pace continued his journey to Louvain, Cologne, and Frankfurt. As the day of the election approached foreign ambassadors were expected to leave Frankfurt. Pace left on 10 June for Mainz, where he remained until Charles was declared emperor on 28 June; see LP III 218–39 passim and J. Wegg *Richard Pace* (London 1932) 142–53.

Albert's answer to this letter is Ep 988.

TO THE MOST REVEREND ALBERT, CARDINAL ARCHBISHOP OF
MAINZ, ETC, FROM ERASMUS, GREETING
Most reverend Prelate and most illustrious Prince, I have no doubt that the small book which I dedicated to your Eminence has reached you. Whether it gives you satisfaction I do not know; it gives none to me, but at that moment   5
it was all I had ready. I shall look about for something else which may be more adequate both to your greatness and to my devotion to you.

Dr Richard Pace, who is on his way to you as the envoy of the king his master, has apart from countless other gifts a remarkable knowledge of both Greek and Latin; he stands very high with his majesty on many counts, has   10

* * * * *

968
4 small book] The *Ratio verae theologiae* (cf Ep 745). From Albert's answer (Ep 988:29–32) it appears that in the letter to Hutten which accompanied the book for Albert (cf Epp 951:8–10, 986 introduction) Erasmus had expressed concern about the two different dedications (cf Ep 976:18n), which he may only just have become aware of; he decided at once to send Albert a copy of Martens' edition. The promise of more to come was fulfilled only by a new preface for another edition of the *Ratio*; see Ep 1365.

great strength of character and a spotless reputation, and is a man made expressly for friendship and popularity. If you give him the honour of your closer acquaintance, I know that you will be very glad to have received this hint from me. In England good literature is triumphant. The king himself, the queen, both cardinals, the bishops almost to a man are whole-hearted   15 in their sympathy and good will and give the cause both resources and prestige. The quarrelsome critics have all been silenced by the king. I hope the same thing will happen in Germany, if your Eminence and others like you lend your favour and encouragement; and this I most earnestly beg you to do. There are some malicious individuals who stick at nothing, especially   20 in this place, where Barbarism when she quitted the earth seems to have left 'her latest footprints.' Though even here such men are growing milder and begin to see what fools they are.

Hutten's gifts are daily more widely recognized, and by your generous kindness to him your Highness is winning much praise, and indeed   25 gratitude, from the learned world. Long may Christ Jesus, who conquered death, preserve you in health and wealth.

Antwerp, 20 May 1519

969 / To Antoon, son of Jan van Bergen   Antwerp, 20 May 1519

This letter was published in the *Farrago*; for the circumstances of its composition see Ep 968 introduction. Antoon was still studying in Louvain with Baerland (cf Ep 760) and may already have planned to go to England (cf Ep 1025 introduction); if so, Pace was likely to receive hospitality and additional recommendations; cf Ep 953:27n.

TO THE ILLUSTRIOUS YOUNG MAN ANTOON VAN BERGEN FROM ERASMUS OF ROTTERDAM, GREETING
Hitherto, my distinguished young friend, I had at any rate one reason for admiring you, that you took delight in honourable studies and honourable conduct beyond the ordinary custom of the nobility. And now I have   5 another, in that I have experienced great kindness from your father. All his

* * * * *

15 both cardinals] Wolsey and Campeggi (cf Ep 961 introduction). For the cultured atmosphere of the English court cf Ep 855.
21 in this place] Louvain (cf Ep 930:12n). That the storms had abated by now is confirmed in Epp 967:61, 969–71, 980:35–7, 983:9–11.
22 'her latest footprints'] When Justice left this world for heaven at the end of the golden age, she lingered among the country folk. Erasmus borrows a phrase from Virgil *Georgics* 2.473, 474.

hopes are centred on your character; this I know clearly from his conversation, and I have no doubt that in every way you will answer your excellent
father's expectations.

Good literature blossoms everywhere, and vainly do the supporters of   10
traditional ignorance struggle against it. In England humane studies are
triumphant, with the support of the king, the cardinals, and the bishops.
The quarrelsome critics who use their voices for evil-speaking only have
been silenced. Here, since we have no such patrons, they are still in full cry
and are even advancing to the attack in printed books; but they are such   15
books as can only betray their own silliness and dullness of mind. Yet even
they grow gradually milder, like men recovering from a severe fever; and
they will be silent once the goodwill of princes has come to our aid. Of
Ferdinand I have great hopes, and I have no mean hopes of you too. Charles
is too far away. As for the lord of Chièvres, small wonder if he has no time   20
for literature, though he is not actively against it. Cardinal Adrian has never
shown much good will towards humane studies, while not their sworn foe
like some men, who think they cannot be left in peace themselves unless
humane studies are suppressed.

The bearer of this, Richard Pace, who is the envoy of the English king   25
and stands high in his favour, is a man whose acquaintance will bring you
great joy if you get to know him well; apart from his open-hearted nature, he
is very good at both Greek and Latin. Best wishes. Give my cordial greetings
to Adriaan van Baerland.

Antwerp, 20 May 1519   30

970 / To Jacopo Bannisio   Brussels, 21 May 1519

This letter was published in the *Farrago*; for its composition and contents see Ep
968 introduction. Bannisio (cf Ep 700) was a Hapsburg diplomat. His life is not
well known, and it is not clear on what new appointment Erasmus wished to
congratulate him. The greetings to Frederick of Saxony (lines 35–6) suggest
that Erasmus expected him to be at Frankfurt in the thick of the election
campaign. Erasmus also knew him to share Pace's taste for the new learning.

* * * * *

969
7 conversation] At Mechelen; cf Epp 926 introduction, 952:66–7.
19 Ferdinand] The brother of King Charles, who was still in Spain; cf Epp
948:201n, 970:16–17.
20 Chièvres] Guillaume de Croy; cf Ep 532:30n.
21 Adrian] Adrian of Utrecht, the future pope; cf Epp 171:16n, 608:13n.
29 Baerland] Adriaan Ælius van Baerland; see Ep 760:16n.

ERASMUS OF ROTTERDAM TO HIS FRIEND JACOPO BANNISIO,
GREETING

Rich as you are in distinctions of every kind, I hear you have been promoted
to a new appointment, and one of the highest standing, on which I send you
my warmest congratulations, nor have I any doubt that in time to come   5
fortune will requite your exceptional merits even more generously. Here we
are storm-tossed by tumults which leave Pan's visitations far behind, such is
the melodrama put on by some of the theology faculty. Nor is any of it fought
out in open field; all is done by trickery and twists and burrowings under
ground. This campaign for the three languages has gone well, and that made   10
them ill. They were afraid that if the New Testament went forward, their
authority would slip back. So they tried everything; but they are thinking
better of it. The New Testament has appeared; it sells – sells very
successfully. One man has had the face to write a pamphlet against me, but it
has done him nothing but harm and given me great satisfaction.   15

      Humane studies would emerge triumphant if only we had such a prince
in our country as they have in England. The king himself is far from ignorant,
extremely intelligent, an open supporter of the humanities, and has silenced
all those who were making trouble. The most reverend the cardinal of York is
reforming the whole system of study, and by his own generosity issues a sort 20
of general invitation to the love of learning; Cardinal Campeggi does the
same, an excellent man and a good scholar. The king's court contains more
distinguished men of learning than any university. I observe that German
princes too show some respect for learning, encouraged by you and others
like you; but we cannot as yet discover how to do likewise. H.S.H. Prince   25
Ferdinand, a young man born (I solemnly aver) for excellence of every kind,
is friendly to me and delighted with what I write; others have assured me,
and he told me so himself, that he has my book on the prince always by him.
They tried to make me his tutor, and he seems to wish for this himself; but
many things dissuade me from life at court, and especially my health, which   30
is so uncertain that unless I can manage it as I think best, I shall soon be in
trouble. Once dead, I should be no more use to the prince than to myself: as it

* * * * *

970
 7 Pan's visitations] Cf *Adagia* III vii 3, and for the 'panics' of the recent past see
    Epp 930:12n, 991:66–7.
13 New Testament] See Ep 864 introduction.
14 one man] Latomus; see Ep 934 introduction.
19 York] Thomas Wolsey; cf Ep 967:40n.
21 Campeggi] See Ep 961 introduction.
22 The king's court] Cf Epp 855, 964 introduction.
28 my book on the prince] Cf Ep 917 introduction.

is, I can do something for him with my pen. My paraphrase on 1 and 2
Corinthians and on Galatians has appeared, and in this field at any rate I win
approval from learned and unlearned alike. If opportunity offers, commend   35
me to the illustrious Frederick Duke of Saxony; I wrote to him lately, and
suppose he has had the letter. Farewell, best of patrons.

If you have the good fortune to meet this envoy from the English king,
Richard Pace, if you do not know him already, get to know him better
without fail. He is a most frank and friendly person. He knows both Greek   40
and Latin very well, and is persona grata on account of his good qualities
with both the king and the cardinals, and indeed with the pope himself.
Farewell once more.

Brussels, 21 May 1519

971 / To Gilles de Busleyden   [Brussels? c 21 May] 1519

Clearly contemporary with Epp 968–70, this letter is written from a place to
which Erasmus had apparently travelled from Antwerp in the company of
Pace. Busleyden, a high dignitary in the Brussels government (cf Ep 686
introduction), was evidently present in the same town, and Erasmus' letter
may have been designed to secure an invitation for Pace and himself on the
following day. The town was probably Brussels, from where Erasmus dated Ep
970. Busleyden was in Brussels on c 16 April; see de Vocht CTL I 363–4. This
letter was published in the *Farrago*.

ERASMUS TO GILLES DE BUSLEYDEN, GREETING
Honoured sir, I came here in hopes of seeing more of Richard Pace, the
English king's representative, a man of great attainments in both Greek and
Latin; but the inclement weather obliges me to stay at home. I send you as a
present a work of Galen's, now speaking better Latin with the aid of Thomas   5
Linacre than ever it did Greek. The last three books will attract you more, for
he spends the first three almost entirely in anointing, bathing, and rubbing
first the child, then the adolescent, and then the adult. My New Testament
has appeared with favourable omens; I should have brought a copy with me,
but forgot it. The theologians grow milder, and almost penitent. I dare not go 10
out, nor dare I invite your Excellency to supper with three eggs on the table.

* * * * *

33 paraphrase] See Epp 916, 956 introductions.
36 lately] Ep 939
42 cardinals] Wolsey and Campeggi

971
5 Galen's] *De sanitate tuenda;* cf Ep 664:29n.

If you do come, the warmth of your welcome will match the modesty of the bill of fare. Farewell. Let me speak with you before I leave.

972 / From Leonardus Priccardus   Aachen, 23 May [1519]

This letter was written after Erasmus' visit to Aachen in September 1518 (cf Epp 867:115–48, 904:9) and was published in the *Farrago*, together with Erasmus' answer, Ep 993.

Leonardus Priccardus, probably Prickert, of Aachen, received his MA at Paris in 1493. He was a canon in Aachen, a friend of Jérôme de Busleyden, and Erasmus' host in November 1520. He died in 1541; see de Vocht *Busleyden* 255–6.

LEONARDUS PRICCARDUS TO ERASMUS OF ROTTERDAM HIS
MOST HONOURED TEACHER, GREETING
One of the cowl-wearing fraternity was spreading the news here the other day among a rabble of the same kidney that some Englishman, I know not who, was lecturing in Greek at Louvain, who is one hundred times the 5
scholar that Rotterdam is and has found holes in more than a hundred places in his recently printed edition of the New Testament, with the intention of publishing your mistakes in a book which is to appear very shortly. For my part I could not believe this monstrous fellow, for all the wondrous holiness of his appearance. He added that all the theologians are against you and 10
argue in opposition, and that they have decided to drum you out of their university by a unanimous resolution, paying not the least regard to orders from the powers that be, since we must obey God rather than princes.

Such and such-like is the rubbish this beastly creature spews forth, and 'like some mad dog runs yelping through the town.' And so, dearest 15
Erasmus, I beg you in heaven's name to be of a good courage: now is the moment, having expounded Jerome in an edition of which no man could ever feel ashamed, to copy his character and his unconquerable resolution. Take my word for it, you will not need to expend so much effort in overthrowing this gentile as the labour and the sleepless nights he had to spend on Rufinus 20

* * * * *

972
4 Englishman] Edward Lee (cf Ep 843 introduction); his notes on Erasmus' New Testament did not appear in print until February 1520; cf Ep 1037.
10 all the theologians] Cf Ep 930:12n.
12 unanimous resolution] Cf CWE 7 preface.
15 'like some mad dog ... town'] Ovid *Ibis* 232
20 on Rufinus] Cf Ep 778:266–9.

and his wiles. Get ready against this Goliath your sling which is God's word
and aim straight at his furrowed forehead the rock that is Christ, for love of
whom you have undertaken the explanation of Scripture. You will lay low
the proud giant on the spot and overthrow all the other gentiles with him, I
mean those theologizers who are said to have conspired against you, as the   25
Holy Spirit assures us in these words of Isaiah: 'They are ashamed and
confounded all of them together; they are gone into confusion that are
contrivers of error.'

Farewell, most desirable Desiderius, and let me have early news of
your health and spirits.   30

From Aachen, 23 May

The precentor, the vice-provost, Schoenraid, and many others send
you greetings and their sincere wishes for victory; they are awaiting a letter
from you, or at least a note. Likewise my colleague Dr Hasebart sends
warmest greetings to you, and Neve.   35

973 / To Richard Foxe   Antwerp, 25 May 1519

Epp 973–4 were addressed to two English prelates with whom Erasmus had
been acquainted since 1506 (cf Epp 187, 192). It rather seems that he had been
out of touch with them but was now reminded of them by the agitation of
Edward Lee, whom he clearly expected to carry some influence, at least with
Foxe (cf Epp 898A introduction, 1099). Both letters were first published in
the *Farrago*, Ep 973 without mention of Lee's name. The name was given,
however, in the *Epistolae ad diversos*, August 1521, after both opponents had
published books each against the other. For Erasmus' presence at Antwerp see
Ep 964 introduction.

ERASMUS TO THE RIGHT REVEREND RICHARD, BISHOP OF
WINCHESTER, GREETING
Right reverend Prelate, if my sincere devotion to you has ever met with your
approval, I have but one request to make of you in return. It is that you
should not lightly lend credence to the falsehoods about me which like some   5
desperate plague are now rife everywhere. If Edward Lee can bring forward

* * * * *

22 furrowed forehead] Varro *Menippean Satires* 134; cf Plautus *Epidicus* 609.
26 Isaiah] Isa 45:16
32 precentor, the vice-provost, Schoenraid] Cf Ep 867:117n, 118n, 123n.
34 Hasebart] A native of the diocese of Thérouanne near Saint–Omer, Aegidius
Hasebart began his study at Louvain in 1483. He became a canon of Aachen and
may have died by 1539.

arguments to prove that his opinion is better than mine, I shall have no quarrel with him. But inasmuch as both here and among his own people, by tongue and pen alike, he and his agents fill every place with malicious rumours, he shows as little care for his own reputation as he does for mine. For a long time he has made no secret of his hostility, although I have never attacked him either in word or deed. He is young, he has a burning desire for reputation; but he would have done better to make a more auspicious start in his pursuit of it. I know your Lordship's wisdom, which does not pass hasty judgments, especially in condemnation. Time will bring all things to light. Truth may be hard-pressed, but she cannot be overcome. If you will use your influence to advise Lee, either to desist entirely from these false accusations, which do his name more harm than mine, or at least to meet me fairly in argument, you will do wonders for his reputation; for now his malice carries him away, like a man frenzied by some mental disease. As for your humble servant, I made some attempt, long ago, to win your good will, but without success; and now I do not ask your good will for myself, but for Lee your countryman. Best wishes to your Lordship, to whom I declare myself entirely devoted.

Antwerp, 25 May 1519

974 / To Thomas Ruthall   Antwerp, 25 May 1519

See Ep 973 introduction.

ERASMUS OF ROTTERDAM TO THE RIGHT REVEREND THOMAS, BISHOP OF DURHAM, GREETING

Right reverend Father in God, we are told by Aristotle that silence is often the solvent of friendship. Unwilling to run this risk myself, especially with such a friend as you, I send you a paraphrase on the Epistle to the Galatians, in which there is a passage on Paul's criticism of Peter which in my view has never yet been adequately explained by any of the ancient commentators. I am well aware that various rumours about me are in circulation. The Philistines feel that humane studies are raising their heads again, and so

* * * * *

973
15 Time] Cf Ep 974:10n.
21 some attempt] Cf Ep 187 and the index of CWE 2.

974
3 Aristotle] *Nicomachean Ethics* 8.5.1; cf *Adagia* II i 26.
5 paraphrase] See Ep 956 introduction.
6 passage] See Ep 956:39n.

they leave no stone unturned; but with the passage of time truth will win the   10
day. I have only one request to make of your Lordship: do not lightly give
credence to the anti-Erasmus party. They are in full cry just now, as though it
were their destiny; but soon they will be ashamed of this distemper, when
they return to their senses, as happened to Ajax. My best wishes to your
Lordship. Pray continue towards your humble servant the favour you have   15
always shown me.

    Antwerp, 25 May 1519

975 / To Antoine Papin   Louvain, [end of May] 1519

This letter and the abbot's reply (Ep 984) were published in the *Farrago* with
conflicting dates. Of the two dates that of this letter is less convincing (cf Ep
967A introduction for an analogous case), and it seems best to assume that this
letter was written shortly before Ep 984 and perhaps sent with a messenger
expected to bring back the requested book.

    The rich abbey of Gembloux, south-east of Brussels, possessed a library
which was already famous in the Middle Ages. It was further enlarged by
Antoine Papin of Ath (d 1541), who had become abbot in 1518 and was
chiefly known for his building activity. Gembloux had joined the Bursfeld
congregation in 1505, and in 1520 Papin sent some of his monks to St Truiden
to help its abbot, Willem Bollart (cf Ep 761:43n), introduce reforms; cf *Gallia
Christiana* (Paris 1715–1875) III 566–7; de Vocht *Busleyden* 445; and Ep 1547 for
another manuscript which Erasmus borrowed from Gembloux.

ERASMUS OF ROTTERDAM TO THE
REVEREND FATHER ANTOINE PAPIN, ABBOT OF GEMBLOUX,
GREETING
From the catalogue of your library, to which I was given access some time
ago, I learn that you possess two very ancient manuscripts containing St   5
Cyprian's opuscula. Now I at least have a great desire to give the world an

    * * * * *

10 no stone unturned] Cf *Adagia* I iv 30.
10 passage of time] Cf *Adagia* II iv 17, with a citation from Sophocles' tragedy *Ajax*
    (646–7). Ajax recovers his senses and despairs at the sight of what he had done
    during a divinely inflicted fit of madness; cf *Adagia* I vii 46; Bietenholz *History
    and Biography* 20–1.

975
5 St Cyprian's] This is the first indication that Erasmus planned to edit him. The
    edition was published by Froben in February 1520 with a dedication to
    Cardinal Lorenzo Pucci (cf Ep 1000), whereas Papin had to be content with
    the publication of Epp 975, 984.

edition of this author, freed from mistakes and separated from the works falsely attributed to him; for among all the Latin writers I find no one who comes closer to the true spirit and energy of the apostles. One feels all through that one is listening to a true pastor and one destined for 10 martyrdom. Yet we theologians allow the works of men like this to fall out of fashion, which makes it easier for us to admire the feeble nonsense of our modern authors. I have no doubt that your Lordship, as a fervent supporter of true piety, is also well disposed to religious studies, and to Cyprian, who is a great religious teacher. I do not ask you to do me this kindness without 15 recompense. Your Cyprian shall come back to you, and come back with interest; and in the mean time I will see to it that posterity is duly informed to whom a great part of this benefit is owing. I have long been in your debt for the venison you sent me, and the debt will be far greater if you send me a Cyprian. My best wishes to your Lordship and to the sacred society 20 of your brethren, and I beg them to commend me to Christ in their spiritual prayers.

Louvain, [1 June] 1519

976 / To Johannes Fabri   Louvain, [c end of May] 1519

This answer to Ep 953 was published in the *Farrago*. It was clearly written shortly after the encounter with Richard Pace on his way to Frankfurt; cf Ep 968 introduction.

ERASMUS OF ROTTERDAM TO THE MOST WORTHY JOHANNES FABRI, VICAR-GENERAL OF THE BISHOP OF CONSTANCE, GREETING

Truly you were born for friendship! Neither the press of business that distracts you on every side nor the great distance that separates us could 5 make you forget your humble friend, and that too when he has been so remiss in his duty towards you. For when I was in Basel, the work of seeing my books through the press left me so little spare time that sometimes I scarcely had the leisure to return the courtesies of a friend and patron of such distinction, to whom it would have been right to render all the services in my 10 power. It showed remarkable generosity to forgive my neglect; and now with great magnanimity you return me thanks. But let me reply to your letter – which was as remarkable for learning as it was for length – in the spirit in which at Basel I habitually return your greetings, and say that of the praise you offer me, which is quite excessive, I will select nothing to keep except the 15 generous spirit which wishes well to my reputation more from bias than good judgment.

I know Beatus Rhenanus dedicated my *Methodus* to you, and I could
easily have been quite content had he only told me what he meant to do
before I had dedicated the book to the archbishop of Mainz. But my dedica-   20
tion was already in the hands of the public before a copy reached Beatus, to
which at that time I had added no dedicatory letter, not wishing to have two
dedications in the New Testament, in case someone might complain that I
was trying to whitewash two walls out of one bucket. And I had so arranged
the shape of my piece that it could either be read separately or be part of the   25
larger undertaking, as I state at the very beginning of that work. In fact, this
idea that came into Rhenanus' head was in my opinion rather unhappy, all
the more so since he is holding locked up in his desk things of his own, with
which he might shed lustre equally on himself and his friends, instead of
using other people's. Not but what here too I should approve of Beatus'   30
keenness if the result had not been unfortunate; for I think it is Fortune that
is to blame, not his intentions. Anyhow, if the result is not what was intended, I will take steps to put this right on another occasion. Nor shall I so
act as to leave posterity in ignorance of our friendship, if any of these trifles
of mine ever reach the ears of posterity.   35

Richard Pace is in capital health and spirits, and a triumphant success
among his own people, being a great favourite with their excellent king; he is
the king's chief secretary, which is a very important office in England. He
was here lately as his king's representative to bring greetings to the Lady
Margaret and Ferdinand and to attend the election of the emperor. The sight   40
of him gave me so much pleasure, no one has approached it for many years
past. Thomas More is of the Privy Council, and so is Colet; Thomas Linacre
* * * * *
976
18 *Methodus*] Erasmus had given the newly enlarged *Ratio verae theologiae* to
   Martens, who published it in November 1518 with a preface to Albert of
   Brandenburg (Ep 745). Meanwhile Erasmus sent another manuscript of the
   text, without his preface, to Basel for inclusion in the New Testament. Thus
   Beatus Rhenanus was not aware of Erasmus' preface to the archbishop when
   he decided to publish with Froben a separate edition of the *Ratio* (January 1519;
   reprinted in April), adding a preface of his own addressed to Fabri.
24 whitewash ... bucket] Cf *Adagia* I vii 3.
28 things of his own] Beatus' *Res Germanicae* did not appear until 1531, but for
   many years he had been acquiring an intimate knowledge of the sources on
   which his great work was based; cf his editions of Tacitus (1519), the *Panegyrics*,
   and Velleius Paterculus (1520): BRE Index bibliographicus nos 46, 48–9, 57.
34 friendship] Epp 953, 976 were published in the *Farrago* of October 1519; for a
   later dedication to Fabri see Ep 1428.
36 Pace] Cf Epp 953:72n, 968 introduction.
42 Privy Council] Colet's appointment to the Privy Council probably dated from
   January 1517; for More's appointment later that year cf Ep 829:6n.

the royal physician. The king himself is a most promising student of philosophy. The queen loves good literature, which she has studied with success since childhood. Who would not wish to pass his life in such a court? 45
Farewell, my honoured friend. From Louvain, 1519

977 / From Kaspar Schalbe   Brussels, 28 May 1519

This letter was reluctantly answered by Ep 981 and published in the *Farrago*. Kaspar Schalbe, probably of Eisenach, matriculated at the University of Erfurt in 1504 and graduated MA in 1510, together with Justus Jonas, in whose company he had just visited Erasmus (cf Ep 963:6n). He was a member of the Erfurt humanist circle and a priest, but subsequently joined the Reformation and married. He is last mentioned in 1526; see Luther w *Briefwechsel* III Ep 587.

TO ERASMUS OF ROTTERDAM, GREATEST OF MEN IN EVERY WAY, FROM KASPAR SCHALBE, GREETING
Through forests infested with brigands and cities infested with plague we have made our way to you, dear Erasmus, Jonas and I, and how well timed, how blest in heaven's name was our arrival! It was a long and tedious 5 journey, but so far are we from regretting it that on our journey, while we were still uncertain where you, the one special pearl of Christendom, were lying hid, we solemnly swore that we would seek you in farthest India or ultimate Thule, to say nothing of Brabant or France. Suffer no more from too low an opinion of yourself – unlike the theologians of the tribe of Aristotle, 10 who all suffer from pride and self-love! If you on your side do not understand how you are the great privilege of this generation given us by Christ himself, I have learnt at home in the silence of my study to know you by your works; and now your living face and your conversation sweet as sugar, as honey, without any affectation (you will be surprised, dear 15 Erasmus) has meant for me almost as much profit as another man might draw from one of your books. I would not inflict my worthless remarks on you did I not wish to have a letter from you as ardently as Jonas, my companion. My life upon it, I could not be torn away from you even if you threatened to drive me away with a stick, unless I have something to bring you back to me, 20 first on my long journey, and still more when the time comes that I return to

* * * * *

45 court] Cf Epp 855, 964 introductions.

977
8 lying hid] See Ep 963:6n.
11 you] Reading *tute*
18 ardently] Cf Ep 967A introduction.

my far-distant home. Why need I waste words to explain how highly I value this journey of ours? So may God love me, as I would not take in exchange Pactolus ten times o'er or solid mountains of gold. Farewell, great Erasmus, and let me have the favour of an answer, even if I have to wait a long time for it. Farewell once more.

Brussels, 28 May 1519

978 / To Georgius Spalatinus   Louvain, 29 May 1519

For the dispatch of this letter, published in the *Farrago*, see Ep 963:6n.

TO THE EXCELLENT THEOLOGIAN GEORGIUS SPALATINUS,
CHAPLAIN TO THE MOST ILLUSTRIOUS DUKE OF SAXONY, FROM
ERASMUS OF ROTTERDAM, GREETING
No, nothing in the way of a letter from you has yet reached me, neither in your own name nor in that of his highness the duke, and I fear they may all have gone astray, for surely something would have arrived by now, unless there has been bad faith somewhere. You can see what a long distance lies between us, and just as though we were at war, the enemies of humane studies are on the watch to intercept a letter. So we must be all the more careful not to entrust letters to the first comer. I was most grateful for the medal, which brought me a truly lifelike portrait of your excellent duke. As for his letter, the prince-bishop of Liège was most anxious to see it. I sent it to him, and the medal as well, and never was able to have another word with the man who conveyed them. All the encouragement, the generosity, the support that his highness has lavished on the promotion of liberal studies I regard as a contribution for my special benefit. Everything I saw in Jonas gave me particular satisfaction. My life upon it, I regard him as a chosen

* * * * *

24 Pactolus ... gold] Cf *Adagia* I vi 75, I ix 15. Pactolus, a river in Lydia, was said to carry gold in its stream.

978
4 letter] When visiting Erasmus, Jonas and Schalbe probably inquired about the fate of Ep 711, from Spalatinus, which had still not arrived; nor had Ep 963, from the elector.
5 I fear ... by now] Translating Allen's reconstruction of a line missing in the printed text
11 medal] Sent by the elector Frederick through Jonas, together with the letter mentioned in the next sentence (cf Ep 963:6n, and for the medal Ep 872:27n), as an acknowledgment for the dedication of Suetonius; cf Epp 586, 979.
12 Liège] Erard de la Marck. He took an interest in Luther (cf Ep 980 introduction), whose cause may well have been mentioned in Frederick's letter.

instrument for the enhancement of Christ's glory in the thick darkness of our times. The gifts of his colleague Schalbe are better known to me from his letters than from the way he speaks. Henceforth the name of Georgius 20 Spalatinus will be enrolled in the list of my special friends, and also among the benefactors to whom I am indebted, whose names I keep not so much on paper as written in my heart. Farewell, dearest Georgius.

Louvain, 29 May 1519

979 / To the Elector Frederick of Saxony   Louvain, 30 May 1519

This is the answer to a letter now lost (cf Epp 963:6n, 978:11n). It was carried by Jonas, who delivered it to Frederick at Frankfurt during the gathering of the electors (cf Ep 968 introduction; *Jonas Briefwechsel* Ep 25). A German translation of Ep 979 in the hand of Spalatinus, evidently made for the convenience of his master, is preserved in Weimar. It is somewhat laboured but accurate. Allen printed it in his notes to Ep 939; cf I. Höss in *Archiv für Reformationsgeschichte* 46 (1955) 209–13. This letter was printed in the *Farrago*.

TO THE MOST ILLUSTRIOUS FREDERICK, DUKE OF SAXONY FROM ERASMUS OF ROTTERDAM, GREETING

Most illustrious Prince, the devotion which led me to dedicate to your Highness my edition of the *Lives of the Caesars* has now, in my opinion, been abundantly repaid by the most friendly letter in which you tell me that the 5 gift was not unwelcome. For when I resolved to dedicate that book to you, I had not yet heard as fully as I since have of the enthusiasm with which you aid the humanities in their continuing fight against the supporters of time-honoured ignorance – a fight in which our enemies, for all their efforts, achieve nothing except to render our victory more splendid and their own 10 folly more notorious. As it is, I consider all the interest, the generosity, and the material assistance which you so nobly lavish on the restoration of liberal studies and the advancement and support of their protagonists as entirely bestowed upon myself. Nor need this policy cause you any misgivings. Literature will not be ungrateful: she will confer upon her champion 15 immortal glory in the three historic tongues. The name of Frederick will one day be more famous for his encouragement of learning than for his splendour of lineage. I myself in future shall not be afraid to dedicate other children of

* * * * *

979
4 *Lives of the Caesars*] by Suetonius; cf Ep 586.
18 other children] No other work by Erasmus is dedicated to Frederick.

my brain to you, since this bold approach of mine has met with success. May
Christle the Almighty preserve your Highness as long as possible to be a   20
blessing to your country and to learning and religion.

Louvain, 30 May 1519

980 / To Martin Luther   Louvain, 30 May 1519

> This answer to Luther's Ep 933 became known at first from the same sources as
> Ep 948 (for subsequent unauthorized printings see Ep 1033 introduction).
> When Erasmus himself published this letter in the *Farrago* and perhaps
> separately in Antwerp (cf NK 2935; Ep 1040), he took care to substitute 'an
> outstanding person' for 'the bishop of Liège' in line 36, but Mosellanus'
> editions retained the original text. The trouble caused was considerable. Pope
> Leo x was alarmed, and Erasmus felt obliged to have recourse to subterfuge (cf
> Epp 1041, 1143; Pastor vii 398–9). Erard de la Marck suffered the indignity of
> being investigated by the Louvain theologians but apparently bore Erasmus no
> ill will (cf Ep 1038). This letter repeats in more cautious terms the position taken
> by Erasmus in Ep 939:69–91, a letter which he had not himself considered
> suitable for publication. In Ep 939 he defended Luther; here he primarily
> defends himself, although the critics were in part identical.

ERASMUS OF ROTTERDAM TO MARTIN LUTHER

Greetings, dearest brother in Christ. Your letter gave me great pleasure: it
displayed the brilliance of your mind and breathed the spirit of a Christian.
No words of mine could describe the storm raised here by your books. Even
now it is impossible to root out from men's minds the most groundless   5
suspicion that your work is written with assistance from me and that I am, as
they call it, a standard-bearer of this new movement. They supposed that
this gave them an opening to suppress both humane studies – for which they
have a burning hatred, as likely to stand in the way of her majesty queen
Theology, whom they value much more than they do Christ – and myself at   10
the same time, under the impression that I contribute something of
importance towards this outburst of zeal. In the whole business their
weapons are clamour, audacity, subterfuge, misinterpretation, innuendo; if
I had not seen it with my own eyes – felt it, rather – I would never have
believed theologians could be such maniacs. One would think it was some   15
disastrous infection. And yet this poisonous virus, starting in a small circle,

* * * * *

980
6 assistance from me] Cf Ep 961:37, CWE 7 preface.

spread to a larger number, so that a great part of this university was carried away by the spreading contagion of this epidemic paranoia.

I assured them that you were quite unknown to me; that I had not yet read your books and could therefore neither disapprove nor approve 20 anything. I merely told them not to make such an offensive uproar in public before they had even read what you have written, and that this was in their own interests, since their judgment ought to carry great weight. I also advised them to consider whether it was a good plan to produce before a casual audience of laymen a distorted account of views which it would be 25 more proper to refute in print or discuss among specialists, especially since all with one voice speak highly of the author's manner of life. I did no good at all: they are so blinded by their own jaundiced, indeed slanderous, disputations. When I think how often we have agreed terms of peace, and how often on some trifling and rash suspicion they have stirred up fresh 30 trouble! And they regard themselves as theologians. Theologians in this part of the world are unpopular at court; and this too they think is my fault. All the bishops are cordially on my side. These men have no confidence in the printed word; their hope of victory lies entirely in malicious gossip. This I despise, for my conscience is clear. Their attitude to you has softened 35 somewhat. They are afraid of my pen, knowing their own record; and, my word, I would paint them in their true colours, as they deserve, did not Christ's teaching and Christ's example point in quite another direction. Fierce wild beasts are tamed by kindness; these men are driven wild if you do anything for them. 40

You have people in England who think well of what you write, and they are in high place. There are some here too, the bishop of Liège among them, who favour your views. As for me, I keep myself uncommitted, so far as I can, in hopes of being able to do more for the revival of good literature. And I think one gets further by courtesy and moderation than by clamour. 45 That was how Christ brought the world under his sway; that was how Paul did away with the Jewish law, by reducing everything to allegory. It is more expedient to protest against those who misuse the authority of the bishops than against the bishops themselves; and I think one should do the same with kings. The universities are not so much to be despised as recalled to 50 more serious studies. Things which are of such wide acceptance that they cannot be torn out of men's minds all at once should be met with argument,

* * * * *

17 university] Cf Epp 930:12n, 961:37n.
29 terms of peace] Cf Epp 946, 1022 introductions.
35 softened] Cf Ep 968:21n.
42 Liège] Erard de la Marck; cf Epp 916, 980 introductions.

close-reasoned forcible argument, rather than bare assertion. Some people's poisonous propaganda is better ignored than refuted. Everywhere we must take pains to do and say nothing out of arrogance or faction; for I think the   55 spirit of Christ would have it so. Meanwhile we must keep our minds above the corruption of anger or hatred, or of ambition; for it is this that lies in wait for us when our religious zeal is in full course.

I am not instructing you to do this, only to do what you do always. I have dipped into your commentary on the Psalms; I like the look of it   60 particularly and hope that it will be of great service. There is a man in Antwerp, the prior of the monastery there, a genuine Christian, who is most devoted to you and was once your pupil, or so he says. He is almost the only one among them all who preaches Christ; the others as a rule preach the inventions of men or their own advantage. I have written to Melanchthon.   65 May the Lord Jesus ever more richly endue you with his spirit every day, for his own glory and the good of mankind. Your letter was not at hand when I wrote this.

Farewell, from Louvain, 30 May 1519

981 / To Kaspar Schalbe   Louvain, 30 May 1519

This answer to Ep 977 was published in the *Farrago*.

ERASMUS OF ROTTERDAM TO HIS FRIEND KASPAR SCHALBE,
GREETING

I ask you, very learned friend Schalbe, is this an invitation or an order? You can see that I have scarce enough leisure to maintain my health, you can see how I am overwhelmed by my researches, and yet you demand a letter. So   5 imperative, so uncontrollable a thing affection is, especially between Germans, and if I try to strive against it, I shall get nowhere. And so I send an answer to your letter, but such an answer that I fear you will say you have

* * * * *

60 commentary] *Operationes in psalmos*, a course of lectures, the first part of which was published in Wittenberg, March 1519 (Luther w v 26–673, Benzing *Lutherbibiliographie* no 516); cf Allen Ep 1127A:96.

62 prior] Jacob Proost (Probst) of Ieper (1486–1562), since 1518 prior of the Augustinian convent in Antwerp. In 1521 he received his licence in theology at Wittenberg. His efforts to propagate the new faith at Antwerp ended with the suppression of his convent in 1522. Subsequently he became a pastor at Bremen; cf de Vocht CTL I 427.

65 Melanchthon] Ep 947

981
5 demand a letter] Cf Ep 941:3n.

not heard from me. Yet if pity for me does not excuse its brevity, at least let it
be excused in consideration of my labours for the public good, which must   10
suffer when I am distracted by private duty such as this; to the individual
recipients they seem things of no account, but the whole burden falls all at
once on me and adds immensely to my load.

Since you do not yield to Jonas in affection, I think it only fair that I
should return yours no less than his. I should deplore your taking a journey   15
so long and so perilous simply for my sake, unless you yourself were actually
so pleased at having done so. If you have reason for this, I do not grudge you
the fruits of it; if it is all imagination, the man who does not feel his troubles is
half-way to a cure. But in one point you show yourself a true German. You
say that sticks and stones would not drive you away unless you are given   20
something to recall your Erasmus to you even at home in your own country.
Have you no shame? Not satisfied with feasting eyes ears and mind on the
pleasure of my company (sweet as honey, so you say), must you carry me off
entirely? And to a country so far away? Why, what small portion of myself
you will carry off, if you take home the picture of my poor body drawn or   25
modelled! The best part of a man like me is to be seen in his books as often as
you please, always assuming there is anything at all of mine that is worth
looking at. Farewell, dearest Kaspar.

Louvain, 30 May 1519

982 / To Helius Eobanus Hessus   Louvain, 30 May 1519

This letter was published in the *Farrago*; for the circumstances of its composition see Ep 963:6n.

ERASMUS OF ROTTERDAM TO EOBANUS HESSUS THE EMINENT
POET, GREETING

Your account of your travels gave me so much pleasure that, after correcting
the printer's errors, I have arranged to have it reprinted here. I was
delighted to see Jonas and Schalbe. All the same, in sending them here you   5
take little thought for my reputation, of which something has always to be
sacrificed as a result of meetings of that kind. Yet you threaten to send me
more visitors of the same sort. Having the benefit of their presence, which
alone provides the opportunity to write, I write for that very reason more
briefly; by other hands it would hardly be safe to write at all, and by these   10

* * * * *

982
3 account of your travels] See Ep 870 introduction.
6 reputation] Because no time is left for scholarly work; cf Epp 941:3n, 991.

men it would be useless, for they can tell you everything by word of mouth better than I could in a letter.

I should prefer that those letters of mine had not been published which you added to your poem; I was in mind to publish them shortly, but in enlarged form. Your poem to the count of Nassau I want to see particularly. He is a supporter of humane letters, and on their account of me also. But our princes know how to be liberal with compliments, not coin. I think not of myself in saying this, for I want nothing, being content with my own lot. Farewell, sincerest of friends.

The moment has come to look around you and choose some subject on which there is much to be said, so that you may show posterity your true stature. Round this you will gather little by little everything of distinction that is furnished by your daily reading. You have not forgotten this, and need no advice from me. Farewell again.

Louvain, 30 May 1519

983 / To Johann Lang   Louvain, 30 May [1519]

> This was clearly one of the letters given to Jonas and Schalbe (cf Ep 963:6n), but unlike the others it was not published in the *Farrago*. It is known from the same source as Ep 872 (Forschungsbibliothek Gotha, MS chart. A 399 f 222 verso), another letter to Lang which Erasmus deemed too bold for publication.

TO THE REVEREND FATHER JOHANN LANG, VICAR OF THE AUGUSTINIANS, WITH SINCERE RESPECTS
Reverend Father, I beg you most emphatically not to judge my feelings towards you by the respect I pay you in the way of correspondence: I am so overwhelmed by letters from all parts that I can scarce find time to read them. I feel great affection for your truly Christian spirit and your defence of true Christianity. I hope that Christ may bless the pious endeavours of yourself and others like you. In these parts the papal party is thus far in full cry, the whole pack being at last of one mind, to do mischief; they are however

* * * * *

14 poem] The *Hodoeporicon*
15 poem to the count of Nassau] Not known to exist now. Erasmus was clearly thinking of a Netherlandish prince, most likely Henry III of Nassau (cf Ep 829:14n), whom he had met at court – Count Henry was one of the tutors of Prince Charles – and who had shown him favour; cf Ep 1092.

983
5 letters] Cf Ep 941:3n.
9 mischief] Cf Ep 930:12n.

somewhat milder than they were, and I hope they will one day be ashamed of   10
their excesses. The best men all support Luther's idea of liberty; his wisdom,
I do not doubt, will ensure that the affair does not issue in discord and
rupture. I believe our objective should be to implant Christ in the hearts of
men, rather than to fight in the arena with men who wear the mask of
Christians, from whom glory or victory will never be won until the tyranny of   15
the Roman See has been abolished, and its hangers-on, Preachers, Carmelites, Minorites – I mean of course the bad ones. I do not see how such an
attempt is to be made without grave disorders. Farewell, Father; I am
conscious how much I owe to your enlightened kindness.

Louvain, 30 May   20
Erasmus of Rotterdam

984 / From Antoine Papin   Gembloux, 30 May [1519]

This answer to Ep 975 was published in the *Farrago*.

ANTOINE PAPIN, ABBOT OF GEMBLOUX, TO ERASMUS OF
ROTTERDAM, GREETING
I send you with the greatest pleasure, my dear Erasmus, such volumes of
Cyprian as I have been able to find in our library, wishing well with all my
heart to the glory of that most saintly man, and to the unremitting study and   5
research which you devote to the unearthing and correcting of sacred texts. I
pray that Christ may prosper and promote your efforts, which cannot be too
highly praised; for while those who print books so full of corruptions that
they are unintelligible and unreadable discourage many people from these
sacred studies, your labours on the other hand will fire many with the wish   10
to pursue them. And so, most learned Father, if there is anything in our
possession that might assist your admirable plan, pray regard what is ours as
yours. Indeed, if you so wish, our whole library shall come over to you en
bloc; we will entrust the whole of it to your sense of honour. Affectionate
best wishes, my very dear friend.   15

Gembloux, 30 May

985 / To Justus Jonas

This letter has been assigned a new date and will now be found as Ep 967A.

* * * * *

10 milder] Cf Ep 968:21n.
15 tyranny of the Roman See] Cf Ep 872:20n.
17 bad ones] Cf Epp 946:4n, 950:31–5; for other conflicts with Carmelites and
Dominicans see the indexes of CWE 5–8.

986 / From Ulrich von Hutten   Mainz, 5 June [1519]

In view of the beginning of this letter the recent correspondence between Erasmus and Hutten requires elucidation. Hutten acknowledged three letters from Erasmus received at short intervals. The first was contemporary with Ep 919, sent together with the book for Albert of Mainz. It is now missing. The second he received during the siege of Tübingen, c 20 April. This was probably Ep 951. The third he received at Bad Cannstadt near Stuttgart, shortly before 21 May (cf Hutten *Opera* I Ep 126). This too is missing. The present letter appears to be primarily in reply to the latter. From the beginning of Ep 999 it appears likely that there had been an earlier answer by Hutten with references to Thomas More. This letter was first published by Hutten in his edition of Erasmus' *Ratio verae theologiae* (Mainz: J. Schöffer [June] 1519). Uncertain as to Erasmus' movements, Hutten entrusted it to Richard Pace (cf Ep 968 introduction). Consequently it did not reach Erasmus until after he had read it in print; see the end of Ep 999, where this letter is briefly answered.

HUTTEN TO HIS FRIEND ERASMUS, GREETING

This endless series of letters from you to me I have never set eyes on. One reached me in the army while we were besieging Tübingen, and it was a very short one; you should be more careful in your choice of men to carry this infinite correspondence. But about the man you sent here with the book that   5
was to be offered to the prince you need not worry: he brought everything safely. Nor was I slow in doing what you wanted, and I found the prince keen on it. Your offering required no puff from me; it was its own sufficient advertisement. When he had read it through quickly, 'There's a subject worthy of Erasmus!' he said. 'May he be with us many years to write like that   10
many times!' And he expressed the warmest wishes for your welfare, for he has high hopes of you, knowing what light you throw on the field of learning and how much you help all who wish to learn. After that, Stromer arrived, for he had married a wife in Saxony and had not followed the court immediately; and while he admires all your work more than one might think   15

* * * * *

986
5 the book] The *Ratio verae theologiae*, sent for Albert of Brandenburg; cf Ep 968:4n.
13 Stromer] Heinrich Stromer (cf Ep 578 introduction). He had married Anna Hummelshain at Leipzig on 24 January 1519; see G. Wustmann *Der Wirt von Auerbachs Keller* (Leipzig 1902) 28–9.

possible, he worships this book above everything. As for Gregor Kopp, the prince's second physician, you have made him a complete Erasmian: he has your books in his hands constantly and reads them more greedily almost than anyone. This gives many people reason to be angry with you: they say you are turning our physicians into divines. You are also coming into   20
disrepute with the lawyers, for sweeping off some men who were all set for their Bartholus; and now they have dropped the law altogether and are having a delightful time reading your books. Having produced the same disastrous effect on the enthusiasm of the theologists, can you wonder if they are not fond of you? They have a sort of right to do this much; it is rare   25
enough for them to do the right thing.

There was a rumour here for a whole month, and I dare say it even reached you, that I had been killed in action. This really was a triumph for those gentry; they were simply delighted. If anything had happened to me, I am sure they would have said it was Christ's answer to their prayers, for I   30
know already that they pray for some harm to befall me. I read Latomus' dialogue, which made me laugh. You must not think you wasted the time you spent in writing your *Apologia*; it did me all the good in the world.

As for what you say about Ferdinand, I am delighted to hear that he loves liberal studies even at his age. You raised my spirits: it made me hope to   35
see the rulers of the world allying themselves with us against barbarism. Cardinal Albert takes our part valiantly; he still treats me generously, and he has a great desire to see you. You are not doing the right thing by not offering to join him; you do not believe me when I keep on proclaiming the very generous feelings he has for you. He has entrusted me with a present,   40
intended to return the honour you have done him. It is a silver-gilt cup, not

* * * * *

16 Kopp] Gregor Kopp (Coppus) of Kalbe, Saxony, was registered at the University of Leipzig in 1500. Like Stromer he was physician to Albert of Brandenburg. At about this time he had helped Hutten with his treatise *De guaiaci medicina* (Mainz: J. Schöffer April 1519); see Hutten *Opera* I 230; Luther w *Briefwechsel* II Ep 257.

22 Bartholus] Bartolo of Sassoferrato, d c 1357. A legal school was called after him, and his name became a synonym for legal professionalism.

31 Latomus' dialogue] *De trium linguarum et studii theologici ratione*; see Ep 934 introduction.

34 Ferdinand] Cf Ep 917 introduction; the following comments may have encouraged Hutten to approach Ferdinand direct; see Ep 1055.

41 cup] A silver-gilt 'loving-cup' (line 45) or a so-called *Deckelbecher*, an artifact popular in the sixteenth century consisting of two identical cups each of which could serve as lid for the other. It reached Erasmus after considerable delay (cf Epp 999 and 1009), and in the last of his wills he left it to Hieronymus Froben (cf Allen XI 364). There is no trace of it now, and of the thirty cups in gold and silver

only very heavy but still more admirable for the workmanship. You will think it a gift worthy of a prince. Though he himself says this is a present for you while you give him a wide berth, and that if you ever come a little closer, he will have much bigger things to give you. He calls this a loving-cup.   45
Personally, I do not know where to send it; they say you are setting off for England. Write and tell me what you want done with the cup, and also what your plans are.

The war went off very well. We have freed Germany from serious danger and widespread anxiety. Why should we be much concerned if the   50
man is still alive? We have stripped him of everything; his life can only be miserable. You shall read the whole story one day. At Stuttgart I met Reuchlin, in a position of great anxiety. The worthy father was afraid of the fury of the troops. But I had arranged with Franz, my chief, to put in a word with the generals in command, so that if Stuttgart had to be taken by assault,   55
orders should be issued throughout the army that Reuchlin's house was not to be touched. You can't think what a great and wonderful service he supposes this to be, though I know perfectly well it was simply my duty to see that such a learned and excellent man should suffer no indignity. In this business particularly Franz showed what a great man he is; for a long time we   60
have never had his like in Germany, and he deserves to be handed down to posterity in something from your pen too. My own hope is that this nation must gain greatly in repute from such a man. There is nothing we admire in Antiquity that he does not zealously imitate. He has the most lively wisdom, lively eloquence too; tackles everything with energy; so tireless that the   65
greatest general would not match him. He never says or does anything mean, and is now engaged on perhaps the most noble enterprise of all. May

* * * * *

in Erasmus' estate only two are known today; see E. Major *Ein Becher aus dem Besitz des Erasmus von Rotterdam* (Basel 1929; reprinted from Historisches Museum Basel *Jahresberichte und Rechnungen* 1928).
46 for England] Cf Ep 964 introduction.
49 the war] Cf Ep 923:27n.
51 man] Ulrich of Württemberg
52 Stuttgart] The town had surrendered on 7 April to the army of the Swabian League under the command of Duke William of Bavaria. Fearing a sack, the aged Reuchlin had buried his books, not knowing, of course, that Hutten and Franz von Sickingen had taken measures to protect him. But the troubles of Stuttgart, and those of Reuchlin, continued; eventually Reuchlin moved to Ingolstadt; cf Ep 1129; Ludwig Geiger *Johann Reuchlin* (Leipzig 1871) 459–61; RE Epp 282–6.
54 Franz] Franz von Sickingen; cf Ep 582:30n.
67 enterprise] Immediately after the campaign in Württemberg Sickingen and his followers were hired by the Hapsburgs and joined an army posted at Höchst

Franz von Sickingen
Engraved portrait by Hieronymus Hopfer, c 1540
Lutherhalle, Wittenberg

God Almighty prosper my hero's plans! While I was there he talked in the most friendly fashion with Reuchlin, who in greeting us called him the Scourge of God. Franz said he would give us all the help he could. In a word, you can see what a support he might be to us; above all, he will not let Reuchlin be suppressed. This must be our great reason for confidence. 70

Farewell, and let me have as soon as possible a long letter on our common interests. How dare you complain that I do not answer, when your own letters are so short? Farewell once more. 75

Mainz, 5 June

987 / From Guillaume Budé   Paris, 10 June [1519]

This letter, published in the *Farrago*, answered both Erasmus' Epp 930 and 954. It was answered by Ep 1004.

BUDÉ TO ERASMUS, GREETING

Luis Vives, a most promising student of the humanities, as I discovered from his conversation, seems to me a keen supporter both of your reputation and of mine, and such an unusually courteous and scholarly person might, I think, prove a most effective link for the future, to support our friendship 5 and hold it together if ever, as happens in human life, any small disagreement, any trace of suspicion I would rather say, should come between us. That any such thing has come between us up to now I for my part will never admit, not even to the priest to whom I entrust the care of my soul.

In passing I must say a word about your letter, which reached me while 10 I was out of town, in which you reassure me quite unneccessarily that you always speak very highly of me, and assert that you are dissatisfied with that letter of yours which you find so long and I so short, for this reason if no other that it seems to have given me some offence. In hopes of relieving you of this suspicion once and for all, since you do not believe me whether I say 15 yes or no, as far as I am concerned you are welcome to let your printers have

* * * * *

near Frankfurt, lest the electors should be tempted by French offers; cf Epp 968 introduction, 1055.

987
2 Vives] Little is known about his brief visit to Paris at this time. On his return he carried this letter for Erasmus (cf Ep 992:2). On 28 June he was not yet back in Louvain; cf Ep 991:93.
11 out of town] In Montpellier (cf Ep 924:20n). In the following comments Budé makes no distinction between Epp 930 and 954.
13 letter of yours] Ep 906

it, if you see no objection; I read it without a trace of ill feeling. If you do not yet know the man I am, I should like to introduce to you even at this late date my somewhat astringent character: I do not like a too respectful approach with a touch of the toady in it, nor would I willingly keep up a friendship on   20 the basis of 'you scratch my back and I'll scratch yours,' any more than I have learnt to put resentment and bitterness on paper. I would rather be accused of untimely humour and some lack of discretion than of the opposite fault. I think it has some reference to this that you say we should 'Cretan with Cretan stand,' as if my views differed from yours or I did not show myself   25 ready to approve what you are trying to do. For my part, as ill luck would have it, I declared war long ago on the lovers of barbarism whom you know so well and engaged them fiercely, but am no longer able to pursue the battle, nor can I throw my weight as I would wish on the side of the good men whose commanding general you are; as though I no longer took sides, I   30 neither give aid to the one side nor harrass the other, although I hate one lot and wish victory to their opponents. This is simply to be a useless burden on the earth as I sink towards old age, as if one were watching a play. As for the question you so much wanted an answer to, what my intentions are, as you put it in one of your notes, I am ashamed to confess my inner feelings; but   35 one thing I do wish, that you should one day be able to know what I feel about the advocacy of all those who professed to be defending scholarship as we understand it.

Please write and let me know if the archbishop who loves you so dearly has sent you anything; for this was done without my knowledge, for good or   40 ill. What follows from this is such that I think it better to stop here and bid you farewell.

Paris, 10 June

* * * * *

24 'Cretan with Cretan stand'] Cf Ep 916:412n.
32 burden on the earth] Homer *Iliad* 18.104
35 notes] Now missing, or in a passage not published by Erasmus. There may be another reference to this in the postscript of Ep 929.
39 archbishop] Through Budé, Archbishop Etienne Poncher had encouraged Erasmus to state his terms for a move to Paris (cf Ep 810:408–19), but it does not seem likely that Erasmus actually did write to Poncher, nor that he received a letter from the archbishop. On the other hand, the royal invitation had recently been repeated by Louis Ruzé; cf Ep 926:37n.

988 / From Albert of Brandenburg   Frankfurt, 13 June 1519

> This letter answers Ep 968 and is answered in turn by Ep 1009; all three were
> published in the *Farrago*.

ALBERT, BY DIVINE MERCY CARDINAL PRIEST OF THE MOST
HOLY ROMAN CHURCH WITH THE TITLE OF ST CHRYSOGONUS,
ARCHBISHOP OF MAINZ AND MAGDEBURG, PRINCE-ELECTOR,
PRIMATE, AND ADMINISTRATOR OF HALBERSTADT, MARGRAVE
OF BRANDENBURG, ETC, TO ERASMUS OF ROTTERDAM,   5
GREETING

Heavy indeed and most necessary on behalf of all men, most learned
Erasmus, is the business which burdens us at this time with such anxious
care, for it is no private concern that occupies us, but we are compelled to
perform our duty of choosing an emperor for the whole world; yet all the time   10
we are actively and willingly mindful of you. Nothing therefore can come
before us so difficult that it can interrupt the reading of your most scholarly
letters when and where soever they arrive. And we beg you sincerely to
interrupt us frequently in this fashion; for be assured that we rejoice
whenever we receive any letter from you.   15

Though this is true of you especially, yet we take no little pleasure at
the same time in the acquaintance of scholars from whatever source. And so
Richard Pace, envoy of the invincible king of England, who is recommended
to us in the first place by his own merit (which was previously not unknown
to us, for we had often heard it spoken of by learned men), secondly by   20
letters from the king his master and the cardinal of York, and lastly by your
testimonial, is dear to us and we give him a warm welcome. Continue upon
your course of enriching Scriptural studies and divine theology with your
admirable endeavours for thus it will come to pass that the most barbarous
nations on earth will be barbarous no longer. With that end in view we wish   25
you all felicity and such success as your heart desires, and we promise you
our aid and comfort towards it.

It is a pleasure to show affection for our friend Hutten, if for no other
reason, because we understand him to be a friend of yours. As regards the
book that you have dedicated to us, there is no cause for concern; we were   30

* * * * *

988
21 York] Thomas Wolsey, the English chancellor, who had given Pace a letter of
   recommendation, received prompt but unenlightening reports on interviews
   Pace had with Albert of Brandenburg at Mainz and Frankfurt between 8 and 12
   May; cf LP III 296–7, 300.

not offended that some other person had given it another dedication, since you yourself had previously intended it for us. We shall shortly be sending a present in return. Till then farewell.

From the imperial city of Frankfurt, 13 June 1519

989 / From Nicolas Bérault   Paris, 20 June [1519]

For the year date of this letter cf Ep 925 introduction. It was published in the *Farrago* and is probably the letter acknowledged by Erasmus in Allen Ep 1002:41–2.

TO THE MOST ELOQUENT THEOLOGIAN ERASMUS OF ROTTERDAM FROM NICOLAS BÉRAULT, GREETING

Some days ago, most learned Erasmus, I gave that excellent and civilized man Francesco Calvo letters for you from Budé, Deloynes, and myself, and I have no doubt that he has surely and certainly delivered them, though perhaps 5 with some delay. And now, though I have nothing else to say, since there is a courier setting out for your part of the world, I could not refrain from writing something in the way of a letter to you, especially because your friend Wilhelm Nesen suggested it and has been obstinately urging me to write; at the same time, I wish to make it clear how much we all look forward to a letter 10 from you, and to induce you to write to that excellent and most learned man, Guillaume Hué, dean of Notre Dame. He is a man who in these lists, if I may use the word, would rather receive a challenge from you than be the challenger; he has considerable experience already in authorship of many kinds and is so devoted to the higher learning, and especially to Scriptural 15 studies, that we have absolutely nobody whom we could set above him. On his behalf I send you greetings provisionally. And I further beg you not to reject the friendship of such an honourable and learned man, who deserves your friendship on many counts, but for this reason especially that he seeks it so keenly and I had almost said, greedily; he would pay a high price for it, 20 were not the friendship of Erasmus open to all and to be had without paying

* * * * *

31 another dedication] Cf Epp 968:4n, 976:18n.
33 present] See Ep 986:41n.

989
4 letters] Cf Epp 819 introduction, 925:3n.
7 courier] Probably Haio Herman of Friesland; cf Ep 1002.
12 Hué] Guillaume Hué (d 31 July 1522) was a canon of Paris with humanist sympathies. Since 1518 he had been dean of the cathedral chapter and thus one of the highest ranking prelates in Paris.

anything. Deloynes, Ruzé, and the others send their greetings. Budé, as I
write this, is in the country with his wife and children; he will be back in
town before long, as soon, I suppose, as his lady, who is expecting a child,
has had her baby and increased the family of Budé. Farewell.   25

Paris, 20 June [1518]

990 / To John Claymond   Louvain, 27 June 1519

John Claymond (c 1468–1537) of Frampton, Lincolnshire, had been a fellow and
later president of Magdalen College, Oxford, until 1517, when Richard Foxe,
bishop of Winchester, persuaded him to take charge of his new foundation,
Corpus Christi. It seems that Erasmus knew him only indirectly and that this
letter, which was published in the *Farrago* shortly after it was written, was an
attempt to establish a personal connection.

ERASMUS OF ROTTERDAM TO THE DISTINGUISHED THEOLOGIAN
DR JOHN CLAYMOND, GREETING
He is an exceptionally wise man, is my lord Richard, bishop of Winchester,
and has always been universally esteemed as such; but let me tell you, good
doctor Claymond, who do so much honour to the ranks of theologians, no   5
act of his has ever proved this more clearly than his consecrating the
magnificent college which he has set up at his own expense expressly to the
three chief tongues, to humane literature, and to classical studies. What
greater service could he have rendered to his fellow men, what monument
could more rightly recommend his name to the undying memory of mankind?   10
So should a pillar of the church, so should a bishop act. And it is a great joy
to me that their eminences Thomas the cardinal of York and Cardinal
Campeggi and (not to become tedious by listing the other names) Henry the
Eighth himself, a monarch second to none of our time in the gifts of true
kingship, have whole-heartedly supported his enterprise. Their authority   15
can suppress with ease the shameless curs that would bark at his heels; their
generosity supplies in good measure the resources that attract energetic
teachers and meet the needs of academic freedom.

* * * * *

25 baby] Probably his second daughter; see M.-M. de la Garanderie *La Correspondance* 185 n 1.

990
7 college] Cf Ep 965:12n. The new college was not, however, strictly speaking
trilingual, unless Hebrew were regarded as implicit in the study of divinity.
12 Thomas] Wolsey; cf Ep 967:40n. For Campeggi see Ep 961.
16 suppress] Cf Ep 948:194–200.

Many parts of the world owe their renown to some famous monument.
It was the vast Colossus gave Rhodes its fame, Caria owes it to the sepulchre 20
of Mausolus, Memphis to the Pyramids, Cnidus to its statue of Venus,
Thebes to its magical figure of Memnon. I foresee that in days to come this
college, like some most holy temple sacred to all that is best in literature, will
be reckoned all over the world to be one of the chief glories of Britain, and
that more men will be drawn to Oxford by the spectacle of that library rich in 25
the three tongues, where no good author is lacking and no bad one finds a
place, than ever were attracted to Rome in olden days by the prospect of so
many marvels.

And furthermore, it is in my view another argument for the wisdom of
the excellent bishop's plan that he should have chosen you in particular, a 30
man whose integrity is nothing new but known from long experience, as the
president of his new college. For one thing, you can bring the weight of your
personal authority to the teaching of these subjects, and for another, you are
in your sole person proof enough that culture and character go well
together. For, as a result of misbehaviour by the few, those who do not wish 35
as well as they should to the humanities maintain that studies of this sort
corrupt human life and wean men away from the Christian religion. And
there are among us, especially in Germany, some younger men whose life is
honourable enough, but whose idea of defending liberal studies is to hold
forth against their opponents with the eloquence of fishwives. 40

Personally I do not deny that one must make allowances for youth and,
if you like, for nationality, especially when men are roused by such bitter
opposition that no language would seem harsh enough for their adversaries.
Yet my view is that your mild and serious, scholarly and cautious attitude
will have far more effect; even those who were lately protesting so loudly 45
and taking the field in opposition will be persuaded thereby to return to their
own lines and will be turned from bitter enemies into loyal champions and

* * * * *

19 monument] The following enumeration is inspired by the traditional seven
    wonders of the ancient world, which include the first three monuments here
    mentioned. The fourth contained a celebrated statue of Venus by Praxiteles.
    An enormous statue of the mythical king Memnon of Ethiopia was the pride of
    Thebes in Egypt.
25 library] Foxe endowed it with a rich collection of books, including Reuchlin's
    De rudimentis hebraicis (Pforzheim 1506) (see Allen VI xx). Claymond was himself
    a great benefactor to the library; cf J.R. Liddell in *The Library* 4th series 18 (1938)
    385–416.
38 younger men] Cf Ep 967:115–23.
40 fishwives] Literally 'out of carts'; cf Ep 949:26n.

defenders. The man who by his own moderation makes the humanities attractive to everyone is far more effective than he who is battling continually with their stubborn and malicious opponents. Is there any form of calumny I 50 have not suffered at the hands of these devotees of barbarism? The disturbance they have excited, the uproar they have aroused, the pits they have dug for innocent feet! I for my part was not wholly destitute of teeth and claws; I had my weapon, had I been willing to use it, nor am I ignorant of the best way of handling monsters of this kind. But I thought it would be 55 more pleasing to Christ, and at the same time more conducive to the advance of liberal studies, either to pacify the protesting party by a policy of moderation or even to give way, until in course of time the energy of these blockheads evaporates or they see the light of their own accord. Nor have I any reason as yet to regret this course. 60

I would not have dared to interrupt you, most learned Claymond, with a letter, had not Cuthbert Tunstall, Thomas More, and Richard Pace extolled with one accord your habitual readiness to be of use, being a man as approachable as you are upright. Encouraged by them, I have taken the liberty of writing in the running hand which I use to keep pace with the flow 65 of my ideas. Farewell.

Louvain, 27 June 1519

991 / To Tranquillus Andronicus Parthenius   [Louvain], 28 June 1519

This letter is addressed to Tranquillus Andronicus Parthenius (Fran Trankvil Andreis) of Trogir west of Split on the Dalmatian coast (1490–1571). After studies in Italy he appeared in Vienna and Ingolstadt (1517–18) and lectured in Leipzig on Quintilian (1518; cf Ep 911:47–9). Probably travelling by way of Erfurt, the point of departure for German pilgrims to Erasmus (cf Ep 963:6n), he arrived in the Netherlands apparently without a letter of introduction and failed to make contact with Erasmus either at Louvain or at Antwerp. This letter seems to be the only document of his visit (cf Ep 947:3n; de Vocht CTL I 321–3). It was evidently written after the Dalmatian had left in anger, perhaps for Paris (line 93n). To placate him, Erasmus offered such excuses as the circumstances seemed to permit, together with frank reproaches for the University of Louvain, and published this letter in the *Farrago*. Over the next twenty-five years Andronicus served as a diplomatic agent in the Balkans, partly on behalf of Ferdinand I. See *Enciklopedija Jugoslavije* (Zagreb 1955–   ) I 101–2.

* * * * *

52 uproar] Cf Ep 930:12n.

ERASMUS OF ROTTERDAM TO TRANQUILLUS PARTHENIUS OF
DALMATIA, GREETING

I had written from Antwerp, most learned Tranquillus, telling them, if you
had not already left, to detain you in Louvain for a few days until my return
or, if that should be impossible, at least to make sure that you did not depart   5
without speaking with me first; and I said I would pay the expense of your
longer stay out of my own pocket. But you were in a hurry to go and left
before my letter arrived; so when I returned to Louvain, I found instead of
my friend Tranquillus two poems, both equally learned and both, it must be
admitted, full of complaints; for one showed that when you left you were   10
annoyed with the university and the other that you were annoyed with me.
In one of them you accuse us all of some sort of barbarous discourtesy
because, when you wished to give us a display of your learning and a lesson
in literature, you were given no opportunity, though other universities
invite people by the prospect of reward to do just what you offered to do   15
gratis of your own free will. In the other you upbraid me as a crass Batavian
who has no use for the Graces, for having refused you an interview, when
the passion to set eyes on me had brought you from afar by most difficult
journeys into an unknown land. I will answer on behalf of us both, but first
let me plead my own case.   20

    To begin with, my dear sir, it is the absolute truth that at the time I was
in Antwerp, absorbed in what I found very troublesome business. But never
have I been so busy as to have refused an interview to a man like yourself,
had I either known you personally or been given an accurate picture of you
by someone else. Instead of a young scholar, friendly and modest, they had   25
described to me some barbarian bombastic character, a Davus or a Geta, some
itinerant busybody – a sort of man from whom I have an aversion such as you
would hardly credit, and by whom I am attacked oftener than I could wish
and than conduces to the progress of my work. This was due to confusion
with another man; for at that time a different person of this kind was seeking   30
publicity in Antwerp. For this sort of visitor therefore, who is both tiresome
and time-consuming, I am sometimes not at home, and again I cannot find the
time, another day I may not be awake, like the man in the old story whose
eyes were closed, but not to everybody. If you find this barely civil, I think it
much more uncivil, while listening to the nonsense these men talk, to neglect   35

* * * * *

991
3 Antwerp] Cf Ep 964 introduction.
16 crass Batavian] Cf *Adagia* III ii 48, IV vi 35.
26 a Davus or a Geta] Barbarian slaves in the comedies of Terence
33 old story] Of the husband, who sometimes connived at his wife's misbehaviour
    and sometimes was inconveniently wide awake; cf *Adagia* i vi 4.

the pressing demands of so many scholars who are always asking me for some assistance in the interest of liberal studies. Had anyone, I will not say painted you to me in your true colours, but merely drawn me an outline, I should have hastened to greet you of my own accord.

So much in my own behalf; it remains to give some answer in the name   40
of Louvain University. You know it is the first and greatest thing in any project to choose the right time to start. You could not have arrived in Louvain at a more unfortunate moment to lecture in the humanities, just when a recent conspiracy was at its height – a conspiracy of certain persons who seem to have vowed their own perdition if they cannot extinguish   45
liberal studies. For this is their idiotic conviction, that if these studies are allowed to acquire any standing, it will mean the weakening of their own authority. All over the world they see not only universities but even princes' courts infected with this new sort of learning; so they strive all the more to keep Louvain immune from the contagion. The whole thing has no support   50
from all the best people. For this disorder took its rise from the most unsubstantial beginnings, in fact from the unfounded suspicions of two or three men. Then, as they are not ashamed to be inconsistent even in a bad cause, they pursue their course for far more flimsy reasons than they used at first. In fact, the whole play depends on two or three leading actors; so you   55
must not spread resentment at this behaviour over the whole university. These men's pertinacity has convinced some people, their impudence has swept others away; some join the cause to win their favour, some out of hope of gain or fear of loss play their part in a production of which they do not approve. The majority clamour for no better reason than because they see   60
many others clamouring. Those who hear the noise from a distance think that the movement has public opinion behind it, especially when they see it advertised with sounding titles like University, Rector, and Faculties. Anyone who watches the play from close at hand or even is familiar in the wings perceives that the whole contraption is moved by two or three.   65
Personally, I would sooner impute such disturbances to a Homeric Ate, to Pan the poets' god or Tisiphone or one of the Furies, or even (as astrologers do) to some untoward concurrence of the heavenly bodies, than I would to the general will.

Another thing, I suspect, that may have done you harm is the innocent   70
way in which you advertised your enthusiasm for me. The chief actors in this

* * * * *

44 recent conspiracy] Cf Ep 930:12n.
66 Ate] Cf Ep 948:27n. The following references to Pan (cf Ep 970:7) and Tisiphone, one of the three Erinyes, etc may have been added to obscure the allusion to Jan Briart Atensis.

play think it an insult to themselves if Erasmus is well spoken of. There may
perhaps have been people who suspected that you had been put up to attack
the theologians with the freedom allowed in verse. I never yet saw any
group of men give more free rein to their own suspicions. A line of yours is   75
going the rounds in Louvain like a proverb: 'Erasmus' eloquent heart I
might not see.' Why they should laugh at this, I do not quite know: it is not
such a bad line as to deserve ridicule, nor is their Erasmus so notoriously
tongue-tied that it is a nine days' wonder if one of his friends calls him
eloquent. There may be ill-natured people here, but not, I think, perverse   80
enough to take pleasure simply in the fact that things have not gone quite as
you intended. But let us leave them to their pleasure, such as it is. I should
like to see you take a more kindly view of this university of ours, which has
its able men and its good young scholars, if only ability were rewarded, and
there were not such violent opposition to more liberal subjects. If I gave you   85
a personal description of these godlike characters, it would not surprise you
to find ancient barbarism blessed with such champions. They are said to be
the target of some attack you are planning; and this, my dear Tranquillus, I
think such a bad idea that I would rather think it cannot be true. They
deserve it, you will say. So be it: let them deserve to swing for it – but I   90
should like you to remember the behaviour proper to professed supporters
of the literature that prides itself on the name of 'the humanities.'

Mind you give my greetings to Luis Vives; if he remembers me, I am
delighted at his good fortune and envious if he has forgotten me. For I hear
he is overjoyed at his escape from this citadel of barbarism, as the phrase   95
goes, and the recovery of his old freedom to work. Farewell, dearest
Tranquillus.

28 June 1519

992 / From Guillaume Budé   Paris, 30 June [1519]

This letter enlarges on points made in Ep 987; it was answered by Ep 1004 and
published in the *Farrago*. Budé entrusted it to Henricus Glareanus and Jacobus
Ceratinus (cf line 5n), who seem to have visited Erasmus about this time.
Nothing certain is known about their visit to Louvain; cf O.F. Fritzsche *Glarean*
(Frauenfeld 1890) 27–9.

* * * * *

93 Vives] He had recently gone to Paris (cf Ep 987:2n). Thus, unlike Erasmus, he
   was, temporarily at least, in the enviable position of being able to forget
   Louvain, that centre of anti-humanist agitation.
95 as the phrase goes] Apparently an echo of Cicero *Pro Fonteio* 20.44

GUILLAUME BUDÉ TO ERASMUS OF ROTTERDAM, GREETING
I had lately sent you a letter by the hand of Luis Vives, a good scholar – to
judge by the two conversations I had with him – and much attached to you.
But now that I have had a visit from Glareanus, accompanied by Jacobus
Ceratinus, who knows Greek and Latin and professes both, I could not   5
escape writing you this letter, they being not unwilling to wait in my house
in the mean time. While I was abroad, I had two letters from you almost in the
same words, and certainly very similar in contents. You seem to disown that
long letter you wrote me and to reject it as fit only for the jakes, for this
reason above all, because it made me annoyed with you. In this you are quite   10
wrong, as you have been wrong before on other matters, and so I made clear
before my departure in a letter beginning 'I have seen the comments you
wrote on my letter.' If you do not believe me even now, you are welcome to
send your letter and mine together to the printers, and I assure you it will be
with my good will. I do not think I have anything to fear from the opinion of   15
educated men; but the tendency of that would be to confirm in any intelligent
and open-minded reader the opinion, were the contents of these letters to be
made public, that there was an element of disloyalty in our friendship, and
that we were writing like this for effect. It is true that I enjoy my joke when I
am writing, and writing perhaps without restraint, but I endure without   20
reluctance, or at least without resentment, if I am paid in my own coin, even
coin of rather dubious value. Being as I am fond of pleasantry by nature, I
have absolutely no wish to be excused from listening to those who repay one
joke with another. In fact, if I wish to be thought an honest man, it follows, I
presume, that I must not take it amiss if people make jokes at my expense that 25
are reasonable and witty.

Do understand, I beg you, that I take the opposite view from you about
exchanges of this sort in writing, between such men at least as have some
experience of life. You think they undermine a firm friendship or are afraid
that others will think so; in my own opinion they confirm and strengthen it at 30
all points. You must realize that no one is further from literature than I am
now. As a result, I value my life at less than half what it is worth and wish for

* * * * *

992
2 letter] Ep 987
5 Ceratinus] Jacob Teyng of Hoorn, hence called Ceratinus, a promising young
   scholar; cf Ep 622:34n.
7 two letters] Epp 930, 954
9 long letter] Ep 906; cf Epp 924, 954.
12 letter beginning] Ep 915
31 I am now] Immersed in court duties and diplomacy; cf Epp 924:20–1, 987:27–9.

nothing except leave to return to the use of my own wits, no matter what the effect on my finances. I relieve you of every vestige of suspicion that I am mildly annoyed, so you need no longer indulge in those unnecessary 35 assurances that you speak of me with respect and so forth. Farewell.

Paris, 30 June

I fear I am delaying Glareanus and his companion longer than I should. Why, I wonder, have you never answered the letter I mentioned just now?

* * * * *

39 letter] Ep 915; at the beginning of Ep 930 Erasmus made it clear that he had no intention of answering it, but see Ep 1004.

TABLE OF CORRESPONDENTS

WORKS FREQUENTLY CITED

SHORT TITLE FORMS

INDEX

WORKS FREQUENTLY CITED

This list provides bibliographical information for works referred to in short-title form in the headnotes and footnotes to Epp 842–992. For Erasmus' writings see the short-title list, pages 421–4. Editions of his lettters are included in the list below.

AK	Alfred Hartmann and B.R. Jenny eds *Die Amerbach-korrespondenz* (Basel 1942–)
Allen	P.S. Allen, H.M. Allen, and H.W. Garrod eds *Opus epistolarum Des. Erasmi Roterodami* (Oxford 1906–58) 11 vols and index
ASD	*Opera omnia Desiderii Erasmi Roterodami* (Amsterdam 1969–)
Auctarium	*Auctarium selectarum aliquot epistolarum Erasmi Roterodami ad eruditos et horum ad illum* (Basel: Froben August 1518)
Benzing *Lutherbibliographie*	Josef Benzing *Lutherbibliographie* (Baden-Baden 1966)
Bierlaire *La familia*	Franz Bierlaire *La familia d'Erasme* (Paris 1968)
Bietenholz *Basle and France*	P.G. Bietenholz *Basle and France in the Sixteenth Century* (Geneva-Toronto 1971)
Bietenholz *History and Biography*	P.G. Bietenholz *History and Biography in the Work of Erasmus of Rotterdam* (Geneva 1966)
Boehmer *Luther*	Heinrich Boehmer *Martin Luther: Road to Reformation* (Meridian Books, New York 1957)
BRE	A. Horawitz and K. Hartfelder eds *Briefwechsel des Beatus Rhenanus* (Leipzig 1886; repr 1966)
Budé *Opera omnia*	Guillaume Budé *Opera omnia* (Basel 1557; repr 1966) 3 vols
CC	*Corpus Christianorum: series latina* (Turnhout 1953–)
CSEL	*Corpus scriptorum ecclesiasticorum latinorum* (Vienna-Leipzig 1866–)
CWE	*Collected Works of Erasmus* (Toronto 1974–)
DBF	*Dictionnaire de biographie française* ed J. Balteau et al (Paris 1932–)
DBI	*Dizionario biografico degli Italiani* ed A.M. Ghisalberti et al (Rome 1960–)
DHGE	*Dictionnaire d'histoire et de géographie ecclésiastiques* ed A. Baudrillart et al (Paris 1912–)
Emden BRUC	A.B. Emden *Biographical Register of the University of Cambridge to AD 1500* (Cambridge 1963)
Emden BRUO	A.B. Emden *Biographical Register of the University of Oxford to AD 1500* (Oxford 1957–9) 3 vols; *Biographical Register of the University of Oxford, AD 1501 to 1540* (Oxford 1974)
Epistolae ad diversos	*Epistolae D. Erasmi Roterodami ad diversos et aliquot aliorum ad illum* (Basel: Froben 31 August 1521)
Farrago	*Farrago nova epistolarum Des. Erasmi Roterodami ad alios et aliorum ad hunc: admixtis quibusdam quas scripsit etiam adolescens* (Basel: Froben October 1519)

M.-M. de la Garanderie   Marie-Madeleine de la Garanderie ed and trans *La*
   La Correspondance   *Correspondance d'Erasme et de Guillaume Budé* (Paris 1967)

Grimm *Buchführer*   H. Grimm 'Die Buchführer des deutschen Kulturbereichs
und ihre Niederlassungsorte in der Zeitspanne 1490 bis um
1550' *Archiv für Geschichte des Buchwesens* 7 (1965–6) 1153–
1772

Harsin *Erard de la*   Paul Harsin *Etude critique sur l'histoire de la principauté de*
   Marck   *Liège* II: *Le règne d'Erard de la Marck 1505–1538* (Liège 1955)

Holborn *Hutten*   Hajo Holborn *Ulrich von Hutten and the German Reformation*
trans R.H. Bainton (Harper Torchbooks, New York 1966)

Höss *Spalatin*   Irmgard Höss *Georg Spalatin, 1484–1545* (Weimar 1956)

Hutten *Opera*   E. Böcking ed *Ulrichi Hutteni opera* (Leipzig 1859–61; repr
1963) 5 vols

Jonas Briefwechsel   *Der Briefwechsel des Justus Jonas* ed Gustav Kawerau (Halle
1884–5; repr 1964) 2 vols

Krause *Eobanus*   Carl Krause *Helius Eobanus Hessus, sein Leben und seine*
Werke (Gotha 1879) 2 vols

LB   J. Leclerc ed *Desiderii Erasmi Roterodami opera omnia* (Leiden
1703–6) 10 vols

LP   *Letters and Papers, Foreign and Domestic, of the Reign of*
Henry VIII ed J.S. Brewer, J. Gairdner, R.H. Brodie (London
1862–1932) 36 vols

Luther w   *D. Martin Luthers Werke: Kritische Gesamtausgabe* (Weimar
1883–)

McConica   J.K. McConica *English Humanists and Reformation Politics*
under Henry VIII and Edward VI (Oxford 1965)

Melanchthon *Werke*   *Melanchthons Werke in Auswahl* ed Robert Stupperich et al
(Gütersloh 1951–)

NDB   *Neue Deutsche Biographie* ed Historische Kommission bei
der Bayerischen Akademie der Wissenschaften (Berlin
1953–)

NK   W. Nijhoff and M.E. Kronenberg eds *Nederlandsche*
Bibliographie van 1500 tot 1540 (The Hague 1923–71)

NNBW   *Nieuw Nederlandsch Biografisch Woordenboek* ed P.C.
Molhuysen et al, 2nd ed (Amsterdam 1974) 10 vols and
Register

Opuscula   W.K. Ferguson ed *Erasmi opuscula: A Supplement to the Opera*
omnia (The Hague 1933)

Opus epistolarum   *Opus epistolarum Des. Erasmi Roterodami per autorem diligenter*
recognitum et adjectis innumeris novis fere ad trientem auctum
(Basel: Froben, Herwagen, and Episcopius 1529)

Pastor   Ludwig von Pastor *The History of the Popes, from the Close*
of the Middle Ages ed and trans R.F Kerr et al, 3rd ed
(London 1938–53) 40 vols

PG   J.P. Migne ed *Patrologiae cursus completus ... series graeca*
(Paris 1857–1912) 162 vols

Phillips   Margaret Mann Phillips *The 'Adages' of Erasmus* (Cambridge
1964)

PL   J.P. Migne ed *Patrologiae cursus completus … series latina*
                            (Paris 1844–1902) 221 vols
RE   L. Geiger ed *Johann Reuchlins Briefwechsel* (Stuttgart 1875;
                            repr 1962)
Reedijk   C. Reedijk ed *The Poems of Desiderius Erasmus* (Leiden 1956)
Rogers   Elizabeth Frances Rogers ed *The Correspondence of Sir
                            Thomas More* (Princeton 1947)
Scheurl's Briefbuch   *Christoph Scheurl's Briefbuch* ed F. von Soden and J.K.F.
                            Knaake (Potsdam 1867–72; repr 1962) 2 vols
Scrinium   *Scrinium Erasmianum: Mélanges historiques publiés …
                            à l'occasion du cinquième centenaire de la naissance d'Erasme* ed J.
                            Coppens (Leiden 1969) 2 vols
Ulmann *Maximilian I*   Heinrich Ulmann *Kaiser Maximilian I* (Stuttgart 1884–91;
                            repr 1967) 2 vols
de Vocht CTL   Henry de Vocht *History of the Foundation and the Rise of the
                            Collegium Trilingue Lovaniense 1517–1550* Humanistica
                            lovaniensia 10–13 (Louvain 1951–5) 4 vols
de Vocht *Busleyden*   Henry de Vocht *Jérôme de Busleyden* Humanistica lovanien-
                            sia 9 (Turnhout 1950)
Volz *Die ersten   Hans Volz 'Die ersten Sammelausgaben von Luther-
  Sammelausgaben*   schriften und ihre Drucker, 1518–20' *Gutenberg Jahrbuch
                            1960* (Mainz 1960) 185–204
Zwingli *Werke*   *Huldreich Zwinglis Sämtliche Werke* ed E. Egli et al, Corpus
                            Reformatorum vols 88–101 (Berlin-Zürich 1905–)

Titles following colons are longer versions of the same, or are alternative titles. Items entirely enclosed in square brackets are of doubtful authorship. For abbreviations, see Works Frequently Cited.

[Acta contra Lutherum: Acta academiae Lovaniensis contra Lutherum *Opuscula*]

Adagia: Adagiorum chiliades 1508 (Adagiorum collectanea for the primitive form, when required) LB II / ASD II-5, 6

Admonitio adversus mendacium: Admonitio adversus mendacium et obtrectationem LB X

Annotationes in Novum Testamentum LB VI

Antibarbari LB X / ASD I-1 / CWE 23

Apologia ad Fabrum: Apologia ad Iacobum Fabrum Stapulensem LB IX

Apologia ad Caranzam: Apologia ad Sanctium Caranzam, or Apologia de tribus locis, or Responsio ad annotationem Stunicae LB IX

Apologia ad viginti et quattuor libros A. Pii LB IX

Apologia adversus Petrum Sutorem: Apologia adversus debacchationes Petri Sutoris LB IX

Apologia adversus monachos: Apologia adversus monachos quosdam hispanos LB IX

Apologia adversus rhapsodias Alberti Pii LB IX

Apologia contra Latomi dialogum: Apologia contra Iacobi Latomi dialogum de tribus linguis LB IX

Apologiae contra Stunicam: Apologiae contra Lopidem Stunicam LB IX

Apologia de 'In principio erat sermo' LB IX

Apologia de laude matrimonii: Apologia pro declamatione de laude matrimonii LB IX

Apologia de loco 'omnes quidem': Apologia de loco 'Omnes quidem resurgemus' LB IX

Apologia invectivis Lei: Apologia qua respondet duabus invectivis Eduardi Lei *Opuscula*

Apophthegmata LB IV

Appendix respondens ad Sutorem LB IX

Argumenta: Argumenta in omneis epistolas apostolicas nova (with Paraphrases)

Axiomata pro causa Lutheri: Axiomata pro causa Martini Lutheri *Opuscula*

Carmina varia LB VIII

Catalogus lucubrationum LB I

Christiani hominis institutum, carmen LB V

Ciceronianus: Dialogus Ciceronianus LB I / ASD I-2

Colloquia LB I / ASD I-3

Compendium vitae Allen I / CWE 4

[Consilium: Consilium cuiusdam ex animo cupientis esse consultum *Opuscula*]

De bello turcico: Consultatio de bello turcico LB V

De civilitate: De civilitate morum puerilium LB I

De concordia: De sarcienda ecclesiae concordia LB V

De conscribendis epistolis   LB I / ASD I-2
De constructione: De constructione octo partium orationis, or Syntaxis   LB I /
    ASD I-4
De contemptu mundi: Epistola de contemptu mundi   LB V / ASD V-1
De copia: De duplici copia verborum ac rerum   LB I / CWE 24
De immensa Dei misericordia: Concio de immensa Dei misericordia   LB V
De libero arbitrio: De libero arbitrio diatribe   LB IX
De praeparatione: De praeparatione ad mortem   LB V / ASD V-1
De pueris instituendis: De pueris statim ac liberaliter instituendis   LB I / ASD I-2
De puero Iesu: Concio de puero Iesu   LB V
De ratione studii   LB I / ASD I-2 / CWE 24
De recta pronuntiatione: De recta latini graecique sermonis pronuntiatione
    LB I / ASD I-4
De tedio Iesu: Disputatiuncula de tedio, pavore, tristicia Iesu   LB V
De virtute amplectenda: Oratio de virtute amplectenda   LB V
Declamatio de morte   LB IV
Declamatiuncula   LB IV
Declarationes ad censuras Lutetiae   LB IX
Detectio praestigiarum: Detectio praestigiarum cuiusdam libelli germanice scripti
    LB X
[Dialogus bilinguium ac trilinguium: Chonradi Nastadiensis dialogus bilinguium ac
    trilinguium   *Opuscula*]
Dilutio: Dilutio eorum quae Iodocus Clithoveus scripsit adversus declamationem
    suasoriam matrimonii
Divinationes ad notata Bedae   LB IX

Ecclesiastes: Ecclesiastes sive de ratione concionandi   LB V
Elenchus in N. Bedae censuras   LB IX
Enchiridion: Enchiridion militis christiani   LB V
Encomium matrimonii (in De conscribendis epistolis)
Encomium medicinae: Declamatio in laudem artis medicae   LB I / ASD I-4
Epigrammata   LB I
Epistola ad Dorpium   LB IX / CWE 3
Epistola ad fratres Inferioris Germaniae: Responsio ad fratres Germaniae Inferioris
    ad epistolam apologeticam incerto autore proditam   LB X
Epistola ad graculos: Epistola ad quosdam imprudentissimos graculos   LB X
Epistola apologetica de Termino   LB X
Epistola consolatoria: Epistola consolatoria virginibus sacris   LB V
Epistola contra pseudevangelicos: Epistola contra quosdam qui se falso iactant
    evangelicos   LB X
Epistola de esu carnium: Epistola apologetica ad Christophorum episcopum
    Basiliensem de interdicto esu carnium   LB IX
Exomologesis: Exomologesis sive modus confitendi   LB V
Explanatio symboli: Explanatio symboli apostolorum sive catechismus
    LB V / ASD V-1
Expostulatio Iesu   LB V

Formula: Conficiendarum epistolarum formula (see De conscribendis epistolis)

Hymni varii   LB V
Hyperaspistes   LB X

Institutio christiani matrimonii   LB V
Institutio principis christiani   LB IV / ASD IV-1

[Julius exclusus: Dialogus Julius exclusus e coelis   *Opuscula*]

Lingua   LB IV / ASD IV-1
Liturgia Virginis Matris: Virginis Matris apud Lauretum cultae liturgia
   LB V / ASD V-1

Methodus: Ratio verae theologiae   LB V
Modus orandi Deum   LB V / ASD V-1
Moria: Moriae encomium, or Moria   LB IV / ASD IV-3

Novum Testamentum: Novum Testamentum 1519 and later (Novum instrumentum
   for the first edition, 1516, when required)   LB VI

Obsecratio ad Virginem Mariam: Obsecratio sive oratio ad Virginem Mariam in
   rebus adversis   LB V
Oratio de pace: Oratio de pace et discordia   LB VIII
Oratio funebris: Oratio funebris Berthae de Heyen   LB VIII

Paean Virgini Matri: Paean Virgini Matri dicendus   LB V
Panegyricus: Panegyricus ad Philippum Austriae ducem   LB IV / ASD IV-1
Parabolae: Parabolae sive similia   LB I / ASD I-5 / CWE 23
Paraclesis   LB V, VI
Paraphrasis in Elegantias Vallae: Paraphrasis in Elegantias Laurentii Vallae
   LB I / ASD I-4
Paraphrasis in Novum Testamentum   LB VII
Paraphrasis in Matthaeum: Paraphrasis in Matthaeum, etc   LB VII
Peregrinatio apostolorum: Peregrinatio apostolorum Petri et Pauli   LB VI, VII
Precatio ad Virginis filium Iesum (in Precatio pro pace)
Precatio dominica   LB V
Precationes   LB V
Precatio pro pace ecclesiae: Precatio ad Iesum pro pace ecclesiae   LB IV, V
Progymnasmata: Progymnasmata quaedam primae adolescentiae Erasmi   LB VIII
Psalmi: Psalmi, or Enarrationes sive commentarii in psalmos   LB V
Purgatio adversus epistolam Lutheri: Purgatio adversus epistolam non sobriam
   Lutheri   LB IX

Querela pacis   LB IV / ASD IV-2

Ratio verae theologiae: Methodus   LB V
Responsio ad annotationes Lei: Liber quo respondet annotationibus Lei   LB IX
Responsio ad collationes: Responsio ad collationes cuiusdam iuvenis gerontodi-
   dascali   LB IX

Responsio ad disputationem de divortio: Responsio ad disputationem cuiusdam
    Phimostomi de divortio   LB IX
Responsio ad epistolam Pii: Responsio ad epistolam paraeneticam Alberti Pii,
    or Responsio ad exhortationem Pii   LB IX
Responsio ad notulas Bedaicas   LB X
Responsio ad Petri Cursii defensionem: Epistola de apologia Cursii   LB X
Responsio adversus febricantis libellum: Apologia monasticae religionis   LB X

Spongia: Spongia adversus aspergines Hutteni   LB X
Supputatio: Supputatio calumniarum Natalis Bedae   LB IX

Vidua christiana   LB V
Virginis et martyris comparatio   LB V
Vita Hieronymi: Vita diui Hieronymi Stridonensis   *Opuscula*

Index

426

Angleberme, Jean Pyrrhus d', professor in Orléans 111; *Militia Francorum regum* 111n

Angst, Wolfgang 152; corrector for Schöffer 256; preface for edition of Livy 324

Antioch, and St Luke 30

Antoninus Pius, emperor, Henry VIII likened to 361

Antwerp: Erasmus' repute in 38; book stolen in 149; Erasmus in 285, 326, 327, 408; criticism of Erasmus 307; Maximilian I in 314; Proost in 393; Augustinian convent 393

Apelles 287

Apostolics, errors of 246

Aquinas. *See* Thomas Aquinas

Ardennes, abbey of St Hubert 174n

Argyropoulos, Johannes: translation of 101; edition of Aristotle *Ethics* 343n

Arians 17. *See also* Arius

Aristarchus, prince of critics 183

Aristophanes, *Acharnians* 244n

Aristotle: ignored by apostles 13; and Thomas Aquinas 23; Eck cites 32; Augustine and 34; theory of memory 58; Linacre's translations 101, 129; Alcionio's versions 128; cited in Italy 246; theologian disciples 388. *See also* Peripatetics
- works: *De generatione animalium* 61n; *Elenchi* 34; *Metaphysica* 34; *Meteorologica* 129; *Nicomachean Ethics* 336n, 343n, 384; *Physica* 34; *Posteriora* 34; *Priora* 34; *Topica* 34

Arius 246. *See also* Arians

Asia Minor: Greek spoken 29; St Paul's conquest of 243

Ateca, Jorge de, confessor to Catherine of Aragon 317–18

Atensis. *See* Briart

Athanasius, St, *Commentary on St Paul* (spurious) 38

Athens, Areopagus of 233

Augsburg: Oecolampadius takes post in 193
- Diet of (1518): Vitellius' speech

103n, 105; Cajetanus' speech 167; Erasmus reports on 171–2; la Marck at 236n

Augustine, St: on Bible texts and versions 5, 5–6, 18, 97; standard of ancients 8; inspired writer 8; on style 9, 10, 11–12; disparages philosophy 13; and Greek heretics 16; and Innocent I 18; mistakes in 23, 26, 28; and 'folly' of Christ 24, 25; theologians and 26; notes lapses in Peter 28; Jerome preferred to 31–5; repute among scholars 32; Erasmus consults 33, 97; deficiencies in 34; and Cicero 34; Origen surpasses 35; on dialectic 84; and religious garb 86; 'Rule' of 88, 183, 184; on eloquence 103; Greeks superior to 181; and Jerome 205–6, 335; and sinners 240–1; Lips urges edition of 259; canons not worthy of his name 260; doctrine of justification 298; and Donatists 299; rejects lust 376
- works: *Ad fratres in eremo* (spurious) 187; Commentary on John 182; *Confessions* 34; *De bono coniugii* 242; *De civitate Dei* 6n, 35, 82; *De doctrina christiana* 9, 12, 18, 34, 84, 103n; *De haeresibus* 16, 17, 187, 246; *De locutionibus* 14; *De ordine* 9; *De trinitate* 34; *Enarratio in Psalmum* 24; letters 80, to Aurelius 187, to Januarius 244, to Macedonius 240, to Publicola 242; *Quaestiones in Heptateuchum* 6n

Augustinian canons; canons regular, unworthy members 260, 376. *See also* Lips

Augustinian friars (Eremites): support Karlstadt at Leipzig 225; Wolsey's reformation of 366; unworthy member 376. *See also* Luther; Lang; Staupitz

Augustus, Octavius, emperor: and Virgil 265; his tragedy *Ajax* 270n; Henry VIII likened to 361

Ausonius, Decimus Magnus 199

Austria: Ferdinand ruler of 251n;

– university; Erasmus warns about
Lee 4n; Erasmus' repute in 38, 307;
Dorp at 49n; parsimony of 52;
Erasmus' work in 106n; Longicampianus at 115, 152n; Cellarius
in 147n; attacks Luther 193n, 294;
Carinus in 257n; Nesen in 257n;
Vives at 272n; Erasmus' troubles in
307, 311; Antoon van Bergen at
330n; enemies of studies in 378,
409; Hasebart at 383n; Erasmus
defends 410
– faculty of theology: Erasmus in 15;
and litigation with la Marck 238,
391n; Latomus in 283n, 285, 290; cen-
sors Hutten's books 325; attributes
others' works to Erasmus 370–1,
391; criticizes Erasmus 380, 381,
382; Luther's books and 391, 392
– College of the Lily: Erasmus at
113n; Haio Herman at 190n; Delft
at 259n; Becker and Castere at
280n
– Collegium Trilingue 52, 110n;
opposition to 67; Baerland at 155n,
156; Buschius seeks post at 155n;
Rescius at 191n; controversies over
277, 283n; Croy a patron of 306n
Low Countries. *See* Burgundian
Netherlands
Lucan 304
Lucas, Jacques, dean of Orléans
– letter to, from Longueil 226
Lucian, *De saltatione* 204
Luke, St 30. *See also* Bible, New
Testament
Lupset, Thomas, lectures at Oxford
367n
Luther, Martin: Pucci works against
95n–96n; confrère of Lang 135n;
in danger 147; Heidelberg disputation 147n; Augsburg disputation
147n; and Cajetanus 167n–168n;
and Froben press 191, 193; admired
by Hollonius 191, 193; Erasmus
wary of 193n; Melanchthon recommends 221; Berquin admires 268n;
Latomus attacks 290; Erasmus de-

fers judgment 292; Capito defends
294; Erasmus defends 296–9;
Erasmus' estimation 309, 368–9;
Leipzig disputation 310n; unnamed
critic 313; Frederick's opinion of
355; works rushed to print 369;
and Louvain 391, 392; support of
good men 396
– works: *Ad Leonum X*, title page *192
illustration*, at Froben press 193n;
'Asteriscs' against Eck 139n;
commentary on Psalms 393; *Ein
Sermon von Ablass und Gnade* 369;
Ninety-five Theses 79n, 137–8,
246n, 282, 296, 351, 369; *Sermo de
poenitentia* 369
– letter from 281
– letter to 391

Maccabees, martyrdom of 2
Mainz: Erasmus in 115; St Victor 115;
Friedlieb in 147; Longicampianus
in 152n; printers in 255; cathedral
school 256; Zobel in 256n
Malaise, Nicolas de, abbot of St
Hubert 156
– letter to 173
Manuzio, Aldo: compared with Froben
53; reported Erasmus' death 57;
Erasmus recalls 126, 129–30;
praised Linacre 128; proposed acad-
emy 129
Manuzio, Paolo, Erasmus greets 130
Marcaeus, Helias
– letter to 2
Marcionites 84
Marck, Antoine de la, abbot of
Beaulieu-en-Argonne
– letter to 333
Marck, Erard de la, prince-bishop of
Liège: vellum copy of *Novum
Testamentum* 41n; relations with
Erasmus 118, 121, 326, 335; patron
of scholars 156, 174; meets Haps-
burgs in Mechelen 269n; seeks tutor
for Ferdinand 272; read Frederick
of Saxony's letter 389; attitude to
Luther 391n, 392

This book

was designed by

A N T J E   L I N G N E R

based on the series design by

A L L A N   F L E M I N G

and was printed by

University

of Toronto

Press